Part IV   Sticky-Price Macroeconomics

Chapter 9   The Income-Expenditure Framework: Consumption and the Multiplier
Box 9.1 Calculating the Consumption Function: An Example
Box 9.2 Calculating the MPE: An Example
Box 9.3 How Fast Does the Economy Move to Equilibrium?: Some Details
Box 9.4 Inventory Adjustment and the Circular Flow: Some Details
Box 9.5 Calculating the Difference between Aggregate Demand and Real GDP: An Example
Box 9.6 The Value of the Multiplier: An Example

Chapter 10   Investment, Net Exports, and Interest Rates
Box 10.1 The Stock Market as an Indicator of Future Investment: Some Tools
Box 10.2 Calculating the Dependence of Aggregate Demand on the Interest Rate: An Example
Box 10.3 A Government Spending Increase and the IS Curve: An Example
Box 10.4 Moving along the IS Curve: An Example

Chapter 11   Extending the Sticky-Price Model: More Analytical Tools
Box 11.1 IS-LM Equilibrium: An Example
Box 11.2 An IS Shock: An Example
Box 11.3 Calculating the Effect of an LM Shock: An Example
Box 11.4 An LM Shock and the Balance of Trade: An Example
Box 11.5 A Change in International Investors' Expectations: An Example

Chapter 12   The Phillips Curve and Expectations
Box 12.1 Forms of Okun's Law: A Tool
Box 12.2 Costs of High Unemployment: Policy Issues
Box 12.3 From Income-Expenditure to the Phillips Curve and the MPRF: Some Details
Box 12.4 Solving for Equilibrium Inflation and Unemployment: Some Details
Box 12.5 Static Expectations of Inflation in the 1960s: An Example
Box 12.6 A High-Pressure Economy under Adaptive Expectations: An Example
Box 12.7 Adaptive Expectations and the Volcker Disinflation: Policy Issues

Part V   Macroeconomic Policy

Chapter 13   Stabilization Policy
Box 13.1 Japan's Liquidity Trap: A Policy
Box 13.2 The Structure of the Economy and the Lucas Critique: The Details
Box 13.3 What are Leading Indicators?: The Details
Box 13.4 The Money Multiplier: A Policy
Box 13.5 The Limits of Stabilization Policy: A Policy
Box 13.6 The Kennedy-Johnson and the Reagan Tax Cuts: A Policy
Box 13.7 Monetary Policy Instruments: A Policy
Box 13.8 The Political Business Cycle and Richard Nixon: A Policy
Box 13.9 Is There a Political Business Cycle?: The Details
Box 13.10 Central Bank Independence: A Policy

Chapter 14   The Budget Balance, the National Debt, and Investment
Box 14.1 The Deficit as an Index of Fiscal Policy: The Details
Box 14.2 The Equilibrium Debt-to-GDP Ratio: An Example
Box 14.3 The U.S. Debt-to-GDP Ratio: The Details

Chapter 15   International Economic Policy
Box 15.1 Currency Arbitrage under the Gold Standard: An Example
Box 15.2 Are Western Europe and the United States Optimal Currency Areas?: An Example

MACROECONOMICS

MACROECONOMICS

J. BRADFORD DeLONG
University of California, Berkeley

Boston   Burr Ridge, IL   Dubuque, IA   Madison, WI   New York   San Francisco   St. Louis
Bangkok   Bogotá   Caracas   Kuala Lumpur   Lisbon   London   Madrid   Mexico City
Milan   Montreal   New Delhi   Santiago   Seoul   Singapore   Sydney   Taipei   Toronto

McGraw-Hill Higher Education

A Division of The **McGraw-Hill** *Companies*

A note on the cover image: We saw a connection to the content of the textbook that might be best expressed by the following comment: "A Mondrian abstract is the most compact imaginable pictorial harmony. . . . At the same time it stretches far beyond its borders so that it seems a fragment of a larger cosmos." (David Sylvester, "About Modern Art: Critical Essays, 1948–1997.")

MACROECONOMICS

Some ancillaries, including electronic and print components, may not be available to customers outside the United States.

This book is printed on acid-free paper.

domestic   1 2 3 4 5 6 7 8 9 0 WCK/WCK 0 9 8 7 6 5 4 3 2 1
international 1 2 3 4 5 6 7 8 9 0 WCK/WCK 0 9 8 7 6 5 4 3 2 1

ISBN 0-07-232848-7

Publisher: *Gary Burke*
Executive sponsoring editor: *Paul Shensa*
Senior developmental editor: *Tom Thompson*
Marketing manager: *Martin D. Quinn*
Project manager: *Jim Labeots*
Senior production supervisor: *Lori Koetters*
Design team lead: *Matthew Baldwin*
Lead supplement producer: *Becky Szura*
Media producer: *Melissa Kansa*
Interior and cover designer: *Maureen McCutcheon*
Cover image: *Piet Mondrian (Pieter Cornelis Mondrian), Dutch, 1872–1944. Lozenge Composition with yellow, black, blue, red, and gray, 1921, oil on canvas, 60 × 60 cm. Gift of Edgar Kaufmann, Jr., 1957.307. Photograph © 2001, The Art Institute of Chicago, All Rights Reserved.*
Typeface: *10/12 Berkeley*
Compositor: *ElectraGraphics, Inc.*
Printer: *Quebecor World Versailles Inc.*

Library of Congress Cataloging-in-Publication Data

De Long, J. Bradford.
    Macroeconomics / J. Bradford DeLong.
      p. cm.
    Includes index.
    ISBN 0-07-232848-7 (alk. paper)
    1. Macroeconomics. I. Title.
    HB172.5 .D435 2002
    339--dc21

                        2001044451

www.mhhe.com

For Ann Marie Marcialle

ABOUT THE AUTHOR

J. Bradford DeLong is professor of economics at the University of California at Berkeley, where he has been teaching since 1995. Before starting to teach at Berkeley, he was deputy assistant secretary for economic policy in the United States Department of the Treasury (1993 to 1995), where an enormous range of issues crossed his desk — from what the Federal Reserve would do next week, to whether the Uruguay Round of the General Agreement on Tariffs and Trade should be ratified, to the macroeconomic implications of the (unsuccessful) health care reform. Before working at the Treasury Department he was an associate professor at Harvard University, where he was both an undergraduate student (B.A. 1982) and a graduate student (Ph.D. 1987). He has also taught at Boston University and MIT.

Professor DeLong is also a research associate of the National Bureau of Economic Research and a visiting scholar at the Federal Reserve Bank of San Francisco. He has been coeditor of the *Journal of Economic Perspectives* since 1996.

Professor DeLong's research interests range from the origins of the Great Depression, to the effect of irrational speculation on stock market values, to whether there is a "new economy," and to, among other things, the causes of long-run economic divergence across nations. He is a prolific writer and has contributed more than 100 articles to publications ranging from the *American Economic Review to Fortune* and *Foreign Affairs* to the *New York Times*. His own web site, http://www.j-bradford-delong.net/, contains a great amount of material — including reviews of books and scholarly articles and analyses of current events — and is widely considered to be one of the best academic web sites on economics available.

Brad DeLong lives in Lafayette, California, with his wife and two children.

PREFACE

I wrote this book out of a sense that it was time for intermediate macroeconomics to spend time in drydock and have the barnacles scraped off its hull. It is more than three-quarters of a century since John Maynard Keynes wrote his *Tract on Monetary Reform,* which first linked inflation, production, employment, exchange rates, and policy together in a pattern that we today can recognize as "macroeconomics." It is two-thirds of a century since John Hicks and Alvin Hansen drew their IS and LM curves. It is more than one-third of a century since Milton Friedman and Ned Phelps demolished the static Phillips curve, and since Robert Lucas, Thomas Sargent, and Robert Barro taught us what rational expectations could mean. All this time, intermediate macroeconomics has become more complicated, as new material is added while old material remains.

It seemed to me that if I could successfully streamline the presentation of material, both traditional and modern, the result would be a more understandable and comprehensible book. I hope that I have succeeded — that this book does move more smoothly through the water than its competitors, and will prove to be a better textbook for third-millennium macroeconomics courses. This conclusion is based on five changes made in the standard presentation of modern macroeconomics. These changes are not radical; rather they are shifts in emphasis and changes of focus. They do not require recasting of courses, but they are very important in bringing the organization of the book into line with what students learning macroeconomics today need to know.

MAJOR INNOVATIONS

The first two changes have to do with *economic growth.*

◆ Provide a more student-friendly way of learning *growth theory.*

◆ Provide sufficient coverage of *growth facts* so that students learn the how and why of both growth over time and growth across countries.

The presentation of long-run growth — both the facts and the theory — in modern macroeconomics textbooks needs to be beefed up, and I have done so. Economic growth is worth much more than one or even two short chapters — here the growth chapters are among the longest in this book. Students have no business leaving macroeconomics courses without understanding the nature and causes of the wealth of nations. They need to see and understand broad cross-country and cross-time patterns: the industrial revolution, the spread of industrialization, the East Asian miracle, and the American century.

Too often undergraduates find the standard presentation of growth theory — with concepts like "output per effective worker" — to be confusing. The more understandable and robust presentation of growth theory in this book focuses on the economy's steady-state capital-output ratio, which is itself a very simple function of the proximate determinants of accumulation: savings rates, depreciation rates, population growth, and labor-augmenting technical change. To make the links between the fundamental determinants of growth and the workings of the economy simpler and more transparent is more than half the battle.

The third change, long overdue, has to do with the *open economy*.

◆ Treat the economy as open from the beginning of the book.

It is time to simply forget about the "closed-economy case" and ask students to analyze an open economy from the very beginning of the book. Even in the United States, virtually every economic policy issue and news event has an important international dimension. Presenting the closed-economy case first gives students a lot of wrong impressions — about the size of the Keynesian multiplier, about the freedom countries have to conduct independent monetary and fiscal policies, about the relationship between savings and investment — that then have to be unlearned in the "open economy macro" chapters. Moreover, moving the international material into the main narrative thread enhances streamlining. All of the "in the closed-economy chapters we said this, but really . . ." passages in the textbook are no longer needed. Throughout the book, save in Chapter 15, the default assumption is that the exchange rate is freely floating. This assumption was not true in the past and may not be true in the distant future, but it is true now and for the foreseeable future and is thus a reasonable working assumption.

The fourth change, also long overdue, has to do with *monetary policy*.

◆ Deal with interest rates, not money stocks.

In today's world, where central banks set interest rates but not money stocks, the LM curve's underlying assumption that the money stock is fixed is artificial. A major reason for giving the LM curve a central place is historical; it allows one to present the Keynesian-monetarist debate of the 1970s as a debate about the relative slopes of IS and LM curves. Steep LM curve or shallow IS curve and monetarists are right — the money stock is the principal determinant of output, unemployment, and inflation. Shallow LM or steep IS curve, and the Keynesians are right. (Never mind that Milton Friedman always thought that this was an unwise and unfair way of presenting the debate.)

However, this debate has been dead for a generation, and conducting much of the discussion of the determination of real GDP in a framework in which the money stock is fixed gives students the wrong intuitions. The LM curve cannot be eliminated: There are monetary regimes under which the central bank does not fix the interest rate. But it can be downplayed. It is much better to downplay the LM curve and focus on the key factors of the position of the IS curve and the real interest rate that is determined by the term structure and central bank policy. This brings the presentation in the textbook much closer to what students will find when they open up the *Wall Street Journal*. This makes our tasks as teachers much easier because there is no longer an artificial gap between the models taught and the actions seen in the world.

Furthermore, the space saved by downplaying the LM curve can be used for a serious discussion of the term structure of interest rates. The Federal Reserve controls short-term, nominal, safe interest rates; and the principal determinants of aggregate demand are long-term, real, risky interest rates. The slippage between these two is a limitation on the government's ability to stabilize the economy. Treating this topic seriously allows us to begin to teach the importance of expectations and the limits of policy relatively early in the book, rather than leaving these topics for the policy chapters at the book's end.

The fifth change has to do with the *Phillips curve* and *aggregate supply*.

◆ **Focus on the Phillips curve — not on the AS-AD diagram.**

The variable on the vertical axis of the aggregate supply–aggregate demand (AS-AD) graph — the price level — is not the best price variable to use in analyzing economic policy. The best price variable is the one on the vertical axis of the Phillips curve, the inflation rate. A very close integration of the AS-AD framework with the Phillips curve helps students follow the thread of the argument better and saves an enormous amount of repetition. After all, the Phillips curve "is" the AS curve with a couple of changes of variables. What point would be served by considering them separately, in different chapters?

Other shifts of emphasis and presentation include Chapter 3, "Thinking Like an Economist," which examines many things about how economists argue and reason that are usually left unexamined, and Chapter 12, "The Phillips Curve and Expectations," which explains that rational, adaptive, and static expectations are not incompatible, but rather different strategies for dealing with the problems of inflation — each of which can be useful in the right economic environment. This book has space for more thorough discussions of the term structure of interest rates and of the workings of international financial markets made possible by the streamlining measures mentioned.

PEDAGOGY

Much of the pedagogical work in this book is aimed at smoothing over what often turn out to be rough spots for the students. One important way that people learn is by watching other people solve problems, and then by repeating the process. Thus, students will note that this book contains a greater-than-usual number of worked examples. This will be especially helpful for those who hesitate before making conceptual leaps.

Boxes provided throughout the book try to reinforce the main narrative without disrupting it. They are an attempt to solve the perennial problem of how to provide additional depth and background to those who need (or want) it without boring or distracting those who wish to move on. *Macroeconomics* contains four kinds of boxes:

◆ *Tools* boxes remind students of some of the algebraic and conceptual tools economists use.

◆ *Details* boxes provide for those who want to dig deeper into a particular subject.

◆ *Policy* boxes provide for those who want to know how the current thread of the book affects the making of economic policy.

◆ *Examples* boxes show how the concepts, ideas, and models of the current main thread of the book can be applied.

To keep students focused on the forest as well as the trees, there are — at strategic points in each chapter — Recap "boxes." These Recaps attempt to put the main ideas of the previous section into a nutshell. They are themselves recapitulated in the end-of-chapter summaries, which are also designed to review the most important concepts presented in the chapter.

The extensive end-of-chapter exercises are divided into two sets, one that is tied to the theoretical material in the book — Analytical Exercises — and a second that is tied to recent events — Policy Exercises. It is important to have policy exercises at the ends of chapters, but since few things turn students off as much as exercises that are obsolete, we have tried to make them current in the book and we will add new ones to our dynamic web site.

And finally, the glossary provides fuller and deeper explanations of economics concepts than is typically found in other books. Once again, for some students such extended definitions are truly useful. And even the extended glossary takes up little space.

STRUCTURE

While the treatment of many, if not all, topics is unique, the structure of the book follows a standard pattern that has served macroeconomists well. **Part I** contains three chapters — Introduction, Measuring the Macroeconomy, and How Economists Think. **Chapter 1** begins with an overview of what macroeconomics is and then quickly focuses on six key variables that together allow one to gain a firm hold on the state of the macroeconomy. These variables are (1) real GDP, (2) the unemployment rate, (3) the inflation rate, (4) the interest rate, (5) the level of the stock market, and (6) the exchange rate. The chapter closes with a quick tour of recent macroeconomic events and macroeconomic policy dilemmas in the world, included both to pique student interest and to give them a sense of the kinds of questions and issues that macroeconomics is supposed to help resolve.

Chapter 2 provides the standard review of national income accounting and other measurement issues, organized around the six key economic variables of Chapter 1. The focus is on the quality of our measurements of these six key variables and what the measurements mean.

Chapter 3, arguably the most innovative material in this section, focuses on how economists view the world. It attempts to provide insight into the kind of "science" economics is and information on the dominance of the circular flow of economic activity in how macroeconomists view the world and on how economists go about building the models that they then use to try to analyze the macroeconomy.

Part II focuses on long-run growth and contains two chapters — The Theory of Economic Growth and The Reality of Economic Growth: History and Prospect. **Chapter 4** focuses on the simple-to-understand capital-output ratio (rather than the more complicated concept of capital-per-effective-worker), how the economy converges to its steady-state equilibrium capital-output ratio, and the effect of technological progress on productivity. Whereas most treatments of growth theory begin with a very artificial economy — no population growth, no technological progress — and do not achieve relative realism until near the end of the discussion, this chapter puts all the balls in play early on. Thus students are unlikely to acquire faulty intuitions about the relationships of economic variables that will plague them later.

Chapter 5 begins with a survey of very long-run economic growth before the industrial revolution, moves on to the industrial revolution itself, and then covers the astonishing economic growth in the United States over the past century and a half that has made America a remarkably rich and productive society from the standpoint of any previous century. It then shifts its focus to patterns of growth and development the world over — including the East Asian miracle, stagnation in Africa, and the convergence of the Organization for Economic Cooperation and Development (OECD) nations to common levels of productivity and industrial structure — before concluding with a discussion of economic policies and how they affect long-run growth. In a sense, Chapter 5 should be part of *everyone's* general education. It is, in summary and compressed form, an inquiry into the nature and causes of the wealth of nations. In my view, intermediate macroeconomics is the most natural place to provide this overview of long-run economic growth.

Part III presents flexible-price, business-cycle macroeconomics with two real-side chapters, Building Blocks of the Flexible-Price Model and Equilibrium in the Flexible-Price Model, and one money and inflation chapter — Money, Prices, and Inflation. Since many of the functions are the same in the flexible-price full-employment model of Part III and the sticky-price model of Part IV, the real-side chapters are written with an eye toward making it clear what changes and what doesn't when we move from flexible- to sticky-price models. **Chapter 6** covers the determination of potential output when wages and prices are flexible; the domestic components of aggregate demand — consumption, investment spending, and government purchases — and the determinants of the final component of aggregate demand, net exports.

Chapter 7 focuses first on how the demand and supply for loanable funds in the flow of funds through financial markets pushes the interest rate to the level at which investment demand equals savings supply, the economy is at full employment, and real GDP equals potential output. It then shows how to use the method of comparative statics to analyze the effects of changes in economic policy and the economic environment on the macroeconomy. It concludes with a section on supply shocks and on "real" business cycles, which are understood as fluctuations in current and expected future productivity and thus in the value of investment spending today.

Chapter 8 moves from the real to the monetary side in the flexible-price framework. It focuses first on the utility of money and on the simple interest–inelastic quantity theory, and it then moves on to consider the determinants of the price level and inflation when money demand is sensitive to the nominal interest rate.

Part IV's presentation of sticky-price macroeconomics is divided into four chapters — The Income-Expenditure Framework; Investment, Net Exports, and Interest Rates; Extending the Sticky-Price Model; and The Phillips Curve and Expectations. This material not only rounds out the sticky-price business-cycle framework but also reaches back to the previous section to explain under what circumstances flexible-price and under what circumstances sticky-price modeling is likely to be appropriate. **Chapter 9** provides the standard treatment of the sticky-price income-expenditure inventory-adjustment model. Its only innovative feature is that, because the model begins with the open-economy case, the calculated value of the multiplier is realistic, as opposed to the grossly inflated multiplier values calculated in closed-economy models with lump-sum taxes, something students then have to unlearn.

Chapter 10 then builds on Chapter 9 to construct the IS curve. An immediate payoff is that the last sections of Chapter 10 use the IS curve, along with changes in the Federal Reserve's interest rate targets, to help students understand macroeconomic fluctuations in the United States in the post–World War II period. It thus demonstrates that the models are actually useful and that they help us understand why the state of the business cycle went as it did in post–World War II America.

Chapter 11 performs three tasks. It asks what determines the interest rate when the Federal Reserve is not following a policy of interest-rate targeting, and then explains that the interest rate and aggregate demand are jointly determined by money demand and the money stock — together summarized in the LM curve — and by the IS curve. It goes on to analyze the impact of changes in the economic environment and economic policy on the exchange rate and the trade balance. It concludes by introducing the concepts of aggregate demand and aggregate supply.

Chapter 12 puts in place the keystone for Parts III and IV. It analyzes not just the determination of real GDP in the sticky-price framework, but also how prices change — how inflation is generated — by the state of aggregate demand relative to potential output. It presents the Phillips curve and the key determinants of the location of the Phillips curve: the natural rate of unemployment on the one hand, and the expected rate of inflation on the other. It then presents the three kinds of inflation expectations we expect to see — static, adaptive, and rational expectations of inflation — and the circumstances under which we expect to see each one. The chapter concludes by outlining the transition from the sticky-price short run to the flexible-price long run: It helps students consider under what circumstances the better answers are generated by using the flexible-price model of Part III, and under what circumstances the better answers are generated by the sticky-price model of Part IV.

Part V, which provides the payoff to all of this model-building work, begins with economic policy in three chapters — Stabilization Policy; The Budget Balance, the National Debt, and Investment; and International Economic Policy. This material allows students to think through the issues and to understand the debates about proper macroeconomic management, both for stabilization and for enhancing economic growth. **Chapter 13** deals with the institutions of macroeconomic policy, the power and limits of stabilization policy, monetary versus fiscal policy, rules versus authorities, and extreme situations such as financial crises.

Chapter 14 covers the government's budget and the government debt, outlining both short-run stabilization and long-run growth implications of the government's budget. And **Chapter 15** takes a look at how fixed exchange rate systems function and how exchange rate regimes have been chosen, and at currency crises.

These chapters are then followed by three more discussions that emphasize the extent to which macroeconomics is an unfinished science. **Chapter 16,** Changes in the Macroeconomy and Changes in Macroeconomic Policy, deals with the fact that because the macroeconomy changes over time, macroeconomists are always aiming at a moving target. **Chapter 17,** The Future of Macroeconomics, focuses on where macroeconomists disagree and on how the science is evolving, even in the absence of structural change in the macroeconomy. Finally, the **Epilogue** sums up the lessons of the book and reminds readers of what we do not know.

FLEXIBILITY

The material in the first section can be compressed to the extent that it truly is review material. However, with the exception of omitting the economic growth material — Chapters 4 and 5, which would be a shame — this book does not lend itself to reordering especially well. The introductory chapters are there for good reason, and the chain of logic and presentation from the start of the flexible-price model in Chapter 6 through the international economic policy discussion in Chapter 15 is a cumulative one.

In my classes I have occasionally shortchanged the chapters after 15, but I don't recommend it. While in government I had many conversations with smart people who could not see why the macroeconomics they had learned 35 years ago did not immediately apply. It proved remarkably hard to teach them that the world had changed and that the way macroeconomists thought about the world had changed. The historical perspectives provided in Chapters 16 and 17 and the Epilogue are (to my way of thinking, at least) worth the effort.

SUPPLEMENTS

◆ For the Instructor

Instructor's Manual Written by David DeJong at the University of Pittsburgh, this useful manual offers a number of general information elements — sample syllabi, web resources, print resources, and some mathematical background (with some homework problems/solutions) — along with the following elements for each chapter — Overview, Annotated Outline, Mathematical Tools, Teaching Tips, Answers to Textbook Exercises, Additional Exercises (and Answers), and Additional Readings.

Test Bank Written by Edward McNertney at Texas Christian University, this manual contains almost 1300 multiple-choice questions categorized by objective, level, type, and source. The print test bank is also available in the latest Diploma test-generating software, ensuring maximum flexibility in test preparation, including the reconfiguring of graphing exercises. This Brownstone program is the gold standard of testing programs.

PowerPoints Prepared by Linda Ghent at Eastern Illinois University, these more than 800 slides contain all of the illustrations from the textbook, along with a detailed, chapter-by-chapter review of the important ideas presented in the book.

Web site Overseen by Scott Simkins, a teacher at North Carolina A&T University who is deeply committed to using the web in the classroom, this site (www.mhhe.com/economics/delong) will contain a host of offerings helpful to all teachers, especially to younger ones — Better Ways to Teach Macro (suggestions for presenting a new approach), a Career Center, Economics on the Web (an annotated list of URLs useful to macroeconomists), a Graphing Library (graphs that can be used to create exercises), some Supplemental Materials (information too timely for the textbook), the entire Instructor's Manual and all the PowerPoints, and finally a link to Brad DeLong's extremely rich and diverse site.

◆ For the Student

Study Guide Prepared by Martha Olney at the University of California, Berkeley, each chapter in this guide begins with an overview and is followed by a set of matching exercises and multiple-choice questions under Basic Definitions. These are followed by two sets of exercises, Manipulation of Concepts and Models and Applying the Concepts and Models. This is followed by some problems for Explaining the Real World and a set of questions under the heading Possibilities to Ponder. Finally, answers and solutions are provided for all exercises and problems.

Software Prepared by Mark Reiman at Pacific Lutheran University, this Windows-based tutorial software allows students to solve exercises by moving graphs and manipulating data in dealing with three key models of macroeconomics — growth, AS/AD, and IS/LM.

Web site The site (www.mhhe.com/economics/delong) contains a host of offerings helpful to students — Quizzes (questions written by the test bank preparer), Graphing exercises (graphs that can be manipulated to solve exercises like those in the textbook), In the News (links to current news articles), Applying the Theory (exercises that test textbook mastery), Working with Data (exercises that help students understand how economists use data), Career Center (job opportunities in economics), Economics on the Web (an annotated list of URLs useful to macroeconomics students), and finally a link to Brad DeLong's extremely rich and diverse site.

ACKNOWLEDGMENTS

I would like to thank, first of all, my students in intermediate macroeconomics — both those who took my courses in years when they were successful and, even more, those who took my courses in years when they were not: Thinking about what went wrong and about why large groups of students did not get it has been a principal spur to this book.

I was privileged to have Martin Feldstein, Olivier Blanchard, and Thomas Sargent as my teachers in the first three macroeconomics courses that I ever took. I thought they were awesome then, and I still think so. I was also lucky enough to have Lawrence Summers as my dissertation advisor. I have surely learned more about macroeconomics from him than from any single other person. Here at Berkeley, those who have had the greatest impact on my macroeconomics teaching are Christina Romer, David Romer, and Marty Olney — especially David, whose powerful arguments about how to teach macroeconomics better I have always found convincing.

I would also like to thank the book team at McGraw-Hill for their professionalism, efficiency, and good humor: Paul Shensa, executive editor; Tom Thompson, development editor; Marty Quinn, marketing manager; Jim Labeots, project manager; Lori Koetters, production supervisor; Matthew Baldwin, designer; and Melissa Kansa, media producer.

Finally, I would like to thank the following reviewers for their excellent suggestions:

David DeJong, *University of Pittsburgh*

Peter Frevert, *University of Kansas*

Michelle Garfinkel, *University of California, Irvine*

Linda Ghent, *Eastern Illinois University*

Barry Haworth, *University of Louisville*

Daniel Himarios, *University of Texas, Arlington*

Barney Hope, *California State University, Chico*

Ruby Kishan, *Southwest Texas State University*

John Lapp, *North Carolina State University*

Anthony Lima, *California State University, Hayward*

Steven McCafferty, *The Ohio State University*

Douglas McMillin, *Louisiana State University*

Starr McMullin, *Oregon State University*

Edward McNertney, *Texas Christian University*

Michael McPherson, *University of North Texas*

Rowena Pecchenino, *Michigan State University*

Uri Possen, *Cornell University*

Plutarchos Sakellaris, *University of Maryland*

Brian Trinque, *University of Texas, Austin*

Anne Villamil, *University of Illinois*

Ping Wang, *Vanderbilt University*

Mark Wohar, *University of Nebraska, Omaha*

Robert Wright, *University of Sterling (UK)*

Jeffrey Zax, *University of Colorado, Boulder*

BRIEF CONTENTS

PART I **PRELIMINARIES**

1 Introduction to Macroeconomics 3

2 Measuring the Macroeconomy 27

3 Thinking Like an Economist 59

PART II **LONG-RUN ECONOMIC GROWTH**

4 The Theory of Economic Growth 87

5 The Reality of Economic Growth: History and Prospect 119

PART III **FLEXIBLE-PRICE MACROECONOMICS**

6 Building Blocks of the Flexible-Price Model 153

Appendix 6A A Closer Look at Consumption 177

Appendix 6B Present Value and Investment 183

7 Equilibrium in the Flexible-Price Model 185

8 Money, Prices, and Inflation 217

PART IV **STICKY-PRICE MACROECONOMICS**

9 The Income-Expenditure Framework: Consumption and the Multiplier 239

10 Investment, Net Exports, and Interest Rates 269

Appendix 10A The Term Premium and Expected Future Interest Rates 295

11 Extending the Sticky-Price Model: More Analytical Tools 299

12 The Phillips Curve and Expectations 329

PART V **MACROECONOMIC POLICY**

13 Stabilization Policy 359

14 The Budget Balance, the National Debt, and Investment 391

15 International Economic Policy 411

16 Changes in the Macroeconomy and Changes in Macroeconomic Policy 439

17 The Future of Macroeconomics 463

Epilogue 477

Glossary 484

Index 508

CONTENTS

PART I PRELIMINARIES

CHAPTER 1
Introduction to Macroeconomics 3
1.1 **Overview** 4
  What Is Macroeconomics? 4
  BOX 1.1 Economic Policy and Political Popularity: Policy 6
  Macroeconomic Policy 6
  BOX 1.2 Macroeconomic Policy and Your Quality of Life: Data 9
  Macroeconomics versus Microeconomics 9
1.2 **Tracking the Macroeconomy** 10
  Economic Statistics and Economic Activity 10
  Six Key Variables 12
  BOX 1.3 U.S. Real GDP per Worker: Data 13
  BOX 1.4 The U.S. Unemployment Rate in the Twentieth Century: Data 15
  BOX 1.5 U.S. Inflation Rates in the Twentieth Century: Data 16
  BOX 1.6 Real Interest Rates: Data 18
  BOX 1.7 The Stock Market: Data 19
  BOX 1.8 The Exchange Rate: Details 20
1.3 **The Current Macroeconomic Situation** 22
  The United States 22
  Europe 23
  Japan 24
  Emerging Markets 25
  Chapter Summary 26
  Key Terms 26
  Analytical Exercises 26
  Policy Exercises 26

CHAPTER 2
Measuring the Macroeconomy 27
2.1 **The Importance of Data** 28
2.2 **The Exchange Rate** 29
  Nominal versus Real Exchange Rates 29
  The Real Exchange Rate 31
  BOX 2.1 Calculating the Real Exchange Rate: An Example 31
2.3 **The Stock Market and Interest Rates** 34
  The Stock Market 34
  Interest Rates 37
  BOX 2.2 Calculating Real Interest Rates: An Example 38
  BOX 2.3 Some Useful Mathematical Tools: Tools 39
2.4 **The Price Level and Inflation** 40
  The Consumer Price Index 40
  Kinds of Index Numbers 40
  BOX 2.4 Calculating Price Indexes: An Example 41
  BOX 2.5 Laspeyres and Paasche Index Numbers: The Details 42
  The Inflation Rate 43
2.5 **Unemployment** 44
  Calculating the Unemployment Rate 44
  Okun's Law 46
  BOX 2.6 Why the Okun's Law Coefficient Is So Large: The Details 48
2.6 **Real GDP** 48
  Calculating Real GDP 49
  Real and Nominal GDP 49
  BOX 2.7 Weighting Goods and Services by Their Market Values: An Example 50

Intermediate Goods, Inventories and
Imputations   50

BOX 2.8 Weighting Goods and
Services by Their Base-Year Values:
An Example   51

Components of Real GDP   53

What Is and Is Not in GDP   54

Chapter Summary   57

Key Terms   57

Analytical Exercises   57

Policy Exercises   58

CHAPTER 3

Thinking Like an Economist   59

3.1   **Understanding Macroeconomics**   60

Economics: Is It a Science?   60

BOX 3.1 Expectations and the
Coming of the Great Depression:
An Example   61

Reliance on Quantitative Models   62

3.2   **The Circular Flow of Economic Activity**   65

The Circular Flow Diagram   65

Different Measures of the Circular Flow   67

BOX 3.2 Accounting Deficiencies and
Statistical Discrepancies: Tools   68

3.3   **Rhetoric Continued: Patterns of Economists'
Thought**   69

Markets   70

Equilibrium   70

Graphs and Equations   70

Building Models   72

Solving Economic Models   73

BOX 3.3 The Production Function: An Example
of a Behavioral Relationship   74

BOX 3.4 Working with Exponents: Some
Tools   75

BOX 3.5 A Sample Equilibrium Condition—The
Capital-Output Ratio: An Example   76

BOX 3.6 Using Arithmetic to Determine
Steady-State Output per Worker: An
Example   77

BOX 3.7 Using Algebra to Determine
Steady-State Output per Worker:
An Example   78

BOX 3.8 Using Graphs and Geometry to
Determine Steady-State Output per Worker:
An Example   79

Chapter Summary   84

Key Terms   84

Analytical Exercises   84

PART II   LONG-RUN ECONOMIC GROWTH

CHAPTER 4

The Theory of Economic Growth   87

4.1   **Sources of Long-Run Growth**   88

Better Technology   88

Capital Intensity   89

4.2   **The Standard Growth Model**   89

The Production Function   90

BOX 4.1 Using the Production Function:
An Example   93

The Rest of the Growth Model   93

BOX 4.2 Investment, Depreciation, and Capital
Accumulation: An Example   96

4.3   **Understanding the Growth Model**   97

How Fast Is the Economy Growing?   98

BOX 4.3 The Growth of Capital per Worker:
An Example   99

BOX 4.4 The Growth of Output per Worker:
An Example   102

Steady-State Growth Equilibrium   103

BOX 4.5 Where the Growth Multiplier Comes
From: The Details   108

BOX 4.6 Converging to the Steady-State
Balanced-Growth Path: An Example   110

Determining the Steady-State Capital-Output
Ratio   111

BOX 4.7 An Increase in Population Growth:
An Example   111

BOX 4.8 An Increase in the Savings Rate:
An Example   114

Chapter Summary   116

Key Terms   116

Analytical Exercises   116

Policy Exercises   117

CHAPTER 5

**The Reality of Economic Growth: History
and Prospect**   119

5.1   **Before Modern Economic Growth**   120

Before the Industrial Revolution   120

Premodern Economic "Growth"   121

The End of the Malthusian Age   122

5.2   **Modern American Economic Growth**   125

American Long-Run Growth, 1800–1973   125

American Economic Growth Since 1973   128

BOX 5.1 Have Real Standards of Living Been Declining?: The Details   130

5.3   **Modern Economic Growth around the World**   132

Divergence, Big Time   132

BOX 5.2 Purchasing-Power-Parity and Real Exchange Rate Comparisons: Some Tools   134

BOX 5.3 Why Have These Economies Converged?: A Policy   135

BOX 5.4 The East Asian Miracle: A Policy   137

BOX 5.5 Postcommunism: A Policy   138

Sources of Divergence   139

Cause and Effect, Effect and Cause   141

5.4   **Policies and Long-Run Growth**   142

Hopes for Convergence   142

Policies for Saving, Investment, and Education   143

Policies for Technological Advance   144

Will Governments Follow Good Policies?   146

Chapter Summary   148

Key Terms   148

Analytical Exercises   148

Policy Exercises   149

PART III FLEXIBLE-PRICE MACROECONOMICS

CHAPTER 6
Building Blocks of the Flexible-Price Model   153

6.1   **Potential Output and Real Wages**   154

The Production Function   154

The Labor Market   156

6.2   **Domestic Spending**   161

Consumption Spending   161

BOX 6.1 Calculating Consumption from Income: An Example   164

Investment Spending   165

BOX 6.2 What Is Investment? Some Details   165

BOX 6.3 Kinds of Investment: Some Details   165

BOX 6.4 How Investment Responds to a Change in Interest Rates: An Example   167

BOX 6.5 The Stock Market: Some Details   168

BOX 6.6 How to Boost Investment: A Policy Issue   168

Government Purchases   169

6.3   **International Trade**   170

Gross Exports   171

BOX 6.7 The J-Curve: Some Details   172

Imports and Net Exports   172

The Exchange Rate   173

6.4   **Conclusion**   175

Chapter Summary   175

Key Terms   176

Analytical Exercises   176

Policy Exercises   176

Appendix 6A A Closer Look at Consumption   177

Appendix 6B Present Value and Investment   183

CHAPTER 7
Equilibrium in the Flexible-Price Model   185

7.1   **Full-Employment Equilibrium**   186

Equilibrium and the Real Interest Rate   186

The Flow of Funds through Financial Markets   187

BOX 7.1 Financial Transactions and the Flow of Funds: Some Details   188

Flow-of-Funds Equilibrium   189

BOX 7.2 Solving for and Verifying the Equilibrium Real Interest Rate: An Example   191

7.2   **Using the Model**   193

Comparative Statics as a Method of Analysis   193

Changes in Fiscal Policy   194

BOX 7.3 A Government Purchases Boom: An Example   197

Investment Shocks: Changes in Investors'
Optimism   199

International Disturbances   200

BOX 7.4 The Effect of a Fall in Confidence in
the Currency: An Example   205

BOX 7.5 The Mexican and East Asian Financial
Crises: Policy Issues   206

7.3   **Supply Shocks**   207

Oil and Other Supply Shocks   207

Real Business Cycles   209

7.4   **Conclusion**   212

Chapter Summary   213

Key Terms   213

Analytical Exercises   214

Policy Exercises   214

CHAPTER 8
Money, Prices, and Inflation   217

8.1   **Money**   218

Money: Liquid Wealth That Can Be
Spent   219

The Usefulness of Money   220

Units of Account   220

8.2   **The Quantity Theory of Money**   221

The Demand for Money   221

The Quantity Equation   222

Money and Prices   222

BOX 8.1 Calculating the Price Level from the
Quantity Equation: An Example   224

BOX 8.2 Different Definitions of the Money
Stock: Some Details   225

Inflation   226

8.3   **The Interest Rate and Money
Demand**   228

Money Demand   228

Money, Prices and Inflation   229

8.4   **The Costs of Inflation**   231

The Costs of Moderate Expected
Inflation   232

The Costs of Moderate Unexpected
Inflation   232

Hyperinflation and Its Costs   233

Chapter Summary   235

Key Terms   235

Analytical Exercises   236

Policy Exercises   236

**PART IV   STICKY-PRICE
MACROECONOMICS**

CHAPTER 9
**The Income-Expenditure Framework:
Consumption and the Multiplier**   239

9.1   **Sticky Prices**   241

Business Cycles   241

The Consequences of Sticky Prices   242

Why Are Prices Sticky?   246

9.2   **Income and Expenditure**   248

Building Up Aggregate Demand   248

BOX 9.1 Calculating the Consumption
Function: An Example   251

BOX 9.2 Calculating the MPE: An
Example   254

Sticky Price Equilibrium   255

BOX 9.3 How Fast Does the Economy Move
to Equilibrium?: Some Details   258

BOX 9.4 Inventory Adjustment and the
Circular Flow: Some Details   259

BOX 9.5 Calculating the Difference
between Aggregate Demand and Real GDP:
An Example   260

9.3   **The Multiplier**   261

Determining the Size of the Multiplier   261

BOX 9.6 The Value of the Multiplier: An
Example   263

Changing the Size of the Multiplier   264

Chapter Summary   265

Key Terms   266

Analytical Exercises   266

Policy Exercises   267

CHAPTER 10
**Investment, Net Exports, and Interest
Rates**   269

10.1   **Interest Rates and Aggregate
Demand**   270

The Importance of Investment   270

Investment and the Real Interest Rate   271

BOX 10.1 The Stock Market as an
Indicator of Future Investment: Some
Tools   275

Exports and Autonomous Spending   275

10.2 The IS Curve 277

Autonomous Spending and the Real Interest Rate 277

From the Interest Rate to Investment to Aggregate Demand 277

The Slope and Position of the IS Curve 280

BOX 10.2 Calculating the Dependence of Aggregate Demand on the Interest Rate: An Example 281

10.3 Using the IS Curve to Understand the Economy 283

Shifting the IS Curve 283

BOX 10.3 A Government Spending Increase and the IS Curve: An Example 283

Moving Along the IS Curve 284

BOX 10.4 Moving Along the IS Curve: An Example 284

Economic Fluctuations in the United States: The IS Curve as a Lens 287

Chapter Summary 292

Key Terms 293

Analytical Exercises 293

Policy Exercises 293

Appendix 10A The Term Premium and Expected Future Interest Rates 295

CHAPTER 11

Extending the Sticky-Price Model: More Analytical Tools 299

11.1 The Money Stock and the Money Market: The LM Curve 300

Money Market Equilibrium 300

The LM Curve 302

The IS-LM Framework 304

BOX 11.1 IS-LM Equilibrium: An Example 304

BOX 11.2 An IS Shock: An Example 306

BOX 11.3 Calculating the Effect of an LM Shock: An Example 308

Classifying Economic Disturbances 310

11.2 The Exchange Rate and the Trade Balance 313

The IS-LM Framework and the International Sector 313

BOX 11.4 An LM Shock and the Balance of Trade: An Example 315

International Shocks and the Domestic Economy 316

BOX 11.5 A Change in International Investors' Expectations: An Example 318

11.3 Aggregate Demand 320

The Price Level and Aggregate Demand 320

Monetary Policy and Aggregate Demand 322

11.4 Aggregate Supply 324

Output and the Price Level 324

Short-Run Aggregate Supply 326

Chapter Summary 327

Key Terms 327

Analytical Exercises 327

Policy Exercises 328

CHAPTER 12

The Phillips Curve and Expectations 329

12.1 Aggregate Supply and the Phillips Curve 330

Unemployment 330

BOX 12.1 Forms of Okun's Law: A Tool 330

BOX 12.2 Costs of High Unemployment: Policy Issues 331

Three Faces of Aggregate Supply 332

The Phillips Curve Examined 333

12.2 Aggregate Demand and Inflation 336

BOX 12.3 From Income-Expenditure to the Phillips Curve and the MPRF: Some Details 337

BOX 12.4 Solving for Equilibrium Inflation and Unemployment: Some Details 338

12.3 The Natural Rate of Unemployment 340

Demography and the Natural Rate 341

Institutions and the Natural Rate 341

Productivity Growth and the Natural Rate 341

The Past Level of Unemployment and the Natural Rate 342

12.4 Expected Inflation 343

The Phillips Curve under Static Expectations 344

BOX 12.5 Static Expectations of Inflation in the 1960s: An Example 345

The Phillips Curve under Adaptive Expectations 345

BOX 12.6 A High-Pressure Economy under Adaptive Expectations: An Example 346

BOX 12.7 Adaptive Expectations and the Volcker Disinflation: Policy Issues 347

The Phillips Curve under Rational Expectations 348

What Kind of Expectations Do We Have? 350

12.5 From the (Sticky Price) Short Run to the (Flexible Price) Long Run 352

Rational Expectations 352

Adaptive Expectations 353

Static Expectations 354

Chapter Summary 354

Key Terms 355

Analytical Exercises 355

Policy Exercises 355

PART V   MACROECONOMIC POLICY

CHAPTER 13
Stabilization Policy 359

13.1 Economic Policy Institutions 360

Monetary Policy Institutions 360

BOX 13.1 Japan's Liquidity Trap: A Policy 363

Fiscal Policy Institutions 364

The History of Economic Policy 367

13.2 The Power and Limits of Stabilization Policy 370

BOX 13.2 The Structure of the Economy and the Lucas Critique: The Details 370

Uncertainty about the Economy 371

BOX 13.3 What Are Leading Indicators? The Details 372

The Money Supply as a Leading Indicator 372

BOX 13.4 The Money Multiplier: A Policy 373

Long Lags and Variable Effects 375

BOX 13.5 The Limits of Stabilization Policy: A Policy 376

13.3 Monetary versus Fiscal Policy 377

Relative Power 377

BOX 13.6 The Kennedy-Johnson and the Reagan Tax Cuts: A Policy 378

Fiscal Policy: Automatic Stabilizers 378

How Monetary Policy Works 379

BOX 13.7 Monetary Policy Instruments: A Policy 379

13.4 Rules versus Authorities 380

Competence and Objectives 380

BOX 13.8 The Political Business Cycle and Richard Nixon: A Policy 381

BOX 13.9 Is There a Political Business Cycle? The Details 382

BOX 13.10 Central Bank Independence: A Policy 383

Credibility and Commitment 384

Modern Monetary Policy 385

13.5 Extreme Situations: Financial Crises 386

Lenders of Last Resort 387

Deposit Insurance and Moral Hazard 388

Chapter Summary 389

Key Terms 389

Analytical Exercises 390

Policy Exercises 390

CHAPTER 14
The Budget Balance, the National Debt, and Investment 391

14.1 Introduction 392

14.2 The Budget Deficit and Stabilization Policy 392

The Budget Deficit and the IS Curve 392

BOX 14.1 The Deficit as an Index of Fiscal Policy: The Details 393

Measuring the Budget Balance 394

14.3 Measuring the Debt and the Deficit 396

Inflation 396

Public Investment 397

Liabilities and Generational Accounting 398

14.4 Analyzing Debts and Deficits 398

Sustainability 398

BOX 14.2 The Equilibrium Debt-to-GDP Ratio: An Example 399

Effects of Deficits 401

BOX 14.3 The U.S. Debt-to-GDP Ratio: The Details 402

Long-Run Effects of Deficits 405

Chapter Summary 408

Key Terms 409

Analytical Exercises   409
Policy Exercises   409

CHAPTER 15
International Economic Policy   411
15.1 The History of Exchange Rates   412
The Classical Gold Standard   412
BOX 15.1 Currency Arbitrage under the Gold Standard: An Example   413
The Collapse of the Gold Standard   416
The Bretton Woods System   417
Our Current Floating-Rate System   418
15.2 How a Fixed Exchange Rate System Works   419
High Capital Mobility   419
Barriers to Capital Mobility   422
15.3 The Choice of Exchange Rate Systems   424
Benefits of Fixed Exchange Rates   424
Costs of Fixed Exchange Rates   425
BOX 15.2 Are Western Europe and the United States Optimal Currency Areas?: An Example   425
15.4 Currency Crises   427
The European Crisis of 1992   427
The Mexican Crisis of 1994–1995   429
The East Asian Crisis of 1997–1998   432
Managing Crises   434
Chapter Summary   437
Key Terms   437
Analytical Exercises   438
Policy Exercises   438

CHAPTER 16
Changes in the Macroeconomy and Changes in Macroeconomic Policy   439
16.1 Changes in the Macroeconomy   440
The Past   440
Future Changes   442
16.2 The History of Macroeconomic Fluctuations   445
Estimating Long-Run Changes in Cyclical Volatility   445
Economic Policy   447
The Great Depression   450

16.3 Macroeconomic Policy: Lessons Learned   453
Stabilization   453
Learning   454
Prospects   454
16.4 Macroeconomic Policy: Lessons Un- or Half-Learned   455
Lessons Unlearned: High European Unemployment   455
Lessons Half-Learned: Japanese Stagnation   458
Lessons Half-Learned: Moral Hazard   459
The Ultimate Lesson   460
Chapter Summary   461
Key Terms   461
Analytical Exercises   462
Policy Exercises   462

CHAPTER 17
The Future of Macroeconomics   463
17.1 The Past of Macroeconomics   464
The Age of John Maynard Keynes   464
The Age of Milton Friedman and Robert Lucas   464
17.2 The Future of Macroeconomics: "Real" Business Cycles   466
One Possible Road   466
The Unevenness of Economic Growth   467
Problems of Real-Business-Cycle Theory   468
Assessment   469
17.3 The Future: New Keynesian Economics   470
Menu Costs   471
Staggered Prices and Coordination Failures   471
Assessment   472
17.4 Debts and Deficits, Consumption and Saving   472
Debts and Deficits: Ricardian Equivalence   472
Consumption and Saving   474
17.5 Does Monetary Policy Have a Long-Run Future?   475
Chapter Summary   476
Key Terms   476
Analytical Exercises   476

Epilogue 477

What Economists Know . . . 478

. . . About the Current State of the
Economy 478

. . . About Long-Run Economic Growth 478

. . . About Business Cycles, Unemployment, and
Inflation in the Long Run 479

. . . About Business Cycles, Unemployment, and
Inflation in the Short Run 480

. . . About the Making of Macroeconomic
Policy 480

**What Economists Don't Know — But Could
Learn** 481

. . . About the Long-Run Relationship
between Kinds of Investment and Productivity
Growth 481

. . . About the Short-Run Determinants of
Investment 481

. . . About the Impact of Government Policy on
the Economy 482

. . . About the Microfoundations of
Macroeconomics 482

What Economists Will Never Know 482

Chasing an Ever-Moving Target 482

Glossary 484

Index 508

LIST OF BOXES

Policy ◆

1.1 Economic Policy and Political Popularity: Policy   6

5.3 Why Have These Economies Converged? A Policy   135

5.4 The East Asian Miracle: A Policy   137

5.5 Postcommunism: A Policy   138

6.6 How to Boost Investment: A Policy Issue   168

7.5 The Mexican and East Asian Financial Crises: Policy Issues   206

12.2 Costs of High Unemployment: Policy Issues   331

12.7 Adaptive Expectations and the Volcker Disinflation: Policy Issues   347

13.1 Japan's Liquidity Trap: A Policy   363

13.5 The Limits of Stabilization Policy: A Policy   376

13.6 The Kennedy-Johnson and the Reagan Tax Cuts: A Policy   378

13.7 Monetary Policy Instruments: A Policy   379

13.8 The Political Business Cycle and Richard Nixon: A Policy   381

13.10 Central Bank Independence: A Policy   383

Tools ◆

2.3 Some Useful Mathematical Tools: Tools   39

3.2 Accounting Deficiencies and Statistical Discrepancies: Tools   68

3.4 Working with Exponents: Some Tools   75

5.2 Purchasing-Power-Parity and Real Exchange Rate Comparisons: Some Tools   134

10.1 The Stock Market as an Indicator of Future Investment: Some Tools   275

12.1 Forms of Okun's Law: A Tool   330

Details ◆

1.8 The Exchange Rate: Details   20

2.5 Laspeyres and Paasche Index Numbers: The Details   42

2.6 Why the Okun's Law Coefficient Is So Large: The Details   48

4.5 Where the Growth Multiplier Comes From: The Details   108

5.1 Have Real Standards of Living Been Declining? The Details   132

6.2 What Is Investment? Some Details   165

6.3 Kinds of Investment: Some Details   165

6.5 The Stock Market: Some Details   168

6.7 The J-Curve: Some Details   172

7.1 Financial Transactions and the Flow of Funds: Some Details   188

8.2 Different Definitions of the Money Stock: Some Details   225

9.3 How Fast Does the Economy Move to Equilibrium? Some Details   258

9.4 Inventory Adjustment and the Circular Flow: Some Details   259

12.3 From Income-Expenditure to the Phillips Curve and the MPRF: Some Details   337

12.4 Solving for Equilibrium Inflation and Unemployment: Some Details   338

13.2 The Structure of the Economy and the Lucas Critique: The Details   370

13.3 What Are Leading Indicators? The Details   372

13.4 The Money Multiplier: Details   373

13.9 Is There a Political Business Cycle? The Details   382

14.1 The Deficit as an Index of Fiscal Policy: The Details   393

14.3 The U.S. Debt-to-GDP Ratio: The Details   402

Data ◆

1.2 Macroeconomic Policy and Your Quality of Life: Data   9

1.3 U.S. Real GDP per Worker: Data   13

1.4 The U.S. Unemployment Rate in the Twentieth Century: Data   15

1.5 U.S. Inflation Rates in the Twentieth Century: Data   16

1.6 Real Interest Rates: Data   18

1.7 The Stock Market: Data   19

Examples ◆

2.1 Calculating the Real Exchange Rate: An Example   31

2.2 Calculating Real Interest Rates: An Example   38

2.4 Calculating Price Indexes: An Example   41

2.7   Weighting Goods and Services by Their Market Values: An Example   50

2.8   Weighting Goods and Services by Their Base-Year Values: An Example   51

3.1   Expectations and the Coming of the Great Depression: An Example   61

3.3   The Production Function: An Example of a Behavioral Relationship   74

3.5   A Sample Equilibrium Condition—The Capital-Output Ratio: An Example   76

3.6   Using Arithmetic to Determine Steady-State Output per Worker: An Example   77

3.7   Using Algebra to Determine Steady-State Output per Worker: An Example   78

3.8   Using Graphs and Geometry to Determine Steady-State Output per Worker: An Example   79

4.1   Using the Production Function: An Example   93

4.2   Investment, Depreciation, and Capital Accumulation: An Example   96

4.3   The Growth of Capital per Worker: An Example   99

4.4   The Growth of Output per Worker: An Example   102

4.6   Converging to the Steady-State Balanced-Growth Path: An Example   110

4.7   An Increase in Population Growth: An Example   111

4.8   An Increase in the Savings Rate: An Example   114

6.1   Calculating Consumption from Income: An Example   164

6.4   How Investment Responds to a Change in Interest Rates: An Example   167

7.2   Solving for and Verifying the Equilibrium Real Interest Rate: An Example   191

7.3   A Government Purchases Boom: An Example   197

7.4   The Effect of a Fall in Confidence in the Currency: An Example   205

8.1   Calculating the Price Level from the Quantity Equation: An Example   224

9.1   Calculating the Consumption Function: An Example   251

9.2   Calculating the MPE: An Example   254

9.5   Calculating the Difference between Aggregate Demand and Real GDP: An Example   260

9.6   The Value of the Multiplier: An Example   263

10.2   Calculating the Dependence of Aggregate Demand on the Interest Rate: An Example   281

10.3   A Government Spending Increase and the IS Curve: An Example   283

10.4   Moving Along the IS Curve: An Example   284

11.1   IS-LM Equilibrium: An Example   304

11.2   An IS Shock: An Example   306

11.3   Calculating the Effect of an LM Shock: An Example   308

11.4   An LM Shock and the Balance of Trade: An Example   315

11.5   A Change in International Investors' Expectations: An Example   318

12.5   Static Expectations of Inflation in the 1960s: An Example   345

12.6   A High-Pressure Economy under Adaptive Expectations: An Example   346

14.2   The Equilibrium Debt-to-GDP Ratio: An Example   399

15.1   Currency Arbitrage under the Gold Standard: An Example   413

15.2   Are Western Europe and the United States Optimal Currency Areas? An Example   425

Preliminaries

Intermediate macroeconomics books usually begin with some preliminary information, and this one is no exception. It begins with an overview of the subject (Chapter 1) that is intended to provide an orientation to the discipline. You need to know, for example, that the field of macroeconomics studies total economic activity, the total number of people employed, and why the overall price level rises and falls.

This information is followed by an overview of the data used by macroeconomists (Chapter 2). Students and other readers need to know what these data are and how they fit together in the national income and product accounts before they can properly begin using the data to understand the state of the economy.

The third preliminary chapter (Chapter 3) is titled "Thinking Like an Economist." Every subject has its own particular patterns of thought and fundamental assumptions — characteristics that make it a separate discipline worth learning. Economists' patterns of thought, however, seem to be difficult for many who are new to the discipline to grasp — perhaps these patterns are, in some way, further from normal day-to-day experience than are those of other disciplines. In any case, Chapter 3 offers a brief introduction to how economists think: their use of abstraction, model building, and of concepts like opportunity cost and rational expectations.

Introduction to Macroeconomics

CHAPTER 1

QUESTIONS

How much richer are we than our parents were at our age?

How much richer will our children be than our grandparents were?

Will changing jobs be easy or hard in five years?

How many of us will *have* jobs in five years?

Will the businesses we work for vanish as demand for the products they make dries up?

Will inflation make us poor by destroying our savings or rich by eliminating our debts?

1.1 OVERVIEW

What Is Macroeconomics?

What exactly is macroeconomics? **Macroeconomics** is the subdiscipline of economics that tries to answer the six questions that begin this chapter. Answers to all these questions depend on what is happening to the economy as a whole, the economy in the large, the *macroeconomy*. "Macro" is, after all, nothing but a prefix for "large." Thus macroeconomics is the branch of economics related to the economy as a whole.

Macroeconomists' principal task is to try to figure out why overall economic activity rises and falls. Why are measures like the total value of all production, the total income of workers and property owners, the total number of people employed, or the unemployment rate higher in some years than in others? Macroeconomists also attempt to understand what determines the level and rate of change of overall prices. The proportional rate of change in the price level has a name you have undoubtedly heard thousands of times: the *inflation rate*. Finally, along the way macroeconomists study other variables — such as interest rates, stock market values, and exchange rates — that play a major role in determining the overall levels of production, income, employment, and prices.

Why Macroeconomics Matters

Why does macroeconomics matter? Why should we care about the questions at the heart of macroeconomics? There are at least three reasons.

Cultural Literacy   First (but least important), macroeconomics is a matter of cultural literacy. Much discussion in newspapers, on television, and at parties concerns the macroeconomy. This should not be surprising: The twentieth-century U.S. economy was, all in all, extraordinarily successful. Today we are on average some 50 percent richer than our parents were when they were our age. If economic growth continues at its recent pace, our children may be five or more times as rich as our grandparents were.

Our modern industrial economy has delivered increases in material prosperity and living standards that no previous generation ever saw. (We discuss this topic at greater length in Chapter 5.) This increasing material prosperity means that the economy has a cultural salience today that it did not have in previous centuries, when productivity was stagnant and material standards of living improved only as fast as a glacier moves.

Thus, if you want to follow and participate in public debates and discussions, you need to know about macroeconomics. If you don't, you won't understand news reports on changes in the economy, such as those listed in Figure 1.1.

Self-Interest   A second (and more important) reason to care about macroeconomics is that the macroeconomy matters to you personally. Each of us is interested in particular issues in *micro*economics. Farmers and bakers are interested in the price of wheat; computer manufacturers and users are interested in the price of microprocessors; and one of us is *very* interested in the price of economics professors. What happens in these individual markets — for wheat, for microprocessors, and for economics professors — shapes the lives of farmers, bakers, computer programmers, and economics professors.

FIGURE 1.1
The Daily Flow of Economic News
Economic news flows past us constantly throughout the day. The total volume of information is overwhelming. Thus one of the major problems of macroeconomics is figuring out how to process all this information — how to make sense of it without drowning in information overload and without throwing valuable news away.

Economies

Thu, 24 May 2001, 10:18am EDT

U.S. Initial Jobless Claims Rise; Number of People Getting Benefits Surges . . .
Taiwan Growth May Be Slowest in 26 Years; Yageo, Others Cutting Workforces...
U.S. Housing Market's Busy Season Shows Few Signs of Slowing as Rates Fall . . .
U.K.'s CBI Lowers Forecast for Growth This Year to 2.1% From Earlier 2.5% . . .
Philippines Central Bank Leaves Key Overnight Interest Rates Unchanged . . .
Japan May Seek to Stem `Inappropriate' Yen Gains, Finance Official Says . . .
German, French Economies Expanded Less Than Expected in First Quarter . . .
Japan's Miyashita Says Proposed Capital Gains Tax Cut Won't Happen Soon . . .
AOL, Internet Service Providers to Benefit From Senate Tax Bill Amendment . . .
U.S. April New Home Sales Fall 9.5%, Signals Emerging Caution Among Buyers . . .
ConAgra to Restate Three Years of Results for False Accounting; SEC Probes . . .
U.S. Stocks Rise, Led by General Electric, Citigroup; Veritas Software Up . . .
Pride International to Acquire Marine Drilling for $1.92 Billion in Stock . . .
Treasuries Gain as Jobless Claims Report Boosts Expectations for Rate Cut . . .
Xoma, Genentech Xanelim Drug Appears to Ease Psoriasis Symptoms in Study . . .
Euro Strengthens on Speculation Central Banks Will Support It After Slide . . .
American Eagle First-Quarter Profit Rises 23% on Higher Sales of Clothing . . .
Gasoline Reaches Record High on Decline in U.S. Supplies of Cleaner Fuel . . .
Ford, Bridgestone/Firestone Attack the Safety of One Another's Products . . .
Argentine Buyout Baron Juan Navarro Looks for Purchases as Economy Slumps . . .

Source: Bloomberg Financial News. www.bloomberg.com/bbn/index.html. May 24, 2001.

What happens in the macroeconomy shapes *everyone's* life. A rise in inflation is sure to enrich debtors (people who have borrowed) and impoverish creditors (people who have lent money to others). An expanding economy will make real incomes rise. A deep recession will increase unemployment and make those who lose their jobs have a hard time finding others. Your bargaining power vis-à-vis your employer (or, on the other side of the table, your bargaining power vis-à-vis your employees) depends on the phase of the business cycle.

Though you cannot control the macroeconomy, you can understand how it affects your opportunities. To some degree, forewarned is forearmed: Whether or not you understand your opportunities may depend on how much attention you pay in this course. The macroeconomy is not destiny: Some people do very well in their jobs and businesses in a recession, and many do badly in a boom. Nevertheless, it is a powerful influence on individual well-being. To paraphrase Russian revolutionary Leon Trotsky, you may not be interested in the macroeconomy, but the macroeconomy is interested in you.

Civic Responsibility   A third important reason to care about macroeconomics is that by working together we can improve the macroeconomy. We get to vote, one of the most precious rights human beings have ever had. In electing our government, we indirectly make macroeconomic policy. As we will see in the next section, the

ECONOMIC POLICY AND POLITICAL POPULARITY: POLICY

Politicians believe strongly that their success at the polls depends on the state of the economy. They think that fairly *and* unfairly they get the credit when the economy does well and suffer the blame when the economy does badly. One of the most outspoken political leaders on this topic was mid-twentieth-century American politician Richard M. Nixon, who publicly blamed his defeat in the 1960 presidential election on the Eisenhower administration's unwillingness to take action against an economic slump:

"The matter was thoroughly discussed by the Cabinet. . . . [S]everal of the Administration's economic experts who attended the meeting did not share [the] bearish prognosis. . . . [T]here was strong sentiment against using the spending and credit powers of the Federal Government to affect the economy, unless and until conditions clearly indicated a major recession in prospect. . . . I must admit that I was more sensitive politically than some of the others around the cabinet table. I knew from bitter experience how, in both 1954 and 1958, slumps which hit bottom early in October contributed to substantial Republican losses in the House and Senate. . . . The bottom of the 1960 dip did come in October . . . the jobless roles increased by 452,000. All the speeches, television broadcasts, and precinct work in the world could not counteract that one hard fact."

Economic historians continue to dispute the causes of the "stagflation" — a combination of relatively high inflation and relatively high unemployment — that struck the American economy in the early 1970s, after Richard Nixon finally became president. Was it the result of his manipulation of economic policy for political goals so that during his 1972 reelection campaign the economy would look better than it had in 1960? The evidence is contradictory. But no matter how much Nixon's policy contributed to stagflation, all observers agree that his major goal was not to create a healthier economy over the long term but to make the economy look good in 1972.

Source: Richard M. Nixon, *Six Crises* (Garden City, NY: Doubleday, 1962), pp. 309–311.

government's macroeconomic policy matters, because it can *accelerate* (or decelerate) long-run economic growth and *stabilize* (or destabilize) the short-run business cycle. In election after election, candidates will present themselves and seek your vote. Those who win will try to manage the macroeconomy. If you are not literate in macroeconomics, you won't be able to distinguish the candidates who might become effective macroeconomic managers from those who are clueless or cynical, promising more than they can deliver. As Box 1.1 describes, some politicians have tried to use macroeconomic policy for their own short-term political gain.

Macroeconomic Policy

Growth Policy

The government's *growth policy* — what it does to accelerate or decelerate long-run economic growth — is surely the most important aspect of macroeconomic policy. Nothing matters more in the long run for the quality of life in an economy than its long-run rate of economic growth.

Consider Argentina, which was once one of the most prosperous nations in the

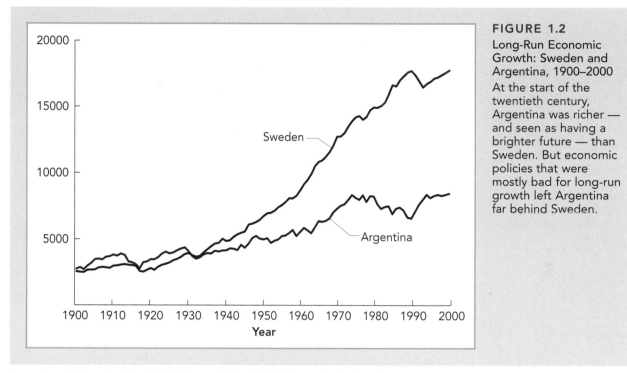

FIGURE 1.2
Long-Run Economic Growth: Sweden and Argentina, 1900–2000
At the start of the twentieth century, Argentina was richer — and seen as having a brighter future — than Sweden. But economic policies that were mostly bad for long-run growth left Argentina far behind Sweden.

Source: Angus Maddison, *Monitoring the World Economy* (Paris: OECD, 1995), as updated by the author.

world. In 1929, for example, it was fifth in the world in the number of automobiles per capita. Yet today Argentina is classified as a "developing" country, and as Figure 1.2 shows, it has fallen far behind rich developed industrial economies like Sweden. Why? Destructive economic policies have retarded Argentina's economic growth. Today Argentines are richer than their predecessors were at the beginning of the twentieth century, but they are not nearly as well off as they might have been had Argentina's economic policies been as good and its economic growth as fast as those in Sweden.

In Scandinavian countries like Norway and Sweden, where throughout the twentieth century economic policies were supportive of growth, the past 100 years have led to extraordinary prosperity. Today economic output per person in Scandinavia is among the highest in the world. According to semiofficial estimates, Scandinavians today are more than six times as wealthy as their predecessors were at the start of the twentieth century.

In the long run, nothing a government can do does more good for the economy than adopting good policies for economic growth.

Stabilization Policy

The second major branch of macroeconomic policy is the government's *stabilization* policy. History does not show a steady, stable, smooth upward trend toward higher production and employment. Typically, levels of production and employment fluctuate above and below long-run growth trends. Production can easily rise several percentage points above the long-run trend or fall 5 percentage points or more below

FIGURE 1.3

The American Business Cycle: Fluctuations in Total Production (Real GDP) Relative to the Long-Run Growth Trend

Since 1960 business-cycle fluctuations have caused the level of production in the United States to fluctuate as much as 8 percent below or 4 percent above the trend level of real GDP.

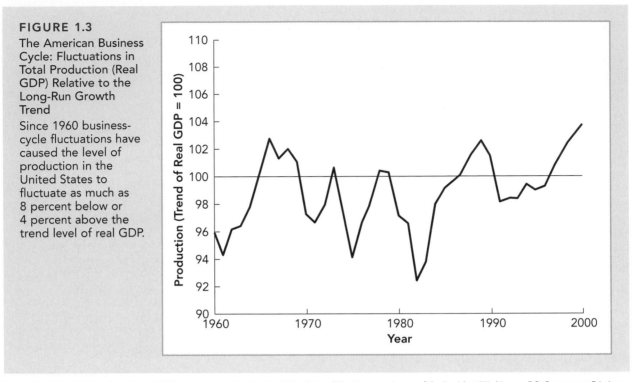

Source: Author's calculations based on real GDP estimates contained in the 2001 edition of *The Economic Report of the President* (Washington, DC: Government Printing Office).

the trend (see Figure 1.3). Unemployment can fall so low that businesses become desperate for workers and will spend much time and money training them. Or it can rise to 10 percent of the labor force in a deep recession, as it did in 1982.

Such fluctuations in production and employment are commonly referred to as *business cycles*. Periods in which production grows and unemployment falls are called *booms*, or macroeconomic **expansions**. Periods in which production falls and unemployment rises are called **recessions** or, worse, **depressions**. Booms are to be welcomed; recessions are to be feared.

Today's governments have powerful abilities to improve economic growth and to smooth out the business cycle by diminishing the depth of recessions and depressions. Good macroeconomic policy can make almost everyone's life better; bad macroeconomic policy can make almost everyone's life much worse (see Box 1.2). For example, policy makers' reliance on the gold standard as the international monetary system during the Great Depression was the source of macroeconomic catastrophe and human misery. Thus the stakes that are at risk in the study of macroeconomics are high.

Business-cycle fluctuations are felt not only in production and employment but also in the overall level of prices. Booms usually bring inflation, or rising prices. Recessions bring either a slowdown in the rate of inflation, or *disinflation* as it is called, or an absolute decline in the price level, called **deflation**. Interest rates, the level of the stock market, and other economic variables also rise and fall with the principal fluctuations of the business cycle.

MACROECONOMIC POLICY AND YOUR QUALITY OF LIFE: DATA

At the end of 1982 the U.S. macroeconomy was in the worst shape since the Great Depression. The unemployment rate was more than 10 percent. In an average week in 1983, some 10.7 million Americans were unemployed — actively seeking work but unable to find a job that seemed worth taking. That year the average unemployed American had already been unemployed for more than 20 weeks. The average household income in the United States was 8 percent below its long-run trend.

By contrast, at the end of 2000 U.S. unemployment was just 4 percent, and average household income was 4 percent above trend. In which year would you rather be trying to find a job?

Bad macroeconomic policy makes years like 1982 and 1983 much more common than years like 1999 and 2000. Although good macroeconomic policy cannot maintain the degree of relative prosperity seen in 2000 indefinitely, it can all but eliminate the prospect of years like 1982 and 1983. ◆

BOX 1.2

Macroeconomics versus Microeconomics

By itself macroeconomics is only half of economics. For more than half a century economics has been divided into two branches, macroeconomics and microeconomics. Macroeconomists examine the economy in the large, focusing on feedback from one component of the economy to another and studying the total level of production and employment. In contrast, **microeconomics**, which was probably the subject of your last economics course, deals with the economy in the small. Microeconomists study the markets for single commodities, examining the behavior of individual households and businesses. They focus on how competitive markets allocate resources to create producer and consumer surplus, as well as on how markets can go wrong.

The two groups of economists also differ in their views of how markets work. Microeconomists assume that imbalances between demand and supply are resolved by changes in prices. Rises in prices bring forth additional supply, and falls in prices bring forth additional demand, until supply and demand are once again in balance. Macroeconomists consider the possibility that imbalances between supply and demand can be resolved by changes in quantities rather than in prices. That is, businesses may be slow to change the prices they charge, preferring instead to expand or contract production until supply balances demand. Table 1.1 summarizes these differences in approach.

In every generation, economists attempt to integrate microeconomics and macroeconomics by providing "microfoundations" for the macroeconomic topics of inflation, the business cycle, and long-run growth. But no one believes that the bridge between microeconomics and macroeconomics has yet been soundly built. Economists are divided roughly evenly between those who think that the failure to successfully integrate microeconomics and macroeconomics is a flaw that urgently needs to be corrected and those who think it is a regrettable but minor annoyance. Thus less knowledge may carry over from microeconomics to macroeconomics than one might expect or hope. Be careful in trying to apply the principles and conclusions of microeconomics to macroeconomic questions — and vice versa.

TABLE 1.1
The Two Branches of Economics

Macroeconomists	Microeconomists
Focus on the economy as a whole.	Focus on the markets for individual commodities and on the decisions of single economic agents.
Spend much time analyzing how total income changes and how changes in income cause changes in other modes of economic behavior.	Hold total income constant.
Spend a great deal of time and energy investigating how people form their expectations and change them over time.	Don't worry much about how decision makers form their expectations.
Consider the possibility that decision makers might change the quantities they produce before they change the prices they charge.	Assume that economic adjustment occurs first through prices that change to balance supply and demand and that only afterward do producers and consumers react to the changed prices by changing the quantities they make, buy, or sell.

RECAP   OVERVIEW

Macroeconomics is that branch of economics related to not the individual markets but the economy as a whole. The government's *growth policy* — what it does to accelerate or decelerate long-run economic growth — is surely the most important aspect of macroeconomic policy. Nothing matters more in the long run for the quality of life in an economy than its long-run rate of economic growth. The second major branch of macroeconomic policy is the government's *stabilization* policy. Typically, levels of production and employment fluctuate above and below long-run growth trends. Periods in which production grows and unemployment falls are called *booms*, or *macroeconomic expansions*. Periods in which production falls and unemployment rises are called *recessions*, or, worse, *depressions*.

1.2 TRACKING THE MACROECONOMY

Economic Statistics and Economic Activity

Macroeconomics could not exist without the economic statistics that are systematically collected and disseminated by governments. Estimates of the value and composition of economic activity, principally those contained in the *national income and product accounts (NIPA)* reported by the U.S. Commerce Department's Bureau of Economic Analysis, are the fundamental data of macroeconomics. We cannot try to explain fluctuations in economic activity unless we know what those fluctuations *are*. But what is economic activity?

Whenever you work for someone and get paid, that is economic activity. Whenever you buy something at a store, that is economic activity. Whenever the government

TABLE 1.2
The Flow of Economic Data, 2000–2001

The items below represent a selection of recent economic data. Most of these data are reported monthly. A few series are reported quarterly — that is, they are calculated four times a year only, once for the January to March period, once for April to June, once for July to September, and once for September to December. (For a detailed description and analysis of what all these numbers mean, consult the Glossary.)

| | 2000 | | | | | | | | | Jan 2001 |
	Apr	May	Jun	Jul	Aug	Sep	Oct	Nov	Dec	Jan 2001
Production										
GDP		5.6Q2			2.2Q3			1.4Q4		
Nonfarm payrolls	410	171	57	–40	–79	195	66	59	19	268
Jobless rate	3.9	4.1	4.0	4.0	4.1	3.9	3.9	4.0	4.0	4.2
Trade gap	29.2	29.6	29.8	31.8	30.1	33.7	33.6	33.0		
Productivity		6.3Q2			3.0Q3			2.4Q4		
Housing starts	1.65	1.59	1.57	1.53	1.52	1.54	1.53	1.57	1.57	
Prices, Inflation										
CPI	0.0	0.1	0.5	0.2	–0.1	0.5	0.2	0.2	0.2	
CPI core	0.2	0.2	0.2	0.2	0.2	0.3	0.2	0.3	0.1	
PPI	–0.4	0.1	0.9	0.1	–0.4	0.8	0.4	0.1	0.0	
PPI core	0.1	0.3	0.0	0.1	0.2	0.2	–0.1	0.0	0.3	
NAPM prices	76.0	65.8	61.2	61.9	56.2	58.1	56.5	57.5	62.2	65.7
CRB index	212	223	224	218	227	225	221	229	229	224
Purchases deflator		2.1Q2			2.0Q3			1.9Q4		
Capacity utiliz.	82.5	82.7	82.7	82.3	82.6	82.4	81.9	81.4	80.6	
Income, Wages										
Personal income	0.6	0.3	0.5	0.2	0.3	1.1	–0.2	0.2	0.4	
Hourly earnings	0.4	0.1	0.3	0.4	0.4	0.2	0.6	0.4	0.4	0.0
Employment costs		1.0Q2			0.9Q3			0.8Q4		
Consumer Spending										
Retail sales	–0.5	0.1	0.4	0.8	–0.0	0.8	–0.1	–0.6	0.1	0.7
Personal spend.	0.2	0.3	0.5	0.6	0.4	0.8	0.3	0.3	0.3	
Home sales	4.88	5.09	5.31	4.82	5.28	5.16	5.00	5.26	4.87	
Manufacturing										
NAPM Index	53.1	53.1	52.1	51.7	49.9	49.6	48.3	47.9	44.3	41.2
Industrial prod.	0.7	0.7	0.5	–0.2	0.7	0.2	–0.3	–0.3	–0.6	
Factory orders	–3.8	4.7	5.2	–8.1	2.0	1.7	–4.0	1.7	1.1	
Inventory ch.		72.0Q2			66.4Q3			61.1Q4		
Equip. and software		17.9Q2			5.6Q3			–4.7Q4		
Financial Markets										
S&P 500	1452	1422	1455	1431	1518	1437	1429	1315	1320	1366
3-month T-bill	5.82	5.99	5.86	6.14	6.28	6.18	6.29	6.36	5.94	5.29
10-year T-note	5.99	6.44	6.10	6.05	5.83	5.80	5.74	5.72	5.24	5.16
30-year T-bond	5.85	6.15	5.93	5.85	5.72	5.83	5.80	5.78	5.49	5.54
Foreign Exchange										
US$-Euro	$0.94	$0.91	$0.95	$0.94	$0.90	$0.87	$0.85	$0.86	$0.90	$0.94
Yen-US$	106	108	106	108	108	107	108	109	112	117

Source: CBS Marketwatch, "Recent Economic Data," cbs.marketwatch.com/news/current/econ_data.htx, Feb. 13, 2001.

taxes you and spends its money to build a bridge, that is economic activity. In general, if a flow of money is involved in a transaction, economists will count that transaction as economic activity. Overall, *economic activity* is the pattern of transactions in which things of real, useful value — resources, labor, goods, and services — are created, transformed, and exchanged. If a transaction does not involve something of useful value being exchanged for money, odds are that NIPA will not count it as part of economic activity.

In the United States, individual economic statistics are released month by month and quarter by quarter, a quarter being a three-month period: a quarter of a year. Thus you will often hear economists and other analysts talk about the "change in inventories in the second quarter." Table 1.2 shows a sample of the kinds of economic data that economists, politicians, and others, including investors in the stock and bond markets, use to assess the course of the economy. The sheer number of statistics is confusing at first glance, but all the statistics either (a) are direct measures of six key economic indicators that together tell most of the story or (b) are primarily useful as partial forecasts of or as factors that help determine the six key indicators of economic activity.

Six Key Variables

You can get a good idea of the pulse of recent economic activity by simply looking at the six key economic variables. Together they summarize the state of the macroeconomy. If you want to be able to say more than "the economy is good" or "the economy is not so good," you need to understand and be able to analyze these six variables:

- Real gross domestic product.
- The unemployment rate.
- The inflation rate.
- The interest rate.
- The level of the stock market.
- The exchange rate.

The first two are the most important: They are directly and immediately connected to people's material well-being. The other four are indicators and controls that are not directly and immediately connected to people's current material well-being, but they profoundly influence the economy's direction. Let's look at each of these indicators more closely.

Real GDP

The first key indicator is the level of *real gross domestic product,* called **real GDP** or often just *GDP* for short. "Real" means that this measure corrects for changes in the overall level of prices. If total spending doubles because the average level of prices doubles but the total flow of commodities does not change, then real GDP does not change. Economic variables are either *real* — that is, they have been adjusted for changes in the price level — or *nominal* — that is, they have not been adjusted for changes in the price level. "Gross" means that this measure includes the replacement of worn-out and obsolete equipment and structures as well as completely new investment. (Gross measures contrast with *net* measures, which include only investments that add to the capital stock. Net measures are better than gross measures, but the information needed to construct them is not reliable.)

U.S. REAL GDP PER WORKER: DATA

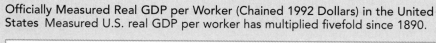

In the year 2000, calculated using 1992 prices, officially measured U.S. real GDP per worker — the total value of all final goods and services produced in the United States divided by the number of workers in the labor force — reached $65,000. The measured productivity of the average American worker had quintupled since 1890, when the standard estimate of 1992-price real GDP per worker was $13,000. Amazingly, this upward leap in economic well-being was accomplished in a little over three generations.

Figure 1.4 shows this upward trend in real GDP per worker. Despite temporary setbacks in recessions and depressions — of which the Great Depression of the 1930s was by far the largest — the principal event of the twentieth century was this quintupling of measured real GDP per worker. Other macroeconomic events visible in the figure include the World War II boom, the 1974–1975 and the 1980–1983 major recessions, the 1990–1991 minor recession, and the two-decade-long period of stagnation from the early 1970s to the early 1990s — a period that saw the 1973 and 1979 sharp oil price increases by OPEC and the large investment-reducing government budget deficits of the 1990s.

Note that this figure says nothing at all about how economic growth was distributed. In fact, the years between 1930 and 1970 saw the middle and working classes diminish the relative income gap between themselves and the rich. The years between 1970 and the present have seen this gap open wider once again.

FIGURE 1.4

Officially Measured Real GDP per Worker (Chained 1992 Dollars) in the United States Measured U.S. real GDP per worker has multiplied fivefold since 1890.

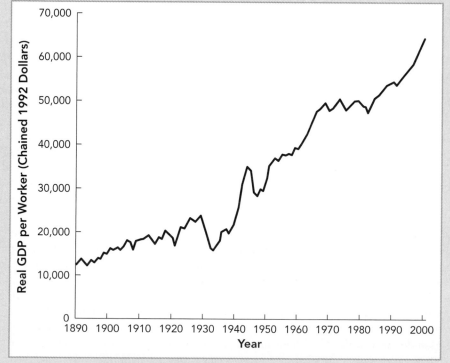

Source: Angus Maddison, *Monitoring the World Economy* (Paris: OECD, 1995), as updated by the author.

"Domestic" means that this measure counts economic activity that happens in the United States, whether or not the workers are legal residents and whether or not the factories are owned by American companies. (Domestic measures contrast with *national* measures, which count all the economic activity conducted by U.S. citizens who are permanent residents and by the companies they own.) Finally, "product" means that real GDP represents the production of *final goods and services*. It includes both *consumption goods* (things that consumers buy, take home or take out, and consume) and *investment goods* (things like machine tools, buildings, highways, and bridges, which boost the country's capital stock and productive capacity). It also includes *government purchases,* things that the government (acting as our collective agent) buys and uses.

Real GDP divided by the number of workers in the economy is the most frequently used summary index of the economy (see Box 1.3). It is a measure of how well the economy produces goods and services that people find useful — the necessities, conveniences, and luxuries of life. It is, however, a flawed and imperfect index. It says nothing, for instance, about the relative distribution of the nation's economic product. And because it measures market prices, not user satisfaction, it is an imperfect measure of material well-being. Nevertheless, **real GDP per worker** remains the best readily available economic index.

The Unemployment Rate

The second key quantity is the **unemployment rate.** The unemployed are people who want to work and are actively looking for jobs but have not yet found one (or have not yet found one that they consider attractive enough to take rather than continue to look for a still better job). The unemployment rate is equal to the number of unemployed people divided by the total labor force, which is the sum of the number of unemployed people and the number of people who have jobs. The U.S. Labor Department's Bureau of Labor Statistics conducts the Current Population Survey, a random survey of America's households, every month. The estimated number of unemployed workers obtained from the survey is then divided by the estimated total labor force, also obtained from the survey. The result is that month's unemployment rate. It is released to the public on the first Friday of the next month.

Most people consider unemployment to be a bad thing, and it usually is. Yet it is important to notice that an economy with no unemployment at all would probably be a badly working economy. Just as an economy needs inventories of goods — goods in transit, goods in process, goods in warehouses and sitting on store shelves — in order to function smoothly, it needs "inventories" of jobs looking for workers (vacancies) and workers looking for jobs (the unemployed). An economy in which each business grabbed the first person who walked through the door to fill a newly open job and in which each worker took the first job offered would be a less productive economy. Workers should be somewhat choosy about what jobs they take. They should decline jobs when they think that "this job pays too little" or "this job would be too unpleasant." Likewise, employers should be choosy about which workers they hire. Such *frictional unemployment* is an inevitable part of the process that makes good matches between workers and firms — matches that pair qualified workers with jobs that use their qualifications.

During recessions and depressions, however, unemployment is definitely not frictional. In these downturns in the business cycle the unemployment rate can rise far above the level resulting from a normal and healthy process of job search. The mar-

THE U.S. UNEMPLOYMENT RATE IN THE TWENTIETH CENTURY: DATA

In the twentieth century the U.S. unemployment rate dipped as low as 1.5 percent during World War II and as high as 25 percent during the Great Depression, the principal macroeconomic catastrophe of the past century. No other recession or depression in the nation's history, not even the depression of the early 1890s, came close to having the Great Depression's devastating impact (see Figure 1.5).

Since World War II, the U.S. unemployment rate has fluctuated between 3 and 10 percent, with the highest rates occurring in the decades of the 1970s and 1980s.

FIGURE 1.5

The U.S. Unemployment Rate Since World War II, the highest rate of unemployment has been the nearly 10 percent of 1982. Before World War II, peaks in unemployment were much higher, especially during the Great Depression of the 1930s.

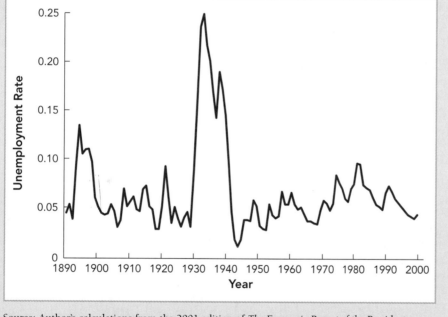

Source: Author's calculations from the 2001 edition of *The Economic Report of the President* (Washington, DC: Government Printing Office) and from Christina Romer, "Spurious Volatility in Historical Unemployment Estimates," *Journal of Political Economy,* Vol. 94 (1986), 1, pp. 1–37.

ket economy breaks down, failing to match workers willing and able to work with businesses that could put their skills and labor power to making useful goods and services. Economists call this type of unemployment *cyclical unemployment.* In the United States during the Great Depression the unemployment rate rose to 25 percent (see Box 1.4). In Germany during the same period, the rate rose to 33 percent.

When the unemployment rate is high, the market economy is not functioning well. The unemployment rate is the best indicator of how well the economy is doing relative to its productive potential.

The Inflation Rate

A third key economic indicator is the **inflation rate**, a measure of how fast the overall price level is rising. If the inflation rate this year is 5 percent, that means that in general things cost 5 percent more this year than they cost last year in money terms, in terms of the symbols printed on dollar bills. A very high inflation rate — more than 20 percent a month, say — can cause massive economic destruction, as the price system breaks down and the possibility of using profit-and-loss calculations to make rational business decisions vanishes. Such episodes of *hyperinflation* are among the worst economic disasters that can befall an economy. But not since the Revolutionary War has the United States experienced hyperinflation. Box 1.5 tracks the inflation rate in the United States over the past century.

U.S. INFLATION RATES IN THE TWENTIETH CENTURY: DATA

In the United States in the twentieth century significant peaks of inflation occurred during World Wars I and II, when overall rates of price increase peaked at more than 20 percent per year (see Figure 1.6). Before World War II, deep recessions like the Great Depression of the 1930s were accompanied by *deflation:* a decline in the level of overall prices that bankrupted businesses and banks, exacerbating the fall in output and employment.

Strangely, moderate inflation rates — a little more than 10 percent a year, say —

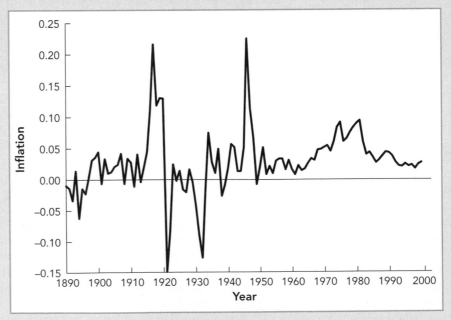

FIGURE 1.6
Inflation in the United States Before 1970, periods when inflation rose above 5 percent were confined to major wars.

Source: Author's calculations from the 2001 edition of *The Economic Report of the President* (Washington, DC: Government Printing Office) and from *Historical Statistics of the United States* (Washington, DC: Government Printing Office, 1975).

are highly unsettling to consumers and business managers. Moderate inflation should not seriously compromise consumers', investors', and managers' ability to determine the best use of their financial resources or to calculate profitability. Yet all these groups are strongly averse to it. Politicians in the industrialized economies have discovered that if they fail to preside over low and stable inflation rates then they are likely to lose the next election.

Since World War II there has been only one single year — in the late 1940s — during which the price level declined. Otherwise, there has been inflation. Post-World War II inflation has come in two varieties: the "creeping" inflation of the 1950s, early and mid-1960s, and 1990s, too small and slow for anyone to pay much attention to it; and the "trotting" inflation of the late 1960s, 1970s, and 1980s — too high to ignore and too tempting a political football for politicians to resist blaming the current government.

The steep decline in inflation that occurred in the early 1980s is called the "Volcker disinflation," after then-Federal Reserve Chair Paul Volcker. Alarmed by the accelerating inflation of the late 1970s and early 1980s, Volcker decided to raise interest rates in order to decrease aggregate demand. In doing so, he risked a deep recession, which came in 1982–1983. But his action did stop the rise in inflation and reduce it back to the creeping range. ◆

The Interest Rate

The fourth key economic indicator is the **interest rate**. Though economists speak of "the" interest rate, there are actually many different interest rates applying to loans of different durations and different degrees of risk. (After all, the person or business entity to whom you lend your money may be unable to pay it back; that is a risk you accept when you make a loan.) The different interest rates often move up or down together, so economists speak of *the* interest rate, referring to the entire complex of different rates. But interest rates do not move in concert all the time. The causes of variations in the *yield curve,* which describes the pattern of interest rates, are an important part of macroeconomics.

The interest rate is important because it governs the redistribution of purchasing power across time. Those people or business enterprises who think they can make good use of additional financial resources borrow, promising to return the purchasing power they use today with interest in the future. Those business enterprises or people who have no immediate use for their financial resources lend, hoping to profit when the borrower returns the borrowed sum — what financiers call the *principal* — with interest.

When economists think about interest rates, they almost always prefer to focus on the *real* interest rate rather than the *nominal* interest rate. The nominal interest rate is the interest rate in terms of money — for example, how many dollars' worth of interest a borrower must pay to borrow a given sum of money for one year. The real interest rate is the interest rate in terms of goods and services — for example, how much purchasing power over goods and services a borrower must pay in order to borrow a given amount of purchasing power for one year. The difference between the two is that nominal interest rates do not take proper account of the effect of inflation; real interest rates do.

Whenever interest rates are low — that is, when money is "cheap" — investment tends to be high, because businesses find that a wide range of possible investments

REAL INTEREST RATES: DATA

Interest rates on long-term debt, like the 10-year notes issued by the U.S. Treasury, are usually higher than interest rates on short-term debt, like the 3-month Treasury bills. Whenever long-term interest rates are shorter than short-term interest rates, the yield curve is said to be "inverted." An inverted yield curve is one of the signals of a possible coming recession.

Interest rates have fluctuated widely in the United States since 1960 (see Figure 1.7). Real interest rates — that is, interest rates adjusted for inflation — have even been negative at times. During the 1970s nominal — money — interest rates were so low and inflation was so high that the interest and principal on a short-term loan bought fewer commodities when the loan was repaid than the original principal could have purchased when the loan was made. In the early 1980s — the Volcker years — interest rates increased radically. Since then they have remained higher than their levels in the 1950s and 1960s.

FIGURE 1.7

U.S. Real Interest Rates, 1960–1999 Since the Volcker disinflation of the early 1980s, real interest rates in the United States have been markedly higher than they were during the 1970s and even the 1960s. The yield curve has also been relatively steeply sloped; that is, the gap between long-term interest rates (like the interest rate on the 10-year U.S. Treasury note) and short-term interest rates (like the interest rate on the three-month U.S. Treasury bill) has been relatively large.

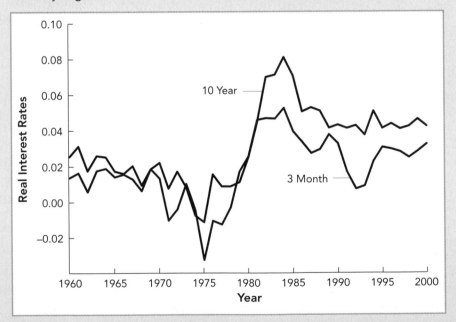

Source: Author's calculations from the 2001 edition of *The Economic Report of the President* (Washington, DC: Government Printing Office) and from *Historical Statistics of the United States* (Washington, DC: Government Printing Office, 1975).

will generate enough cash to pay the interest on borrowed money, repay the principal of the loan, and still produce a profit. Whenever interest rates are high — that is, when money is "dear" — investment tends to be low, because businesses find that most possible investments will not generate enough cash flow to repay the principal and the high interest. Box 1.6 shows changes in real interest rates in the United States since 1960.

The Stock Market

The *level of the* **stock market** is the key economic indicator you hear about most often — you hear about it every single day unless you try hard to avoid the news. The level of the stock market is an index of expectations for the future. When the

THE STOCK MARKET: DATA

For more than a century and a quarter, the United States has had a thick market in equities — the "stocks" of a corporation, pieces of paper that indicate ownership of its shares. One of the major indexes that tracks the performance of the stock market as a whole is Standard and Poor's composite index, the S&P 500. Figure 1.8 plots the *real* value — that is, the value adjusted for inflation — of this stock market index over time.

FIGURE 1.8

Real Stock Index Prices Since 1997 real stock index prices have far exceeded their standard, conventional valuation of 15 times earnings. Economists differ over whether this phenomenon is due to (a) an irrational speculative mania, (b) an increased tolerance for risk, or (c) expectations of rapid future economic growth on the part of investors.

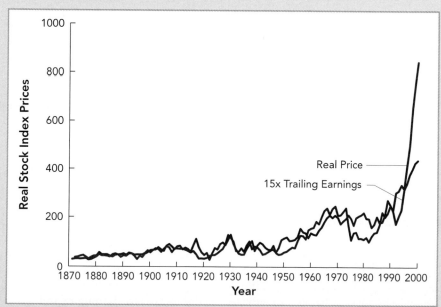

Source: Author's calculations from data in Robert Shiller, *Market Volatility* (Cambridge: MIT Press, 1987), as subsequently extended by Shiller. www.yale.edu/~rshiller/.

Over the past century, on average, a share of stock has traded for about 15 times its past year's, or "trailing," earnings per share. Earnings per share are calculated by dividing a corporation's annual profits by the number of shares of stock the corporation has outstanding. The 15-times-earnings figure is only an average: Companies with good prospects for growth sell for more than 15 times their earnings, and corporations seen as being in decline sell for less.

There are some years in which expectations of the future of the economy are relatively depressed, and stock indexes like the S&P 500 sell for much less than the 15 times earnings rule of thumb. Consider 1982, when the stock market as a whole was worth 40 percent less than 15 times earnings.

stock market is high, investors expect economic growth to be rapid, profits to be high, and unemployment to be relatively low. (Note, however, that there is an element of tail chasing in the stock market. Perhaps it would be more accurate to say that the stock market is high when average opinion expects that average opinion will expect that future economic growth will be rapid.) Conversely, when the stock market is low, investors expect the economic future to be relatively gloomy.

At times, such as the end of the 1960s or the end of the 1990s, the stock market appears significantly overvalued compared to its standard historical patterns. During such episodes investors are implicitly forecasting a major boom and continued rapid productivity growth. If their forecasts turn out to be wrong, these investors will be severely disappointed with their stock market investments. Box 1.7 shows the course of the U.S. stock market over the past century.

The Exchange Rate

The sixth and last key economic quantity is the **exchange rate**. The *nominal exchange rate* is the rate at which the monies of different countries can be exchanged for one another. The *real exchange rate* is the rate at which the goods and services produced in different countries can be exchanged for one another.

The exchange rate governs the terms on which international trade and investment take place. When the domestic currency is *appreciated,* its value in terms of other currencies is high. Foreign-produced goods are relatively cheap for domestic buyers, but domestic-made goods are relatively expensive for foreigners. In these circumstances imports are likely to be high; exports are likely to be low. When the domestic currency is *depreciated,* the opposite is the case. Domestically made goods are cheap for foreign buyers. Thus exports are likely to be high. But domestic consumers' and investors' power to purchase foreign-made goods is limited. Thus im-

THE EXCHANGE RATE: DETAIL

The terms on which people in one country can buy goods and services made in other countries and sell the goods and services they make themselves are summarized in the exchange rate. The nominal exchange rate tells how many units of foreign currency can be bought with 1 unit of the domestic currency; it is the value of a foreign currency. The real exchange rate adjusts for differences in the rate of inflation between countries. Thus it measures the relative price of tradeable goods: how much in the way of foreign-produced goods can be bought with 1 unit of domestically produced goods.

FIGURE 1.9

The U.S. Real Exchange Rate: The Dollar against a Composite Index of Foreign Currencies The most significant fluctuation in the U.S. exchange rate came during the large depreciation of foreign currencies in the early and mid-1980s. By 1985 foreign-made goods were less than two-thirds as expensive relative to U.S.-made goods than they had been at the start of the decade.

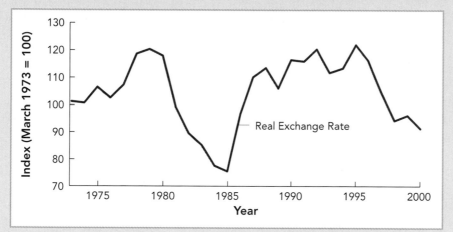

Source: Author's calculations from the 2001 edition of *The Economic Report of the President* (Washington, DC: Government Printing Office).

Before the early 1970s, the U.S. exchange rate was *fixed* vis-à-vis other major currencies in the Bretton Woods system. The U.S. Treasury stood ready to buy or sell dollars in exchange for other currencies at fixed parities determined by each country's posted valuation of its currency in terms of gold.

Since the early 1970s the U.S. exchange rate has been *floating* — free to move up or down in response to the market forces of supply and demand (see Figure 1.9). When U.S. interest rates are relatively high compared to those of other countries — as in the early 1980s — the dollar *appreciates.* In such a case the dollar becomes much more valuable, as many people try to invest in America to capture the high interest rates. We then say that the value of the exchange rate is relatively low. The exchange rate is defined as the value (in terms of dollars) of foreign currency: When the relative value of the dollar rises, the value in dollars of foreign currency falls.

When U.S. interest rates fall relative to those in other countries, the dollar tends to *depreciate,* to fall in value, so U.S. goods are cheap to buy and easy to sell. When the dollar's value is low and the dollar has depreciated, the exchange rate — the value in dollars of foreign currency — is relatively high.

ports are likely to be low. Box 1.8 details the effects of changes in the U.S. exchange rate since 1977.

Real GDP, the unemployment rate, the inflation rate, the interest rate, the stock market, and the exchange rate — these are the 6 key economic indicators. Know the values of these key variables in context — both their relative levels today and their recent trends — and you have a remarkably complete picture of the current state of the macroeconomy.

RECAP   TRACKING THE MACROECONOMY

Know and understand six key variables, and you understand most of what there is to know about the state of the macroeconomy. The first key variable is the level of real GDP — the real inflation-adjusted value of goods and services. The second key variable is the unemployment rate: The fraction of the labor force that is out of work. The third key variable is the inflation rate — a measure of how rapidly the overall price level is changing. The fourth key variable is the interest rate. When economists think about interest rates, they almost always prefer to focus on the real interest rate rather than the *nominal* interest rate. The fifth key variable is the level of the stock market. The level of the stock market is a good indicator of investor confidence and of the likely future pace of investment spending. The sixth and last key variable is the exchange rate — the price at which goods made here at home are exchanged for goods made abroad.

1.3 THE CURRENT MACROECONOMIC SITUATION

The United States

As of the late spring of 2001, the U.S. macroeconomy seemed poised to continue its expansion, albeit at a slower pace than during the second half of the 1990s. The United States was still in the long expansion that had begun at the beginning of the 1990s — the longest business cycle expansion, and period of time without a recession, in history. Most observers expected real GDP in the United States economy to grow at about 1.5 percent in 2001 — a pace that would see the unemployment rate rise a few tenths of a percentage point — and at about 3.0 percent in 2002.

The fears that had been common during the winter that the United States economy teetered on the brink of a recession were largely gone. The consensus of observers of the economy was that the Federal Reserve had overdone it and raised interest rates too far and too fast in late 1999 and 2000. But the Federal Reserve had swiftly and substantially lowered interest rates in the winter of 2001. The three-month money-market nominal interest rate that had been 6.74 percent per year in the summer of 2000 was 3.95 percent per year by the late spring of 2001, and further cuts were generally expected. Economists expected these Federal Reserve rate cuts to boost investment spending and growth by the end of 2001, or the beginning of 2002. Thus forecasters' central projections saw U.S. growth accelerating a bit in late 2001 as Federal Reserve interest rate cuts and front-loaded tax cuts began to have their effect on total spending.

The Federal Reserve had shown itself ready and anxious to take steps to fight any slowdown. The larger recessions of the post-World War II period had all come to pass because the Federal Reserve was more concerned with fighting inflation than with avoiding recession. In the winter of 2001, however, inflation continued to be less than 2 percent per year and was not seen as a threat by anyone.

The U.S. growth slowdown at the very end of 2000 had been preceded by a remarkable decade-long economic boom. Policy makers and economists advocating the Clinton deficit-reduction program in the early 1990s had claimed that deficit reduction would make possible a high-investment economic expansion, which would then become a high productivity growth expansion. Up until 1996 there had been no signs that high investment was leading to high productivity growth. But by the late summer of 1999 productivity growth had been strong for four years in a row. Perhaps political claims in the early 1990s that deficit reduction would ignite a high-investment and high-productivity growth recovery were coming true. Perhaps the U.S. economy was simply benefiting from the sudden wave of rapid productivity growth driven by the technological revolutions in data processing and data communications. More likely is that both possibilities were somewhat true, and that they reinforced each other — higher investment allowed businesses to more rapidly take advantage of technological advances in data processing and data communications.

In the United States the strong growth in production and sales in the second half of the 1990s had pushed the unemployment rate down to a level — 4 percent — not seen in a generation. A tight labor market was good news for workers: Employers appeared eager to pour resources into training them for their jobs. Yet the tight labor market and the strong demand for employees was not showing up in strong real wage growth. This low inflation proved a puzzle to economists: Practically all had confidently forecast (using their estimates of the Phillips Curve relationship between inflation and unemployment) that unemployment below 5 percent would surely lead to accelerating inflation. Yet it had not done so.

There are, however, two sources of weakness in the U.S. economy. First, the stock market remains very high, and there are fears (i) that the stock market may crash, and (ii) that a stock market crash would harm consumer confidence, reduce consumption spending, and send the economy into a recession. Thus the Federal Reserve has to maintain financial stability while not artificially boosting the stock market further. Second, the U.S. exchange rate — the value of foreign currency and goods — is low, which means that the value of the dollar is high. Should foreign exchange speculators lose confidence in the dollar, the value of foreign currency could rise far and fast, possibly causing macroeconomic problems.

Economists are very good at pointing out economic situations that are inconsistent with fundamental values — policies, imbalances, or balance sheet problems such that they cannot possibly last, and are bound to end, perhaps in a crisis. The value of the stock market and the value of the exchange rate as of the late spring of 2001 appear at odds with fundamentals, and possible sources of financial crises in the future. But, as economist Rudiger Dornbusch has written, "to get to the crisis takes longer than you think, and then it happens faster than you would have thought."

Europe

As of the late spring of 2001, economic growth in the 11 countries belonging to the European Monetary Union, and having the newly formed euro for their principal currency, was slowing but not slowing as fast as people had feared. Rising oil prices and rising interest rates (in large part a result of the fear on the part of the newly formed European Central Bank that its currency, the euro, had depreciated too far) had reduced growth in late 2000 below what had been forecast, and real GDP growth for 2001 was forecast at between 2.0 and 2.5 percent.

There was certainly room for economic expansion in Europe. The preceding year had seen consumer prices throughout the euro zone rise by less than 2 percent. Economic forecasters were projecting 3 percent real GDP growth for 2001. Unfortunately, such a rate of growth would have little or no effect at reducing European unemployment, which remained stuck near 10 percent. The challenge for European policy remained one of avoiding rises in inflation while attempting to reduce western Europe's distressingly high and stubborn rate of unemployment.

For the first time in decades in Europe there was hope that the next decade will bring a reduction, not an increase in unemployment. Changes in policy are making the European labor market more flexible, and in the long run making it easier for firms to change the number of workers they employ should make it easier for workers to find jobs and lower unemployment. Western Europe is perhaps half a decade behind the United States in its adoption of data processing and data communications technology, and so the productivity growth acceleration experienced by the United States in the late 1990s should be visible in western Europe in the decade of the 2000s.

With the formation of its new currency, the euro, monetary policy in Europe is now being made by a new institution, the European Central Bank. It is being very closely watched as it establishes its operating procedures and its fundamental rules of thumb to guide policy.

Japan

Japan ended 2000 with an annual real GDP growth rate of 1.8 percent. This is an astonishingly low growth rate given the large amount of unused capacity in the Japanese economy and the extraordinarily low levels of nominal short-term interest rates in Japan. One reason for the low growth rate is that people are unsure whether prices have further to fall: Japan is actually undergoing deflation, with prices falling by 0.7 percent in 2000. Real GDP growth in Japan for 2001 is projected to be only 1.4 percent, certainly less than the rate of growth of potential output.

The start of the 1990s saw the collapse of the Japanese stock and real estate markets, the end of the so-called "bubble economy." The 1990s as a whole saw the breakdown of the Japanese model of economic growth, as the economy stagnated for much of the decade. Now there is a general recognition that Japan faces a structural economic crisis. But there is no political consensus on what is to be done, and the major political steps that need to be taken to restore growth — restructuring the Japanese financial system, and deregulating transportation and distribution — are not being taken.

The Bank of Japan is now pursuing a policy of making short-term safe nominal interest rates as close to zero as it can. But U.S. short-term safe nominal interest rates were zero in the Great Depression, and that did not help the U.S. economy recover and did not boost U.S. investment. What matters for investment spending is not a low short-term safe nominal interest rate but a low long-term risky real interest rate, and that remains high as long as bond traders fear that (i) the low interest rate policy will not last very long, (ii) many companies may go bankrupt and never repay the money they borrow, and (iii) prices may decline, turning low nominal interest rates into high inflation-adjusted real interest rates.

Perhaps it is time for the Japanese government to pursue a policy of thoroughgoing inflation to boost demand that has been extremely sluggish for nearly a decade. But the conventional wisdom is that Japanese demand and production are unlikely to pick up until ongoing "structural" problems — in particular the fear of lenders that those who want to borrow from them are really bankrupt — are resolved. Requiring businesses to declare the true value of their real estate holdings is commonly pointed to as the key blockage to investment, higher demand, and economic recovery.

Moreover, Japan's public finances are becoming unstable. The budget deficit is huge, officially-reported public debt is more than annual GDP and rising, and there are many unfunded pension and other liabilities of the Japanese government that are not on the official balance sheet. A government that has obligations that it cannot meet from its normal tax revenue is a government that is likely to resort, at some time in the future, to high inflation to balance its finances.

Emerging Markets

As of the spring of 2001, the financial crisis in East Asia had been over for nearly two years. The panic that started in 1997 on the part of investors in New York, Frankfurt, London, and Tokyo, and the consequent withdrawal of their money from emerging market economies, imposed very high costs: Massive bankruptcies, high interest rates, increases in unemployment, falls in production. However, foreign investors appear to have regained confidence in East Asian economies. Recovery and growth are rapid throughout the region, save in Indonesia.

Moreover, growth continues through the rest of the emerging markets of the world, with growth continuing to be exceptionally fast in China and India. Together those two countries make up 40 percent of the world's population.

But the slowdown in growth in the world economy's industrial core, especially in the United States, is not good for emerging market economies. It is hard for their exports to expand if incomes in the industrial core are not rising. In addition, as of the spring of 2001 there were ongoing but localized financial crises in Argentina and Turkey, and the fear of other crises elsewhere discouraged investment and slowed growth.

Nevertheless, consensus forecasts were for real GDP growth to average 4.0 percent in 2001 and 5.0 percent in 2002 in emerging markets outside the world economy's industrial core. From one perspective, this glass is half full: The world's poor countries are growing faster than the rich, and closing the gap. From a second perspective, this glass is nearly empty: The gap is being closed at a glacial pace, and not being closed at all in large chunks of South America, in Africa, in much of the Middle East, and in Indonesia.

RECAP   THE CURRENT MACROECONOMIC SITUATION

As of the late spring of 2001, economic forecasters expected U.S. growth to resume. They expected Federal Reserve rate cuts to boost investment spending and growth starting at the end of 2001. They expected European unemployment to remain high, but European growth to continue.

Japan ended 2000 with an annual real GDP growth rate of 1.8 percent. This is an astonishingly low growth rate given the large amount of unused capacity in the Japanese economy, and the extraordinarily low levels of nominal short-term interest rates in Japan. But what matters for investment spending is not a low short-term safe nominal interest rate but a low long-term risky real interest rate, and that requires confidence that policy will be continued, confidence that companies will not go bankrupt, and confidence that prices will not decline.

Last, forecasts were for real GDP growth to average 4.0 percent in 2001 and 5.0 percent in 2002 in emerging markets outside the world economy's industrial core.

Chapter Summary

1. Macroeconomics is the study of the economy in the large — the determination of the economywide levels of production, employment and unemployment, and inflation or deflation.

2. There are three key reasons to study macroeconomics: to gain cultural literacy, to understand how economic trends affect you personally, and to exercise your responsibility as a voter and citizen.

3. The six key variables in macroeconomics are real GDP, the unemployment rate, the inflation rate, the interest rate, the level of the stock market, and the exchange rate.

Key Terms

macroeconomics (p. 4)

expansion (p. 8)

recession (p. 8)

depression (p. 8)

deflation (p. 8)

microeconomics (p. 9)

real GDP (p. 12)

real GDP per worker (p. 14)

unemployment rate (p. 14)

inflation rate (p. 16)

interest rate (p. 17)

stock market (p. 19)

(real) exchange rate (p. 20)

Analytical Exercises

1. What are the key differences between microeconomics and macroeconomics?

2. Why are real GDP and the unemployment rate important macroeconomic variables?

3. Why are the interest rate and the level of the stock market important economic variables?

4. Roughly, what was the highest level that the U.S. inflation rate reached in the twentieth century? What was the highest *peacetime* unemployment rate?

5. Roughly, how much higher is *measured* real GDP per worker today than it was in 1973?

Policy Exercises

1. What was the rate of real GDP growth in the United States in 2000?

2. What is the current unemployment rate?

3. What is the current inflation rate? If you find more than one inflation rate listed, are they consistent with each other?

4. What is the current level of the stock market? How does it compare to the level of the stock market at the beginning of 2000?

5. How does the current level of the stock market compare with the historical average, roughly 15 times a stock market index's trailing earnings?

Measuring the Macroeconomy

CHAPTER

QUESTIONS

What key data do macroeconomists look at?

How are key macroeconomic data estimated and calculated?

What is the difference between nominal and real values?

How are stock market values related to interest rates?

How are interest rates related to the price level and the inflation rate?

How is unemployment related to total production?

What is right — and what is wrong — with the key measure of economic activity, real GDP?

2.1 THE IMPORTANCE OF DATA

Economics is a *social* science: It is about us, about what we do. Thus it shares with other social sciences one important source of information: introspection. We can ask ourselves "Why did I do that?" or "If I had done that, what would I have been thinking?" We can ask other people, and listen to their answers ("I did that because . . ."). In most of the other social sciences, the overwhelming source of information is introspection, either our own or other people's.

Economists are in a better position than most other social scientists as far as their sources of information are concerned. Everything that passes through the economy is priced and sold. Thus economists have quantitative data to work with: prices, quantities, and values. Having quantitative data allows economists to do more than many other social scientists. They can use theories to make not just qualitative but quantitative forecasts ("The change from Carter- to Reagan-era fiscal policy reduced the growth rate of the U.S. economy by 0.3 percent per year."). With data they can

TABLE 2.1
The Six Key Economic Variables

Variable	Details	Importance
Real GDP	Rough synonyms include GNP, NNP, NDP, national income, aggregate demand, and total production.	The principal measure of material well-being and economic productivity.
Unemployment rate	As reported, omits "discouraged workers" who would like to work but have stopped looking for jobs.	The principal measure of how far production is falling short of potential output; a measure of the relative distribution of economic well-being.
Inflation rate	Most economists think officially reported statistics overstate the true increase in the nominal cost of living by 0.5 to 1 percent per year.	The proportional rate of change of the price level. Central banks today view their principal mission as ensuring price stability — keeping the rate of inflation low enough that nobody worries about it much.
Interest rate	The most important interest rates are "real" — those that control for the effects of inflation — and long-term.	The real long-term interest rate is the principal determinant of the level of investment and a principal determinant of future production growth
Stock market	A broad index like the S&P is better than a narrow index like the Dow-Jones.	The stock market summarizes into one single index a large number of influences on investment, including investors' optimism, expected future profits, and the real interest rate.
Exchange rate	Once again, the most important rate is the real rate.	The exchange rate determines the relative price of foreign-made goods in terms of home-produced goods. Economists usually work with an index of the value of the dollar against an average of all other currencies and call it *the* exchange rate.

test theories, comparing what was actually the case to what various theories would have predicted.

The most important macroeconomic data are, of course, the six key variables introduced in Chapter 1:

- Real GDP (gross domestic product).
- The unemployment rate.
- The inflation rate (that is, the proportional rate of change in the price level).
- The interest rate.
- The level of the stock market.
- The exchange rate.

Learn about these six measurements of the economy — what their current values are, what their trends have been over time, what their future values are projected to be, how they are calculated, and what they mean — and you will have an excellent knowledge of the state of the economy. Table 2.1 summarizes the major features of these key economic variables. Let's see how they are calculated, but in reverse order — starting with the exchange rate and ending with real GDP.

RECAP   THE IMPORTANCE OF DATA

In most of the other social sciences, the overwhelming source of information is introspection — either our own or other people's. Economists have the advantage that everything that passes through the economy is priced and sold. Thus economists have quantitative data to work with: Prices, quantities, and values. Having quantitative data allows economists to do more than many other social scientists. Especially important is the ability to measure the six key variables — real GDP, the unemployment rate, the inflation rate, the interest rate, the stock market, and the exchange rate.

2.2 THE EXCHANGE RATE

Nominal versus Real Exchange Rates

The **nominal exchange rate** is the relative price of two different kinds of money, as set in the *foreign exchange market*. Domestic exporters earn foreign currency when they export — sell goods to people abroad. Foreign producers earn domestic currency when they sell us imports — sell their goods to people here. Both then have a problem. Domestic exporters can't pay domestic workers with foreign currency; foreign producers can't pay foreign workers with domestic currency. Foreign producers need to trade the dollars they have earned for money that is useful to them; domestic exporters need to trade the foreign currency they have earned for dollars they can use.

How do foreign producers and domestic exporters solve this problem? They turn to the foreign exchange market, where those who have foreign currency but want dollars exchange it for dollars and those who have dollars but want foreign currency exchange dollars for other currencies. Those with foreign currency who want dollars include not only domestic exporters but also foreigners wishing to invest in the

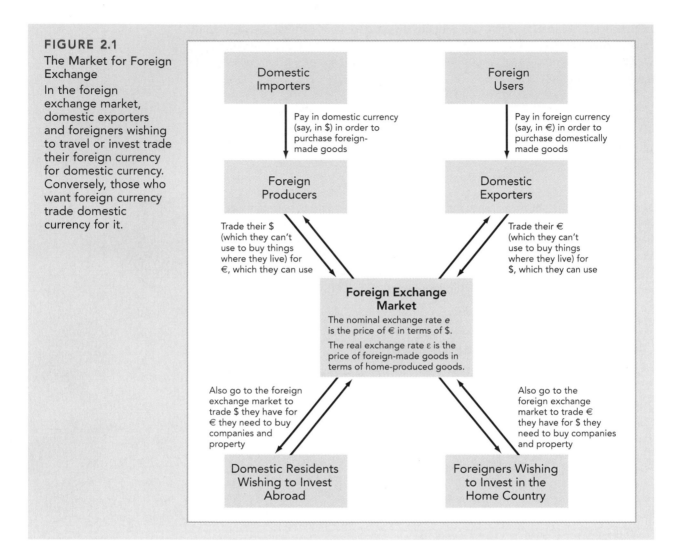

FIGURE 2.1

The Market for Foreign Exchange

In the foreign exchange market, domestic exporters and foreigners wishing to travel or invest trade their foreign currency for domestic currency. Conversely, those who want foreign currency trade domestic currency for it.

Domestic Importers

Pay in domestic currency (say, in $) in order to purchase foreign-made goods

Foreign Producers

Trade their $ (which they can't use to buy things where they live) for €, which they can use

Foreign Users

Pay in foreign currency (say, in €) in order to purchase domestically made goods

Domestic Exporters

Trade their € (which they can't use to buy things where they live) for $, which they can use

Foreign Exchange Market

The nominal exchange rate *e* is the price of € in terms of $.

The real exchange rate ε is the price of foreign-made goods in terms of home-produced goods.

Also go to the foreign exchange market to trade $ they have for € they need to buy companies and property

Also go to the foreign exchange market to trade € they have for $ they need to buy companies and property

Domestic Residents Wishing to Invest Abroad

Foreigners Wishing to Invest in the Home Country

United States. Those with dollars who want foreign currency include not only foreigners who have sold Americans imports but also American residents who wish to invest abroad. (See Figure 2.1.)

If the nominal exchange rate between the dollar (the currency of the United States) and the euro (the currency of the European Union) is $1.20 = €1.00, then a single euro costs $1.20 in U.S. currency. It takes less than one euro — 0.83 euro and change — to buy a single dollar.

Economists, however, are more interested in the **real exchange rate**: the nominal rate adjusted for changes in the value of the currency. The nominal — the money — exchange rate can change without affecting the pattern of cross-national trade. When the real exchange rate — the rate in terms of goods and services — changes, the pattern of cross-national trade must change as well.

Suppose a burst of inflation doubled the price level in the United States, so everything that once cost $1 in the United States now costs $2, everything that used to cost $2 now costs $4, and so on. Suppose also that the nominal exchange rate changed from $1.20 = €1.00 to $2.40 = €1.00. Before the burst of inflation you could sell goods in Europe for €0.83 (and change), turn the euros into $1.00, and buy American goods. After the burst of inflation you could sell goods in Europe for €0.83 (and change), turn the euros into $2.00, and buy the exact same American goods as before. The change in the nominal exchange rate has offset the change in the U.S. price level. In this case the real exchange rate — the rate at which goods trade for goods — has not changed. The terms at which the goods of one country are traded for the goods of another are the same.

Now suppose that a burst of inflation doubled the price level in the United States but that $1.20 still exchanges for €1.00 on the foreign exchange market. Has the exchange rate changed? The nominal exchange rate has not changed: 0.83 (plus change) euros will still get you a paper dollar; $1.20 will still get you a euro. However, that paper dollar will buy only as many goods in the United States as 50 cents would have bought before. The doubling of the U.S. price level, coupled with the unchanged nominal exchange rate, means that the same quantity of U.S.-made goods will buy twice as many European-made goods. Thus the real exchange rate has halved.

Of course, if the price levels in different countries do not change, then there is no distinction between a change in the nominal exchange rate and a change in the real exchange rate. If the nominal exchange rate doubled — changed from $1.20 = €1.00 to $2.40 = €1.00 — but the price levels in the United States and Europe remained the same, then investors would need twice as many dollars to buy the same amount of foreign currency. Thus it would cost twice as many U.S.-made goods to buy the same amount of foreign-made goods. The real exchange rate would have doubled.

The Real Exchange Rate

Calculating the Real Exchange Rate

To calculate the real exchange rate ε, you need to know three pieces of information. First, you need to know the price level in the home country — call it P, for price. Second, you need to know the price level abroad — call it by P^*. (It is conventional

---

CALCULATING THE REAL EXCHANGE RATE: AN EXAMPLE

Suppose that the index of the U.S. price level is 120, the index of the foreign (the euro) price level is 83.333, and the nominal exchange rate (the price of the foreign currency in dollars) is $1.20 = €1. Then the real exchange rate would be

$$\varepsilon = e \times \frac{P}{P^*} = 1.2 \times \frac{120}{83.333} = 1.2 \times 1.44 = 1.73$$

Now suppose the U.S. price level were to rise to 150, the foreign price level were to rise to 100, and the price of foreign currency were to fall to parity — $1.00 = €1. In that case the real exchange rate would be:

$$\varepsilon = e \times \frac{P}{P^*} = 1.0 \times \frac{150}{100} = 1.0 \times 1.5 = 1.5$$

That is all there is to calculating real exchange rates.

BOX 2.1

in macroeconomics to let asterisks stand for values in foreign countries.) Third, you need to know the nominal exchange rate — call it *e*, for exchange. You can then calculate the value of the real exchange rate by multiplying the nominal exchange rate by the ratio of the home price level to the foreign price level:

$$\varepsilon = e \times \frac{P}{P*}$$

Box 2.1 illustrates how the process works.

Calculating the Overall Exchange Rate: Index Numbers

If you open up a newspaper in search of *the* exchange rate for the dollar, you will not find it. Instead, you will find a list of rates similar to the one in Table 2.2 but with many more entries — one line for almost every country on the globe.

There is an exchange rate for the dollar against each and every other currency — a dollar-Swiss franc exchange rate, a dollar-yen exchange rate, a dollar-euro exchange rate, a dollar-pound exchange rate, a dollar-Canadian dollar exchange rate, a dollar-Mexican peso exchange rate, and more than 100 more for all the other currencies. Which of these is *the* exchange rate?

In this situation economists do what they usually do when they are confronted with too much variety. They take an average and hope that deviations from the average will cancel each other out. In other words, they construct an **index number** to stand in place of the more than 100 exchange rates of the U.S. dollar against other currencies. The usual approach is to take a trade-weighted average, in which each currency receives a weight equal to its share of total U.S. trade.

Let's go through the steps of calculating an index number for the exchange rate. To keep this example simple, we will restrict ourselves to the U.S. exchange rate vis-à-vis the six largest other industrial countries. First, we set the *base year* to be 1992, meaning that all exchange rates that we average will be relative to their value in 1992. They will all be of the form

TABLE 2.2
Sample Exchange Rates

Currency	Value	Change	High	Low
Australian dollar*	0.6465	–0.0002	0.6467	0.6467
British pound*	1.60200	–0.00210	1.60410	1.60250
Canadian dollar	1.49000	–0.00010	1.49170	1.49100
The euro*	1.06080	0.00000	1.06100	1.06080
French franc	6.1783	0.0000	6.1783	6.1783
German mark	1.8425	0.0000	1.8425	1.8421
Italian lira	1824.00	0.00	1824.00	1824.00
Japanese yen	109.85	–0.15	110.01	109.90
New Zealand dr*	0.5180	–0.0007	0.5186	0.5186
Swiss franc	1.5065	+0.0002	1.5065	1.5060

* U.S. dollars per currency unit; otherwise, currency units per U.S. dollar.

$$\frac{\text{Exchange rate in this year}}{\text{Exchange rate in 1992}}$$

Furthermore, each exchange rate's weight in the index will be the share of U.S. trade with that particular country's economy in 1992. Thus the index number can be represented by the equation

$$\text{Index} = \sum_{\text{all countries}} \left(\frac{\text{exchange rate in this year}}{\text{exchange rate in 1992}} \times \text{share of trade in 1992} \right)$$

where Σ — the Greek capital letter sigma — stands for "sum" or "add up," the parentheses to the right of sigma tell what is to be summed, and the notation beneath sigma tells the range over which the sum applies. The equation says, "For all of these countries, add up the products of their exchange rates this year divided by their exchange rates in 1992 and multiplied by their share of total trade with the United States in 1992."

By convention, economists usually set the value of an index number in its base year to 100. To do this, simply multiply the equation for the index by 100:

$$\text{Index} = 100 \times \sum_{\text{all countries}} \left(\frac{\text{exchange rate in this year}}{\text{exchange rate in 1992}} \times \text{share of trade in 1992} \right)$$

Table 2.3 shows the results of this calculation for the year 1995. Figure 2.2 presents the exchange rate index from 1992 to 1998.

We have gone step-by-step through the process of defining the exchange rate, distinguishing between real and nominal exchange rates, calculating real exchange rates, and calculating a weighted average to arrive at *the* exchange rate. Both the calculation of index numbers and the distinction between real and nominal quantities will come up over and over again in this book. So pay attention.

TABLE 2.3
Calculating the Exchange Rate Index for 1995

Country	Exchange Rate (Value of Foreign Currency) 1992	Exchange Rate (Value of Foreign Currency) 1995	Rate in 1995/ Rate in 1992	Share of 1992 Trade	Contribution to Index
Canada	0.781	0.729	0.933	0.332	0.310
Japan	0.008	0.011	1.349	0.249	0.337
Britain	1.766	1.579	0.894	0.124	0.111
France	0.189	0.201	1.062	0.097	0.103
Germany	0.640	0.698	1.091	0.111	0.121
Italy	0.001	0.001	0.756	0.086	0.065
				Sum:	1.047
				x 100 =	
				Value of index	104.674

FIGURE 2.2

The Exchange Rate Index, 1992–1998

In 1998 the real exchange rate for the U.S. dollar was some 11 percent below its level in 1992. In 1998 a given amount of foreign-made goods could be used to purchase only 89 percent as many U.S.-made goods as it could have purchased in 1992.

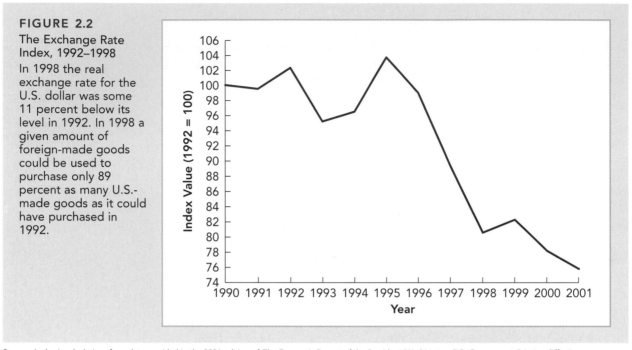

Source: Author's calculations from data provided in the 2001 edition of *The Economic Report of the President* (Washington, DC: Government Printing Office).

RECAP   THE EXCHANGE RATE

Domestic exporters earn foreign currency when they export — sell goods to people abroad. Foreign producers earn domestic currency when they sell us imports — sell their goods to people here. Both then have a problem. Domestic exporters can't pay domestic workers with foreign currency. Foreign producers can't pay foreign workers with domestic currency. Domestic producers need to trade the foreign currency they have earned for dollars they can use. They turn to the foreign exchange market, where those who have foreign currency but want dollars exchange it for dollars, and those who have dollars but want foreign currency exchange dollars for other currencies.

2.3 THE STOCK MARKET AND INTEREST RATES

The Stock Market

We don't have to calculate the value of an index for the stock market because news agencies perform that task for the public. The best — the most representative — index of the U.S. stock market is probably Standard and Poor's composite index, usually called the S&P 500. The index you will hear about most, however, is the Dow-Jones Industrial Average (DJIA). But if the DJIA tells a different story from the S&P, ignore it; it is less representative of the market than is the S&P 500.

Although we don't have to assemble and calculate a stock market index, we do have to divide the numbers reported in the news by some measure of the price level — usually either the *GDP deflator or the consumer price index (CPI)*. If both the price level and the (nominal) value of the stock market double, a representative share of stock is worth no more in real terms. To arrive at real magnitudes, economists *deflate* nominal magnitudes like a stock index by some measure of the price level in order to arrive at *real* magnitudes. In this case we are most interested in the real value of the stock market.

The Usefulness of Knowledge about the Stock Market

Current stock market indexes are the easiest economic statistics to get. But what good is knowing the real value of the stock market to a macroeconomist? The stock market is a sensitive indicator of the relative optimism or pessimism of investors, and therefore it is a good forecaster of future investment spending.

To see why, we need to think about the mechanisms underlying the stock market. Most investors in the stock market face a choice between holding stocks and holding bonds. *Stocks* are shares of ownership of a corporation, and give you ownership of that corporation's profits or earnings. *Bonds* are debts that the corporation owes you. A bond is a piece of paper that gives you periodic interest payments and, at the bond's maturity, returns to you the principal amount of the bond.

It is clear what the rate of return is on money invested in bonds. It is simply the interest payment the bond issuer makes divided by the price of the bond. Call this real rate of interest in the economy r. If you invest in shares of stock, what is your rate of return? You paid a price P^s (P for price, s for stock) for each share. The corporation reports earnings E^s per share. Some of those earnings will be paid out directly to shareholders in the form of dividends. Others will be retained and reinvested, boosting the corporation's fundamental value. Both components increase shareholder wealth, and together they are the return on the investment in stocks. Thus an investor in stocks gets a return on each dollar invested of

$$\frac{E^s}{P^s}$$

Which will the investor prefer to hold, stocks or bonds? Saying that investors will prefer stocks if E^s/P^s is greater than r is not quite right. Investments in stocks are risky. The company might go bankrupt, its reported earnings might be rigged, or the market might go down. As compensation for this risk, investors in stocks demand an extra return called the *risk premium,* or σ^s (the Greek lowercase letter sigma, with s for stocks as a superscript). So investors will want to hold only stocks if

$$\frac{E^s}{P^s} > r + \sigma^s$$

Investors will want to hold safer bonds if

$$\frac{E^s}{P^s} < r + \sigma^s$$

And investors will hold both stocks and bonds if

$$\frac{E^s}{P^s} = r + \sigma^s$$

Since in the world outside the classroom we see investors holding both stocks *and* bonds — some holding one, some holding the other, and some holding both — it is

FIGURE 2.3
Calculating the Value
of a Basket of Stocks

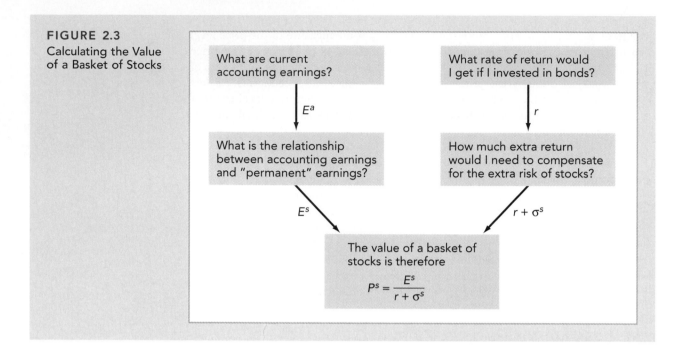

this last equation that must be true. If we turn this equation around, the value of stocks is equal to corporate earnings divided by the sum of the real interest rate on bonds and the risk premium:

$$P^s = \frac{E^s}{r + \sigma^s}$$

However, there is one more complication. The accounting earnings reported in the financial press — call them E^a — are not the earnings E^s that belong in the numerator of the stock valuation equation. The financial press reports what the firm's accountants have calculated, but investors are interested in some long-run average of expected future earnings. In order to apply the stock-price valuation formula, you also need an estimate of the relationship between the current earnings E^a that you see in the newspaper and "permanent" earnings E^s. (See Figure 2.3.)

The Stock Market Summarizes a Lot of Information
The real value of the stock market sums up, in one number that is reported every day:
- The current level of earnings, or profits.
- Whether investors are optimistic (expecting long-run earnings to be above today's level) or pessimistic (expecting long-run earnings to be below today's level), and how optimistic or pessimistic they are.
- The current cost of capital — whether money is cheap and easy to borrow (in which case r is low) or expensive (in which case r is high).
- Attitudes toward risk — whether people are strongly averse to the risks involved in entrepreneurship (in which case σ^s is high) or willing to gamble on new industries and new businesses (in which case σ^s is low).

These are the factors that determine whether corporate managers are willing to undertake investments to boost their companies' capital stocks. Thus the stock market summarizes all the information relevant to the economywide level of investment spending. Its usefulness as a summary of all the information relevant to determining investment spending is the reason it is one of the six key variables of macroeconomics.

Interest Rates

The interest rate is the price at which purchasing power can be shifted from the future into the present — borrowed today with a promise to pay it back with interest in the future. Interest is not a single lump sum but an ongoing stream of payments made over time. Thus it is what economists call a *flow* variable. A flow variable cannot be measured simply as a quantity; it must be measured as a quantity per unit of time. In the case of the interest rate, it is measured not as a percentage of the amount borrowed, the principal, but as a *percentage per year.*

Economists like to talk about "the" interest rate in the same way that they like to talk about "the" exchange rate. But just as there are a large number of different exchange rates, there are a large number of interest rates. Loans of higher risk carry higher interest rates: Whomever you lent your money to might not pay it back — that is a risk you accepted when you lent in the first place. Loans of different duration carry different interest rates as well. Moreover, differences in tax treatment — whether and when you have to pay taxes on interest earned from bonds — also lead to differences in interest rates.

Thus even with respect to U.S. government bonds — the ultimate in safe investments — there is no single interest rate. Table 2.4 shows a small sample of the interest rates quoted on U.S. Treasury securities with maturities between a few months and 30 years. Note that the price quoted depends on whether you are buying or selling: Market makers need their margin. For instance, you can buy a 30-year Treasury bond that pays annual interest of $5.375 for every $100 of initial "face value" at a price of 99 7/32 dollars — $99.21875 — for each $100 of face value. But if you want to sell that same bond you could get only 99 5/32 dollars — $99.15625.

Moreover, the interest rates published in the newspaper are nominal rates: They tell how much money you earn in interest per year if you lend out a sum of dollars now and collect the principal at the loan's maturity. You will not be surprised to

TABLE 2.4
Treasury Yield Curve

Term	Coupon	Maturity	Years	Bid	Ask	Chg	Yield
3mo	—	05/17/01	0.25	4.92	/ 90	+.01	5.071
6mo	—	08/16/01	0.50	4.80	/ 78	+.04	5.007
1yr	—	11/29/01	0.79	4.61	/ 59	+.04	4.824
2yr	4¾	01/31/03	1.96	99–29	/ 31	−03	4.785
5yr	5¾	11/15/05	4.75	103–14	/ 16	−07	4.927
10yr	5	02/15/11	10.00	99–09	/ 11	−04	5.093
30yr	5⅜	02/15/31	30.00	99–05	/ 07	−06	5.432

Source: CBS Marketwatch, cbs.marketwatch.com/data/newsroom/mwb_tres.htx?source=htx/http2_mw, Feb. 14, 2001.

learn that economists are interested instead in the real interest rate: how much purchasing power over goods and services you get in the future in return for trading away your purchasing power over goods and services today.

When we calculate real exchange rates, or real stock values, or real GDP, we divide the nominal exchange rate or stock index value or nominal GDP level by the

BOX

2.2

CALCULATING REAL INTEREST RATES: AN EXAMPLE

Why subtract the inflation rate from the nominal interest rate? Suppose you borrow $10 million for one year at a nominal interest rate of 8 percent per year. Suppose further that the annual inflation rate is also 8 percent, so the price level will rise by 8 percent between now and next year. Thus whatever goods you want to buy will be more expensive. Let's say you want to buy cheap television sets priced at $200 a set this year; they will cost $216 a set by next year.

Right now when you borrow, you get $10 million. Next year you will have to pay back $10.8 million — $10 million principal and $800,000 interest. You borrow enough now to buy 50,000 TV sets. Next year, when you pay back your loan with interest, you will pay the lender $10.8 million, just enough money to buy 50,000 cheap TV sets. Thus you will return the same purchasing power over goods and services as what you borrowed, making a real interest rate of zero (see Figure 2.4).

Suppose the inflation rate had been 4 percent, so the price of a standard basket of goods and services, and of the cheap TV sets you are buying, will rise from $200 to $208 next year. You borrow $10 million, enough to buy 50,000 cheap TV sets. Next year, when you pay back your loan with its 8 percent annual interest, you will pay the lender $10.8 million, enough money to buy 51,923 TV sets. The extra 1,923 TV sets are a 3.846 percent increase in purchasing power over goods and services. Thus you will return 3.846 percent more purchasing power than you borrowed. However, to keep things simple, economists round the percentage off and call it a 4 percent real interest rate. (You will find that economists often round off numbers, drop small terms from equations, and generally do whatever they can to make things simpler.)

Thus the rule: To calculate a *real* interest rate, subtract the inflation rate from the *nominal* interest rate.

FIGURE 2.4
The Real versus the Nominal Interest Rate

At an 8%-per-year interest rate, $1 now is equivalent to $1.08 a year from now.   **8%**

But an 8%-per-year inflation rate means that . . .   **–8%**

The real interest rate is zero: $1.08 a year from now gives just as much purchasing power over goods and services as $1 today.   **= 0**

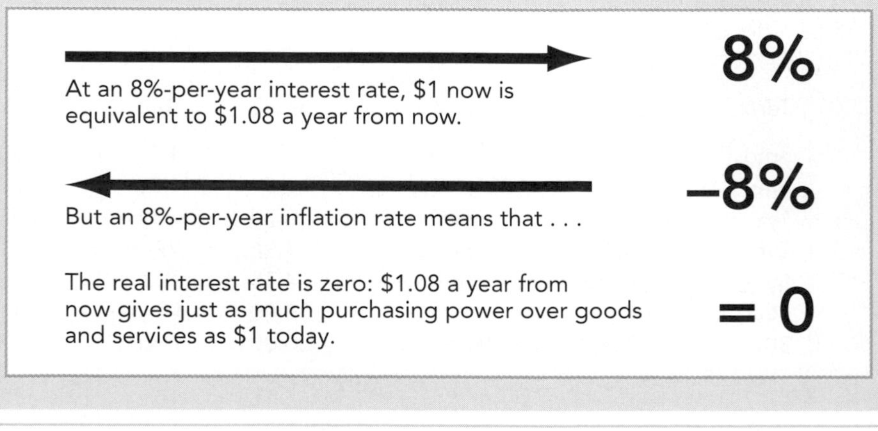

price level, but that is not what we do to calculate real interest rates. Instead of dividing the nominal interest rate by the price level, we *subtract* the inflation rate — the percentage rate of change in the price level — from the nominal interest rate to get the real interest rate. Box 2.2 explains the reason for this procedure, and Box 2.3

SOME USEFUL MATHEMATICAL TOOLS: TOOLS

BOX

2.3

In saying that the real interest rate is the nominal interest rate minus the inflation rate, we are using one of three mathematical tools that will make life a lot easier throughout this course. They are all *approximations*. But they are all close enough for our purposes, and they make life simpler. They are as follows:

1. *The growth-of-a-product rule:* The proportional change of a *product* is equal to the *sum* of the proportional changes of its components.

2. *The growth-of-a-quotient rule:* The proportional change of a *quotient* is equal to the *difference* between the proportional changes of its components.

3. *The growth-of-a-power rule:* The proportional change of a *quantity raised to a power* is equal to the *proportional change in the quantity times the power* to which it is raised.

As we just saw in calculating the real interest rate, these three rules are only approximations: An 8 percent increase in a nominal sum of money and a 4 percent increase in the price level produce not a 4 percent but a 3.846 percent increase in real purchasing power over goods and services. But that is close enough.

To illustrate the first, product, rule, suppose we have two variables, P (price) and Q (quantity) that together are multiplied to make up E (expenditure), $E = P \times Q$. Then,

Proportional change in E = proportional change in P + proportional change in Q

Thus if real production Q is growing at 5 percent per year, and the price level P is growing at 2 percent per year, then total nominal expenditure E will be growing at a proportional rate of 5 percent + 2 percent = 7 percent per year.

To illustrate the second, quotient, rule, start out with E (expenditure) and Q (quantity) so that when we divide them we get P (price), $E/Q = P$. Then,

Proportional change in P = proportional change in E – proportional change in Q

Thus if nominal expenditure E is growing at 7 percent per year and real production Q is growing at 5 percent per year, then the price level P must be growing at a proportional rate of 7 percent – 5 percent = 2 percent per year.

To illustrate the third, power, rule, suppose that real GDP Y is equal to the economy's capital stock K raised to a power — K^α, K raised to the power α. (Recall that $X^{0.5}$ is the square root of X, that $X^1 = X$, and that $X^2 = X \times X$.) Then,

Proportional change in $Y = \alpha \times$ proportional change in K

Thus if α equals 0.5, and thus $Y = K^{0.5}$, and if the capital stock K is growing at 6 percent per year, real GDP Y will be growing at 0.5×6 percent = 3 percent per year.

You may hear people say that a background in calculus is needed to understand intermediate macroeconomics. That is not true. In fact, 95 percent of what calculus is used for in intermediate macroeconomics is contained in these three mathematical tools. (Of course, calculus is needed if you want to understand just *why* they work.)

generalizes by explaining a few more mathematical tricks that are useful when we are shifting between levels and growth rates.

> ### RECAP   THE STOCK MARKET AND INTEREST RATES
>
> We don't have to calculate an index for the stock market because news agencies perform that task for the public already. We do, however, have to divide the numbers reported in the news by some measure of the price level in order to adjust for inflation and determine the real value of the stock market. To arrive at real magnitudes, economists *deflate* nominal magnitudes like a stock index by some measure of the price level in order to arrive at *real* magnitudes. In this case we are most interested in the real value of the stock market. Note that when we calculate real interest rates, we do not divide the nominal interest rate by the price level. Instead we *subtract* the inflation rate — the percentage rate of change in the price level — from the nominal interest rate to get the real interest rate.

2.4 THE PRICE LEVEL AND INFLATION

The Consumer Price Index

The idea that economists need to measure the **price level** and to use it to calculate real quantities has come up several times already. Estimating the price level and its proportional rate of change — the inflation rate — is at the heart of macroeconomics.

The most frequently seen measure of the overall price level is the consumer price index, or CPI. (Other measures of prices include the producer price index of prices paid not by consumers but by companies, the economywide GDP deflator, and the domestic purchases deflator.) The CPI is calculated and reported once a month by the **Bureau of Labor Statistics**. It is an expenditure-weighted index, in which each good or service receives a weight equal to its share in total expenditure in the base year. (See Box 2.4 for a sample calculation.)

The Bureau of Labor Statistics changes the basket of **goods and services** used in constructing the CPI on a somewhat irregular basis. It updates the basket every five years if it has the money in its budget to do so; if not, it updates the basket every 10 years. Statisticians try to keep the weighted "market basket" of goods and services used in calculating the index reasonably close to the goods and services consumers are currently buying. If it were not, the CPI would be of doubtful relevance. Who would care about the rate of change in the price of a statistical market basket that didn't represent what consumers were really buying?

Kinds of Index Numbers

Using relative expenditure levels in a fixed base year as the weights in a price index produces a kind of index that economists call a *Laspeyres index*. The CPI is a Laspeyres price index. Another type of index, a *Paasche index*, is in a sense the opposite of a Laspeyres index. A Laspeyres index of production or consumption counts up the current dollar value of what is produced or consumed and divides by what the value of what is produced or consumed would have been if all commodities had

CALCULATING PRICE INDEXES: AN EXAMPLE

One standard example economists use to illustrate how a price index is calculated is an index for consumers of fruit (perhaps because calculating indexes allows economists to really add apples and oranges). Suppose that in the base year a consumer buys $4.50 worth of oranges at a price of $0.75 a pound, $4.20 worth of apples at $1.20 a pound, $0.90 worth of pears at $0.90 a pound, and $0.40 worth of bananas at $0.40 a pound. Then, with a total of $10 spent on fruit in the base year, the price index for fruit will be given by

$$\text{Price index for fruit} = \frac{\text{price of oranges today}}{\text{price of oranges in base year}} \times \text{orange index weight}$$

$$+ \frac{\text{price of apples today}}{\text{price of apples in base year}} \times \text{apple index weight}$$

$$+ \frac{\text{price of pears today}}{\text{price of pears in base year}} \times \text{pear index weight}$$

$$+ \frac{\text{price of bananas today}}{\text{price of bananas in base year}} \times \text{banana index weight}$$

$$= \frac{\text{price of oranges today}}{\$0.75} \times 45 + \frac{\text{price of apples today}}{\$1.20} \times 42$$

$$+ \frac{\text{price of pears today}}{\$0.90} \times 09 + \frac{\text{price of bananas today}}{\$0.40} \times 04$$

We multiply the total annual expenditure on each fruit by 100 so that in the base year the price index will be equal to 100, as is customary for economists to do.

Now consider a year in which, as shown in Table 2.5, the price of oranges has risen to $1.50, the price of apples has fallen to $1.00, and the prices of pears and bananas have not changed. The overall fruit price index will be

$$\text{Price index for fruit} = \frac{\$1.50}{\$0.75} \times 45 + \frac{\$1.00}{\$1.20} \times 42 + \frac{\$0.90}{\$0.90} \times 09 + \frac{\$0.40}{\$0.40} \times 04 = 138$$

TABLE 2.5
Calculating a Price Index for Fruit: An Example

Fruit	Base-Year Expenditure	Base-Year Price (per Pound)	Subsequent-Year Price (per Pound)
Oranges	$4.50	$0.75	$1.50
Apples	4.20	1.20	1.00
Pears	0.90	0.90	0.90
Bananas	0.40	0.40	0.40

---

sold for their prices in the base year. The expenditure weights in a Paasche index are variable: If expenditures on a particular good rise this year and make it a large part of the current dollar value, then that good's weight in the price index will rise too.

The second most-often-seen indicator of the price level, the GDP deflator, is a Paasche index. Box 2.5 compares the pluses and minuses of these two kinds of price indexes.

In general, a Laspeyres index overstates price increases. In the real world, when some items become expensive, consumers *substitute* and buy other items that remain cheap. But a Laspeyres index, because it is based on a fixed market basket of goods and services, does not take account of this substitution. Thus it suffers from what economists call *substitution bias,* and it tends to overstate changes. A Paasche index, on the other hand, understates the increase in fruit prices. It calculates the difference between the price today of the *fruit you bought* and the price back in the base year. The Paasche index takes account of substitution. But it doesn't take account of the fact that the substituted items are less valued than the items they replace. The Paasche index reports, in the example of Box 2.5, that the skyrocketing price of oranges has no effect on fruit prices. Yet it makes no sense to say that a frost that makes oranges completely unaffordable has no effect on the price of fruit.

BOX 2.5

LASPEYRES AND PAASCHE INDEX NUMBERS: THE DETAILS

To see the difference between a Laspeyres and a Paasche index, return to our fruit example in Box 2.4. Suppose the prices of apples, pears, and bananas remain at their base-year levels, but surprise frosts destroy the orange crops in both Florida *and* California. The price of oranges skyrockets to $8.25 a pound (see Table 2.6), so no one buys any oranges — instead, consumers double their purchases of apples, pears, and bananas to 7 pounds of apples, 2 pounds of pears, and 2 pounds of bananas.

The CPI for fruit, a Laspeyres index, would then be

$$\text{Price index for fruit} = \frac{\$8.25}{\$0.75} \times 45 + \frac{\$1.20}{\$1.20} \times 42 + \frac{\$0.90}{\$0.90} \times 09 + \frac{\$0.40}{\$0.40} \times 04 = 550$$

According to this index, the price of fruit is five and a half times as high as that in the base year.

The deflator for fruit, a Paasche index, would be

- Total nominal expenditure on fruit in the frost year: $11
- Cost of buying those pieces of fruit in the base year: $11
- Dividing the first number by the second, we discover that the price of fruit has not changed from its base-year value, 100.

TABLE 2.6
Two Different Kinds of Indexes: An Index Number Example

Fruit	Base-Year Expenditure	Base-Year Price (per Pound)	Subsequent-Year Price (per Pound)
Oranges	$4.50	$0.75	$8.20
Apples	4.20	1.20	1.20
Pears	0.90	0.90	0.90
Bananas	0.40	0.40	0.40

So which is the "correct" price index? The answer is "neither." There is no final and definitive resolution to this "index number problem." All price indexes are imperfect. All try to summarize in a single number what is inherently a multidimensional reality of many prices changing in different directions and different proportions.

To strike a balance between the two types of indexes and their two types of biases, the Commerce Department's **Bureau of Economic Analysis** and the Labor Department's Bureau of Labor Statistics have begun to move toward hybrid indexes. To reduce substitution bias, the Bureau of Labor Statistics has begun using geometric averages — multiply two numbers together and take the square root — instead of arithmetic averages. And the Bureau of Economic Analysis has begun using a procedure called *chain weighting* to construct its indexes.

With chain weighting, each year's proportional change in the index is calculated using a different base year. For instance, the percentage change in the index from 1999 to 2000 is calculated using the average of 1999 and 2000 as the base; the change from 2000 to 2001 will be calculated using the average of 2000 and 2001 as the base; and the change from 2001 to 2002 will be calculated using the average of 2001 and 2002 as the base. The results of these calculations are then "chained" together to make up the index.

The Inflation Rate

The CPI is reported once a month in the form of the percentage change in consumer prices over the preceding month. "Consumer prices in November rose 0.3 percent above their level in October," a newscaster will say. Eventually, 12 monthly changes in consumer prices over the course of the year are added up and become that year's **inflation** rate. "The consumer price inflation rate in 1999 was 2.7 percent," the newscaster will say.

Because the inflation rate is a measure of the rate of change in prices over time, it is a *flow* variable. When we speak of the inflation rate, we speak of it as such-and-such percent *per year*. Speaking of the inflation rate without reference to a measure of time is incomplete. But people do, and we always assume that when the time measure is omitted, the inflation percentage is an annual rate.

What the inflation rate is at any moment depends on which price level it is based on. The CPI-based inflation rate will not be exactly the same as the GDP-deflator-based inflation rate. Figure 2.5 plots four different measures of inflation in the United States: the GDP deflator, a CPI for all urban consumers (the CPI-U), a CPI using an experimental method of taking account of housing prices (the CPI-U-X1), and a CPI that omits the volatile prices of food and energy, which can cause severe transitory fluctuations in the overall index (the CPI-U ex F&E).

RECAP   THE PRICE LEVEL AND INFLATION

Already the idea that economists need to measure the price level and to use it to calculate real quantities has come up several times. Estimating the price level and its proportional rate of change — the inflation rate — is at the heart of macroeconomics. The most frequently seen measure of the overall price level is the Consumer Price Index, or CPI. It is a fixed weight — a Laspeyres index of prices. Each good or service receives a weight equal to its share in total expenditure in the base year. And periodically the base year is moved forward in time.

FIGURE 2.5
Different Measurements of U.S. Inflation, 1960–2000
Different measures of inflation tell slightly different stories about inflation. But all tell the same broad story: Differences are small relative to the large swings in the inflation rate from one decade to another.

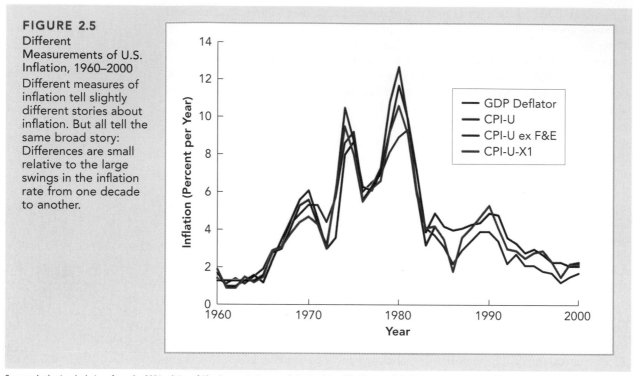

Source: Author's calculations from the 2001 edition of *The Economic Report of the President* (Washington, DC: Government Printing Office).

2.5 UNEMPLOYMENT

Calculating the Unemployment Rate

The unemployment rate is a key indicator of economic performance. An economy with persistent high unemployment is wasting its productive resources: Its level of output is below its productive potential. Such an economy surely has a lower level of social welfare than otherwise might easily be attained. Being unemployed is not pleasant, nor is fearing unemployment for no other reason than the turning of the wheel of the business cycle.

Keeping unemployment low is one of the chief goals of macroeconomic policy. Yet in the course of the business cycle unemployment rises and falls. Figure 2.6 shows the annual unemployment rate in the United States during the second half of the twentieth century. It shows the large variation in unemployment. Even though the second half of the twentieth century saw nothing like the extraordinary peaks of unemployment in the Great Depression, the unemployment rate still varied from a low of less than 4 percent of the labor force to a high of almost 10 percent of the labor force.

Every month the Labor Department's Bureau of Labor Statistics (BLS) sends interviewers to talk to 60,000 households in a nationwide survey called the Current Population Survey (CPS). The BLS uses the CPS data to estimate the unemployment rate — the fraction of people who (a) wanted a job, (b) looked for a job, but (c) could not find an acceptable job. Statisticians classify the people who are interviewed into four categories:

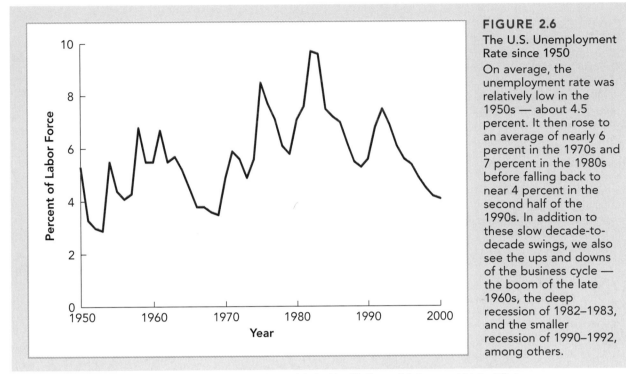

FIGURE 2.6
The U.S. Unemployment Rate since 1950
On average, the unemployment rate was relatively low in the 1950s — about 4.5 percent. It then rose to an average of nearly 6 percent in the 1970s and 7 percent in the 1980s before falling back to near 4 percent in the second half of the 1990s. In addition to these slow decade-to-decade swings, we also see the ups and downs of the business cycle — the boom of the late 1960s, the deep recession of 1982–1983, and the smaller recession of 1990–1992, among others.

Source: Author's calculations from the 2001 edition of *The Economic Report of the President* (Washington, DC: Government Printing Office).

1. Those who were employed in some sort of job when interviewed.
2. Those who were out of the labor force and did not want a job immediately.
3. Those who did want a job immediately but had not been looking for one because they did not think they could find one.
4. Those who did want a job immediately, had been looking, but had not found a job they would take.

According to the BLS definition of the unemployment rate, the *labor force* is group 1 plus group 4 — those who had jobs plus those who were looking for jobs:

$$\text{Labor force} = \text{employed} + \text{looking for work}$$

The unemployment rate is the numer of unemployed — those in group 4 — divided by the total labor force:

$$\text{Unemployment rate} = \frac{\text{looking for work}}{\text{labor force}} = \frac{\text{looking for work}}{\text{employed} + \text{looking for work}}$$

In contrast to the inflation rate, which is a *flow* variable, the unemployment rate is a *stock* variable. Saying that the current unemployment rate is 4 percent, with no reference to a measure of time, makes perfect sense.

The official unemployment rate may well underestimate the real experience of unemployment. Someone in group 3, who wants a job but has given up looking, certainly feels unemployed and may well feel as unemployed as someone in group 4. Perhaps these *discouraged workers* should be included in the unemployment rate. Furthermore, some people in group 1 have part-time jobs but want full-time jobs.

FIGURE 2.7
U.S. Unemployment
Rates by Demographic
Group, 1960–2000
The higher a group's
average unemployment
rate, the more the
group's unemployment
rate rises in recessions
(and falls in booms).
Recessions — times of
high and rising
unemployment — are
unusually difficult for
teenage and African-
American workers.

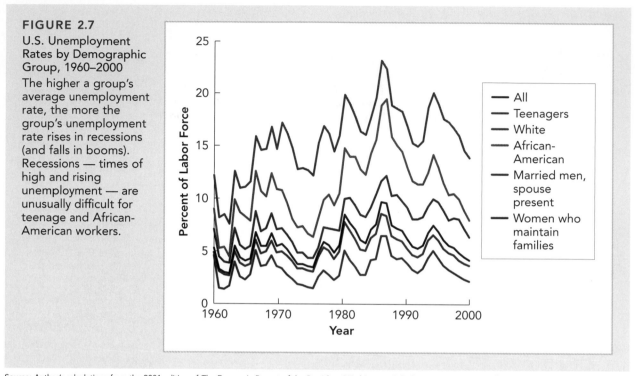

Source: Author's calculations from the 2001 edition of *The Economic Report of the President* (Washington, DC: Government Printing Office).

Perhaps these *part-timers for economic reasons* should be counted as unemployed, or as half-unemployed.

Economists have noted striking and persistent variations in unemployment by demographic group and class. Teenagers age 16 to 19 have higher unemployment rates than adults, African-Americans have higher unemployment rates than whites, and high school dropouts have higher unemployment rates than those who have postgraduate degrees. For most of the post-World War II period (but not recently) women have had higher unemployment rates than men. Significantly, recessions don't just raise the unemployment rate; they disproportionately raise the unemployment rate among these high-unemployment groups. Figure 2.7 contrasts the unemployment rates of various groups of workers.

The question "How long is the typical person who loses his or her job unemployed?" is hard to answer because it is an ambiguous one. Most people who become unemployed on any one day — say, July 16, 2001 — remain unemployed for only a short time; more than half find a job within a month. Yet of all the people who are unemployed on July 16, 2001, some three-quarters of them will be unemployed for more than two months before they find another job.

Okun's Law

In the United States since World War II, the unemployment rate has been tightly coupled with the rate of growth of real GDP in a relationship called Okun's law (see Figure 2.8). From any one year to the next, the very simple equation

Percentage change in real GDP = percentage growth in potential output −
(2.5 × percentage = point change in unemployment rate)

fits the data very well. According to Okun's law, unemployment falls (rises) when real GDP grows faster (slower) than potential output. Specifically, in the United States a 1-percentage-point fall in unemployment is associated with an extra 2.5 percentage points of growth in real GDP. For example, in a year in which potential output grew 2.5 percent and unemployment fell by 1 percentage point, real GDP would grow by fully 5 percent.

Because of Okun's law, if you know what is happening to real GDP relative to potential output, you have a good idea of what is happening to the unemployment rate, and vice versa. Box 2.6 explains the details of Okun's law at greater length.

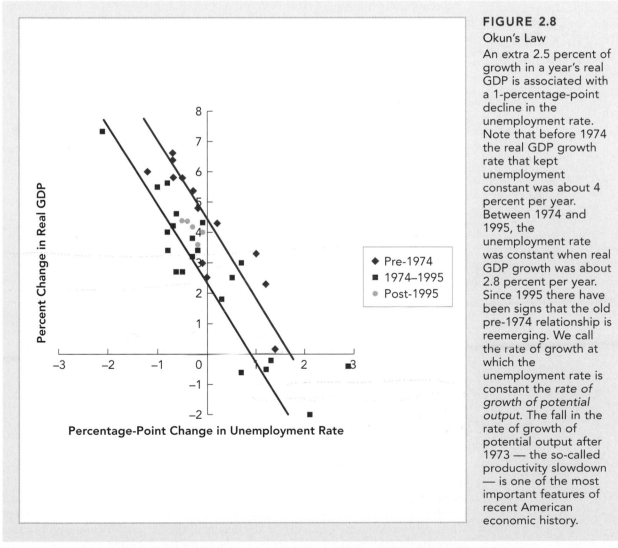

FIGURE 2.8

Okun's Law

An extra 2.5 percent of growth in a year's real GDP is associated with a 1-percentage-point decline in the unemployment rate. Note that before 1974 the real GDP growth rate that kept unemployment constant was about 4 percent per year. Between 1974 and 1995, the unemployment rate was constant when real GDP growth was about 2.8 percent per year. Since 1995 there have been signs that the old pre-1974 relationship is reemerging. We call the rate of growth at which the unemployment rate is constant the *rate of growth of potential output*. The fall in the rate of growth of potential output after 1973 — the so-called productivity slowdown — is one of the most important features of recent American economic history.

Source: Author's calculations from the 2001 edition of *The Economic Report of the President* (Washington, DC: Government Printing Office).

WHY THE OKUN'S LAW COEFFICIENT IS SO LARGE: THE DETAILS

Okun's law posits not a 1-to-1 relation but a 2.5-to-1 relationship between real GDP growth and the unemployment rate. That is, a 1-percentage-point fall in the unemployment rate is associated not with a 1 but a 2.5 percent boost in the level of production.

Why is the Okun's law coefficient so large? Why isn't it the case that a 1-percentage-point fall in unemployment produces a 1 percent rise in output, or even less? One answer is that the unemployment rate, as officially measured, does not count discouraged workers. In a recession, the number of people at work falls, the number of people looking for work rises, and the number of people who are not looking for work because they doubt they could find jobs — but who would be working if business conditions were better — rises. Because the conventionally measured unemployment rate does not include these discouraged workers, more than a 1 percent rise in real GDP is needed to reduce the unemployment rate by 1 percentage point.

Moreover, when business returns to normal, firms' initial response is not to hire more employees but to ask existing employees to work longer hours. So average hours of work per week go up, and the unemployment rate falls by less than one would otherwise expect.

Finally, in some industries, employing more workers increases production by more than a proportional amount: Product design and setup need to be done only once, no matter how much is produced. Thus businesses that have *economies of scale* do not need twice as many workers to produce twice as much output.

RECAP   THE UNEMPLOYMENT RATE

The unemployment rate is a key indicator of economic performance. An economy with persistent high unemployment is wasting its productive resources: its level of output is below its productive potential. Moreover, the official unemployment rate may well underestimate the real experience of unemployment in the American economy.

2.6 REAL GDP

Sixth and last of the key economic variables is **real GDP**, the most frequently used measure of economic performance. You will see other measures of total production and total income as well. All of them are close cousins of real GDP: GNP (gross national product), NNP (net national product), NDP (net domestic product), and NI (national income). And you will hear commentators refer to "total output," "total production," "national product," "total income," and "national income." Except when you are focusing explicitly on the details of the national income and product accounts (**NIPA**), treat all these terms as synonyms for real GDP.

Calculating Real GDP

Real GDP is calculated by adding up the value of all final goods and services produced in the economy. Because it measures the rate at which goods and services are produced, real GDP is a flow variable; it is usually expressed as an annual amount. Often, however, you will not hear the phrase "per year." But when you hear that real GDP in the fourth quarter of 2002 was such and such, remember that such a statement means that the flow of production in the fourth quarter was such and such *per year.* And when you hear that real GDP in the fourth quarter of 2002 grew at so-and-so percent, remember that such a statement means that real GDP in the fourth quarter grew at so-and-so percent *per year* — the difference between real GDP in the third quarter and real GDP in the fourth quarter is only one-quarter of the reported annual growth rate.

What are the final goods and services that make up GDP? A *final good or service* is something that is not used further in production during the course of the year. Thus final goods and services include:

- Everything bought by consumers.
- Everything bought by businesses not as an input for further production but as an investment to increase the business's capital stock and expand its future production capacity.
- Everything bought by the government.

Because GDP measures *product* and not *spending,* it includes a balancing item, *exports minus imports.* Because imported goods bought by consumers, installed as pieces of investment, or bought by the government were not made in the United States, they are not part of gross domestic product, so imports need to be subtracted from GDP. Because exported goods bought by foreigners were made in the United States, they *are* part of GDP and need to be added to the total.

Real and Nominal GDP

When economists add up final goods and services produced in the year to calculate GDP, how do they weight each good or service? The answer is that they use market value — what people paid for a good or service — in the calculation of *nominal* GDP. Box 2.7 presents a stylized, hypothetical example of how this is done.

In 2000 nominal GDP (that is, GDP measured at 2000 prices) was $9.99 trillion; in 1999 nominal GDP (that is, measured at 1999 prices) was $9.30 billion. Thus the growth rate of nominal GDP between 1999 and 2000 was 7.4 percent. But it is clear this *nominal* measure of GDP, in which current-year prices are used to weight the final goods and services produced and to calculate growth rates, is not a good measure of productivity or material output. It confuses changes in the overall price level — inflation or deflation — with changes in total production. Suppose production in the next year stayed unchanged but prices doubled; nominal GDP would double. Suppose production doubled but prices stayed the same; nominal GDP would also double. While nominal GDP does not distinguish between these two sources of increase in total expenditure, we need to distinguish between them. Hence economists favor real GDP — the value of final goods and services weighted by the prices of some particular base year. Box 2.8 illustrates the weighting of goods and services in terms of base-year prices.

Whenever you hear a statement such as "Real GDP in 1999 was 8.88 trillion 1996 dollars," remember that "1996 dollars" means that 1996 is the base year of the

WEIGHTING GOODS AND SERVICES BY THEIR MARKET VALUES: AN EXAMPLE

How do economists weight goods and services by their market values? Recall the discussion of the CPI earlier in this chapter (see page 41) in which the representative consumer bought 11.5 pounds of fruit:

Fruit	Quantity (Pounds)	Price (per Pound)
Oranges	6	$0.75
Apples	3.5	1.20
Pears	1	0.90
Bananas	1	0.40

If these quantities were the final goods and services produced in a particular year — let's call it year 1 — and we then wanted to measure the GDP of fruit, we simply multiply the quantities produced by their market prices:

$$\text{GDP} = 6 \text{ lbs. oranges} \times \$0.75/\text{lb.} + 3.5 \text{ lbs. apples} \times \$1.20/\text{lb.} +$$
$$1 \text{ lb. pears} \times \$0.90/\text{lb.} + 1 \text{ lb. bananas} \times \$0.40/\text{lb.}$$
$$= \$10.00$$

The nominal GDP of fruit in year 1 is $10.

calculation. When measured using 1996 prices, GDP in 1999 — real GDP — was not $9.30 trillion but only $8.88 trillion. The difference, the gap between $9.30 and $8.88, was due to price inflation between 1996 and 1999. Real GDP between 1995 and 1996 rose by only 2.5 percent, not 4.5 percent.

As has been noted above (see page 43), economists construct an alternative index number for the rate of inflation, the GDP deflator, from nominal GDP and real GDP. The procedure is

1. Calculate nominal GDP.
2. Calculate real GDP.
3. Divide the first number by the second; the quotient is the GDP deflator.

The GDP deflator is a Paasche index — the kind of index that tends to understate the effect on the price level of a rise in the price of a particular good. While the GDP deflator takes account of purchasers' ability to substitute away from items that have increased prices, it does not take account of the reduction in utility — the implicit cost to consumers — of settling for second best.

Intermediate Goods, Inventories, and Imputations

Intermediate Goods

GDP is defined as the market value of final goods and services produced. Thus so-called *intermediate goods* — goods sold to another business for use in further

WEIGHTING GOODS AND SERVICES BY THEIR BASE-YEAR VALUES: AN EXAMPLE

Recall the hypothetical example in Box 2.7. Assume that in the year following year 1 — year 2 — the prices and quantities of fruit produced are as follows:

Fruit	Quantity (Pounds)	Price (per Pound)
Oranges	8	$1.00
Apples	3.5	1.20
Pears	1	0.50
Bananas	1	0.40

Now we can calculate nominal GDP of fruit in both year 1 and year 2 and real GDP of fruit (at year 1 prices) in both year 1 and year 2:

- Nominal GDP of fruit in year 1: $10.00
- Real GDP of fruit in year 1 (at year 1 prices): $10.00
- Nominal GDP of fruit in year 2: $13.10
- Real GDP of fruit in year 2 (at year 1 prices): $11.50

The nominal quantity grows by 31 percent between year 1 and year 2. The real quantity grows by only 15 percent between year 1 and year 2. The difference is inflation, the change in the price level.

BOX 2.8

production — are excluded from GDP. A product made by one business and sold to another will eventually show up in the national income and product accounts and be counted as part of GDP. It will show up when the second business sells its product (which will by then embody the value added by the first producer) to a consumer, an investor, a foreign purchaser, or the government. Meanwhile, because the value of an intermediate good is included in the price of the final good that the intermediate good is used to make, its value must be excluded from GDP.

For example, if a builder buys wood from a lumber mill to build a house, the value of the wood becomes part of the value of the house. To count the sale of the wood to the home builder as well as the sale of the newly built house to its purchaser would be to count the wood twice. And what would happen if the builder bought the lumber mill and thus no longer had to buy finished wood? GDP should not go down just because two businesses have merged.

One way to think about intermediate goods is that GDP represents the economic value added at every stage of production. The value added by any one business is equal to the total value of the firm's products minus the value of the materials and intermediate goods the firm purchases. In computing value added from start to finish, each intermediate good and service enters the calculation twice: once with a plus sign, when the value added of the business that made the good is calculated, and once with a minus sign, when the value added of the business that uses the good is calculated. Using this value-added approach, every good and service in the economy cancels out except those that are *not* sold to other businesses for use in the production process. The goods whose values do not cancel out are the *final goods and services* — consumption goods, goods purchased by the government, goods purchased as part of investment, and net exports.

Inventories

What happens if the production process is not finished when the end of the year rolls around and the Commerce Department's Bureau of Economic Analysis (BEA) closes the books on that year's GDP calculation? Some intermediate goods will not have been used to produce goods for final sale. The value has already been added in making the intermediate good, but no final good that embodies that value has yet been sold. The NIPA finesses this problem by treating inventories at the end of a period as a special kind of final good, a form of investment. A business that produces intermediate goods or final goods and doesn't sell them by the end of the year is treated as having "purchased" those goods for itself as part of its capital stock. The general rule is that whenever a business increases its end-of-period inventory, that increase is counted as a component of investment and of final demand.

What happens the next year when the final goods are finished and sold? The value of those final goods sold becomes part of the next period's GDP. But the intermediate goods that went into them are counted as a negative investment, a disinvestment, in inventory. Thus the intermediate goods left over from this year and used next year are *subtracted* from next year's GDP.

Imputations

What about goods and services that are produced and consumed but not sold in the marketplace? Such goods and services lack prices and market values; how are they counted in GDP? In some cases national income accounts estimate — they guess, really — what goods or services would have sold for on the market if there had been a market.

The largest such "imputation" in the NIPA is found in housing. When somebody rents an apartment or a house, the rent he or she pays to the landlord becomes part of GDP as the purchase of "housing services" by the renter. When a landlord rents a house to a tenant, the landlord is selling a service — the usefulness of having a roof over the renter's head — just as a barber is selling a service when a customer gets a haircut. Thus rent is one item in consumer spending on services. Accountants enter it as a component of expenditure in the FIRE (finance, insurance, and real estate) sector, a large component of consumer demand.

However, a little more than half of all Americans own their own houses and are their own landlords. These homeowners do not write a monthly rent check to themselves. Counting renter-occupied housing as part of GDP but ignoring owner-occupied housing would not be consistent. Therefore GDP includes the *imputed* rent on owner-occupied dwellings — the amount the BEA thinks that owner-occupied apartments and houses would rent for if they were rented out.

The inclusion of the cost of goods and services bought by the government may also be understood as an imputation. Since citizens do not directly pay firefighters, police officers, judges, and other government employees, the value of what the government spends on firefighting — in wages, insurance, materials, and so forth — is counted in GDP.

Components of Real GDP

How does the Bureau of Economic Analysis construct its measure of real GDP? The BEA includes in its measure of real GDP, which we will always denote by Y in equations and diagrams, the values of the following:

- Goods and services that are ultimately bought and used by households (except for newly constructed buildings); these goods and services are termed **consumption spending** (denoted C).

- Goods and services (including newly constructed buildings) that become part of society's business or residential capital stock; these goods and services are termed **investment spending** (denoted I). Gross investment spending is divided into two parts: the capital consumption allowance, or the depreciation of worn-out or obsolete capital; and net investment, which increases the total capital stock. Investment can be divided into four components: houses and apartments (residential structures), other buildings and infrastructure (nonresidential structures), machines (producers' durable equipment), and, as noted above, the change in business inventories (see Table 2.7).

- **Government purchases** (denoted G). Note that government purchases do not include any payments the government makes that are not payment for a good or service provided to the government.

- **Net exports** (denoted NX) are a balancing item included in GDP: the GDP total needs to be adjusted for the difference between exports and imports to make the national income and product accounts consistent.

Accountants add up all these components to arrive at GDP (see Table 2.8). This definition of GDP, the national income identity, is one of the most fundamental bases of macroeconomics:

$$Y = C + I + G + NX$$

This is the equation that you will write down more than any other during any macroeconomics course.

Goods (and services) produced abroad but consumed or used in the United States are imports. Goods (and services) produced in the United States and shipped abroad to be consumed or used there are gross exports. The distinction between gross exports and net exports is similar to the distinction between gross investment and net

TABLE 2.7
Components of Investment, Third Quarter of 2000

Category of Investment	Annual Rate (Billions)
Total private gross investment spending	$1,364
Residential structures	376
Nonresidential structures	246
Producers' durable equipment	685
Change in business inventories	57

Source: Author's calculations from the 2001 edition of *The Economic Report of the President* (Washington, DC: Government Printing Office).

TABLE 2.8
Components of GDP, Third Quarter of 2000

Category of Investment	Annual Rate (Billions)
Total GDP	$8,574
Consumption spending	5,847
Investment spending	1,364
Government purchases	1,492
Net exports	−166

Source: Author's calculations from the 2001 edition of *The Economic Report of the President* (Washington, DC: Government Printing Office).

investment. Gross exports are exports before the counterbalancing factor of imports has been subtracted. Most often gross exports are less important than net exports — the difference between gross exports and imports, the net flow of goods into or out of the United States.

The final component of the national income identity, net exports, has been growing in relative size and importance. In the years just after World War II, imports into and exports from the United States were about 5 percent of GDP. The United States was then more or less a closed economy. Macroeconomics textbooks gave short shrift to international trade and finance: It was not very important. Today imports into and exports from the United States are about 15 percent of GDP, three times as large a share as the percentage 50 years ago. The American economy is no longer a closed economy, and so international economics issues can no longer be downplayed.

What Is and Is Not in GDP

Depreciation and Net Output

Real GDP is a very imperfect measure of total economic activity, or material well-being. Some things that are included in GDP should not be, and some things that are not included in GDP should be. For example, every year a portion of the nation's capital stock loses value. It wears out or becomes obsolete, so it is no longer worth keeping it operating because the cost of doing so is higher than the value of the goods the capital produces. Replacing such worn-out or obsolete capital is as much a cost of production to a business (or a government) as is meeting the business's payroll. Such replacement is surely not an *increase* in the nation's capital stock. Yet GDP counts *all* investment — including this replacement investment — in its measure of total economic activity, for the measure of investment included in real GDP is gross investment.

Why is replacement investment included in real GDP? Why is it seen not as a cost of doing business but as the near-equivalent of building a new factory to expand the business's productive capacity? Depreciation expenditures are counted in real GDP because the statisticians who compile the NIPA have no confidence in their estimates of economywide depreciation. A better measure of economic activity is net domestic product (NDP), which includes only net investment and excludes depreciation. However, the national income accountants prefer to focus attention on measures that they think are reasonably accurate, and so they downplay the (poorly measured) NDP and play up the GDP estimate.

Government Purchases

Government purchases of goods and services are also counted in GDP. The government uses the goods and services it purchases: It builds roads, provides police protection and courts, runs schools, issues weather reports, maintains the national parks, maintains the armed services, and so on.

Many of these services, if they were provided by private businesses, would be counted as intermediate goods — things that are not of final value themselves but are aids to private-sector production. As such, they would be excluded from the GDP. Think about it. Suppose two companies made a contract that a certain arbitrator would be the judge of any disputes that arose between them, and suppose they paid the arbitrator a retainer. The services of the private judge that they hired would be classified in the NIPA as an intermediate good and would not be included in the final goods and services added up to calculate GDP.

Nevertheless, *all* government purchases of goods and services are counted as part of GDP, including the money the government collects in taxes and then pays to its own judges, bailiffs, and clerks, many of whom decide business-to-business disputes. A large number of government purchases fall into this category. They are counted as part of GDP, but they would not be counted had they been made for analogous substantive purposes by private businesses.

What Isn't in GDP but Should Be

Moreover, many expenditures excluded from the NIPA, and thus from GDP, probably should not be. Production that takes place within the household is excluded from GDP. That is, the work family members do to keep their own households going, for which they are not paid, is excluded from GDP.

This exclusion warps our picture of the U.S. economy. In 2000 some 129 million Americans, male and female, worked a total of about 206 billion paid hours (and some 7 million Americans spent a total of 5 billion hours looking for jobs). But many Americans — most of them adult women — also spent at least 100 billion hours performing services, such as cooking, cleaning, shopping, and chauffeuring, that would count as employment and would count in GDP if they were receiving pay for them rather than doing them for their own families. As Figure 2.9 shows, only a little more than 30 percent of American women were counted in the labor force in 1948, even though most of them would have said that they worked full days. Within-the-household production has never been counted as part of GDP. When the NIPA system was set up, economists believed that it would be difficult or impossible to obtain reasonable, credible, defensible estimates of the economic value of within-the-household production.

Yet the exclusion of within-the-household production makes a difference not just for the level of national product but for its rate of growth. Over time the border between paid market and unpaid nonmarket, within-the-household work has shifted. Be suspicious of economic growth rates based on total GDP, GDP per capita, or GDP per adult, because they are distorted by the shifting dividing line between what people do and how they arrange their work. A meal cooked is a meal cooked whether it is part of the market paid work of a restaurant chef or part of the unpaid work of a homemaker. Over time the share of meals prepared in the first way has grown, while the share of meals prepared in the second way has shrunk. This shift in the dividing line between home cooking and dining out has raised measured GDP, but the shift by itself is not an increase in society's wealth.

FIGURE 2.9
Labor-Force Participation Rates by Gender, 1948–1996
The paid-labor-force participation rates of men and women have been converging for a generation, as male labor-force participation has fallen slightly and female participation has grown rapidly. What were the counterparts of the women who worked for wages in 1996 doing back in 1948? They were working, but not for wages. And their work then wasn't counted as part of GDP.

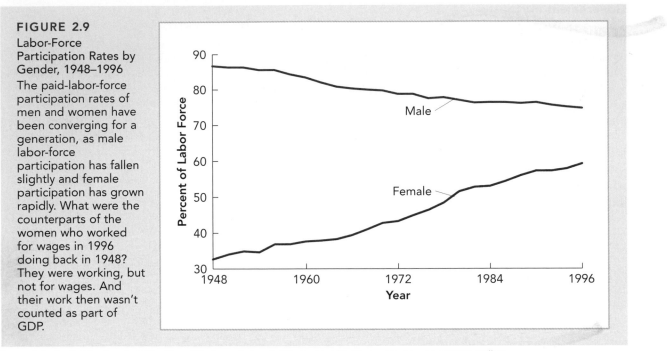

Source: Author's calculation from the 2001 edition of *The Economic Report of the President* (Washington, DC: Government Printing Office).

Depletion, Pollution, and "Bads"

The NIPA system makes no allowance for the depletion of scarce natural resources. To the extent that an economy produces a high income in the act of using up valuable natural resources, that income is not true GDP at all but the depletion of natural resources. Kuwait, Qatar, and Saudi Arabia have high levels of measured real GDP per worker, but much of their income arises not out of sustainable production but out of the sale of limited and depletable natural resources. A better system would have a category for the depletion of natural resources.

Moreover, the NIPA contains no category for the production of "**bads**" — things that you would rather *not* have. Producing more smog does not diminish GDP. The extra cases of lung cancer produced by cigarette smoking do not diminish GDP (indeed, they raise the medical care sector's contribution to GDP). If the demand for locks and alarm systems rises because crime increases, GDP increases. As noted before, GDP is a measure of only the economy's level of productive effort, not of well-being.

RECAP   REAL GDP

Real GDP is calculated by adding up the value of all final goods and services produced in the economy. Because it measures the rate at which goods and services are produced, real GDP is a flow variable: Remember that real GDP is measured as the value of goods and services produced *per year.* Real GDP has four components: (i) everything bought by consumers, (ii) everything bought by firms to increase their capital stock, (iii) everything bought by the government (including the time of bureaucrats), and (iv) net exports.

Chapter Summary

1. Because economics studies goods and services that flow through the market and are bought and sold with prices attached, economists have a lot of quantitative data to work with.

2. The real exchange rate is the relative price at which two countries' goods exchange for each other. You calculate it by adjusting the nominal exchange rate for changes in the price levels in the two countries.

3. The level of the stock market is a valuable summary index of a range of factors that affect investment: the current level of profits, investors' optimism or pessimism, the real rate of interest, and attitudes toward risk.

4. Real interest rates are much more important variables to keep track of than are nominal interest rates. You calculate the real interest rate by subtracting the rate of inflation from nominal interest rates.

5. The most commonly seen measure of the price level is the consumer price index (CPI). The proportional rate of change of the price level is called the inflation rate.

6. Unemployment and total output are linked through Okun's law: a 1-percentage-point change in the unemployment rate comes with a 2.5 percent change in the level of output in the opposite direction.

7. Real GDP is the most commonly seen measure of the overall level of economic activity. It is the value — calculated using market prices in some chosen base year — of all final goods and services produced in a year.

8. The line between GDP and not GDP is principally the result of economists' beliefs in the 1940s and 1950s about what it would be possible to measure easily. It is not the result of a set of principled decisions about what kinds of activities should and should not be included in a measure of material welfare.

Key Terms

nominal exchange rate (p. 29)
real exchange rates (p. 30)
index number (p. 32)
price level (p. 40)
Bureau of Labor Statistics (p. 40)

goods and services (p. 40)
Bureau of Economic Analysis (p. 43)
inflation (p. 43)
real GDP (p. 48)
NIPA (p. 48)

consumption spending (p. 53)
investment spending (p. 53)
government purchases (p. 53)
net exports (p. 53)
"bads" (p. 56)

Analytical Exercises

1. Are capital goods — large turbine generators, jet airliners, bay-spanning bridges — intermediate goods or final goods? How are they included in GDP?

2. How do the labor and other factors of production that go into producing intermediate goods ultimately get counted in GDP?

3. Explain whether or not and why the following items are included in the calculation of GDP:
   a. Increases in business inventories.
   b. Sales of existing homes.
   c. Fees earned by real estate agents on selling existing homes.

   d. Income earned by Americans living and working abroad.
   e. Purchases of IBM stock by your brother.
   f. Purchase of a new tank by the Department of Defense.
   g. Rent that you pay to your landlord.

4. Which interest rate concept — the nominal interest rate or the real interest rate — do lenders and borrowers care more about? Why?

5. Which is the more important measure for assessing an economy's performance, real GDP or nominal GDP?

Policy Exercises

1. In 1979 the (short-term) nominal interest rate on three-month Treasury bills averaged 10 percent, and the GDP deflator rose from 50.88 to 55.22. What was the annual rate of inflation in 1979? What was the real interest rate in 1979?

   a. Were real interest rates higher in 1979 or in 1998, when the (short-term) nominal interest rate on three-month Treasury bills was 4.8 percent and the inflation rate was 2.6 percent?

   b. Which interest rate concept — the nominal interest rate or the real interest rate — do lenders and borrowers care more about? Why?

2. In 1998 the GDP deflator rose at an annual rate of 2.6 percent, and the short-term interest rate on three-month Treasury bills averaged 4.8 percent. What was the (short-term) nominal interest rate in 1998? What was the (short-term) real interest rate in 1998?

3. In 1992 the implicit GDP deflator (in 1992 dollars) was equal to 100; in 1993 it was equal to 102.64. What was the annual rate of inflation between 1992 and 1993? In 1993 the implicit GDP deflator (in 1992 dollars) was equal to 102.64; in 1994 it was 105.09. What was the annual rate of inflation between 1993 and 1994?

4. In 1992 both nominal GDP and real GDP (measured in 1992 dollars) were equal to $6.2444 trillion. By 1997 nominal GDP had risen to $8.1109 trillion, and the implicit GDP deflator had risen to 111.57. What was real GDP in 1997? What was the average rate of real GDP growth between 1992 and 1997?

5. Use the data in the following table to answer the questions below:

	Real GDP* (trillions)	Labor Force (millions)
1960	$2.2629	69.6
1970	3.3976	82.8
1980	4.615	106.9
1990	6.1363	125.8

* In 1992 dollars.

What was real GDP per worker in 1960, 1970, 1980, and 1990? How fast did real GDP per worker grow between 1960 and 1970? Between 1970 and 1980? Between 1980 and 1990?

Thinking Like an Economist

CHAPTER

QUESTIONS

Is economics a science?

What do economists mean by a *model*?

Why do economists use mathematical models so much?

What patterns and habits of thought must you learn to successfully think like an economist?

3.1 UNDERSTANDING MACROECONOMICS

Every new subject requires new patterns of thought; every intellectual discipline calls for new ways of thinking about the world. After all, that is what makes it a *discipline*: a discipline that allows people to think about a subject in some new way. Economics is no exception.

In a way, learning an intellectual discipline like macroeconomics is similar to learning a new language or being initiated into a club. Economists' way of thinking allows us to see the economy more sharply and clearly than we could in other ways. (Of course, it can also cause us to miss certain relationships that are hard to quantify or hard to think of as purchases and sales; that is why economics is not the only social science, and we need sociologists, political scientists, historians, psychologists, and anthropologists as well.) In this chapter we will survey the intellectual landmarks of economists' system of thought, in order to help you orient yourself in the mental landscape of macroeconomics.

Economics: Is It a Science?

If you are coming to economics from a background in the *natural* **sciences**, you probably expect economics to be something like a natural science, only less so: To the extent that it works, it works more or less like chemistry, though it does not work as well. Economic theories are unsettled and poorly described. Economists' predictions are often wrong.

If you hold these opinions, you are half-right. While economics is a science, it is not a *natural* science. It is a *social* science. Its subject is not electrons or elements but human beings: people and how they behave. This subject matter has several important consequences. Some of them make economics easier than a natural science, some of them make economics harder than a natural science, and some of them just make it different.

First, because economics is a social science, debates within economics last a lot longer and are *much* less likely to end in a clear consensus than are debates in the natural sciences. The major reason is that different people have different views of what makes a free, a good, a just, or a well-ordered society. They look for an economy that harmonizes with their vision of what a society should be. They ignore or explain away facts that turn out to be inconvenient for their particular political views. People are, after all, only human.

Economists *try* to approach the objectivity that characterizes most work in the natural sciences. After all, what is is, and what is not is not. Even if wishful thinking or predispositions contaminate the results of a single study, later studies can correct the error. But economists never approach the unanimity with which physicists embraced the theory of relativity, chemists embraced the oxygen theory of combustion, and biologists rejected the Lamarckian inheritance of acquired characteristics. Biology departments do not have Lamarckians. Chemistry departments do not have phlogistonists. But economics departments do have a wide variety of points of view and schools of thought.

Second, the fact that economics is about people means that economists cannot ethically undertake large-scale experiments. Economists cannot set up special situations in which potential sources of disturbance are reduced to a minimum, then observe what happens, and generalize from the results of the experiment (where sources of disturbance are absent) to what happens in the world (where sources of disturbance are common). Thus the experimental method, the driver of rapid progress in many of the natural sciences, is lacking in economics. This flaw makes economics harder to analyze, and it makes economists' conclusions much more tentative and subject to dispute, than is the case with natural sciences.

Third, the subjects economists study — people — have minds of their own. They observe what is going on around them, plan for the future, and take steps to avoid future consequences that they foresee and fear will be unpleasant. At times they simply do what they want, just because they feel like doing it. Thus in economists' analyses the present often depends not just on the past but on the future as well — or on what people expect the future to be. Box 3.1 presents one example of this: how people's **expectations** of the future and particularly their fear that there might be a depression contributed to the coming of the Great Depression of the 1930s.

This third wrinkle makes economics in some sense very hard. Natural scientists can always assume the arrow of causality points from the past to the future. In

BOX 3.1

EXPECTATIONS AND THE COMING OF THE GREAT DEPRESSION: AN EXAMPLE

An important example of how people's expectations can change the course of economic events comes from the stock market crash of 1929. The crash changed what Americans expected about the future of the economy, and the shifts in spending caused by their changed expectations played a key role in causing the greatest economic depression in American history, the Great Depression.

On October 29, 1929, the price of shares traded on the New York Stock Exchange suffered their largest one-day percentage drop in history. Stock values bounced back a bit initially, but by the end of the week they were down by more than a quarter (see Figure 3.1). Gloom fell over Wall Street. Many people had lost a lot of money.

FIGURE 3.1
The Stock Market, 1928–1932

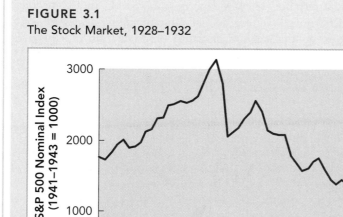

Source: J. Bradford DeLong and Andrei Shleifer, "Closed End Fund Discounts: A Yardstick of Small-Investor Sentiment," *Journal of Portfolio Management* 18:2 (Winter 1992), pp. 46–53.

At that time stock ownership was confined to the rich. Middle-class Americans owned little stock. Nonetheless, the crash affected their perceptions of the economy: Bad times were coming. Because people expected the economic future to be dimmer, many cut back on spending, especially on big-ticket consumer durables. The 1920s had been the first decade in which consumer credit was widely available to finance purchases of cars, refrigerators, stoves, and washing machines. With the economic future uncertain, spending on consumer durables collapsed. It made sense to borrow to buy a consumer durable only if you were confident that you could make the payments and pay off the loan. If you thought the economic future might be bad, you had a powerful incentive to avoid debt. And in the short run the easiest way to avoid debt is to refrain from purchasing large consumer durables on credit.

You can probably guess what happened in the months after the crash. Most people simply stopped buying big-ticket items like cars and furniture. This massive drop in demand reduced new orders for goods. The drop in output generated layoffs in many industries. Even though most people's incomes had not yet changed, their expectations of their future income had.

The drop in demand produced by this shift in expectations helped bring on what people feared; it put America on the path to the Great Depression. The Great Depression happened in large part because people expected something bad to happen. Without that pessimistic shift in expectations triggered by the crash of 1929, there would have been no Great Depression.

economics people's expectations of the future mean that the arrow of causality often points the other way, from the (anticipated) future back to the present.

Reliance on Quantitative Models

In spite of the political complications, the nonexperimental nature, and the peculiar problems of cause and effect in economics, the discipline remains a *quantitative* science. Most of the relationships that economists study come quantified. Thus economics makes heavy use of arithmetic and algebra, while political science, sociology, and most of history do not. Economics makes heavy use of arithmetic to measure economic variables of interest. Moreover, economists use mathematical *models* to relate these variables.

The American economy is complex: 130 million workers, 10 million firms, and 90 million households buying and selling $24 trillion worth of goods and services per year. Economists must simplify it. To understand this complex phenomenon, they restrict their attention to a few **behavioral relationships** — cause-and-effect links between economic quantities — and a handful of **equilibrium conditions** — conditions that must be satisfied for economic activity to be stable and for supply and demand to be in balance. They attempt to capture these behavioral relationships and equilibrium conditions in simple algebraic equations and geometric diagrams. Then they try to apply their equations and graphs to the real world, while hoping that their simplifications have not made the model a distorted and faulty guide to how the real-world economy works.

Among economists, the process of reducing the complexity and variation of the real-world economy to a handful of equations is known as "building a **model**." Using models to understand what is going on in the complex real-world economy has been a fruitful intellectual strategy. But model building tends to focus on the variables and relationships that fit easily into the algebraic model. It overlooks other factors.

An Emphasis on the Abstract

Economics might have developed as a descriptive science, like sociology or political science. If so, courses in economics would concentrate on economic institutions and practices and the institutional structure of the economy as a whole. But it has not; it has instead become a more abstract science that emphasizes general principles applicable to a variety of situations. Thus a large part of economics involves a particular set of tools: a unique way of thinking about the world that is closely linked with the analytical tools economists use and that is couched in a particular technical language and a particular set of data. While one can get a lot out of sociology and political science courses without learning to think like a sociologist or a political scientist (because of their focus on institutional description), it is not possible to get much out of an economics course without learning to think like an economist.

The Rhetoric of Economics

Surrounding the models economists build a special *rhetoric:* a set of analogies and metaphors that economists use to help laypeople grasp the functioning of the macroeconomy. Metaphors and analogies are the basic stuff of human thought. To understand something we do not know, we will often compare it to something we do know. Economics is no exception. In economics, curves "shift" and money has a "velocity." When the central bank raises interest rates and throws people out of work, economists say that this "pushes the economy down the Phillips curve." Conversely, when the central bank lowers interest rates and the economy booms, economists say that this "pushes the economy up the Phillips curve" — as if the economy were a dot on a diagram drawn on a piece of paper, constrained to move along a particular curve called the Phillips curve, and monetary policy really did push the dot up and to the left (see Figure 3.2).

As a student you should be conscious of (and a little critical of) the rhetoric of economics for two reasons. First, if you don't understand the metaphors, much of economics may simply be incomprehensible. All will become clear, or at least clearer, if you are conscious of the metaphors. For example, there is a central dominant metaphor in macroeconomics, the *circular flow metaphor,* without which discussions of the "velocity" of money are simply incomprehensible. The circular flow metaphor compares the process of spending throughout the economy to the flow of a liquid. Thus if the total amount of spending increases but the quantity of money does not, the money must be "flowing" faster than it did in the past, since a fixed quantity of pieces of money are changing hands more often. Hence money must have a higher *velocity.* Without the concept of spending as a *circular flow* of purchasing power, references to the velocity of money will make no sense.

Much of the rhetoric of economics can be reduced to four dominant concepts:

- The image of the **circular flow** of purchasing power through the economy — the circular flow of economic activity.

- The use of the word "market" to describe intricate and decentralized processes of exchange, as if all the workers and all the jobs in the economy really were being matched in a single open-air market.

- The idea of **equilibrium:** that economic processes tend to move the economy into some sort of balance and to keep the economy at this point of balance.

FIGURE 3.2
Pushing the Economy Up the Phillips Curve
Between 1986 and 1989 the Federal Reserve's expansionary monetary policy reduced interest rates and increased total spending. Increased total spending meant that unemployment fell from 7 percent in 1986 to 5.3 percent in 1989. As unemployment fell, inflation rose from 2.6 percent in 1986 to 4.4 percent in 1989. Economists talk about this change by saying, "Between 1986 and 1989 the Federal Reserve's expansionary monetary policy pushed the economy up and to the left along the Phillips curve" (which depicts the short-run relationship between unemployment and inflation).

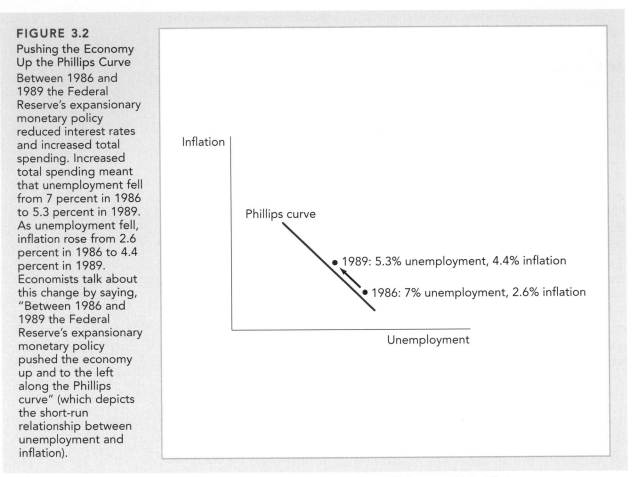

Source: Author's calculations from the 1999 edition of *The Economic Report of the President* (Washington, DC: Government Printing Office).

- The use of graphs and diagrams as an alternative to equations and arithmetic in expressing economic relationships. Economists identify equations with geometric curves, situations of equilibrium with points where curves cross, and changes in the economic environment or in economic policy with shifts in the positions of particular curves.

We will look next at the circular flow of economic activity. The market, equilibrium, and the relationship between graphs and equations will be covered in later sections.

RECAP   UNDERSTANDING MACROECONOMICS

While economics is a science, it is not a *natural* science. It is a *social* science. The subjects economists study — people — have minds of their own, and think ahead. Thus in economics it is common for the (expected) future to influence the past, and chains of causation can get very tangled. Economics might have developed as a descriptive science, like sociology or political science. It didn't. Economics, instead, developed as an abstract, simplifying, model-oriented discipline.

3.2 THE CIRCULAR FLOW OF ECONOMIC ACTIVITY

When economists speak of the "circular flow" of economic activity, they have a definite picture in mind. They see patterns of spending, income, and production as liquid flowing through various sets of pipes. In this extended metaphor, categories of agents in the economy — all businesses, the government, all households — are the pools into and out of which the fluid of purchasing power (i.e., money) flows.

Thus economists think of economic activity — the pattern of production and spending in the economy — as a circular flow of purchasing power through the economy. The circular flow metaphor allows them confidently to predict that changes in one part of the economy will affect the whole and to explain what the likely effects will be. It allows them to simplify economic behavior, to understand the entire set of decisions made by different agents in different parts of the economy by thinking of a few typical decisions made by abstract representative agents.

The Circular Flow Diagram

Figure 3.3 shows a simplified diagram of the circular flow. It omits the government and international trade. Nevertheless, it is a good starting point for our discussion. In this figure, money payments flow from firms to households as businesses pay their workers and their owners for their labor and capital. This is the "income side" of the circular flow: Firms buy the *factors of production* capital and labor from the households that own them. Money payments then flow from households to firms as households buy goods. This is the "expenditure side" of the circular flow: Households buy *final goods and services* from businesses. Note that these flows balance: The purchasing power that firms earn by selling their goods is the same as the purchasing power that firms spend by buying factors of production, and the incomes of households are equal to their total expenditures.

This simplified diagram is expanded in Figure 3.4 to take account of the roles of the government, financial markets, and international trade and investment. But the core idea of a balanced circular flow of purchasing power is still present. Along the

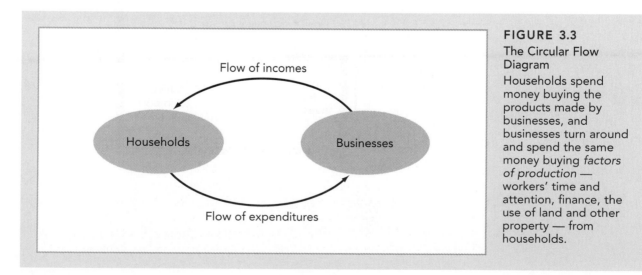

FIGURE 3.3
The Circular Flow Diagram
Households spend money buying the products made by businesses, and businesses turn around and spend the same money buying *factors of production* — workers' time and attention, finance, the use of land and other property — from households.

FIGURE 3.4

The Circular Flow of Economic Activity

This version of the circular flow is complicated by the addition of the government and financial markets to the diagram. Not all final goods and services are bought by households. Some are bought by the government, which taxes to raise resources to finance itself. Some are bought by businesses seeking to invest, which raise the needed resources by issuing stock, issuing bonds, and borrowing — all of which take place in *financial markets.* This version is also complicated by its recognizing that there is a world outside, a world that buys the products of domestic businesses and that invests through domestic financial markets.

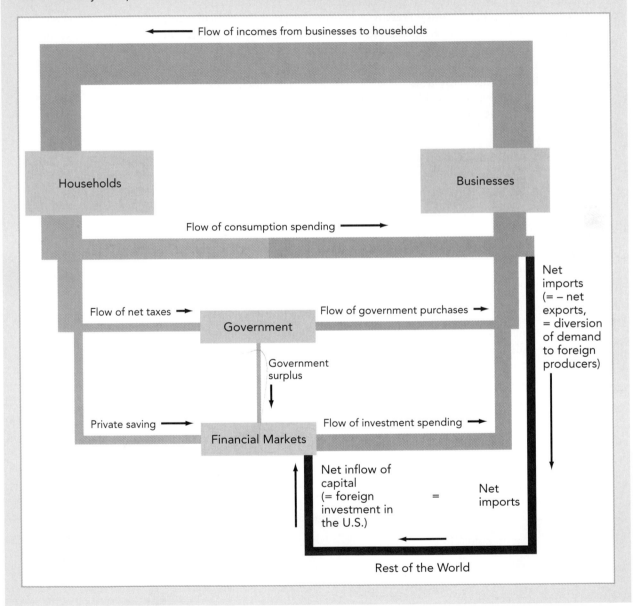

Flow of incomes from businesses to households

Households

Businesses

Flow of consumption spending

Net imports (= − net exports, = diversion of demand to foreign producers)

Flow of net taxes   Flow of government purchases

Government

Government surplus

Private saving   Flow of investment spending

Financial Markets

Net inflow of capital (= foreign investment in the U.S.)   =   Net imports

Rest of the World

top of the diagram there is still the flow of incomes to households from businesses as they purchase labor and other factors of production from the households that own them. All these components of business expenditure — rent, wages, salaries, benefits, interest, and profits — become the components of *household income*. Toward the bottom left of the diagram are the uses of household incomes — consumption spending, savings, and taxes. Consumption spending flows directly to businesses as households purchase consumption goods. Total taxes flow to the government, which uses some of this revenue to make transfer payments — classified here as negative taxes — back to households, uses most of them for government purchases, and sends the remaining *government budget surplus* into financial markets as the government uses its budget surplus to buy back bonds.

Households save the portion of their incomes that is left over after taxes and consumption spending. These savings flow into financial markets as they are put into banks and mutual funds. Businesses seeking to invest draw on the pool of savings to gain financing for purchasing capital goods to expand their productive capacity. Exports serve as an addition to (and imports a subtraction from) total demand for domestically made products.

Thus at the bottom right we have the components of *aggregate demand*: consumption spending, investment spending, government purchases, and net exports (which are, in the United States today, net imports, a subtraction from GDP, because imports are greater than gross exports).

Within the *business sector,* businesses buy and sell intermediate goods from each other as they strive to produce goods and services and make profits. Within the *household sector,* households buy and sell assets from and to one another. These within-the-business-sector and within-the-household-sector transactions are important components of the economy. But because they net out to zero within the business sector or within the household sector, they are not counted as part of the circular flow of economic activity.

To better grasp the circular flow of economic activity, look at one particular part of the circular flow, a dollar paid out by a business as a dividend to a shareholder. The dollar is payment for use of a factor of production, the capital invested in the business by the shareholder. When the dividend check is deposited, it becomes part of the shareholder's household income. Suppose the household doesn't spend it but simply keeps the money in the bank, thus saving it. The bank will notice that it has an extra dollar on deposit and will loan that dollar out to a business in need of cash to build up its inventory. That business will then spend the dollar buying goods and services as it builds up its inventory. As soon as the dollar shows up as a component of business investment spending, the circular flow is complete. The dollar's worth of purchasing power has flowed from the business sector to the household sector, then flowed as part of the flow of savings into the financial markets, and finally flowed out of the financial markets and back to the business sector as part of business investment spending.

Different Measures of the Circular Flow

Income, production, and expenditure can be measured at three different points in the circular flow:

1. At the point where consumers, exporters, the government, and firms that are making investments purchase goods and services from businesses. This measurement is real GDP, or total output. It is the total economywide

production of goods and services. It is the expenditure-side measure of the circular flow.

2. At the point in the circular flow where businesses pay households for the factors of production. Businesses need labor, capital, and natural resources, all factors of production owned directly or indirectly by households. When businesses buy them, they provide households with incomes. This measurement is called *total income* or *national income*. It is the income-side measure of the circular flow.

3. At the point where households decide how to use their income. How much do they save? How much do they pay in taxes? How much do they spend on consumption goods? This measure of the circular flow of economic activity is the "uses-of-income" measure.

The measure used most often is the expenditure-side measure: the gross domestic product produced by firms and demanded by purchasers. It is estimated by summing the four components of spending (and sales) — consumption, government purchases, investment, and net exports. If we compare the expenditure-side measure of GDP with the income-side or uses-of-income-side measure, we will find that, aside from differences created by different accounting conventions, they are equal (see Box 3.2). They are equal because the circular flow principle is designed into the national income and product accounts (NIPA). Every expenditure on a final good or service is accounted for as a payment to a business. Every dollar payment that flows into a business is then accounted for as paid out to somebody. It can be paid out as income — wages, fringe benefits, profits, interest, or rent — or as an expenditure on

BOX
3.2

ACCOUNTING DEFINITIONS AND STATISTICAL DISCREPANCIES: TOOLS

Because of the technical details of national income accounting, the different measures of the circular flow do not exactly balance. First, there is the *statistical discrepancy*. All pieces of GDP reported by the Commerce Department are estimates. All estimates are imperfect. It is not unusual for $100 billion a year to go "missing" in the circular flow; as Table 3.1 shows, this happened in the third quarter of 2000.

TABLE 3.1
Measures of the U.S. Circular Flow (in Billions of Dollars per Year), Third Quarter of 2000

Gross domestic product	$8,574
Minus: Depreciation	−912
Equals: Net domestic product	$7,662
Minus: Net factor incomes paid abroad	−64
Equals: Net national product	$7,598
Minus: Net indirect taxes	−693
Plus: Net subsidy to government enterprises	+25
Plus: Statistical discrepancy	+102
Equals: National income	$7,032

Source: Author's calculations from the 2001 edition of *The Economic Report of the President* (Washington, DC: Government Printing Office).

Second, different measurements of the circular flow differ because of differences in exact accounting definitions. For example, measures of net domestic product and national income (NI) exclude depreciation expenditures, but gross domestic product includes them. NI excludes indirect business taxes, but the product measures include them. Domestic product measures include, and national product measures exclude, incomes earned in the United States by people who are not citizens or permanent residents. National product measures include, and domestic product measures exclude, incomes earned abroad by U.S. citizens and permanent residents.

goods or services of another business that then, in turn, purchases factors of production.

What if you want to withdraw your income from the circular flow? Suppose, for instance, that you simply take the dollar bills you receive and use them to buy something old and precious from another household — a bar of gold, say. And suppose you keep the bar of gold in your basement. Doesn't that break the circular flow? The answer is that it does not. You no longer have your income, but the household that you bought the gold bar from does. That household will then either spend it on consumption goods, save it, or have it taxed away.

What if you decided to hide the dollar bills in your basement? Doesn't that break the circular flow? The answer, again, is that it does not. The Bureau of Engraving and Printing will notice that the total number of dollar bills circulating in the economy has dropped. It will print up more dollar bills and hand them to the Treasury. The government will spend these extra dollar bills, and thus replace the ones you have hidden. The net effect is the same as it would be if you had saved the dollar bills by lending them out to the government through the purchase of a Treasury bond. There are only two differences between buying a Treasury bond and your basement storage scheme: (1) You have a stack of dollar bills in your basement rather than a piece of paper with the words "Treasury bond" written on it. (2) The government does not pay interest on the dollar bills stacked in your basement, but it does pay interest on its bonds. In the circular flow diagram, you have saved your income, but you have saved it in a relatively pointless way by making the government an interest-free loan.

RECAP   THE CIRCULAR FLOW OF ECONOMIC ACTIVITY

Money flows from households to firms as households buy goods. This is the "expenditure side" of the circular flow: Households buy *final goods and services* from businesses. Businesses then turn around and buy factors of production from households. These payments make up household income. This is the "income side" of the circular flow. The circular flow principle is that the two flows must match: In the economy as a whole, expenditure must equal income.

3.3 RHETORIC CONTINUED: PATTERNS OF ECONOMISTS' THOUGHT

Besides the circular flow of economic activity, three other concepts dominate the rhetoric of economics: markets, equilibrium, and graphs and diagrams. Let's look at each of these in turn.

Markets

Economists often speak as if all economic activity took place in great open-air marketplaces like those of medieval merchant cities. Contracts between workers and bosses are made in the "labor market." All the borrowing of money from and the depositing of money into banks take place in the "money market." Supply and demand balance in the "goods market." Indeed, in the market squares of preindustrial trading cities you could survey the buyers and sellers and form a good idea of what was being sold and for how much.

In using the open-air markets of centuries past as a metaphor for the complex processes of matching and exchange that take place in today's modern industrial economy, economists are assuming that information travels fast enough and buyers and sellers are well informed enough for prevailing prices and quantities to be as they would be if we actually could walk around the perimeter of a marketplace and examine all buyers and sellers in an hour. In most cases this bet that a decentralized matching process is like an open-air market will be a good intellectual bet to make. But sometimes (for example, in situations of so-called *structural unemployment*) it may not be.

Equilibrium

Economists spend most of their time searching for the state of *equilibrium* — a point or points of balance at which some economic quantity is neither rising nor falling. The dominant metaphor is that of an old-fashioned scale whose two pans are in balance. The search for equilibrium is an attempt to simplify the problem of understanding how the economy will behave. Economists' questions are much easier to analyze if we can identify "points of rest" where the pressures for economic quantities to rise and fall are evenly balanced. Once the potential points of rest have been identified, economists can figure out how fast economic forces will push the economy to those points of equilibrium. The search for points of equilibrium, followed by an analysis of the speed of adjustment to equilibrium, is the most common way of proceeding in any economic analysis.

Do not, however, forget that this pattern of thought is merely an aid to understanding economic theories and principles. It is not the theories and principles themselves. The theories and principles, in turn, are just aids to understanding the reality; they are not themselves the reality.

Graphs and Equations

In the seventeenth century, the French philosopher and mathematician René Descartes spent much of his life demonstrating that graphs and equations are two different representations of the same reality. Specifically, an algebraic equation relating two variables can also be represented as a curve drawn on a graph. Each of the variables in the equation can be thought of as one of the axes of the graph. The set of points whose *x*-axis value is the first variable and whose *y*-axis value is the second — that is, the set of points for which the equation holds — makes up a line or curve on the graph. That line or curve is the equation (see Figure 3.5). Thus the solution to a set of two equations is the point on the graph where the two curves that represent the equations intersect. Moreover, you can just as easily move back in the other direction, by thinking of a curve in terms of the equation that generates it. Today economists make very extensive use of these ideas from Descartes' **Analytic Geometry**.

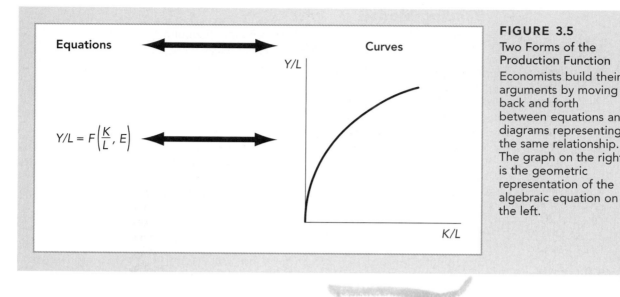

FIGURE 3.5
Two Forms of the Production Function
Economists build their arguments by moving back and forth between equations and diagrams representing the same relationship. The graph on the right is the geometric representation of the algebraic equation on the left.

Just after the end of World War II Professor Paul Samuelson of MIT discovered that many of his students were much more comfortable manipulating diagrams than solving algebraic equations. With diagrams, they could *see* what was going on in a hypothetical economy. Thinking of how a particular curve would shift was often easier than thinking of the consequences of changing the value of the constant term in an equation.

When economists translate their algebraic equations into analytical geometric diagrams, they do two things that may annoy you. First, economists (like mathematicians) think of a "line" as a special kind of "curve" (and it is: it is a curve with zero curvature). So you may find words — in this book, in your lecture, or in your section — referring to a "Phillips curve," but when you look at the accompanying diagram, you see that it is a straight line. Do not let this bother you. Economists use the word "curve" to preserve a little generality.

If you find analytic geometry easy and intuitive, then Samuelson's intellectual innovation will make macroeconomics more accessible to you. Behavioral relationships become curves that shift about on a graph. Conditions of economic equilibrium become dots where curves describing two behavioral relationships cross (and thus both behavioral relationships are satisfied). Changes in the state of the economy become movements of a dot. Understanding economic theories and arguments becomes as simple as moving lines and curves around on a graph and looking for the place where the correct two curves intersect. And solving systems of equations becomes easy, as does changing the presuppositions of the problem and noting the results.

If you are not comfortable with analytic geometry, then you need to find other tools to help you think like an economist. Remember that the graphs are merely *tools* to aid your understanding. If they don't, then you need to concentrate on understanding and manipulating the algebra or understanding and using the verbal descriptions of a problem. Use whatever method feels most comfortable. Grab hold of what makes most sense to you, and recognize that all three approaches are ways of reaching the same conclusions.

Building Models

Simplification is the essence of model building. Economists use simple models for two reasons. First, no one really understands excessively complicated models, and a model is of little use if economists cannot understand the logic behind its prediction. Second, the predictions generated by simple models are nearly as good as the ones generated by more complex models. While the economic models used by the Federal Reserve or the Congressional Budget Office are more complicated than the models presented in this textbook, in essence they are cousins of the models used here.

You may have heard that economics is more of an art than a science. This means that the rules for effective and useful model building — for omitting unnecessary detail and complexity while retaining the necessary and important relationships — are nowhere written down. In this important respect, economists tend to learn by doing or by example. But there are fundamental steps that almost every successful construction of a macroeconomic model follows. They include the use of representative agents, a focus on opportunity costs in understanding agents' decisions, and careful attention to the effect of people's expectations on events.

Representative Agents

One simplification that macroeconomists, but not microeconomists, invoke constantly is that all participants in the economy are the same or, rather, that the differences between businesses and workers do not matter much for the issues macroeconomists study. Thus macroeconomists analyze a situation by examining the decision making of a single **representative agent** — be it a business, a worker, or a saver. They then generalize to the economy as a whole from what would be the rational decisions of that single representative agent.

The use of representative agents makes macroeconomics simpler, yet it also makes some questions very hard to analyze. Consider unemployment: The key concept is that some workers have jobs but others do not. If one has adopted the simplifying assumption of a single representative worker, how can one worker represent both those who are employed and those who are not?

The assumption of a representative agent is also useless when the relative *distribution* of income and wealth among people in the economy is important. Most of the time our judgments about social welfare are influenced by distribution. Consider an economy in which everyone works equally hard, but 1 million lucky people receive $1,000,000 a year in income and 99 million receive $10,000 a year in income. Now consider an economy in which all 100 million people work equally hard and each receives $80,000 a year in income. Almost all of us would think that the second was a better — a happier and a fairer — economy, even though total income in the first economy amounts to $10.9 trillion and total income in the second economy amounts to only $8 trillion. As noted above, every discipline sees some things clearly and some things fuzzily. Distribution and its impact on social welfare are an area that macroeconomics has trouble bringing into focus.

Opportunity Cost

Perhaps the most fundamental principle of economics is that there is always a choice. But making a choice excludes the alternatives. If you keep your wealth in the form of easily spendable cash, you pass up the chance to keep it earning interest in the form of bonds. If you keep your wealth in the form of interest-earning bonds, you pass up the capability of immediately spending it on something that suddenly strikes your fancy. If you spend on consumption goods, you pass up the opportunity to save. Economists use the term **opportunity cost** to refer to the value of the best alternative that you forgo in making any particular choice.

At the root of every behavioral relationship is somebody's decision. In analyzing such decisions, economists always think about the decision maker's opportunity costs. What else could the decision maker do? What opportunities and choices does the decision maker foreclose by taking one particular course of action? Many students make economics a lot harder than it has to be by not remembering that this opportunity-cost way of thinking is at the heart of every behavioral relationship in an economic model.

The Focus on Expectations

Many times the opportunity cost of taking some action today is not an alternative use of the same resources today but a forgone opportunity to save one's resources for the future. A worker trying to decide whether to quit a job and search for another will be thinking about future wages after a successful search. A consumer trying to decide whether to spend or save will be thinking about what interest rate savings will earn in the future.

No one, however, knows the future. At best people can form rational and reasonable expectations of what the future might be. Hence nearly every behavioral relationship in macroeconomic models depends on *expectations of the future*. Expectations formation is a central, perhaps the central, piece of macroeconomics. Every macroeconomic model must explain the amount of time people can spend thinking about the future, the information they have available, and the rules of thumb they use to turn information into expectations.

Economists tend to consider three types of expectations:

- *Static expectations,* in which decision makers simply don't think about the future.
- *Adaptive expectations,* in which decision makers assume that the future is going to be like the recent past.
- *Rational expectations,* in which decision makers spend as much time as they can thinking about the future, and know as much (or more) about the structure and behavior of the economy as the model builder does.

The behavior of an economic model will differ profoundly depending on what kind of expectations economists build into the model.

Solving Economic Models

Behavioral Relationships and Equilibrium Conditions

When economists are trying to analyze the implications of how people *act* — say, how the overall level of production would change with a larger capital stock — they almost always write an equation that represents a *behavioral relationship*. This behavioral relationship states how the effect (the total level of production) is related to the cause (the available capital stock). The economist usually draws a diagram to help visualize the relationship and writes it down verbally: "A larger capital stock means that the average employee will have more machines and equipment to work with, and this will increase total production per worker. But increases in capital will probably be subject to *diminishing returns to scale*, so the gain in production from increasing the capital stock per worker from $40,000 to $80,000 will be less than the gain in production from increasing the capital stock per worker from $0 to $40,000."

Box 3.3 fleshes out this example of a behavioral relationship, in this case the *production function*.

In addition to analyzing behavioral relationships, economists consider *equilibrium conditions* — conditions that must be true if the economy is to be in balance. If an equilibrium condition does not hold, then the state of the economy must be changing rapidly, moving toward a state of affairs in which the equilibrium condition *does* hold. In microeconomics the principal equilibrium condition is that supply

THE PRODUCTION FUNCTION: AN EXAMPLE OF A BEHAVIORAL RELATIONSHIP

One of the key behavioral relationships in macroeconomics is the *production function*, which specifies the relationship between the economy's productive resources. The production function relates:

- The economy's capital-labor ratio (how many machines, tools, and structures are available to the average worker), written K/L (K for capital and L for labor).
- The level of technology or efficiency of the labor force, written E.
- The level of real GDP per worker, written Y/L (Y for real GDP or total output and L for the number of workers in the economy).

An economist could write the production function in this general, abstract form:

$$\frac{Y}{L} = F\left(\frac{K}{L}, E_t\right)$$

This formula states that the level of output per worker is some *function, F,* of K/L and E_t; that is, the level of output per worker depends in a systematic and predictable way on the capital-labor ratio and the efficiency of labor in the current year. But this abstract form does not specify the particular form of this systematic and predictable relationship.

Alternatively, an economist could write the production function in a particular algebraic form, for example, the Cobb-Douglas form which is convenient to use (Box 3.4 explains why):

$$\frac{Y}{L} = \left(\frac{K}{L}\right)^{\alpha} \times E_t^{1-\alpha}$$

This equation states: "Take the capital-labor ratio, raise it to the exponential power α, and multiply the result by the efficiency of labor E_t raised to the exponential power $(1-\alpha)$. The result is the level of output per worker that the economy can produce." While this equation is more particular than the abstract form $Y/L = F(K/L, E_t)$, it remains flexible: The parameter α could have any of a wide range of different values, and the efficiency of labor E_t could have any value. This Cobb-Douglas algebraic form still stands for a whole family of possible production functions. The values chosen for E and α will tell us exactly which production function is the real one and thus what the behavioral relationship is between the economy's resources and its output. Once we know the values of E and α, we can calculate what the output per worker will be for every possible value of capital per worker.

Why do economists choose to write the production function in this particular algebraic form? Ease of use is the key reason. This form of the production function makes a lot of calculations *much* simpler and more straightforward than other forms.

WORKING WITH EXPONENTS: SOME TOOLS

What is the point behind the use of the Cobb-Douglas production function, with all its exponents:

$$\frac{Y}{L} = \left(\frac{K}{L}\right)^{\alpha} \times E_t^{1-\alpha}$$

Recall that exponents greater than 1 are a means of repeated multiplication. Thus 2^1 is 2 multiplied by itself once, that is, 2; 2^2 is 2 times itself twice, that is, $2 \times 2 = 4$; 2^3 is 2 times itself three times, that is, $2 \times 2 \times 2 = 8$. Recall that exponents between 1 and zero are a way of taking roots. Thus $2^{0.5}$ is the square root of 2, and $2^{1/3}$ is the cube root of 2.

Whenever the Cobb-Douglas production function is used, the *parameters* that are the exponents will be between zero and 1. In fact, in most applications of this production function the parameter α will be something like ½. Raising the capital-labor ratio to the α power is something like taking the square root of the capital-labor ratio. So the production function will state that output per worker is proportional to the square root of the capital-labor ratio. This function (a) is easy to calculate or look up for particular cases, (b) is one with which we have a lot of experience, (c) is an increasing function (so it fits the intuitive requirement that more capital is useful), and (d) is a function with diminishing returns — the higher the capital stock, the less valuable is the next investment in expanding the capital stock still further. Thus a lot of features that economists would like a sensible behavioral relationship between the capital-labor ratio and output per worker to have are already built into the Cobb-Douglas production function.

Moreover, there is an additional advantage to using the Cobb-Douglas production function. It makes calculating growth rates easy. Recall from Chapter 2 the rule of thumb for calculating the growth rate of a quantity raised to a power: *The proportional change of a quantity raised to a power is equal to the proportional change in the quantity times the power to which it is raised.*

Output per worker is proportional to the capital-output ratio raised to the power α. Thus if nothing else is changing and if we know the growth rate of the capital-labor ratio, we can immediately calculate the growth rate of output per worker. If α is ½ and if the capital-labor ratio is growing at 4 percent per year, then output per worker is growing at

$$\frac{1}{2} \times 4\% = 2\% \text{ per year}$$

must equal demand. If it does not, then buyers who find themselves short are frantically raising their bids (and prices are rising) or sellers who find themselves with excess inventory are frantically trying to shed it (and prices are falling). Only if supply equals demand can the price in a market be stable. In macroeconomics, the supply-must-equal-demand equilibrium condition is the most important, but there are other important equilibrium conditions too. Box 3.5 provides an example of one: the equilibrium condition required for *balanced growth*.

As we have seen, economists solve models by combining behavioral relationships with equilibrium conditions. If the equilibrium conditions are not satisfied, then the economy cannot be stable. Someone's expectations must turn out to be false, or

A SAMPLE EQUILIBRIUM CONDITION — THE CAPITAL-OUTPUT RATIO: AN EXAMPLE

An important equilibrium condition that is not of the supply-must-equal-demand form is the equilibrium condition for *balanced growth,* which plays a big part in Chapter 4. This equilibrium condition relates the following economic variables:

- The share of total income in the economy that is saved and invested, written *s.*
- The proportional rate of growth of the labor force, written *n.*
- The proportional rate of growth of the efficiency of the labor force, written *g.*
- The depreciation rate — the rate at which capital wears out — written δ (Greek lowercase letter delta).

Growth will be *balanced* if, and only if, the ratio of the economy's stock of capital *K* to its level of output *Y* is constant. This equilibrium condition holds if, and only if, the capital-to-output ratio *K/Y* is equal to

$$\frac{K}{Y} = \kappa^* = \frac{s}{n + g + \delta}$$

The capital-output ratio must be equal to the economy's savings rate *s* divided by the sum of the population growth rate *n,* the labor efficiency growth rate *g,* and the depreciation rate δ.

If the capital-output ratio is lower than this value, it will grow because net investment will be high relative to the capital stock. If the capital-output ratio is higher than this value, it will shrink because net investment will be low relative to the capital stock. In either case, the capital-output ratio will converge to its *balanced-growth equilibrium* level over time.

Thus this balanced-growth capital-output-ratio equation satisfies the two requirements for being an equilibrium condition. If the economy does not satisfy the equilibrium condition, it will be heading toward it. If the economy satisfies the equilibrium condition, it will remain in the same place.

---

someone's plans for what to buy and sell must be unsatisfied. If the behavioral relationships are not satisfied, the relationships are not behavioral. The behavioral relationships *must* be satisfied. Economists hope that the simplified behavioral relationships of models are a good enough match to actual behavior. And they hope that the *actual* economy moves to equilibrium rapidly enough that the only situations they need to consider are those in which the equilibrium conditions hold.

Boxes 3.6, 3.7, and 3.8 present three views of how economic models are put together. All three boxes show how to solve an economic model: how to combine the behavioral relationship of the production function with the balanced-growth equilibrium condition to determine the value of steady-state output per worker in the economy. But they do so in three different ways. Box 3.6 uses arithmetic to arrive at a particular solution for a particular production function determined by particular parameter values. Box 3.7 uses algebra to derive a more general solution that holds for a wide range of parameter values. And Box 3.8 uses graphical techniques — Descartes' idea that anything that can be done with equations can also be done with curves on a graph.

USING ARITHMETIC TO DETERMINE STEADY-STATE OUTPUT PER WORKER: AN EXAMPLE

Using simple arithmetic, we can combine the production function (a behavioral relationship) with the balanced-growth equilibrium condition to calculate the economy's equilibrium level of output per worker.

Suppose the efficiency of labor E is \$10,000 a year, the diminishing-returns-to-investment parameter α is $\frac{1}{2}$, the savings rate s is 25 percent of total output, the population growth rate n and the labor efficiency growth rate g are each 1 percent per year, and the depreciation rate δ is 3 percent per year. In that case the balanced-growth capital-output ratio K/Y will be

$$\kappa^* = \frac{s}{n + g + \delta} = \frac{25\%}{1\% + 1\% + 3\%} = 5$$

If $K/Y = 5$, then $K = 5 \times Y$ and $K/L = 5 \times Y/L$. Thus, in this economy, the equilibrium capital stock per worker will be five times output per worker:

$$\frac{K}{L} = 5 \times \frac{Y}{L}$$

Given the current efficiency of labor, the production function is

$$\frac{Y}{L} = \left(\frac{K}{L}\right)^{\alpha} \times E_t^{1-\alpha}$$

$$\frac{Y}{L} = \left(\frac{K}{L}\right)^{0.5} \times 10{,}000^{0.5} = \sqrt{\frac{K}{L}} \times 100$$

What is the equilibrium? In equilibrium, both the behavioral relationship and the equilibrium condition hold. To solve these two equations together, substitute one into the other:

$$\frac{K}{L} = 5 \times \frac{Y}{L} = 5 \times \sqrt{\frac{K}{L}} \times 100$$

$$\frac{K}{L} = 500 \times \sqrt{\frac{K}{L}}$$

$$\sqrt{\frac{K}{L}} = 500$$

$$\frac{K}{L} = 250{,}000$$

and so

$$\frac{Y}{L} = \sqrt{\frac{K}{L}} \times 100$$

$$\frac{Y}{L} = 50{,}000$$

In its balanced-growth equilibrium, the level of output per worker is \$50,000 a year, and the balanced-growth level of the capital stock per worker is \$250,000.

USING ALGEBRA TO DETERMINE STEADY-STATE OUTPUT PER WORKER: AN EXAMPLE

Box 3.6 showed how to use arithmetic to calculate the economy's steady-state-growth equilibrium level of output per worker for particular values of the parameters E and α (E = $10,000 a year, and α = ½). But if we wanted to find the answer for another set of values of these two parameters, we would have to do the whole process all over again. We can save a lot of work in the long run if we are willing to use algebra instead of arithmetic.

Once again, start with the behavioral relationship:

$$\frac{Y}{L} = \left(\frac{K}{L}\right)^{\alpha} \times E^{1-\alpha}$$

This equation states the influence of the capital-labor ratio K/L on output per worker Y/L. But our equilibrium condition doesn't address the capital-labor ratio K/L; it is phrased in terms of the capital-output ratio K/Y. So we need to rewrite the equation using the fact that $K/L = K/Y \times Y/L$ — that is, the capital-labor ratio is equal to the capital-output ratio times output per worker. We proceed as follows:

$$\frac{Y}{L} = \left(\frac{Y}{L} \times \frac{K}{Y}\right)^{\alpha} \times E^{1-\alpha}$$

Dividing both sides of this equation by $(Y/L)^{\alpha}$, we obtain

$$\left(\frac{Y}{L}\right)^{1-\alpha} = \left(\frac{K}{Y}\right)^{\alpha} \times E^{1-\alpha}$$

Raising both sides to the $1/(1 - \alpha)$ power produces an equation that we can work with:

$$\frac{Y}{L} = \left(\frac{K}{Y}\right)^{\frac{\alpha}{1-\alpha}} \times E$$

There is an important general principle here: If a behavioral relationship and an equilibrium condition refer to different variables, the first step is to rewrite one or the other so that both refer to the same thing.

Now we can determine the balanced-growth equilibrium level of output per worker by substituting the equation for the balanced-growth equilibrium condition into our reworked equation for the production function:

$$\frac{Y}{L} = \left(\frac{s}{n + g + \delta}\right)^{\frac{\alpha}{1-\alpha}} \times E$$

Thus if the efficiency of labor E_t is $10,000 a year, the diminishing-returns-to-investment parameter α is ½, the savings rate s is 25 percent of total output, the population growth rate n and labor efficiency growth rate g are both 1 percent per year, and the depreciation rate δ is 3 percent per year, we can calculate the equilibrium level of output per worker as

$$\frac{Y_t}{L_t} = \left(\frac{.25}{.01 + .01 + .03}\right)^{\frac{.5}{1-.5}} \$10{,}000 = 5^1 \times \$10{,}000 = \$50{,}000$$

Notice that this is the same answer we arrived at using arithmetic in Box 3.6. But now we have a general equation that can be used with any set of parameter values. To answer the question, "What would output per worker be if everything else was the same but the efficiency of labor was doubled?" we could simply substitute the new parameter values into our algebraic answer:

$$\frac{Y}{L} = \left(\frac{s}{n + g + \delta}\right)^{\frac{\alpha}{1-\alpha}} \times E$$

And immediately say, "Output per worker doubles." ◆

USING GRAPHS AND GEOMETRY TO DETERMINE STEADY-STATE OUTPUT PER WORKER: AN EXAMPLE

To avoid using algebra to solve the problem in Box 3.7, or just to understand what our algebraic manipulations are telling us, we can turn to René Descartes' tools and use analytic geometry. We can think about our behavioral relationship, the production function, as a curve on a graph, with output per worker on the vertical axis and capital per worker on the horizontal axis (see Figure 3.6). This curve always slopes upward: Increasing the amount of capital per worker increases the amount of output per worker. However, as capital per worker increases, the curve's slope decreases: Diminishing returns to scale mean that each new increase in capital yields less additional output than the one before.

On the graph in Figure 3.6, our equilibrium condition — that the capital-output ratio K/L be equal to the steady-state value of $s/(n + g + \delta)$ in terms of the parameters of the economy — is simply a line with a constant slope, for which capital per worker is the appropriate constant multiple of output per worker. Diminishing returns to capital guarantee that eventually the slope of the production function curve will fall below the slope of the equilibrium-condition line. Thus the two curves must cross. The point where they cross is the equilibrium.

FIGURE 3.6
Equilibrium Output per Worker

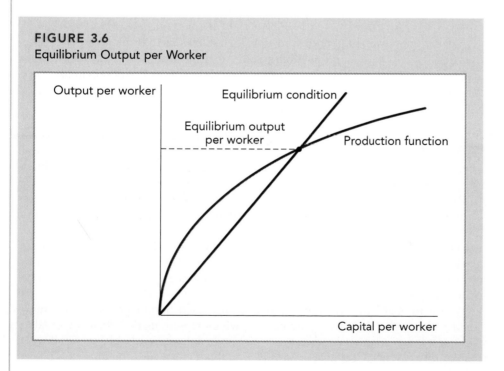

If we knew the parameter values and had a steady hand, we could solve for the balanced-growth value of output per worker simply by finding the point on the graph where the curves cross, and reading off the *x*-axis and *y*-axis values.

Even if we don't have a steady hand and don't know the parameter values, the diagram is still worth drawing. Diagrams allow for qualitative if not quantitative predictions. For example, consider an increase in the equilibrium capital-output ratio. It will reduce the slope of the equilibrium-condition line. You can immediately draw an equilibrium-condition line with a lesser slope on Figure 3.6, and see that such a change pushes the equilibrium point up and to the right along the production function. Diagrams allow us to visualize the effect of a change in a way that equations do not.   ◆

The Advantages of Algebra

Model building is a powerful way of thinking, if the details that you omit are indeed unnecessary and if the factors emphasized are the most important factors. Algebraic equations are the *best* way to summarize cause-and-effect behavioral relationships in economics. Because so many economic concepts are easily quantified, arithmetic might seem a more natural choice, but arithmetic quickly reaches its limits. For example, to know what the level of output per worker would be for each of a great number of possible levels of the capital stock per worker and the efficiency of labor, you would need to carry around a huge table. Table 3.2 shows just a tiny part of what would be required. It is much better to remember and to work with a single algebraic equation, like this one:

$$\frac{Y}{L} = \left(\frac{K}{L}\right)^{0.5} \times 10,000^{1-0.5}$$

Algebra, moreover, has another advantage. It allows us to think about the consequences of a host of different possible systematic relationships by replacing the fixed and known coefficients like $10,000 and 0.5 with unspecified and potentially varying parameters, in this case E and α:

$$\frac{Y}{L} = \left(\frac{K}{L}\right)^{\alpha} \times E^{1-\alpha}$$

Using algebra to analyze this single equation allows us to manipulate and analyze all at once, in shorthand form, all the systematic relationships corresponding to different parameter values and all the tables that they summarize.

Do you want to analyze a situation in which boosting capital per worker raises output per worker at almost the same rate indefinitely? You can do that with a value of α that is near 1. Do you want to analyze a situation in which boosting capital per worker beyond an initial minimal level does little to raise potential output per worker? You can do that with a value of α near zero. Do you want to analyze an intermediate case? You can do that, too, with an intermediate value of the parameter α that shows how quickly a diminishing marginal product to investment sets in. Do you want to analyze a productive economy, in which output per worker is high? Then pick a high value of the parameter E, which represents the efficiency of labor. Do you want to analyze a poor economy, close to subsistence levels, in which even mammoth amounts of capital per worker would not create an affluent society? Then

TABLE 3.2
A Small Part of a Very Large and Cumbersome Table

Output per Worker	Capital per Worker	Efficiency of Labor
$ 0	$ 0	$ 5,000
$ 7,071	$ 10,000	$ 5,000
$10,000	$ 20,000	$ 5,000
$12,247	$ 30,000	$ 5,000
$14,142	$ 40,000	$ 5,000
$15,811	$ 50,000	$ 5,000
$17,321	$ 60,000	$ 5,000
$18,708	$ 70,000	$ 5,000
$20,000	$ 80,000	$ 5,000
$21,213	$ 90,000	$ 5,000
$22,361	$100,000	$ 5,000
$ 0	$ 0	$ 5,000
$10,000	$ 10,000	$10,000
$14,142	$ 20,000	$10,000
$17,321	$ 30,000	$10,000
$20,000	$ 40,000	$10,000
$22,361	$ 50,000	$10,000
$24,495	$ 60,000	$10,000
$26,458	$ 70,000	$10,000
$28,284	$ 80,000	$10,000
$30,000	$ 90,000	$10,000
$31,623	$100,000	$10,000

pick a low value of the parameter E. Figure 3.7 shows some of the results of manipulating both α and E in the production function. Figures 3.8 and 3.9, for example, show in graphs the same flexibility of the production function in response to different parameter values as Figure 3.7 showed in algebra.

It is easy moving back to the specific when you want to consider a particular case with a particular set of parameter values. Just substitute the numerical values for that particular case ($10,000 and 0.5) for the abstract parameters (E and α).

It is possible to pass — even do well in — a macroeconomics course without feeling comfortable with all the algebra. In this book we generally go through each topic three times: once in words, stating the logic of the argument and telling which quantities influence which others; once in algebra; and once in diagrams that represent the algebraic and verbal relationships. If you don't understand a concept the first time it is presented, you have two more chances. Recognize, however, that words, equations, and diagrams are simply three ways of presenting the same material. They should agree. So a discrepancy between your understanding of the algebra, the diagrams, and the words is a sign that something is wrong with your understanding.

FIGURE 3.7

A Single Equation, a Host of Relationships

A single algebraic equation can represent a host of different relationships between capital per worker and output per worker. Each of those relationships in turn represents a host of possible values of capital per worker and efficiency of labor and the resulting values of output per worker.

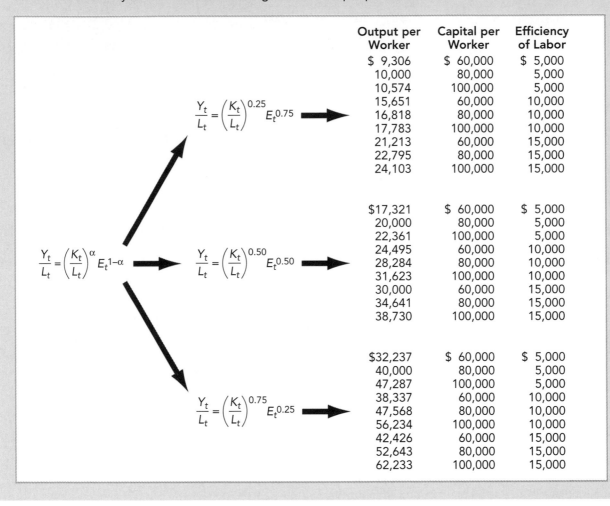

Output per Worker	Capital per Worker	Efficiency of Labor
$ 9,306	$ 60,000	$ 5,000
10,000	80,000	5,000
10,574	100,000	5,000
15,651	60,000	10,000
16,818	80,000	10,000
17,783	100,000	10,000
21,213	60,000	15,000
22,795	80,000	15,000
24,103	100,000	15,000
$17,321	$ 60,000	$ 5,000
20,000	80,000	5,000
22,361	100,000	5,000
24,495	60,000	10,000
28,284	80,000	10,000
31,623	100,000	10,000
30,000	60,000	15,000
34,641	80,000	15,000
38,730	100,000	15,000
$32,237	$ 60,000	$ 5,000
40,000	80,000	5,000
47,287	100,000	5,000
38,337	60,000	10,000
47,568	80,000	10,000
56,234	100,000	10,000
42,426	60,000	15,000
52,643	80,000	15,000
62,233	100,000	15,000

$$\frac{Y_t}{L_t} = \left(\frac{K_t}{L_t}\right)^{\alpha} E_t^{1-\alpha}$$

$$\frac{Y_t}{L_t} = \left(\frac{K_t}{L_t}\right)^{0.25} E_t^{0.75}$$

$$\frac{Y_t}{L_t} = \left(\frac{K_t}{L_t}\right)^{0.50} E_t^{0.50}$$

$$\frac{Y_t}{L_t} = \left(\frac{K_t}{L_t}\right)^{0.75} E_t^{0.25}$$

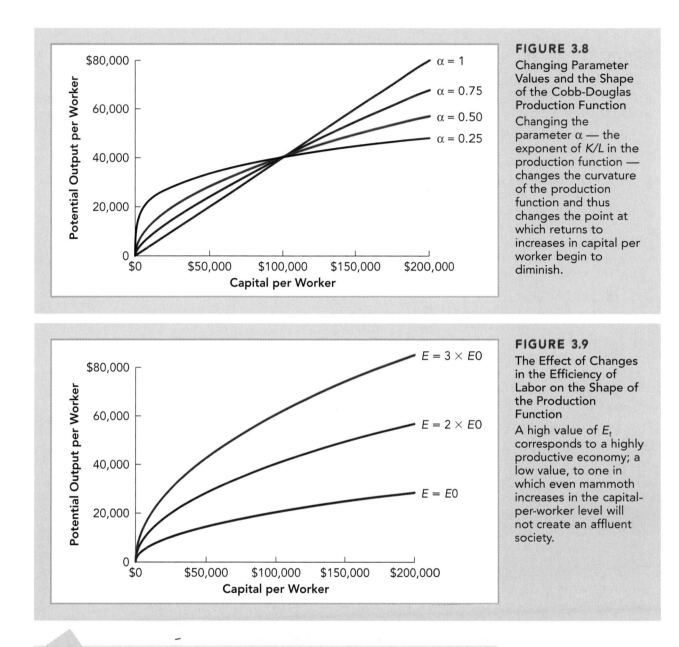

FIGURE 3.8

Changing Parameter Values and the Shape of the Cobb-Douglas Production Function

Changing the parameter α — the exponent of K/L in the production function — changes the curvature of the production function and thus changes the point at which returns to increases in capital per worker begin to diminish.

FIGURE 3.9

The Effect of Changes in the Efficiency of Labor on the Shape of the Production Function

A high value of E_t corresponds to a highly productive economy; a low value, to one in which even mammoth increases in the capital-per-worker level will not create an affluent society.

RECAP PATTERNS OF ECONOMIC THOUGHT

Economists' patterns of thought are different from those found in most other social science courses. Economists use models, and stress simple models, for no one really understands excessively complicated models and a model is of little use if you cannot understand the logic behind it. Economists consider two types of relationships between variables in building their models — *behavioral relationships* and *equilibrium conditions* — conditions that must be true if the economy is to be in balance. They base their behavioral relationships on an analysis of representative agents' *opportunity costs*. And they use algebraic equations to describe both kinds of relationships between variables.

Chapter Summary

1. Economists' ways of thinking are strange — peculiar to their intellectual discipline.

2. Economics is abstract. Today's economics courses focus more on analytic tools and chains of reasoning and less on institutional descriptions.

3. Economics is a relatively mathematical subject because so much of what it analyzes can be measured. Thus economists use arithmetic to count things and use algebra because it is the best way to analyze and understand arithmetic.

4. When macroeconomists build models, they usually follow four key strategies:

- Strip down a complicated process to a few econo-mywide behavioral relationships and equilibrium conditions.

- Simplify — ignore differences between people in the economy

- Look at opportunity costs as ways to understand behavioral relationships.

- Focus on expectations of the future, and how such expectations affect the present.

Key Terms

science (p. 60)

expectations (p. 61)

behavioral relationships (p. 62)

equilibrium conditions (p. 62)

model (p. 62)

circular flow (p. 63)

equilibrium (p. 63)

analytic geometry (p. 70)

representative agents (p. 72)

opportunity cost (p. 73)

Analytical Exercises

1. What do you think a science is? List five characteristics that you think a science *must* have. Which of these does economics satisfy?

2. List five characteristics that you think a science must *not* have? Which of these does economics satisfy?

3. Why does the fact that economic agents take actions today that depend on their expectations of the future make economics an extra-hard subject?

4. What do economists mean when they say that it is time to "build a model" of a situation or a problem?

5. List four metaphors that you have heard people use in talking about the economy that are now, or were at the time, obscure to you.

6. In what sense can a line on a graph be an equation?

7. What advantage do models with symbolic parameters (which can later be varied or specified) have over models in which the parameters are specific numbers hard-wired into the equations of the model?

8. What are behavioral relationships? List five behavioral relationships that you have encountered in previous economics courses.

9. What are equilibrium conditions? List some equilibrium conditions that you have encountered in previous economics courses.

10. Which do you think is the best measure of the circular flow of economic activity: GDP, NDP, NNP, or national income? Why?

Long-Run Economic Growth

Long-run economic growth is the subject of this two-chapter part. Chapter 4 covers the theory of growth, and Chapter 5 covers the world-wide pattern of economic growth. Long-run economic growth is *the* most important topic in macroeconomics. Standards of living in the United States today are at least five times what they were at the end of the nineteenth century. Successful economic growth has meant that almost all citizens of the United States today live better, and we hope happier, lives than even the rich elite of a century ago. The study of long-run economic growth aims at understanding its sources and causes and at determining what government policies will promote or retard long-run economic growth.

The study of long-run growth is also a separate module that is not very closely connected to the study of business cycles, recessions, unemployment, inflation, and stabilization policy that make up the bulk of the subject matter of macroeconomics courses and of this book. Any discussion of economic policy has to refer to long-run economic growth: The effect of a policy on long-run growth is its most important element. But the models used and the conclusions reached in Part II will by and large not be used in subsequent parts. Starting in Chapter 6, our attention turns from growth to business cycles.

Why, then, include this two-chapter part on long-run growth? The principal reason is that long-run economic growth is such an important topic that it must be covered.

The Theory
of Economic Growth

CHAPTER

QUESTIONS

What are the principal determinants of long-run economic growth?

What equilibrium condition is useful in analyzing long-run growth?

How quickly does an economy head for its steady-state growth path?

What effect does faster population growth have on long-run growth?

What effect does a higher savings rate have on long-run growth?

4.1 SOURCES OF LONG-RUN GROWTH

Ultimately, long-run economic growth is *the* most important aspect of how the economy performs. Material standards of living and levels of economic productivity in the United States today are about four times what they are today in, say, Mexico because of favorable initial conditions and successful growth-promoting economic policies over the past two centuries. Material standards of living and levels of economic productivity in the United States today are at least five times what they were at the end of the nineteenth century and more than ten times what they were at the founding of the republic. Successful economic growth has meant that most citizens of the United States today live better, along almost every dimension of material life, than did even the rich elite in preindustrial times.

It is definitely possible for good and bad policies to accelerate or retard long-run economic growth. Argentines were richer than Swedes in the years before World War I began in 1914, but Swedes today have perhaps four times the material standard of living and the economic productivity level of Argentines. Almost all this difference is due to differences in growth policies — good policies in the case of Sweden, bad policies in the case of Argentina — for there were few important differences in initial conditions at the start of the twentieth century to give Sweden an edge.

Policies and initial conditions work to accelerate or retard growth through two principal channels. The first is their impact on the available level of *technology* that multiplies the efficiency of labor. The second is their impact on the **capital intensity** of the economy — the stock of machines, equipment, and buildings that the average worker has at his or her disposal.

Better Technology

The overwhelming part of the answer to the question of why Americans today are more productive and better off than their predecessors of a century or two ago is "better technology." We now know how to make electric motors, dope semiconductors, transmit signals over fiber optics, fly jet airplanes, machine internal combustion engines, build tall and durable structures out of concrete and steel, record entertainment programs on magnetic tape, make hybrid seeds, fertilize crops with better mixtures of nutrients, organize an assembly line for mass production, and do a host of other things that our predecessors did not know how to do a century or so ago. Perhaps more important, the American economy is equipped to make use of all these technological discoveries.

Better technology leads to a higher level of **efficiency of labor** — the skills and education of the labor force, the ability of the labor force to handle modern machine technologies, and the efficiency with which the economy's businesses and markets function. An economy in which the efficiency of labor is higher will be a richer and a more productive economy. This technology-driven overwhelming increase in the efficiency with which we work today is the major component of our current relative prosperity.

Thus it is somewhat awkward to admit that economists know relatively little about better technology. Economists are good at analyzing the consequences of advanced technology, but they have less to say than they should about the sources of such technology. (We shall return to what economists do have to say about the sources of better technology toward the end of Chapter 5.)

Capital Intensity

The second major factor determining the prosperity and growth of an economy — and the second channel through which changes in economic policies can affect long-run growth — is the *capital intensity* of the economy. How much does the average worker have at his or her disposal in the way of capital goods — buildings, freeways, docks, cranes, dynamos, numerically controlled machine tools, computers, molders, and all the others? The larger the answer to this question, the more prosperous an economy will be: A more capital-intensive economy will be a richer and a more productive economy.

There are, in turn, two principal determinants of capital intensity. The first is the *investment effort* being made in the economy: the share of total production — real GDP — saved and invested in order to increase the capital stock of machines, buildings, infrastructure, and other human-made tools that amplify the productivity of workers. Policies that create a higher level of investment effort lead to a faster rate of long-run economic growth.

The second determinant is the *investment requirements* of the economy: the amount of new investment that goes to simply equipping new workers with the economy's standard level of capital or to replacing worn-out and obsolete machines and buildings. The ratio between the investment effort and the investment requirements of the economy determines the economy's capital intensity.

This chapter focuses on the intellectual tools that economists use to analyze long-run growth. It outlines a relatively simple framework for thinking about the key growth issues. Thus, this chapter looks at the theory. The following chapter looks at the facts of economic growth.

Note that, as mentioned above, the tools have relatively little to say about the determinants of technological progress. They do, however, have a lot to say about the determinants of the capital intensity of the economy. And they have a lot to say about how evolving technology and the determinants of capital intensity together shape the economy's long-run growth.

> **RECAP   SOURCES OF LONG-RUN GROWTH**
>
> Ultimately, long-run economic growth is *the* most important aspect of how the economy performs. Two major factors determine the prosperity and growth of an economy: the pace of technological advance and the capital intensity of the economy. Policies that accelerate innovation or that boost investment to raise capital intensity accelerate economic growth.

4.2 THE STANDARD GROWTH MODEL

Economists begin to analyze long-run growth by building a simple, standard model of economic growth — a *growth model*. This standard model is also called the Solow model, after Nobel Prize–winning MIT economist Robert Solow. Economists then use the model to look for an *equilibrium* — a point of balance, a condition of rest, a state of the system toward which the model will converge over time. Once you have found the equilibrium position toward which the economy tends to move, you can use it to understand how the model will behave. If you have built the right model, it will tell you in broad strokes how the economy will behave.

In economic growth economists look for the *steady-state balanced-growth equilibrium*. In a steady-state balanced-growth equilibrium the capital intensity of the economy is stable. The economy's capital stock and its level of real GDP are growing at the same proportional rate. And the capital-output ratio — the ratio of the economy's capital stock to annual real GDP — is constant.

The Production Function

The first component of the model is a behavioral relationship called the **production function**. This relationship tells us how the productive resources of the economy — the **labor force**, the **capital** stock, and the level of technology that determines the efficiency of labor — can be used to determine and produce the level of output in the economy. The total volume of production of the goods and services that consumers, investing businesses, and the government want is limited by the available resources. The production function tells us how available resources limit production.

Tell the production function what resources the economy has available, and it will tell you how much the economy can produce. Abstractly, we write the production function as

$$\frac{Y}{L} = F\left(\frac{K}{L}, E\right)$$

This says that **output per worker** (*Y/L*) — real GDP *Y* divided by the number of workers *L* — is systematically related, in a pattern prescribed by the form of the function *F*(), to the economy's available resources: the capital stock per worker (*K/L*) and the current efficiency of labor (*E*) determined by the current level of technology and the efficiency of business and market organization.

The Cobb-Douglas Production Function

As long as the production function is kept at the abstract level of an *F*()—one capital letter and two parentheses — it is not of much use. We know that there is a relationship between resources and production, but we don't know what that relationship is. So to make things less abstract, and more useful, henceforth we will use one particular form of the production function. We will use the so-called Cobb-Douglas production function, a functional form that economists use because it makes many kinds of calculations relatively simple. The Cobb-Douglas production function states that

$$\frac{Y}{L} = \left(\frac{K}{L}\right)^{\alpha} \times E^{1-\alpha}$$

The economy's level of output per worker (*Y/L*) is equal to the capital stock per worker *K/L* raised to the exponential power of some number α and then multiplied by the current efficiency of labor *E* raised to the exponential power $1-\alpha$.

The efficiency of labor *E* and the number α are *parameters* of the model. The parameter α is always a number between zero and 1. The best way to think of it is as the parameter that governs how fast diminishing returns to investment set in. A level of α near zero means that the extra amount of output made possible by each additional unit of capital declines very quickly as the capital stock increases, as Figure 4.1 shows.

By contrast, a level of α near 1 means that the next additional unit of capital makes possible almost as large an increase in output as the last additional unit of capital, as

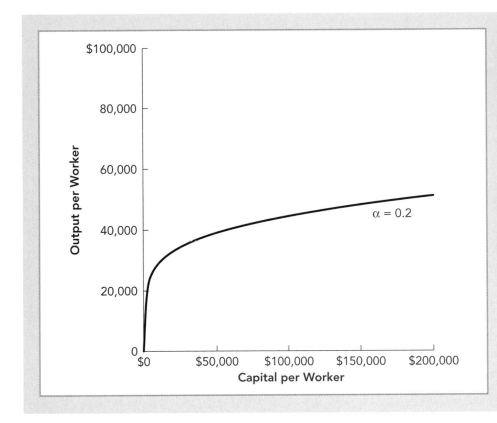

FIGURE 4.1
The Cobb-Douglas
Production Function
for Parameter α Near
Zero
When the parameter α
is close to zero, there
are sharply declining
marginal returns to
increasing capital per
worker: An increase in
capital per worker
produces much less in
increased output than
the last increase in
capital per worker.
Diminishing returns to
capital accumulation
set in rapidly and
ferociously.

Figure 4.2 shows. When α equals 1, output is proportional to capital: Double the stock of capital per worker, and you double output per worker as well. When the parameter α is near to but less than 1, diminishing returns to capital accumulation set in, but they do not set in rapidly or steeply. And as α varies from a high number near 1 to a low number near zero, the force of diminishing returns gets stronger.

The other parameter, E, tells us the current level of the efficiency of labor. A higher level of E means that more output per worker can be produced for each possible value of the capital stock per worker. A lower value of E means that the economy is very unproductive: Not even huge amounts of capital per worker will boost output per worker to achieve what we would think of as prosperity. Box 4.1 illustrates how to use the production function once you know its form and parameters — how to calculate output per worker once you know the capital stock per worker.

The Cobb-Douglas production function is flexible in the sense that it can be tuned to fit any of a wide variety of different economic situations. Figure 4.3 shows a small part of the flexibility of the Cobb-Douglas production function. Is the level of productivity high? The Cobb-Douglas function can fit with a high initial level of the efficiency of labor E. Does the economy rapidly hit a wall as capital accumulation proceeds and find that all the investment in the world is doing little to raise the level of production? Then the Cobb-Douglas function can fit with a low level — near zero — of the diminishing-returns-to-capital parameter α. Is the speed with which diminishing returns to investment set in moderate? Then pick a moderate value of α, and the Cobb-Douglas function will once again fit.

FIGURE 4.2

The Cobb-Douglas Production Function for Parameter α Equal 1

When α = 1, output per worker is proportional to capital per worker: Doubling capital per worker doubles output per worker. There are no diminishing returns to capital accumulation. When the parameter α is near to but less than 1, diminishing returns to capital accumulation set in slowly and gently.

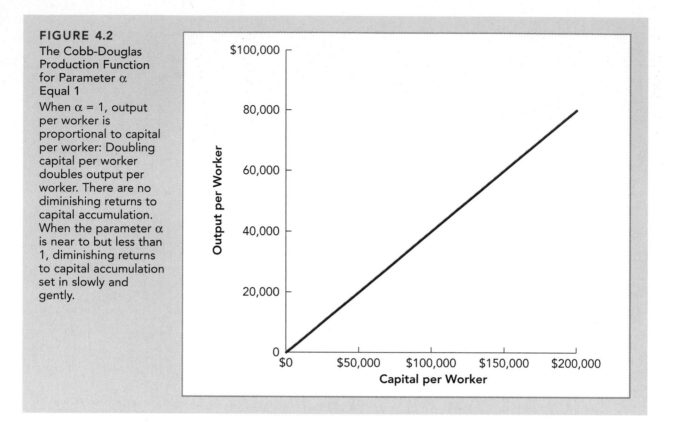

FIGURE 4.3

The Cobb-Douglas Production Function Is Flexible

By changing α — the exponent of the capital-labor ratio (K/L) in the algebraic form of the production function — you change the curvature of the production function and thus the extent of diminishing returns to further increases in capital per worker. Raising the parameter α decreases the speed with which the returns to increased capital accumulation diminish.

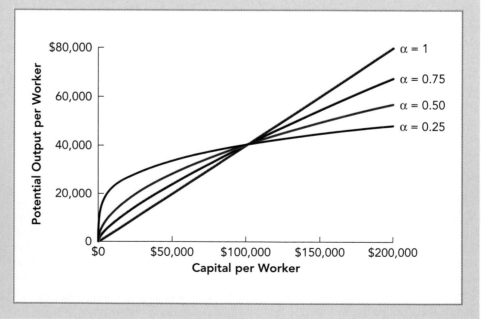

USING THE PRODUCTION FUNCTION: AN EXAMPLE

For given values of E (say, 10,000) and α (say, 0.3), this production function tells us how the capital stock per worker is related to output per worker. If the capital stock per worker is \$250,000, then output per worker will be

$$\frac{Y}{L} = \$250{,}000^{0.3} \times 10{,}000^{0.7}$$
$$= \$41.628 \times 630.958$$
$$= \$26{,}265$$

And if the capital stock per worker is \$125,000, then output per worker will be

$$\frac{Y}{L} = \$125{,}000^{0.3} \times 10{,}000^{0.7}$$
$$= \$33.812 \times 630.958$$
$$= \$21{,}334$$

Note that the first \$125,000 of capital boosted production from \$0 to \$21,334, and that the second \$125,000 of capital boosted production from \$21,334 to \$26,265, less than one-quarter as much. These substantial diminishing returns should not be a surprise: The value of α in this example — 0.3 — is low, and low values are supposed to produce rapidly diminishing returns to capital accumulation.

Nobody expects anyone to raise \$250,000 to the 0.3 power in her or his head and come up with 41.628. That is what calculators are for! This Cobb-Douglas form of the production function, with its fractional exponents, carries the drawback that we cannot expect students (or professors) to do problems in their heads or with just pencil and paper. However, this form of the production function also carries substantial benefits: By varying just two numbers — the efficiency of labor E and the diminishing-returns-to-capital parameter α — we can consider and analyze a very broad set of relationships between resources and the economy's productive power.

In fact, this particular Cobb-Douglas form of the production function was developed by Cobb and Douglas for precisely this purpose: By judicious choice of different values of E and α, it is simple to "tune" the function so that it can capture a large range of different kinds of behavior.

No economist believes that there is, buried somewhere in the earth, a big machine that forces the level of output per worker to behave exactly as calculated by the algebraic production function above. Instead, economists think that the Cobb-Douglas production function is a simple and useful approximation. The process that does determine the level of output per worker is an immensely complex one: Everyone in the economy is part of it, and it is too complicated to work with. Using the Cobb-Douglas production function involves a large leap of abstraction. Yet it is a useful leap, for using this approximation to analyze the economy will lead us to approximately correct conclusions.

The Rest of the Growth Model

The rest of the growth model is straightforward. First comes the need to keep track of the quantities of the model over time. We do so by attaching to each variable — such as the capital stock, efficiency of labor, output per worker, or labor force — a subscript telling what year it applies to. Thus K_{1999} will be the capital stock in year 1999. If we want to refer to the efficiency of labor in the current year (but don't care what the current year is), we use t (for "time") as a stand-in for the numerical value of the current year. Thus we write E_t. And if we want to refer to the efficiency of labor in the year after the current year, we write E_{t+1}.

Population Growth

Second comes the pattern of labor-force growth. We assume — once again making a simplifying leap of abstraction — that the **labor force** L of the economy is growing at a constant proportional rate given by the value of a parameter n. (Note that n does not have to be the same across countries and can shift over time in any one country.) Thus we can calculate the growth of the labor force between this year and the next with the formula

$$L_{t+1} = (1 + n) \times L_t$$

Next year's labor force will be n percent higher than this year's labor force, as Figure 4.4 shows. Thus if this year's labor force is 10 million and the growth rate parameter n is 2 percent per year, then next year's labor force will be

$$
\begin{aligned}
L_{t+1} &= (1 + n) \times L_t \\
&= (1 + 2\%) \times L_t \\
&= (1 + 0.02) \times 10 \\
&= 10.2 \text{ million}
\end{aligned}
$$

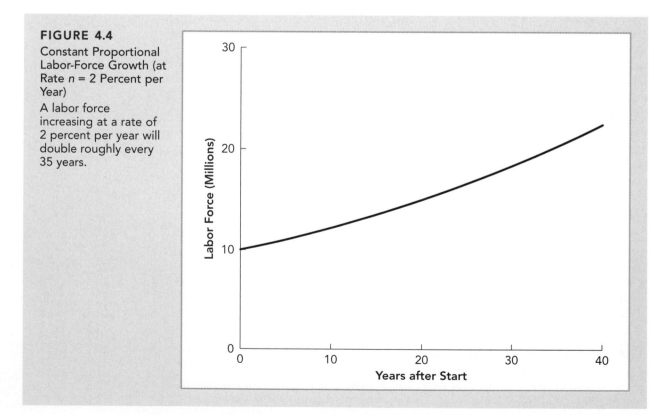

FIGURE 4.4

Constant Proportional Labor-Force Growth (at Rate n = 2 Percent per Year)

A labor force increasing at a rate of 2 percent per year will double roughly every 35 years.

We assume that the rate of growth of the labor force is constant not because we believe that labor-force growth is unchanging but because the assumption makes the analysis of the model simpler. The trade-off between realism in the model's description of the world and simplicity as a way to make the model easier to analyze is one that economists always face. They usually resolve it in favor of simplicity.

Efficiency of Labor

Assume, also, that the efficiency of labor E is growing at a constant proportional rate given by a parameter g. (Note that g does not have to be the same across countries and can shift over time in any one country.) Thus between this year and the next year

$$E_{t+1} = (1 + g) \times E_t$$

Next year's level of the efficiency of labor will be g percent higher than this year's level, as Figure 4.5 shows. Thus if this year's efficiency of labor is $10,000 per worker and the growth rate parameter g is 1.5 percent per year, then next year the efficiency of labor will be

$$\begin{aligned} E_{t+1} &= (1 + g) \times E_t \\ &= (1 + 0.015) \times \$10,000 \\ &= \$10,150 \end{aligned}$$

Once again this assumption is made because it makes the analysis of the model easier, not because the rate at which the efficiency of labor grows is constant.

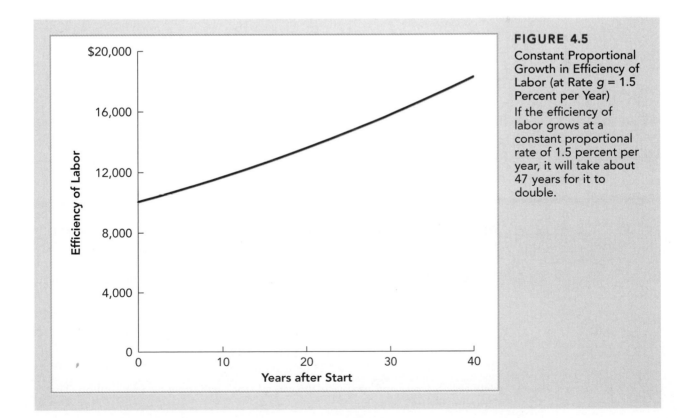

FIGURE 4.5

Constant Proportional Growth in Efficiency of Labor (at Rate g = 1.5 Percent per Year)

If the efficiency of labor grows at a constant proportional rate of 1.5 percent per year, it will take about 47 years for it to double.

Savings and Investment

Last, assume that a constant proportional share, equal to a parameter s, of real GDP is saved each year and invested. S is thus the economy's **savings rate**. Such gross investments add to the capital stock, so a higher amount of savings and investment means faster growth for the capital stock. But the capital stock does not grow by the full amount of *gross* investment. A fraction δ (the Greek lowercase letter *delta*, for "**depreciation**") of the capital stock wears out or is scrapped each period. Thus the actual relationship between the capital stock now and the capital stock next year is

$$K_{t+1} = K_t + (s \times Y_t) - (\delta \times K_t)$$

The level of the capital stock next year will be equal to the capital stock this year plus the savings rate s times this year's level of real GDP minus the depreciation rate δ times this year's capital stock, as Figure 4.6 shows. Box 4.2 illustrates how to use this capital accumulation equation to calculate the capital stock.

FIGURE 4.6

Changes in the Capital Stock

Gross investment adds to and depreciation subtracts from the capital stock. Depreciation is a share α of the current capital stock. Investment is a share s of current production.

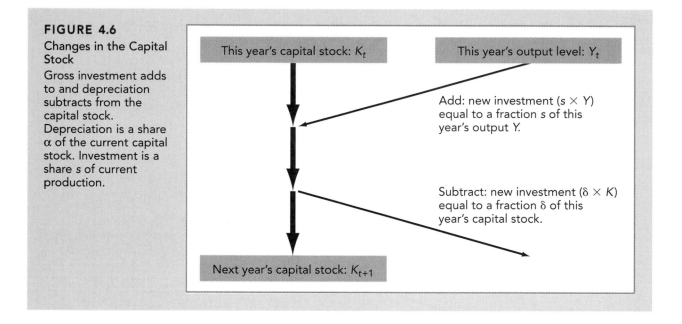

This year's capital stock: K_t

This year's output level: Y_t

Add: new investment ($s \times Y$) equal to a fraction s of this year's output Y.

Subtract: new investment ($\delta \times K$) equal to a fraction δ of this year's capital stock.

Next year's capital stock: K_{t+1}

INVESTMENT, DEPRECIATION, AND CAPITAL ACCUMULATION: AN EXAMPLE

Suppose that the current level of output in the economy is $8 trillion a year and the current year's capital stock in the economy is $24 trillion. As Figure 4.7 shows, a savings rate s of 20 percent and an annual depreciation rate δ of 4 percent would mean that next year's capital stock will be

$$
\begin{aligned}
K_{t+1} &= K_t + (s \times Y_t) - (\delta \times K_t) \\
&= \$24 + (0.2 \times \$8) - (0.04 \times \$24) \\
&= \$24 + \$1.6 - \$0.96 \\
&= \$24.64 \text{ trillion}
\end{aligned}
$$

Between this year and next year the capital stock will grow by $640 billion. That is a proportional growth rate of 2.667 percent.

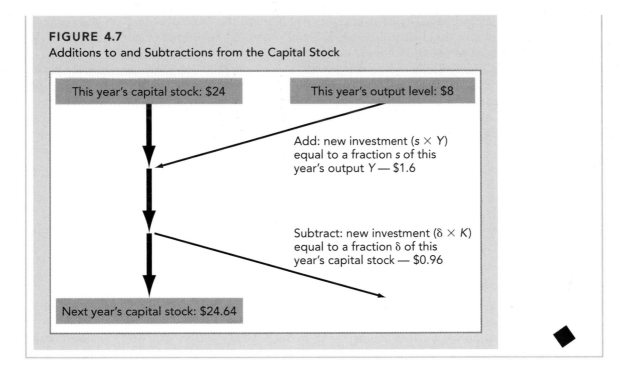

FIGURE 4.7
Additions to and Subtractions from the Capital Stock

This year's capital stock: $24

This year's output level: $8

Add: new investment ($s \times Y$) equal to a fraction s of this year's output Y — $1.6

Subtract: new investment ($\delta \times K$) equal to a fraction δ of this year's capital stock — $0.96

Next year's capital stock: $24.64

That is all there is to the growth model: three assumptions about rates of population growth, increases in the efficiency of labor, and investment, plus one additional equation to describe how the capital stock grows over time. Those factors plus the production function make up the growth model. It is simple. But understanding the processes of economic growth that the model generates is more complicated.

RECAP   THE STANDARD GROWTH MODEL

When the economy's capital stock and its level of real GDP are growing at the same proportional rate, its capital-output ratio — the ratio of the economy's capital stock to annual real GDP — is constant and the economy is in equilibrium — on its steady-state balanced growth path. The standard growth model analyzes how this steady-state balanced growth path is determined by five factors: The level of the efficiency of labor, the growth rate of the efficiency of labor, the economy's savings rate, the economy's population growth rate, and the capital stock depreciation rate.

4.3 UNDERSTANDING THE GROWTH MODEL

Economists' first instinct when analyzing any model is to look for a point of equilibrium. They look for a situation in which the quantities and prices being analyzed are stable and unchanging. And they look for the economic forces that can push an out-of-equilibrium economy to one of its points of equilibrium. Thus microeconomists talk about the equilibrium of a particular market. Macroeconomists talk (as we will later in the book) about the equilibrium value of real GDP relative to potential output.

In the study of long-run growth, however, the key economic quantities are never stable. They are growing over time. The efficiency of labor is growing; the level of output per worker is growing; the capital stock is growing; the labor force is growing. How, then, can we talk about a point of equilibrium where things are stable if everything is growing?

The answer is to look for an equilibrium in which everything is growing together, at the same proportional rate. Such an equilibrium is one of *steady-state balanced growth*. If everything is growing together, then the relationships between key quantities in the economy are stable. And the material in this chapter will be easier if we focus on one key ratio: the **capital-output ratio**. Thus our point of equilibrium will be one at which the capital-output ratio is constant over time and toward which the capital-output ratio will converge if it should find itself out of equilibrium.

How Fast Is the Economy Growing?

We know that the key quantities in the economy are growing. The efficiency of labor is, after all, increasing at a proportional rate g. And we know that it is technology-driven improvements in the efficiency of labor that have generated most of the increases in our material welfare and economic productivity over the past few centuries.

Determining how fast the quantities in the economy are growing is straightforward if we remember our three mathematical rules:

- The proportional growth rate of a product — $P \times Q$, say — is equal to the sum of the proportional growth rates of the factors, that is, the growth rate of P plus the growth rate of Q.

- The proportional growth rate of a quotient — E/Q, say — is equal to the difference of the proportional growth rates of the dividend (E) and the divisor (Q).

- The proportional growth rate of a quantity raised to an exponent — Q^y, say — is equal to the exponent (y) times the growth rate of the quantity (Q).

The Growth of Capital per Worker

Begin with capital per worker. To reduce the length of equations, let's use the expression $g(k_t)$ to stand for the proportional growth rate of capital per worker. The proportional growth rate is simply the amount that output per worker will be next year minus the amount it is this year, all divided by the output per worker this year:

$$g(k_t) = \frac{(K_{t+1} / L_{t+1}) - (K_t / L_t)}{K_t / L_t}$$

Capital per worker is a quotient: It is the capital stock divided by the labor force. Thus the proportional growth rate of capital per worker is the growth rate of the capital stock minus the growth rate of the labor force, as Figure 4.8 shows.

The growth rate of the labor force is simply the parameter n. The growth rate of the capital stock is a bit harder to calculate. We know that it is

$$\frac{K_{t+1} - K_t}{K_t}$$

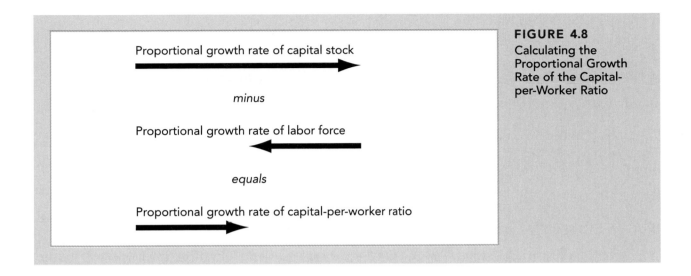

FIGURE 4.8
Calculating the Proportional Growth Rate of the Capital-per-Worker Ratio

And we know that we can write next year's capital stock as equal to this year's capital stock plus gross investment minus depreciation:

$$K_{t+1} = K_t + (s \times Y_t) - (\delta \times K_t)$$

If we substitute in for next year's capital stock and rearrange, we have

$$\frac{[K_t + (s \times Y_t) - (\delta \times K_t)] - K_t}{K_t} = \frac{s \times Y_t}{K_t} - \delta\frac{K_t}{K_t} = \frac{s \times Y_t}{K_t} - \delta$$

Then we see that the proportional growth rate of capital per worker is

$$g(k_t) = \frac{s}{K_t / Y_t} - \delta - n$$

To make our equations look simpler, let's give the capital-output ratio K/Y a special symbol: κ (the Greek letter *kappa*). Thus we can write that the proportional growth rate of capital per worker is

$$g(k_t) = \frac{s}{\kappa_t} - \delta - n$$

This says that the growth rate of capital per worker is equal to the savings share of GDP (s) divided by the capital-output ratio (κ), and minus the depreciation rate (δ), and minus the labor-force growth rate (n). Box 4.3 presents calculations of what the growth rate of capital-per-worker is for sample parameter values. A higher rate of

THE GROWTH OF CAPITAL PER WORKER: AN EXAMPLE

Suppose that the proportional growth rate of the labor force n is 2 percent per year, or 0.02. Suppose also that the depreciation rate δ is 4 percent per year and the savings rate is 20 percent. We can then calculate what the proportional rate of growth of capital per worker will be for each possible level of the capital-output ratio. Simply substitute the values of depreciation, labor-force growth, and the savings rate into the equation for the growth rate of capital per worker:

$$g(k_t) = \frac{s}{\kappa_t} - \delta - n$$

to get

$$g(k_t) = \frac{0.20}{\kappa_t} - 0.04 - 0.02$$

Then if the current capital-output ratio is 5, the growth rate of capital per worker will be

$$g(k_t) = \frac{0.20}{5} - 0.04 - 0.02 = 0.04 - 0.04 - 0.02 = -0.02$$

At minus 2 percent per year, the capital-per-worker ratio is shrinking. By contrast, if the current capital-output ratio is 2.5, the growth rate of capital per worker will be

$$g(k_t) = \frac{0.20}{2.5} - 0.04 - 0.02 = 0.08 - 0.04 - 0.02 = +0.02$$

At plus 2 percent per year, the capital-per-worker ratio is growing.

Figure 4.9 depicts these results graphically.

FIGURE 4.9

Capital-per-Worker Growth as a Function of the Capital-Output Ratio
The growth rate of capital per worker is plotted here as a function of the capital-output ratio for the following parameter values: labor-force growth rate n of 0.02, depreciation rate δ of 0.04, and savings rate s of 0.20. The higher the capital-output ratio, the lower is the growth rate of capital per worker.

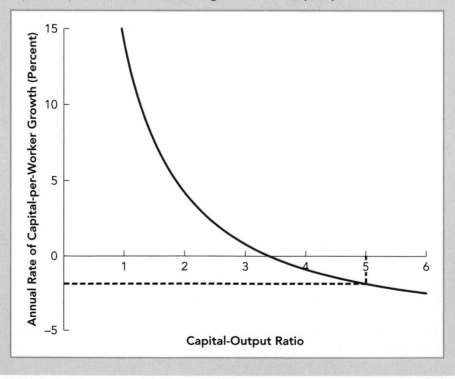

labor-force growth will reduce the rate of growth of capital per worker: Having more workers means the available capital has to be divided up more ways. A higher rate of depreciation will reduce the rate of growth of capital per worker: More capital will rust away. And a higher capital-output ratio will reduce the proportional growth rate of capital per worker: The higher the capital-output ratio, the smaller is investment relative to the capital stock.

The Growth of Output per Worker

Our Cobb-Douglas form of the production function tells us that the level of output per worker is

$$\frac{Y_t}{L_t} = \left(\frac{K_t}{L_t}\right)^\alpha \times E_t^{1-\alpha}$$

Output per worker is the product of two terms, each of which is a quantity raised to an exponential power. So using our mathematical rules of thumb, the proportional growth rate of output per worker — call it $g(y_t)$ to once again save space — will be, as Figure 4.10 shows

- α times the proportional growth rate of capital per worker.
- Plus $(1 - \alpha)$ times the rate of growth of the efficiency of labor.

The rate of growth of the efficiency of labor is simply g. And the previous section calculated the growth rate of capital per worker $g(k)$: $s/\kappa_t - \delta - n$. So simply plug these expressions in

$$g(y_t) = \left[\alpha \times \left(\frac{s}{\kappa_t} - \delta - n\right)\right] + [(1 - \alpha) \times g]$$

And simplify a bit by rearranging terms:

$$g(y_t) = g + \left\{\alpha \times \left[\frac{s}{\kappa_t} - (n + g + \delta)\right]\right\}$$

FIGURE 4.10
Calculating the Growth Rate of Output per Worker
The growth rate of output per worker is a weighted average of the growth rates of capital per worker and efficiency of labor.

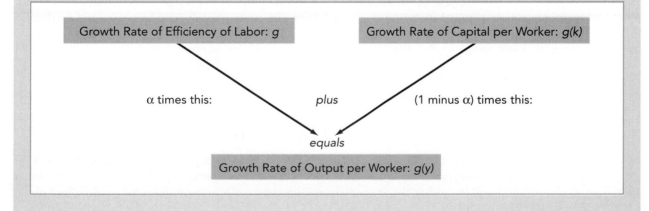

THE GROWTH OF OUTPUT PER WORKER: AN EXAMPLE

Suppose that we are analyzing an economy in which the growth rate of the efficiency of labor g is 0.02, the diminishing-returns-to-investment parameter α is 0.5, the labor-force growth rate n is 0.02, the depreciation rate δ is 0.04, and the savings rate s is 0.3. Then we can determine the current proportional rate of growth of output per worker by substituting the values of the parameters into the equation

$$g(y_t) = g + \left\{ \alpha \times \left[\frac{s}{\kappa_t} - (n + g + \delta) \right] \right\}$$

to get

$$g(y_t) = 0.02 + \left\{ 0.5 \times \left[\frac{0.3}{\kappa_t} - (0.02 + 0.02 + 0.04) \right] \right\}$$

If the capital-output ratio is 3, then the proportional rate of growth of output per worker will be

$$g(y_t) = 0.02 + \left\{ 0.5 \times \left[\frac{0.3}{3} - (0.02 + 0.02 + 0.04) \right] \right\} = 0.02 + 0.5 \times 0.02 = 0.03$$

It will be 3 percent per year.

If the capital-output ratio is 6, then the proportional rate of growth of output per worker will be

$$g(y_t) = 0.02 + \left\{ 0.5 \times \left[\frac{0.3}{6} - (0.02 + 0.02 + 0.04) \right] \right\} = 0.02 + 0.5 \times -0.03 = 0.005$$

It will be ½ percent per year.

Box 4.4 shows how to calculate the growth rate of output per worker in a concrete case.

The Growth of the Capital-Output Ratio

Now consider the capital-output ratio κ_t. It is the key ratio that we will focus on because the economy will be in equilibrium when it is stable and constant. The capital-output ratio is equal to capital per worker divided by output per worker. So its proportional growth rate is the difference between their growth rates:

$$g(\kappa_t) = g(k_t) - g(y_t) = \left(\frac{s}{\kappa_t} - \delta - n \right) - \left\{ g + \alpha \times \left[\frac{s}{\kappa_t} - (n + g + \delta) \right] \right\}$$

This simplifies to

$$g(\kappa_t) = (1 - \alpha) \times \left[\frac{s}{\kappa_t} - (n + g + \delta) \right]$$

Thus the growth rate of the capital-output ratio depends on the balance between the *investment requirements* $(n + g + \delta)$ and the *investment effort* (s) made in the economy. The higher the investment requirements, the lower will be the growth rate of the capital-output ratio, as Figure 4.11 illustrates.

FIGURE 4.11
Growth of the Capital-Output Ratio
The proportional growth rates of both capital per worker and output per worker are decreasing functions of the capital-output ratio. The higher the capital-output ratio, the slower is growth. The rate of growth of the capital-output ratio itself is also a decreasing function of the capital-output ratio: The gap between capital-per-worker and output-per-worker growth is large and positive when the capital-output ratio is low and negative when the capital-output ratio is high.

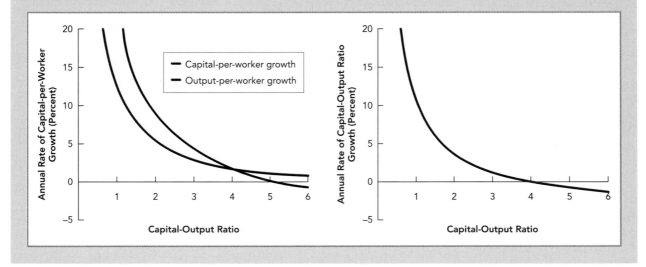

Steady-State Growth Equilibrium

The Capital-Output Ratio

From the growth rate of the capital-output ratio,

$$g(\kappa_t) = (1 - \alpha) \times \left[\frac{s}{\kappa_t} - (n + g + \delta) \right]$$

we can see that whenever the capital-output ratio κ_t is greater than $s/(n + g + \delta)$, the growth rate of the capital-output ratio will be negative. Output per worker will be growing faster than capital per worker, and the capital-output ratio will be shrinking. By contrast, we can see that whenever the capital-output ratio κ_t is *less* than $s/(n + g + \delta)$, the capital-output ratio will be growing. The capital stock per worker will be growing faster than output per worker, as Figure 4.12 shows.

What happens when the capital-output ratio κ_t is equal to $s/(n + g + \delta)$? Then the growth rate of the capital-output ratio will be zero. It will be stable, neither growing nor shrinking. If the capital-output ratio is at that value, it will stay there. If the capital-output ratio is away from that value, it will head toward it. No matter where the capital-output ratio κ_t starts, it will head for, **converge** to, home in on its steady-state balanced-growth value of $s/(n + g + \delta)$ (see Figure 4.13).

Thus the value $s/(n + g + \delta)$ is the *equilibrium level* of the capital-output ratio. It is a point at which the economy tends to balance and to which the economy converges. The requirement that the capital-output ratio equal this equilibrium level becomes our equilibrium condition for balanced economic growth.

FIGURE 4.12

Growth of the Capital-Output Ratio as Function of the Level of the Capital-Output Ratio

The value of the capital-output ratio at which its rate of change is zero is an *equilibrium*. If the capital-output ratio is at that equilibrium value, it will stay there. If it is away from that equilibrium value, it will head toward it.

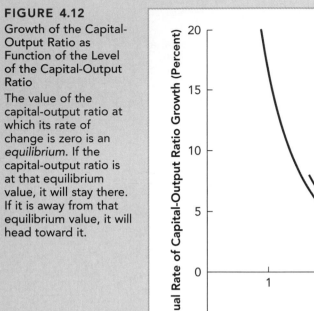
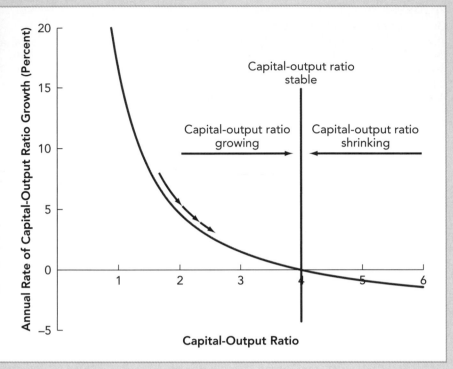

FIGURE 4.13

Convergence of the Capital-Output Ratio to Its Steady-State Value

If the capital-output ratio starts at a value different from its steady-state equilibrium value, it will head toward equilibrium. The figure shows the paths over time of the capital-output ratio for parameter values of *s* = 0.28, *n* = 0.02, *g* = 0.015, δ = 0.035, and α = 0.5 and for initial starting values of 1, 3, and 6. The steady-state capital-output ratio κ^* is 4.

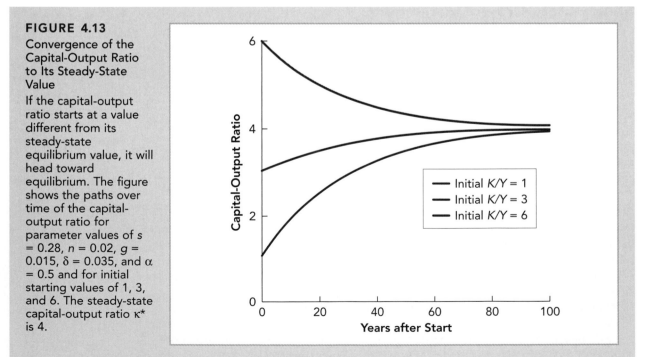

To make our future equations even simpler, we can give the quantity $s/(n + g + \delta)$ — the equilibrium value of the capital-output ratio — the symbol κ^*:

$$\kappa^* = \frac{s}{n + g + \delta}$$

Other Quantities

When the capital-output ratio κ_t is at its steady-state value of

$$\kappa^* = \frac{s}{n + g + \delta}$$

the proportional growth rates of capital per worker and output per worker are stable too. Output per worker is growing at a proportional rate g:

$$g(y_t) = g$$

The capital stock per worker is growing at the same proportional rate g:

$$g(k_t) = g$$

The total economywide capital stock is then growing at the proportional rate $n + g$: the growth rate of capital per worker plus the growth rate of the labor force. Real GDP is also growing at rate $n + g$: the growth rate of output per worker plus the labor force growth rate.

The Level of Output per Worker on the Steady-State Growth Path

When the capital-output ratio is at its steady-state balanced-growth equilibrium value κ^*, we say that the economy is on its **steady-state growth path**. What is the level of output per worker if the economy is on this path? We saw the answer to this in Chapter 3. The requirement that the economy be on its steady-state growth path was then our equilibrium condition:

$$\frac{K_t}{Y_t} = \kappa^* = \frac{s}{n + g + \delta}$$

In order to combine it with the production function,

$$\frac{Y_t}{L_t} = \left(\frac{K_t}{L_t}\right)^\alpha \times E_t^{1-\alpha}$$

we first rewrote the production function to make capital per worker the product of the capital-output ratio and output per worker:

$$\frac{Y_t}{L_t} = \left(\frac{Y_t}{L_t} \times \frac{K_t}{Y_t}\right)^\alpha \times E_t^{1-\alpha}$$

Dividing both sides by $(Y/L)^\alpha$,

$$\left(\frac{Y_t}{L_t}\right)^{1-\alpha} = \left(\frac{K_t}{Y_t}\right)^\alpha \times E_t^{1-\alpha}$$

and then raising both sides to the $1/(1 - \alpha)$ power produce an equation for the level of output per worker:

$$\frac{Y_t}{L_t} = \left(\frac{K_t}{Y_t}\right)^{\frac{\alpha}{1-\alpha}} \times E_t$$

FIGURE 4.14
Calculating Steady-
State Output per
Worker along the
Steady-State Growth
Path.

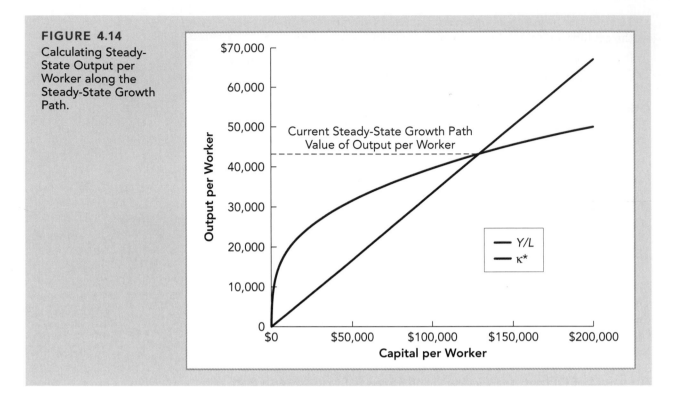

Substitute the equilibrium condition into this transformed form of the production function. The result is that, as long as we are on the steady-state balanced-growth path,

$$\frac{Y_t}{L_t} = \left(\frac{s}{n+g+\delta}\right)^{\frac{\alpha}{1-\alpha}} \times E_t = \kappa^{*\frac{\alpha}{1-\alpha}} \times E_t$$

Is the algebra too complicated? There is an alternative, diagrammatic way of seeing what the steady-state capital-output ratio implies for the steady-state level of output per worker. It is shown in Figure 4.14. Simply draw the production function for the current level of the efficiency of labor E_t. Also draw the line that shows where the capital-output ratio is equal to its steady-state value, κ^*. Look at the point where the curves intersect. That point shows what the current level of output per worker is along the steady-state growth path (for the current level of the efficiency of labor).

Anything that increases the steady-state capital-output ratio will rotate the capital-output line to the right. Thus it will raise steady-state output per worker. Anything that decreases the steady-state capital-output ratio rotates the capital-output line to the left. It thus lowers steady-state output per worker.

If we define

$$\lambda = \frac{\alpha}{1-\alpha}$$

and call λ the *growth multiplier* (discussed in Box 4.5), then output per worker along the steady-state growth path is equal to the steady-state capital-output ratio raised to the growth multiplier times the current level of the efficiency of labor:

$$\left(\frac{Y_t}{L_t}\right)_{ss} = \kappa^{*\lambda} \times E_t$$

Thus calculating output per worker when the economy is on its steady-state growth path is a simple three-step procedure:

1. Calculate the steady-state capital-output ratio, $\kappa^* = s/(n + g + \delta)$, the savings rate divided by the sum of the population growth rate, the efficiency of labor growth rate, and the depreciation rate.

2. Amplify the steady-state capital-output ratio κ^* by the growth multiplier. Raise it to the $\lambda = \alpha/(1 - \alpha)$ power, where α is the diminishing-returns-to-capital parameter.

3. Multiply the result by the current value of the efficiency of labor E_t, which can be easily calculated because the efficiency of labor is growing at the constant proportional rate g.

The fact that an economy converges to its steady-state growth path makes analyzing the long-run growth of an economy relatively easy as well:

1. Calculate the steady-state growth path, shown in Figure 4.15.

2. From the steady-state growth path, forecast the future of the economy: If the economy is on its steady-state growth path today, it will stay on that path in the future (unless some of the parameters — n, g, δ, s, and α — shift). If the economy is not on its steady-state growth path today, it is heading for that path and will get there soon.

Thus long-run economic forecasting becomes simple.

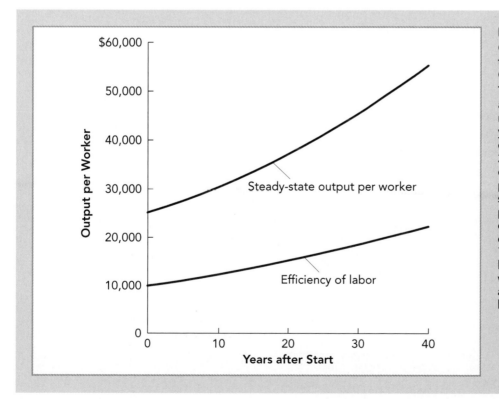

FIGURE 4.15

Output per Worker on the Steady-State Growth Path

The parameter values are labor-force growth rate n at 1 percent per year; increase in the efficiency of labor g at 2 percent per year; depreciation rate δ at 3 percent per year; savings rate s at 37.5 percent; and diminishing-returns-to-capital parameter α at ⅓. The efficiency of labor and output per worker grow smoothly along the economy's balanced-growth path.

WHERE THE GROWTH MULTIPLIER COMES FROM: THE DETAILS

Why is the steady-state capital-output ratio raised to the (larger) power of $\alpha/(1 - \alpha)$ rather than just the power α? The power used makes a big difference when one applies the growth model to different situations.

The reason is that an increase in the capital-output ratio increases the capital stock both directly and indirectly. For the same level of output you have more capital. And because extra output generated by the additional capital is itself a source of additional savings and investment, you have even more capital. The impact of the additional capital generated by anything that raises κ^* — an increase in savings, a decrease in labor force, or anything else — is thus multiplied by these positive feedback effects.

Figure 4.16 shows the effect of this difference between α and $\alpha/(1 - \alpha)$. An increase in the capital-output ratio means more capital for a given level of output, and that generates the first-round increase in output: amplification by the increase in capital raised to the power α. But the first-round increase in output generates still more capital, which increases production further. The total increase in production is the proportional increase in the steady-state capital-output ratio raised to the (larger) power $\alpha/(1 - \alpha)$.

FIGURE 4.16
The Growth Multiplier: Effect of Increasing Capital-Output Ratio on Steady-State (SS) Output per Worker

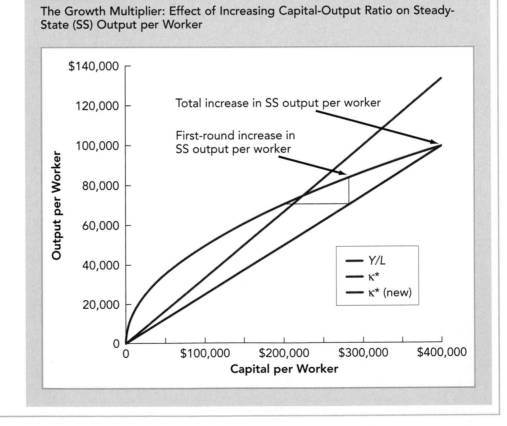

How Fast Does the Economy Head for Its Steady-State Growth Path?

Suppose that the capital-output ratio κ_t is not at its steady-state value κ^*? How fast does it approach its steady state? Even in this simple growth model we can't get an exact answer. But if we are willing to settle for approximations and confine our attention only to small differences beween the current capital-output ratio κ_t and its steady-state value κ^*, then we can get an answer. The growth rate of the capital-output ratio will be approximately equal to a fraction $[(1 - \alpha) \times (n + g + \delta)]$ of the gap between the steady-state and its current level.

For example, if $(1 - \alpha) \times (n + g + \delta)$ is equal to 0.04, the capital-output ratio will close approximately 4 percent of the gap between its current level and its steady-state value in a year. If $(1 - \alpha) \times (n + g + \delta)$ is equal to 0.07, the capital-output ratio will close 7 percent of the gap between its current level and its steady-state value in a year. A variable closing 4 percent of the gap each year between the ratio's current and steady-state values will move the ratio halfway to its steady-state value in 18 years. A variable closing 7 percent of the gap each year will move the ratio halfway to its steady-state value in 10 years. (See, for example, Figure 4.17.)

This finding generalizes as long as we remember that it is only an approximation and is only approximately valid for relatively small proportional deviations of the capital-output ratio from its steady-state value. Yet this approximation allows us to make much better medium-run forecasts of the dynamic of the economy:

- An economy that is not on its steady-state growth path will close a fraction $[(1 - \alpha) \times (n + g + \delta)]$ of the gap between its current state and its steady-state growth path in a year.

Box 4.6 illustrates how to use this approximation.

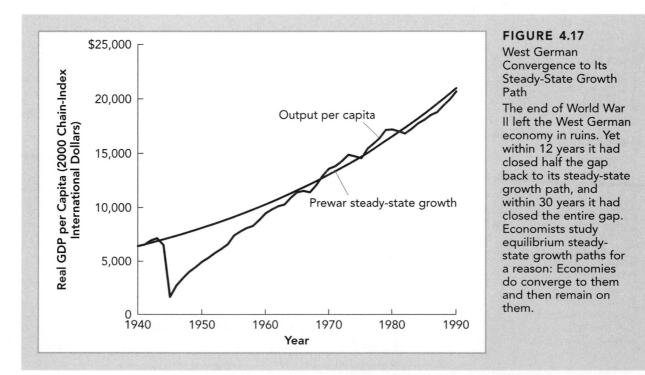

FIGURE 4.17

West German Convergence to Its Steady-State Growth Path

The end of World War II left the West German economy in ruins. Yet within 12 years it had closed half the gap back to its steady-state growth path, and within 30 years it had closed the entire gap. Economists study equilibrium steady-state growth paths for a reason: Economies do converge to them and then remain on them.

Source: J. Bradford DeLong and Barry Eichengreen, "The Marshall Plan: History's Most Successful Structural Adjustment Programme," in Rüdiger Dornbusch, Willhelm Nolling, and Richard Layard, eds., *Postwar Economic Reconstruction and Lessons for the East Today* (Cambridge: MIT Press, 1993), pp. 189–230.

CONVERGING TO THE STEADY-STATE BALANCED-GROWTH PATH: AN EXAMPLE

Consider an economy with parameter values of population growth $n = 0.02$, efficiency of labor growth $g = 0.015$, depreciation $\delta = 0.035$, and diminishing-returns-to-investment parameter $\delta = 0.5$ — the economy whose capital-output ratio is shown in Figure 4.11. This economy would, if off its steady-state growth path, close a fraction of the gap between its current state and its steady state each year:

$$(1 - \alpha) \times (n + g + \delta) = (1 - 0.5) \times (0.02 + 0.015 + 0.035) = 0.5 \times 0.07 = 0.035$$

This 3.5 percent rate of convergence would allow the economy to close half of the gap to the steady state in 20 years.

Thus short- and medium-run forecasting becomes simple too. All you have to do is predict that the economy will head for its steady-state growth path and calculate what the steady-state growth path is.

FIGURE 4.18

Labor-Force Growth and GDP-per-Worker Levels

The average country with a labor-force growth rate of less than 1 percent per year has an output-per-worker level that is nearly 60 percent of the U.S. level. The average country with a labor-force growth rate of more than 3 percent per year has an output-per-worker level that is only 20 percent of the U.S. level. But countries are poor not just because they have fast labor-force growth rates; to some degree they have fast labor-force growth rates because they are poor. Nevertheless, high labor-force growth rates are a powerful cause of relative poverty in the world today.

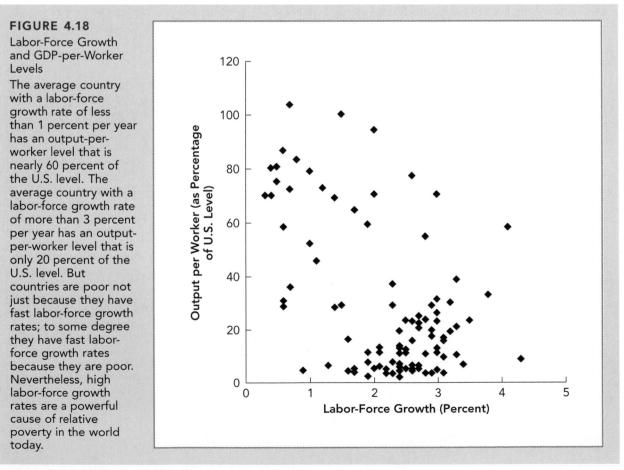

Source: Author's calculations from the Penn World Table data constructed by Alan Heston and Robert Summers, www.nber.org.

Determining the Steady-State Capital-Output Ratio

Labor-Force Growth

The faster the growth rate of the labor force, the lower will be the economy's steady-state capital-output ratio. Why? Because each new worker who joins the labor force must be equipped with enough capital to be productive and to, on average, match the productivity of his or her peers. The faster the rate of growth of the labor force, the larger the share of current investment that must go to equip new members of the labor force with the capital they need to be productive. Thus the lower will be the amount of investment that can be devoted to building up the average ratio of capital to output.

A sudden and permanent increase in the rate of growth of the labor force will lower the level of output per worker on the steady-state growth path. How large will the long-run change in the level of output be, relative to what would have happened had population growth not increased? It is straightforward to calculate if we know what the other parameter values of the economy are.

How important is all this in the real world? Does a high rate of labor-force growth play a role in making countries relatively poor not just in economists' models but in reality? It turns out that it is important, as Figure 4.18 shows. Of the 22 countries in the world with GDP-per-worker levels at least half of the U.S. level, 18 have labor-force growth rates of less than 2 percent per year, and 12 have labor-force growth rates of less than 1 percent per year. The additional investment requirements imposed by rapid labor-force growth are a powerful reducer of capital intensity and a powerful obstacle to rapid economic growth. Box 4.7 shows just how powerful these effects are.

AN INCREASE IN POPULATION GROWTH: AN EXAMPLE

Consider an economy in which the parameter α is $\frac{1}{2}$ — so the growth multiplier $\gamma = \alpha/(1 - \alpha)$ is 1 — in which the underlying rate of productivity growth g is 1.5 percent per year, the depreciation rate δ is 3.5 percent per year, and the savings rate s is 21 percent. Suppose that the labor-force growth rate suddenly and permanently increases from 1 to 2 percent per year.

Then before the increase in population growth the steady-state capital output ratio was

$$\kappa^*_{old} = \frac{s}{n_{old} + g + \delta} = \frac{.21}{.01 + .015 + .035} = \frac{.21}{.06} = 3.5$$

After the increase in population growth, the new steady-state capital-output ratio will be

$$\kappa^*_{new} = \frac{s}{n_{new} + g + \delta} = \frac{.21}{.02 + .015 + .035} = \frac{.21}{.07} = 3$$

Before the increase in population growth, the level of output per worker along the old steady-state growth path was

$$\left(\frac{Y_t}{L_t}\right)_{ss,old} = (\kappa^*)^\lambda \times E_t = 3.5^1 \times E_t$$

After the increase in population growth, the level of output per worker along the new steady-state growth path will be

$$\left(\frac{Y_t}{L_t}\right)_{ss,new} = (\kappa^*)^\lambda \times E_t = 3.0^1 \times E_t$$

BOX
4.7

Divide the second of the equations by the first:

$$\frac{(Y_t / L_t)_{\text{ss,new}}}{(Y_t / L_t)_{\text{ss,old}}} = \frac{3.0^1 \times E_t}{3.5^1 \times E_t} = 0.857$$

And discover that output per worker along the new steady-state growth path is only 86 percent of what it would have been along the old steady-state growth path: Faster population growth means that output per worker along the steady-state growth path has fallen by 14 percent.

In the short run this increase in labor-force growth will have no effect on output per worker. Just after population growth increases, the increased rate of population growth has had no time to increase the population. It has had no time to affect the actual capital-labor ratio. But over time the economy will converge to the new, lower steady-state growth path, and output per worker will be reduced by 14 percent relative to what it would otherwise have been. (See Figure 4.19.)

FIGURE 4.19

Effects of a Rise in Population Growth on the Economy's Growth Path
Although a sudden change in one of the parameters of the economic growth model causes a sudden change in the location of the economy's steady-state growth path, the economy's level of output per worker does not instantly jump to the new steady-state value. Instead, it converges to the new steady-state value only slowly, over considerable periods of time.

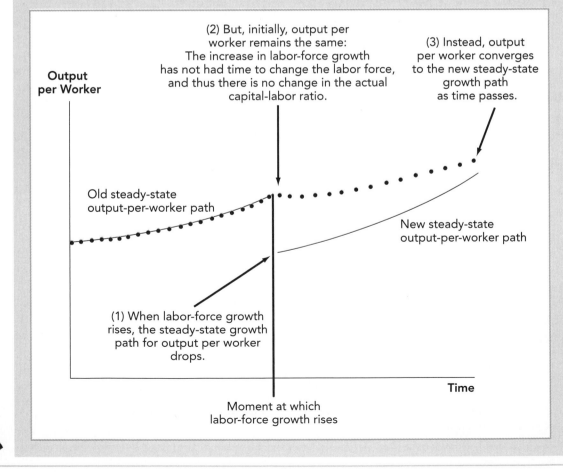

Depreciation and Productivity Growth

Increases or decreases in the depreciation rate will have the same effects on the steady-state capital-output ratio and on output per worker along the steady-state growth path as will increases or decreases in the labor-force growth rate. The higher the depreciation rate, the lower will be the economy's steady-state capital-output ratio. Why? Because a higher depreciation rate means that the existing capital stock wears out and must be replaced more quickly. The higher the depreciation rate, the larger the share of current investment that must go to replacing the capital that has become worn out or obsolete. Thus the lower will be the amount of investment that can be devoted to building up the average ratio of capital to output.

Increases or decreases in the rate of productivity growth will have effects similar to those of increases or decreases in the labor-force growth rate on the steady-state capital-output ratio, but they will have very different effects on the steady-state level of output per worker. The faster the growth rate of productivity, the lower will be the economy's steady-state capital-output ratio. The faster the productivity growth, the higher is output now. But the capital stock depends on what investment was in the past. The faster the productivity growth, the smaller is past investment relative to current production and the lower is the average ratio of capital to output. So a change in productivity growth will have the same effects on the steady-state capital-output ratio as will an equal change in labor-force growth.

But a change in productivity growth will have very different effects on output per worker along the steady-state growth path. Output per worker along the steady-state growth path is

$$\left(\frac{Y_t}{L_t}\right)_{ss} = \kappa^{*\lambda} \times E_t$$

While an increase in the productivity growth rate g lowers κ^*, it increases the rate of growth of the efficiency of labor E, and so in the long run it does not lower but raises output per worker along the steady-state growth path.

The Savings Rate

The higher the share of national product devoted to savings and gross investment, the higher will be the economy's steady-state capital-output ratio. Why? Because more investment increases the amount of new capital that can be devoted to building up the average ratio of capital to output. Double the share of national product spent on gross investment, and you will find that you have doubled the economy's capital intensity — doubled its average ratio of capital to output.

One good way to think about it is that the steady-state capital-output ratio is the point at which the economy's investment effort and its investment requirements are in balance. Investment effort is simply s, the share of total output devoted to savings and investment. Investment requirements are the amount of new capital needed to replace depreciated and worn-out machines and buildings (a share of total output equal to $\delta \times \kappa^*$), plus the amount needed to equip new workers who increase the labor force (a share of total output equal to $n \times \kappa^*$), plus the amount needed to keep the stock of tools and machines at the disposal of workers increasing at the same rate as the efficiency of their labor (a share of total output equal to $g \times \kappa^*$). So double the savings rate and you double the steady-state capital-output ratio. (See Box 4.8.)

How important is all this in the real world? Does a high rate of savings and investment play a role in making countries relatively rich not just in economists'

AN INCREASE IN THE SAVINGS RATE: AN EXAMPLE

To see how an increase in savings changes output per worker along the steady-state growth path, consider an economy in which the parameter α is $\frac{1}{2}$ — so $\lambda = \alpha/(1 - \alpha)$ is 1 — in which the underlying rate of labor-force growth is 1 percent per year, the rate of productivity growth g is 1.5 percent per year, and the depreciation rate δ is 3.5 percent per year. Suppose that the savings rate s was 18 percent, and suddenly and permanently rises to 24 percent.

Then before the increase in savings, the steady-state capital-output ratio was

$$\kappa^*_{\text{old}} = \frac{s_{\text{old}}}{n + g + \delta} = \frac{.18}{.01 + .015 + .035} = \frac{.18}{.06} = 3$$

After the increase in savings, the new steady-state capital-output ratio will be

$$\kappa^*_{\text{new}} = \frac{s_{\text{new}}}{n + g + \delta} = \frac{.24}{.01 + .015 + .035} = \frac{.24}{.06} = 4$$

Before the increase in savings, the level of output per worker along the old steady-state growth path was

$$\left(\frac{Y_t}{L_t}\right)_{\text{ss,old}} = \kappa^{*\lambda} \times E_t = 3.0^1 \times E_t$$

After the increase in savings, the level of output per worker along the new steady-state growth path will be

$$\left(\frac{Y_t}{L_t}\right)_{\text{ss,new}} = \kappa^{*\lambda} \times E_t = 4.0^1 \times E_t$$

Divide the second of the equations by the first:

$$\frac{(Y_t / L_t)_{\text{ss,new}}}{(Y_t / L_t)_{\text{ss,old}}} = \frac{4.0^1 \times E_t}{3.0^1 \times E_t} = 1.333$$

And discover that output per worker along the new steady-state growth path is 133 percent of what it would have been along the old steady-state growth path: Higher savings mean that output per worker along the steady-state growth path has risen by 33 percent.

The increase in savings has no effect on output per worker immediately. Just after the increase in savings has taken place, the economy is still on its old, lower steady-state growth path. But as time passes it converges to the new steady-state growth path corresponding to the higher level of savings, and in the end output per worker is 33 percent higher than it would otherwise have been. ◆

models but in reality? It turns out that it is important indeed, as Figure 4.20 shows. Of the 22 countries in the world with GDP-per-worker levels at least half of the U.S. level, 19 have investment shares of more than 20 percent of output. The high capital-output ratios generated by high investment efforts are a very powerful source of relative prosperity in the world today.

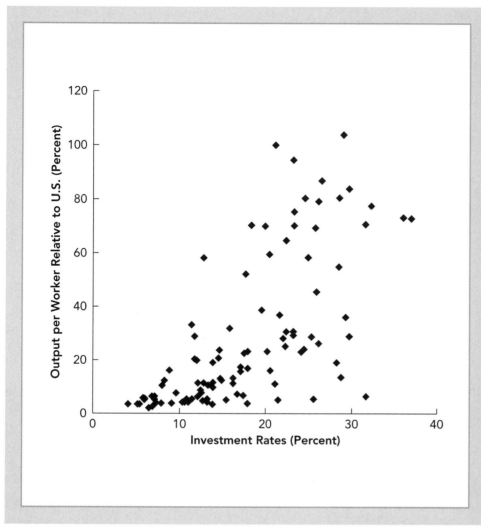

FIGURE 4.20
National Investment Shares and GDP-per-Worker Levels
The average country with an investment share of output of more than 25 percent has an output-per-worker level that is more than 70 percent of the U.S. level. The average country with an investment share of output of less than 15 percent has an output-per-worker level that is less than 15 percent of the U.S. level. This is not entirely due to a one-way relationship from a high investment effort to a high steady-state capital-output ratio: Countries are poor not just because they invest little; to some degree they invest little because they are poor. But much of it is. High savings and investment rates are a very powerful cause of relative wealth in the world today.

Source: Author's calculations from the Penn World Table data constructed by Alan Heston and Robert Summers, www.nber.org.

RECAP   UNDERSTANDING THE GROWTH MODEL

A few rules of thumb help us understand the growth model. Double the savings rate and you double the steady-state capital-output ratio, and increase the level of GDP per worker by a factor of 2 raised to the $(\alpha/(1 - \alpha))$ power. An increase in the population growth rate lowers the steady-state capital-output ratio by an amount proportional to its increase in the economy's investment requirements — the sum of depreciation, labor force growth, and efficiency of labor growth. As it lowers the steady-state capital-output ratio it lowers the steady-state growth path of output per worker as well. An increase in the efficiency of labor growth rate lowers the steady-state capital-output ratio, but raises the steady-state growth path of output per worker.

Chapter Summary

1. One principal force driving long-run growth in output per worker is the set of improvements in the efficiency of labor springing from technological progress.

2. A second principal force driving long-run growth in output per worker is the increases in the capital stock which the average worker has at his or her disposal and which further multiplies productivity.

3. An economy undergoing long-run growth converges toward and settles onto an equilibrium steady-state growth path, in which the economy's capital-output ratio is constant.

4. The steady-state level of the capital-output ratio is equal to the economy's savings rate divided by the sum of its labor-force growth rate, labor efficiency growth rate, and depreciation rate.

Key Terms

capital intensity (p. 88)

efficiency of labor (p. 88)

production function (p. 90)

labor force (p. 90)

capital (p. 90)

output per worker (p. 90)

savings rate (p. 96)

depreciation (p. 96)

capital-output ratio (p. 98)

convergence (p. 103)

steady-state growth path (p. 105)

Analytical Exercises

1. Consider an economy in which the depreciation rate is 3 percent per year, the rate of population increase is 1 percent per year, the rate of technological progress is 1 percent per year, and the private savings rate is 16 percent of GDP. Suppose that the government increases its budget deficit — which had been at 1 percent of GDP for a long time — to 3.5 percent of GDP and keeps it there indefinitely.
   a. What will be the effect of this shift in policy on the economy's steady-state capital-output ratio?
   b. What will be the effect of this shift in policy on the economy's steady-state growth path for output per worker? How does your answer depend on the value of the diminishing-returns-to-capital parameter α?
   c. Suppose that your forecast of output per worker 20 years in the future was $100,000. What is your new forecast of output per worker 20 years hence?

2. Suppose that a country has the production function
$$Y_t = K_t^{0.5} \times (E_t \times L_t)^{0.5}$$

   a. What is output Y considered as a function of the level of the efficiency of labor E, the size of the labor force L, and the capital-output ratio K/Y?
   b. What is output per worker Y/L?

3. Suppose that with the production function
$$Y_t = K_t^{0.5} \times (E_t \times L_t)^{0.5}$$
the depreciation rate on capital is 3 percent per year, the rate of population growth is 1 percent per year, and the rate of growth of the efficiency of labor is 1 percent per year.
   a. Suppose that the savings rate is 10 percent of GDP. What is the steady-state capital-output ratio? What is the value of output per worker on the steady-state growth path written as a function of the level of the efficiency of labor?
   b. Suppose that the savings rate is 15 percent of GDP. What is the steady-state capital-output ratio? What is the value of output per worker on the steady-state growth path?

c. Suppose that the savings rate is 20 percent of GDP. What is the steady-state capital-output ratio? What is the value of output per worker on the steady-state growth path?

4. What happens to the steady-state capital-output ratio if the rate of technological progress increases? Would the steady-state growth path of output per worker for the economy shift upward, downward, or remain in the same position?

5. Discuss the following proposition: "An increase in the savings rate will increase the steady-state capital-output ratio and so increase both output per worker and the rate of economic growth in both the short run and the long run."

6. Would the steady-state growth path of output per worker for the economy shift upward, downward, or remain the same if capital were to become more durable — if the rate of depreciation on capital were to fall?

7. Suppose that a sudden disaster — an epidemic, say — reduces a country's population and labor force but does not affect its capital stock. Suppose further that the economy was on its steady-state growth path before the epidemic.
   a. What is the immediate effect of the epidemic on output per worker? On the total economywide level of output?
   b. What happens subsequently?

8. According to the marginal productivity theory of distribution, in a competitive economy the rate of return on a dollar's worth of capital — its profits or interest — is equal to capital's marginal productivity. With the production function what is the marginal product of capital? How much is total output (*Y*, not *Y/L*) boosted by the addition of an extra unit to the capital stock?

$$\frac{Y_t}{L_t} = \left(\frac{K_t}{L_t}\right)^\alpha E_t^{1-\alpha}$$

9. According to the marginal productivity theory of distribution, in a competitive economy the rate of return on a dollar's worth of capital — its profits or interest — is equal to capital's marginal productivity. If this theory holds and the marginal productivity of capital is indeed

$$\frac{dY}{dK} = \alpha \times \frac{Y}{K}$$

how large are the total earnings received by capital? What share of total output will be received by the owners of capital as their income?

10. Suppose that environmental regulations lead to a slowdown in the rate of growth of the efficiency of labor in the production function but also lead to better environmental quality. Should we think of this as a "slowdown" in economic growth or not?

Policy Exercises

1. In the mid-1990s during the Clinton presidency the United States eliminated its federal budget deficit. The national savings rate was thus boosted by 4 percent of GDP, from 16 percent to 20 percent of real GDP. In the mid-1990s, the nation's rate of labor-force growth was 1 percent per year, the depreciation rate was 3 percent per year, the rate of increase of the efficiency of labor was 1 percent per year, and the diminishing-returns-to-capital parameter α was ⅓. Suppose that these rates continue into the indefinite future.
   a. Suppose that the federal budget deficit had remained at 4 percent indefinitely. What then would have been the U.S. economy's steady-state capital-output ratio? If the efficiency of labor in 2000 was $30,000 per year, what would be your forecast of output per worker in 2040?
   b. After the elimination of the federal budget deficit, what would be your calculation of the U.S. economy's

steady-state capital-output ratio? If the efficiency of labor in 2000 was $30,000 per year, what would be your forecast of output per worker in 2040?

2. How would your answers to the above question change if your estimate of the diminishing-returns-to-capital parameter α was not ⅓ but ½ and if your estimate of the efficiency of labor in 2000 was not $30,000 but $15,000 a year?

3. How would your answers to question 1 change if your estimate of the diminishing-returns-to-capital parameter α was not ⅓ but ⅔?

4. What are the long-run costs as far as economic growth is concerned of a policy of taking money that could reduce the national debt — and thus add to national savings — and distributing it as tax cuts instead? What are the long-run benefits of such a policy? How can we decide whether such a policy is a good thing or not?

5. At the end of the 1990s it appeared that because of the computer revolution the rate of growth of the efficiency of labor in the United States had doubled, from 1 percent per year to 2 percent per year. Suppose this increase is permanent. And suppose the rate of labor-force growth remains constant at 1 percent per year, the depreciation rate remains constant at 3 percent per year, and the American savings rate (plus foreign capital invested in America) remains constant at 20 percent per year. Assume that the efficiency of labor in the United States in 2000 was $15,000 per year and that the diminishing-returns-to-capital parameter α was $1/3$.
   a. What is the change in the steady-state capital-output ratio? What is the new capital-output ratio?
   b. Would such a permanent acceleration in the rate of growth of the efficiency of labor change your forecast of the level of output per worker in 2040?

6. How would your answers to the above question change if your estimate of the diminishing-returns-to-capital parameter α was not $1/3$ but $1/2$ and if your estimate of the efficiency of labor in 2000 was not $30,000 but $15,000 a year?

7. How would your answers to question 5 change if your estimate of the diminishing-returns-to-capital parameter α was not $1/3$ but $2/3$?

8. Output per worker in Mexico in the year 2000 was about $10,000 per year. Labor-force growth was 2.5 percent per year. The depreciation rate was 3 percent per year, the rate of growth of the efficiency of labor was 2.5 percent per year, and the savings rate was 16 percent of GDP. The diminishing-returns-to-capital parameter α is 0.5.
   a. What is Mexico's steady-state capital-output ratio?
   b. Suppose that Mexico today is on its steady-state growth path. What is the current level of the efficiency of labor E?
   c. What is your forecast of output per worker in Mexico in 2040?

9. In the framework of the question above, how much does your forecast of output per worker in Mexico in 2040 increase if:
   a. Mexico's domestic savings rate remains unchanged but the nation is able to finance extra investment equal to 4 percent of GDP every year by borrowing from abroad?
   b. The labor-force growth rate immediately falls to 1 percent per year?
   c. Both a and b happen?

10. Consider an economy with a labor-force growth rate of 2 percent per year, a depreciation rate of 4 percent per year, a rate of growth of the efficiency of labor of 2 percent per year, and a savings rate of 16 percent of GDP. If the savings rate increases from 16 to 17 percent, what is the proportional increase in the steady-state level of output per worker if the diminishing-returns-to-capital parameter α is $1/3$? $1/2$? $2/3$? $3/4$?

The Reality
of Economic Growth:
History and Prospect

CHAPTER

QUESTIONS

What is modern economic growth?

What was the post-1973 productivity slowdown? What were its causes?
Is the productivity slowdown now over?

Why are some nations so (relatively) rich and other nations so (relatively) poor?

What policies can speed up economic growth?

What are the prospects for successful and rapid economic development in tomorrow's world?

5.1 BEFORE MODERN ECONOMIC GROWTH

Before the Industrial Revolution

If we take the scattered and imperfect information we have about the global economy from the distant past to today, we see a pattern like that depicted in Table 5.1.

Until 1800 the growth rates of human populations were glacial. Population growth between 5000 B.C. and A.D. 1800 averaged less than one-tenth of a percent per year. (Nevertheless, the cumulative magnitude of population growth was impressive, carrying the number of human beings alive on the planet from perhaps 5 million in 5000 B.C. to 900 million in 1800 — 7000 years is a long time.) Until 1500, as best we can tell, there had been next to *no* growth in output per worker for the average human for millennia. Even in 1800 the average human had a material standard of living (and an economic productivity level) at best twice that of the average human in the year 1. The problem was not that there was no technological progress. There was. Humans have long been ingenious. Warrior, priestly, and bureaucratic elites in 1800 lived much better than their counterparts in previous millennia had lived. But just because the ruling elite lived better does not mean that other people lived any better.

Only after 1800 do we see large sustained increases in worldwide standards of living. After 1800 human numbers grew as the population explosion took hold. It carried the total population to 6 billion in October 1999. Population growth on a world scale accelerated from a rate of 0.2 percent per year between 1500 and 1800 to 0.6 percent per year between 1800 and 1900, 0.9 percent per year between 1900 and 1950, and 1.9 percent per year between 1950 and 1975 before the first slowing of the global rate of population growth — 1.6 percent per year from 1975 to 2000.

Average rates of material output per capita, which grew at perhaps 0.15 percent per year between 1500 and 1800, grew at roughly 1 percent per year worldwide between 1800 and 1900 and at an average pace of about 2 percent per year worldwide between 1900 and 2000, as Figure 5.1 shows.

TABLE 5.1
Economic Growth through Deep Time

Year	Population*	GDP per Capita†
−5000	5	$ 130
−1000	50	160
1	170	135
1000	265	165
1500	425	175
1800	900	250
1900	1625	850
1950	2515	2030
1975	4080	4640
2000	6120	8175

* Millions.

† In year-2000 international dollars.

Source: Joel Cohen, *How Many People Can the Earth Support?* (New York: Norton, 1995).

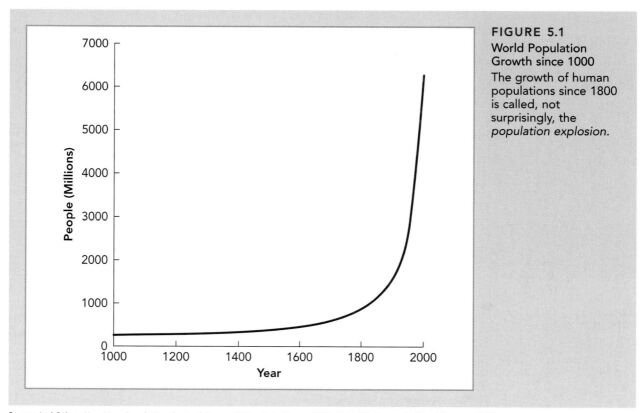

FIGURE 5.1
World Population Growth since 1000
The growth of human populations since 1800 is called, not surprisingly, the *population explosion.*

Source: Joel Cohen, *How Many People Can the Earth Support?* (New York: Norton, 1995); United Nations and Michael Kremer of MIT.

Premodern Economic "Growth"

Why were there no sustained increases in the material productivity of human labor before 1500? Because improved technology quickly ran aground on resource scarcity. As human populations grew, the stocks of known natural resources had to be divided among more and more people: Miners had to exploit lower-quality metal ores, farmers had to farm lesser-quality agricultural land, and forests vanished. Who alive today has ever seen one of the cedars of Lebanon? In spite of technological progress, resource scarcity meant that the efficiency of labor was little, if any, greater in A.D. 1500 than in 1500 B.C.

One of the oldest ideas in economics is that increases in technology inevitably run into natural-resource scarcity and so lead to increases in the numbers of people but not in their standard of living or productivity. This idea was introduced late into economics by Thomas R. Malthus, who was to become the first academic professor of economics (Adam Smith had been a professor of moral philosophy) at the East India Company's Haileybury College.

Malthus saw a world in which inventions and higher living standards led to increases in the rate of population growth. With higher living standards women ovulated more frequently, and more pregnancies were successfully carried to term. Better-nourished children (and adults) had a better chance of resisting diseases. Moreover, when incomes were high, new farmsteads were relatively plentiful, and getting the permission of one's father or elder brother to marry was easier. For these reasons, both social and biological, a higher standard of living before 1800 led to a faster rate of population increase. And the faster rate of population growth increased natural-resource scarcity and lowered productivity until once again people were so poor and malnourished that population growth was roughly zero.

The End of the Malthusian Age

Technology

We clearly no longer live in a **Malthusian age**. For at least 200 years improvements in the efficiency of labor made possible by new technologies and better organizations have *not* been neutralized by natural-resource scarcity. (But a Malthusian age may return: Project twentieth-century population growth rates forward and calculate that the year 2200 population of the earth will be 93 billion; it requires skill and ingenuity to argue today that **resource scarcity** will not be a dominant feature of such a world).

What caused the end of the Malthusian age? How did humanity escape from the trap in which invention and ingenuity increased the numbers but not the material well-being of humans?

The key is that even in the Malthusian age the pace at which inventions occurred increased steadily. First of all, the population grew. Inventions made communication easier; especially after the invention of printing, knowledge could spread widely and quickly. More people meant more inventions: Two heads are greater than one. The rate of technological progress slowly increased over the millennia. By about 1500 it passed the point at which **natural-resource scarcity** could fully offset it. Sustained increases not just in population but in the productivity of labor followed.

The Demographic Transition

At first the rise in material standards of living brought sharp increases in the rate of population growth: the population explosion. But as material standards of living rose far above subsistence, countries began to undergo the **demographic transition**, sketched out in Figure 5.2.

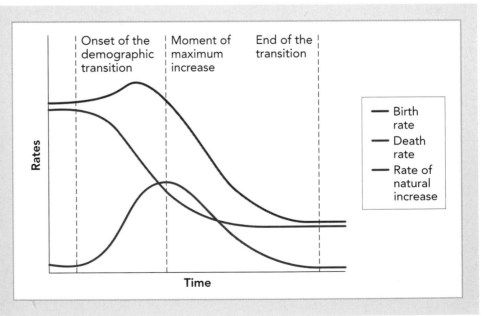

FIGURE 5.2

Stylized Picture of the Demographic Transition

The demographic transition sees, first, a rise in birth rates and a sharp fall in death rates as material standards of living increase above subsistence levels. But after a while birth rates start to decline rapidly too. The end of the demographic transition sees both birth and death rates at a relatively low level and the population nearly stable.

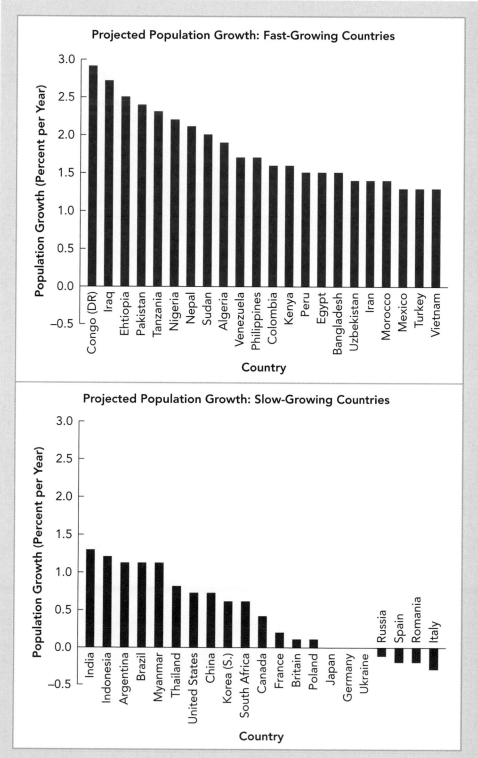

Source: United Nations.

FIGURE 5.3
Expected Population Growth Rates, 1997–2015
The population of India is projected to grow at 1.3 percent and that of China at 0.7 percent per year over the next generation. Demographers today believe that the world population has at most one more doubling to undergo before the demographic transition will have taken hold throughout the world.

Birth control meant that those who did not wish to have more children could exercise their choice. Parents began to find more satisfaction in having a few children and paying a great deal of attention to each. The resources of the average household continued to increase, but the number of children born fell. The long-run relationship between levels of productivity and population growth rates was not — as Malthus thought — a spiral of ever-faster population growth rates as material standards of living increased. Instead, population growth rates peaked and began to decline.

In the world today not all countries have gone through their demographic transitions. Many countries are not rich enough to have begun the population growth declines seen in the second half of the demographic transition. Countries such as Nigeria, Iraq, Pakistan, and the Congo are currently projected to have population growth rates in excess of 2 percent per year over the next generation, as Figure 5.3 shows. But there is also a large group of developing countries like Thailand, China, Korea, and South Africa in which population growth over the next generation is projected to be less than 1 percent per year. And in the industrialized countries — like Japan, Italy, and Germany — populations are projected to stay nearly the same over the next generation.

The Industrial Revolution

The century after 1750 saw the **Industrial Revolution** proper: the invention of the steam engine, the spinning jenny, the power loom, the hydraulic press, the railroad locomotive, the water turbine, and the electric motor, as well as the hot-air balloon, gas lighting, photography, and the sewing machine. But the Industrial Revolution

FIGURE 5.4

Industrialized Areas of the World, 1900

Perhaps the most important lesson to draw from this short look at economic history is that economists' standard growth models apply to a relatively narrow slice of time. For instance, the growth model discussed in Chapter 4 does not illuminate very much regarding the period before 1800, yet it is very useful in analyzing what has happened over the past two centuries, as well as what is going on today with respect to the growth of different national economies.

Industrializing areas

Source: Steven Dorwick and J. Bradford DeLong, "Globalization and Convergence," in Jeffrey Williamson et al., eds. *Globalization in Historical Perspective* (Chicago: University of Chicago Press, forthcoming).

was not just a burst of inventions. It was an economic transformation that revolutionized the *process* of invention as well. Since 1850 the pace of invention and innovation has further accelerated: steel making, the internal combustion engine, pasteurization, the typewriter, the cash register, the telephone, the automobile, the radio, the airplane, the tank, the limited-access highway, the photocopier, the computer, the pacemaker, nuclear weapons, superconductivity, genetic fingerprinting, and the human genome map. The coming of the Industrial Revolution marked the beginning of the era of modern economic growth: the era in which it was expected that new technological leaps would routinely revolutionize industries and generate major improvements in living standards.

The fact that Britain was the center of the Industrial Revolution meant that for a century, from 1800 to 1900, British levels of industrial productivity and British standards of living were the highest in the world. It also meant that English (rather than Hindi, Mandarin, French, or Spanish) became the world's de facto second language. But the technologies of the Industrial Revolution did not remain narrowly confined to Britain. Their spread was rapid to western Europe and the United States. It was less rapid — but still relatively thorough and complete — to southern and eastern Europe and, most interesting perhaps, Japan, as shown in Figure 5.4.

RECAP   BEFORE MODERN ECONOMIC GROWTH

Up until 1800 human populations grew very slowly, and human living standards were stagnant. After 1800 we see sustained rises in living standards. And after 1800 human numbers grew as the population explosion took hold and carried our total population to 6 billion in October 1999. At first the rise in material standards of living brought sharp increases in the rate of population growth: The population explosion. But as material standards of living rose far above subsistence, countries began to undergo the *demographic transition*; population growth rates peaked and began to decline toward stability.

5.2 MODERN AMERICAN ECONOMIC GROWTH

Before 1500 human material standards of living and productivity levels rose at perhaps 0.01 percent per year. Between 1500 and 1800 they rose faster in the areas that were to become the industrial core of the modern world economy — first northwestern Europe and then northwestern Europe's settler colonies in North America — rising at a rate of perhaps 0.2 percent per year. The first half of the nineteenth century saw leading-edge economies' levels of productivity rise at about 0.5 percent per year, and the second half of the century saw productivity accelerate still further.

American Long-Run Growth, 1800–1973

The Pace of Economic Growth

Focus on the pace of long-run growth in what has been the world's leading-edge economy for the past 100 years: the United States. Growth in the years before and after the Civil War was faster than it had been in the first half of the nineteenth century. It accelerated still further as a second wave of industrialization took hold, fueled by new inventions and innovations such as steel making, organic chemicals manufacture, oil, the internal combustion engine, pasteurization, the typewriter, the cash register, and the telephone. The accelerated pace of invention and economic growth has been maintained ever since.

Throughout the nineteenth century and the first three-quarters of the twentieth century the *measured* pace of **productivity growth** continued to accelerate. The measured growth rate of output per worker rose from perhaps 0.5 percent per year between 1800 and 1870 to about 1.6 percent per year between 1870 and 1929, on the eve of the Great Depression, as is shown in Figure 5.5. Growth slowed slightly during the Great Depression and World War II decades — a measured growth rate of 1.4 percent per year from 1929 to 1950. But then it accelerated: The growth rate of output per worker between 1950 and 1973 in the United States was 2.1 percent per year.

Moreover, it is likely that *true* output-per-worker growth since 1870 has been even faster. Many economists believe that official estimates overstate inflation and understate real economic growth by 1 percent per year, in large part because national income accountants have a very hard time valuing the boost to productivity and standards of living generated by the invention of new goods and services. So for the rate of output per worker growth since 1870, perhaps we should be thinking of 2 to 2.5 percent per year instead of 1.5 percent per year.

If so, then those of us living in the United States today have a level of productivity — a material standard of living — somewhere between 14 and 25 times that of

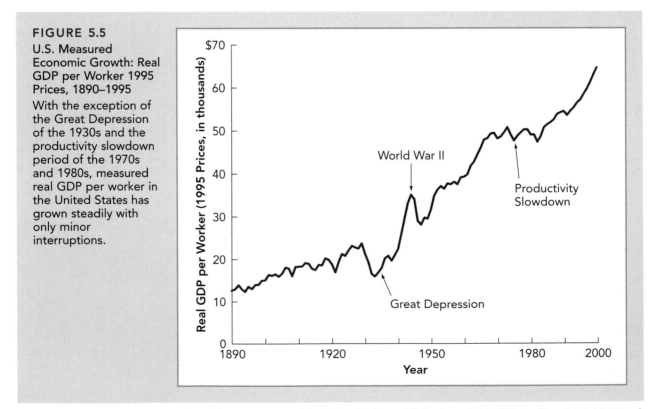

FIGURE 5.5

U.S. Measured Economic Growth: Real GDP per Worker 1995 Prices, 1890–1995

With the exception of the Great Depression of the 1930s and the productivity slowdown period of the 1970s and 1980s, measured real GDP per worker in the United States has grown steadily with only minor interruptions.

Source: Author's calculations from the 2001 edition of *The Economic Report of the President* (Washington, DC: Government Printing Office) and from *Historical Statistics of the United States* (Washington, DC: Government Printing Office, 1975).

TABLE 5.2
Labor-Time Costs of Commodities, 1895–1997

| Commodity | Time to Earn (Hours)* | | Productivity Multiple |
	1895	1997	
Horatio Alger books (6 vols.)	21.0	0.6	35.0
One-speed bicycle	260.0	7.2	36.1
Cushioned office chair	24.0	2.0	12.0
100-piece dinner set	44.0	3.6	12.2
Hairbrush	16.0	2.0	8.0
Cane rocking chair	8.0	1.6	5.0
Solid gold locket	28.0	6.0	4.7
Encyclopedia Britannica	140.0	4.0	35.0
Steinway piano	2400.0	1107.6	2.2
Sterling silver teaspoon	26.0	34.0	0.8
Oranges (dozen)	2.0	0.1	20.0
Ground beef (1 lb.)	0.8	0.2	4.0
Milk (1 gal.)	2.0	0.25	8.0
Television	∞	15.0	∞
Plane ticket: SFO-BOS	∞	20.0	∞
Antibiotic strep-throat cure	∞	1.0	∞
Dental x-ray	∞	2.0	∞
Laptop computer	∞	70.0	∞

* Time needed for an average worker to earn the purchase price of the commodity.

Source: 1895 Montgomery Ward catalogue.

our counterparts in the late nineteenth century. For middle-class and richer consumers today such an estimate does not seem at all unreasonable. It takes only one-eighth as much time to earn the money to buy a hairbrush, one-twelfth as much time to earn the money to buy a chair, and one-thirty-fifth as much time to earn the money to buy a book today as it did in 1895 (see Table 5.2). And in 1895, no matter how long you worked, you couldn't earn enough money to buy a plane ticket, a TV, a portable CD player, a laptop computer, an automatic washing machine, an electric blender, or a microwave oven.

For the relatively poor of the world, or even of the United States, it is not reasonable to say that their incomes and material standards of living have multiplied to so great an extent. An invention or innovation has no effect on people's material standard of living if they cannot afford to acquire it.

Structural Change

Modern economic growth is also a shift in the kinds of things we do at work and play and in the way we live. In the immediate aftermath of the Civil War perhaps half of all Americans were farmers. Today less than 2 percent of American workers are farmers and farm laborers: There are more gardeners, groundskeepers, and growers and maintainers of ornamental plants in the United States today than there are food-growing farmers and farm laborers. In the second half of the nineteenth century

Americans traveled by foot, horse, wagon, train, and riverboat; at the end of the twentieth century, they traveled by foot (rarely), bicycle (rarely), automobile, bus, train, boat, and plane. Most Americans in the second half of the nineteenth century were literate, but very few had finished anything equivalent to today's high school. Modern economic growth is the large-scale shift of employment from agriculture to manufacturing and now to services. And it is the creation of large business organizations. At the start of the nineteenth century, a business with 100 people was a very large organization for its time.

Between approximately 1890 and 1930, or perhaps 1890 and 1950, a host of innovative technologies and business practices were adopted in the United States. Europeans speak of "Fordism": taking the part — Henry Ford's assembly lines in Detroit and his mass production of the Model-T Ford — for the whole. The fact that other industrial economies were unable to fully adopt American technologies of mass production and mass distribution in the first half of the twentieth century gave the United States a unique level of industrial dominance and technological leadership in the years after 1950.

Three main factors explain America's position at the leading edge of technology in the world economy throughout the twentieth century:

- *The United States had an exceptional commitment to education* — to schooling everyone (everyone who was white, that is; and boys more than girls) even in the largely rural economy of the nineteenth century and to making the achievement of a high school diploma the rule rather than the exception in the cities of the early twentieth century.

- *The United States was of extraordinarily large size* — the largest market in the world. Thus the nation could take advantage of potential economies of scale in ways that other, smaller economies could not match.

- *The United States was extraordinarily rich in natural resources,* particularly energy. To the extent that energy-intensive and natural-resource-intensive industries were at the heart of early-twentieth-century industrial growth, the U.S. was again well-positioned.

American Economic Growth Since 1973

The Productivity Growth Slowdown

In 1973 the steady trend of climbing rates of productivity growth stopped cold. Between 1973 and 1995 *measured* growth in output per worker in the U.S. economy grew at only 0.6 percent per year. The slowdown did not affect the U.S. economy alone: It hit — to different degrees and with different effects — the other major economies of the world's industrial core in western Europe, Japan, and Canada as well (see Table 5.3).

What caused the **productivity slowdown**? Observers have pointed to four factors — oil prices, the baby boom, increased problems of economic measurement, and environmental protection expenditures — and there are no doubt others.

The argument that the productivity slowdown can be explained by expenditures on environmental protection is a branch of the "problems-of-measurement" argument. When the price of electricity goes up because power companies switch to burning higher-priced low-sulfur coal or install sulfur-removing scrubbers in their chimneys, they are producing not just electric power but electric power plus cleaner air. But the NIPA does not count pollution reduction as a valued economic output.

TABLE 5.3
The Magnitude of the Post-1973 Productivity Slowdown in the G-7 Economies

Country	Output-per-Worker Annual Growth (%)	
	1950–1973	1973–1995
United States	2.1	0.6
Canada	2.7	1.6
Japan	7.4	2.6
Britain	2.4	1.8
Germany (West)	5.7	2.0
France	4.4	1.5
Italy	4.9	2.3

Source: Author's calculations from the 2001 edition of *The Economic Report of the President* (Washington, DC: Government Printing Office).

America has spent a fortune on environmental protection in the past generation, and has in gross received big benefits from this investment, but the gains aren't included in measured GDP.

The argument that the productivity slowdown can be explained by problems of economic measurement is a bit subtle. Few doubt that these problems lead to understatements of the rate of economic growth. But to account for a *slowdown* in economic growth, the problems of measurement must have gotten *worse*. They must be worse now than they were three decades ago.

In the 1970s the baby-boom generation of Americans began to enter the labor force. This generation is very large. I should know: I was born in 1960, the year in which more Americans were born than in any year either before or since. The relatively young labor force had many more workers with little experience than did the labor force of the 1960s and 1950s. Some economists argue that this fall in the average level of labor-force experience generated the productivity slowdown. Others point out that the baby-boom generation had little experience but a lot of education and that in the past education had been a powerful *booster* of productivity. The average level of education in the labor force increased quite rapidly as the baby-boom generation entered the economy.

The last explanation of the productivity slowdown is the tripling of world oil prices by the OPEC cartel in 1973, in the wake of the third Arab-Israeli war. Productivity growth slowed at almost exactly the same time that oil prices skyrocketed. Economists hypothesized that in response to the tripling of world oil prices firms began redirecting their capital expenditures from capital that produced more output to capital that used less energy; firms retired a large share of their most energy-intensive capital and began to substitute workers for energy use wherever possible.

The problem with this explanation is twofold. First, since 1986 real oil prices have been *lower* than they were before 1973; hence the productivity slowdown should have ended a decade ago. Second, energy costs are not *that* large a share of the typical business's costs. By now the productivity slowdown has mounted to more than one-quarter of total output. How can even the tripling of the price of a commodity that accounts for less than 4 percent of costs lead to a more than 25 percent reduction in output? This makes no sense.

The causes of the productivity slowdown remain uncertain, and the slowdown itself remains a mystery.

Effects of the Productivity Slowdown

At a growth rate of 2.1 percent per year, output per worker doubles every 34 years. At a growth rate of 0.6 percent per year, output per worker takes 120 years to double — three and a half times as long. Social psychologists tell us that 40-year-olds feel happiest not when their incomes are high but when their incomes are high relative to those of their households when they were growing up. Before 1973, when economic growth was more rapid, most American voters felt much richer than their parents and hence were more willing to invest in social welfare programs and other liberal political initiatives. Since 1973, slower growth has made Americans feel much less well off than they had expected they would be. It is clear that growth slowed sharply as a result of the productivity slowdown. But it is not clear whether growth stopped for large numbers of Americans. Box 5.1 analyzes what we know about the

BOX

5.1

HAVE REAL STANDARDS OF LIVING BEEN DECLINING? THE DETAILS

For some categories of workers (such as males in their twenties with just a high school education), the post-1973 productivity slowdown has been accompanied by stagnant or declining real wages. Yet offsetting this are many improvements in the

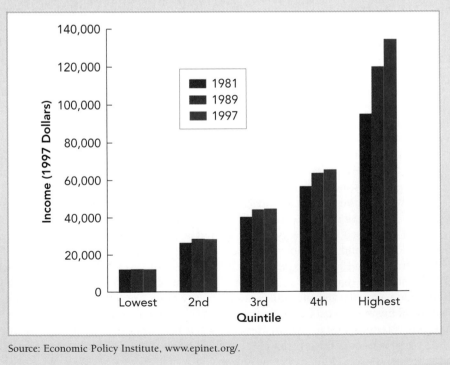

FIGURE 5.6
Measured Real Mean Household Income, by Quintile
The era of the productivity slowdown saw not just slow growth but a widening of the American distribution of income.

Source: Economic Policy Institute, www.epinet.org/.

quality of life — from cleaner air to the convenience of automated teller machines — that the NIPA system cannot measure. If we accept the Boskin Commission estimates of unmeasured growth in material well-being that centered around 1 percent per year, then true total product-per-worker growth in the United States has slowed not to the 0.6 percent per year recorded in official statistics for 1973–1995 but to 1.6 percent per year.

This is still a substantial drop from the estimated 3.1 percent per year that the same adjustment produces for growth before 1973. And increased income inequality has produced declines in real income or near stagnation for some groups (see Figure 5.6). But it is not true that America's output per worker has stagnated over the past generation. Whether we as a society have distributed the gains in productivity to persons and households and to private and public uses wisely and appropriately — that is another question.

"true" pace of economic growth during the productivity slowdown. The consequences of this are uncertain: Former president Jimmy Carter saw it as the origin of a national "malaise." Liberals have blamed it for a rightward shift in politics. Conservatives have blamed it for a rush to security and an unwillingness to undertake bold libertarian experiments. All have seen it as a cause of more (not necessarily unjustified) skepticism toward the government and its programs.

The End of the Productivity Slowdown

As computers improved and spread throughout the U.S. economy in the 1970s and 1980s, economists kept waiting to see the wonders of computing show through in national productivity. But that didn't happen. The productivity growth slowdown continued throughout the 1970s and 1980s. This surprising phenomenon came to be called the "computer paradox" after Robert Solow's famous 1987 observation: "We see the computer age everywhere except in the productivity statistics."

Since 1995, however, productivity growth in the American economy has accelerated once again to a pace of 2.1 percent per year. Half a decade is a very short time on which to pin any long-run trend, but there is certainly reason to hope that the productivity slowdown has come to an end.

The U.S. economy has benefited from a stunning investment boom since 1992. Between 1992 and 1998 real GDP rose by an average of 3.6 percent per year, and business fixed investment soared at a 10.1 percent average rate — almost three times as fast. As a consequence, the share of business fixed investment in GDP jumped from 9.2 percent to 13.2 percent, with much of the additional investment going into computers and related equipment. At least one major economic forecasting business attributes the recent acceleration in productivity growth to this investment boom, a huge share of which is driven by the rapidly falling price of computers.

There is every reason to expect that technological progress in the computer and communications sectors will continue, and there is every reason to expect that these useful technologies will continue to diffuse throughout the economy. Thus the best bet in forecasting future productivity growth is to make future projections on the basis of what has happened in the past half-decade. If these projections are accurate, then the productivity slowdown has been brought to an end, and it is the technological revolution in computers and communications that has ended it. But that is a subject for the end of this book.

RECAP   MODERN AMERICAN ECONOMIC GROWTH

Over the past two centuries measured economic growth in the United States has raised output per worker at an average pace of between 1.5 and 2.0 percent per year. Moreover, it is likely that *true* output per worker growth since 1890 has been even faster. Many economists believe that official estimates overstate inflation and understate real economic growth by 1.0 percent per year, in large part because national income accountants have a very hard time valuing the boost to productivity and standards of living generated by the invention of new goods and services, and new types of goods and services.

Accompanying this increase in productivity and living standards is structural change: The move from the country to the city, the large-scale shift of employment from agriculture to manufacturing and now to services, and the creation of large business organizations. Starting in 1973 the steady trend of climbing rates of productivity growth stopped cold: Between 1973 and 1995 measured growth in output per worker in the U.S. economy grew at only 0.6 percent per year. Since 1995, however, productivity growth in the American economy has accelerated once again to a pace of 2.1 percent per year, the result of an investment boom, the rapidly falling prices of data processing and data communications equipment, and technological advances.

5.3 MODERN ECONOMIC GROWTH AROUND THE WORLD

Divergence, Big Time

The industrial core of the world economy saw its level of material productivity and standard of living explode in the nineteenth and twentieth centuries. Elsewhere the growth of productivity levels and standards of living and the spread of industrial technologies were slower. As the industrialized economies grew while industrial technologies spread slowly elsewhere, the world became a more and more unequal place. As development economist Lant Pritchett puts it, the dominant feature of world economic history is "**divergence**, big time." In terms of relative incomes and productivity levels, the world today is more unequal and more *divergent* than ever before, as Figure 5.7 shows.

Those who live in relatively poor regions of the world today have higher material living standards than did their predecessors who lived in those regions a century ago. But the relative gap vis-à-vis the industrial core has grown extraordinarily and extravagantly. In the first half of the nineteenth century the average inhabitant of an average country had perhaps one-half the material standard of living of a citizen of the world's leading industrial economy. Today the average inhabitant of an average country has only one-sixth the material standard of living and productivity level of the leading nation. (Box 5.2 provides some insight into the difficulties of making such comparisons.)

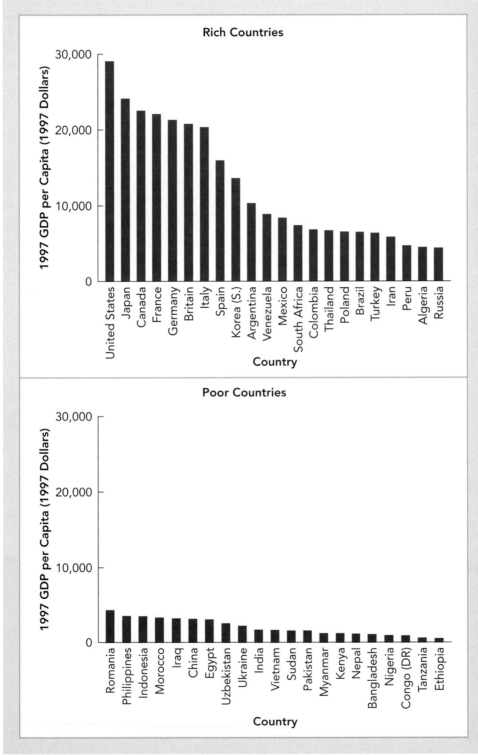

FIGURE 5.7
World Distribution of Income, Selected Countries

In some places modern economic growth has taken hold and propelled levels of productivity and living standards upward. In other places people on average live little, if any, better than their ancestors did. The world is a more unequal place, in relative income terms, than it has been since there were some human tribes that had fire and others that did not.

Source: Author's calculations from Alan Heston's and Robert Summer's Penn World Table, www.nber.org.

PURCHASING-POWER-PARITY AND REAL EXCHANGE RATE COMPARISONS: SOME TOOLS

When our focus is on comparing standards of living, either across time or across countries, we get much more meaningful figures by correcting current (and even average trend) exchange rates for differences in *purchasing power parity (PPP)*. The differences between estimates of relative income levels based on current exchange rates and estimates based on PPP calculations can be very large. On a purchasing-power-parity basis GDP per worker in the United States today is some 13 times GDP per worker in India; by contrast, on an average exchange rate basis GDP per worker in the United States today is more than 70 times the level in India.

PPP-based calculations attempt (as the name applies) to translate one currency into another at a rate that preserves average purchasing power. But current exchange rates do not preserve purchasing power. If you exchange your dollars in the United States for rupees in India you will find that your rupees in India will buy about the same amount of internationally traded manufactured goods as your dollars would have bought in the United States. (Unless, of course, you try to buy something that the Indian government has decided to put up a trade barrier against.) But your rupees in India will buy you vastly more in the way of personal services, the products of skilled craftspeople, and any other labor-intensive goods and services.

Why? International arbitrage keeps the exchange rate at the level that makes easily traded manufactured goods roughly equally expensive. If they weren't, someone could make an easy fortune by shipping them from where they were cheap to where they were dear. But how — in this world of stringent immigration restrictions — can a cook in Bangalore take advantage of the fact that there is fierce demand in Marin County, north of San Francisco, for caterers who can prepare a good curry? Because relative productivity levels in labor services are much more equal than relative productivity levels in manufacturing, living standards throughout the world are more equal than exchange rate–based calculations suggest.

The Exception: OECD Economies

It is not inevitable that there be such divergence. The United States — with its 14- to 25-fold increase in output per worker over the years since 1870 — has not been the fastest-growing economy in the world. A number of other economies at different levels of industrialization, development, and material productivity a century ago have now *converged,* and their levels of productivity, economic structures, and standards of living today are very close to those of the United States (see Box 5.3). The six largest of these converging economies and the United States make up the so-called Group of Seven, or G-7, economies, whose leaders gather for annual summit meetings. The six non-U.S. members' steady process of convergence to the U.S. level from 1950 until 1990 is shown in Figure 5.8.

Most of these economies were significantly poorer than the United States in 1870 and even in 1950. The Japanese economy, for example, went from a level of output per capita equal to 16 percent of the U.S. level in 1950 to 84 percent of the U.S. level in 1992 — before falling steeply backward during Japan's recent recession. Italian levels of GDP per capita have gone from 30 to 65 percent of the U.S. level; German

WHY HAVE THESE ECONOMIES CONVERGED?: A POLICY

By and large the economies that have converged are those that belong to the Organization for Economic Cooperation and Development (OECD), which was started shortly after World War II, in the days of the Marshall Plan, as a group of countries that received (or gave) Marshall Plan aid to help rebuild and reconstruct after the war. Countries that received Marshall Plan aid adopted a common set of economic policies: large private sectors freed of government regulation of prices, investment with its direction determined by profit-seeking businesses, large social insurance systems to redistribute income, and governments committed to avoiding mass unemployment.

The original OECD members all wound up with mixed economies. In these, markets direct the flow of resources, while governments stabilize the economy, provide social insurance safety nets, and encourage entrepreneurship and enterprise. The member nations arrived at this setup largely due to good luck, partly due to the Cold War, and partly as a result of post–World War II institutional reforms.

This configuration was essentially the price countries had to pay for receiving Marshall Plan aid. The U.S. executive was unwilling to send much aid to countries that it thought were likely to engage in destructive economic policies, largely because it did not believe that it could win funding from the Republican-dominated Congress for a Marshall Plan that did not impose such strict *conditionality* upon recipients. By contrast, countries that were relatively rich after World War II but did not adopt OECD-style institutional arrangements — such as Argentina and Venezuela — lost relative ground.

As the OECD economies became richer, they completed their demographic transitions: Population growth rates fell. The policy emphasis on entrepreneurship and enterprise boosted national investment rates, so the OECD economies all had healthy investment rates as well. These factors boosted their steady-state capital-output ratios. And the diffusion of technology from the United States did the rest of the job in bringing OECD standards of economic productivity close to the U.S. level.

---

levels, from 40 to 75 percent; Canadian levels, from 70 to 85 percent; and British levels, from 60 to 70 percent in the past half-century. Moreover, as Box 5.4 shows, the East Asian economies have also "converged."

The Rule: Divergence behind the Iron Curtain

But convergence is the exception. Divergence is the rule. And perhaps the most important driving force behind divergence is communism: Being unlucky enough to have been ruled by communists in the twentieth century is a virtual guarantee of relative poverty.

There used to be a snaky geographic line across Eurasia that Winston Churchill had once called the "Iron Curtain." On one side were regimes that owed their allegiance to Karl Marx and to Marx's viceroys on earth. On the other side were regimes that claimed, in the 1946–1989 Cold War, to be of the "free world" — regimes that were, if not good, at least less worse. Walk this geographic line, shown in Figure 5.9, from Poland to Korea and then hop over to the only Western hemisphere communist satellite — Cuba — looking first left at the level of material welfare in the communist

FIGURE 5.8

Convergence among the G-7 Economies: Output per Capita as a Share of U.S. Level

In 1950 GDP per capita levels in the six nations that now are America's partners in the G-7 varied from 20 percent of the U.S. level (Japan) to 70 percent of the U.S. level (Canada). Today estimates of GDP per capita place levels in all six at more than 65 percent of the U.S. level — and they would be even closer to the U.S. level if the measurements took account of the shorter average work year abroad.

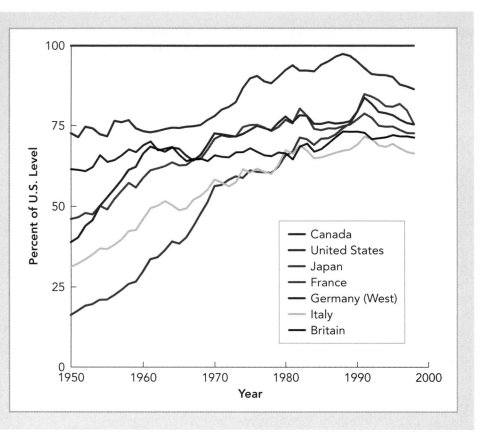

Source: Author's calculations.

FIGURE 5.9
The Iron Curtain

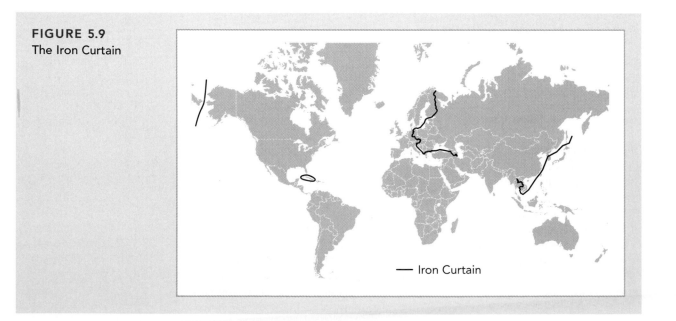

THE EAST ASIAN MIRACLE: POLICY

The story of extraordinarily successful economies goes beyond the original OECD nations. The economies of the "East Asian miracle" have over the past two generations exhibited stronger growth than has ever before been seen anywhere in the world. They have not yet converged to the standards of living and levels of economic productivity found in the world economy's industrial core, but they are converging.

Immediately before World War II the regions that are now South Korea, Hong Kong and Singapore, and Taiwan had output-per-worker levels less than one-tenth the level of the United States. Today Singapore's GDP per capita is 90 percent, Hong Kong's is 70 percent, Taiwan's is 50 percent, and South Korea's is 45 percent of the U.S. level. A second wave of East Asian economies — Malaysia and Thailand — now average more than one-quarter of the U.S. level of GDP per capita.

The successful East Asian economies share a number of similarities with the OECD economies in terms of economic policy and structure. Resource allocation decisions are by and large left to the market. Governments regard the encouragement of entrepreneurship and enterprise as a major goal. And high savings and investment rates are encouraged by a number of different government policies.

Yet there are also a number of differences vis-à-vis the OECD. Governments in East Asia have been more aggressive in pursuing *industrial policy* and somewhat less aggressive in establishing social insurance systems than have the OECD economies. However, they have also had more egalitarian income distributions and hence less need for redistribution and social insurance. They have subsidized corporations that they believe are strategic for economic development, thinking that their bureaucrats know better than the market — heresy to economists. (However, it is worth noting that they have focused subsidies on the companies that have proved successful at exporting goods to other countries, so their bureaucrats have in a sense been rewarding the judgment of *foreign* markets.) The examples of successful catching up suggest that growth could have been faster in the world economy. Economies — even very poor ones — *can* rapidly adopt modern machine technologies and move their productivity levels close to first-world leading-edge standards. ◆

countries and then right at the level of material welfare in the noncommunist countries. The location of the Iron Curtain is a historical accident: It is where Stalin's Russian armies stopped after World War II, where Mao's Chinese armies stopped in the early 1950s, and where Giap's Vietnamese armies stopped in the mid-1970s.

Notice as you walk that to your right, outside the Iron Curtain, the countries are far better off in terms of GDP per capita (see Table 5.4). They are not necessarily better off in education, health care, or the degree of income inequality. If you were in the poorer half of the population, you probably received a better education and had access to better medical care in Cuba than in Mexico. But the countries fortunate enough to lie outside what was the Iron Curtain were and are vastly more prosperous. Depending on how you count and how unlucky you are, 40 and 94 percent of the potential material prosperity of a country was annihilated if it happened to fall under communist rule in the twentieth century. The fact that a large part of the globe was under communist rule in the twentieth century is one major reason for the world's *divergence*. A failure to successfully aid post-communist economies in

TABLE 5.4
The Iron Curtain: GDP-per-Capita Levels of Matched Pairs of Countries

East-Bloc Country	GDP per Capita	Matched West-Bloc Country	GDP per Capita	Relative Gap (%)
North Korea	$ 700	South Korea	$13,590	94
China	3,130	Taiwan	14,170	78
Vietnam	1,630	Philippines	3,520	54
Cambodia	1,290	Thailand	6,690	81
FSR Georgia	1,960	Turkey	6,350	69
Russia	4,370	Finland	20,150	78
Bulgaria	4,010	Greece	12,769	69
Slovenia	11,800	Italy	20,290	42
Hungary	7,200	Austria	22,070	67
Czech Republic	10,510	Germany	21,260	51
Poland	6,520	Sweden	19,790	67
Cuba	3,100	Mexico	8,370	63

Source: Author's calculations from Alan Heston's and Robert Summer's Penn World Table, www.nber.org.

POSTCOMMUNISM: POLICY

The demolition of the Berlin Wall and the elimination of the Iron Curtain have not significantly improved the situation in what are euphemistically and optimistically called "economies in transition" (from socialism to capitalism, that is). Figuring out how to move from a stagnant, ex-communist economy to a dynamic, growing one is very difficult, and no one has ever done it before.

A few of the economies in transition appear to be on the path toward rapid convergence with western Europe: Slovenia, Hungary, the Czech Republic, and Poland have already successfully maneuvered through enough of the transition phase to have advanced their economies beyond the point reached before 1989. It seems clear that their economic destiny is to become, effectively, part of western Europe. Slovakia, Lithuania, Latvia, and Estonia appear to have good prospects of following their example.

Elsewhere, however, the news is bad. Whether reforms have taken place step-by-step or all at once, whether ex-communists have been excluded from or have dominated the government, and whether governments have been nationalist or internationalist, the results have been similar. Output has fallen, corruption has been rife, and growth has not resumed. Material standards of living in the Ukraine today are less than half of what they were when General Secretary Gorbachev ruled from Moscow.

Economists debate ferociously the appropriate economic strategy for unwinding the inefficient centrally planned Soviet-style economy. The fact that such transition has never been undertaken before should make advice-givers cautious. And one other observation should make advice givers depressed: The best predictor of whether an eastern European country's transition will be rapid and successful or not appears to be its distance from western European political and financial capitals like Vienna, Frankfurt, and Stockholm.

their transition would be a further blow, and as Box 5.5 discusses, "transition" is not going well.

The Rule: Divergence in General

Even if attention is confined to noncommunist-ruled economies, there still has been enormous divergence in relative output-per-worker levels over the past 100 years. Since 1870, the ratio of richest to poorest economies has increased sixfold. In 1870 two-thirds of all countries had GDP per capita levels between 60 and 160 percent of the average. Today the range that includes two-thirds of all countries extends from 35 to 280 percent of the average.

Sources of Divergence

The principal cause of the extraordinary variation in output per worker between countries today is differences in their respective steady-state capital-output ratios. Two secondary causes are, first, openness to creating and adapting the technologies that enhance the efficiency of labor as measured by levels of development two generations ago and, second, the level of education today.

Productivity two generations ago is a good indicator of the level of technological knowledge that had been acquired as of a half-century ago. The level of education today captures the country's ability to invent and acquire further technological expertise today. Without education, inventing new and adopting foreign technological knowledge are simply not possible.

Global Patterns

Together these factors — the determinants of capital-output ratios and the two determinants of access to technology — account for the bulk of the differences between countries in their relative productivity levels.

The determinants of the steady-state balanced-growth capital-output ratio play a very powerful role. A higher share of investment in national product is powerfully correlated with relative levels of output per worker. No country with an investment rate of less than 10 percent has an output-per-worker level even 20 percent of that of the United States. No country with an investment share of less than 20 percent has an output-per-worker level greater than 75 percent of the U.S. level.

A high level of labor-force growth is correlated, albeit less powerfully, with a low level of output per worker. The average country with a labor-force growth rate of more than 3 percent per year has an output-per-worker level of less than 20 percent of the U.S. level. The average country with a labor-force growth rate of less than 1 percent has an output-per-worker level that is greater than 60 percent of the U.S. level.

Together these determinants of the steady-state capital-output ratio can, statistically, account for up to half of the variation in national economies' levels of productivity per worker in the world today. The power of these factors is central to the theoretical model of economic growth presented in Chapter 4 and should not be underestimated. Indeed, their power is the reason we spent so much space on the standard growth model in Chapter 4.

But the factors stressed in Chapter 4 are not the only major determinants of relative wealth and poverty in the world today. Differences in the efficiency of labor are as important as differences in steady-state capital-output ratios. Differences in the efficiency of labor arise from the differential ability of workers to handle and utilize modern technologies. The efficiency of labor is high where education levels are high

— so workers can use the modern technologies they are exposed to — and where economic contact with the industrial core is high — so workers and managers are exposed to the modern technologies invented in the world's R&D laboratories.

Schooling is the variable that has the strongest correlation with output per worker. Countries that have an average of four to six years of schooling have output-per-worker levels that average 20 percent of the U.S. level. Those with an average level of schooling of more than 10 years have output-per-worker levels of 65 percent of the U.S. level, as Figure 5.10 shows.

There is no single best indicator of a country's exposure to — and thus ability to adopt and adapt — the technologies invented in the industrial core that amplify the efficiency of labor. Some economists like Jeffrey Sachs and Andrew Warner of Harvard focus on trade and foreign investment as the main sources of increased efficiency and technological capability. Others like Charles Jones and Robert Hall of Stanford focus on geographic and climatic factors that have influenced migration and still influence trade and intellectual exchange. Still others like Ken Sokoloff and Stan Engerman or Andrei Shleifer, Rafael La Porta, Florencio Lopez-di-Silanes, and Robert Vishny focus on institutions of governance and their effect on entrepreneurship as the key variable. But as much as economists dispute which variables are most important as determinants of technology transfer and the efficiency of labor, all agree that all these variables are important indeed to understanding why our world today is the way it is.

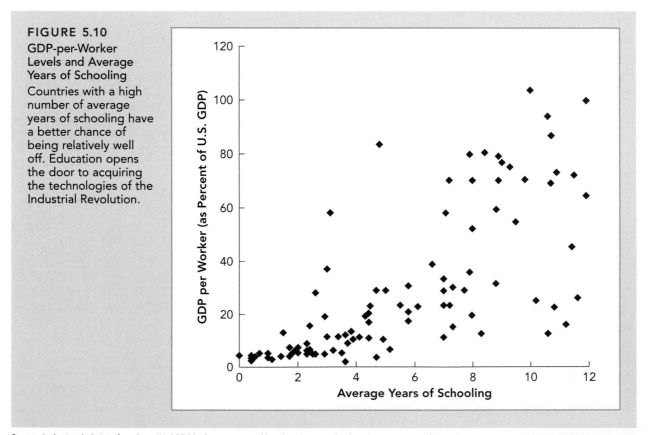

FIGURE 5.10
GDP-per-Worker Levels and Average Years of Schooling
Countries with a high number of average years of schooling have a better chance of being relatively well off. Education opens the door to acquiring the technologies of the Industrial Revolution.

Source: Author's calculations from Penn World Table data constructed by Alan Heston and Robert Summers, www.nber.org/.

Cause and Effect, Effect and Cause

All the factors discussed above are both causes and effects. High population growth and low levels of output per worker go together both because rapid population growth reduces the steady-state capital-output ratio and because poor countries have not yet undergone their demographic transitions. This interaction — in which a high rate of population growth reduces the steady-state capital-output ratio and a low steady-state capital-output ratio means that the demographic transition is not far advanced — creates a vicious spiral that reinforces relative poverty.

Moreover, demography is not the only vicious spiral potentially present. A poor country must pay a high relative price for the capital equipment it needs to acquire in order to turn its savings into productive additions to its capital stock. This should come as no surprise. The world's most industrialized and prosperous economies are the most industrialized and prosperous because they have attained very high levels of manufacturing productivity: Their productivity advantage in unskilled service industries is much lower than that in capital- and technology-intensive manufactured goods. The higher relative price of machinery in developing countries means that poor countries get less investment — a smaller share of total investment in real GDP — out of any given effort at saving some fixed share of their incomes.

Moreover, to the extent that education is an important kind of investment, a good education is much harder to provide in a poorer country. Even primary education requires at its base a teacher, some books, and a classroom — things that are relatively cheap and easy for a rich country to provide but expensive for a poor country. In western Kenya today the average primary school classroom has 0.4 book per pupil.

But there is also the possibility for virtuous circles. Anything that increases productivity and sets the demographic transition in motion will reduce the rate of growth of the labor force, increase the amount of investment bought by any given amount of savings, and make education easier.

How important are these vicious spirals and virtuous circles? It is hard to look at the cross-country pattern of growth over the past century without thinking that such vicious spirals and virtuous circles *must* have been very important. Otherwise, the massive divergence in relative productivity levels seems inexplicable.

RECAP   MODERN ECONOMIC GROWTH AROUND THE WORLD

The industrial core of the world economy saw its level of material productivity and standards of living explode in the nineteenth and twentieth centuries. Elsewhere the growth of productivity levels and standards of living and the spread of industrial technologies were slower, and the gap between rich and poor countries has widened enormously over the past century.

High population growth and low levels of output per worker go together both because rapid population growth reduces the steady-state capital-output ratio, and because poor countries have not yet undergone their demographic transitions which lower population growth. Low investment rates and low levels of output per worker go together both because low investment reduces the steady-state capital output ratio, and because poor countries face adverse terms of trade and high prices for capital goods that make investment difficult and expensive. Thus the obstacles to rapid growth in many poor countries in the world today are overwhelming.

5.4 POLICIES AND LONG-RUN GROWTH

Hopes for Convergence

Relative and Absolute Stagnation

Always keep in mind that in the context of economic growth "stagnation" and "failure" are relative terms. Consider Argentina once again, for it has been one of the world's most disappointing performers in terms of economic growth in the twentieth century. Argentina has experienced substantial economic growth. *Officially measured* labor productivity or national product per capita in Argentina today is perhaps three times what it was in 1900. True productivity, taking adequate account of the value of new commodities, is higher. But the much more smoothly running engine of capitalist development in Norway — no more, and probably less, rich and productive than Argentina in 1900 — has multiplied *measured* national product per capita there by a factor of nine.

A pattern of productivity growth like Argentina's is heartbreakingly slow when compared to what, reasonably, might have been and was achieved by the world's industrial leaders. What is bad about falling behind, or falling further behind, is not that second place is a bad place to be — it is false to think that the only thing that matters is to be top nation and that it is better to be poor but first than rich but second. What is bad about falling behind is that the world's industrial leaders provide an easily viewable benchmark of how things might have been different and of how much better things might have been. There was no destiny keeping Buenos Aires today from looking like and having its people as rich as those of Paris, Toronto, or Sidney.

Half Empty and Half Full

In many respects, it is decidedly odd that the world distribution of output per worker is as unequal as it is. World trade, migration, and flows of capital should all work to move resources and consumption goods from where they are cheap to where they are dear. As they travel with increasing speed and increasing volume as transportation and communication costs fall, these commodity and factor-of-production flows should erode differences in productivity and living standards between national economies. Moreover, most of the edge in standards of living and productivity levels held by the industrial core is no one's private property but, instead, is the common intellectual and scientific heritage of humankind. Hence every poor economy has an excellent opportunity to catch up with the rich by adopting and adapting from this open storehouse of modern machine technology.

We can view this particular glass either as half empty or as half full. Half full is that much of the world has already made the transition to sustained economic growth. Most people today live in economies that, while far poorer than the leading-edge postindustrial nations of the world's economic core, have successfully climbed onto the escalator of economic growth and thus the escalator to modernity. The economic transformation of most of the world is less than a century behind that of the leading-edge economies — only an eyeblink behind from the perspective of the six millennia since the spread of agriculture out of the Middle East's fertile crescent.

Moreover, perhaps we can look forward to a future in which convergence of relative income levels will finally begin to take place. The bulk of humanity is now achieving material standards of living at which the demographic transition takes hold. As population growth rates in developing countries fall, their capital-output ratios will begin to rise quickly. With tolerable government, reasonable security of property, and better ways of achieving an education, their output-per-worker levels and material standards of living will converge to the world's leading edge.

Half empty is that we live today in the most unequal age — in terms of the divergence in the life prospects of children born into different economies — that the world has ever seen. One and a half billion people today live in economies that have *not* made the transition to intensive economic growth and have *not* climbed onto the escalator to modernity. It is very hard to argue that the median inhabitant of Africa is *any* better off in material terms than his or her counterpart of a generation ago.

Policies for Saving, Investment, and Education

It is certainly possible for a government to adopt policies that boost national savings, improve the ability to translate savings into productive investment, and accelerate the demographic transition.

Savings and Investment

Policies that ensure savers get reasonable rates of return on their savings have the potential to boost the savings rate. By contrast, systems of economic governance in which profits are diverted into the hands of the politically powerful through restrictions on entrepreneurship tend over time to diminish savings, as do economic policies that divert the real returns to savings into the hands of financiers or the government through inflation. Government deficits also have the potential to reduce the savings rate: Unless consumers and investors are farsighted enough to recognize that a government deficit now means a tax increase later, a government that spends more than it raises in revenue must borrow — and the amount borrowed is not a contribution to total national savings because it is not available to fund investment.

A number of potential policies work to boost investment for a given amount of savings. Policies that welcome foreign investors' money have the potential to cut a decade or a generation off the time needed to industrialize — if the foreign-funded capital is used wisely. Free-trade policies that allow businesses to freely earn and spend the foreign exchange they need to purchase new generations of machinery and equipment are an effective way of boosting investment. Policies that impose heavy tariffs or require scarce import licenses in order to purchase foreign-made capital equipment are a sure sign that a country will not get its money's worth out of a given nominal savings share but will, instead, find that real investment remains low. Indeed, many of the most successful *developmental states* have done the opposite. They have provided large subsidies to fund investment and expansion by businesses that have demonstrated their competence and productivity by successfully exporting and thus competing in the world market.

Education

Universal education, especially of girls, pays a twofold benefit. Investments are more likely to be productive with a better-educated workforce to draw on; hence investments are more likely to be made. Educated women are likely to want at least as much education for their children as they had, and they are likely to have relatively attractive opportunities outside the home — so the birthrate is likely to fall.

It is certainly the case that the developing countries of the world appear, for the most part, to be going through the demographic transition faster than the economies of today's industrial core did in the past three centuries. Thus current estimates of the world's population in 2050 are markedly lower than the estimates of a decade ago. Ten years ago the projected global population in 2050 was 16 billion or more;

today it is 12 billion or less. This is due, in part at least, to rapid expansions in educational attainment in today's developing economies.

A high level of educational attainment also raises the efficiency of labor both by teaching skills directly and by making it easier to advance the general level of technological expertise. A leading-edge economy with a high level of educational attainment is likely to have more inventions. A follower economy with a high level of educational attainment is likely to have a more successful time at adapting to local conditions the inventions and innovations from the industrial core of the world economy. How large these effects are at the macroeconomic level is uncertain, but that they are there nobody doubts.

The East Asian economies, especially, provide examples of how uncorrupt and well-managed developmental states can follow macroeconomic policies that accelerate economic growth and convergence. These economies, which have provided incentives to accelerate the demographic transition and boost savings and investment, have managed to close the gap vis-à-vis the world economy's industrial core faster than anyone would have believed possible.

Policies for Technological Advance

Without better technology, increases in capital stock produced by investment rapidly run into diminishing returns. And without improvements in the "technologies" of organization, government, and education, productivity stagnates.

Somewhat surprisingly, economists have relatively little to say about what governs technological progress. Why did better technology raise living standards by 2 percent annually a generation ago but by less than 1 percent today? Why did technology progress by only 0.25 percent per year in the early 1800s? Improving literacy, communications, and research and development may help explain faster progress since the Industrial Revolution than before it and faster progress in the twentieth than in the nineteenth century. Yet, as noted above, as important a feature of recent economic history as the post-1973 productivity slowdown remains largely a mystery.

Invention and Innovation

Economists note that technological progress has two components: science (solid-state physics and the invention of the transistor, the mapping of the human genome, the discovery that potassium nitrate, sulfur, and charcoal when mixed together and exposed to heat have interesting properties) and research and development that leads to successful innovation. About pure science economists have almost nothing to say. About research and development, and the innovations it generates, economists have rather more to say.

Economists note that perhaps 75 percent of all U.S. scientists and engineers work on research and development for private firms. R&D spending amounts to about 3 percent of GDP in the United States and other advanced industrial economies. One-fifth of total gross investment is research and development. More than half of net investment is research and development — investments in knowledge, as opposed to investments in machinery, equipment, structures, and infrastructure.

Businesses conduct investments in R&D to increase their profits. Firms spend money on R&D for reasons analogous to those that lead them to expand their capacity or improve their factories. If the expected present value of profits from an R&D project at the prevailing rate are greater than the costs of the project, then the business will spend money on the project. If not, then it will not.

Rivalry and Excludibility

But there are features of technology that make thinking about the R&D process more complicated than thinking about other types of investment. First and most important, research and development is a public good. A firm that has discovered something — a new and more profitable process, a new and better way of organizing the factory, a new type of commodity that can be produced — will not reap the entire social benefit from its discovery. Other businesses can examine the innovation — the product, the process, the method of organization — and copy it. They can probably do so for a much lower cost than it took to research and develop the innovation in the first place.

By contrast, a firm that has just spent a large sum to buy and move into a new building does not have to worry that any firm will use that building as well. As a commodity, a building — or a machine, or even the skills and experience inside a worker's head — is both rival and excludable. To say that a commodity is *rival* means that if one firm is using it, another firm cannot do so: I cannot use that hammer to pound this nail if you are now using it to pound that other nail. To say that a commodity is *excludable* means that the "owner" of the commodity can easily monitor who is using it and can easily keep those whom he or she does not authorize from using it.

Most physical commodities are (or, with the assistance of the legal system, can easily be made) both rival and excludable. But by their nature ideas are not. Ideas are definitely not rival — there is nothing in the physical universe that makes it impossible for me to use the same idea you are using. And ideas are hard to make excludable as well: How can you keep me from thinking what I want to think?

Patents and Copyrights

To protect ideas and intellectual property in general, countries have **patent laws and copyrights**. In fact, one of the few enumerated powers that the U.S. Constitution gives Congress is the power to set up limited-term patent and copyright laws. *Patents give a firm that has discovered something new the right to exclude anyone else from using that discovery for a period of years.* But even the strictest patent and copyright laws are incomplete. Often the most valuable part of the R&D process is figuring out not how to do something but whether or not it (or something very close to it) can be done at all. Once a patent has been granted, other firms can and do search for alternative ways of making it or ways of making something close to it that are not covered by the patent.

Governments seeking to establish patent laws face a difficult dilemma. If their patent laws are strong, then much of the modern technology in the economy will be restricted in use: either restricted to being used only by the inventor or restricted because the inventor is charging other firms high licensing fees to use the technology (or not letting them use it at all). There is no social cost involved in letting everyone use the idea or the process or the innovation, once it is discovered. Information, after all, wants to be free. Thus a government that enacts strict patent laws is pushing the average level of technology used in its factories and businesses at some particular moment far below the level that could be achieved at that particular moment.

On the other hand, if the patent laws are weak and thus provide little protection to inventors and innovators, then the profits that inventors and innovators earn will be low. Why then should businesses devote money and resources to research and development? They will not. And the pace of innovation, and thus of technological improvement, will slow to a crawl.

This dilemma cannot be evaded. The profits from innovation come because the innovator has a monopoly right to the innovation — and hence the rest of the economy is excluded from using that item of technology. Reduce the degree of exclusion to lower the deadweight loss from using less-than-best-practice technology, and you will find that you have reduced the rewards to research and development (and thus presumably the pace of R&D as well). Increase the strength of the patent system to raise the rewards to research and development, and you will find that you have increased the gap between the average technology used in the economy and the feasible best practice.

Moreover, technological progress depends on more than the *appropriability* of research — the extent to which the increased productivity made possible by innovation boosts the profits of the innovating firm. It also depends on the productivity of research: how much in the way of new productivity-enhancing inventions is produced by a given investment in R&D? Economists don't know much about the interactions among product development, applied research, and basic research, so they have little to say about how to improve the productivity of research and the pace of productivity growth.

Will Governments Follow Good Policies?

That governments *can* assist in growth and development does not mean that governments *will*. The broad experience of growth in developing economies — outside the East Asian Pacific Rim, outside the OECD — has been that governments often *won't*. Over the past two decades many have argued that typical systems of regulation in developing countries have retarded development by

- Embarking on "prestige" industrialization programs that keep resources from shifting to activities in which the country had a long-run comparative advantage.

- Inducing firms and entrepreneurs to devote their energies to seeking rents by lobbying governments, instead of seeking profits by lowering costs.

- Creating systems of regulation and project approval that have degenerated into extortion machines for manufacturing bribes for the bureaucrats.

Many governments — particularly unelected governments — are not *that* interested in economic development. Giving valuable industrial franchises to the nephews of the dictator; making sure that members of your ethnic group are in key places to extort bribes; or taking the foreign exchange that would have been spent importing productive machinery and equipment and using it instead to buy more modern weapons for the army — these can seem more attractive options. In the absence of political democracy, the checks on a government that does not seek economic development are few.

Moreover, checks on government that do exist may not be helpful. In a nondemocracy, or a shaky semidemocracy, there are two possible sources of pressure on the government: riots in the capital and coups by the soldiers. Even a government that seeks only the best for its people in terms of economic growth will have to deal with these sources of pressure and will have to avoid riots in the capital and coups by the soldiers.

Coups by the soldiers are best avoided by spending money on the military. Riots in the capital are best avoided by making sure that the price of food is low and that influential opinion leaders in the capital are relatively happy with their material standards of living. Thus governments find themselves driven to policies that redistribute income from the farms to the cities, from exporting businesses to urban consumers of imported goods, from those who have the power to invest and make the economy grow to those who have the power to overthrow the government.

If the rulers have the worst of motives, government degenerates into *kleptocracy*: rule by the thieves. If government has the best of motives, it is still hard to avoid policies that diminish saving and retard the ability to translate savings into productive investment. W. W. Rostow recounts a visit by President Kennedy to Indonesia in the early 1960s; Kennedy talked about economic development and a South Asian Development Bank to provide capital for Indonesia's economic growth. Indonesia's then-dictator Sukarno responded, "Mr. President, development takes too long. Give me West Irian [province, the western half of the island of New Guinea, to annex] instead."

Taken as a group, the poor countries of the world have *not* closed any of the gap relative to the world's industrial leaders since World War II.

Neoliberalism

Much thinking about the proper role of government in economic growth over the past two decades has led to conclusions that are today called *neoliberal*. The government has a sphere of core competencies — administration of justice, maintenance of macroeconomic stability, avoidance of deep recessions, some infrastructure development, provision of social insurance — at which it is effective. But there is a large area of potential activities in which governments (or, at least, governments that do not have the bureaucratic honesty and efficiency needed for a successful *developmental state*) are more likely to be destructive than constructive — hence the neoliberal recommendation that governments attempt to shrink their role back to their core competencies and thus to deregulate industries and privatize public enterprises. Whether such policies will in fact lead to convergence rather than continued divergence is still an open question.

RECAP POLICIES AND LONG-RUN GROWTH

Most people today live in economies that, while far poorer than the leading-edge post-industrial nations of the world's economic core, have successfully climbed onto the escalator of economic growth and thus the escalator to modernity. A follower economy with a higher level of educational attainment is likely to have a much more successful time at adapting to local conditions inventions and innovations from the industrial core of the world economy. Thus education appears to be a key policy for successful economic growth outside the industrial core. Inside the industrial core, without better technology increases in the capital stock produced by investment rapidly run into diminishing returns. One-fifth of total gross investment is research and development. More than half of net investment is research and development — investments in knowledge, as opposed to investments in machinery, equipment, structures, and infrastructure.

That governments *can* assist in growth and development does not mean that governments *will*. Many governments — particularly unelected governments — are not *that* interested in economic development. In the absence of political democracy, the checks on a government that does not seek economic development are few.

Chapter Summary

1. Before the commercial revolution — before 1500 or so — economic growth was very slow. Populations grew at a glacial pace. And as best we can tell there were no significant increases in standards of living for millennia before 1500: Humanity was caught in a Malthusian trap.

2. The way out of the Malthusian trap opened about 1500. Thereafter populations grew, and standards of living and levels of material productivity grew as well.

3. The Industrial Revolution was the start of the current epoch: the epoch of modern economic growth. Beginning in the mid-eighteenth century the pace of invention and innovation ratcheted up. Key inventions replaced muscle with machine power, and material productivity levels boomed.

4. Modern economic growth is well-described by the growth model in Chapter 4, which is why we spent so much time on it. Output per worker and capital per worker increase at a pace measured in percent per year, a pace that is extraordinarily rapid in long-term historical perspective.

5. Looking across nations, the world today is an astonishingly unequal place in relative terms. The relative gap between rich and poor nations in material productivity is much greater than it has ever been before.

6. Combining the determinants of the steady-state capital-output ratio with the proximate determinants — the level of technological knowledge in a country after World War II and its average level of educational attainment — accounts for the overwhelming bulk of variation in the relative wealth and poverty of nations today.

7. Macro policies to increase economic growth are policies to accelerate the demographic transition (through education), to boost savings rates, to boost the amount of real investment that a country gets for a given savings effort, and (again through education) to boost the rate of invention or of technology transfer.

8. What are the prospects for successful rapid development in tomorrow's world? Do you see the glass as half empty or half full?

Key Terms

Malthusian age (p. 122)

resource scarcity (p. 122)

natural-resource scarcity (p. 122)

demographic transition (p. 122)

Industrial Revolution (p. 124)

productivity growth (p. 126)

productivity slowdown (p. 128)

divergence (p. 132)

patent laws and copyrights (p. 145)

intellectual property (p. 145)

Analytical Exercises

1. Why do many economists think that the consumer price index overstates the true rate of inflation?

2. Would an increase in the saving and investment share of U.S. total output raise growth in productivity and living standards?

3. Many observers project that by the end of the twenty-first century the population of the United States will be stable. Using the Solow growth model, what would such a downward shift in the growth rate of the labor force do to the growth of output per worker and to the growth of total output (consider both the effect on the steady-state growth path and the transition from the "old" positive population growth to the "new" zero population growth steady-state growth path)?

4. What are the arguments for having a strong patent system to boost economic growth? What are the arguments for having a weak system of protections of intellectual property? Under what systems do you think that

the first will outweigh the second? Under what circumstances do you think that the second will outweigh the first?

5. What steps do you think that international organizations — the UN, the World Bank, or the IMF — could take to improve political leaders' incentives to follow growth-promoting policies?

6. Suppose somebody who hasn't taken any economics courses asks you why humanity escaped from the Malthusian trap — of very low standards of living and slow population growth rates that nevertheless put pressure on available natural resources and kept output per worker from rising — in which humanity found itself between 8000 B.C. and A.D. 1800. What answer would you give?

7. Suppose somebody who hasn't taken any economics courses asks you why some countries are so very, very much poorer than others in the world today. What answer would you give?

8. The *endogenous growth theorists*, led by Stanford's Paul Romer, argue that it is a mistake to separate the determinants of the efficiency of labor from investment — that investments both raise the capital-worker ratio and increase the efficiency of labor as workers learn about the new technology installed with the purchase of new, modern capital goods. If the endogenous growth theorists are correct, is the case for government policies to boost national savings and investment rates strengthened or weakened? Why?

9. Suppose that population growth depends on the level of output per worker, so

$$n = 0.0001 \times \left[\left(\frac{Y}{L} \right) - \$200 \right] \qquad (1)$$

The population growth rate n is zero if output per worker equals $200, and each $100 increase in output per worker raises the population growth rate by 1 percent per year. Suppose also that the economy is in its Malthusian regime, so the rate of increase of the efficiency of labor E is zero and output per worker is given by

$$\frac{Y_t}{L_t} = \left(\frac{s}{n + \delta} \right)^{\frac{\alpha}{1-\alpha}} E_0 \qquad (2)$$

with the diminishing-returns-to-investment parameter $\alpha = 0.5$, the depreciation rate $\delta = 0.04$, and the efficiency of labor $E_0 = \$100$.

a. Suppose that the savings rate s is equal to 8 percent per year. Graph (on the same set of axes) steady-state output-per-worker (Y/L) as a function of the population growth rate n from equation (2) and the population growth rate n as a function of output per worker (Y/L) from equation (1).

b. Where do the curves cross? For what levels of output per worker Y/L and population growth n is the economy (i) on its steady-state path and (ii) at its Malthusian rate of population growth?

c. Suppose that the savings rate rises by an infinitesimal amount — say, by one-hundredth of 1 percentage point, from 0.08 to 0.0801. Calculate approximately how the equilibrium position of the economy will change. By how much, and in which direction, will steady-state output per worker change? By how much, and in which direction, will the population growth rate change?

10. Suppose we have our standard growth model with $s = 20$ percent, $n = 1$ percent, $g = 1$ percent, and $\alpha = 3$ percent. Suppose also that the current level of the efficiency of labor E is $10,000 per year and the current level of capital per worker is $50,000. Suppose further that the parameter α in the production function

$$\frac{Y_t}{L_t} = \left(\frac{K_t}{L_t} \right)^\alpha \times E_t^{1-\alpha}$$

is equal to 1: $\alpha = 1$.

a. What can you say about the future growth of output per worker in this economy? Can you write down an equation for what output per worker will be at any date in the future?

b. Suppose that the savings rate s is not 20 but 15 percent. How will the future growth of output per worker be different?

c. Why aren't the normal tools of analysis and rules of thumb of the growth model of much use when $\alpha = 1$? (Consider the shape of the production function and what that says about diminishing returns to investment.)

Policy Exercises

1. Look in the back of this book at the rate of growth of real GDP per worker in the United States over the past

10 years. Guess what the average magnitude of annual fluctuations in growth about its trend rate are. How

large was the "trend" component of growth in the past year? How large was the "cycle" component of growth in the past year?

2. Pick an industrialized country, an upper-middle-income developing country, a lower-middle-income developing country, and a poor country from the tables in the back of the book. What have been their relative rates of economic growth over the past five years? Are your countries representative in light of the discussion in this chapter?

3. Look at the relative purchasing-power-parity levels of GDP per worker for the G-7 economies — Germany, France, Britain, Italy, Canada, Japan, and the United States. Have the nations drawn closer together in levels of GDP per worker in the past five years?

4. What items of news have you read about in the past week that you would classify as shifts in macro policies that encourage growth?

5. What items of news have you read about in the past week that you would classify as shifts in macro policies that discourage growth?

6. What items of news have you read about in the past week that you would classify as shifts in micro policies that encourage growth?

7. What items of news have you read about in the past week that you would classify as shifts in micro policies that discourage growth?

8. Do you believe that over the next three decades the lower-income countries of the world will catch up to — or at least draw nearer in relative terms to — the high-income countries? Why or why not?

Flexible-Price
MACROECONOMICS

PART

This part looks from a direction opposite to the long-run view of the economy presented in Part II. The chapters in this part take a "snapshot" of the economy, looking at the economy over such a short period of time that its productive resources are effectively fixed. They examine not growth but levels. The key questions are:

1. What determines the equilibrium level of real GDP (Y)?

2. What economic forces keep real GDP (Y) at its equilibrium level?

3. What determines the composition of real GDP — the division of production and spending between consumption goods (C), investment goods (I), government purchases (G), and net exports (NX)?

Part III answers these questions in the flexible-price case, in which markets clear — every buyer finds a willing seller and every seller finds a willing buyer. This assumption means, most importantly, that labor supply equals demand: No firms wanting to hire workers are left unsatisfied, and no workers willing to work are left permanently unemployed. (In Part IV, we analyze the case in which prices are sticky, real GDP is not always equal to potential output, and unemployment can rise high above frictional levels.)

Chapter 6 assembles the building blocks of what will become the flexible-price model of the macroeconomy. Chapter 7 puts these building blocks together and assembles the model. It also demonstrates how to use the model to analyze the level and components of real GDP. Chapter 8 turns the focus of attention from production to the price level and shows how to analyze the determinants of the price level and inflation in the flexible-price case.

Building Blocks of the Flexible-Price Model

CHAPTER

QUESTIONS

What is a full-employment analysis?

What keeps the economy at full employment when wages and prices are flexible?

What determines the level of consumption spending?

What determines the level of investment spending?

What determines the level of net exports?

What determines the level of the exchange rate?

In the previous two chapters we have looked at long-run growth — at how the economy develops and evolves over periods as long as generations. In this chapter we shift our point of view and take a "snapshot" of the economy, looking at it over such a short period that its productive resources are fixed.

In this short-period analysis, the key questions are three: What determines the equilibrium level of real GDP (Y)? What are the economic forces that keep real GDP (Y) at its equilibrium value? And what determines the division of real GDP between consumption spending (C), investment spending (I), government purchases (G), and net exports (NX)? This chapter, Chapter 6, answers the first two questions. If wages and prices are sufficiently flexible (as we assume they are here in Part III), then markets clear: Quantities demanded are equal to quantities supplied. In particular, the labor market clears: Employment is equal to the labor force (save for some "frictional" unemployment), and production is equal to potential output. Should production not be equal to potential output, rising or falling real wages will quickly lower or raise firms' demands for labor and bring the economy back to equilibrium.

The third question cannot be fully answered in this chapter. What this chapter does is assemble the building blocks needed to answer it. The full answer, however, comes only in Chapter 7.

6.1 POTENTIAL OUTPUT AND REAL WAGES

In the flexible-price model of the macroeconomy, two sets of factors determine the levels of potential (and actual) output and of real wages: the production function and the balance of supply and demand in the labor market.

The Production Function

Chapter 4 introduced the **production function**, the rule that tells us how much the economy can produce given its available productive resources. In the Cobb-Douglas form of the production function, as we learned, potential output (Y^*) is determined by the size of the labor force (L), the economy's capital stock (K), the efficiency of labor (E), and a parameter α that tells us how fast returns to investment diminish. The production function tells us that potential output is

$$Y^* = K^{\alpha}(LE)^{1-\alpha}$$

The graph in Figure 6.1 shows one slice of this production function — the relationship between the capital stock K and potential output Y^*, holding labor L and the efficiency of labor E fixed.

In Chapters 4 and 5 all the variables in the production function had the subscript t, indicating the year they referred to. Because we were looking at changes over time, keeping track of which year we were talking about was important. In this chapter we are looking at the economy at one instant, not over time, and so we do not have to keep track of the year. To reduce clutter in the equations, we will drop the subscripts and speak simply of the labor force L, the capital stock K, the efficiency of labor E, and the level of potential output Y^*.

The assumption that wages and prices are flexible was commonly made by the so-called classical economists, who wrote before World War II. Thus this assumption is also called the *classical assumption*. The classical assumption guarantees that markets work — that prices adjust rapidly to eliminate gaps between the quantities

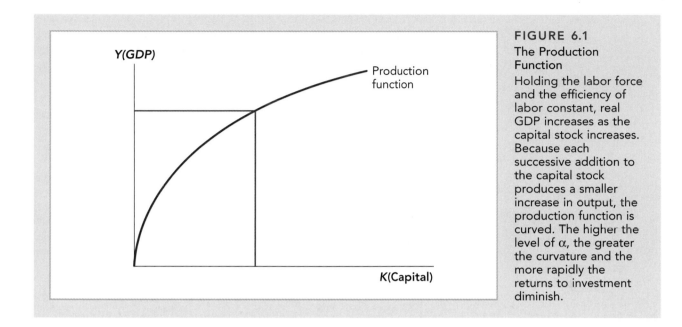

FIGURE 6.1

The Production Function
Holding the labor force and the efficiency of labor constant, real GDP increases as the capital stock increases. Because each successive addition to the capital stock produces a smaller increase in output, the production function is curved. The higher the level of α, the greater the curvature and the more rapidly the returns to investment diminish.

demanded and the quantities supplied. Thus no businesses find their inventories of unsold goods piling up, and there is full employment: Everyone who wants a job (at the market-clearing level of wages) can get a job, and every business that wants to hire a worker (at the market-clearing level of wages) can hire a worker. Because of full employment, actual output is equal to potential output: There is no gap between the economy's productive potential and the level of output the economy produces.

The classical assumption made in Chapters 6, 7, and 8 means that Part III is devoted to full-employment flexible-price macroeconomics. The flexible-price assumption it is not always a good one, however. Experience has shown that a market economy does not always work well and does not always produce full employment. So in Part IV we will drop it and make instead the "Keynesian" assumption that wages and prices are sticky (see Table 6.1).

TABLE 6.1
Classical Flexible-Price versus Keynesian Sticky-Price Analyses

Issue	Classical	Keynesian
Wages and prices	Fully flexible	Can be "sticky" or fixed
Expectations	Consistent with full employment	Volatile — can take a number of forms
Labor market	Always in equilibrium with full employment	Can be out of equilibrium, causing involuntary unemployment
Effect of shocks to aggregate demand	Change in the composition but not the level of GDP	Change in the composition and the level of GDP

If the classical flexible-price assumption is not always a good one to make, why make it at all? It *is* a good assumption if wages and prices are relatively flexible and have enough time to adjust in order to balance supply and demand. The classical assumption simplifies the analysis of several issues, making it easier to grasp how the macroeconomy works. In general it is better to start with the simpler cases before looking at more complicated ones. Moreover, the way an economy functions under the flexible-price assumption provides a useful baseline against which to assess economic performance. Nevertheless, we must remember that Part III presents only one model of the economy: the classical model. The Keynesian sticky-price model behaves very differently in a number of ways.

The Labor Market

When markets work well, what keeps the economy at full employment and actual production equal to potential output? One way to look at this issue is that the answer lies in the adjustment of prices and supply and demand in the **labor market**. When the supply of and demand for labor balance, real GDP will equal potential output.

Labor Demand

Economists try to suppress every detail and difference that does not matter to the overall result in order to simplify the analysis and focus it on the important factors that count. Because differences between businesses will not matter, let's think about an economy with K typical — identical — competitive firms, each of which owns 1 unit of the economy's capital stock. Each of these firms hires L workers and pays each worker the same wage W. Each firm sells Y units of its product at a per-unit price P. The typical firm does not control either the wages it must pay or the prices it receives; those are determined by the market. The firm tries to make as much money as it can. The firm's profits are simply its revenues minus its costs, and its only costs are the wages it pays to workers. Therefore

$$\text{Profits} = \text{revenues} - \text{costs}$$
$$= (P \times Y) - (W \times L)$$

To figure out how many workers to hire, the firm follows two simple rules:

1. Hire workers to boost output.
2. Stop hiring when the extra revenue from the output produced by the last worker hired just equals his or her wage.

The value of the output produced by the last worker hired is the product price P times the **marginal product of labor (MPL)**. The cost of hiring the last worker is his or her wage W. The firm will keep hiring until

$$(P \times \text{MPL}) - W = 0$$

What is the marginal product of labor? The typical firm owns 1 unit of capital, and its output is what can be made by that single unit of capital and the firm's workers according to the production function

$$Y_{\text{firm}} = F(1, L_{\text{firm}})$$

The marginal product of labor is the difference between what the firm can produce with its current labor force L_{firm} and what it would produce if it hired one more worker (see Figure 6.2):

$$\text{MPL} = F(1, L_{\text{firm}} + 1) - F(1, L_{\text{firm}})$$

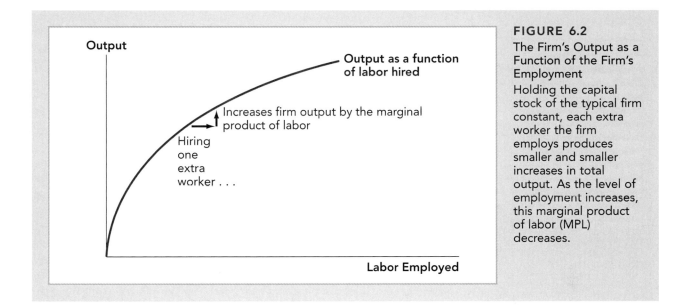

FIGURE 6.2
The Firm's Output as a Function of the Firm's Employment
Holding the capital stock of the typical firm constant, each extra worker the firm employs produces smaller and smaller increases in total output. As the level of employment increases, this marginal product of labor (MPL) decreases.

Because we want a form of the MPL that is simple to work with, we will consider the Cobb-Douglas production function. The MPL for the Cobb-Douglas production function is

$$\text{MPL} = K_{\text{firm}}{}^\alpha \times E^{1-\alpha}(L_{\text{firm}} + 1)^{1-\alpha} - K_{\text{firm}}{}^\alpha \times E^{1-\alpha}L_{\text{firm}}{}^{1-\alpha}$$

Again, we take how much the firm would produce if it hired one more worker and subtract how it produces now, with its current labor force. Since the firm has only 1 unit of capital, we can rewrite this equation as

$$\text{MPL} = 1^\alpha \times E^{1-\alpha}(L_{\text{firm}} + 1)^{1-\alpha} - 1^\alpha \times E^{1-\alpha}L_{\text{firm}}{}^{1-\alpha}$$
$$= E^{1-\alpha}[(L_{\text{firm}} + 1)^{1-\alpha} - L_{\text{firm}}{}^{1-\alpha}]$$

The term inside the brackets looks like the rate of growth of a variable growing by 1 unit (the firm's labor force L_{firm}) and then raised to a power (the term $1 - \alpha$). We have a standard rule of thumb for dealing with such a situation (look again, in Chapter 2, at Box 2.3, "Useful Mathematical Tools"). The proportional growth rate of a variable raised to a power is the proportional growth rate of the variable multiplied by the power to which the variable is raised. This tells us that the term inside the brackets is

$$[(L_{\text{firm}} + 1)^{1-\alpha} - L_{\text{firm}}{}^{1-\alpha}] = (1 - \alpha) \times \frac{1}{L_{\text{firm}}{}^\alpha}$$

So the MPL is

$$\text{MPL} = \frac{(1 - \alpha)E^{1-\alpha}}{L_{\text{firm}}{}^\alpha}$$

There is nothing deep in this math. Indeed, the Cobb-Douglas function was carefully tweaked so that it would yield such simple forms for quantities like the MPL. That is why economists use it so often. If the Cobb-Douglas production function produced more complicated expressions, we would not use it.

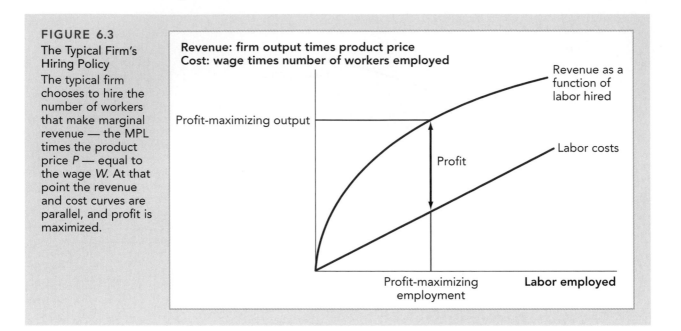

FIGURE 6.3
The Typical Firm's Hiring Policy
The typical firm chooses to hire the number of workers that make marginal revenue — the MPL times the product price *P* — equal to the wage *W*. At that point the revenue and cost curves are parallel, and profit is maximized.

Revenue: firm output times product price
Cost: wage times number of workers employed

Revenue as a function of labor hired

Profit-maximizing output

Labor costs

Profit

Profit-maximizing employment

Labor employed

As Figure 6.3 shows, the firm hires workers up to the point where the product price times the marginal product of labor equals the wage:

$$(P \times MPL) - W = 0$$

Substituting for the MPL in this equation, we get

$$P \times \frac{(1-\alpha)E^{1-\alpha}}{L_{\text{firm}}{}^{\alpha}} = W$$

Next, we rearrange this equation to see that the typical firm's demand for workers is

$$L_{\text{firm}} = \left[\frac{(1-\alpha)E^{1-\alpha}}{W/P}\right]^{1/\alpha}$$

Because there are *K* firms in the whole economy, total economywide employment is equal to *K* times the typical firm's demand for labor:

$$L^d = K\left[\frac{(1-\alpha)E^{1-\alpha}}{W/P}\right]^{1/\alpha}$$

Labor Market Equilibrium

In the section above we calculated economywide labor demand. But what is the labor supply? The answer is simple: It is the number of workers who want to work. The labor market will be in equilibrium when firms' total demand for workers is equal to the labor force.

Can the labor market not be in equilibrium if wages and prices are flexible? Think about what would happen if labor supply were not equal to demand. Suppose there are more workers than firms want to hire at current wages and prices. Then some of the unemployed will underbid the employed workers, offering to take their jobs and

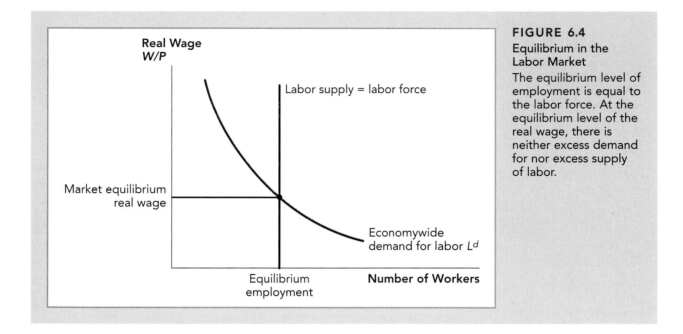

FIGURE 6.4
Equilibrium in the Labor Market
The equilibrium level of employment is equal to the labor force. At the equilibrium level of the real wage, there is neither excess demand for nor excess supply of labor.

work for less. The workers who are employed will respond by offering to accept lower wages to keep their jobs. The wage W will decline relative to the price level P, and the **real wage** W/P will fall. As the real wage falls, firms will hire more workers.

Suppose firms want to hire more workers than there are people in the labor force. Some firms will try to bid workers away from other firms by offering higher wages. The real wage W/P will rise. As the real wage rises, employers will reduce the quantity of labor they demand. Thus, in **labor market equilibrium**, labor demand L^d will equal the labor force L (see Figure 6.4):

$$L = L^d = K\left[\frac{(1-\alpha)E^{1-\alpha}}{W/P}\right]^{1/\alpha}$$

Labor demand is equal to the labor force when the real wage W/P is

$$\frac{W}{P} = [(1-\alpha)E^{1-\alpha}]\left(\frac{K}{L}\right)^{\alpha} = (1-\alpha)\frac{Y}{L}$$

and each of the K firms in the economy employs L/K workers. As long as wages and prices are flexible enough for this adjustment process to work, the economy will remain at full employment.

Note that a full-employment economy is not necessarily the best or even a good economy. The real incomes of people who don't own chunks of the capital stock are their real wages: $W/P = (1-\alpha) \times (Y/L)$. If α is large, their real incomes will be small, and social welfare may be low.

Employment and Output

When the labor market is in equilibrium, the typical firm produces a level of output equal to

$$Y_{\text{firm}} = 1^{\alpha}E^{1-\alpha}(L/K)^{1-\alpha}$$

FIGURE 6.5

In a Full-Employment Economy, Real GDP Equals Potential Output

When the economy is at full employment, the level of employment is equal to the labor force and real GDP is equal to potential output.

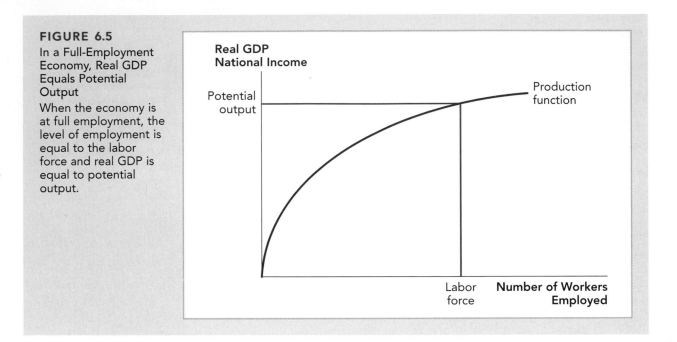

Because there are K firms, total output Y is simply K times the typical firm's output: $Y = K \times Y_{\text{firm}}$. This is the same *potential output, Y^*,* in the Cobb-Douglas form of the production function analysis

$$Y = K \times Y_{\text{firm}} = K \times 1^{\alpha}E^{1-\alpha}(L/K)^{1-\alpha} = K^{\alpha}E^{1-\alpha}L^{1-\alpha}$$

$$= K^{\alpha}(LE)^{1-\alpha} = Y^*$$

The conclusion is clear: If markets work well — if wages and prices are flexible and adjust to balance supply and demand, and if markets are competitive — then the actual level of production in the economy Y will equal the economy's **potential output** Y^*, as Figure 6.5 shows.

RECAP   POTENTIAL OUTPUT AND REAL WAGES

A flexible-price economy is a full-employment economy: Wages are flexible enough to keep supply and demand in balance in the labor market. Because there are enough jobs for all the workers who want to work at the prevailing market-clearing wage, real GDP in a flexible-price economy is always equal to potential output and unemployment is not a problem. This classical model of the macroeconomy is the polar opposite of the Keynesian model, where prices and wages are sticky, markets do not always clear with supply and demand in balance, high unemployment is possible, and there are gaps between real GDP and potential output.

6.2 DOMESTIC SPENDING

In Chapters 2 and 3 we saw via the national income identity that total spending is divided into four components:

- Consumption spending (*C*)
- Investment spending (*I*)
- Government purchases (*G*)
- Net exports, the balancing item (*NX*)

These four components add up to national income, which is the same as according to the circular flow principle, is the same as aggregate demand (*E*) and real GDP, *Y* (see Figure 6.6):

$$C + I + G + NX = Y$$

In this section we look at the determinants of the three domestic components of spending, *C, I,* and *G*. We discuss international trade in a later section.

Consumption Spending

Individual households make the spending and saving decisions that ultimately determine the flow of consumption spending. In this section we first examine how households divide their income up among taxes, saving, and consumption spending. Then we will see how consumption spending varies in response to changes in income and in other aspects of the economic environment.

The Household's Decisions

The wages of workers plus the profits of property owners (rent, interest, dividends, and retained earnings) add up to national income. Because at this level of analysis we are uninterested in any accounting distinctions between national income and real GDP, we use the letter *Y* to represent both. (Recall that the circular flow principle guarantees that whatever businesses produce and sell must show up as income for households.)

Households pay some of their income to the government in net taxes — taxes less transfer payments from the government — which we write as *T*. To keep the analysis

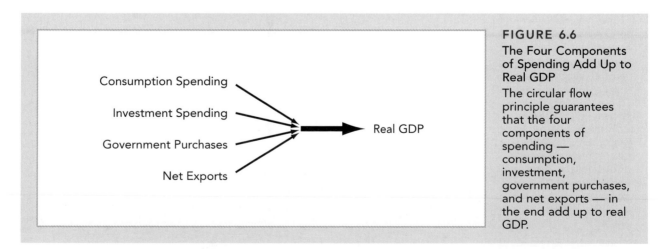

FIGURE 6.6

The Four Components of Spending Add Up to Real GDP

The circular flow principle guarantees that the four components of spending — consumption, investment, government purchases, and net exports — in the end add up to real GDP.

simple, throughout this book we will assume that net taxes are equal to the constant average tax rate t multiplied by national income:

$$T = t \times Y$$

In the real world taxes are not proportional to income. Our tax system is somewhat progressive, which means that richer taxpayers on average pay more of their income in taxes than do the relatively poor. Once again, however, the complications induced by the fact that our tax system is not proportional to income are not central to the analysis, so we follow economists' standard practice of simplifying wherever possible.

The amount left after households pay their taxes is their **disposable income**, written Y^D:

$$Y^D = Y - T = (1 - t)Y$$

Households also save some of their income to boost their wealth and future spending. We represent private household savings by S^H — S for "savings" and H for "household." (Note that household savings include the retained earnings of corporations: The NIPA treats undistributed corporate earnings that are retained by the corporation as if they were distributed to the shareholding households and then immediately reinvested back into the corporation.) As Figure 6.7 shows, households spend the rest of their income — everything that is not saved or paid to the government in taxes — buying consumption goods:

$$C = Y^D - S^H = Y - T - S^H$$

In the United States today, consumption spending C — purchases by households for their own use, from pine nuts and flour to washing machines and automobiles — accounts for roughly two-thirds of GDP. We will break consumption spending down into a baseline level of consumption (defined as the value of a parameter C_0) and a fraction (a parameter C_y) of disposable income Y^D, or a fraction $C_y \times (1 - t)$ of total income Y:

$$C = C_0 + C_y \times Y^D = C_0 + C_y \times (1 - t)Y$$

Thus we assume that consumption spending C is a linear function of real GDP Y.

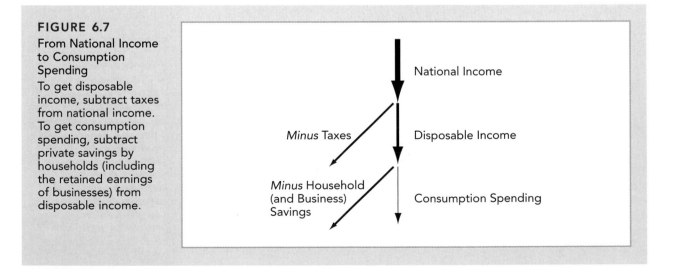

FIGURE 6.7
From National Income to Consumption Spending
To get disposable income, subtract taxes from national income. To get consumption spending, subtract private savings by households (including the retained earnings of businesses) from disposable income.

National Income

Minus Taxes

Disposable Income

Minus Household (and Business) Savings

Consumption Spending

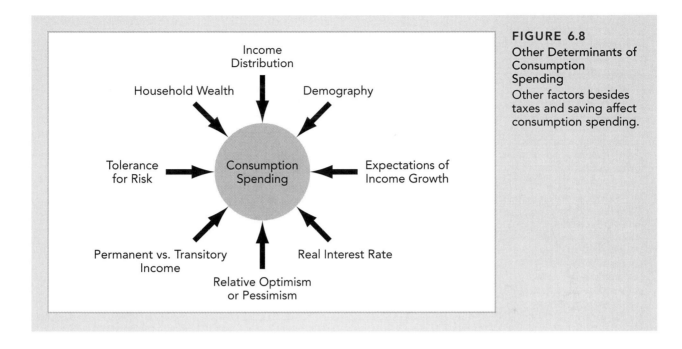

FIGURE 6.8
Other Determinants of Consumption Spending
Other factors besides taxes and saving affect consumption spending.

Notice that in writing this particular **consumption function**, we have once again followed the economists' principle (or vice) of ruthless simplification. In this complicated world, consumption spending does not depend on disposable income alone. As Figure 6.8 shows, other factors affecting it include changes in the real interest rate, household total stock market and real estate wealth, the demographic structure of the population, income distribution, consumers' relative optimism, expected future income growth, tolerance for risk, and whether consumers see changes in disposable income as transitory or permanent. (If consumers expect an income increase to be transitory, they will save most of it and spend only a little; if they expect an income increase to be permanent, they will spend most of it.) But here and throughout the book we will sweep these complications under the rug. We will think about only baseline consumption C_0, the marginal propensity to consume C_y, and disposable income Y^D as the determinants of consumption spending (although we will occasionally sneak in other factors by saying that they change baseline consumption C_0).

The Marginal Propensity to Consume

The baseline level of consumption, the parameter C_0, is the amount households would spend on consumption goods if they had no income at all. That is, it is the amount by which they would draw down their wealth in the absence of income in order to keep body and soul together.

The **marginal propensity to consume (MPC)**, the same parameter C_y in the consumption function, is the amount by which consumption spending rises in response to a $1 increase in disposable income (see Figure 6.9). We are sure that C_y is greater than zero: If incomes rise, households will use some of their extra income to boost their consumption spending. We are also sure that C_y is less than 1: As incomes rise, households will increase their savings as well; they will not spend all their extra income on consumption goods.

FIGURE 6.9

The Consumption Function

Consumption spending depends on the level of disposable income and two parameters: C_y (the marginal propensity to consume, or MPC) and C_0 (the baseline level of consumption). If we know both these parameters and the value of disposable income Y^D, we can plot the level of consumption spending at each possible level of disposable income.

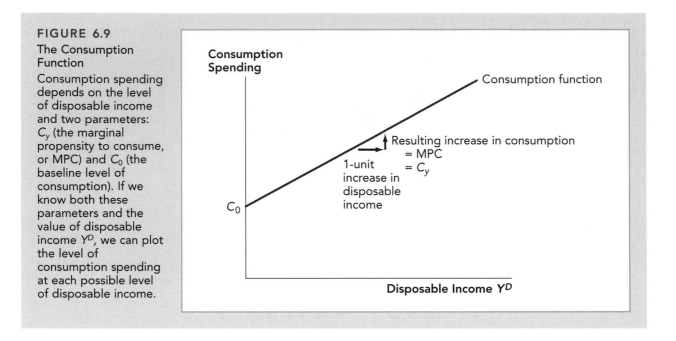

The value of the marginal propensity to consume also depends on how long people expect the change in income to last. As discussed in Appendix 6A, if people expect the change in income to be *permanent*, then the MPC is likely to be relatively large. If they expect the change in income to be *transitory* — and think their income next year will revert back to its normal pattern — the MPC is likely to be relatively small. With these two parameters, C_0 and C_y, we can calculate what the total level of consumption spending will be for each possible level of disposable income Y^D (see Box 6.1).

BOX 6.1

CALCULATING CONSUMPTION FROM INCOME: AN EXAMPLE

If we know the parameters C_0 (the baseline level of consumption), C_y (the marginal propensity to consume, or MPC), and t (the tax rate), we can calculate the level of consumption spending C for any level of total national income Y using the equation

$$C = C_0 + C_y \times Y^D = C_0 + C_y \times (1 - t)Y$$

Suppose the tax rate t is 25 percent, the total national income Y is $10 trillion, the baseline level of consumption C_0 is $2 trillion, and the marginal propensity to consume C_y is 0.6. We first calculate disposable income — how much households have left after paying their taxes. Disposable income is equal to $(1 - t)Y$, which for these parameter values and this level of national income is

$$(1 - 0.25) \times \$10 \text{ trillion} = \$7.5 \text{ trillion}$$

We can then calculate consumption:

$$\begin{aligned} C &= C_0 + C_y \times \$7.5 \text{ trillion} \\ &= \$2 \text{ trillion} + 0.6 \times \$7.5 \text{ trillion} \\ &= \$6.5 \text{ trillion} \end{aligned}$$

What will happen if disposable income rises from $7.5 trillion to $8 trillion? Consumption spending will rise from $6.5 trillion to $6.8 trillion — an amount equal to the marginal propensity to consume, 0.6, times the change in disposable income, $0.5 trillion.

◆

Investment Spending

In the United States today investment spending averages roughly 17 percent of GDP. But investment spending is the most volatile and variable component of GDP. (*Note:* Economists' definition of "investment spending" is probably not what you think it is; Boxes 6.2 and 6.3 explain how economists define and calculate investment spending.)

WHAT IS INVESTMENT? SOME DETAILS

When economists use the term "investment," they mean something different from what most people mean by the word. Most people use it to mean activity such as buying a stock or bond, a certificate of deposit, or commodity futures. But such purchases do not directly increase the economy's capital stock or have any place in the national income and product accounts.

When economists use the term "investment" or "investment spending," they are talking about transactions that add to the capital stock and increase potential output. Such transactions include the purchase and installation of new business machinery and equipment, the construction and purchase of a new building (or the repair of an old one), and a change in business inventories.

◆

KINDS OF INVESTMENT: SOME DETAILS

Economists categorize investment in two different ways. The first distinction they draw is between gross investment and net investment. *Gross investment* is the total sum of spending on machines, construction (houses, factories, office buildings, roads, dams, and bridges), and additions to inventories.

Some of gross investment adds to the capital stock of machines, goods in process, buildings, and other structures that amplify productivity. The rest of gross investment replaces worn-out and obsolete pieces of capital. The amount of gross investment spending that increases the capital stock is called *net investment*. The amount of investment spending that replaces obsolete and worn-out capital is called *depreciation* or capital *consumption*.

Economists also categorize investment according to use, as follows:

1. Residential construction
2. Nonresidential construction
3. Equipment investment
4. Inventory investment

To some degree, these four subcategories of investment have different determinants and different consequences. But in order to simplify and construct a useful model, we ignore those differences.

◆

Fluctuations in economywide investment spending have two sources. First is the interest rate: The higher the real interest rate, the lower is investment spending. A higher real interest rate makes investment projects more expensive for firms to undertake, so they undertake fewer of them. Second is business managers' and investors' confidence — what John Maynard Keynes called their "animal spirits." The higher their confidence, the higher is investment spending. Optimistic managers and investors are more willing to bet their careers and fortunes on the belief that an expansion of productive capacity or some other investment will pay off.

Why Firms Invest

A business invests because its managers believe that the investment project will be profitable: The appropriately discounted return on the investment must be greater than the investment's cost. The higher the interest rate, the lower is the appropriately discounted return on the investment project. The higher the interest rate, the smaller is the number of potential investment projects that will be profitable. Thus a lower interest rate leads to higher investment spending.

How many investment projects will a higher interest rate discourage? How much lower will investment be if the interest rate is higher? Analyzing these questions is beyond the scope of this book. (Appendix 6B, however, presents the key concept of *present value,* a tool used in finance to assess whether an investment project is worth undertaking at the prevailing interest rate.)

The interest rate most relevant to determining investment is the long-term, real, risky interest rate. The relevant interest rate is long-term because investment projects affect the business's profits and costs for a long time to come. The relevant interest rate is real — that is, inflation-adjusted — because an investment project gives the business that undertakes it a real, physical asset, not a financial claim denominated in dollars. The relevant interest rate is risky because investment projects are risky. In calculating whether investment projects are worthwhile, be sure to compare apples to apples. Discount the long-term, real, risky profits anticipated from undertaking an investment project by the long-term, real, risky interest rate.

The Investment Function

To model the inverse relationship between the level of investment spending and the long-term, real, risky interest rate, set investment spending I equal to the baseline level of investment (the value of the parameter I_0) minus the **real interest rate** r times the slope of the investment function parameter I_r (see Figure 6.10):

$$I = I_0 - I_r \times r$$

Box 6.4 shows how to use this **investment function** equation to calculate the level of investment spending at a particular interest rate. Box 6.5 presents an alternative way of thinking about the investment function — one that focuses on the stock market, not on interest rates.

Notice the pattern used for parameters so far: C_0, C_y, I_0, I_r. This should make the symbols used in algebraic equations clearer and easier to remember. The capital letter in the name of each parameter tells you what variable is on the left-hand side of the equation in which the parameter appears. A C means that the parameter is part of an equation determining the level of consumption spending C; an I means that the parameter is part of an equation determining the level of investment spending I; and so forth. The subscript tells you the variable by which the parameter is multiplied in

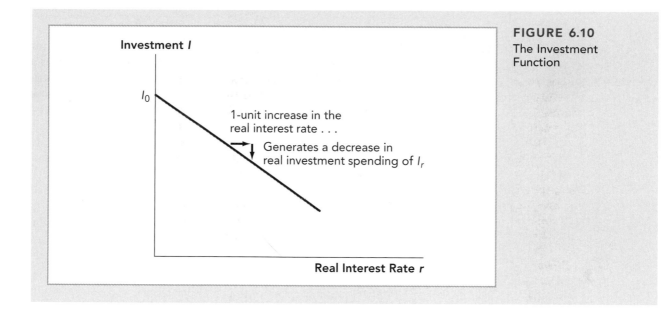

FIGURE 6.10
The Investment
Function

Investment *I*

I_0

1-unit increase in the
real interest rate . . .

Generates a decrease in
real investment spending of I_r

Real Interest Rate *r*

HOW INVESTMENT RESPONDS TO A CHANGE IN INTEREST RATES: AN EXAMPLE

From the parameters I_0 (the baseline level of investment) and I_r (the responsiveness of investment to a change in real interest rates) we can calculate the level of investment spending for each possible value of the real interest rate r.

For example, suppose that I_0 is $2 trillion and that I_r is $10,000 billion. Then we can use the equation

$$I = I_0 - I_r \times r$$

to calculate that if the real interest rate is 5 percent, then the level of investment spending is $1.5 trillion:

$$I = \$2 \text{ trillion} - \$10,000 \text{ billion} \times 0.05 = \$1.5 \text{ trillion}$$

If the real interest rate is 10 percent, the level of investment spending is $1 trillion:

$$I = \$2 \text{ trillion} - \$10,000 \text{ billion} \times 0.10 = \$1 \text{ trillion}$$

And if the real interest rate is 0 percent, the level of investment spending is $2 trillion:

$$I = \$2 \text{ trillion} - \$10,000 \text{ billion} \times 0 = \$2 \text{ trillion}$$

BOX

6.4

that equation. For example, I_r is the amount by which investment spending I changes in response to a change in the real interest rate r.

Like the consumption function, the investment function is an enormous simplification of real-world investment patterns. In the real world, firms' investment decisions depend not only on the real interest rate but also on how much money the

THE STOCK MARKET: SOME DETAILS

An alternative way of looking at investment — one that would complicate our models too much for us to use it here — sees the level of investment spending as a function of the level of the stock market. Think about what determines stock market values. Most investors in the stock market face a choice between holding *stocks* — shares of ownership of a corporation that also give you ownership of that corporation's profits or earnings — or holding *bonds:* pieces of paper that represent loans that pay interest. If you invest your money in bonds, you earn the real interest rate *r.* If you invest in shares of stock, your return is equal to your share of the profits of the companies in which you have invested.

When expected future profits are high, investors find stocks more attractive than bonds and thus bid up stock prices. When the real interest rate falls, investors also find stocks more attractive than bonds and bid up stock prices. In either case, the stock market will rise. However, when expected future profits are high, businesses invest more. When the real interest rate falls, businesses find investment projects cheaper and also invest more. The same things that determine the value of the stock market also determine the level of investment spending. The stock market and investment move together: What raises or lowers one raises or lowers the other.

The only significant difference is that causes of fluctuations in investment affect the stock market first and investment spending second. The stock market is thus a very useful leading indicator of investment spending. Keep a close watch on the stock market if you want to forecast the level of investment spending. ◆

firms have available. Total profits are also an important determinant of investment. In the real world, some components of investment — construction, for example — are very sensitive to changes in the real interest rate. Other components of investment — for example, inventory investments by small firms with little access to

HOW TO BOOST INVESTMENT: A POLICY ISSUE

As we saw in Chapters 4 and 5, a high level of saving and investment is one of the keys to a prosperous economy. The higher the share of GDP devoted to investment spending, the higher is the steady-state capital-output ratio and the richer is the economy.

Governments seeking to boost investment have two major tools at their disposal. First, they can lower real interest rates (or induce the central bank to lower them). If real interest rates are lowered, more investment projects will be undertaken and investment spending will rise. Second, governments can try to raise the baseline level of investment by encouraging private decision makers. They can exhort and reassure them — although the tactic sometimes backfires, as in President Herbert Hoover's repeated declaration during the Great Depression that "prosperity is just around the corner." More important, policy makers can try to reduce or eliminate sources of risk. Instilling confidence that the economy will be stable and risks will be managed is perhaps the best way to boost investment by encouraging optimism.

outside sources of funding — are not. Box 6.6 discusses two tools government policy makers sometimes have at their disposal to change the level of investment.

Government Purchases

The federal government buys the labor of government employees — judges, air traffic controllers, customs inspectors, FBI agents, National Oceanic and Atmospheric Administration researchers, and others — as well as military hardware, sections of the interstate highway system, and other goods and services. All these expenditures make up the **government purchases** component of GDP. Such government purchases of goods and services add up to about 25 percent of GDP, counting together the purchases of the local, state, and federal governments.

Note that government *spending* is larger than government *purchases*. In addition to buying goods and services (including the work-time of its employees), the government also spends by transferring money to citizens through Social Security and other programs, disability benefits, food stamps, and other **transfer payments.** Because transfer payments do not themselves represent demand for final goods and services, they do not show up directly as a portion of GDP in the government purchases total G. Rather, transfer payments show up in the NIPA as negative taxes. The variable T — taxes — represents **net taxes**, taxes less transfer payments. It is the net amount by which the government's tax and transfer system reduces disposable income. (See Figure 6.11.)

As noted above, in this book we assume net taxes T, taxes less transfers, are equal to the average tax rate t times GDP Y:

$$T = tY$$

We do not inquire into what determines either government purchases G or the average tax rate t. We leave that for the political scientists. We do look at what happens when government spending G or the tax rate t changes.

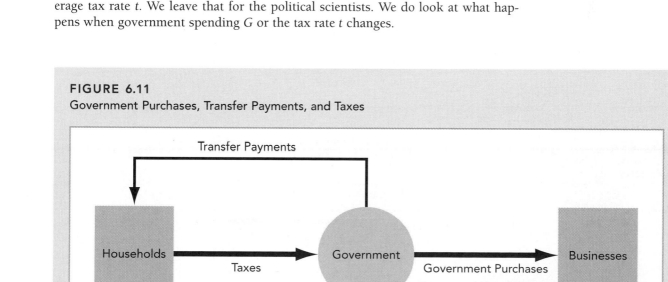

FIGURE 6.11
Government Purchases, Transfer Payments, and Taxes

6.3 INTERNATIONAL TRADE

The final component of GDP is **net exports** — the difference between gross exports and **imports**. **Gross exports** are made up of goods and services that are produced in the home country and then sold abroad. GDP is a measure of production, and since gross exports are part of production, they need to be counted in GDP. But first imports need to be subtracted from GDP, as Figure 6.12 shows. Not all the goods and services that make up consumption, investment, and government purchases are produced domestically. Consumption, for instance, includes spending on Chinese toys, Irish computers, Brazilian coffee, and Scottish tweeds as well as on domestically made goods. So adding up C, I, and G overestimates domestic demand for U.S.-made products. By adding *net* rather than *gross* exports to $C + I + G$, economists (a) take account of goods made domestically that are sold to foreigners and don't show up in $C + I + G$ and (b) correct $C + I + G$ for the amount of foreign-made goods it counts.

FIGURE 6.12
Gross Exports, Imports, and Net Exports

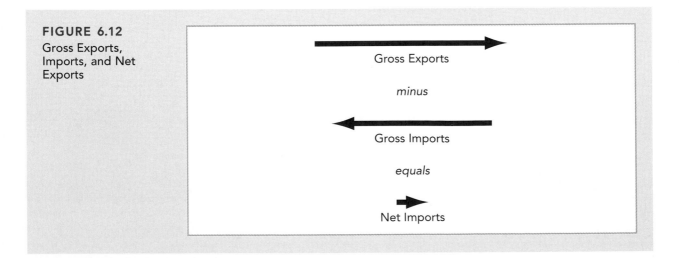

Gross Exports

The volume of gross exports from the United States depends on two variables. The first is the real GDP of our trading partners — call it Y^f, for "foreign GDP." The second is the real exchange rate — call it ε. The higher the value of the real exchange rate — the more expensive the foreign currency — the cheaper are U.S.-made goods to foreigners, and the more of them they buy, as Figure 6.13 shows.

Thus the function for gross exports GX is

$$GX = (X_f \times Y^f) + (X_\varepsilon \times \varepsilon)$$

Here, just as in the investment and consumption equations, X_ε and X_f are parameters that help determine gross exports. X_f is the increase in exports generated by an increase in foreign GDP. It is the proportion of foreign income spent on our exports. X_ε is the increase in exports produced by a rise in the real exchange rate ε.

In the real world, the relationship between the real exchange rate and exports is not as simple as the gross exports function. Many determinants of gross exports are suppressed in order to keep the model simple. Moreover, there are substantial lags in the process. A change in the real exchange rate has little or no effect on gross exports this year but will have effects on gross exports one, two, and three years into the future, as Box 6.7 explains.

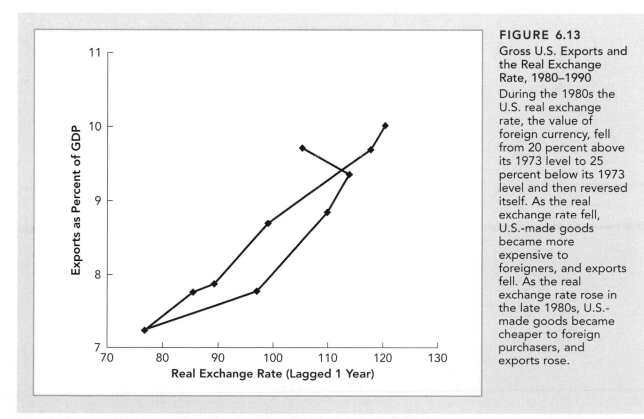

FIGURE 6.13

Gross U.S. Exports and the Real Exchange Rate, 1980–1990

During the 1980s the U.S. real exchange rate, the value of foreign currency, fell from 20 percent above its 1973 level to 25 percent below its 1973 level and then reversed itself. As the real exchange rate fell, U.S.-made goods became more expensive to foreigners, and exports fell. As the real exchange rate rose in the late 1980s, U.S.-made goods became cheaper to foreign purchasers, and exports rose.

Source: The 2001 edition of *The Economic Report of the President* (Washington, DC: Government Printing Office).

THE J-CURVE: SOME DETAILS

Trade links across countries take time to create, time to modify, and time to destroy. So while a depreciation of the U.S. real exchange rate causes an increase in foreign purchases of U.S. goods, a year or more will pass before we see the change in the volume of trade. In the short run, a rise in the real exchange rate — an increase in the value of foreign currency — may see a fall, not a rise, in exports. Economists call this the *J curve,* because the plot of exports over time after a rise in the exchange rate looks a little like a "J." The real exchange rate — the value of foreign currency — began to rise very steeply in 1986, but as Figure 6.14 shows, real exports in 1986 were flat. It was not until 1987 and 1988 that the increased competitiveness of U.S. exporters led to an export boom.

FIGURE 6.14

The J Curve in the 1980s
Changes in export volumes lag behind changes in the real exchange rate by a year or more.

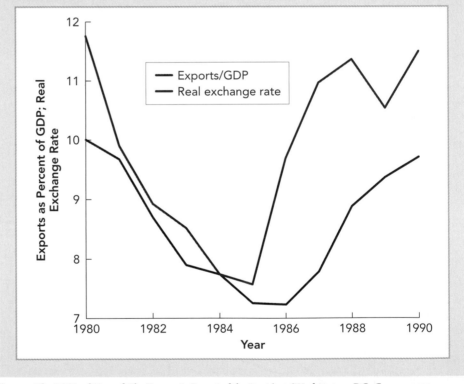

Source: The 2001 edition of *The Economic Report of the President* (Washington, DC: Government Printing Office).

Imports and Net Exports

The value of demand for **imports** — for products produced abroad — depends on domestic real GDP: The higher the real GDP, the more money consumers and investors spend on imports.

The *quantity* of imports demanded depends as well on the real exchange rate ε. The higher the real exchange rate — the higher the value of foreign currency — the more expensive are foreign-made goods and the fewer of them do domestic consumers and investors buy. However, we are interested not in the quantity but in the value of imports. When because of exchange rate movements the quantity of imports demanded is high, the value of a typical import is low. So the value of imports is largely independent of the real exchange rate.

Therefore we simplify and model gross imports *IM* as a constant share — a share that is the propensity to import IM_y — of real GDP *Y*:

$$IM = IM_y \times Y$$

Net exports *NX* are the difference between gross exports and imports. Thus they depend on the real exchange rate, ε; on real GDP abroad, Y^f; and on real GDP here at home, *Y*:

$$NX = GX - IM = (X_f \times Y^f) + (X_\varepsilon \times \varepsilon) - (IM_y \times Y)$$

The Exchange Rate

We have seen that the exchange rate is an important determinant of net exports. But what determines the exchange rate?

Consider foreign exchange speculators whose job it is to trade currencies and make money. They spend their days glued to computer terminals, watching the prices of bonds denominated in different currencies flash across the screen. They buy and sell bonds and stocks of different countries and governments denominated in different currencies — dollars, euros, pounds, yen, pesos, ringgit, and more than 100 others. Their lives are ruled by greed and fear, as sketched out in Figure 6.15:

- *Greed:* Suppose a trader sees higher interest rates paid on the bonds of U.S. companies denominated in dollars than on those of German companies denominated in euros. In this case, there is money to be made by selling ("going short") German companies' bonds, buying ("going long") U.S. companies' bonds, and pocketing the extra interest.

- *Fear:* Suppose that the trader is long on dollar-denominated bonds and short on euro-denominated bonds and the U.S. exchange rate rises. At a higher real exchange rate, each dollar is worth fewer euros; whatever profits were expected

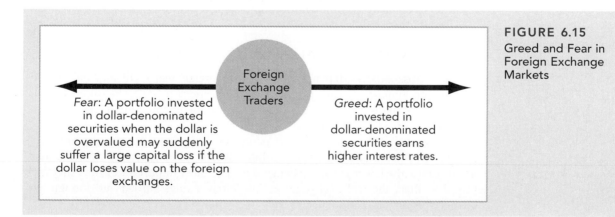

FIGURE 6.15
Greed and Fear in Foreign Exchange Markets

from the interest rate spread are wiped out by the capital loss caused by the exchange rate movement. If today's value of the exchange rate is different from long-run historical trends, the fear that exchange rates will return to their normal relationships and impose large foreign exchange losses will be immense.

The greater the difference in interest rates in favor of dollar-denominated securities, the higher is the greed factor. And the higher the greed factor, the lower must be the value of the exchange rate in order for fear to offset greed. The enormously liquid, enormously high-volume, enormously volatile foreign exchange markets settle at the point where greed and fear balance. Thus the real exchange rate ε is equal to the average foreign exchange trader's opinion ε_0 of what the exchange rate should be if there were no interest rate differentials minus a parameter ε_r times the interest rate differential between domestic real interest rates r and foreign real interest rates r^f:

$$\varepsilon = \varepsilon_0 - \varepsilon_r \times (r - r^f)$$

The longer that interest rate differentials are expected to continue, and the more slowly that real exchange rates are expected to revert to trend, the higher ε_r will be and the larger will be the effect of a given interest rate differential on the exchange rate.

Remember: The exchange rate is the value of foreign currency. If foreign currency becomes more valuable, the exchange rate rises; if domestic currency becomes more valuable, the exchange rate falls. Often you will hear people talk of an appreciation or revaluation of the dollar or of a depreciation or devaluation of the dollar. An *appreciation* or *revaluation* of the dollar is a reduction in the value of the exchange rate. A *depreciation* or *devaluation* of the dollar is an increase in the value of the exchange rate.

If we take the equation for net exports

$$NX = GX - IM = (X_f \times Y^f) + (X_\varepsilon \times \varepsilon) - (IM_y \times Y)$$

and substitute into it the equation for the value of the exchange rate, the result is the relatively unappetizing

$$NX = GX - IM = (X_f \times Y^f) + (X_\varepsilon \times \varepsilon_0) - (X_\varepsilon \times \varepsilon_r \times r) + (X_\varepsilon \times \varepsilon_r \times r^f) - (IM_y \times Y)$$

This equation is unappetizing because it is complex. It is nevertheless valuable because it contains a lot of information. It tells us directly how domestic and foreign interest rates affect net exports, without requiring that we go through the intermediate step of calculating the real exchange rate. This direct equation is sometimes valuable because removing the exchange rate means that (for the moment at least) we have one less thing to keep track of. Tweaking a model to rid it of complicating variables is a standard technique of economists.

RECAP   INTERNATIONAL TRADE

Gross exports depend positively on foreign real GDP and on the exchange rate. Imports depend positively on domestic real GDP. The difference between gross exports and imports is net exports, which is the fourth and last component of aggregate demand.

In turn, the exchange rate depends on a number of factors, the most important of which is the domestic real interest rate. The higher the domestic real interest rate, the lower is the exchange rate. The most important of the other factors that affect the real exchange rate are interest rates abroad and foreign exchange speculators' confidence.

6.4 CONCLUSION

Needless to say, the short-run flexible-price analysis begun in this chapter is not complete. The chapter has focused only on the building blocks of the analysis. What determines the division of real GDP between its four components is explained in Chapter 7. Moreover, recall that this chapter has presented only a short-run, snapshot view of the economy. It has not discussed the impact of changes in policy and in the economic environment on economic growth. That was done in Chapters 4 and 5 (refer to them to analyze how changes in investment spending ultimately affect productivity).

Moreover, this chapter has ignored the nominal financial side of the economy — money, prices, and inflation — entirely. That topic will be covered in Chapter 8.

Last, but not least, the flexible-price analysis of this part, Part III, is itself not a complete analysis of even the short-run real side of the economy. It needs to be supplemented by the analysis of what happens when prices are sticky. That analysis is carried out in Part IV.

Chapter Summary

1. This chapter has begun the analysis of a flexible-price, full-employment economy in the short run — a period short enough that potential output is fixed, but long enough for flexible wages and prices to bring supply and demand into balance and thus markets into equilibrium.

2. When the economy is at full employment, the level of real GDP is equal to potential output, which is the level of output generated by the production function of Chapter 4 from the current stocks of labor and capital and the current efficiency of labor.

3. When wages and prices are flexible, the working of the labor market keeps the economy at full employment. If labor demand is less than the size of the labor force, falling wages raise employment; if labor demand is greater than the size of the labor force, rising wages lower employment.

4. The level of consumption spending is determined by many things, but the most important of them are four: Real GDP (or national income) Y, the average tax rate t, the baseline level of consumption C_0, and household's marginal propensity to consume (MPC) C_y. National income and the tax rate together determine disposable income Y^D:

$$Y^D = (1 - t)Y$$

Disposable income, the baseline level of consumption, and the MPC together determine the level of consumption according to the consumption function:

$$C = C_0 + C_y \times Y^D$$

or

$$C = C_0 + C_y \times (1 - t)Y$$

5. The level of investment spending is primarily determined by two factors: Business managers' degree of optimism, which powerfully affects the baseline level of investment spending I_0, and the real interest rate r, for the higher is the real interest rate the lower is investment spending. The simple investment function is:

$$I = I_0 - I_r \times r$$

6. The stock market is a useful indicator of the future value of investment spending. Its value depends on the same factors — the degree of optimism about future profits and the real interest rate.

7. The exchange rate is determined by foreign exchange traders' view of the long-run equilibrium value of the exchange rate and the interest rate differential between investments at home and investments abroad.

8. Net exports are determined by the level of the exchange rate, the level of real GDP (which determines the level of imports), and the level of real GDP abroad (which affects the level of exports).

Key Terms

production function (p. 154)

labor market (p. 156)

marginal product of labor (MPL) (p. 156)

labor supply (p. 158)

labor market equilibrium (p. 158)

real wage (p. 159)

potential output (p. 160)

disposable income (p. 162)

consumption function (p. 163)

marginal propensity to consume (MPC) (p. 163)

real interest rate (p. 166)

investment function (p. 166)

government purchases (p. 169)

transfer payments (p. 169)

net taxes (p. 169)

imports (p. 170)

net exports (p. 170)

gross exports (p. 170)

Analytical Exercises

1. In the full-employment model, what determines the level of real GDP?

2. In the economy as a whole, what makes labor demand equal to the labor force?

3. What happens if the parameter C_0 in the consumption function rises?

4. What happens to net exports if foreign exchange speculators become more optimistic about the long-run real value of the domestic currency?

5. What happens to net exports if interest rates abroad rise?

Policy Exercises

1. Suppose an economy with the standard Cobb-Douglas production function

$$Y^* = K^\alpha (L\,E)^{1-\alpha}$$

has a diminishing-returns-to-scale parameter α equal to $1/3$, a value of the labor force L equal to 100 million workers, a value of the capital stock K equal to $40 trillion, and an efficiency of the labor force E equal to $50,000. What is the value of potential output Y^*? What is the value of potential output per worker Y^*/L? What is the market-clearing real wage (in dollars per year) at which the economy is at full employment, with neither unemployed workers nor excess demand for labor?

2. In an economy at full employment with an unchanging diminishing-returns-to-scale parameter α and output per worker growing at 3 percent per year, at what rate must the real wage be growing in order to maintain full employment?

3. What would you expect has happened to real investment in the United States over the past five years, given that the real value of the stock market has doubled during that time?

4. Over the past decade foreign exchange speculators have become much more confident in the long-run value of the dollar. What would you suspect has happened to net exports over the past decade?

5. Consumers whose stock market wealth has multiplied over the past decade have recently started pulling money out of the stock market to enhance their standard of living. What kind of shift in which parameter of the consumption function could be used to model this phenomenon?

A Closer Look at Consumption

6A

6A.1   PERMANENT AND TRANSITORY INCOME

One of the most important factors omitted from our consumption function is the distinction between permanent and transitory income. Your *permanent income* is the average level that you expect your level of income to be in the future. Your *transitory income* is the difference between your income now and your permanent income. Milton Friedman was the very first to point out that not this year's income but permanent income is likely to be the main determinant of consumption.

The Budget Constraint

Think of a consumer trying to decide how much to spend in two periods only — now and the future. Suppose that he or she can save (or borrow) in the present for the future at a real interest rate r. And suppose that the now and the future are not necessarily the same length of time: The future period is some parameter θ times the length of the present period. In the present the typical consumer decides how much to spend and how much to save. Income Y_{now}, consumption C_{now}, and saving S are linked by

$$S = Y_{now} - C_{now}$$

In the future, the consumer adds his or her future income to savings — which have in the meantime grown because they have earned real interest at rate r — and spends the total (you can't take it with you, after all!):

$$\theta \times C_{future} = \theta \times Y_{future} + (1 + r)S$$

Combining these two equations produces what economists call the *present value* form of the *consumer's budget constraint*:

$$C_{now} + [\theta C_{future}/(1 + r)] = Y_{now} + [\theta Y_{future}/(1 + r)]$$

Total consumption spending now and in the future must equal total income in the two periods. Future income and consumption count a little bit less — are

FIGURE 6A.1

The Budget Constraint
You can read off income in the present and the future from the circle showing the consumer's income in both periods. By borrowing and lending, the consumer is free to choose levels of consumption in the present and the future corresponding to any point along the budget-constraint line. The slope of the budget line corresponds to the real interest rate. The higher the real interest rate, the steeper is the line — the more you can boost consumption in the future by cutting back and saving today.

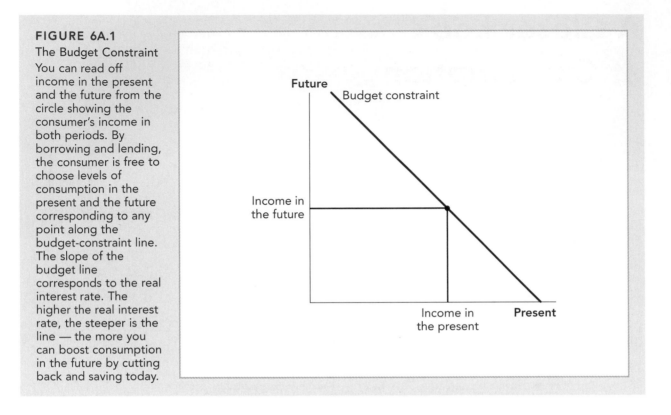

"discounted" by the real interest rate — in order to turn them into "present values" before adding them to current consumption. Because savings earn interest, you must put aside only $1/(1 + r)$ dollars today in order to be able to spend 1 dollar on consumption in the future. Hence 1 dollar of consumption — or income — in the future has a "present value" of only $1/(1 + r)$ dollars today.

We can show this budget constraint on a diagram that plots the present on the horizontal axis and the future on the vertical axis (see Figure 6A.1). By borrowing or saving the consumer can redistribute consumption across time.

The Marginal Utility of Consumption

A representative consumer modeled by an economist will try to arrange his or her consumption now and in the future to maximize his or her utility. And any representative consumer in a model built by an economist will have a very simple utility function to maximize, such as

$$U = C_{\text{now}}^{\gamma} \times C_{\text{future}}^{(1-\gamma)}$$

Where γ — the Greek letter "gamma" — is the parameter of the utility function. It governs how much the consumer values consumption now as opposed to consumption in the future.

If the marginal utility of per unit of time consumption (MUC) today is more than $(1 + r)/\theta$ times the MUC in the future, the consumer can increase his or her total utility a bit by cutting consumption in the future by an average of $(1 + r)/\theta$ dollars, reducing savings now by 1 dollar and increasing consumption now by 1 dollar. If the marginal utility of consumption today is less than $(1 + r)/\theta$ times the MUC in the future, the consumer can increase his or her total utility a bit by boosting consumption in the future by $(1 + r)/\theta$ dollars, increasing savings now by 1 dollar and cutting consumption now by 1 dollar. Thus if the consumer is behaving like a proper agent in an economist's model, it must be that

$$\frac{\text{MUC}_{\text{now}}}{\text{MUC}_{\text{future}}} = \frac{1 \times r}{\theta}$$

What is the marginal utility of consumption now? Just as with the marginal product of labor, it is the change in utility produced by adding 1 more unit of consumption now:

$$\text{MUC}_{\text{now}} = [(C_{\text{now}} \times 1)^{\gamma} \times C_{\text{future}}^{-\gamma}] - (C_{\text{now}} \times C_{\text{future}}^{1-\gamma})$$

which can be simplified to

$$\text{MUC}_{\text{now}} = [(C_{\text{now}} \times 1)^{\gamma} \times C_{\text{now}}] \times C_{\text{future}}^{1-\gamma}$$

Once again we can use our rule for the growth rate of a quantity raised to a power — in this case C_{now} growing at the proportional rate of $1/C_{\text{now}}$ — and thus evaluate the marginal utility of consumption. It is

$$\text{MUC}_{\text{now}} = \gamma \, (C_{\text{now}})^{\gamma-1} \times C_{\text{future}}^{1-\gamma}$$

Similarly, the marginal utility of consumption in the future is

$$\text{MUC}_{\text{future}} = (1 - \gamma \, (C_{\text{now}})^{\gamma} \times C_{\text{future}}^{-\gamma}$$

Thus if the consumer if behaving as expected,

$$\frac{1 + r}{\theta} = \frac{\gamma \, (C_{\text{now}})^{\gamma-1} \times C_{\text{future}}^{1-\gamma}}{(1 - \gamma)C_{\text{now}}^{\gamma} \times C_{\text{future}}^{-\gamma}} = \frac{\gamma C_{\text{future}}}{(1 - \gamma)C_{\text{now}}}$$

or

$$C_{\text{future}} = \frac{(1 + r) \times (1 - \gamma)}{\theta\gamma} \times C_{\text{now}}$$

This equation tells us that the consumer spends a fraction γ of the present value of his or her total income on current consumption:

$$C_{\text{now}} = \gamma \times \left(Y_{\text{now}} + \frac{\theta Y_{\text{future}}}{1 + r}\right)$$

He or she spends the rest on future consumption. Once again, there is nothing especially "deep" in this simple result. Economists use this particular utility function often because it produces simple results.

Note that using this equation, a \$1 increase in transitory income — in Y_{now} but not in Y_{future} — would lead to a γ dollar increase in consumption today. But a \$1 increase in permanent income — in both Y_{now} and Y_{future} — would generate an increase in consumption in the present of

$$\Delta C_{\text{now}} = \gamma \times \left(1 + \frac{\theta}{1 + r}\right)$$

Thus the marginal propensity to consume is much larger if a change in income is permanent than if it is transitory. When an increase is transitory, consumers tend to smooth out their consumption over time by saving the bulk of the windfall, as shown in Figures 6A.2 and 6A.3. If consumers do not believe a change in income will be permanent, they will not adjust their spending now by very much.

For example, in the late 1960s President Lyndon Johnson proposed and Congress passed the Vietnam War income surtax. The surtax, a 10 percent increase in federal taxes, was imposed in an attempt to reduce consumption spending and so reduce

FIGURE 6A.2
Consumption Smoothing
Consumers try to smooth consumption over time. If their income is unusually high in the present, they will spend little of the excess and save most of it.

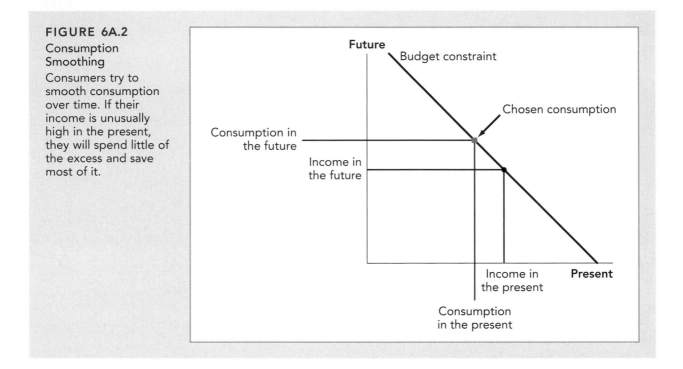

FIGURE 6A.3
The Effect of an Increase in Transitory Income
A change in transitory income — a change in income in the present but not the future — leads to a change in consumption in the present that is only a small fraction of the change in today's income.

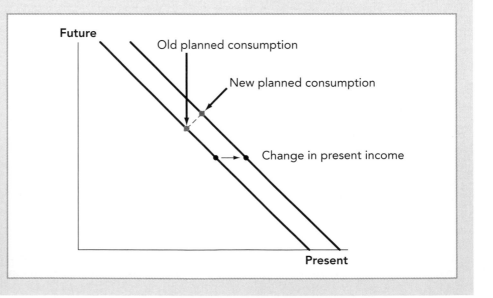

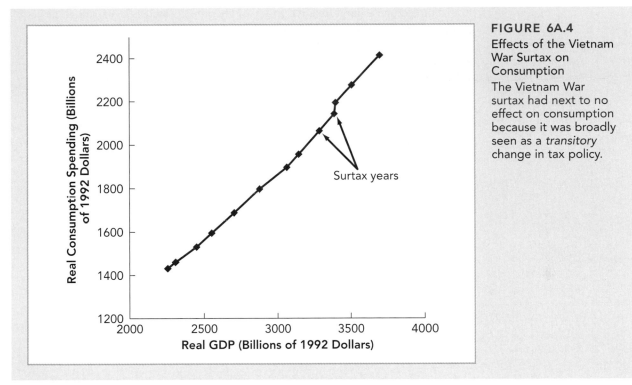

FIGURE 6A.4
Effects of the Vietnam War Surtax on Consumption
The Vietnam War surtax had next to no effect on consumption because it was broadly seen as a *transitory* change in tax policy.

Source: The 1999 edition of *Economic Report of the President* (Washington, DC: Government Printing Office).

inflationary pressures during the Vietnam War. But President Johnson sold the surtax to Congress (and to the public) by promising that it would be a short-term, temporary measure with no permanent effects. He was convincing. Because everyone believed that the tax increase was short-term and temporary, it had no effect on consumers' beliefs about their permanent income. Everyone saw it as a change in transitory income only. And so it had next to no effect on consumption spending, as you can see in Figure 6A.4.

6A.2 CONSUMPTION AND THE REAL INTEREST RATE

An increase in the real interest rate makes saving more profitable: It means a higher rate of return earned on wealth saved and invested. Consumer saving is equal to after-tax income minus consumption. Does this mean that consumption spending is powerfully affected by the real interest rate and that an increase in the real interest rate decreases consumption spending? Probably not. An increase in the real interest rate does increase the rate of return on savings, and this induces a consumer to *substitute* saving for consumption in the present. But return to the expression for consumption spending now — C_{now} — derived earlier in this appendix:

$$C_{now} = \gamma \times \left(Y_{now} + \frac{\theta Y_{future}}{1 + r} \right)$$

If current income is large relative to future income — as it is if we are thinking of people saving for their retirement — then a change in the real interest rate r has no effect on current consumption spending. Thus it has no effect on current saving — the difference between current income and current consumption.

Why not? Because an increase in saving doesn't just make it more attractive to substitute saving for consumption today. An increase in the real interest rate also increases consumers' total lifetime wealth: Their permanent income is boosted because they earn higher returns on the money that they do save. This higher *permanent income* increases consumption in the present — and so reduces current saving. Which effect dominates? Is the income effect stronger, or is the substitution effect stronger? For consumers with low future incomes, the two effects almost cancel out. For consumers with high future incomes, they do indeed save more. But consumers with high future incomes had little reason to save to begin with, so even a large proportional increase in their saving has little effect on total economywide saving.

As a result, most economists think that these two effects roughly balance each other. They believe that changes in real interest rates have a small negative effect on consumption spending and a small positive effect on savings. But the effect of the real interest rate on consumption spending is not large enough to be worth the extra complication it would add to our models here.

Present Value
and Investment

How should you decide whether an investment is worth making? Suppose that you are on the investment committee of a business and that brought before you is a proposal to make a $100 million investment this year that will pay off by creating $130 million worth of real inflation-adjusted value five years hence.

If the real interest rate is 5 percent and if you take the $100 million and invest it in the bond market, after one year you will have $100 × (1 + 5 percent) = $105 million. After two years, you will have $105 × (1 + 5 percent) = $110.25 million; after three years, $110.25 × (1 + 5 percent) = $115.76 million; and after five years, $127.63 million of real inflation-adjusted purchasing power. Thus you will make more money in risk-adjusted, inflation-adjusted expected-value terms by undertaking the investment project than by undertaking the next-best alternative, so the investment project is worthwhile.

If the real interest rate is 6 percent, however, the answer will be different. At 6 percent, after five years you will have $100 × (1.06)^5 = $133.8 million in inflation-adjusted purchasing power. The investment project will lose money compared to the next-best alternative, so it should not be undertaken.

Such comparisons are easier if you use an economists' concept called *present value*. The present value is the amount of wealth that you would have to set aside today and invest at the real interest rate to generate some particular amount of purchasing power in the future. If the real interest rate is 5 percent per year, to have $130 million of inflation-adjusted purchasing power in five years you would have to take $101.85 million today, put it aside, and let it compound in the bond market: $101.85 × (1.05)^5 = $130 million. Thus the *present value* of $130 million in five years at an interest rate of 5 percent is $101.85 million.

To calculate the present value $PV of a sum of inflation-adjusted purchasing power $SUM to be received *n* years in the future at an interest rate of *r* percent per year, you *discount* the future sum back to the present at the rate *r* using the formula

$$\$PV = \frac{\$SUM}{(1 + r)^n}$$

because $PV in the bond market at an interest rate of r for n years will compound to $SUM. (If whether or not the $SUM will actually be paid in the future is subject to more than the usual amount of risk found in the bond market, the present value will be lower: you can either risk-adjust the $SUM to a lower value or risk-adjust the discount rate r by adding a risk premium σ, and discounting at $r + \sigma$.)

With present value, the decisions of business investment committees become easier. One investment project will be a better use of resources than another only if the first has a higher present value than the second.

Most investment projects don't yield returns in the shape of a single, lump-sum payment n years into the future. Most yield a stream of profits each year for a prolonged period. Thus more useful than the formula for the present value of a $SUM n years in the future is the $STREAM formula for the present value of a stream of payments each year from now into the indefinite future:

$$\$PV = \frac{\$STREAM}{r}$$

Think of how much a flow of real purchasing power of $1 million per year each year into the indefinite future is worth. If you wanted to receive such an annual flow, how much would you have to put into the bond market today? $1/r$ million invested in the bond market yields an annual flow of real purchasing power of $1 million per year. Thus an investment project that you expect to yield a cash flow of $STREAM in real purchasing power per year each year has a present value of $STREAM/$r$.

You can see from these financial formulas how important the real interest rate is for determining whether investments are worthwhile or not. If an investment project promises a long-running stream of returns — as in the example above — a small change in the real interest rate can have an enormous impact on present value.

These topics are pursued further in finance courses, but not in intermediate macroeconomics.

Equilibrium in the Flexible-Price Model

CHAPTER 7

QUESTIONS

When wages and prices are flexible, what economic forces keep total production equal to aggregate demand?

Why does the flow of funds through financial markets have to balance?

What are the components of savings flowing into financial markets?

What is a comparative-statics analysis?

What are supply shocks?

What are real business cycles?

7.1 FULL-EMPLOYMENT EQUILIBRIUM

Equilibrium and the Real Interest Rate

The first section of Chapter 6 showed that, under the flexible-price full-employment classical assumptions, GDP and national income Y equal potential output Y^*:

$$Y = Y^*$$

The rest of Chapter 6 set out the determinants of each of the components of total spending. We saw that the exchange rate is a function of (a) the real interest rate differential between home and abroad and (b) foreign exchange traders' opinions:

$$\varepsilon = \varepsilon_0 - \varepsilon_r \times (r - r^f)$$

We saw the determinants of consumption spending:

$$C = C_0 + C_y \times (1 - t) \times Y$$

of investment spending:

$$I = I_0 - I_r \times r$$

and of net exports:

$$NX \ (X_f \times Y^f) + (X_\varepsilon \times \varepsilon_0) - (X_\varepsilon \times \varepsilon_r \times r) + (X_\varepsilon \times \varepsilon_r \times r^f) - (IM_y \times Y)$$

We left the determination of government purchases to the political scientists:

$$G = G$$

These four components add up to aggregate demand, or total expenditure, which we can write E if we want to emphasize that, conceptually, demand is not quite the same as real GDP Y. However, the circular flow principle guarantees that in equilibrium aggregate demand E will add up to real GDP Y:

$$C + I + G + NX = E = Y$$

But the determinants of each of the components of total spending E seem to have nothing at all to do with the production function that determines the level of real GDP Y. How does aggregate demand add up to potential output? Can we be sure that all the output businesses think they can sell when they hire more workers is in fact sold? The answer is that in the flexible-price full-employment classical model of this section, the real interest rate r plays the key balancing role in making sure that the economy reaches and stays at equilibrium.

If we look at all the determinants of all the components of total spending, we see that the components depend on four sets of factors:

- *Factors that are part of the domestic economic environment* (such as consumers' and investors' baseline spending C_0 and I_0 and government purchases G).
- *Factors that are determined abroad* (such as foreign real GDP Y^f and exchange speculators' view of the long-run "fundamental" value of the exchange rate ε_0).
- *The level of real GDP Y itself* (which is a determinant of consumption spending and imports).
- *The real interest rate.*

Of all these factors, only one — the real interest rate — is a price determined by supply and demand here at home. So if market forces are to cause the components of total spending to add up to real GDP, those market forces must work through the interest rate.

To understand what makes aggregate demand equal to potential output, we need to look at the market in which the interest rate functions as the price: the market for loanable funds. When you lend money, the interest rate is the price you charge and the price the borrower pays. Thus we need to look at the flow of loanable funds through the financial markets, the places where household savings and other inflows into financial markets are balanced by outflows to firms seeking capital to expand their productive capacity. The equilibrium we are looking for is one in which supply equals demand in the financial markets. According to the circular flow principle, if financial markets are in equilibrium, then the sum of all the components of spending is equal to real GDP.

The Flow of Funds through Financial Markets

The circular flow principle ensures that if supply equals demand in the flow of funds through **financial markets**, then aggregate supply (real GDP Y, equal to potential output Y^*) is equal to aggregate demand (the sum of all the components of total spending: $C + I + G + NX$). To see this, begin by assuming that real GDP is equal to potential output Y^* and that the circular flow principle holds — real GDP is equal to aggregate demand:

$$Y^* = Y = C + I + G + NX$$

Then rewrite this expression by moving everything except for investment spending I to the left-hand side:

$$Y^* - C - G - NX = I$$

Now include taxes T in the left-hand side by adding and subtracting it:

$$(Y^* - C - T) + (T - G) - NX = I$$

Note that the right-hand side is simply investment, the net flow of purchasing power out of the financial markets as firms raise money to build factories and structures and boost their productive capacity. The left-hand side is equal to **total savings**: the flow of purchasing power into financial markets as households, the government, and foreigners seek to save by committing their money to buy valuable financial assets here at home (see Figure 7.1). Thus we see that whenever the circular flow principle holds, the supply and demand in the flow of funds through financial markets balances as well. (Although, as Box 7.1 points out, the relationship is not direct.)

The $Y^* - C - T$ inside the first set of parentheses is private savings. Because national income is equal to potential output, Y^* is just total household income. Take income, subtract consumption spending, subtract taxes, and what is left is **private savings**: the flow of purchasing power from households into the financial markets.

The $T - G$ inside the second set of parentheses is **public savings**: the government's budget surplus (or government dissaving, the government's budget deficit, if G happens to be larger than T). It is the flow of funds from the government into the financial markets.

The last term — minus net exports, $-NX$ — is the **capital inflow**, the net flow of purchasing power that foreigners channel into domestic financial markets. As Figure 7.2 illustrates, minus net exports are the excess of dollars earned by foreigners selling imports into the home country over and above the amount of dollars foreigners

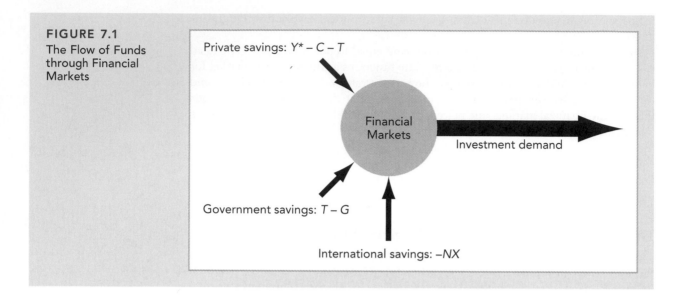

FIGURE 7.1
The Flow of Funds through Financial Markets

> **FINANCIAL TRANSACTIONS AND THE FLOW OF FUNDS: SOME DETAILS**
>
> Notice that the relationship between the flows of funds into and out of financial markets is indirect. When the government runs a surplus, the government does not directly lend money to a business that wants to build a new factory. Instead, it uses the surplus to buy back some of the bonds that it previously issued. The bank that owned those bonds then takes the cash and uses it to buy some other financial asset — perhaps bonds issued by a corporation. The chain of transactions within financial markets comes to an end only when some participant makes a loan to an investing company or buys a newly issued bond or stock and so transfers purchasing power to the company actually undertaking an investment.
>
> Similarly households or foreigners using financial markets to save rarely buy newly issued corporate bonds or shares of stock that are part of an initial public offering that transfer purchasing power directly to a company undertaking investment. Instead, they usually purchase already-existing securities or simply deposit their wealth in a bank. The relationship between the flows of funds into and out of financial markets is indirect, but it is very real.

BOX 7.1

need to buy our exports. If net exports are less than zero, foreigners have some dollars left over. They then have to do something with these extra dollars. Foreigners find dollars useful in only two ways: for buying our exports (but if net exports are less than zero, there aren't enough exports to soak up all the dollars they earn) and for buying property here — land, stocks, buildings, bonds. So this last term is the net flow of purchasing power into domestic financial markets by foreigners wishing to park some of their savings here. (When net exports are positive, this term is the net amount of domestic savings diverted into overseas financial markets).

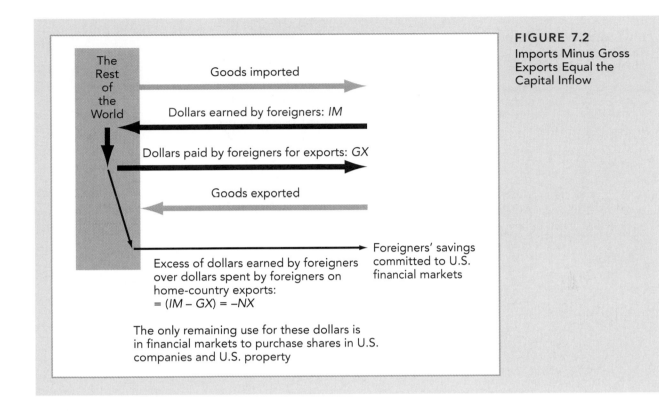

FIGURE 7.2
Imports Minus Gross Exports Equal the Capital Inflow

Flow-of-Funds Equilibrium

We have established that the three terms on the left-hand side of the equation

$$(Y^* - C - T) + (T - G) - NX = I$$

are the three flows of purchasing power into the financial markets: private savings, government savings, and international savings. Added together they make up the supply of loanable funds. The demand for loanable funds is simply investment spending. And the price of loanable funds is the real interest rate, as Figure 7.3 illustrates.

What happens if the flow of funds does not balance — if at the current long-term real interest rate r the flow of savings into the financial markets exceeds the demand by corporations and others for purchasing power to finance investments? If the left-hand side is greater than the right, some financial institutions — banks, mutual funds, venture capitalists, insurance companies, whatever — will find purchasing power piling up as more money flows into their accounts than they can find good securities and other investment vehicles to commit it to. They will try to underbid their competitors for the privilege of lending money or buying equity in some particular set of investment projects. How do they underbid? They underbid by saying that they will accept a lower interest rate than the market interest rate r. Thus if the flow of savings exceeds investment, the interest rate r falls. As r falls, the number and value of investment projects that firms and entrepreneurs find it worthwhile to undertake rises. (See Figure 7.4.)

FIGURE 7.3
Equilibrium in the Flow of Funds

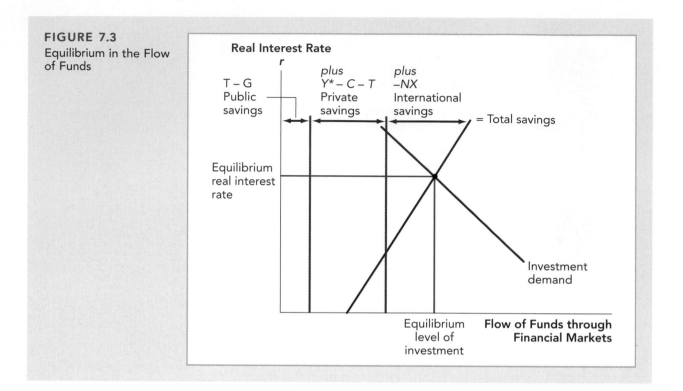

FIGURE 7.4
Excess Supply of Savings in the Flow of Funds

When the interest rate is such that there is an excess supply of savings, some savers will offer to accept a lower interest rate and the interest rate will drop.

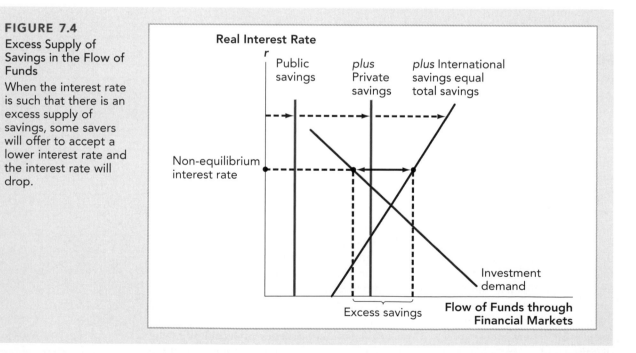

The process will stop when the interest rate r adjusts to bring about equilibrium in the loanable funds market. The flow of savings into the financial markets will then be just equal to the flow of purchasing power out of financial markets and into the hands of firms and entrepreneurs using it to finance investment.

Solving the Model

At what level of the real interest rate will the flow of funds through financial markets be in equilibrium? At what level will the real interest rate be stable? To determine the flow-of-funds equilibrium, look more closely at the supply of and demand for funds. First, let's look at the determinants of the supply of private savings:

$$Y^* - C - T = [1 - t - (1 - t)C_y]Y^* - C_0$$

Second, let's look at the determinants of public savings:

$$T - G = tY^* - \overline{G}$$

Third, let's look at the determinants of international savings:

$$-NX = IM_y Y + X_\varepsilon \varepsilon_r r - X_f Y^f - X_\varepsilon \varepsilon_0 - X_\varepsilon \varepsilon_r r^f$$

These three added together make up the flow-of-funds supply of savings. Note that in Figures 7.3 and 7.4 the supply of savings is upward-sloping: When the interest rate r rises, the total savings flow increases. An increase in the real interest rate attracts foreign capital into domestic financial markets.

The flow-of-funds demand is simply the investment function:

$$I = I_0 - I_r r$$

Equilibrium is, of course, where the supply and demand curves cross — where the supply of savings is equal to investment demand. What is the equilibrium interest rate? It is the level at which the supply of savings is equal to investment demand. To get an explicit expression for the interest rate, begin by writing out the determinants of all the pieces of savings:

$$\{[1 - t - (1 - t)C_y]Y^* - C_0\} + (tY^* - \overline{G}) + (IM_y Y + X_\varepsilon \varepsilon_r r - X_f Y^f - X_\varepsilon \varepsilon_0 - X_\varepsilon \varepsilon_r r^f) = I_0 - I_r r$$

Group all the terms that depend on Y^* on the left of the left-hand side, all the terms that are constant in the middle of the left-hand side, and all the terms that depend on international factors on the right of the left-hand side, and move all the terms with the real interest rate r over to the right-hand side:

$$\{1 - [(1 - t)C_y - IM_y]\}Y^* - (C_0 + I_0 + \overline{G}) - (X_f Y^f + X_\varepsilon \varepsilon_0 + X_\varepsilon \varepsilon_r r^f) = -(I_r + X_\varepsilon \varepsilon_r)r$$

And divide by $-(I_r + X_\varepsilon \varepsilon_r)$ to determine the equilibrium real interest rate r:

$$r = \frac{(C_0 + I_0 + \overline{G}) - (X_f Y^f + X_\varepsilon \varepsilon_0 + X_\varepsilon \varepsilon_r r^f) - \{1 - [(1 - t)C_y - IM_y]\}Y^*}{I_r + X_\varepsilon \varepsilon_r}$$

Box 7.2 shows how to use this equation to find the equilibrium real interest rate given values for the parameters of this flexible-price model of the macroeconomy.

SOLVING FOR AND VERIFYING THE EQUILIBRIUM REAL INTEREST RATE: AN EXAMPLE

Given the parameters of the flexible-price model and the value of potential GDP, it is straightforward to calculate the equilibrium real interest rate r by substituting the parameters into the formula

$$r = \frac{(C_0 + I_0 + \overline{G}) + (X_f Y^f + X_\varepsilon \varepsilon_0 + X_\varepsilon \varepsilon_r r^f) - \{1 - [(1 - t)C_y - IM_y]\}Y^*}{I_r + X_\varepsilon \varepsilon_r}$$

For example, when parameter values are:

Potential output $Y^* = \$10{,}000$ billion

Baseline consumption $C_0 = \$3{,}000$ billion

Baseline investment $I_0 = \$1{,}000$ billion

Government purchases $G = \$2{,}000$ billion

Tax rate $t = 25$ percent

MPC $C_y = 0.67$

Propensity to import $IM_y = 0.2$

Abroad, $X_f = 0.1$ and $Y^f = \$10{,}000$ billion

Foreign exchange speculators' long-run view $\varepsilon_0 = 100$

Sensitivity of exports to the exchange rate $X_\varepsilon = 10$

Sensitivity of investment to the interest rate $I_r = 9{,}000$

Sensitivity of the exchange rate to the interest rate $\varepsilon_r = 600$

Then replacing each of the parameters with its value produces

$$r = \frac{(3{,}000 + 1{,}000 + 2{,}000) + (0.1 \times 10{,}000 + 10 \times 100) - \{1 - [(1 - 0.25) \times 0.67 - 0.2]\} \times 10{,}000}{9{,}000 + 600 \times 10}$$

$$= \frac{6{,}000 + 2{,}000 - 0.7 \times 10{,}000}{15{,}000}$$

$$= \frac{1{,}000}{15{,}000} = 0.0667$$

Thus we have an equilibrium real interest rate of 6.67 percent per year.

Is the economy in fact in equilibrium when the real interest rate is 6.67 percent per year? Yes. At that level of the interest rate:

- Private savings equal –\$500 billion (yes, they are less than zero — households are drawing down their wealth in order to finance high current consumption), as you can see by substituting the parameters into the equation that determines private saving.

$$Y^* - C - T = [1 - t - (1 - t)C_y]Y^* - C_0$$

- Government savings equal \$500 billion, as you can see by subtracting government purchases from taxes.

- The capital inflow from abroad — minus net exports — equals \$400 billion, as you can see by substituting the parameter values and a real interest rate of 6.67 percent into the equation:

$$-NX = IM_y Y + X_\varepsilon \varepsilon_r r - X_f Y^f - X_\varepsilon \varepsilon_0 - X_\varepsilon \varepsilon_r r^f$$

that determines minus net exports.

- These three components of saving add up to \$400 billion.

- Investment is equal to \$400 billion.

Thus the flow of funds through financial markets balances.

Looking at the components of real GDP:

- Consumption spending equals \$8,000 billion.

- Investment spending equals \$400 billion.

- Government purchases equal \$2,000 billion.

- Net exports equal –$400 billion.
- All these add up to $10,000 billion: the level of potential output

Total spending — aggregate demand — is indeed equal to real GDP.

RECAP   FULL-EMPLOYMENT EQUILIBRIUM

    In the flexible-price model real GDP is equal to potential output. But real GDP is also equal to aggregate demand, the sum of consumption, investment, government purchases, and net exports. The determinants of aggregate demand seem to have nothing to do with potential output. What makes aggregate demand add up to the economy's productive potential? The key is that in the flexible-price model the real interest rate is the price that adjusts in order to keep real GDP equal to aggregate demand and potential output. The real interest rate is the price that equilibrates the market for loanable funds — the place where savings flow into and investment financing flows out of financial markets.

7.2 USING THE MODEL

Comparative Statics as a Method of Analysis

The flexible-price full-employment model we have built gives us the capability to determine the level and composition of real GDP and national income. If we know the economic environment and economic policy, we can use the model to determine the equilibrium real interest rate, either by solving the algebraic equations or by drawing the flow-of-funds diagram and looking for the point where supply balances demand, or by doing both. We can then calculate the equilibrium values of a large number of economic variables — real GDP, consumption spending and investment spending, imports and exports, the real exchange rate, and more. In fact, three of the six key economic variables — real GDP, the exchange rate, and the real interest rate — come directly from the model. (We will see how to calculate the price level and the inflation rate in Chapter 8.) In a flexible-price model like this one the unemployment rate is not interesting, for the economy is always at full employment. And we have seen that the stock market is proportional to and a leading indicator of investment spending.

    However, the model so far gives us the capability to calculate not just the current equilibrium position of the economy but also how that equilibrium will change in response to changes in the economic environment or in economic policy. To do so, we use a method of analysis economists call **comparative statics**. We determine the response of the economy to some particular shift in the environment or policy in three steps. We first look at the initial equilibrium position of the economy without the shift. We then look at the equilibrium position of the economy with the shift. We then identify the difference in the two equilibrium positions as the change in the economy in response to the shift.

    Let's see how the model can be used to analyze the consequences of three disturbances to the economy: (a) changes in fiscal policy, in the government's tax and spending plans, (b) changes in investors' relative optimism, and (c) changes in the international economic environment.

Changes in Fiscal Policy

Suppose the economy is in equilibrium when policy makers decide to increase annual government purchases by the amount ΔG. (As before, Δ, the Greek capital letter *delta,* stands for "change.") Let's look at what happens to the components of aggregate demand one by one.

The change in government purchases has no effect on consumption. Because potential output does not change, national income does not change. Neither national income, baseline consumption, the tax rate, nor the marginal propensity to consume shifts, so there is no effect on the consumption function

$$C = C_0 + C_y(1 - t)Y$$

Thus

$$\Delta C = 0$$

While the shift in government purchases has no *direct* effect on investment, there will be an indirect effect. Investment depends on the interest rate, and the interest rate will change as a result of the change in government purchases. So from the investment function

$$I = I_0 - I_r r$$

we can conclude that the level of investment spending will change by

$$\Delta I = - I_r \Delta r$$

That is, the shift in investment spending will be equal to the sensitivity of investment to the interest rate times the shift in the equilibrium real interest rate.

Nothing in the international economic environment changes. Nor does the level of potential output change. So looking at the net exports function,

$$NX = X_f Y^f + X_\varepsilon \varepsilon_0 - X_\varepsilon \varepsilon_r r + X_\varepsilon \varepsilon_r r^f - IM_y Y$$

it is clear that here, as well, the only shift will be a proportional change in response to the shift in the equilibrium real interest rate:

$$\Delta NX = - (X_\varepsilon \varepsilon_r \Delta r)$$

Finally, real GDP Y does not change because potential output does not change, and this is a full-employment model with real GDP always equal to potential output:

$$\Delta Y = \Delta Y^* = 0$$

Putting all these pieces together, we have assembled the relevant components of aggregate demand in "change" form. We can see that as government purchases shift, the other components of aggregate demand will have to shift with it:

$$\Delta Y = \Delta I + \Delta G + \Delta NX$$

$$0 = -I_r \Delta r + \Delta G - X_\varepsilon \varepsilon_r \Delta r$$

By putting the change in the real interest rate on the left-hand side of the equation and everything else on the right, we discover that the shift in government purchases means that the equilibrium real interest rate must change by

$$\Delta r = \frac{\Delta G}{I_r + X_\varepsilon \varepsilon_r}$$

To understand this answer, look at the flow-of-funds diagram in Figure 7.5. More government purchases mean less government savings. This shortfall in savings creates a gap between investment demand and savings supply: The interest rate rises. The rising interest rate lowers the quantity of funds demanded for investment financing and increases international savings flowing into domestic financial markets. The flow-of-funds market settles down to equilibrium at a new, higher equilibrium interest rate r with a new, lower level of investment. On the flow-of-funds diagram, the increase in government purchases and the consequent reduction in government savings have shifted the flow-of-funds supply curve to the left. The equilibrium position in the diagram has moved up and to the left along the investment curve.

Once the change in the equilibrium interest rate has been calculated, determining what happens to the rest of the economy is straightforward. Simply substitute the change in the equilibrium interest rate into the model's behavioral relationships and calculate the changes in the equilibrium levels of the components of GDP and in the equilibrium level of the real exchange rate. There is no effect on the level of real GDP Y or on consumption spending C:

$$\Delta Y = 0$$
$$\Delta C = 0$$

The change in government purchases G is equal to itself. This change was the trigger that shifted the economy's equilibrium position:

$$\Delta G = \Delta G$$

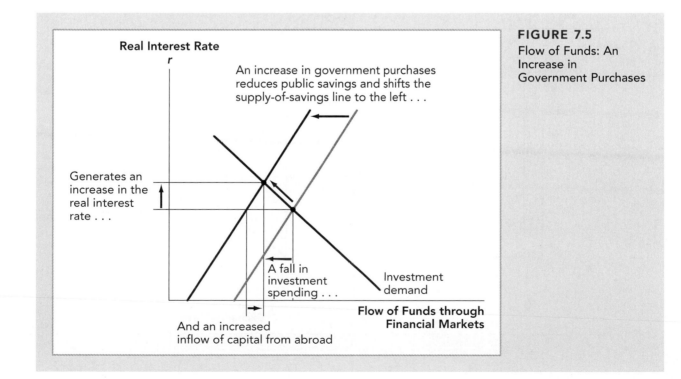

FIGURE 7.5
Flow of Funds: An Increase in Government Purchases

The change in investment spending is the interest sensitivity of investment I_r times the change in the equilibrium real interest rate, which we already calculated above:

$$\Delta I = -I_r \times \Delta r = \frac{-I_r}{I_r + X_\varepsilon \varepsilon_r} \Delta G$$

The changes in net exports and in the exchange rate are also equal to their sensitivities to the real interest rate times the change in the equilibrium real interest rate:

FIGURE 7.6
The Interest Rate, the Exchange Rate, and the Capital Inflow

Why does a rise in the domestic interest rate increase the flow of savings into the loanable funds market? Start in the upper left panel of the figure, where the total savings and investment demand curves cross to determine the equilibrium level of investment spending and the real interest rate. That real interest rate then helps determine the real exchange rate, as shown in the upper right panel: The higher the real interest rate, the lower is the real exchange rate. That real exchange rate then helps determine net exports, as shown in the lower right panel. And the value of net exports is the inverse of international savings, the capital inflow into the flow of funds. Thus the total savings curve slopes upward: The higher the interest rate, the lower the exchange rate, and the lower net exports, the more international savings flow into domestic financial markets.

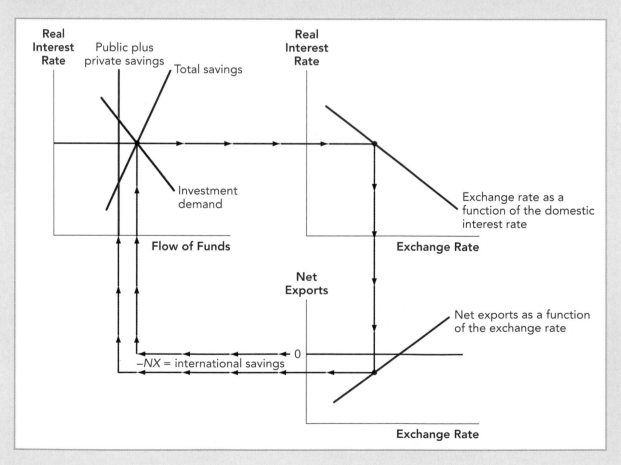

$$\Delta NX = \frac{-X_\varepsilon \varepsilon_r}{I_r + X_\varepsilon \varepsilon_r} \Delta G$$

$$\Delta \varepsilon = \frac{-X_\varepsilon}{I_r + X_\varepsilon \varepsilon_r} \Delta G$$

The overall picture of the changes generated by the increase in government purchases is clear. The increase in government purchases has led to a shortfall in savings and a rise in real interest rates. The higher real interest rates have led to lower investment and to an appreciation in the home currency: a lower level of ε. This exchange rate appreciation has led to a decline in net exports. The declines in net exports and in investment spending just add up to the increase in government purchases, so the level of GDP is unchanged and still equal to potential output — as we assumed it would be.

Note that the fall in investment is not as large as the rise in government purchases. The increase in government purchases reduced the flow of domestic savings into financial markets, but the increased flow of foreign-owned capital into the market partially offset this reduction. The extra savings from abroad kept the decline in investment from being as large as the rise in government purchases, as Figure 7.6 shows. Box 7.3 provides a numerical example of this process at work.

A GOVERNMENT PURCHASES BOOM: AN EXAMPLE

BOX 7.3

Assume that the parameters of the model are:

$t = 0.33$	Tax rate of one-third of income.
$I_r = 9{,}000$	A 1-percentage-point fall in the interest rate raises investment spending by \$90 billion a year.
$C_y = 0.75$	A marginal propensity to consume of three-quarters.
$\varepsilon_r = 10$	With an initial value for the real exchange rate ε set at the traditional indexed value of 100, a 1 percentage point change in the interest rate difference vis-à-vis abroad generates a 10 percent shift in the exchange rate.
$X_\varepsilon = 600$	A 1 percent change in the exchange rate leads to a \$6 billion–a-year change in exports.

Suppose that there is a sudden increase in government purchases of \$150 billion a year. This boom in spending increases the equilibrium real interest rate by 1 percentage point:

$$\Delta r = \frac{\Delta G}{I_r + X_\varepsilon \varepsilon_r} = \frac{\$150}{9{,}000 + 600 + 10} = \frac{150}{15{,}000} = 0.01 = 1\%$$

As a result, the equilibrium values of the other variables in the economy will change by

$$\Delta G = \Delta G = +\$150 \text{ billion}$$

$$\Delta I = \frac{-I_r}{I_r + X_\varepsilon \varepsilon_r} \Delta G = \frac{-9{,}000}{9{,}000 + 600 \times 10} \$150 = -\$90 \text{ billion}$$

$$\Delta C = 0$$

$$\Delta NX = \frac{-X_\varepsilon \varepsilon_r}{I_r + X_\varepsilon \varepsilon_r} \Delta G = \frac{-(600 \times 10)}{9{,}000 + 600 \times 10} \$150 = -\$60 \text{ billion}$$

$$\Delta \varepsilon = \frac{-\varepsilon_r}{I_r + X_\varepsilon \varepsilon_r} \Delta G = \frac{-10}{9{,}000 + 600 \times 10} \$150 = -0.1 = -10\% \text{ change}$$

FIGURE 7.7
Flow-of-Funds: A $150 Billion Increase in Government Purchases

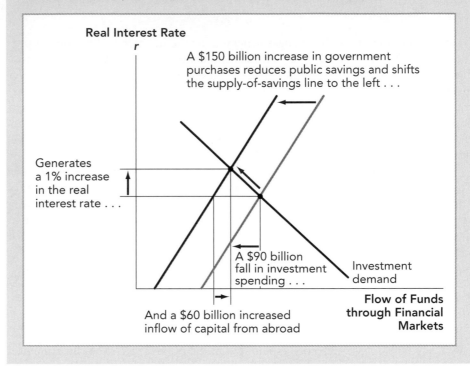

In sum, the $150 billion increase in annual government purchases shifts the economy's equilibrium by raising the real interest rates by 1 percent. Such an increase in the real interest rate carries with it a 10 percent fall in the exchange rate. The interest rate increase reduces investment spending by $90 billion a year. The exchange rate decline reduces net exports by $60 billion a year.

Some additional insight into this example can be gained by looking at the flow-of-funds diagram in Figure 7.7. The increase in government spending shifts the supply-of-loanable-funds curve to the left by $150 billion. Given the slopes of the loanable funds supply and the investment demand curves, the result of this leftward shift is a $90 billion fall in annual investment — and a 1-percentage-point rise in the real interest rate.

Given this 1-percentage-point rise in the real interest rate, it is straightforward to determine the resulting change in the exchange rate, as shown in Figure 7.8, and thus the change in net exports.

What if this model economy had experienced a change not in government spending but in tax rates? A hint: The effects of a cut in tax rates are very similar but not quite identical to an increase in government spending. A tax cut increases household incomes, and households then divide their increased disposable incomes, spending some of the increase on consumption and saving the rest.

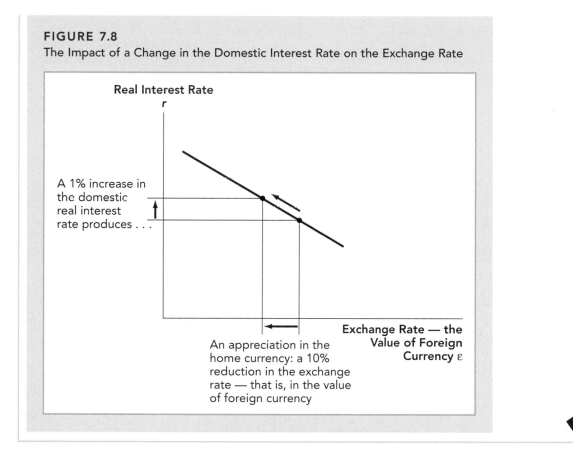

FIGURE 7.8
The Impact of a Change in the Domestic Interest Rate on the Exchange Rate

Investment Shocks: Changes in Investors' Optimism

Suppose the economy is in equilibrium, when domestic businesses become more optimistic about the future and increase the amount they wish to spend on new plant and equipment. What would be the effect of this shift on the economy? It would produce a domestic investment boom — a rise ΔI_0 in the value of I_0 in the investment equation:

$$I = I_0 - I_r r$$

While the increased optimism of investors increases investment, it is going to be associated with an increase in interest rates, so total investment spending will increase by an amount less than the rise in I_0:

$$\Delta I = \Delta I_0 - I_r \times \Delta r$$

The increase in the domestic interest rate will change the exchange rate and net exports, but the other variables in the model will be unaffected. Government spending and consumption spending are unchanged; foreign income, foreign interest rates, and foreign exchange traders' long-run expectations are unchanged.

Thus the changes in the national income identity are straightforward:

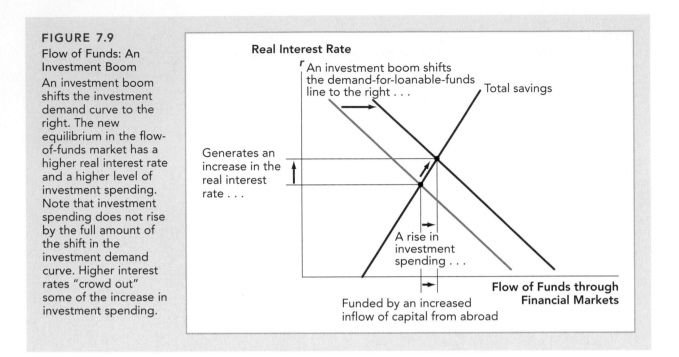

FIGURE 7.9

Flow of Funds: An Investment Boom

An investment boom shifts the investment demand curve to the right. The new equilibrium in the flow-of-funds market has a higher real interest rate and a higher level of investment spending. Note that investment spending does not rise by the full amount of the shift in the investment demand curve. Higher interest rates "crowd out" some of the increase in investment spending.

$$\Delta I + \Delta NX = 0$$
$$(\Delta I_0 - I_r \times \Delta r) + (-X_\varepsilon \varepsilon_r \times \Delta r) = 0$$

For this to be true, the change in the equilibrium real interest rate must be

$$\Delta r = \frac{\Delta I_0}{I_r + X_\varepsilon \varepsilon_r}$$

As Figure 7.9 shows, the investment boom has shifted the demand-for-loanable-funds curve to the right and increased the equilibrium real interest rate. The increased equilibrium interest rate leads to no change in consumption spending or in government purchases; it leads to a fall in the exchange rate and in net exports, as Figure 7.10 shows. Nevertheless investment spending rises:

$$\Delta C = 0$$
$$\Delta G = 0$$
$$\Delta \varepsilon = \frac{-\varepsilon_r \Delta I_0}{I_r + X_\varepsilon \varepsilon_r}$$
$$\Delta NX = \frac{-X_\varepsilon \varepsilon_r \Delta I_0}{I_r + X_\varepsilon \varepsilon_r}$$
$$\Delta I = \Delta I_0 - I_r \times \frac{\Delta I_0}{I_r + X_\varepsilon \varepsilon_r} = \frac{X_\varepsilon \varepsilon_r \Delta I_0}{I_r + X_\varepsilon \varepsilon_r}$$

International Disturbances

An Increase in Foreign Interest Rates

Now consider a disturbance from abroad: an upward jump in the foreign real interest rate r^f by an amount Δr^f. This increase has an immediate impact on the exchange rate, changing it by

FIGURE 7.10

The International Consequences of an Investment Boom

A change in business managers' optimism that shifts the investment demand curve to the right triggers a rise in the real interest rate, a fall in the exchange rate, a fall in net exports, and in increase in foreigners' funding of domestic investment. Thus the higher domestic interest rate pulls foreign funds into the country to finance higher desired domestic investment.

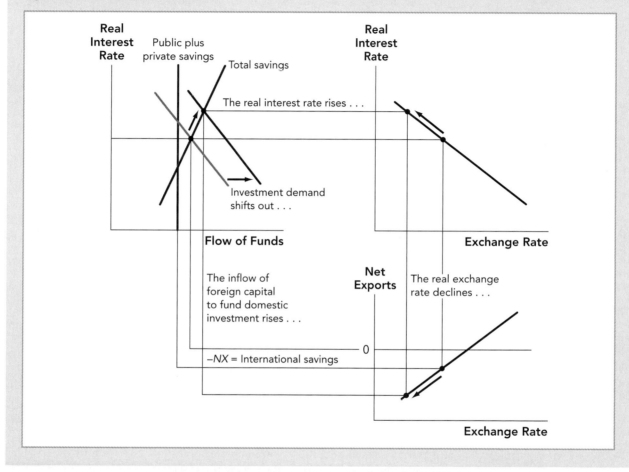

$$\Delta\varepsilon = -\varepsilon_r(\Delta r - \Delta r^t)$$

As a result, net exports shift by

$$\Delta NX = -X_\varepsilon\varepsilon_r(\Delta r - \Delta r^t)$$

As net exports rise, the inflow of foreign funds to finance domestic investment falls. The supply of savings in the flow-of-funds diagram shifts to the left, and the domestic interest rate rises.

Consumption spending and government purchases will not be affected by the rise in overseas interest rates, the fall in the exchange rate, and the rise in the domestic interest rate that it triggers. Nothing has happened to affect any of the determinants of consumption spending or government purchases. Investment spending, however, will be affected by the shift in the equilibrium domestic interest rate. As the economy responds to this shift, the changes in the national income identity will be

$$\Delta I + \Delta NX = 0$$

$$-I_r \Delta r - X_\varepsilon \varepsilon_r (\Delta r - \Delta r^f) = 0$$

Therefore the shift in the equilibrium domestic real interest rate r is

$$\Delta r = \frac{X_\varepsilon \varepsilon_r \Delta r^f}{I_r + X_\varepsilon \varepsilon_r}$$

From this change in the domestic interest rate and the value Δr^f for the change in the foreign interest rate, we can calculate the shifts in the equilibrium values of the components of GDP and in the equilibrium real exchange rate. As we have seen, there are no changes in consumption spending or government purchases:

$$\Delta C = 0$$
$$\Delta G = 0$$

Investment will fall by the sensitivity of investment spending to the interest rate times the change in the equilibrium real interest rate:

$$\Delta I = -I_r \times \frac{X_\varepsilon \varepsilon_r \Delta r^f}{I_r + X_\varepsilon \varepsilon_r}$$

The shift in the exchange rate will be proportional to the difference between the shifts in the domestic and the foreign interest rates; the shift in net exports will be proportional to the shift in the exchange rate:

$$\Delta \varepsilon = \frac{-\varepsilon_r}{I_r + X_\varepsilon \varepsilon_r} X_\varepsilon \varepsilon_r \Delta r^f + \varepsilon_r \Delta r^f = \frac{I_r \varepsilon_r \Delta r^f}{I_r + X_\varepsilon \varepsilon_r}$$

$$\Delta NX = \frac{-X_\varepsilon \varepsilon_r}{I_r + X_\varepsilon \varepsilon_r} X_\varepsilon \varepsilon_r \Delta_r^f + X_\varepsilon \varepsilon_r \Delta r^f = \frac{I_r X_\varepsilon \varepsilon_r \Delta r^f}{I_r + X_\varepsilon \varepsilon_r}$$

Again, the quickest way to understand the shift in the economy's equilibrium is to use the flow-of-funds diagram. The rise in the foreign interest rate reduces the amount of capital that foreigners want to devote to domestic investments. It shifts the flow-of-funds supply curve to the left, as Figure 7.11 shows. As a result, the economy's equilibrium moves up and to the left along the investment demand curve. The new equilibrium has a higher domestic interest rate and a lower value for investment.

GDP remains equal to potential output. The domestic interest rate rises less than the change in the foreign interest rate, raising the real exchange rate as shown in Figure 7.12. Thus the economy's level of net exports grows by as much as the level of domestic investment shrinks.

A Decline in Confidence in the Currency

Suppose the economy is in equilibrium when there is a change in foreign exchange speculators' confidence in the currency and thus in the long-run value of the exchange rate ε_0. What will happen? The shift in the exchange rate will be

$$\Delta \varepsilon = \Delta \varepsilon_0 - \varepsilon_r \Delta r$$

because the exchange rate is affected not just by foreign exchange speculators' beliefs but also by the domestic real interest rate, and the domestic interest rate will change because the change in the exchange rate will alter the flow of funds through financial markets. The change in net exports, and thus in the inflow of capital, will be proportional to the change in the exchange rate:

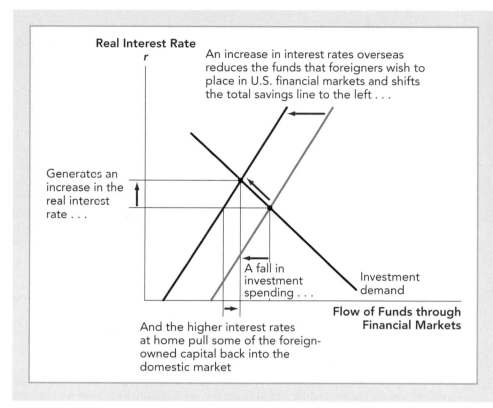

Real Interest Rate
r

An increase in interest rates overseas reduces the funds that foreigners wish to place in U.S. financial markets and shifts the total savings line to the left . . .

Generates an increase in the real interest rate . . .

A fall in investment spending . . .

Investment demand

Flow of Funds through Financial Markets

And the higher interest rates at home pull some of the foreign-owned capital back into the domestic market

FIGURE 7.11
Flow of Funds: An Increase in Interest Rates Abroad
A rise in foreign interest rates diminishes foreigners' willingness to finance domestic investment and shifts the flow-of-funds savings supply curve to the left. The economy's equilibrium moves up and to the left along the investment demand curve. The new equilibrium has a higher real interest rate and lower investment spending.

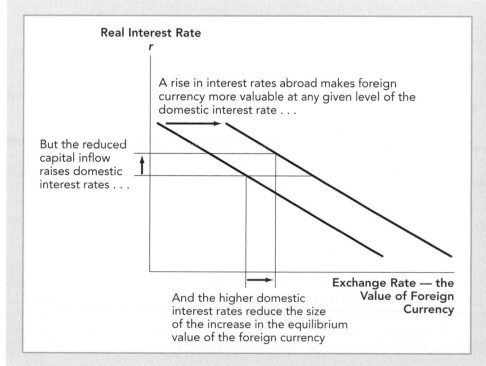

Real Interest Rate
r

A rise in interest rates abroad makes foreign currency more valuable at any given level of the domestic interest rate . . .

But the reduced capital inflow raises domestic interest rates . . .

Exchange Rate — the Value of Foreign Currency

And the higher domestic interest rates reduce the size of the increase in the equilibrium value of the foreign currency

FIGURE 7.12
The Real Exchange Rate and Domestic Interest Rates
A rise in foreign real interest rates raises the value of the exchange rate, but not by as much as one would expect from the change in foreign interest rates alone. Domestic interest rates rise as well and partially offset the effect of changing foreign interest rates on the exchange rate.

$$\Delta NX = X_\varepsilon \Delta\varepsilon_0 - X_\varepsilon \varepsilon_r \Delta r$$

The changing domestic interest rate will shift the level of domestic investment spending as well. Thus the relevant changes in the national income identity are

$$\Delta I + \Delta NX = 0$$

$$-I_r \Delta r + (X_\varepsilon \Delta\varepsilon_0 - X_\varepsilon \varepsilon_r \Delta r) = 0$$

This means that the change in the equilibrium domestic interest rate r is

$$\Delta r = \frac{X_\varepsilon \Delta\varepsilon_0}{I_r + X_\varepsilon \varepsilon_r}$$

Using this formula, we can calculate the shift in the equilibrium value of the components of real GDP and the shift in the value of the exchange rate. Once again, consumption spending and government purchases are unchanged:

$$\Delta C = 0$$
$$\Delta G = 0$$

The change in investment spending is equal to the interest sensitivity of investment spending times the change in the real interest rate:

$$\Delta I = \frac{-I_r}{I_r + X_\varepsilon \varepsilon_r} X_\varepsilon \Delta\varepsilon_0$$

The shift in the real exchange rate is generated both by the shift in foreign exchange speculators' expectations and by the shift in the equilibrium real interest rate; the shift in net exports is proportional to the shift in the real exchange rate:

$$\Delta\varepsilon = \frac{-\varepsilon_r}{I_r + X_\varepsilon \varepsilon_r} X_\varepsilon \Delta\varepsilon_0 + \Delta\varepsilon_0 = \frac{I_r \Delta\varepsilon_0}{I_r + X_\varepsilon \varepsilon_r}$$

$$\Delta NX = \frac{-X_\varepsilon \varepsilon_r}{I_r + X_\varepsilon \varepsilon_r} X_\varepsilon \Delta\varepsilon_0 + X_\varepsilon \Delta\varepsilon_0 = \frac{I_r X_\varepsilon \Delta\varepsilon_0}{I_r + X_\varepsilon \varepsilon_r}$$

Why does a decrease in foreign exchange speculators' long-run confidence — for an increase in ε_0 is a belief that the long-run value of the currency will be lower — have these effects? The shift in confidence means that at current exchange and interest rates, foreign exchange speculators wish to pull their money out of the home currency; they are not happy using their money to finance domestic investment. Thus on the flow-of-funds diagram in Figure 7.13 the savings supply curve shifts to the left. Once again, the equilibrium point moves up and to the left along the investment demand curve. Once again, the economy comes to rest at a point with a higher domestic interest rate and a lower value for investment. The equilibrium value of the exchange rate is higher, and so is the value of net exports. Box 7.4 provides a numerical example of this process.

The four cases we have analyzed here are not exhaustive. There are many other changes in the economic environment or in economic policy that the flexible-price model is useful for analyzing. Think of these four as examples of how to proceed: identify the components of real GDP that are going to change, determine the change in the equilibrium real interest rate, and then use the change in that rate and the triggering shift in the economic environment to calculate the postchange state of the economy.

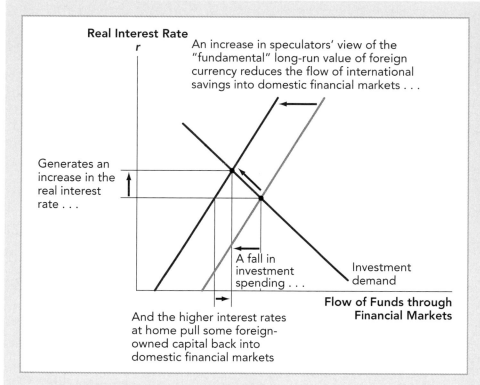

Real Interest Rate

r

An increase in speculators' view of the "fundamental" long-run value of foreign currency reduces the flow of international savings into domestic financial markets . . .

Generates an increase in the real interest rate . . .

A fall in investment spending . . .

Investment demand

Flow of Funds through Financial Markets

And the higher interest rates at home pull some foreign-owned capital back into domestic financial markets

FIGURE 7.13

Flow of Funds: A Decline in Exchange Rate Confidence

If foreign exchange traders lose confidence in the long-run value of the domestic currency, the effects on the domestic economy are very similar to the effects of a rise in foreign interest rates: The value of the exchange rate rises, and the savings supply curve shifts to the left.

THE EFFECT OF A FALL IN CONFIDENCE IN THE CURRENCY: AN EXAMPLE

BOX

7.4

Suppose the parameters describing the economy are the ones used in Box 7.3:

$t = 0.33$	Tax rate of one-third.
$I_r = 9,000$	A 1-percentage-point fall in the interest rate raises investment spending by $90 billion a year.
$C_y = 0.75$	A marginal propensity to consume of three-quarters.
$\varepsilon_r = 10$	With an initial value for the real exchange rate ε set at the traditional indexed value of 100, a 1-percentage-point change in the interest rate difference vis-à-vis abroad generates a 10 percent shift in the exchange rate.
$X_\varepsilon = 600$	A 1 percent change in the exchange rate leads to a $6 billion–a-year change in exports.

Suppose further that the initial value of the exchange rate ε is 100 and that the long-run exchange rate expectation ε_0 is also 100. What happens if this economy is hit by a sudden loss in confidence in the long-run value of its currency, a rise in ε_0 from 100 to 120?

Consumption and government purchases do not change, so the relevant changes in the national income identity are

$$\Delta Y^* = 0 = \Delta I + \Delta NX$$

The changes in investment and net exports are

$$\Delta I = -I_r \times \Delta r$$
$$\Delta NX = X_\varepsilon \times \Delta \varepsilon = X_\varepsilon \times \Delta \varepsilon_0 - X_\varepsilon \times \varepsilon_r \times \Delta r$$

With these particular parameter values:

$$\Delta I = -9,000 \times \Delta r$$
$$\Delta NX = 600 \times \Delta \varepsilon = 600 \times 0.20 - 600 \times 10 \times \Delta r$$
$$0 = \Delta I + \Delta NX$$

Substituting the values from the first two into the third:

$$0 = -9,000 \times \Delta r + 600 \times 0.20 - 600 \times 10 \times \Delta r$$
$$0 = 120 - 15,000 \times \Delta r$$
$$\Delta r = 0.008 = 0.8\%$$

The real interest rate rises by eight-tenths of a percentage point. Thus investment falls by $72 billion and net exports rise by $72 billion:

$$\Delta I = -9,000 \times 0.8 = -72$$
$$\Delta NX = 600 \times 20 - 600 \times 10 \times 0.8 = +72$$

And the new equilibrium value of the real exchange rate is

$$\varepsilon = \varepsilon_0 + \varepsilon_r \times (r^f - r) = 120 + 10 \times (-0.8) = 112$$

Higher interest rates offset the loss of confidence in the currency, and so the exchange rate — the value of foreign currency — increases by a little more than half of the change in currency traders' expectations. ◆

THE MEXICAN AND EAST ASIAN FINANCIAL CRISES: POLICY ISSUES

At the end of 1994, currency traders and international investors lost confidence in the Mexican peso. In the middle of 1997, they lost confidence in virtually all the currencies of the rapidly growing developing economies of East Asia.

Sharp rises in real interest rates, falls in domestic investment, and declines in the value of the affected domestic currencies followed in both crises. Some commentators railed against these changes. From the right, the editorial page of the *Wall Street Journal,* for example, denounced the International Monetary Fund (IMF) and the U.S. Treasury for advising the affected countries that the values of their domestic currencies should depreciate and the home-currency value of foreign currencies, the exchange rate, should rise. From the left, other economists denounced the IMF and the U.S. Treasury for advising countries to allow the real interest rate to rise.

There are complicated and delicate issues involved in crisis management. But our analysis above of the consequences of a collapse in foreign exchange trader confidence in the currency should make us skeptical of both positions. Our analysis strongly suggests that both the *Wall Street Journal,* which attacked the IMF from the right, and the economists who attacked the IMF from the left were wrong. In our flexible-price model the fall in exchange rate confidence and the resulting decline in international investment *must* lead to a rise in domestic interest rates and a fall in investment. There is no alternative equilibrium in which this does not happen. The fall in exchange rate confidence and the decline in international investment *must* also lead to a rise in the exchange rate and a rise in net exports. There is no alternative equilibrium in which this doesn't happen.

There is a legend that King Canute's advisers told him that he was so powerful that he could command the tides to stop. Our analysis of the consequences of a collapse of exchange rate confidence suggests that — unless confidence can be restored — those who demand that such a crisis be resolved without a rise in the exchange rate and a rise in domestic interest rates are giving advice as good as that given to King Canute.

RECAP   USING THE MODEL

To use the flexible-price model to understand the economy, begin by drawing the flow-of-funds diagram and calculating the equilibrium real interest rate. You can then use the equilibrium real interest rate and your knowledge of the economic environment to calculate the equilibrium values of a large number of economic variables — real GDP, consumption spending and investment spending, imports and exports, the real exchange rate, and more. You can also use the model to calculate how the economy's equilibrium will change in response to changes in the environment or in policy. Doing so involves using a method called comparative statics: Look first at the initial equilibrium position of the economy without the shift. Look second at the equilibrium position of the economy with the shift. Then identify the difference in the two equilibrium positions as the dynamic change in the economy in response to the shift.

7.3 SUPPLY SHOCKS

So far we have assumed that the level of potential output is fixed. Whatever shocks have affected the economy, they have had no effect on *aggregate supply,* no effect on potential output. But there are shocks to a flexible-price full-employment economy that change aggregate supply. **Supply shocks** like the 1973 tripling of world oil prices reduce potential output. Inventions and innovations can be positive productivity shocks that increase the level of potential output.

We can use the full-employment model to analyze the effects of a supply shock on the economy. However, the effects of a supply shock are different in one important respect from the effects of the demand or international shocks we analyzed above. In response to a supply shock the level of GDP *does* change — even in this full-employment chapter — because the level of potential GDP has changed. In each case, call the resulting supply-shock-driven change in potential output ΔY^*.

Oil and Other Supply Shocks

In 1973 the world price of oil tripled. In response to the 1973 Arab-Israeli War, the Organization of Petroleum Exporting Countries exerted its market power to restrict the worldwide supply of oil and raise the price. Capital- and energy-intensive production processes that had made economic sense and been profitable with oil costing less than $3 a barrel became unproductive and unprofitable with oil costing $10 a barrel. Thus potential output fell because it was now more profitable to use technologies that economized on oil by intensively using other factors of production such as labor, and so the efficiency of labor E in the production function fell.

Looking at the changes in the national income identity,

$$\Delta C + \Delta I + \Delta G + \Delta NX = \Delta Y^*$$

we find them more complex than those in the case of the demand shocks because the change in real GDP is not zero. If we expand the changes form of the national income identity by substituting for each component of GDP the equation for its determinants, we produce

$$[C_y(1 - t)\Delta Y^*] - I_r\Delta r + (-X_\varepsilon\varepsilon_r\Delta r - IM_y\Delta Y^*) = \Delta Y^*$$

We can regroup and solve this equation for the change Δr in the equilibrium interest rate:

$$\Delta r = \left[\frac{1 - C_y(1 - t) + IM_y}{I_r + X_\varepsilon\varepsilon_r} \Delta Y^*\right]$$

A negative value for ΔY^* — an adverse supply shock, one that lowers the level of potential output and GDP — generates an *increase* in the domestic real interest rate. Why? Because a fall in GDP due to an oil price increase or some other adverse supply shock reduces incomes and so reduces the flow of private savings into financial markets. (Although a decline in incomes carries with it a decline in consumption, and in net exports, but these declines do not match the decline in income, so domestic savings fall.)

As Figure 7.14 shows, the fall in domestic savings shifts the savings supply curve to the left, raising the real interest rate and reducing investment. As before, the increase in the domestic real interest rate makes foreigners more willing to invest in the home country. It increases the flow of foreign savings (which partly offsets the leftward shift in the savings supply curve), reduces net exports, and lowers the exchange rate (lowers the value of foreign currency).

By now it must seem as though every shock that affects a full-employment economy does one of four things:

- Shifts the savings supply curve to the left (raising domestic interest rates and lowering investment).
- Shifts the savings supply curve to the right (lowering domestic interest rates and raising investment).
- Shifts the investment demand curve to the left (lowering investment and lowering domestic interest rates).
- Or shifts the investment demand curve to the right (raising investment and raising domestic interest rates).

If you think this, you are right. Every shock to the economy will affect the flow of funds in one of the above four ways. Analyzing the effect of a shock on savings and investment is key to understanding its economywide impact.

Outside the flow of funds, however, different kinds of shocks have other, less similar effects. From the change in the level of GDP and the change in the interest rate, it is straightforward to calculate the effect of the supply shock on the other economic variables:

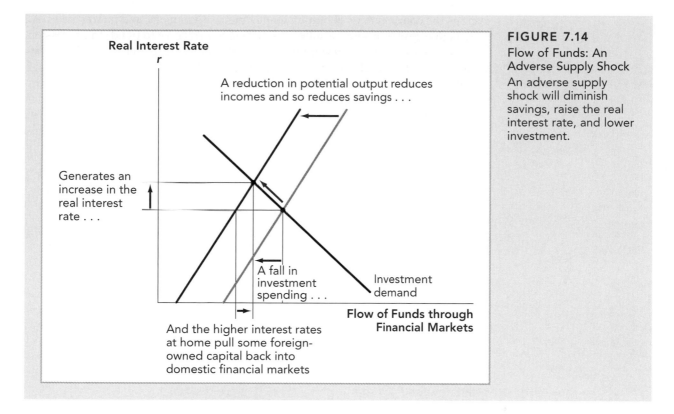

FIGURE 7.14
Flow of Funds: An Adverse Supply Shock
An adverse supply shock will diminish savings, raise the real interest rate, and lower investment.

$$\Delta C = C_y(1 - t)\Delta Y^*$$

$$\Delta I = I_r\left[\frac{1 + IM_y - C_y(1 - t)}{I_r + X_\varepsilon\varepsilon_r}\Delta Y^*\right]$$

$$\Delta G = 0$$

$$\Delta NX = \left(X_\varepsilon\varepsilon_r\left[\frac{1 + IM_y - C_y(1 - t)}{I_r + X_\varepsilon\varepsilon_r}\right] - IM_y\right)\Delta Y^*$$

$$\Delta\varepsilon = \varepsilon_r\left[\frac{1 + IM_y - C_y(1 - t)}{I_r + X_\varepsilon\varepsilon_r}\Delta Y^*\right]$$

An adverse supply shock — a negative value for ΔY^* — leads to declines in consumption, investment, and net exports; it leads to an appreciation of the home currency and thus to a reduction in the value of foreign currency — in the exchange rate. It also leads to a rise in the price level and an acceleration of inflation (topics covered in the next chapter).

Real Business Cycles

The mid-twentieth century economist Joseph Schumpeter was the most powerful exponent of the belief that changes in technology are the principal force driving business cycles. Schumpeter saw technological progress as inherently lumpy: There were five-year periods during which a great deal of new technology diffused rapidly throughout the economy. These were booms. There were five-year periods during which the pace of technological innovation and diffusion was much slower. These were periods of relative stagnation. Schumpeter saw the key feature of the business cycle as the comovements of output, employment, investment, and interest rates: All were high together in a boom; all were low together (relative to trend) in a recession.

It is easy to see how uneven invention and innovation patterns could generate such **real business cycles** — business cycles driven by the fundamental technological dynamic of the economy. Suppose that the most common shift in technology involves (a) a sudden step up in the efficiency of labor, accompanied by (b) a sudden rise in investment demand as it becomes more profitable for a business to enlarge its capital stock. Such a shock has a supply component — an increase ΔY^* in this year's potential output — and an investment demand component — an increase ΔI_0 in this year's investment demand.

How does the economy's full-employment equilibrium shift in response to such a combined shock? We simply add together the effects of a supply shock, outlined immediately above, and the effects of an investment boom driven by investors' increasing optimism, outlined in the previous section. The change in the equilibrium domestic real interest rate from a supply shock is

$$\Delta r = \left[\frac{1 - C_y(1-t) + IM_y}{I_r + X_\varepsilon \varepsilon_r} \Delta Y^* \right]$$

The change from an investment demand shock is

$$\Delta r = \frac{\Delta I_0}{I_r + X_\varepsilon \varepsilon_r}$$

Adding them together, the change in the equilibrium interest rate from this Schumpeterian technology shift is

$$\Delta r = - \frac{[1 - C_y(1-t) + IM_y]}{I_r + X_\varepsilon \varepsilon_r} \Delta Y^* + \frac{\Delta I_0}{I_r + X_\varepsilon \varepsilon_r}$$

The increased profitability of investment expands investment demand, shifting the investment demand curve to the right. But the positive technology shock does more than just make investment more profitable: It boosts the current efficiency of labor as well. Higher productivity means higher incomes, which mean more savings, which shift the total savings line to the right as well. The increase in investment demand tends to raise the interest rate; the increase in savings caused by higher incomes tends to lower it. Which dominates? Suppose that the investment demand condition dominates. Then the domestic real interest rate will rise, as Figure 7.15 shows.

It is then straightforward to calculate the changes in the components of aggregate demand:

$$\Delta C = C_y(1-t)\Delta Y^*$$

$$\Delta I = \frac{X_\varepsilon \varepsilon_r}{I_r + X_\varepsilon \varepsilon_r} \Delta I_0 + I_r \frac{[1 - C_y(1-t) + IM_y]}{I_r + X_\varepsilon \varepsilon_r} \Delta Y^*$$

$$\Delta G = 0$$

$$\Delta NX = \left\{ X_\varepsilon \varepsilon_r \frac{[1 - C_y(1-t) + IM_y]}{I_r + X_\varepsilon \varepsilon_r} - IM_y \right\} \Delta Y^* - \frac{X_\varepsilon \varepsilon_r \Delta I_0}{I_r + X_\varepsilon \varepsilon_r}$$

The change in the equilibrium level of the exchange rate is

$$\Delta \varepsilon = \left\{ \varepsilon_r \frac{[1 - C_y(1-t) + IM_y]}{I_r + X_\varepsilon \varepsilon_r} - IM_y \right\} \Delta Y^* - \frac{\varepsilon_r \Delta I_0}{I_r + X_\varepsilon \varepsilon_r}$$

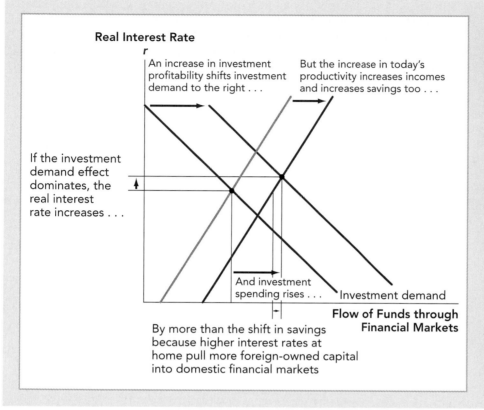

FIGURE 7.15

Flow of Funds: A Schumpeterian Combined Productivity-and-Investment Shock

Higher productivity today and optimism about future technological developments affect both the supply and the demand curves in the market for loanable funds. It is plausible to conclude that the economy will boom, with real GDP and investment rising, domestic real interest rates rising, the exchange rate falling, and capital flowing in to finance domestic investment. This pattern is the standard pattern seen in a business-cycle boom.

As long as the shock shifts the investment demand curve in Figure 7.15 to the right by more than it shifts the total savings line, the value of the exchange rate will fall.

Thus this positive-technology shock to both the efficiency of labor and the profitability of investment has produced:

- A rise in output.
- A sharp rise in investment.
- A decline in the exchange rate: an decrease in the value of foreign currency and an increase in the value of domestic currency.
- A decrease in net exports: an increase in the flow of foreign capital into the country to finance domestic investment.

These shifts in the economy are typically found in a business-cycle boom. Perhaps these Schumpeterian forces are the principal cause of the booms and recessions that we see in our economy.

Most economists, however, would be skeptical of the claim that most of our business cycles are such *real business cycles*. There is one characteristic feature of the boom phase of the business cycle as defined by Schumpeter that the model cannot produce: a fall in unemployment. This chapter's model, after all, is one in which the economy is always at full employment, so how could the model produce an increase in employment correlated with its technology-driven boom?

Some economists speculate that the pattern of unemployment found in the business cycle is due to movements in the level of real wages. When real wages are higher than expected or than average, more people are willing to work for wages. When real wages are temporarily lower than their average trend, some workers choose to forgo working for a month or a season or a year. According to this approach, unemployment is high whenever a significant fraction of labor-force members have looked at their employment opportunities, found that they were being offered unusually low wages, and decided to do something other than work for a while.

There is, however, a serious problem with this approach. Few of the cyclically unemployed in a business-cycle slump choose to describe themselves as "voluntarily unemployed." They see themselves not as people making a rational economic decision to spend a lot more time being leisurely but as people who want to work — who would be eager to work if only someone would hire them at the wages others are being paid — but who can't find work because there is excess supply in the labor market.

A second problem is that real-business-cycle theory explains booms — rapid rises in output — as the result of the rapid diffusion of technology and a sharp increase in the efficiency of labor. But how can it describe recessions or depressions, during which production does not grow at all but declines? Does the efficiency of labor decline because of technological regress? Are we supposed to believe that production was lower in 1991 than in 1990 because businesses had forgotten how to use their most productive modes of operation? This seems unlikely. Thus the Schumpeterian approach may well provide a correct theory of booms — or at least some booms. It is harder to see how it could provide an accurate account of recessions and depressions or of the high levels of cyclical unemployment found in times of recession and depression.

RECAP   SUPPLY SHOCKS

There are shocks to a flexible-price macroeconomy that change the level of potential output. For example, in 1973 the world price of oil tripled, and capital- and energy-intensive production processes that had made economic sense and been profitable with oil costing less than $3 a barrel became unproductive and unprofitable with oil costing $10 a barrel. Thus potential output fell. An adverse supply shock will reduce potential output, will in all likelihood raise real interest rates, and is likely to lead to a rise in the price level as well.

Another type of shock that changes the level of potential output is a technology shock. The economist Joseph Schumpeter was the most powerful exponent of the belief that changes in technology are the principal force driving business cycles. It is easy to see how uneven invention and innovation patterns could generate such real business cycles as producers and investors respond to changing technology and investment opportunities. It is harder to see how changes in technology could cause large-scale unemployment or the production declines that occur in recessions and depressions.

7.4 CONCLUSION

This chapter has analyzed a flexible-price macroeconomy in the *short run* — a time in which neither labor nor capital stocks have an opportunity to change. It has taken a snapshot of the economy in equilibrium at a point in time. It has asked how the equilibrium would be different if the economic environment or economic policy were different. It has at times implicitly talked about the dynamic evolution of the economy in the short run by describing the economy as shifting from one equilibrium to another in response to a change in policy or in the environment.

The flexible-price model presented here is very powerful. It allows us to say a great deal about the way various kinds of shocks will affect the economy and the composition of total spending and output as long as full employment is maintained. It has even, in its discussions of supply shocks and of Schumpeterian real business cycles, dipped into analyzing not just changes in the composition of demand but changes in the level of production.

Nevertheless, it is worth stressing what this chapter has not done:

- It has not discussed the impact of changes in policy and the economic environment on economic growth — that was done in Part II, Chapters 4 and 5. Refer to those chapters to analyze how changes in savings ultimately affect productivity and material standards of living in the long run.

- It has ignored the nominal financial side of the economy — money, prices, and inflation — completely. That topic will be covered in Chapter 8.

- It has maintained the full-employment assumption — that notion will be relaxed in Part III, the chapters starting with Chapter 9.

Chapter Summary

1. When the economy is at full employment, real GDP is equal to potential output.

2. In a flexible-price full-employment economy, the real interest rate shifts in response to changes in policy or the economic environment to keep real GDP equal to potential output.

3. The real interest rate balances the supply of loanable funds committed to financial markets by savers with the demand for funds to finance investments. The circular flow principle guarantees that when the savings supply equals investment, aggregate demand and real GDP will equal potential output.

4. Supply shocks are sharp, sudden changes in costs — like the world oil price increase of 1973 — that shift the efficiency of labor as changed prices cause businesses to economize on or intensively use labor.

5. Real-business-cycle theory attempts to use this chapter's model to account for changes not just in the short-run composition of real GDP but in the short-run level of real GDP as well. It may be (and it may not be) a good theory for booms, or for some booms, but it is hard to see how it could ever be a good explanation of recessions or depressions.

Key Terms

financial markets (p. 187)

total savings (p. 187)

private savings (p. 187)

public savings (p. 187)

capital inflow (p. 187)

comparative statics (p. 193)

supply shocks (p. 207)

real business cycles (p. 210)

Analytical Exercises

1. Suppose that in the flexible-price full-employment model the government increases taxes and government purchases by equal amounts. The tax increase reduces consumption spending. What happens qualitatively (tell the direction of change only) to investment, net exports, the exchange rate, the real interest rate, and potential output?

2. What happens according to the flexible-price full-employment model if the intercept C_0 of the consumption function rises. Explain qualitatively (tell the direction of change only) what happens to consumption, investment, net exports, the exchange rate, the real interest rate, and potential output.

3. Explain qualitatively the direction in which consumption, investment, government purchases, net exports, the exchange rate, the real interest rate, and potential output move in the flexible-price full-employment model if the government raises taxes.

4. Give three examples of changes in economic policy or in the economic environment that would shift the total savings curve on the flow-of-funds diagram to the left.

5. Give three examples of changes in the economic environment or in economic policy that would increase the equilibrium real exchange rate.

Policy Exercises

1. Suppose that the relevant parameters of the economy are:

   $t = 0.33$ Tax rate of one-third.

   $I_r = 90$ A 1-percentage-point fall in the interest rate raises investment spending by $90 billion a year.

   $C_y = 0.75$ A marginal propensity to consume of three-quarters.

   $\varepsilon_r = 10$ With an initial value for the real exchange rate ε set at the traditional indexed value of 100, a 1-percentage-point change in the interest rate difference vis-à-vis abroad generates a 10 percent shift in the exchange rate.

   $X_\varepsilon = 6$ A 10 percent change in the exchange rate leads to a $60 billion–a-year change in exports.

   And suppose that an irrational exuberance causes a stock market boom that leads consumers to increase their spending by $200 billion at a constant level of disposable income. What would be the increase in interest rates in response to such an exuberance-driven consumption boom?

2. In the economy presented in question 1, suppose that total GDP is $10 trillion and that the government does not want real interest rates to rise and investment to fall in response to the stock market–generated consump-

tion boom. What kinds of policies can the government undertake? How successful will they be?

3. When President Bill Clinton took office, he spent essentially all his political capital on his first-year effort to raise taxes and cut spending by $300 billion a year in an economy with an annual GDP of $6 trillion. What, qualitatively and quantitatively, does the flexible-price full-employment model say should have been the consequences of these policies if the relevant parameters of the economy are those given in question 1?

4. Consider two economies. In one, the relevant parameters are:

   $Y^* = \$10,000$ In billions; potential output equals $10 trillion.

   $t = 0.33$ Tax rate of one-third.

   $I_r = 90$ A 1-percentage-point fall in the interest rate raises investment spending by $90 billion a year.

   $C_y = 0.75$ A marginal propensity to consume of three-quarters.

   $\varepsilon_r = 10$ With an initial value for the real exchange rate ε set at the traditional indexed value of 100, a 1-percentage-point change in the interest rate difference vis-à-vis abroad generates a 10 percent shift in the exchange rate.

$X_\varepsilon = 6$ A 10 percent change in the exchange rate leads to a $60 billion–a-year change in exports.

In the other, the relevant parameters are:

$Y^* = \$10,000$ In billions; potential output equals $10 trillion.

$t = 0.33$ Tax rate of one-third.

$I_r = 90$ A 1-percentage-point fall in the interest rate raises investment spending by $90 billion a year.

$C_y = 0.5$ A marginal propensity to consume of one-half.

$\varepsilon_r = 10$ With an initial value for the real exchange rate ε set at the traditional indexed value of 100, a 1-percentage-point change in the interest rate difference vis-à-vis

abroad generates a 10 percent shift in the exchange rate.

$X_\varepsilon = 6$ A 10 percent change in the exchange rate leads to a $60 billion–a-year change in exports.

Compare the effects of a $100 billion increase in government purchases on these two economies. In which economy do interest rates go up by more? In which economy does investment go down by more?

5. During the 2000 presidential campaign, candidate George W. Bush favored using the federal budget surplus to fund tax cuts while candidate Albert Gore favored using the federal budget surplus to retire parts of the national debt. Which candidate's economic policies *seem* likely to lead to lower interest rates? To higher investment spending? To lead to a lower value of the exchange rate?

Money, Prices, and Inflation

QUESTIONS

What do economists mean by "money"?

Why is money useful?

What do economists mean when they say that money is a unit of account?

What determines the price level and the inflation rate?

Why would a government ever generate hyperinflation — a condition in which prices rise by more than 20 percent a *month*?

What determines the level of money demand?

What determines the level of the money supply?

Why is inflation seen as something to be avoided?

8.1 MONEY

Newspaper and television commentators devote a lot of attention to **inflation.** Inflation disrupts the economy in a number of different ways. Moreover, even when inflation is absent, fear that it will emerge has a powerful effect on the economy. The actions of economic policy-making agencies like the Federal Reserve are tightly constrained by fear that certain courses of action will lead to inflation.

As Figure 8.1 shows, the United States experienced an episode of relatively mild inflation — prices rising at between 5 and 10 percent per year — in the 1970s. Although relatively mild, that inflation was large enough to cause significant economic and political trauma. Avoiding a repeat of the inflation of the 1970s remains a major goal of economic policy even today, a quarter of a century later.

Many countries have experienced inflations that are *not* mild. In Russia in 1998 the price level rose at a rate of 60 percent. In Germany in 1923 prices rose at a rate of 60 percent per *week*. So-called **hyperinflations** have been seen in many other countries in this century, from Argentina to Ukraine, from Hungary to China. They are extremely destructive, inflicting severe damage on the ability of **money** to grease the wheels of the social mechanism of exchange that is the market economy. The system of prices and market exchange breaks down, and production can fall to a small fraction of potential output.

Chapters 6 and 7 did not discuss the determination of the level of prices and the inflation rate. They did not have to. It was perfectly possible to figure out what the real interest and exchange rates, the level of real GDP, and the division of real GDP into its

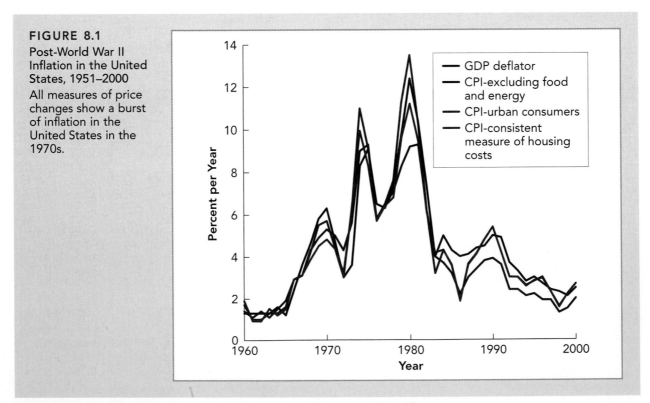

FIGURE 8.1

Post-World War II Inflation in the United States, 1951–2000

All measures of price changes show a burst of inflation in the United States in the 1970s.

Source: The 2001 edition of *The Economic Report of the President* (Washington, DC: Government Printing Office).

components were without mentioning the overall price level or the rate of inflation. And there was no feedback from production and output back to the price level.

The power to analyze real variables without referring to the price level is a special feature of the flexible-price full-employment model of the economy. Economists call it the *classical dichotomy:* Real variables (such as real GDP, real investment spending, or the real exchange rate) can be analyzed and calculated without thinking of nominal variables such as the price level. Economists also speak of it as the property whereby money is **neutral** or is a *veil* — a covering that does not affect the shape of the face underneath.

Starting in Chapter 9 the classical dichotomy will not hold. Money will not be neutral: The determination of the price level and its changes will be intimately tied up with fluctuations in production and employment. This is because Chapter 9 introduces prices that are sluggish, or sticky, or that are fixed. Hence they cannot adjust smoothly and instantaneously to changes in nominal variables like the **money stock** and the **price level**. But here in Part II prices are flexible, and the **classical dichotomy** holds.

This chapter explores what determines the overall level of prices and the rate of inflation (or deflation) in our flexible-price full-employment model of the macroeconomy. This topic is worth examining for two reasons. First, it provides a useful baseline analysis against which to contrast the conclusions of future chapters. Second, whenever we look over relatively long spans of time — decades, perhaps — wages and prices *are* effectively flexible, they *do* have time to move in response to shocks, and the flexible-price assumption is a fruitful and useful one.

Money: Liquid Wealth That Can Be Spent

When noneconomists use the word "money," they may mean a number of things: "She has a lot of money" usually means that she is wealthy; "He makes a lot of money" usually means that he has a high income. When economists use the word "money," however, they mean something different. To economists, *money* is wealth that is held in a readily spendable form. Money is that kind of wealth that you can use immediately to buy things because others will accept it as payment. Today the economy's stock of money is made up of:

- Coins and currency that are transferred by handing the cash over to a seller (almost everyone will accept cash as payment for goods and services).
- Checking account balances that are transferred by writing a check (which most people will accept as payment for goods and services).
- Other assets — like savings account balances — that can be turned into cash or demand deposits nearly instantaneously, risklessly, and costlessly.

Why do economists adopt this special definition of money? I do not know. Giving household words special definitions is probably a bad thing to do, since it can cause confusion and misunderstanding. Yet economists do so not only for "money" but also for terms such as "investment" and "utility."

Whether assets that can be quickly and cheaply turned into cash (savings account balances, money market mutual funds, liquid Treasury securities, and so on) are included in the money stock is a matter of taste and judgment. At what level of cost and inconvenience is an asset no longer "readily spendable"? There is no clear answer. Thus economists have a number of different measures of the money stock — identified by symbols like H, M1, M2, M3, and L — each of which draws the line around a different set of assets that it counts as wealth readily *enough* spent to be "money."

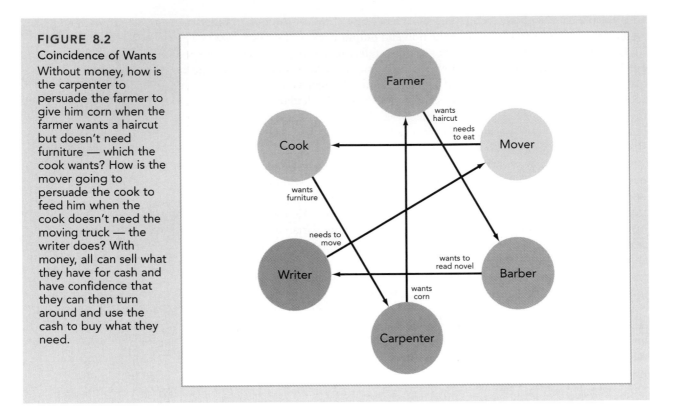

The Usefulness of Money

In our world all you need to carry out a market transaction — whether you want to buy or sell some good or service — is either to have money yourself (if you want to buy) or to deal with a purchaser who has money (if you want to sell). In a barter economy, an economy without the social convention of money, market exchange would require the so-called *coincidence of wants:* You would have to have physically in your possession some good or service that another person wants, and that person would have to have in his or her possession some good or service that you want. As Figure 8.2 shows, finding consumption goods to satisfy the coincidence of wants would get remarkably complicated very quickly. Without money, an extraordinary amount of time and energy would be spent simply arranging the goods one needed to trade.

Units of Account

There is one other feature worth noting. The same assets that serve as the most common form of readily spendable purchasing power also serve as *units of account*. Dollars or euros or yen are not only what we use to settle transactions but also what we use to quote prices to one another. At some times and places the functions of money as a **medium of exchange** and as a **unit of account** have been separated, but today they almost invariably go together.

This is a potential cause of trouble. Anything that alters the real value of the domestic money in terms of its purchasing power over goods and services will also alter the real terms of existing contracts that use money as the unit of account. The effect of changes in the price level on contracts that have used the domestic money as a unit of account is a principal source of the social costs of inflation and deflation. The effect of changes in the exchange rate on contracts that have used foreign monies as units of account is a principal source of the social costs of currency crises.

RECAP   MONEY

To an economist, "money" is wealth that is held in a readily spendable form. Money is that kind of wealth that you can use immediately to buy things because others will accept it as payment. Money is useful because in its absence we would have a barter economy and market exchange would require the so-called *coincidence of wants*. Without money, an extraordinary amount of time and energy would be spent simply arranging the goods one needed to trade.

The same assets that serve as the most common form of readily spendable purchasing power also serve as *units of account*. Dollars or euros or yen are not only what we use to settle transactions but also what we use to quote prices to one another. This is a potential cause of trouble. The effect of changes in the price level on contracts that have used the domestic money as a unit of account is a principal source of the social costs of inflation and deflation. The effect of changes in the exchange rate on contracts that have used foreign monies as units of account is a principal source of the social costs of currency crises.

8.2 THE QUANTITY THEORY OF MONEY

The Demand for Money

People have a *demand* for money just as they have a demand for any other good. They want to hold a certain amount of wealth in the form of readily spendable purchasing power because the stuff is useful. The more money in your portfolio, the easier it is to buy things. Too little money makes life pointlessly difficult. You have to waste time running to the bank for extra cash or waste energy and time liquidating pieces of your portfolio before you can carry out your normal daily transactions.

Nevertheless, you don't want to have too much of your wealth in the form of readily spendable purchasing power. Cash sitting in your pocket is not earning interest at the bank. Wealth you do not want to spend for five years could earn a higher return as a certificate of deposit or as an investment in the stock market than as cash in your checking account.

Figure 8.3 summarizes the reasons for and opportunity cost of holding money. The higher the flow of spending, the more money the households and businesses in the economy will want to hold. How much more? That depends on the transactions technology of the economy: what businesses will take credit cards, how easy it is to get checks approved, how long the float is, and so forth. In this section of the chapter, however, we ignore all other determinants of money demand and focus on the flow of spending as *the* principal determinant of money demand.

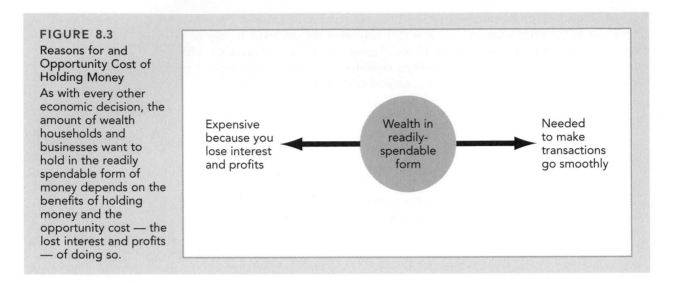

FIGURE 8.3

Reasons for and Opportunity Cost of Holding Money

As with every other economic decision, the amount of wealth households and businesses want to hold in the readily spendable form of money depends on the benefits of holding money and the opportunity cost — the lost interest and profits — of doing so.

The Quantity Equation

The theory that the only important determinant of the demand for money is the flow of spending is called the **quantity theory of money**. It is summarized in either the Cambridge (England) money-demand function

$$M = \frac{1}{V} \times (P \times Y)$$

or the (American) quantity equation

$$M \times V = (P \times Y)$$

In either form of the quantity theory, $P \times Y$ represents the total nominal flow of spending. For each dollar of spending on goods and services, households want to hold $1/V$ dollars' worth of money. The parameter V — a constant, or perhaps growing slowly and predictably (in this section of the chapter only — later on things become more complicated!) — is the **velocity** of money. The velocity of money is a measure of how "fast" money moves through the economy: how many times a year the average unit of money shows up in someone's income and is then used to buy a final good or service that counts in GDP.

Money and Prices

The Price Level

Together, the quantity theory of money and the full-employment assumption allow us to determine the price level in the flexible-price model of the macroeconomy. Real GDP Y is equal to potential output: $Y = Y^*$. The velocity of money V is determined by the sophistication of the banking system and the social conventions that govern payment and settlement. For the "M1" concept of money — currency plus checking account deposits — the current velocity V is about 8.5: Businesses and households want to hold about \$1 of their wealth in the form of M1 for every \$8.50 of real GDP produced. Changes in financial sophistication have raised velocity over time. In the years

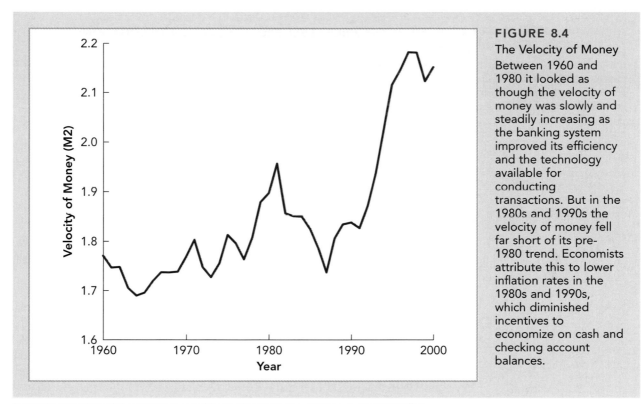

FIGURE 8.4
The Velocity of Money
Between 1960 and 1980 it looked as though the velocity of money was slowly and steadily increasing as the banking system improved its efficiency and the technology available for conducting transactions. But in the 1980s and 1990s the velocity of money fell far short of its pre-1980 trend. Economists attribute this to lower inflation rates in the 1980s and 1990s, which diminished incentives to economize on cash and checking account balances.

Source: The 2001 edition of *The Economic Report of the President* (Washington, DC: Government Printing Office).

immediately after World War II, the M1 velocity of money was only 3. For the M2 concept, velocity is considerably lower (see Figure 8.4).

Thus if we know real GDP Y, the velocity of money V, and the money stock M, we can calculate that the price level is

$$P = \left(\frac{V}{Y}\right) \times M$$

Box 8.1 presents an example of such a quantity-theory calculation.

Should the price level be momentarily higher than the quantity equation predicts, households and businesses will notice that they have less wealth in the form of readily spendable purchasing power than they want. They will cut back on purchases for a little while to build up their liquidity. As they cut back on purchases, sellers will note that demand is weak and will cut their prices, so the price level will fall.

Should the price level be momentarily lower than the quantity equation value, households and businesses will note that they have more wealth in the form of money than they want, so they will accelerate their purchases to reduce their money balances. Sellers will note that demand is strong and will raise their prices, so the price level will rise. As long as prices are flexible, the economy's price level will remain at its quantity-theory equilibrium. Transitory fluctuations in the velocity of money mean that day-to-day or even year-to-year changes in the money stock are not mirrored in equivalent proportional changes in the price level. But on a decade-to-decade time scale the quantity theory of money is a very reliable guide to and predictor of large movements in

CALCULATING THE PRICE LEVEL FROM THE QUANTITY EQUATION: AN EXAMPLE

It is straightforward to use the quantity theory of money

$$P = \left(\frac{V}{Y}\right) \times M$$

to calculate the price level. For example, in the third quarter of 1998 real GDP (in chained 1992 dollars) was equal to $7,566 billion, the M1 measure of the money stock was equal to $1,072 billion, and the velocity of money was equal to 7.964. Therefore:

$$P = \left(\frac{7.964}{\$7,556}\right) \times \$1,072 = 1.1284$$

In the third quarter of 1998 the price level was equal to 112.84 percent of its 1992 level, which works out to an average rate of inflation of about 2.14 percent per year from 1992 to 1998.

Had velocity grown an additional 10 percent between 1992 and 1998, the price level would have grown an additional 10 percent as well if the money stock and real GDP were unchanged from their historical values. Had the money stock grown by an additional 10 percent between 1992 and 1998, the price level would have grown by an additional 10 percent as well if velocity and real GDP were unchanged from their historical values. And had real GDP grown by an additional 10 percent between 1992 and 1998, this would have reduced the 1998 price level by 10 percent relative to its historical value if velocity and the money stock were unchanged from their historical values.

prices. Using the quantity theory in this way requires that we know the level of the money stock, however. What determines the level of the money stock?

The Money Stock

Determination of the money stock is the basic task of *monetary policy*. In the United States the **Federal Reserve**, the nation's central bank, determines the money stock.

The **central bank** directly determines the **monetary base**, the sum of currency in circulation and of deposits at the Federal Reserve's 12 branches. When the central bank wants to reduce the monetary base, it sells short-term government bonds and accepts currency or deposits at its regional branches as payment. The currency is then removed from circulation and stored in a basement somewhere; the deposits the central bank receives as payment are then erased from its books. Thus the monetary base declines. When the Federal Reserve wants to increase the monetary base, it buys short-term government bonds, paying for them with currency or by crediting the seller with a deposit at the Federal Reserve. These transactions are called **open-market operations**, because the Federal Reserve buys or sells bonds on the open market. (See Figure 8.5.) The procedures that govern when and how the U.S. central bank, the Federal Reserve, undertakes these transactions are decided at periodic meetings of the *Federal Open Market Committee (FOMC)*.

Although the Federal Reserve directly controls the monetary base, the other

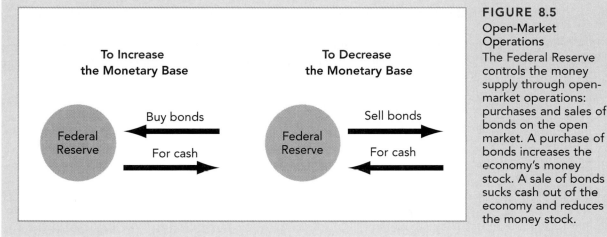

FIGURE 8.5
Open-Market Operations
The Federal Reserve controls the money supply through open-market operations: purchases and sales of bonds on the open market. A purchase of bonds increases the economy's money stock. A sale of bonds sucks cash out of the economy and reduces the money stock.

measures of the money stock are determined by the interaction of the monetary base with the banking sector. Banks accept checking and savings account deposits. They lend out the purchasing power deposited in the bank, earn interest, and provide the depositor with a claim to wealth in readily spendable form. But the central bank limits commercial banks' ability to accept deposits. It requires that commercial banks redeposit at the Federal Reserve a certain proportion of their total deposits. Financial institutions find it prudent to hold extra liquid reserves in case an unexpectedly large number of depositors seek to withdraw their money. There is nothing worse for a financial institution than to be unable to meet its depositors' demands for money. Thus, as Box 8.2 shows, broader measures of the money stock are larger than but limited in their growth by the size of the monetary base, the regulatory **reserve requirements** imposed on banks and other financial institutions, and financial institutions' extremely powerful incentive never to get caught without enough cash to satisfy depositors' demands.

In this chapter (and later chapters too) we sweep these complications under the rug. We assume that the central bank can easily set the money stock at whatever level it wishes. (Although these subjects are given short shrift in this book, they are explored in great depth in money and banking textbooks by authors such as Rick Mishkin, Glenn Hubbard, and Steve Cecchetti.)

Table 8.1 summarizes the definitions of the money stock.

DIFFERENT DEFINITIONS OF THE MONEY STOCK: SOME DETAILS

The different definitions of the money stock all draw the line separating "money" from "not-money" in different places. Economists' definition of "money" considers any wealth held in the form of readily spendable purchasing power to be money. But ready spendability is, to some degree at least, a thing found in the eye of the beholder.

The narrowest definition of money — called "H" for "*h*igh-powered money," or sometimes "B" for "monetary *b*ase" — includes only cash and deposits at branches of the Federal Reserve. The assets that make up the monetary base are special

BOX
8.2

because only they can serve as reserves to satisfy the Federal Reserve's requirement that institutions that accept deposits also maintain funds to cover any emergency spike in withdrawals.

The narrowest commonly used definition of money is M1, which consists of currency plus checking account deposits, traveler's checks, and any other deposits at institutions from which the depositor can demand his or her money back and get it instantaneously. Almost anyone will accept M1-type money as a means of payment for almost any purchase. M2 adds to M1 wealth held in the form of savings accounts, wealth held in relatively small term deposits, and money held in money market mutual funds. Some of the money included in M2 cannot be spent without paying a penalty for early withdrawal. Moreover, if the bank wants, it has the legal right to delay a withdrawal for a period of time. M2-type money is a little bit less spendable than M1-type money.

There are also broader definitions of money. One of the broadest is M3, which includes large term deposits and institutional money market fund balances. Still larger is L, which includes savings bonds and Treasury bills. But a large chunk of these assets is not readily spendable. Have you ever tried to buy something with a savings bond or a Treasury bill?

TABLE 8.1
Measures of the Money Stock

Concept of Money	Assets Included in Concept	Amount, 1998 (in Billions)
C	Currency.	$ 460
H	Monetary base: assets that can serve as *reserves* for banks; equals currency plus reserve deposits at Federal Reserve Banks	514
M1	Currency plus checking account deposits and traveler's checks	1,092
M2	M1 plus savings account deposits, small time deposits, and household money market funds	4,412
M3	M2 plus institutional money market funds, eurodollar accounts, large time deposits, and repurchase agreements	5,982
L	M3 plus short-term Treasury securities and other liquid financial assets	7,065

Source: The 2001 edition of *The Economic Report of the President* (Washington, DC: Government Printing Office).

Inflation

The quantity equation

$$P = \left(\frac{V}{Y}\right) \times M$$

leads immediately to an equation for the inflation rate π — the proportional rate of change of the price level — if you recall our rule from Chapter 2 about how to calculate the proportional growth rates of products or quotients. Put simply, the proportional growth rate of a product is the sum of the growth rates of the terms multiplied together; the proportional growth rate of a quotient is the difference between the growth rates of the individual terms. Thus

inflation = velocity growth rate + money growth rate – real GDP growth rate

To write this relationship in more compact form, use a lowercase m and v for the proportional growth rates of the money stock and velocity and use a lowercase y for the growth rate of real GDP. Then

$$\pi = m + v - y$$

If the proportional growth rate of real GDP is 4 percent per year, the velocity of money V increases at a proportional rate of 2 percent per year, and the money stock M grows at 5 percent per year, then

$$\pi = 5\% + 2\% - 4\% = 3\%$$

The inflation rate is 3 percent per year.

Most changes in the rate of inflation are due to changes in the rate of growth of the money stock. It is rare that there are substantial and persistent changes in y, the rate of growth of real GDP. The variable v, the rate of growth of velocity, is determined by the slow pace of institutional and technological change in the banking system. But m, the rate of growth of the money stock, can change quickly and substantially. Thus if you see a large and persistent change in inflation, odds are that it is due to a change in the rate of growth of the money stock.

If the Federal Reserve keeps the money stock relatively stable, prices will be relatively stable and inflation will be low. If the Federal Reserve lets the money stock grow more quickly, then prices will be unstable and inflation will be relatively high. But at a year-to-year time scale the relationship is not very close.

RECAP   THE QUANTITY THEORY OF MONEY

People want to hold a certain amount of wealth in the form of readily spendable purchasing power because the stuff is useful. The more money in your portfolio, the easier it is to buy things. However, you don't want to have too much of your wealth in the form of readily spendable purchasing power. Cash sitting in your pocket is not earning interest at the bank. Wealth you do not want to spend for five years could earn a higher return as a certificate of deposit or as an investment in the stock market than as cash in your checking account.

The theory that the only important determinant of the demand for money is the flow of spending is the quantity theory of money, $M \times V = P \times Y$, where $P \times Y$ represents the total nominal flow of spending. For each dollar of spending on goods and services, households want to hold $1/V$ dollars' worth of money. The parameter V, a constant or perhaps growing slowly and predictably, is the velocity of money. The velocity of money is a measure of how "fast" money moves through the economy: how many times a year the average unit of money shows up in someone's income and is then used to buy a final good or service that counts in GDP.

8.3 THE INTEREST RATE AND MONEY DEMAND

Money Demand

In this section we think more systematically about the determinants of money demand. Because the real world is more complicated than the simplest quantity theory implies, representing the velocity of money as a constant or slowly moving steady trend is misleading. In the real world, inflation is not always proportional to money growth.

As Figure 8.6 shows, in the 1980s in the United States both inflation and the velocity of money fell sharply, but money growth in the 1980s was as fast as it had been in the 1970s. Inflation fell even though money growth did not. In the first half of the 1990s there were further rapid declines in velocity, which meant that even relatively high money growth did not trigger accelerating inflation. The second half of the 1990s saw equally rapid increases in velocity, so nominal money supply growth had to dip well below zero in order to keep inflation from rising.

Economic theory suggests that money demand should be *inversely* related to the nominal interest rate, which is the sum of the real interest rate and the current inflation rate. The cash in your purse or wallet does not earn interest. Your checking account balances earn little or no interest as well. As a result, their purchasing power

FIGURE 8.6

Money Growth and Inflation Are Not Always Parallel

In the 1960s and 1970s the correlation between money growth and inflation was strong and robust. In the 1980s and 1990s this correlation broke down.

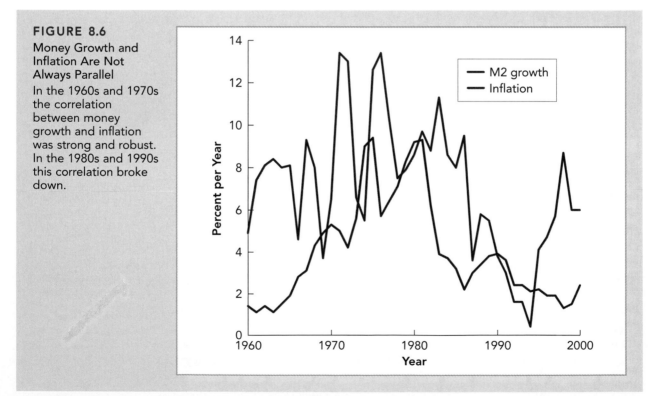

Source: The 2001 edition of *The Economic Report of the President* (Washington, DC: Government Printing Office).

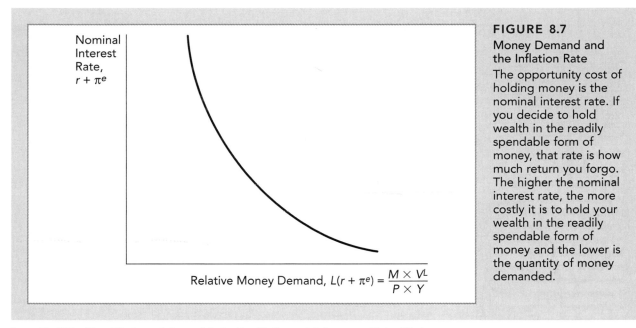

FIGURE 8.7
Money Demand and the Inflation Rate
The opportunity cost of holding money is the nominal interest rate. If you decide to hold wealth in the readily spendable form of money, that rate is how much return you forgo. The higher the nominal interest rate, the more costly it is to hold your wealth in the readily spendable form of money and the lower is the quantity of money demanded.

Source: The 2001 edition of *The Economic Report of the President* (Washington, DC: Government Printing Office).

over real goods and services erodes at the rate of inflation. The expected real return on keeping your money in readily spendable form is $-\pi^e$, the negative of the expected inflation rate π^e.

By contrast, were you to take a dollar out of your checking account and invest it, its real return would be the real interest rate r. The difference between the rate of return on money balances and the rate of return on other assets is the *opportunity cost* of holding money. This opportunity cost is the sum of the inflation rate π^e and the real interest rate r, that is, the nominal interest rate i. The higher the opportunity cost of holding money, the lower is the demand for money balances, as Figure 8.7 shows. Economic theory thus tells us that the velocity of money will be a function like

$$V = V^L \times [V_0 + V^i \times (r + \pi^e)]$$

where V^L is the financial technology-driven trend in the velocity of money, and $V_0 + V_i(r + \pi^e)$ captures the dependence of the demand for money on the nominal interest rate. The higher the nominal interest rate $i = r + \pi^e$, the higher is the velocity function V and the lower is the demand for money.

Such a function for velocity means that the demand for nominal money balances is

$$M = \frac{P \times Y}{V^L \times [V_0 + V_i \times (r + \pi^e)]}$$

Money, Prices, and Inflation

Because the level of money demand depends on the current rate of inflation, we need to keep track of two equations to determine the behavior of money, prices, and inflation. The first comes directly from the money-demand function and is the equation for the price level:

$$M = \frac{P \times Y}{V^L \times [V_0 + V_i \times (r + \pi^e)]}$$

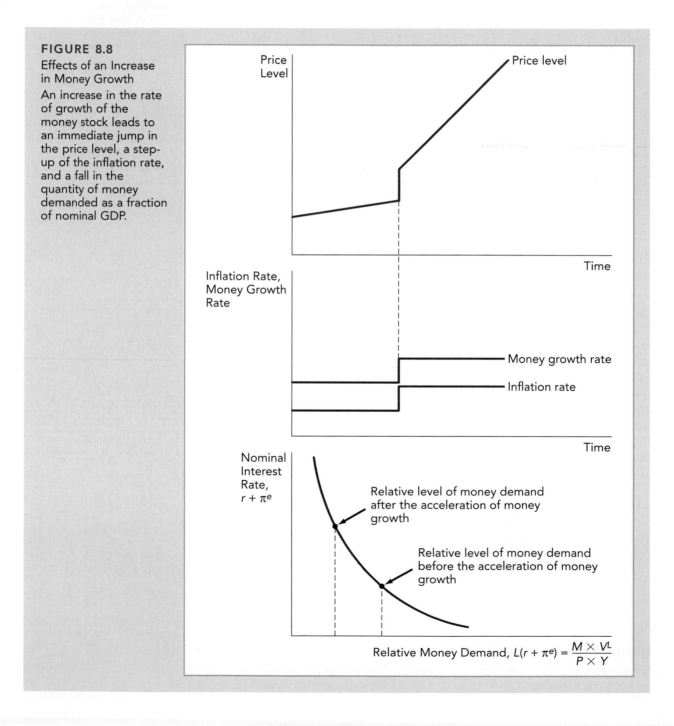

FIGURE 8.8

Effects of an Increase in Money Growth

An increase in the rate of growth of the money stock leads to an immediate jump in the price level, a step-up of the inflation rate, and a fall in the quantity of money demanded as a fraction of nominal GDP.

The second comes from the rate of change of the demand for money. If inflation is constant and the proportional rate of change of the velocity trend is v, then as before

$$\pi = m + v - y$$

Thus if the rate of growth of the money stock is +6 percent per year, the velocity trend is +1 percent per year, and real GDP growth is +4 percent per year, inflation is 3 percent per year.

Suppose that the rate of growth of the money stock suddenly increases permanently from 6 to 10 percent per year. When the economy settles down, the new inflation rate will be 4 percent per year higher — 7 percent instead of 3 percent per year. But at an inflation rate of 7 percent per year, the opportunity cost of holding money is higher. If the real interest rate is stable at 3 percent per year, then the opportunity cost of holding money has just jumped from 6 to 10 percent per year.

A higher opportunity cost of holding money will raise the velocity of money. If the money stock and real GDP remain fixed, this increase in the velocity of money will cause the price level to jump suddenly and discontinuously, as is shown in Figure 8.8! By how much will the price level jump? That depends on how sensitive money demand is to changes in the nominal interest rate. The more sensitive is money demand to the nominal interest rate, the larger will be the sudden jump in the price level.

Thus in the flexible-price macroeconomy, a change in the rate of growth of the money stock not only changes the long-run inflation rate, but also causes an immediate jump in the price level at the moment that households and businesses become aware that the rate of money growth has changed.

> **RECAP   THE INTEREST RATE AND MONEY DEMAND**
>
> The real world is more complicated than the quantity theory implies. The velocity of money is not a constant or a trend but depends on the nominal interest rate and other factors. The higher the nominal interest rate, the higher is the velocity of money.
>
> Because the nominal interest rate depends on the inflation rate, an increase in the growth rate of the money stock will have an amplified effect on the price level. First, the price level will rise because there is more money. Second, the velocity of money will increase because inflation and nominal interest rates are higher — and this increase in the velocity of money will generate a further increase in the price level.

8.4 THE COSTS OF INFLATION

Why should we care whether the central bank controls the money supply so that inflation is low and stable or lets the money supply expand rapidly and produce high and unpredictable inflation? One reason *not* to care about inflation is the fear that inflation makes us directly and significantly poorer. Any claim by a politician that inflation is the "cruelest tax" because its higher prices rob Americans of the benefits of their wages is not coherent. Inflation raises all nominal prices and wages in the economy. The higher nominal prices that a worker has to pay because of inflation are, on average (but only on average), offset by the higher nominal wages that his or her employer can pay because of inflation. Higher living standards come from better technology and more capital-intensive production processes, not from reduced inflation.

Inflation does have costs, but they are subtle. For the most part, the costs of moderate inflation appear to be relatively small, smaller than one would guess given the strength of today's political consensus that price stability is a very desirable goal.

The Costs of Moderate Expected Inflation

The costs of *expected inflation* are especially small. Expected inflation raises the nominal interest rate, which you will recall is equal to the real interest rate plus the rate of inflation. Since the nominal interest rate is the opportunity cost of holding money balances, when the rate is high, you devote more time and energy to managing your cash balances. From the viewpoint of the economy as a whole, this extra time and energy is just wasted. Nothing useful is produced, and valuable resources that could be used to add to output or be simply spent on enjoying yourself are used up.

Expected inflation wastes time and energy in other ways as well. Firms find that they must spend resources changing their prices not because of any change in their business but simply because of inflation. Households find that it is harder to figure out what is a good buy and what is a bad one as inflation pushes prices away from what they had perceived normal prices to be. The most serious costs of expected inflation surely come from the fact that our tax laws are not designed to deal well with inflation. Lots of productive activities are penalized, and lots of unproductive ones rewarded, simply because of the interaction of inflation with the tax system. The fact that debt interest is treated as a cost means that in times of high inflation it is artificially cheap to finance businesses by issuing bonds or borrowing at the bank, and so businesses adopt debt-heavy capital structures that may make the economy more vulnerable to financial crises and that certainly increase the amount of resources wasted paying bankruptcy lawyers, as businesses with lots of debt tend to go bankrupt relatively easily.

Nevertheless when the rate of inflation is low — perhaps less than 10 percent per year, probably less than 5 percent per year, and certainly less than 2 percent per year — these costs are too small to worry about because they are counterbalanced by benefits. Suppose the central bank wants to push the real interest rate below zero in some economic crisis? It cannot do so unless there is some inflation in the economy, because nominal interest rates cannot be less than zero and the real interest rate is the difference between the nominal interest rate and the inflation rate. Many economists and psychologists have speculated that worker morale is greatly harmed if worker wages are clearly and unambiguously cut. A small amount of inflation may then grease the wheels of the labor market, allowing for wage adjustment without the damaging effect on morale of explicit wage cuts.

The Costs of Moderate Unexpected Inflation

Unexpected inflation does have significant and worrisome costs, for unexpected inflation redistributes wealth from creditors to debtors. Creditors receive much less purchasing power than they had anticipated if a loan falls due during a time of significant inflation. Debtors find the payments they must make much less burdensome if they borrow over a period of significant inflation. The process works in reverse as well: If inflation is less than had been expected, creditors receive a windfall and debtors go bankrupt. Most people are averse to risk. We buy insurance, after all. People who are averse to risk dislike uncertainty and unpredictability — and unexpected inflation certainly creates uncertainty and unpredictability.

Yet perhaps the economic costs of moderate unexpected inflation are relatively low. Why don't debtors and creditors want to insure themselves against inflation risk by *indexing* their contracts and using some alternative, more stable unit of account? In economies with high and variable inflation, we do see such indexation. The fact that we do not see it in countries with moderate and low inflation suggests that the costs of inflation to individual debtors and creditors (though perhaps not to society as a whole) must be relatively low.

Nevertheless, there is a powerful political argument that the costs of moderate inflation are high. Voters do not like moderate inflation. The 1970s saw government after government in the industrialized world voted out of office. Polls showed that voters interpreted the rising rates of inflation as signs that the political parties in power were incompetent at managing the economy. Since the end of the 1970s, no major political party in the industrialized world has dared run on a platform of less price stability and more inflation.

Hyperinflation and Its Costs

The costs of inflation mount to economy-destroying levels during episodes of *hyperinflation,* when inflation rises by more than 20 percent *per month.* Hyperinflations arise when governments attempt to obtain extra revenue by printing money but overestimate how much they can raise. For some governments, printing money is an important source of revenue. Most governments tax their citizens or borrow from people who think that the government will pay them back. But if a government finds that it does not have the administrative reach to increase its explicit tax take and that no one will lend to it, it can simply print money and use the bills hot off the press to purchase goods and services.

Where do the resources — the power to buy goods and services — that the government acquires by printing money come from? A government that finances its spending by printing money is actually financing its spending by levying a tax on holdings of cash. Suppose I have $500 in cash in my pocket when the government suddenly announces it has printed up enough extra dollar bills to double the economy's cash supply. With Y and V unchanged, doubling the money supply doubles the price level. The $500 in my pocket will buy only as much after the government's money-printing spree as $250 would have bought before. The situation is as if the government levied a special one-time 50 percent tax on cash holdings.

Where did the 250 real dollars in my pocket go? The government has them: It now has 500 newly printed dollars, even if each of them is worth half a preinflation dollar in real terms. Clearly, printing money can be easier than imposing a 50 percent explicit tax. To collect an explicit tax, a government needs an entire wealth-tracking, money-collecting, compliance-monitoring bureaucracy. To print money, all the government needs is a printing press, some ink, some paper, and a working connection to the electric power grid.

Almost everyone agrees that this **inflation tax** — also called **seigniorage** because the right to coin money was originally a right reserved to certain feudal lords, certain *seigneurs* — is a bad policy. One of the first principles of public finance is that

FIGURE 8.9

The Inflation Tax

The "inflation tax" is a way for the government to get command over goods and services just as much as is any other tax. Those who pay the inflation tax are those who hold assets that lose value in the event of inflation.

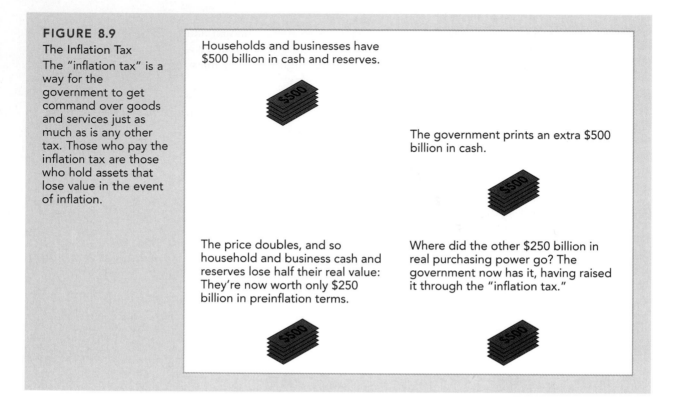

Households and businesses have $500 billion in cash and reserves.

The government prints an extra $500 billion in cash.

The price doubles, and so household and business cash and reserves lose half their real value: They're now worth only $250 billion in preinflation terms.

Where did the other $250 billion in real purchasing power go? The government now has it, having raised it through the "inflation tax."

taxes should be broad-based and lie relatively lightly on economic activity. The inflation tax is a heavy tax on a narrow base of economic activity, the activity of holding money. Moreover, the inflation tax is a heavy tax on one small slice of money holding: cash and deposits at the central bank. (See Figure 8.9.)

Other components of the money stock — your checking account, say — are not a potential source of purchasing power for the government through the inflation tax. Suppose that you deposited your money in your checking account and the bank then took that purchasing power and used it to buy an office building. If the price level doubles, you have lost half the real value of your checking account, but the gainer in real terms is not the government. The gainer in real terms is the bank, which now finds the value of the office building it owns is twice as large relative to the value of the money it owes to its depositors. Not only is an inflation tax a bad tax, but in its operation it disrupts the rest of the financial system as well.

For these reasons, the inflation tax is resorted to only by a government that is falling apart and lacks the administrative capacity to raise money in any other way. Even so, such a government usually finds out afterward that the costs of the inflation tax and hyperinflation outweigh the benefits. Eventually prices rise so rapidly that the monetary system breaks down. People would rather deal with each other in barter terms than use a form of cash whose value is shrinking measurably every day. GDP starts to fall as the economy begins to lose the benefits of the division of labor. In the end the government finds that its currency is next to worthless. It runs the printing presses faster and faster and yet finds that the money it prints buys less and less. At the end of the German hyperinflation of the 1920s, 1 trillion marks were needed to buy what 1 mark had bought less than 10 years before.

RECAP THE COSTS OF INFLATION

The economic costs of expected moderate inflation are small. They are largely the costs of extra trips to the bank and of time and resources wasted in the socially unproductive activity of keeping one's money balance near its target level. The economic costs of moderate unexpected inflation are larger. It redistributes wealth unexpectedly between debtors and creditors and increases risk. Largest, however, are the political costs of moderate inflation: Voters seem to use inflation as a sign that the government's economic policy is not sound.

If you look for high economic costs of inflation, you must turn your attention to episodes of hyperinflation. In a hyperinflation a government without the ability to tax or borrow resorts to printing money to buy goods and services. The inflation rate rises to 20 percent per month or more. The price mechanism breaks down as people resort to barter. And production falls.

Chapter Summary

1. By "money" economists mean something special: wealth in the form of readily spendable purchasing power.

2. Without money it is hard to imagine how our economy could successfully function. The fact that everyone will accept money as payment for goods and services is necessary for the market economy to function.

3. Money is not only a medium of exchange, but also a unit of account — a yardstick that we use to measure values and to specify contracts.

4. Money demand is determined by (a) businesses' and households' desire to hold wealth in the form of readily spendable purchasing power in order to carry out transactions, and (b) businesses' and households' recognition that there is a cost to holding money — wealth in the form of readily spendable purchasing power pays little or no interest.

5. The velocity of money is how many transactions a given piece of money manages to facilitate in a year. The principal determinant of the velocity of money is the economy's "transactions technology": the organization of its financial system.

6. The stock of money is determined by the central bank.

7. The price level is equal to the money stock times the velocity of money divided by the level of real GDP.

8. The inflation rate is equal to the proportional growth rate of the money stock plus the proportional growth rate of velocity minus the proportional growth rate of real GDP.

9. Governments cause hyperinflations because printing money is a way of taxing the public, and a government that cannot tax any other way will be strongly tempted to resort to it.

Key Terms

inflation (p. 218)

hyperinflation (p. 218)

money (p. 218)

neutrality (p. 219)

money stock (p. 219)

price level (p. 219)

classical dichotomy (p. 219)

medium of exchange (p. 220)

unit of account (p. 220)

quantity theory of money (p. 222)

velocity (p. 222)

Federal Reserve (p. 224)

central bank (p. 224)

monetary base (p. 224)

open-market operations (p. 224)

reserve requirements (p. 225)

inflation tax (p. 233)

seigniorage (p. 233)

Analytical Exercises

1. Economists say that a government can raise real revenue — real power to buy goods and services — through the "inflation tax." Who is it that pays this tax? How is it that the government collects it?

2. Suppose that real GDP is $10,000 billion, the velocity of money is 5, and the money stock is $2,500 billion. What is the price level?

3. Suppose that the rate of labor-force growth is 1 percent per year, the rate of growth of the efficiency of labor is 3 percent per year, the economy is on its steady-state growth path, and the velocity of money is increasing at 1 percent per year. Suppose also that the Chair of the Federal Reserve calls you into his or her office and asks how fast money growth should be to achieve a stable price level. What answer do you give?

4. Suppose that the rate of labor-force growth is 3 percent per year, but the efficiency of labor is stable and the economy is on its steady-state growth path. Suppose also that the rate of growth of the nominal money stock is 10 percent per year. Do you think that it is likely that the inflation rate is less than 5 percent per year? Why or why not?

5. What would the Federal Reserve have to do if it wanted to raise the monetary base today by $10 billion? What do you guess would happen to the price of short-term government bonds if the Federal Reserve did this?

Policy Exercises

1. In early September 1998 the U.S. monetary base was $500 billion. Suppose that the U.S. government decided to raise $250 billion in real purchasing power (in the dollars of September 1998) through the inflation tax. What would happen to the price level?

2. In the third quarter of 1998 nominal GDP was $8,574 billion. The monetary base H was $494 billion; M1 was $1,072 billion; and M2 was $4,210 billion. Calculate the velocities of the monetary base, M1, and M2.

3. Between 1990 and 1998 M1 increased from $826 billion to $1,092 billion, while nominal GDP increased from $5,744 billion to $8,507 billion. What was the average annual rate of increase of the M1 money stock? Of nominal GDP? Of M1 velocity?

4. Between 1980 and 1990, and between 1990 and 1998 M1 increased from $409 billion to $826 billion to $1,092 billion; M2 rose from $1,601 billion to $3,280 billion to $4,412 billion; and M3 rose from $1,992 billion to $4,066 billion to $5,983 billion, while nominal GDP rose from $2,784 billion to $5,744 billion to $8,507 billion. Calculate the average annual rates of increase of M1, M2, M3, and nominal GDP $P \times Y$ between 1980 and 1990 and between 1990 and 1998. Calculate the average annual rates of increase of the velocity of M1, M2, and M3 between 1980 and 1990 and between 1990 and 1998. How constant do these velocity trends appear to be both across time and across different measures of the money stock?

5. Suppose that you were told that the rate of inflation was about to decline significantly over the next decade. Would you expect the velocity of money to rise unusually fast, behave normally, or fall over the course of the decade?

Sticky-Price
MACROECONOMICS

PART IV

Chapters 4 through 8 do not give a complete picture of the macro-economy. In Chapters 4 through 8, growth is smooth from year to year. But in the real world growth is not. In Chapters 4 through 8, supply and demand in the labor market are always in balance. But in the real world the labor market is not always in equilibrium.

To understand these business-cycle fluctuations in economic growth and unemployment, we need a model that does not require that employment be full and real GDP equal to potential output. The full-employment model of Part III is not of help because its flexible-price assumption guarantees full employment. Here in Part IV, therefore, we need to break this flexible-price assumption to build a useful model of the business cycle.

From this point forward prices will be "sticky": They will not move freely and instantaneously in response to changes in demand and supply. We will use this sticky-price model to account for business-cycle fluctuations.

Building this sticky-price model of the macroeconomy is the task of Part IV. Chapter 9 focuses on how, when prices are sticky, the inventory adjustment process is the key to understanding how GDP can fall below or rise above potential output. Chapter 10 analyzes how changes in the interest rate affect investment, exports, and GDP. Chapter 11 focuses on equilibrium in the money market and the balance of aggregate demand and aggregate supply. Chapter 12 focuses on expectations and inflation. It links the sticky-price model of Part IV back to the flexible-price model of Part III by analyzing which model is most useful in what sets of circumstances.

The Income-Expenditure Framework: Consumption and the Multiplier

CHAPTER

QUESTIONS

What are "sticky" prices?

What factors might make prices sticky?

When prices are sticky, what determines the level of real GDP in the short run?

When prices are sticky, what happens to real GDP if some component of aggregate demand falls?

When prices are sticky, what happens to real GDP if some component of aggregate demand rises?

What determines the size of the spending multiplier?

Over the past decade real GDP in the American economy has grown at an average rate of 3.8 percent per year. At the same time, the American unemployment rate has fluctuated around an average level consistent with stable inflation — a *natural rate of unemployment* — of 4.5 percent. (Note, however, that this natural rate of unemployment is not a constant: It moves slowly over time.) And the inflation rate in the United States has averaged about 2.5 percent per year.

If Chapters 4 through 8 gave a complete picture of the macroeconomy, economic growth would be smooth. Real GDP would grow 3.8 percent — the current rate of growth of potential GDP — year after year, not just on average. The unemployment rate would remain steady at its *natural rate* of approximately 4.5 percent. And inflation would be steady as well, determined by the rates of growth of potential output and the money stock and on the velocity of money.

If such were the case, the analysis in Chapters 4 and 5 would provide a complete picture of how potential output grew over time. The analysis in Chapters 6 and 7 would explain why real GDP equals potential output and how national income is divided among the different components of aggregate demand. The analysis in Chapter 8 would detail how the price level and the inflation rate are determined. It would be the last chapter in this textbook. Your survey of macroeconomics would be finished.

But Chapters 4 through 8 do not give a complete picture of the macroeconomy. Growth is not at all smooth; on a year-to-year time scale, it is not even guaranteed. In 1982 real GDP was not 3.8 percent more but 2.1 percent less than it was in 1981 (see Figure 9.1). Between 1979 and 1982 the unemployment rate rose by 4.1 per-

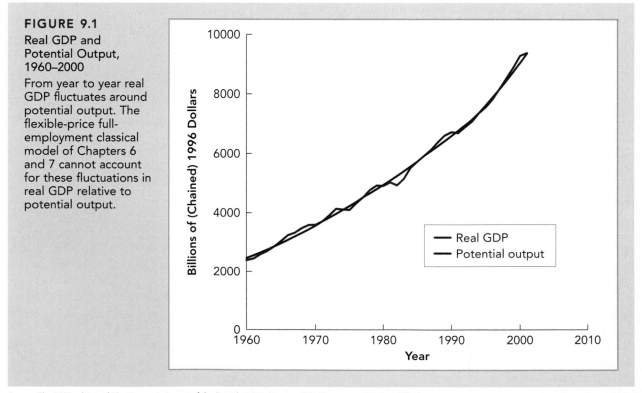

FIGURE 9.1
Real GDP and Potential Output, 1960–2000

From year to year real GDP fluctuates around potential output. The flexible-price full-employment classical model of Chapters 6 and 7 cannot account for these fluctuations in real GDP relative to potential output.

Source: The 2001 edition of *The Economic Report of the President* (Washington, DC: Government Printing Office).

centage points, and it rose again by 2.2 percentage points between 1989 and 1992. Unemployment may have been only 4 percent at the end of 2000, but it was 7.6 percent in the middle of 1992. Inflation at the end of 2000 may have been only 2.8 percent per year, but in 1981 it was 9.4 percent.

These fluctuations in growth are called *business cycles*. A business cycle has two phases: an exciting expansion or boom phase as production, employment, and prices all grow rapidly, and a subsequent recession or depression phase during which inflation falls or prices slump, unemployment rises, and production falls. During booms, output grows faster than trend, investment spending amounts to a higher-than-average share of GDP, unemployment falls, and inflation usually accelerates. During recessions, output falls, investment spending is a low share of real GDP, unemployment rises, and inflation usually decelerates.

9.1 STICKY PRICES

Business Cycles

To understand business cycles, we need a model that does not guarantee always-full employment and in which real GDP does not always equal potential output. Business cycles, after all, are not fluctuations in potential output but fluctuations of actual production around potential output. Thus the full-employment model of Chapters 6 through 8 is of no help because its assumption that **prices are flexible** guarantees full employment. The flexible-price assumption allowed us to start our analysis by noting that the labor market would clear with the supply of workers equal to the demand for labor and that as a result firms would fully employ the labor force and thus real GDP and household income would be equal to potential output.

From this point forward, however, we need to break this flexible-price assumption in order to build a more useful model of the business cycle. Thus prices will be "sticky": They will not move freely and instantaneously in response to changes in demand and supply. Instead, prices will remain fixed at predetermined levels as businesses expand or contract production in response to changes in demand and costs. As you will see, such sticky prices make a big difference in economic analysis; they will drive a wedge between real GDP and potential output and between the supply of workers and the demand for labor. We will then be able to use this sticky-price model to account for business-cycle fluctuations.

Building this **sticky-price** model of the macroeconomy will take up all of Part IV. In this chapter, we will focus on how, when prices are sticky, firms hire or fire workers and expand or cut back production on the basis of whether their inventories are falling or rising. Inventory adjustment is the key to understanding how the level of real GDP can fall below and fluctuate around potential output. Chapter 10 focuses on how changes in the Federal Reserve–controlled interest rate affect the levels of investment, exports, and real GDP in the sticky-price model.

Chapter 11 begins to cover the monetary side of the sticky-price model. First, it analyzes equilibrium in the money market; second, it analyzes how the balance between aggregate demand and aggregate supply determines the price level in the sticky-price model. The last chapter of Part IV, Chapter 12, focuses on expectations and inflation. By the end of Chapter 12 we will have linked up the sticky-price model of Part IV with the flexible-price model of Part III. We will understand the sorts of situations for which the sticky-price model is appropriate. And we will understand under what sets of circumstances wages and prices are flexible enough and have enough time to adjust for the flexible-price model to be the most useful way of analyzing the macroeconomy.

At each stage in the building of our sticky-price macroeconomic model, the preceding topic serves as a necessary foundation. The analysis of inflation and expectations in Chapter 12 rests on the analysis of aggregate demand and aggregate supply in Chapter 11. The analysis of monetary equilibrium and aggregate demand in Chapter 11 rests on the analysis of how changes in interest rates affect investment, exports, and real GDP in Chapter 10. And the analysis of Chapter 10 in turn rests on the analysis of income, expenditure, and equilibrium in a sticky-price economy carried out here in Chapter 9.

Up to this point this book has not been *cumulative*. You could understand the long-run growth analysis in Chapters 4 and 5 without a firm grasp of the introductory material in Chapters 1 through 3. You could understand the flexible-price analysis in Chapters 6 and 7 without a firm grasp of either the introductory or the long-run growth chapters. And you could understand Chapter 8 without having read anything earlier in the book. But from this point on, this book becomes very cumulative indeed: Chapter 10 is incomprehensible without a firm grasp of Chapter 9; Chapter 11 is incomprehensible without a firm grasp of Chapter 10; Chapter 12 is incomprehensible without a firm grasp of Chapter 11; and the chapters that follow 12 require it as well.

The Consequences of Sticky Prices

Flexible-Price Logic

To preview the difference between the flexible-price and the sticky-price models, let us analyze a decline in consumers' propensity to spend under both sets of assumptions. Suppose there is a sudden fall in the parameter C_0 that determines the baseline level of consumption in the consumption function

$$C = C_0 + C_y \times Y$$

At any given level of national income Y, consumers wish to save more and spend less. To make this concrete, suppose that the function for annual consumption spending (in billions of dollars) declines from

$$C = 2000 + 0.5 \times Y$$

to

$$C = 1800 + 0.5 \times Y$$

In the full-employment model of Chapters 6 through 8, a $200 billion fall in annual consumption spending would have no impact on *real* GDP. No matter what the flow of aggregate demand, because nominal wages and prices are flexible the labor market would still reach its full-employment equilibrium as shown in Figure 9.2. And because the economy remains at full employment, real GDP would equal potential output.

The fall in consumption spending would have an effect on the economy — just not on the level of real GDP. As we saw in Chapters 6 and 7, a fall in consumption spending means an increase in savings. As consumption falls, the savings supply curve shifts rightward on the flow-of-funds diagram, as Figure 9.3 shows. Thus a fall in consumption spending reduces the equilibrium interest rate in the flow-of-funds market. It also increases the equilibrium level of investment and net exports by $200 billion a year, the amount necessary to keep GDP equal to potential output.

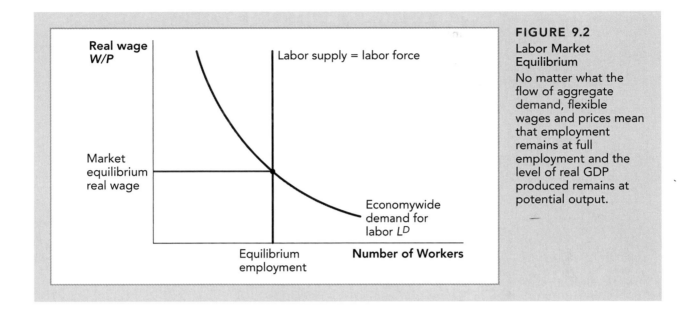

FIGURE 9.2
Labor Market Equilibrium
No matter what the flow of aggregate demand, flexible wages and prices mean that employment remains at full employment and the level of real GDP produced remains at potential output.

Moreover, as we saw in Chapter 8, such a fall in the real rate has consequences for money demand. Changes in households' and businesses' total demand for money M can be triggered by a change in the price level P, real GDP Y, the banking system structure-driven trend in the velocity of money V^L, or the dependence of velocity on the nominal interest rate. The higher the nominal interest rate i — which equals the real interest rate r plus the expected future inflation rate π^e — the lower are

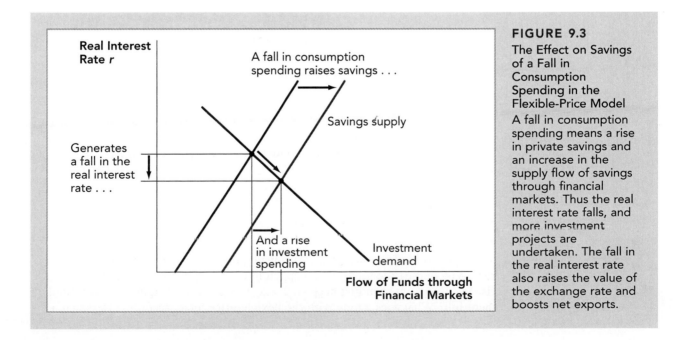

FIGURE 9.3
The Effect on Savings of a Fall in Consumption Spending in the Flexible-Price Model
A fall in consumption spending means a rise in private savings and an increase in the supply flow of savings through financial markets. Thus the real interest rate falls, and more investment projects are undertaken. The fall in the real interest rate also raises the value of the exchange rate and boosts net exports.

households' and businesses' demand to hold their wealth in the readily spendable and liquid form of money:

$$M = \frac{P \times Y}{V^L \times [V_0 + V_i \times (r + \pi^e)]}$$

If we rearrange this equation to solve for the equilibrium price level P,

$$P = \left(\frac{M}{T}\right) \times \{V^L \times [V_0 + V_i \times (r + \pi^e)]\}$$

we see that a fall in the nominal interest rate means a fall in velocity and carries with it a fall in the price level. As households and businesses try to divert some of their spending to build up their stocks of liquid money, their actions put downward pressure on prices, restoring equilibrium in the money market.

Thus these are the flexible-price-model consequences of a fall in consumers' desired baseline spending:

- Consumption falls.
- Savings rise.
- The real interest rate falls.
- Investment rises.
- The value of the exchange rate rises.
- The price level declines.

Sticky-Price Logic

If wages and prices are sticky, the analysis is different. The first consequence of consumers' cutting back their spending will be a fall in the aggregate demand for goods. Consumer spending has fallen, yet nothing has happened to change the flow of spending on investment goods, the flow of net exports, or the flow of government purchases.

As businesses see spending on their products begin to fall, they will not cut their nominal prices (remember, prices are sticky). Instead, they will respond to the fall in the quantity of their products demanded by reducing their production, They want to avoid accumulating unsold and unsellable inventory. As they reduce production, they will fire some of their workers, and the incomes of the fired workers will drop. By how much will total national income drop? It will fall by the amount of the fall in consumption spending: $200 billion a year. (Moreover, because the decline in incomes leads to a further decline in consumption as households that have lost income cut back on their spending, national incomes and real GDP will fall by more than the decline in C_0. This *multiplier* process is discussed later on in the chapter.)

In sum, the consequences of a fall in consumption spending under the sticky-price assumption are:

- Consumption falls.
- Production and employment decline.
- National income declines.

In the flexible-price model, when consumption falls, investment and net exports rise. Why doesn't the same thing happen in the sticky-price model? Why doesn't a rise in investment spending keep GDP equal to potential output and keep employment full? What goes wrong with the flexible-price logic, according to which a fall

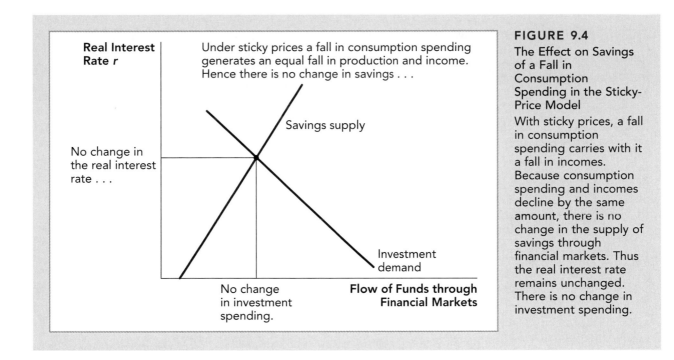

FIGURE 9.4
The Effect on Savings of a Fall in Consumption Spending in the Sticky-Price Model
With sticky prices, a fall in consumption spending carries with it a fall in incomes. Because consumption spending and incomes decline by the same amount, there is no change in the supply of savings through financial markets. Thus the real interest rate remains unchanged. There is no change in investment spending.

in consumption spending generates an increase in savings that then boosts both investment spending and net exports?

The answer is that as firms cut back production and employment, total income falls. A fall in total income reduces savings (if consumption is held constant) just as a fall in consumption raises savings (if income is held constant). Under the sticky-price assumption that effects on savings of the fall in consumption and the fall in income cancel each other out, there is no change in the flow of savings. Thus there is no rightward shift in the position of the savings supply curve on the flow-of-funds diagram in Figure 9.4. There is no fall in interest rates to trigger higher investment (and a higher value of the exchange rate and expanded net exports). There is nothing to offset the fall in consumption spending and keep GDP from falling below potential output.

Why doesn't this sticky-price unemployment-generating logic work when prices are flexible? The answer is that when flexible-price firms see a fall in aggregate demand spending, they respond not by cutting production and employment but by cutting the nominal prices they charge and the nominal wages they pay. Since prices and wages both fall, the real incomes households earn remain constant. Thus a fall in consumption spending does induce a rise in savings — hence a fall in the real interest rate, a rise in investment spending, an increase in the value of the exchange rate, and a rise in net exports.

Expectations and Price Stickiness

Note that price stickiness causes problems only in the short run. If managers, workers, consumers, and investors had time to foresee a fall in consumption and gradually adjust their wages and prices to it, even considerable stickiness in prices would not be a problem. With sufficient advance notice unions and businesses would strike wage bargains, and businesses could adjust their selling prices to make sure demand matches productive capacity. Both the stickiness of prices and the failure to accurately foresee changes far enough in advance are needed to create business cycles.

Thus one way to think about it is that the analysis in Part IV is a short-run analysis and the analysis in Part III is a longer-run analysis although still not as long-run as the analysis of Part II. In the short run, prices are sticky; shifts in policy or in the economic environment that affect the components of aggregate demand will affect real GDP and employment. In the long run, prices are flexible and workers, bosses, and consumers have time to react and adjust to changes in policy or the economic environment. Thus in the long run, such shifts do not affect real GDP or employment.

Why do we need a sticky-price short-run model as well as the model? Why isn't it good enough to say that once wages and prices have fully adjusted (however long that takes), unemployment will be back at its natural rate and real GDP will be equal to potential output? The most famous and effective criticism of such let's-look-only-at-the-long-run analyses was made by John Maynard Keynes on page 88 of his 1924 *Tract on Monetary Reform*. Criticizing one such long-run-only analysis, Keynes wrote: "In the long run [it] is probably true. . . . But this *long run* is a misleading guide to current affairs. *In the long run* we are all dead. Economists set themselves too easy, too useless a task if in tempestuous seasons they can only tell us that when the storm is long past the ocean will be flat once more."

Where is the line that divides the short run from the long run? Do we switch from living in the short run of Part IV to the long run of Part III on June 19, 2005? No, we do not. The long run is an analytical construct. A change can be considered "long run" if enough people see it coming far enough in advance and have had time to adjust to it — to renegotiate their contracts and change their standard operating procedures accordingly. The length of the long run, and thus how many of us will be dead before it comes, depends in turn on the degree of price stickiness and the process by which people form their expectations — both key topics for research in modern macroeconomics.

Why Are Prices Sticky?

Why don't prices adjust quickly and smoothly to maintain full employment? Why do businesses respond to fluctuations in demand first by hiring or firing workers and accelerating or shutting down their production lines? Why don't they respond first by raising or lowering their prices.

Economists have identified any number of reasons that prices could be sticky, but they are uncertain which are most important. Some likely explanations are:

- Managers and workers find that changing prices or renegotiating wages is costly and hence best delayed as long as possible.
- Managers and workers lack information and so confuse changes in total economywide spending with changes in demand for their specific products.
- The level of prices is as much a sociological as an economic variable — determined as much by what values people think are "fair" as by the balance of supply and demand. Workers take a cut in their wages as an indication that their employer does not value them — hence managers avoid wage cuts because they fear the consequences for worker morale.

- Managers and workers suffer from simple "money illusion"; they overlook the effect of price-level changes when assessing the impact of changes in wages or prices on their real incomes or sales.

Let's look more closely at each of these likely explanations. Economists call the costs associated with changing prices "**menu costs,**" a shorthand reference to the fact that when a restaurant changes its prices, it must print up a new menu. In general, changing prices or wages may be costly for any of a large number of reasons. Perhaps people want to stabilize their commercial relationships by signing long-term contracts. Perhaps reprinting a catalog is expensive. Perhaps customers find frequent price changes annoying. Perhaps other firms are not changing their prices and what matters most to a firm is its price relative to the prices of competitors. Hence managers and workers prefer to keep their prices and wages stable as long as the shocks that affect the economy are relatively small — or, rather, as long as the change they might want to make in their prices and wages is small.

A second source of price stickiness is misperception of real and nominal price changes. If managers and workers lack full information about the state of the economy, they may be unsure whether a change in the flow of spending on *their* products reflects a change in overall aggregate demand or a change in demand for their particular products. If it is the latter, they *should* respond by changing how much they produce, not necessarily by changing the price. If it is the former, they should respond by changing their price in accord with overall inflation, not by changing how much they produce.

If managers are uncertain which it is, they will split the difference. Hence firms will lower their prices less in response to a downward shift in total nominal demand than the flexible-price macroeconomic model would predict. If they keep their prices too high, they will have to fire workers and cut back production. **Imperfect information** is a possible source of sticky prices.

Yet a third reason why prices and wages are sticky is that workers and managers are really not the flinty-eyed rational maximizers of economic theories. In real life, work effort and work intensity depend on whether workers believe they are being treated fairly. A cut in nominal wages is almost universally perceived as unfair; wages depend on social norms that evolve slowly. Thus wages are by nature sticky. And if wages are sticky, firms will find that their best response to shifts in demand is to hire and fire workers rather than to change prices.

Last, workers, consumers, and managers confuse changes in nominal prices with changes in real (that is, inflation-adjusted) prices. Firms react to higher nominal prices by thinking falsely that it is more profitable to produce more — even though it isn't because their costs have risen in proportion. Workers react to higher nominal wages by searching more intensively for jobs and working more overtime hours, even though rises in prices have erased any increase in the real purchasing power of the wage paid for an hour's work. Such **money illusion** is a powerful generator of price stickiness and business-cycle fluctuations.

All these factors are potential sources of price stickiness. Your professor may have strong views about which is most important, but I believe that our knowledge is more limited. I am not sure the evidence is strong enough to provide clear and convincing support for any particular single explanation as the most important one. A safer position is to remain agnostic about the causes of sticky wages and prices, and so we will focus on analyzing their effects.

The full-employment model of Chapters 6 through 8 does not help explain business cycles because its assumption that prices are flexible guarantees that real GDP is always equal to potential output. In order to build a more useful model of the business cycle, we need to assume that prices are sticky. If prices are sticky, the first consequence of a shock like consumers cutting back their spending will be a fall in the aggregate demand for goods. As businesses see spending on their products begin to fall, they will not cut their nominal prices but will reduce production and fire workers to avoid accumulating unsold and unsellable inventory. Thus output can fall below potential output, and unemployment can rise above its natural rate.

9.2 INCOME AND EXPENDITURE

If prices are sticky, higher aggregate demand boosts production, and this boosts incomes. Higher incomes give a further boost to consumption, and this in turn boosts aggregate demand some more. Thus any shift in a component of aggregate demand upward or downward leads to an *amplified* shift in total production because of the induced shift in consumption, as Figure 9.5 shows. The early-twentieth-century British economist John Maynard Keynes was one of the first to stress the importance of this *multiplier* process.

While in booms the multiplier process induces an upward spiral in production, in bad times it is a source of misery. The downward shock is amplified as those who have been thrown out of work cut back on their consumption spending in turn. Because consumption spending is more than two-thirds of aggregate demand, this multiplier effect can be significant because the positive-feedback loop is so large.

Building Up Aggregate Demand

In the remainder of this chapter we will see how the level of aggregate demand is determined in the sticky-price macroeconomic model. We will use a bottom-up ap-

FIGURE 9.5
The Multiplier Process
In the multiplier process, an increase in spending causes an increase in production and incomes, which leads to a further increase in spending. This positive-feedback loop amplifies the effect of any initial shift.

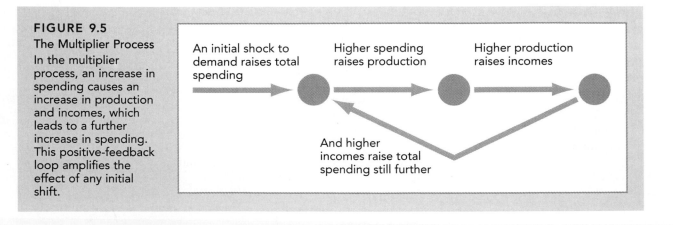

An initial shock to demand raises total spending

Higher spending raises production

Higher production raises incomes

And higher incomes raise total spending still further

proach, building aggregate demand or planned expenditure *E* on domestically produced products up from the determinants of each of its components, consumption spending *C,* investment spending *I,* government purchases *G,* and net exports *NX:*

$$E = C + I + G + NX$$

As long as prices are sticky, the level of real GDP is determined by the level of aggregate demand

$$Y = E$$

and not by the level of potential output

$$Y = Y^*$$

The Consumption Function

The two-thirds of GDP that is consumption spending is spending by households on things they find useful: services such as haircuts, nondurable goods such as food, and durable goods such as washing machines. As incomes rise, consumption spending rises with them, increasing demand and setting the multiplier process in motion. As we saw in Chapter 6, consumption spending does not rise dollar for dollar with total incomes. The share of an extra dollar of disposable income that is added to consumption spending is the **marginal propensity to consume (MPC)**, as shown in Figure 9.6, the parameter C_y in the consumption function equation. The share of an extra dollar of national income that shows up as additional consumption spending is equal to the marginal propensity to consume times the share of income that escapes taxes: $(1 - t)C_y$ in the **consumption function** equation:

$$C = C_0 + C_y (1 - t)Y$$

If changes in incomes are considered permanent, the MPC will be high: A \$1 increase in incomes will lead to an increase in consumption of as much as 80 cents. But if changes in income are considered transitory, the MPC will be low: A \$1 increase in incomes will lead to an increase in consumption of only 30 cents or so.

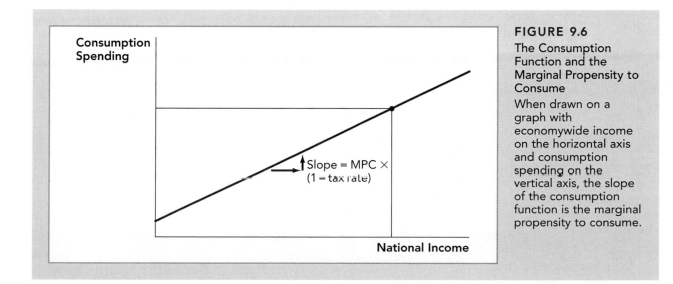

FIGURE 9.6

The Consumption Function and the Marginal Propensity to Consume

When drawn on a graph with economywide income on the horizontal axis and consumption spending on the vertical axis, the slope of the consumption function is the marginal propensity to consume.

Transitory increases in income have only a small effect on consumption because people seek to smooth out their consumption spending over time.

For reasonably long-lasting shifts in the level of income, the MPC C_y is roughly 0.6. That is, 60 cents of every extra dollar of disposable income shows up as higher consumption. But remember that, as shown in Figure 9.7, the slope of the con-

FIGURE 9.7

Consumption as a Function of After-Tax Disposable Income

Three different factors drive the wedge between GDP and consumption spending. The first is depreciation: goods produced that merely replace obsolete and worn-out capital and so are a component of total cost rather than total income. The second is the tax system — both direct and indirect taxes. The third is private savings.

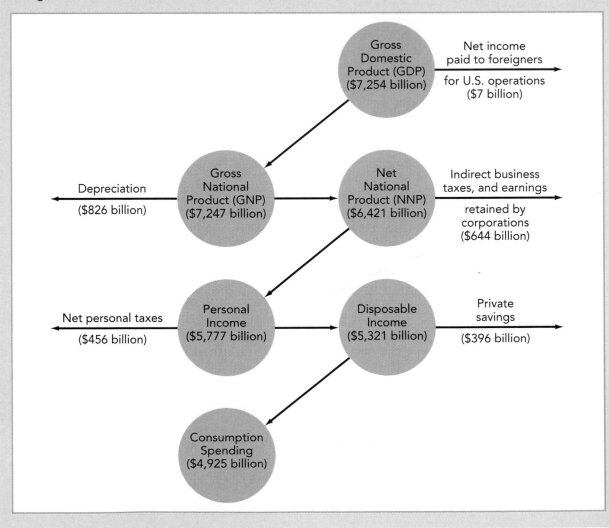

Source: The 2001 edition of *The Economic Report of the President* (Washington, DC: Government Printing Office).

CALCULATING THE CONSUMPTION FUNCTION: AN EXAMPLE

Suppose statistical evidence tells us that the marginal propensity to consume out of disposable income C_y is 0.75. Suppose further that taxes amount to 40 percent of national income and that when real GDP — total national income — equals \$8 trillion, consumption equals \$5.5 trillion.

The fact that C_y is 0.6 and that the average tax rate t is 0.4 allows us to fill in some of the parameters in the consumption function:

$$C = C_0 + C_y \times (1 - t) \times Y$$
$$= C_0 + 0.75 \times (1 - 0.4) \times Y$$
$$= C_0 + 0.45 \times Y$$

We also know that when national income Y equals \$8 trillion, consumption C equals \$5.5 trillion:

$$\$5.5 = C_0 + 0.45 \times \$8$$
$$= C_0 + \$3.6$$
$$\$1.9 = C_0$$

So the numerical form of the consumption function is

$$C = \$1.9 + 0.45 \times Y$$

sumption function is smaller than the parameter C_y because the tax system means that a \$1 increase in national income is a less-than-\$1 increase in disposable income.

Box 9.1 shows how to use the consumption function and its parameters — the MPC and the tax rate — to calculate what consumption spending is.

The Other Components of Aggregate Demand

The determinants of the other components of aggregate demand — investment spending, government purchases, and net exports — are familiar from Chapter 6.

The level of investment spending, I, is determined by the real interest rate and assessments of profitability made by business investment committees:

$$I = I_0 - I_r \times r$$

In our model we represent these determinants by making investment spending I a function of the real interest rate r and of the parameters I_0 and I_r, the baseline level of investment spending and the interest sensitivity of investment.

The level of government purchases G is set by politics. Net exports are equal to gross exports (a function of the real exchange rate ε and the level of foreign real GDP Y^f) minus imports. Imports are a function of national income Y:

$$NX = GX - IM = (X_f Y^f + X_\varepsilon \varepsilon) - IM_y Y$$

Figure 9.8 shows the relative sizes of these four components of aggregate demand.

Autonomous Spending and the Marginal Propensity to Expend

Let's take the equation for aggregate demand

$$E = C + I + G + NX$$

FIGURE 9.8

Components of Aggregate Demand

By far the largest component of GDP is made up of consumption spending. Government purchases come second, and gross investment comes third. For the past two decades the United States has imported more than it has exported; hence net exports have been negative, not a contribution to but a subtraction from GDP.

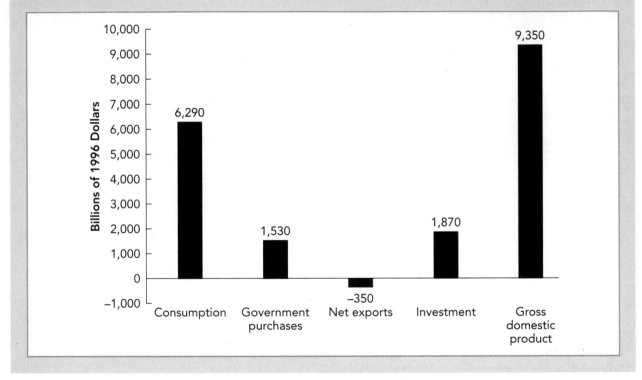

Source: The 2001 edition of *The Economic Report of the President* (Washington, DC: Government Printing Office).

and replace the two components of aggregate demand that depend directly on national income Y with their determinants:

$$E = [C_0 + C_y(1 - t)Y] + I + G + (GX - IM_yY)$$

We can now classify the components of aggregate demand into two groups. The first group is so-called **autonomous spending**, which we will call A. Autonomous spending is made up of the components of aggregate demand that do *not* depend directly on national income Y. The second group includes all the other components of aggregate demand. It is equal to the **marginal propensity to expend (MPE)** on domestic goods times the level of national income Y. Thus with these new definitions of

$$A = C_0 + I + G + GX$$

and

$$MPE = C_y(1 - t) - IM_y$$

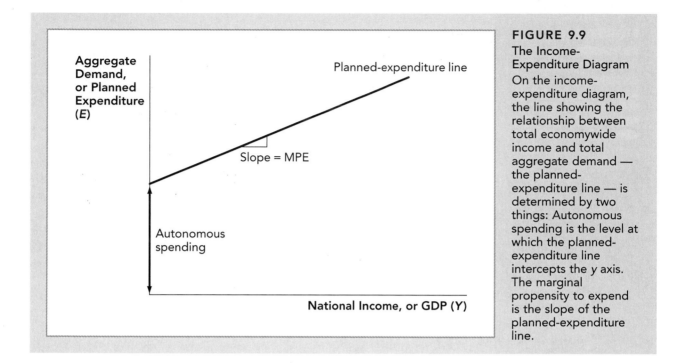

FIGURE 9.9
The Income-Expenditure Diagram
On the income-expenditure diagram, the line showing the relationship between total economywide income and total aggregate demand — the planned-expenditure line — is determined by two things: Autonomous spending is the level at which the planned-expenditure line intercepts the y axis. The marginal propensity to expend is the slope of the planned-expenditure line.

we can rearrange our equation for aggregate demand to fit these new definitions:

$$E = (C_0 + I + G + GX) + [C_y(1 - t) - IM_y] \times Y$$

and rewrite aggregate demand in the more compact form

$$E = \overset{\curvearrowright}{A} + MPE \times Y$$

which Figure 9.9 graphs. Aggregate demand or planned-expenditure is plotted on the vertical axis, and national income or real GDP is plotted on the horizontal axis of this **income-expenditure diagram**. In Figure 9.9, the intercept of the **planned-expenditure** or aggregate demand line is the level of **autonomous spending** A; the slope of the planned-expenditure or aggregate demand line is the **marginal propensity to expend MPE**.

A change in the value of any determinant of any component of autonomous spending — the baseline levels of consumption C_0, investment I_0, or government purchases G; the real interest rate r; and foreign-determined variables like foreign interest rates r^f, foreign levels of real income Y^f, or speculators' view of exchange rate fundamentals ε_0 — will shift the planned-expenditure line up or down. The higher the autonomous spending, the further from the x axis the planned-expenditure line will be (see Figure 9.10).

Changes in the marginal propensity to consume C_y, the tax rate t, or the propensity to spend on imports IM_y will change the MPE and the slope of the planned-expenditure line. The higher the MPE, the steeper is the slope of the planned-expenditure line (see Figure 9.11). Box 9.2 provides an example of how to calculate the MPE.

FIGURE 9.10

An Increase in Autonomous Spending

An increase in autonomous spending shifts the planned-expenditure line upward.

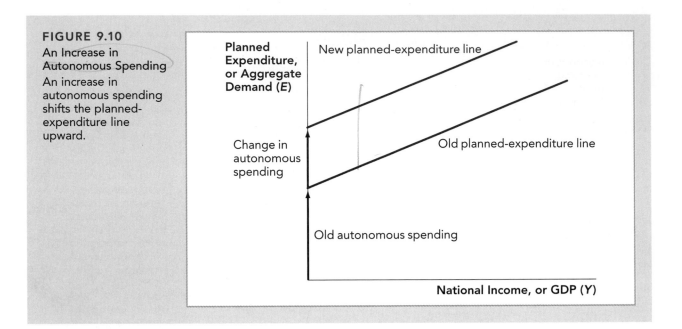

FIGURE 9.11

An Increase in the Marginal Propensity to Expend

A change in the marginal propensity to expend changes the slope of the planned-expenditure line.

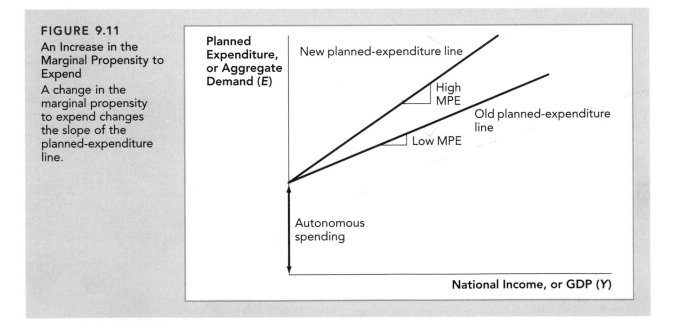

BOX 9.2

CALCULATING THE MPE: AN EXAMPLE

In the planned-expenditure function

$$E = A + MPE \times Y$$

the marginal propensity to expend (MPE) will be less than the slope of the consumption function $C_y(1 - t)$ because of the effect on the economy of imports. The MPE is

$$E = A + MPE \times Y$$

Thus if the marginal propensity to consume C_y is 0.75 and the tax rate is 40 percent, the 0.45 slope of the consumption function is an upper bound to the MPE. If imports are 15 percent of real GDP, then

$$MPE = [C_y(1 - t) - IM_y]$$
$$= [0.75 \times (1 - 0.4) - 0.15]$$
$$= 0.45 - 0.15 = 0.30$$

[handwritten: .2, .25]

Such relatively small values of the MPE are typical for modern industrialized economies, which have substantial amounts of international trade (that is, relatively high values for IM_y), large social-democratic social-insurance states (that is, relatively high values for t), and deep and well-developed financial systems that provide ample room for household borrowing and lending to smooth out consumption (that is, relatively small values for C_y as well). However, in the past, in relatively closed economies, or in economies with undeveloped financial systems, the MPE can be significantly higher.

Sticky-Price Equilibrium

The economy will be in equilibrium when planned expenditure equals real GDP — which is, according to the circular flow principle, the same as national income. Under these conditions there will be no short-run forces pushing for an immediate expansion or contraction of national income, real GDP, and aggregate demand.

On the income-expenditure diagram, the points at which planned expenditure equals national income are a line running up and to the right at a 45-degree angle with respect to the x axis, as Figure 9.12 shows. This line covers all the possible points of equilibrium. The actual equilibrium will be that point at which planned expenditure is equal to national income. The point where this planned-expenditure line intersects the 45-degree equilibrium-condition line is the economy's equilibrium.

In algebra, the equilibrium values of aggregate demand E and real GDP or national income Y must satisfy both

$$E = A + MPE \times Y$$

and

$$E = Y$$

Substituting Y for E in the first of these equations and regrouping, the solution is

$$Y = E = \frac{A}{1 - MPE}$$

[handwritten: $\frac{6 \text{ trillion}}{1 - [.6(1-.25)] - .2}$ $\frac{6}{.75} = 8$]

If the numerical values of the parameters of the planned expenditure function

$$E = A + MPE \times Y$$

are $A = \$5,600$ billion and MPE = 0.3, then planned expenditure as a function of real GDP is

$$E = 5,600 + 0.3 \times Y$$

[handwritten margin notes: $\sim PE$; $C_y(1-t) - IM_y$]

FIGURE 9.12

Equilibrium on the Income-Expenditure Diagram, 1996

On the income-expenditure diagram, the equilibrium point of the economy is that point where aggregate demand (as a function of total product) is equal to total product.

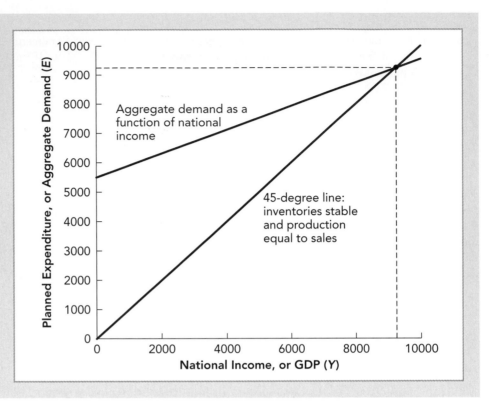

FIGURE 9.13

Inventory Adjustment and Equilibrium: Goods Market Equilibrium and the Income-Expenditure Diagram

If the economy is not at its equilibrium point, then either total production exceeds aggregate demand (in which case inventories are rising) or aggregate demand exceeds total production (in which case inventories are falling).

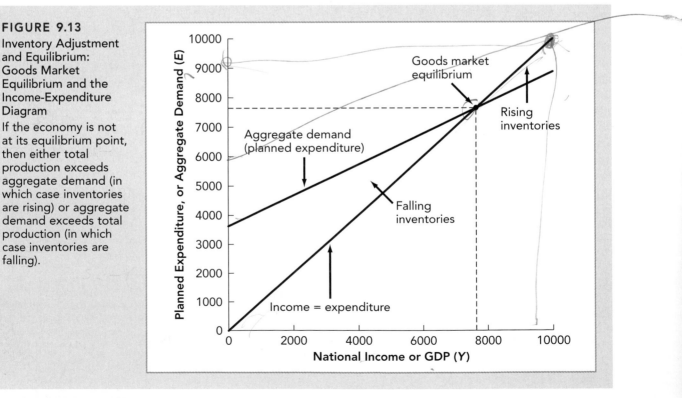

The equilibrium level of real GDP and aggregate demand is then

$$Y = \$8,000 \text{ billion}$$

If the economy is not on the 45-degree line, then aggregate demand E does not equal real GDP Y. If Y is greater than E, there is excess supply of goods. If E is greater than Y, there is excess demand for goods. In neither case is the economy in equilibrium.

In the first case, in which production exceeds demand, inventories are rising rapidly and firms unwilling to accumulate unsold and unsellable inventories are about to cut production and fire workers (see Figure 9.13). In the second case, in which demand exceeds production, inventories are falling rapidly. Businesses are selling more than they are making. Some businesses will respond to the fall in inventories by boosting prices, trying to earn more profit per good sold. But the bulk of businesses will respond to the fall in inventories by expanding production to match demand. They are about to hire more workers. Real GDP and national income are about to expand.

Now suppose that businesses see their inventories falling and respond by boosting their production to equal last month's planned expenditure. Will such an increase bring the economy into goods market equilibrium, with planned expenditure equal to total income and real GDP? The answer is that it will not. To boost production, firms must hire workers, paying more in wages and causing household incomes to rise. When income rises, total spending rises as well. Thus the increase in production and income generates a further expansion in aggregate demand.

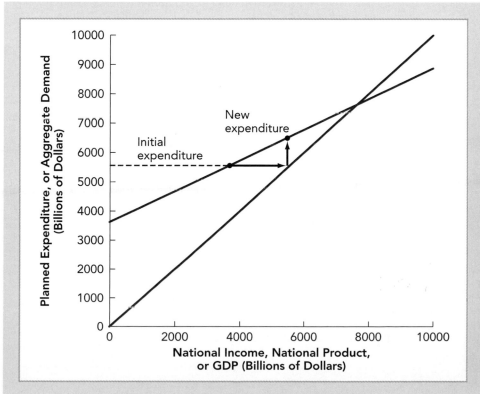

FIGURE 9.14

The Inventory Adjustment Process: An Income-Expenditure Diagram

If planned expenditure is greater than total production and inventories are falling, businesses will hire more workers and increase production.

Even after production has increased to close the initial gap between aggregate demand and national income, the economy will still not be in equilibrium, as Figure 9.14 shows. Inventories will be falling even though hiring more workers has increased production. Because hiring more workers has also boosted total income and further increased aggregate demand, production will have to expand by a *multiple* of the initial gap in order to stabilize inventories. The process will come to an end, with aggregate demand equal to national income, only when both have risen to the level at which the planned-expenditure line crosses the 45-degree income-equals-expenditure line. And the process works in reverse if planned expenditure is below national income.

BOX

9.3

HOW FAST DOES THE ECONOMY MOVE TO EQUILIBRIUM? SOME DETAILS

At any one particular moment the economy does not have to be in short-run equilibrium. Aggregate demand can exceed real GDP, and national income and inventories can fall, for periods as long as a year. There *are* strong forces pushing the economy toward short-run equilibrium. Businesses do not like to lose money by producing things that they cannot sell or by not having things on hand that they could sell. But it takes at least months, usually quarters, and possibly more time for businesses to expand or cut back production

For example, between the summer of 1990 and the summer of 1991 inventories fell for five straight quarters. Real GDP was less than aggregate demand as businesses decided that their high levels of inventories were too large given the economic uncertainties created by the Iraqi invasion of Kuwait and the subsequent recession. Between the winter of 1994 and the summer of 1995, for six quarters, inventories rose. For a year and a half GDP was greater than aggregate demand. (See Figure 9.15.)

FIGURE 9.15

Inventories as the Balancing Item: Inventory Investment in the 1990s

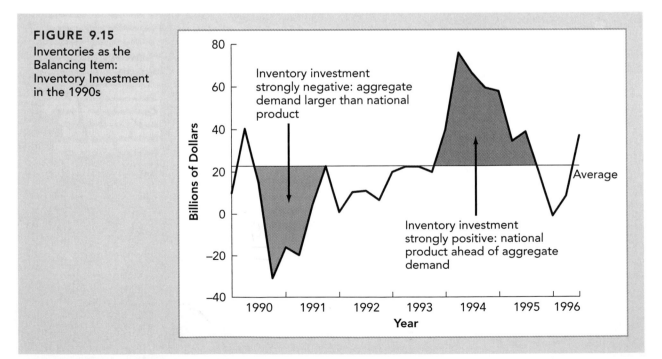

Source: The 2001 edition of *The Economic Report of the President* (Washington, DC: Government Printing Office).

INVENTORY ADJUSTMENT AND THE CIRCULAR FLOW: SOME DETAILS

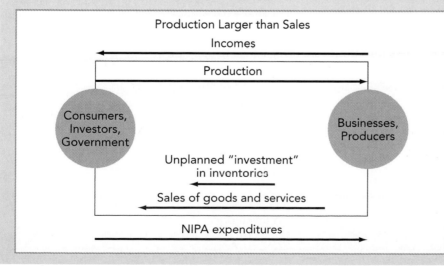

The economy can be out of equilibrium, with planned expenditure either higher or lower than national income and GDP. Yet by the definition of the circular flow, economywide total expenditure always equals national income or GDP. We would think that total expenditure is the same thing as aggregate demand. So isn't there a contradiction here?

The answer is that statisticians who compile the national income and product accounts (NIPA) define "total expenditure" in a peculiar way. When production is greater than spending and inventories pile up unexpectedly, the national income accountants say the producing company has made an "investment expenditure": It has spent money increasing its inventory.

Suppose Mammoth Motors produces an extra 100,000 cars, valued at $15,000 each, which it then fails to sell. Mammoth thus has the unpleasant surprise of seeing its inventory rise by 100,000 cars: an unexpected inventory increase of $1.5 billion. For Mammoth this is a disaster — it spent a huge sum making things it could not sell that are now sitting in parking lots across the nation. But NIPA statisticians record this as an "expenditure" by Mammoth: an investment in inventories of $1.5 billion. Never mind that Mammoth certainly did not want to make this "investment."

The NIPA system is set up to call every change in every business's inventory a positive or negative "investment expenditure" by that business in order to make the circular flow principle hold by definition. Thus from the NIPA point of view (save for accounting definitions and the statistical discrepancy), national income and GDP have to be equal to total expenditure.

FIGURE 9.16

The Circular Flow and Aggregate Demand
If planned expenditure is below total income, even though planned spending is less than production, national income accountants define things so that the circular flow principle — according to which spending is equal to production — holds. Unplanned business inventory accumulation is counted as spending. Thus it is important to remember that aggregate demand is equal to *planned* expenditure — not to total spending, as the NIPA reports it.

Production Larger than Sales

Incomes

Production

Consumers, Investors, Government

Businesses, Producers

Unplanned "investment" in inventories

Sales of goods and services

NIPA expenditures

We do not want to pick a fight with the national income accountants, but we do want to be able to speak of production greater than demand or demand greater than production. So we finesse the issue by making a subtle distinction between the investment spending that goes into our macroeconomic model and the investment spending recorded by the NIPA. Our investment spending I is *planned* investment spending: It is what businesses wanted to do. Thus our concept of aggregate demand is total *planned* expenditure, which is different from actual expenditure whenever some business finds itself unexpectedly accumulating or decumulating inventories. (See Figure 9.16.)

CALCULATING THE DIFFERENCE BETWEEN AGGREGATE DEMAND AND REAL GDP: AN EXAMPLE

Suppose that our planned-expenditure function has numerical values for its coefficients, so that in trillions

$$E = A + MPE \times Y$$
$$= \$5.6 + 0.3 \times Y$$

Suppose, first, that the current level of real GDP Y is $7.5 trillion. Then aggregate demand — total *planned* expenditure — is

$$E = \$5.6 + 0.3 \times \$7.5$$
$$= \$7.85$$

And business inventories are being drawn down at a rate

$$\frac{\Delta \text{ inventories}}{\Delta \text{ time}} = Y - E = -\$350 \text{ billion per year}$$

Suppose, second, that the current level of total real GDP Y is $9.5 trillion. Then total planned expenditure is

$$E = \$5.6 + 0.3 \times \$8.5$$
$$= \$8.35$$

And business inventories are being added to at a rate of

$$\frac{\Delta \text{ inventories}}{\Delta \text{ time}} = \$350 \text{ billion per year}$$

However, if the current level of total national income (and of real GDP) Y is $9 trillion, then total planned expenditure is

$$E = \$5.6 + 0.3 \times \$8.0$$
$$= \$8.0$$

And business inventories are stable:

$$\frac{\Delta \text{ inventories}}{\Delta \text{ time}} = \$0$$

9.3 THE MULTIPLIER

Determining the Size of the Multiplier

Suppose something happens to change the level of planned-expenditure at every possible level of total income. Anything that affects the level of autonomous spending will do. What would happen to the equilibrium level of total income and real GDP?

An upward shift in the planned-expenditure line would increase the equilibrium level of total income. At the prevailing level of national income, planned expenditure would be larger than real GDP. Businesses would find themselves selling more than they were making, and their inventories would fall. In response, businesses would boost production to try to keep inventories from being exhausted, and production would expand. How much production would expand depends on the magnitude of the change in autonomous spending and the value of the spending **multiplier.**

The value of the multiplier depends on the slope of the planned-expenditure line, the marginal propensity to expend (MPE). The higher the MPE, the steeper is the planned expenditure line and the greater is the multiplier. A large multiplier can amplify small shocks to spending patterns into large changes in total production and income, as Figure 9.17 shows.

To calculate the multiplier, recall the simplified equation for planned expenditure

$$E = A + MPE \times Y$$

and the equilibrium condition

$$Y = E$$

Substitute the second into the first, and solve for Y:

$$Y = \frac{A}{1 - MPE}$$

Thus if autonomous spending changes by an amount ΔA, equilibrium real GDP changes by

$$\Delta Y = \frac{1}{1 - MPE} \times \Delta A$$

FIGURE 9.17

The Multiplier Effect

An increase in autonomous spending will generate an amplified increase in the equilibrium level of national income. Why? Because planned expenditure will rise not just by the increase in autonomous spending but by the increase in autonomous spending plus the marginal propensity to expend times the increase in the equilibrium level of national income.

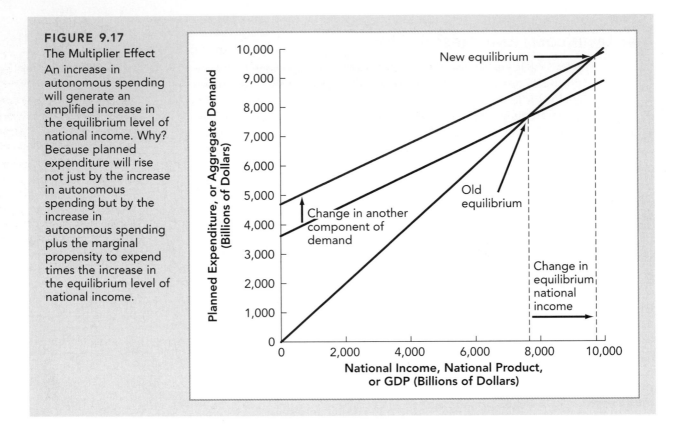

And if we want to express the denominator of this fraction in terms of the basic parameters of the model, it is

$$\Delta Y = \frac{1}{1 - [C_y(1 - t) - IM_y]} \times \Delta A$$

This factor, $1/(1 - MPE) = 1/\{1 - [C_y(1 - t) - IM_y]\}$ is the *multiplier:* It multiplies the upward shift in the planned-expenditure line as a result of the increase in autonomous spending into a change in the equilibrium level of real GDP, total income, and aggregate demand.

Why the factor $1/(1 - MPE)$? Think of it this way: The MPE — the marginal propensity to expend — is the slope of the planned-expenditure line. A \$1 increase in national income raises the equilibrium level of planned expenditure by \$1, because expenditure has to go \$1 higher to balance income and production. As Figure 9.18 shows, it also raises the level of planned expenditure by \$MPE. Thus a \$1 increase in the level of total income closes \$(1 − MPE) of the gap between planned expenditure and total income. To close a full initial gap of \$$\Delta A$ between planned expenditure and national income, the equilibrium level of national income must increase by $\Delta A/(1 - MPE)$.

Because autonomous spending is influenced by a great many factors,

$$A = C_0 + (I_0 - I_r \times r) + G + (X_f \times Y^f + \varepsilon_r \times \varepsilon_0 - \varepsilon_r \times r + \varepsilon_r \times r^f)$$

almost every change in economic policy or the economic environment will set the multiplier process in motion.

FIGURE 9.18

Determining the Size of the Multiplier

An increase ΔA in national income and total production raises the level of aggregate demand consistent with equilibrium by ΔA, but it also raises the level of planned expenditure by the MPE $\times \Delta A$. A ΔA dollar increase in national income and total production reduces the gap between total production and planned expenditure by only (1 − MPE) ΔA. Hence the increase in the equilibrium level of national income produced by a change ΔA in autonomous spending is not ΔA but $\Delta A/(1 − MPE)$ — ΔA times the value of the multiplier.

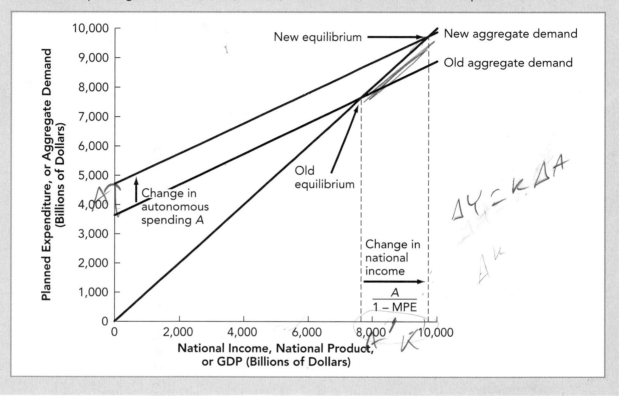

THE VALUE OF THE MULTIPLIER: AN EXAMPLE

Suppose that the planned-expenditure function has values for its parameters of $A =$ $5.6 trillion and MPE = 0.3, so that

$$E = A + MPE \times Y$$
$$= \$5.6 + 0.3 \times Y$$

Then the equilibrium value of total income (and of real GDP) Y is $9 trillion, for only at $Y = \$9$ trillion is planned expenditure equal to real GDP.

Now suppose that autonomous spending A increases by an amount of $100 billion, or $0.1 trillion:

$$\Delta A = \$0.1$$

Then the planned-expenditure function is

$$E = \$5.7 + 0.3 \times Y$$

and the equilibrium value of total income (and real GDP) Y is $9.143.

BOX

9.6

The change in Y divided by the change in autonomous spending is

$$\frac{\Delta Y}{\Delta A} = 1.43$$

This is equal to

$$1.43 = \frac{1}{1 - 0.3} = \frac{1}{1 - MPE}$$

which we saw above is the definition of the multiplier.

Changing the Size of the Multiplier

One factor that tends to minimize the multiplier is the government's *fiscal automatic stabilizers*. The government doesn't levy a total lump-sum tax. Instead the government imposes roughly proportional (actually slightly progressive) taxes on the economy, so government tax collections are equal to a tax rate t times the level of GDP Y: the total tax take equals $t \times Y$.

This means that the government collects more in tax revenue when GDP is relatively high. The collection of extra revenue dampens swings in after-tax income and thus reduces consumption. Similarly, the government collects less in tax revenue when GDP is relatively low; thus after-tax income is higher than that under lump-sum taxes, and this higher income boosts consumption. Because the fall in consumption is smaller, the multiplier is smaller. Disturbances to spending are not amplified as much as they used to be, and so shocks to the economy tend to cause smaller business cycles.

The automatic working of the government's tax system (and, to a lesser extent, its social welfare programs) function as an *automatic stabilizer,* reducing the magnitude of fluctuations in real GDP and unemployment. With a proportional tax system the multiplier is

$$\frac{\Delta Y}{\Delta A} = \frac{1}{1 - MPE} = \frac{1}{1 - [C_y(1 - t) - IM_y]}$$

If the government levied lump-sum taxes, the multiplier would be

$$\frac{\Delta Y}{\Delta A} = \frac{1}{1 - MPE} = \frac{1}{1 - (C_y - IM_y)}$$

How large are fiscal automatic stabilizers in the United States today? When national product and national income drop by a dollar, income tax and social security tax collections fall automatically by at least one-third of a dollar. Thus, the fall in consumers' disposable income is only two-thirds as great as the fall in national income, and the fall in consumption is only two-thirds as large as it would be without fiscal automatic stabilizers.

An economy that is more open to world trade will also have a smaller multiplier than will a less open economy. The more open the economy, the greater is the marginal propensity to expend on imports. The more of every extra dollar of income spent on imports, the less is left to be devoted to planned expenditure on *domestic products* — and therefore the smaller is the multiplier. If the share of imports in GDP is large, the potential change in the multiplier from an open economy

$$\frac{\Delta Y}{\Delta A} = \frac{1}{1 - MPE} = \frac{1}{1 - [C_y(1 - t) - IM_y]}$$

to that from a closed economy

$$\frac{\Delta Y}{\Delta A} = \frac{1}{1 - MPE} = \frac{1}{1 - [C_y(1 - t)]}$$

can be considerable. In modern industrialized economies where the share of imports in real GDP is certainly more than 10 percent, any calculation of the multiplier must take into account the effects of world trade.

RECAP   THE MULTIPLIER

If prices are sticky, higher aggregate demand boosts production, and this boosts incomes. Higher incomes give a further boost to consumption, and this in turn boosts aggregate demand some more. Thus any shift in a component of aggregate demand upward or downward leads to a multiplied shift in total production. The early-twentieth-century British economist John Maynard Keynes was one of the first to stress the importance of this multiplier process. The multiplier arises because aggregate demand E is equal to autonomous spending E times the marginal propensity to expend MPE times national income Y: $E = A + MPE \times Y$.

In equilibrium aggregate demand E equals national income Y, which is true if and only if $Y = [1/(1 - MPE)] \times A$. The term $1/(1 - MPE)$ is the value of the multiplier.

Chapter Summary

1. Business-cycle fluctuations can push real GDP away from potential output and push unemployment far away from its average rate.

2. If prices were perfectly and instantaneously flexible, there would be no such thing as business-cycle fluctuations. Hence macroeconomics must consist in large part of models in which prices are sticky.

3. There are a number of reasons that prices might be sticky: menu costs, imperfect information, concerns of fairness, or simple money illusion. All seem plausible. None has overwhelming evidence of importance vis-à-vis the others.

4. In the short run, while prices are sticky, the level of real GDP is determined by the level of aggregate demand.

5. The short-run equilibrium level of real GDP is that level at which aggregate demand as a function of national income is equal to the level of national income, or real GDP.

6. Two quantities summarize planned expenditure as a function of total income: the level of autonomous spending and the marginal propensity to expend (MPE).

7. The level of autonomous spending is the intercept of the planned-expenditure function on the income-expenditure diagram. It tells us what the level of planned expenditure would be if national income were zero.

8. The MPE is the slope of the planned-expenditure function on the income-expenditure diagram. It tells us how much planned expenditure increases for each $1 increase in national income.

9. The value of the MPE depends on the tax rate t, the marginal propensity to consume (MPC), and the share of spending on imports IM_y. In algebra, $MPE = C_y(1 - t) - IM_y$.

10. In the simple macro models, an increase in any component of autonomous spending causes a more-than-proportional increase in real GDP. This is the result of the multiplier process.

11. The size of the multiplier depends on the marginal propensity to expend (MPE): the higher the MPE, the higher is the multiplier. The value of the multiplier is

$$\frac{\Delta Y}{\Delta A} = \frac{1}{1 - MPE}$$

Key Terms

flexible prices (p. 241)

sticky prices (p. 241)

menu costs (p. 247)

imperfect information (p. 247)

money illusion (p. 247)

marginal propensity to consume (MPC) (p. 249)

consumption function (p. 249)

income-expenditure diagram (p. 253)

planned expenditure function (p. 253)

autonomous spending (p. 253)

marginal propensity to expend (MPE) (p. 253)

multiplier (p. 261)

Analytical Exercises

1. Describe, in your own words, the factors that determine the slope of the planned-expenditure curve.

2. Suppose that government purchases increase by $100 billion but there are no other changes in economic policy or the economic environment.
    a. What effect does this increase in government purchases have on the location of the planned-expenditure line?
    b. What effect does this increase in government purchases have on the planned-expenditure function?
    c. What effect does this increase in government purchases have on the equilibrium level of aggregate demand, national income, and real GDP?

3. Consider an economy in which prices are sticky, the marginal propensity to consume out of disposable income C_y is 0.6, the tax rate t is 0.25, and the share of national income spent on imports IM_y is 20 percent.
    a. Suppose that total autonomous spending is $6 trillion. Graph planned expenditure as a function of total national income.
    b. Determine the equilibrium level of national income and real GDP.
    c. What is the value of the multiplier?
    d. Suppose that total autonomous spending increases

by $100 billion to $6.1 trillion. What happens to the equilibrium level of national income and real GDP Y?

4. Suppose that prices are sticky; the marginal propensity to consume out of disposable income C_y is 0.9. Suppose further that the economy is closed — the share of national income spent on imports is zero — and that the tax rate is 12.5 percent.
    a. What is the marginal propensity to expend?
    b. What is the value of the multiplier?
    c. What level of autonomous spending would be needed to attain a level of equilibrium aggregate demand equal to $10 trillion?

5. Classify the following changes into two groups: those that increase equilibrium real GDP and those that decrease real GDP.
    An increase in consumers' desire to spend today.
    An increase in interest rates overseas.
    A decline in foreign exchange speculators' confidence in the value of the home currency.
    A fall in real GDP overseas.
    An increase in government purchases.
    An increase in managers' expectations of the future profitability of investments.
    An increase in the tax rate.

Policy Exercises

1. Suppose that the economy is at its full-employment level of output of $8 trillion, with government purchases equal to $1.6 trillion, the net tax rate equal to 20 percent, and the budget in balance.

   a. Suppose that adverse shocks to consumption and investment lead real GDP to fall to $7.5 trillion. What is the level of taxes collected? What is the government's budget deficit?

   b. Suppose that favorable shocks to consumption and investment lead real GDP to rise to $9.5 trillion. What is the level of taxes collected? What is the government's budget balance?

   c. Most economists like to calculate a "full-employment budget balance," equal to government purchases minus what tax collections would be if the economy were at full employment, and to take that balance as their summary measure of the short-run effect of government taxes and spending on the level of real GDP. What advantages does such a full-employment budget measure have over the actual budget as a measure of economic policy? What disadvantages does it have?

2. Suppose that the economy is short of its full-employment level of GDP, $8 trillion, by $500 billion, with the MPC out of disposable income equal to 0.6, the import share IM_y equal to 0.2, and the tax rate t equal to 25 percent.

   a. Suppose the government wants to boost real GDP up to full employment by cutting taxes. How large a cut

in the tax rate is required to do so? How large a cut in total tax collections is produced by this cut in the tax rate?

   b. Suppose the government wants to boost real GDP up to full employment by increasing government spending. How large an increase in government spending is required to do so?

   c. Can you account for any asymmetry between the answers to *a* and *b*?

3. Think about the four possible sources of price stickiness mentioned in this chapter: money illusion, "fairness" considerations, misperceptions of price changes, and menu costs. What have you read or seen in the past two months that strike you as examples of any of these four phenomena? In your opnion, which of the four sources seems most likely to be the most important?

4. What changes in the economy's institutions can you think of that would diminish price stickiness and increase price flexibility? What advantage in terms of the size of the business cycle would you expect to follow from such changes in institutions? What disadvantages do you think that such institutional changes might have?

5. Suppose the government wants to increase real GDP by $500 billion. How would you suggest the government go about accomplishing this goal?

Investment, Net Exports, and Interest Rates

CHAPTER 10

QUESTIONS

How are the determinants of investment different in a sticky-price and in a flexible-price model?

How are the determinants of net exports different in a sticky-price and in a flexible-price model?

How do changes in interest rates affect the equilibrium level of production and income in a sticky-price model?

What is the IS *curve?* What use is it?

What determines the equilibrium level of real GDP when the central bank's policy is to keep the real interest rate constant?

10.1 INTEREST RATES AND AGGREGATE DEMAND

The Importance of Investment

The changes in investment spending shown in Figure 10.1 are the principal driving force behind the business cycle. Without exception, reductions in investment have played a powerful role in every single recession and depression. Increases in investment have spurred every single boom. Thus if we can understand the causes and consequences of changes in investment spending, we will understand most of what we need to know about business cycles.

The Role of Investment

From this point forward our analysis of investment spending will differ from the analysis in the flexible-price model of Chapters 6 and 7. The investment function looks the same in both models, but the process by which the economy reaches equilibrium is different. Hence the investment function plays a very different role in the two models.

In the flexible-price model in Chapters 6 and 7, the **real interest rate** was a market-clearing price. It was pushed up or down by supply and demand to equate the flow of savings into financial markets (from households and businesses, the government, and foreigners) to the flow of investment funding out of financial markets (to finance increases in the capital stock). Supply and demand in the loanable funds market determined the interest rate. In the flexible-price model, the level of savings determined the level of investment, and the strength of investment demand determined the interest rate.

FIGURE 10.1

Investment as a Share of Real GDP, 1970–2000

The substantial year-to-year swings in investment are one of the principal drivers of the business cycle. When investment booms, the economy as a whole booms too.

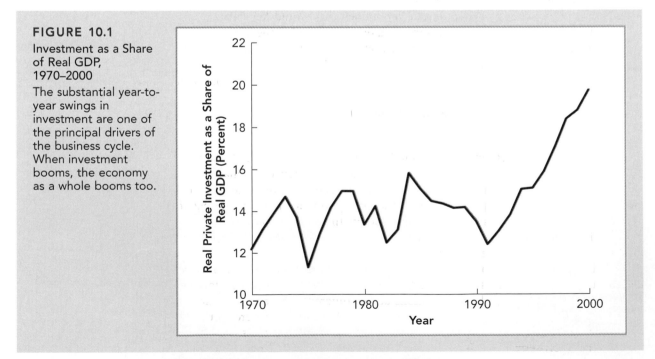

Source: The 2001 edition of *The Economic Report of the President* (Washington, DC: Government Printing Office).

In the sticky-price model, the interest rate is not set in the loanable funds market. Instead, it is set directly by the central bank or indirectly by the combination of the stock of money and the liquidity preferences of households and businesses. The interest rate then determines the level of investment, which then plays a key role in **autonomous spending**. Together, autonomous spending and the multiplier determine the level of output.

"What happened to equilibrium in the loanable funds market?" you may ask. In a sticky-price model the fact that businesses match the quantity they produce to aggregate demand *automatically* creates balance in the financial market, no matter what the interest rate. Any interest rate can be an equilibrium interest rate because the inventory-adjustment process has already made savings equal to investment.

Sources of Fluctuations in Investment

Fluctuations in investment have two sources. Some are triggered by changes in the real interest rate r. A lower real interest rate means higher investment spending, and a higher interest rate means lower investment spending. Other fluctuations are triggered by shifts in investors' expectations about future growth, profits, and risk. These two sources of fluctuations in investment correspond, respectively, to (1) changes in investment spending I produced by the interest sensitivity of investment parameter I_r times changes in r, and (2) changes in the baseline level of investment I_0 in the **investment function**

$$I = I_0 - I_r \times r$$

Both sources of fluctuation are important, but neither is clearly more important than the other.

Investment and the Real Interest Rate

A business that undertakes an investment project always has alternative uses for the money. One alternative would be to take the money that would have been spent building the factory or buying the machines and place it instead in the financial markets — that is, lending it out at the market real rate of interest. Thus the *opportunity cost* of an investment project is the **real interest rate**. The higher the interest rate, the fewer the number and value of investment projects that will return more than their current cost, and the lower the level of investment spending. But which interest rate is the relevant one? There are many different interest rates.

The Long-Term Interest Rate

The interest rate that is relevant for determining investment spending is a long-term interest rate. Investments are durable and long-lasting. Whenever a manager considers undertaking an investment project, he or she must compare the potential profits from the project to the opportunity to make money from a *long-term* alternative commitment of the funds elsewhere. The interest rate that is the opportunity cost of undertaking an investment project is the interest rate on a long-term loan for a period of a decade or more: the **long-term interest rate**.

This distinction matters, because long- and **short-term interest rates** are different and do not always move in step. Figure 10.2 shows a standard chart that plots the interest rate on bonds of different durations at two different moments. Looking at the shifts over time in such a *yield curve* chart shows that different interest rates do not always fluctuate together. It also shows that long-term interest rates are usually higher than short-term ones. In late 1992, for example, the yield curve was very steep: Long-term loans carried much, much higher interest rates than short-term

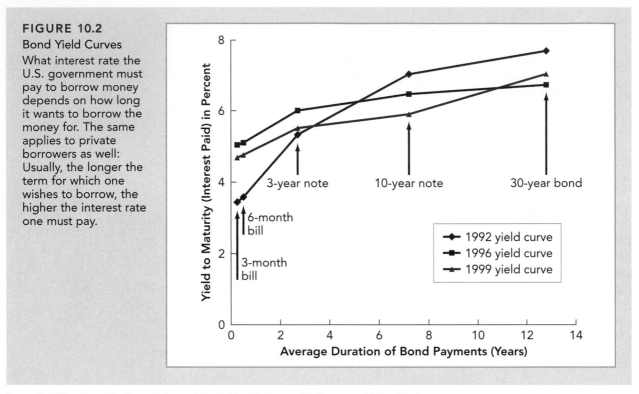

FIGURE 10.2

Bond Yield Curves

What interest rate the U.S. government must pay to borrow money depends on how long it wants to borrow the money for. The same applies to private borrowers as well: Usually, the longer the term for which one wishes to borrow, the higher the interest rate one must pay.

Source: The 2001 edition of *The Economic Report of the President* (Washington, DC: Government Printing Office).

loans. The premium in the interest rate that the market charges on long-term loans vis-à-vis short term loans is called the *term premium.*

As this chapter's appendix explains, when Wall Street bond traders expect short-term interest rates to rise in the future, the term premium is large. When they expect short-term interest rates to fall steeply, the term premium is negative. Financiers call such a rare happening an *inverted term structure.*

The Real Interest Rate

The interest rate that is relevant for investment spending decisions is not the nominal but the **real interest rate**. The nominal prices a business charges rise with inflation. If a business is willing to invest when the interest rate is 5 percent and inflation is 2 percent per year (and so the real interest rate is 3 percent per year), then the business should also be willing to invest when the interest rate is 10 percent and inflation is 7 percent per year (and so the real interest rate is still 3 percent per year). Figure 10.3 shows both nominal and real interest rates in the United States. There is a big difference between the two.

The Risky Interest Rate

Lending money to a business always carries an element of risk. Perhaps the borrower will go bankrupt before the loan is due. Perhaps the creditors will find themselves last, or nearly last, in line as a small amount of leftover postbankruptcy assets are divided up. Financial institutions lending money are keenly interested in the financial health of those to whom they lend. The riskier they believe the loan is — the larger

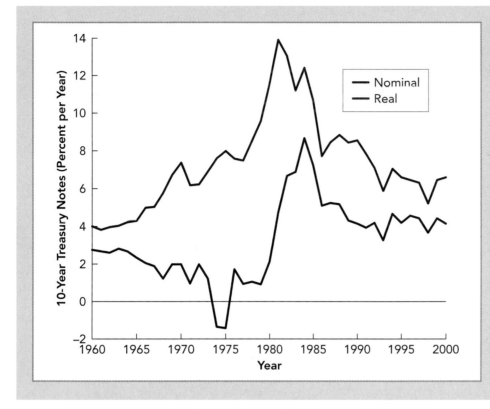

FIGURE 10.3
Gaps between Real and Nominal Interest Rates
Most borrowers and lenders care not about the nominal interest rate — the interest rate in terms of money — but about the real interest rate on loans — the interest rate in terms of goods. The difference between the nominal and the real interest rates is the inflation rate.

Source: Author's calculations and 2001 edition of *The Economic Report of the President* (Washington, DC: Government Printing Office).

the possibility of a bankruptcy or a debt rescheduling appears to be — the higher is the interest rate that lenders will demand to compensate them for risk.

The interest rate that a firm faces is the interest rate charged to risky borrowers, not the interest rate charged to safe borrowers (like the U.S. government) to whom people lend when they want to sleep easily at night. The premium that lenders charge for loans to companies rather than to safe government borrowers is called the *risk premium*. (See Figure 10.4.) Financial and economic disturbances — like the default of the Russian government in August 1998 — can cause large and swift moves in the risk premium. The **risky interest rate** does not move in step with the **safe interest rate**.

Thus to determine the level of investment spending, take the baseline level of investment I_0 (determined by businesses' optimism, expected economic growth, and a bunch of other factors for which the level of the stock market serves as a convenient thermometer). Subtract from this baseline level the interest sensitivity of investment parameter I_r times the relevant interest rate r. The relevant interest rate must be *long-term* because most investments are long-term. The relevant interest rate must be *real* because investment projects are real assets: Their value rises with inflation. And the relevant interest rate must be *risky* because businesses borrowing to invest may go bankrupt. In the investment function

$$I = I_0 - I_r \times r$$

the relevant interest rate r is the long-term, real, risky interest rate, as is plotted in Figure 10.5.

FIGURE 10.4

The Risk Premium: Safe and Risky Interest Rates

Loans that are not made to the U.S. government are risky: lenders charge a risk premium that depends both on their tolerance for risk and on the amount of risk involved when they lend to other organizations. This risk premium is not constant but varies over time.

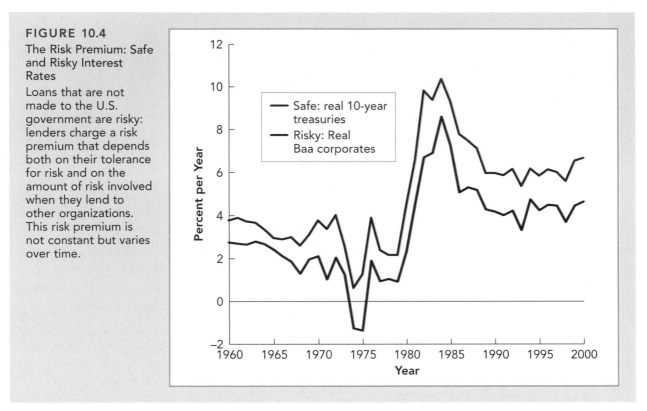

Source: The 2001 edition of *The Economic Report of the President* (Washington, DC: Government Printing Office).

The interest rate can be directly observed: It is what the newspapers print every day in their analyses of the bond market. But is there any easy way to observe the rest of the determinants of investment spending — all of those that are packed into the baseline level of investment spending I_0? Box 10.1 tells us how.

FIGURE 10.5

Investment as a Decreasing Function of the Long-Term, Real, Risky Interest Rate

The baseline level of investment I_0 tells us what the level of investment would be if the real interest rate were zero. The interest rate sensitivity parameter I_r tells us how much investment is discouraged by a 1-unit increase in the long-term, real, risky interest rate.

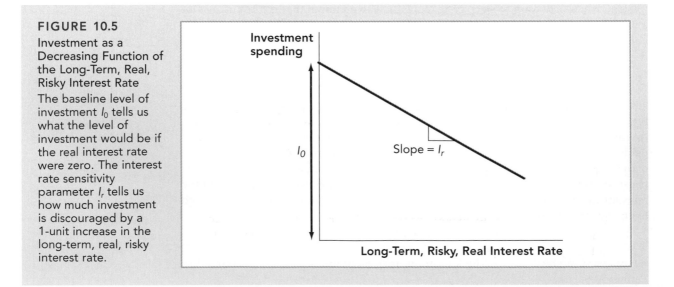

THE STOCK MARKET AS AN INDICATOR OF FUTURE INVESTMENT: SOME TOOLS

Recall from Chapter 2 that if investors in the stock market are acting rationally, the level of the stock market P^s will be equal to

$$P^s = E^a \times \left(\frac{E^s}{E^a}\right) \times \left(\frac{1}{r + \sigma^s}\right)$$

where

- E^a is the accounting earnings corporations report.
- E^s/E^a is the ratio of the long-run "permanent" earnings investors expect to today's accounting earnings. It is a measure of optimism, of expected future growth.
- r is the long-term real interest rate on bonds.
- s is the risk premium investors require to invest in stocks rather than in less risky assets.

Thus the stock market sums up — in one easy-to-find number, reported daily — the real interest rate r plus the same important influences — profitability, expected growth, and attitudes toward risk — that determine the baseline level of investment I_0.

Think of it this way: An investor deciding whether or not to commit his or her portfolio to stocks (rather than bonds) is making more or less the same decision as that made by a business's investment committee deciding whether to build a factory. The purchase of a share of stock gives you title to a share in the ownership of past investments — factories, buildings, inventories, and organizations — that have been undertaken by one company. The same things that determine whether it is a good idea to undertake the construction of a new factory also determine whether it is a good idea to spend money to acquire title to a share of an old factory. And the conclusions reached by investors in the stock market that we observe every day in stock price fluctuations are likely to be much the same as the conclusions reached by businesses' investment committees.

The higher the stock market, the higher is the likely future level of investment spending.

Exports and Autonomous Spending

Investment spending is not the only component of autonomous spending that is affected by the real interest rate. In the planned-expenditure function

$$E = A + MPE \times Y$$

autonomous spending includes gross exports as well:

$$A = C_0 + I + G + GX$$

As we saw in Chapter 6, gross exports depend on foreign total incomes Y_f and the real exchange rate ε. So we can expand the determinants of gross exports in the expression for autonomous spending:

$$A = C_0 + (I_0 - I_r \times r) + G + (X_f Y^f + X_\varepsilon \times \varepsilon)$$

As we also saw in Chapter 6, the real exchange rate ε depends on the domestic real interest rate r (as well as on foreign exchange speculators' opinions of fundamentals and foreign interest rates):

$$\varepsilon = \varepsilon_0 - \varepsilon_r \times (r - r^f)$$

Substituting the determinants of the exchange rate into the autonomous spending equation

$$A = C_0 + (I_0 - I_r \times r) + G + (X_f Y^f + X_\varepsilon \varepsilon_0 + X_\varepsilon \varepsilon_r \times r^f) - X_\varepsilon \varepsilon_r \times r$$

it becomes clear that there are two components of autonomous spending affected by changes in the real interest rate. A higher real interest rate reduces autonomous spending by reducing exports ($X_\varepsilon \varepsilon_r \times r$) as well as by reducing investment ($I_r \times r$). Figure 10.6 presents a graphical summary of how changes in the real interest rate affect exports and thus autonomous spending.

Why does a higher domestic interest rate reduce exports? A higher real interest rate makes investing in the home country more attractive: Foreign exchange speculators try to take advantage of this opportunity to earn higher returns by shifting their portfolio holdings to include more home-currency-denominated assets. This increase in demand for home-currency-denominated assets and decrease in demand for foreign-currency-denominated assets drives down the exchange rate, which is the value of foreign currency.

A lower value of foreign currency makes exports more expensive to foreigners: Their currency buys less here because it is less valuable. It diminishes their ability

FIGURE 10.6

From the Real Interest Rate to the Change in Exports

A change in the real interest rate has larger effects on aggregate demand than changes through investment alone: a change in the real interest rate changes the exchange rate and thus changes net exports as well.

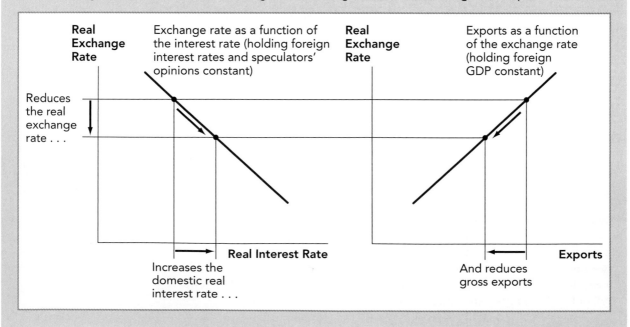

to purchase exports. Since exports are a part of autonomous spending, a rise in the real interest rate diminishes autonomous spending through this channel as well. Thus a change in interest rates has a bigger effect on output than one would think from the effect of interest rates on investment alone.

RECAP   INTEREST RATES AND AGGREGATE DEMAND

> The investment function in the sticky-price model looks the same as it does in the flexible-price model, but it plays a very different role. In the flexible-price model the real interest rate is a market-clearing price. Supply and demand in the loanable funds market determine the interest rate. The level of savings determines the level of investment, and the strength of investment demand determines the interest rate. In the sticky-price model, the interest rate is not set in the loanable funds market but is set directly by the central bank. The interest rate then determines the level of investment, which then plays a key role in autonomous spending. Together, autonomous spending and the multiplier determine the level of output. In a sticky-price model the fact that businesses match the quantity they produce to aggregate demand *automatically* creates balance in the financial market, no matter what the interest rate. Any interest rate can be an equilibrium interest rate because the inventory-adjustment process always forces savings equal to investment.

10.2 THE IS CURVE

Autonomous Spending and the Real Interest Rate

If we put the two interest rate terms in the equation for autonomous spending together

$$A = [C_0 + I_0 + G + (X_f Y^f + X_\varepsilon \varepsilon_0 + X_\varepsilon \varepsilon_r r^f)] - (I_r + X_\varepsilon \varepsilon_r) \times r$$

we see that a 1-percentage-point increase in interest rates reduces autonomous spending by an amount $(I_r + X_\varepsilon \varepsilon_r)$, as Figure 10.7 shows.

Think back to the **income-expenditure diagram** of Chapter 9. Recall that the equilibrium level of real GDP depended on the level of autonomous spending. Because a change in the real interest rate changes autonomous spending, it will change the equilibrium level of real GDP.

From the Interest Rate to Investment to Aggregate Demand

By how much does a change in the interest rate change equilibrium real GDP? The effect will be equal to the interest sensitivity of autonomous spending $(I_r + X_\varepsilon \varepsilon_r)$ times the multiplier of Chapter 9. This relationship between the level of the real interest rate and the equilibrium level of real GDP has a name that was coined by economist John Hicks more than 60 years ago: the "**IS curve**," where *IS* stands for "investment-saving." The IS curve is a workhorse tool that macroeconomists and macroeconomics courses use very, very frequently.

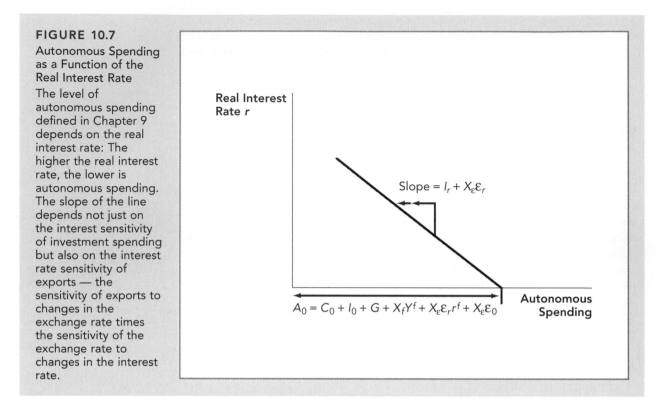

FIGURE 10.7

Autonomous Spending as a Function of the Real Interest Rate

The level of autonomous spending defined in Chapter 9 depends on the real interest rate: The higher the real interest rate, the lower is autonomous spending. The slope of the line depends not just on the interest sensitivity of investment spending but also on the interest rate sensitivity of exports — the sensitivity of exports to changes in the exchange rate times the sensitivity of the exchange rate to changes in the interest rate.

To construct the IS curve, we must first draw a diagram with equilibrium real GDP on the horizontal axis and the real interest rate on the vertical axis, as in Figure 10.8. We begin by picking a value for the real interest rate and then determine the level of autonomous spending at that real interest rate. Then we plug the corresponding level of autonomous spending into an income-expenditure diagram and draw the resulting planned-expenditure line. The point where the planned-expenditure line crosses the 45-degree line is the point at which aggregate demand equals national income. That is the value of equilibrium real GDP corresponding to our initial choice of the real interest rate.

The interest rate we started with and the real GDP level we ended with make up a single point on the IS curve. We repeat the process for as many different possible interest rates as we need. Plotting the points on the IS diagram and connecting them produces the IS curve.

The algebra of the IS curve is straightforward, if a little crowded and complicated. We start from the formula for autonomous spending in terms of the factors underlying aggregate demand:

$$A = [C_0 + I_0 + G + (X_f Y^f + X_\varepsilon \varepsilon_0 + X_\varepsilon \varepsilon_r r^f)] - (I_r + X_\varepsilon \varepsilon_r) \times r$$

Then we divide the determinants of autonomous spending into those that don't depend on the interest rate and those that do, calling the first set of determinants "baseline autonomous spending," or A_0:

$$A_0 = [C_0 + I_0 + G + (X_f Y^f + X_\varepsilon \varepsilon_0 + X_\varepsilon \varepsilon_r r^f)]$$
$$A = A_0 - (I_r + X_\varepsilon \varepsilon_r) \times r$$

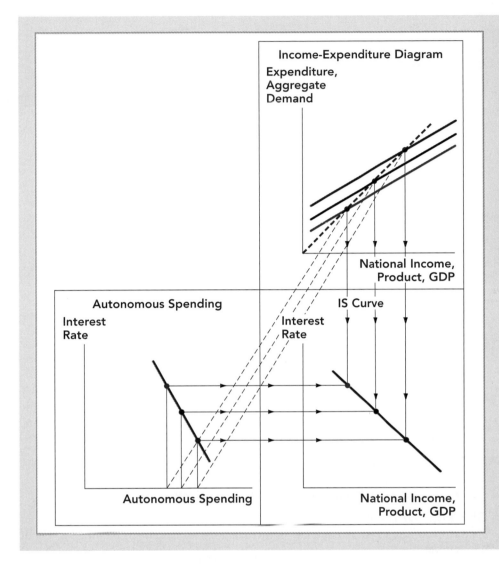

FIGURE 10.8
The IS Curve
For each possible value of the real interest rate, there is a different level of autonomous spending. For each level of autonomous spending, the income-expenditure process generates a different equilibrium level of real GDP. The IS curve tells us what equilibrium level of real GDP corresponds to each possible value of the real interest rate.

We recall from the income-expenditure analysis in Chapter 9 that real GDP is equal to autonomous spending A divided by 1 minus the MPE:

$$Y = \frac{A}{1 - MPE}$$

Replacing A with its components, we see that real GDP Y is

$$Y = \frac{A_0}{1 - MPE} - \frac{I_r + X_\varepsilon \varepsilon_r}{1 - MPE} \times r$$

This equation can be expanded if we want to express the MPE and the baseline level of autonomous spending A_0 in terms of the underlying model parameters and policy variables:

$$Y = \frac{[C_0 + I_0 + G + (X_f Y^f + X_\varepsilon \varepsilon_0 + X_\varepsilon \varepsilon_r r^f)]}{1 - [C_y(1 - t) - IM_y]} - \frac{I_r + X_\varepsilon \varepsilon_r}{1 - [C_y(1 - t) - IM_y]} \times r$$

FIGURE 10.9

The IS Curve

The position of the IS curve summarizes all the determinants of equilibrium real GDP and how the level of equilibrium real GDP shifts in response to shifts in the interest rate.

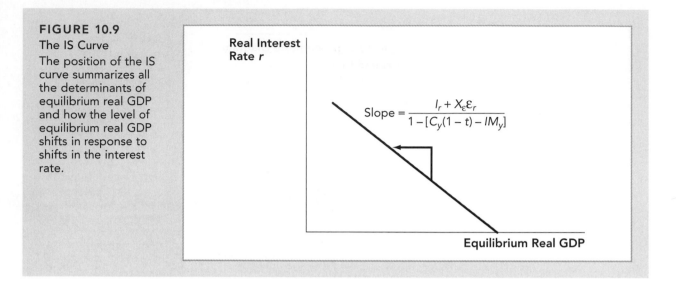

In this IS curve equation, the first set of terms is the horizontal *intercept* of the IS curve: the value that real GDP would attain if the real interest rate were zero. The second set of terms determines the *slope* of the IS curve: the responsiveness of equilibrium real GDP to changes in the long-term, risky, real interest rate, as in Figure 10.9.

Because the expanded form of the IS-curve equation is complex and next to impossible to remember, its main use is as a reference. Look at it from time to time (and especially before exams) to remind yourself of the factors that determine the intercept and the slope of the IS curve.

The Slope and Position of the IS Curve

The Slope of the IS Curve

The slope of the IS curve depends on three factors, all clearly visible in its algebraic expression:

$$\text{IS slope} = -\frac{1}{1 - [C_y(1 - t) - IM_y]} \times (I_r + X_\varepsilon \varepsilon_r)$$

The first term is simply the multiplier: $1/(1 - MPE)$. The larger the multiplier, the larger is the impact on aggregate demand set in motion by a given change in investment spending. The slope of the IS curve also depends on how large a change in investment is generated by a change in interest rates (the I_r term) and on how large a change in exports is generated by a change in the real interest rate (the product of the interest rate sensitivity of the exchange rate and the exchange rate sensitivity of exports $X_\varepsilon \times \varepsilon_r$). Thus anything that affects the multiplier will change the slope of the IS curve as well. Anything that affects the responsiveness of investment to a change in real interest rates will change the slope of the IS curve. Anything that changes how large a swing in real exchange rates is induced by a change in interest rates will change the slope of the IS curve. And anything that affects how sensitive exports are to the exchange rate will change the slope of the IS curve. Box 10.2 shows how to combine these to calculate the slope of the IS curve.

BOX
10.2

CALCULATING THE DEPENDENCE OF AGGREGATE DEMAND ON THE INTEREST RATE: AN EXAMPLE

To calculate how much a change in the interest rate will shift the equilibrium level of aggregate demand, you need to know four things:

- The marginal propensity to spend and thus the multiplier $[1/(1 - MPE)]$.
- The interest sensitivity of investment I_r.
- How much a change in the interest rate will affect the exchange rate (ε_r).
- How much a change in the exchange rate will affect exports (X_ε).

Suppose that you know that the marginal propensity to expend is 0.5 and the interest sensitivity of investment is 100: a 1-percentage-point rise in the interest rate decreases annual investment by $100 billion. Then the direct effects of interest rates on investment coupled with the multiplier would lead you to conclude that a 1-percentage-point increase in the interest rate will decrease equilibrium aggregate demand by $200 billion acting through the investment channel alone.

But there is another channel through which interest rates affect aggregate demand: the export channel. If a 1-percentage-point change in the interest rate reduces the exchange rate by 10 percent, and if each 1-percentage-point reduction in the exchange rate reduces exports by $5 billion, then there will be an additional decrease of $2 \times 5 \times 10 = \$100$ billion in aggregate demand through the exports channel.

Thus the total decline in equilibrium annual aggregate demand from a 1-percentage-point increase in the interest rate will be $300 billion. That will be the slope of the IS curve.

The Position of the IS Curve

The position of the IS curve depends on the baseline level of autonomous spending A_0 times the multiplier $1/(1 - MPE)$.

$$\frac{A_0}{1 - MPE} = \frac{[C_0 + I_0 + G + (X_f Y^f + X_\varepsilon \varepsilon_0 + X_\varepsilon \varepsilon_r r^f)]}{1 - [C_y(1 - t) - IM_y]}$$

Anything that changes any of the non-interest-dependent components of autonomous spending will shift the position of the IS curve. An increase in government spending G will shift the IS curve to the right and raise the equilibrium level of real GDP for any fixed value of the real interest rate, as Figure 10.10 shows. An increase in the baseline level of investment spending I_0 or consumption spending C_0 will do the same. Other events that shift the IS curve to the right include increases in income overseas Y^f, increases in foreign exchange speculators' expectations ε_0, and increases in foreign interest rates r^f.

Moving the Economy to the IS Curve

What happens if the current level of real GDP and the interest rate is not on the IS curve? If the economy is above the IS curve on the diagram, then real GDP is higher than planned expenditure. Inventories are rising rapidly and unexpectedly. So businesses cut back production. Employment, real GDP, and national income fall. If the economy is below the IS curve, aggregate demand is higher than total production. Inventories fall. Firms try to expand production in order to meet unexpectedly high

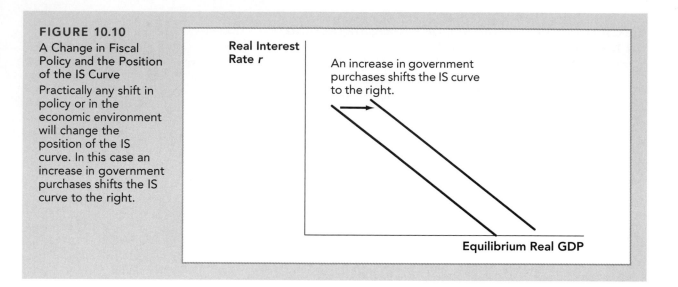

FIGURE 10.10

A Change in Fiscal Policy and the Position of the IS Curve
Practically any shift in policy or in the economic environment will change the position of the IS curve. In this case an increase in government purchases shifts the IS curve to the right.

demand. As they do, real GDP, employment, and national income rise, as Figure 10.11 shows.

The process that pulls the economy back to the IS curve works relatively slowly, over months, quarters, or possibly even years. Firms respond to increases in inventories by contracting (and to decreases in inventories by raising) production. As was noted in Chapter 9, the economy can stay away from its equilibrium on the income-expenditure diagram for a substantial time, all the while with inventories building up or falling. And if the economy is away from its equilibrium level of real GDP on the income-expenditure diagram, it is not on the IS curve either.

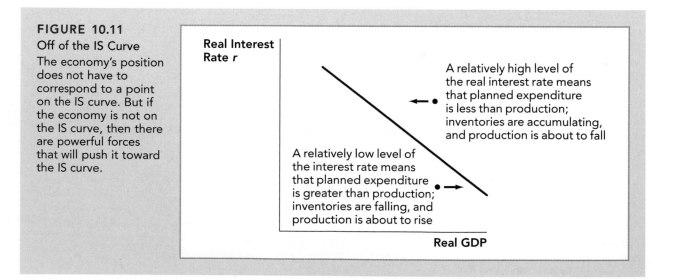

FIGURE 10.11

Off of the IS Curve
The economy's position does not have to correspond to a point on the IS curve. But if the economy is not on the IS curve, then there are powerful forces that will push it toward the IS curve.

RECAP   THE IS CURVE

> The higher the real interest rate, the lower are the investment spending and net exports components of autonomous spending and the lower is real GDP in the sticky-price model. The relationship between the real interest rate and real GDP is called the IS relationship. When plotted on a graph with real GDP on the horizontal axis and the real interest rate on the vertical axis, it is called the IS curve. The IS curve is downward-sloping. Its horizontal intercept is equal to baseline autonomous spending — what autonomous spending A would be if the interest rate were zero — times the multiplier. Its slope is equal to the multiplier $(1/(1 - MPE))$ times the sum of two terms: (a) the interest sensitivity of investment spending I_r, and (b) the product of the exchange rate sensitivity of gross exports and the interest sensitivity of the exchange rate $X_\varepsilon \times \varepsilon_r$.

10.3 USING THE IS CURVE TO UNDERSTAND THE ECONOMY

Shifting the IS Curve

We have seen that anything that affects the non-interest-dependent components of autonomous spending shifts the position of the IS curve. Changes that increase baseline autonomous spending shift the IS curve to the right and raise equilibrium real GDP (if interest rates are constant). Changes that reduce baseline autonomous spending shift the IS curve to the left and reduce equilibrium real GDP (if interest rates are held constant).

For example, two kinds of changes in government policy directly affect the position of the IS curve. A shift in tax rates changes both the position and the slope of the IS curve. And a change in the level of government purchases shifts the IS curve to the right or the left. It thus increases or decreases the equilibrium level of real GDP associated with each possible level of the real interest rate. (See Box 10.3.)

BOX 10.3 A GOVERNMENT SPENDING INCREASE AND THE IS CURVE: AN EXAMPLE

It is straightforward to calculate the effect on equilibrium aggregate demand of an increase in a component of baseline autonomous spending such as government purchases. For example, suppose that in the economy the initial MPE is equal to 0.5, the baseline level of autonomous spending is $5 trillion, a 1-percentage-point decline in the real interest rate raises investment spending by $110 billion and exports by $15 billion, and the real interest rate is fixed at 4 percent. Then the initial equilibrium level of annual real GDP is

$$Y = \frac{A_0}{1 - MPS} - \frac{I_r + X_\varepsilon \varepsilon_r}{1 - MPS} \times r = \frac{\$5}{1 - 0.5} - \frac{\$0.11 + \$.015}{1 - 0.5} \times 4 = \$10 - \$0.25 \times 4 = \$9 \text{ trillion}$$

And suppose that annual government purchases are then raised by $\Delta G = \$200$ billion.

Since government purchases are a component of baseline autonomous spending A_0, the increase in equilibrium aggregate demand is straightforward to calculate as long as the central bank does not change the real interest rate r:

$$\Delta Y = \frac{\Delta A_0}{1 - MPE} - \frac{I_r + X_\varepsilon \varepsilon_r}{1 - MPE} \times \Delta r = \frac{\$0.2}{1 - 0.5} - \frac{\$0.11 + \$.015}{1 - 0.5} \times 0 = \$0.4 \text{ trillion}$$

Real equilibrium aggregate demand rises by $400 billion.

Moving Along the IS Curve

Changes in the level of the real interest rate r will move the economy either left and upward or right and downward along the IS curve: A higher real interest rate will produce a lower level of aggregate demand. A lower real interest rate will produce a higher level of aggregate demand and equilibrium real GDP. The Federal Reserve can control — target — interest rates to a considerable degree. Such an **interest rate–targeting** central bank can stimulate the economy by cutting interest rates (see Box 10.4 and Figure 10.12) and can contract the economy by raising interest rates.

How does the Federal Reserve control interest rates? It does so by buying and selling short-term government bonds for cash in *open-market operations,* so-called because they are carried out in the "open market" and the Federal Reserve really does not care who it buys from or sells to. Whenever the Federal Reserve buys government bonds in return for cash, it increases the total amount of cash in the hands of the public and reserves in the hands of the banking system, as Figure 10.13 shows. Banks with the extra reserves use them to try to increase their deposits. Thus such

MOVING ALONG THE IS CURVE: AN EXAMPLE

Suppose that the staff projections of the Federal Reserve predict that if current policies are continued, real GDP will be only $9 trillion at a time for which estimates of potential output are $10.5 trillion. The Federal Open Market Committee (FOMC) might well decide that it is time to lower interest rates to close such a "deflationary gap."

Suppose further that the staff estimates that the marginal propensity to spend is 0.5, that a 1-percentage-point fall in the real interest rate generates an extra $110 billion in annual investment spending, that a 1-percentage-point fall in the real interest rate produces a 5 percent rise in the real exchange rate — the value of foreign currency — and that each 1 percent rise in the real exchange rate raises exports by $3 billion.

Such estimates of the structure of the economy imply that the slope of the IS curve is

$$\text{IS slope} = \frac{I_r + X_\varepsilon \varepsilon_r}{1 - MPS} = \frac{\$11,000 + 5 \times \$300}{1 - 0.5} = \$25,000$$

So to boost equilibrium real GDP by $500 billion by moving the economy along the IS curve, the real interest rate has to be reduced by 0.02 — by 2 percentage points.

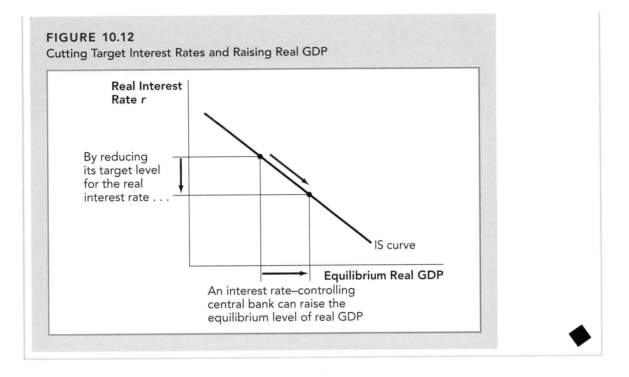

FIGURE 10.12
Cutting Target Interest Rates and Raising Real GDP

an expansionary open-market operation increases the economy's stock of money: It increases the quantity of assets — checking account deposits and cash — that are readily spendable purchasing power.

Banks, businesses, and households take a look at the larger quantity of money — wealth in the form of readily spendable purchasing power — that they hold. At the previous level of interest rates this is more money than they want to hold in their portfolios. So households, businesses, and banks try to use this money to buy assets, such as bonds, that pay higher yields than cash. As they do so, they push the price of bonds up and the interest rate down. Thus an expansionary open-market operation reduces interest rates in the economy. The same process works in reverse to push interest rates up when the Federal Reserve sells bonds for cash on the open market. Box 10.4 shows how central bankers would go about trying to calculate the size of the change in interest rates needed to properly manage the economy.

Difficulties

There are, however, some difficulties in attempting to control aggregate demand by manipulating interest rates. First, our knowledge of the structure of the economy is imperfect. Perhaps at any particular moment the slope of the IS curve is half what the Federal Reserve staff believes or is twice what the Federal Reserve staff believes. Second, even when policies do have their expected effects, these effects do not necessarily arrive on schedule. As economist Milton Friedman often says, economic policy works with long *and* variable lags.

Moreover, the interest rates that the Federal Reserve can control are *short-term, nominal, safe* interest rates. The interest rate that determines where the economy in equilibrium is along the IS curve is the long-term, real, risky interest rate. Even if

FIGURE 10.13
Open-Market
Operations
The Federal Reserve
changes interest rates
by changing the
quantity of liquid
money in the economy
through open-market
operations: purchases
or sales of U.S.
government bills,
notes, and bonds for
cash on the open
market.

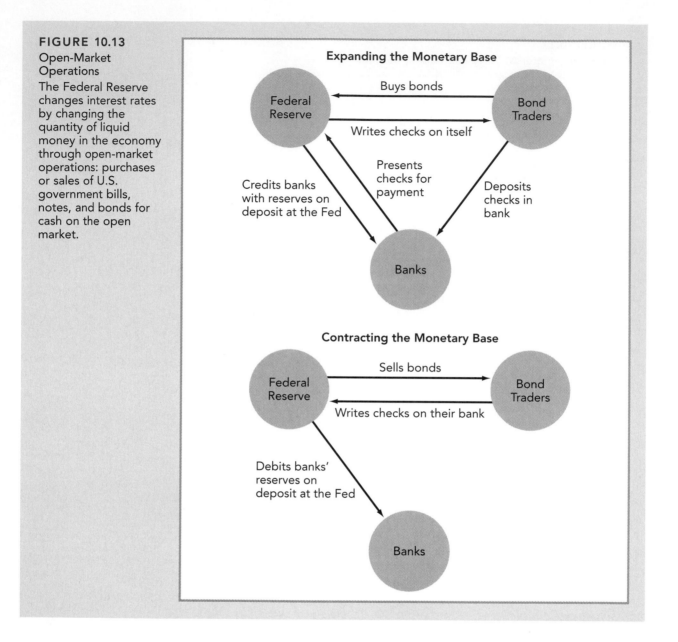

the government and central bank attain their target interest rate and even if the effects of changes in the interest rate are exactly as predicted and arrive exactly on schedule, there is a lot of potential slippage: Changes in the term premium between short and long interest rates, changes in the rate of inflation, and changes in the risk premium will each carry the economy to a point on the IS curve other than the point that the Federal Reserve wanted.

What determines the value of the *term premium* — the gap between short-term and long-term interest rates? Appendix 10A shows that the major determinant is expectations of future monetary policy. Long-term interest rates will be high relative to

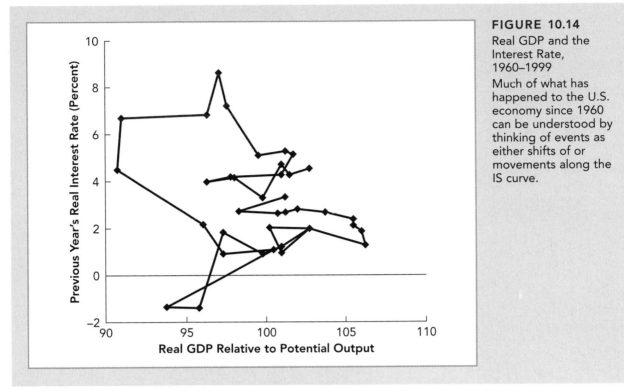

FIGURE 10.14
Real GDP and the Interest Rate, 1960–1999
Much of what has happened to the U.S. economy since 1960 can be understood by thinking of events as either shifts of or movements along the IS curve.

Source: Author's calculations and 2001 edition of *The Economic Report of the President* (Washington, DC: Government Printing Office).

short-term interest rates if people expect short-term interest rates to be raised in the future; long-term interest rates will be lower relative to short-term interest rates if people expect short-term rates to be lowered in the future.

Economic Fluctuations in the United States: The IS Curve as a Lens

How useful is the IS curve in understanding economic fluctuations in the United States over the past generation or so? If we plot on a graph the points corresponding to the long-term real interest rate and output relative to potential attained by the U.S. economy since 1960, we see that the economy has been all over the map — or at least all over the diagram (see Figure 10.14). Yet we can make sense of what has happened using shifts in and along the IS curve. That in fact is what the IS curve is for. It is a useful tool, which is why we have spent so many pages developing it. In the next four sections we will apply the IS curve to gain insight into business-cycle fluctuations in each of the past four decades.

The 1960s

The 1960s saw a substantial rightward shift of the IS curve. Increased optimism on the part of businesses, the Kennedy-Johnson cut in income taxes, and the extra government expenditures needed to fight the Vietnam War all increased aggregate

FIGURE 10.15

Shifting Out and
Moving along the IS
Curve, 1960s

The Vietnam War, the
Kennedy-Johnson tax
cut, and an increase in
business optimism
about the future all
shifted the IS curve to
the right between the
start of the 1960s and
the second half of the
decade.

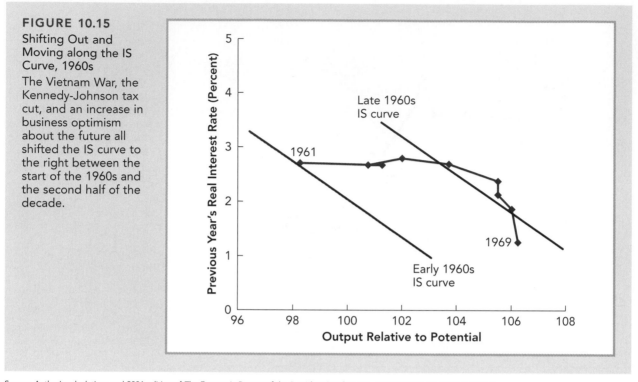

Source: Author's calculations and 2001 edition of *The Economic Report of the President* (Washington, DC: Government Printing Office).

demand. The IS curve shifted rightward by perhaps 5 percent of potential output in the 1960s, as Figure 10.15 shows.

The late 1960s also saw a movement downward and to the right along the IS curve, as real interest rates declined. In large part real interest rates declined by accident. The Federal Reserve did not fully gauge the amount by which inflation was rising. Rising inflation increased the gap between the nominal interest rates directly controlled by monetary policy and the real interest rates that determine aggregate demand. The Federal Reserve did not recognize this as it was happening and thus allowed real interest rates to drift downward.

The Late 1970s

The second half of the 1970s saw the level of real GDP in the U.S. significantly below the level of potential output. As Figure 10.16 shows, from 1977 to 1979 the U.S. economy moved down and to the right along the IS curve. However, the expansion of output toward potential was accompanied by unexpectedly high and rising inflation. This rise in inflation was further fueled by a supply shock: the sudden rise in oil prices triggered by the Iranian revolution.

A sudden shift in Federal Reserve policy occurred in 1979 when Paul Volcker became Chair of the Federal Reserve, replacing G. William Miller. Under Miller fighting inflation had been a relatively low priority. Under Volcker fighting inflation became the highest priority of all. The Federal Reserve raised annual real interest rates step-by-step from 1979 to 1982 up to nearly 5 percent. The increase in real interest rates moved the economy up and to the left along the end-of-the-1970s position of

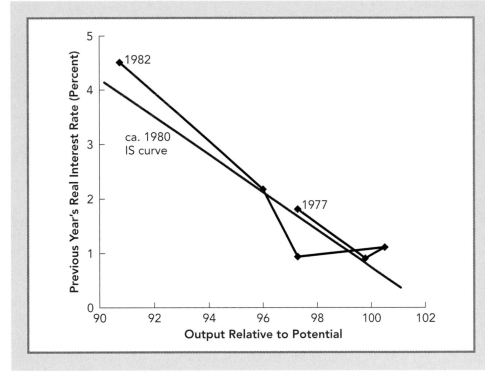

FIGURE 10.16
Moving along the IS Curve, Late 1970s
Sharp rises in real interest rates at the end of the 1970s after Paul Volcker became Chair of the Federal Reserve pushed the U.S. economy up and to the right along the IS curve.

Source: Author's calculations and 2001 edition of *The Economic Report of the President* (Washington, DC: Government Printing Office).

the IS curve: The unemployment rate reached nearly 10 percent in 1982, and real GDP fell to only 91 percent of the economy's potential output.

The 1980s

The election of Ronald Reagan in 1980 was followed by a massive fiscal expansion. Military spending was increased and income taxes were cut in a series of steps that became effective between 1982 and 1985. The result of these increases in government purchases and cuts in taxes was an enormous government deficit and an outward shift in the IS curve. A simultaneous increase in investor optimism triggered by falling inflation combined with the government's fiscal stimulus to shift the IS curve outward relative to potential output by at least 12 percent. (See Figure 10.17.)

The Federal Reserve responded to this outward shift in the IS curve by raising real interest rates. It sought in the first half of the 1980s to ensure that the success it had achieved in reducing inflation did not unravel. The Federal Reserve feared that a rapid return of real GDP to potential GDP would put upward pressure on inflation once more — hence the rise in real interest rates to make sure that the large Reagan-era fiscal expansion did not have too great an effect.

As inflation remained low throughout the mid and late 1980s, Federal Reserve policymakers gained confidence. They became increasingly optimistic that higher real GDP levels relative to potential would not reignite inflation. Between 1985 and 1980 successive step-by-step reductions in real interest rates carried the U.S. economy back to full employment, and carried it down and to the right along the IS curve. (See Figure 10.18.)

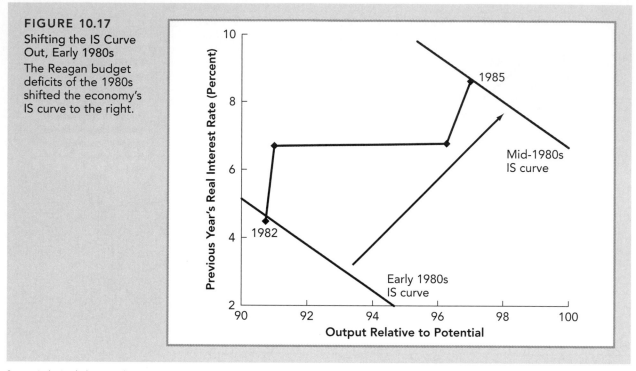

FIGURE 10.17
Shifting the IS Curve Out, Early 1980s
The Reagan budget deficits of the 1980s shifted the economy's IS curve to the right.

Source: Author's calculations and 2001 edition of *The Economic Report of the President* (Washington, DC: Government Printing Office).

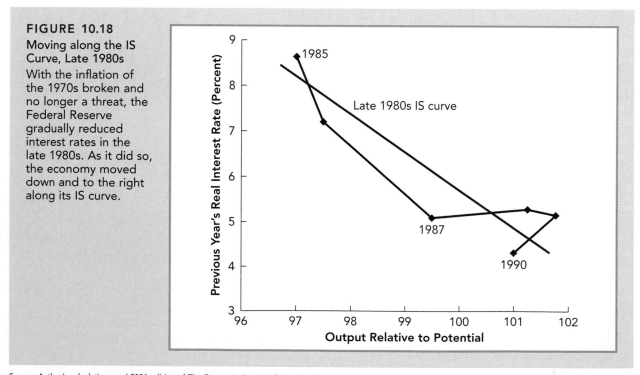

FIGURE 10.18
Moving along the IS Curve, Late 1980s
With the inflation of the 1970s broken and no longer a threat, the Federal Reserve gradually reduced interest rates in the late 1980s. As it did so, the economy moved down and to the right along its IS curve.

Source: Author's calculations and 2001 edition of *The Economic Report of the President* (Washington, DC: Government Printing Office).

The 1990s

The principal maker of economic policy since the late 1980s has been Federal Reserve Chair Alan Greenspan — appointed and reappointed by three successive presidents, Reagan, Bush, and Clinton. Greenspan is somewhat of a paradox: a Federal Reserve Chair whom all trust to be a ferocious inflation fighter, yet one who — in the policies that he has chosen — has frequently seemed willing to risk higher inflation in order to achieve higher economic growth or to avoid a recession.

Immediately after taking office Greenspan faced a challenge: the sudden stock market crash of October 1987. How large an effect would this crash have on aggregate demand? What would it do to investment spending? How much of a leftward shift in the IS curve would be generated by the sudden change in investors' expectations about the future that triggered the stock market crash? No one knew. If the crash turned out to be the harbinger of a large leftward shift in the IS curve, then an unchanging monetary policy would lead to a significant recession. So the Greenspan-led FOMC lowered interest rates and expanded the monetary base, hoping that this shift in monetary policy would offset any leftward shift in the IS curve and avoid a recession.

In point of fact, the stock market crash of 1987 had next to no effect on investment spending or aggregate demand. Economists have still not come up with a convincing story for why its effects were so small. The two years after 1987 saw higher output relative to potential and saw lower unemployment rates. The years between 1987 and 1990 did not see real interest rates rising — as they usually do in the latter stages of an expansion — but real interest rates that were stable or falling.

As the unemployment rate fell, inflation accelerated. The economy moved up and to the left along the Phillips curve. In 1988 and 1989, inflation moved up from 3 to 4 percent. The Federal Reserve found that it had successfully avoided any chance of a (big) recession in 1988 in the aftermath of the stock market crash, but only at the price of letting inflation rise above 4 percent per year. In the second half of 1990 there came a sudden leftward shift in the IS curve: The Iraqi invasion of Kuwait served as a trigger for firms to reduce investment, as they waited to see whether the world economy was about to experience another long-run upward spike in oil prices. The U.S. economy slid into recession at the end of 1990. The Federal Reserve, worried about the upward creep in inflation in the late 1980s, took no steps to reduce real interest rates as the economy slid into the recession. (See Figure 10.19.)

During the recession inflation fell to $2\frac{1}{2}$ percent. Unemployment rose to a peak of 7.6 percent — in the late spring of 1992, just in time to be salient for the 1992 presidential election. Recovery began in mid-1992.

Soon thereafter Greenspan made another decision to risk higher inflation in order to accomplish other goals. In 1993 he signaled that if Congress and the president took significant steps to reduce the budget deficit, then the Federal Reserve would try as best as it could to maintain lower interest rates — a shift in the policy mix that would keep the target level of production and employment unchanged but that with lower interest rates would promise higher investment and faster productivity growth: an "investment-led recovery."

This time the gamble turned out extremely well. As fiscal policy tightened in 1994 and beyond, interest rates remained significantly lower than they had been in the 1980s even though output recovered to potential. Moreover, this time there was no significant acceleration of inflation, even though by the end of the 1990s unemployment had fallen to the lowest level in a generation.

FIGURE 10.19
The Recession of
1990–1992

A sharp inward shift in
the IS curve triggered
a recession at the
beginning of the
1990s.

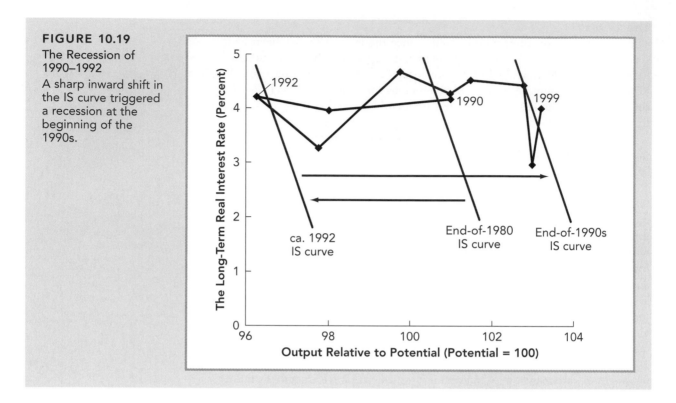

RECAP   USING THE IS CURVE TO UNDERSTAND THE ECONOMY

We have seen that anything that affects the non-interest-dependent components of autonomous spending shifts the position of the IS curve. Changes that increase baseline autonomous spending shift the IS curve to the right and raise equilibrium real GDP. Changes that reduce baseline autonomous spending shift the IS curve to the left and reduce real GDP. Changes in the level of the real interest rate r will move the economy either left and upward or right and downward along the IS curve: A higher real interest rate will produce a lower level of aggregate demand. A lower real interest rate will produce a higher level of aggregate demand and equilibrium real GDP. The Federal Reserve can control — target — interest rates to a considerable degree. Such an interest rate–targeting central bank can stimulate the economy by cutting interest rates and can contract the economy by raising interest rates.

Chapter Summary

1. In the sticky-price model the investment function is the same as in the flexible-price model. But in the flexible-price model the level of savings determines investment,

and the investment function determines the real interest rate. In the sticky-price model the real interest rate is determined outside the IS framework, and the level of the real interest rate powerfully affects the level of real GDP.

2. The international sector of the sticky-price model is essentially the same as the international sector of the flexible-price model.

3. The income-expenditure diagram takes autonomous spending as given and then determines the equilibrium level of real GDP, aggregate demand, and national income as functions of autonomous spending and the marginal propensity to spend.

4. The IS curve incorporates the effect of changing inter-

est rates on autonomous spending and adds this effect to the income-expenditure diagram.

5. The IS curve slopes downward because a higher interest rate lowers both investment and exports, and these reductions in autonomous spending in turn lower aggregate demand and equilibrium real GDP.

6. When the central bank's policy involves targeting the real interest rate, then the position of the IS curve and the central bank's interest rate target together determine the equilibrium level of aggregate demand and real GDP.

Key Terms

autonomous spending (p. 271)

investment function (p. 271)

real interest rate (p. 271)

long-term interest rate (p. 271)

short-term interest rate (p. 271)

risky interest rate (p. 273)

safe interest rate (p. 273)

income-expenditure diagram (p. 277)

IS curve (p. 277)

interest rate targeting (p. 284)

Analytical Exercises

1. Why does an expansion of government purchases have an amplified impact on the equilibrium level of real GDP? Suppose that the central bank does not target interest rates but instead keeps the money stock constant. Is it still the case that an expansion of government purchases will cause a greater than one-for-one increase in the equilibrium level of real GDP?

2. Explain why the IS curve slopes downward. Is its slope steeper in a closed economy, with no international trade, or in an open economy?

3. For each of the following, decide whether the IS curve shifts in and to the left, shifts out and to the right, or stays unchanged:
   The tax rate decreases.
   Foreign interest rates rise.
   Businesses become more optimistic about future demand.

Consumers desire to save a greater proportion of their income for the future.
The central bank lowers the short-term nominal interest rate it controls.
The term premium rises.
Foreign exchange speculators become more pessimistic about the long-run value of domestic currency.

4. Suppose that the government and central bank together want to keep GDP constant but raise the rate of investment. What policies can they follow to achieve this?

5. Suppose that the level of investment spending does not depend at all on the interest rate. Does this mean that the IS curve is vertical? If not, how can it be that central-bank changes in the real interest rate affect the equilibrium level of real GDP?

Policy Exercises

1. Suppose that the consumption, investment, net exports, and exchange rate functions are:

$$Y = C + I + G + NX$$
$$C = C_0 + C_y(1 - t)Y = \$3,000 + 0.5(1 - 0.4)Y$$

$$I = I_0 - I_r r = \$1,200 - \$100r$$
$$GX = X_f Y^f + X_\varepsilon \varepsilon = 0.1 Y^f + \$4\varepsilon$$
$$IM = IM_y Y = .2Y$$
$$NX = GX - IM$$
$$\varepsilon = 100 + 10(r^f - r)$$

Derive the IS curve for this economy: real GDP as a function of all the unspecified variables in the economy. Suppose that the foreign interest rate r^f is 5 percent, that total foreign income Y^f is \$10,000, and that government spending G is \$3,000. What then is equilibrium annual real GDP if the central bank sets the real interest rate at 3 percent? At 5 percent? At 7 percent?

2. Suppose that the economy is the same as in problem 1 except for the fact that it is a closed economy. There are no imports and no exports: $IM_y = 0$, $X_f = 0$, and $X_\varepsilon = 0$. Derive the IS curve for this economy. What is equilibrium annual real GDP if the central bank sets the interest rate at 3 percent? At 5 percent? At 7 percent?

3. In which of the two economies — the open economy of problem 1 or the closed economy of problem 2 — do you think that changes in interest rates have larger effects on the equilibrium level of real GDP? Explain your answer.

4. Suppose that the short-term nominal interest rate — the one the central bank actually controls — is 3 percent. But also suppose that the inflation rate is zero, that the term premium is 4 percent, and that the risk premium is 3 percent.

a. What is the real interest rate relevant for the IS curve?

b. Suppose that the IS equation of the economy is $Y = \$10,000 - 300 \times r$. What is the equilibrium level of real GDP?

c. Suppose that the central bank wants to use monetary policy to raise Y to \$9,000. Can it do so by open-market operations that lower the short-term nominal interest rate? Explain why or why not. What other policy steps can you think of that the government and central bank could take to raise equilibrium real GDP to \$9,000?

5. Suppose that the consumption, investment, net exports, and exchange rate functions are:

$$Y = C + I + G + NX$$
$$C = C_0 + C_y(1 - t)Y = \$3,000 + 0.5(1 - 0.4)Y$$
$$I = I_0 - I_r r = \$1,200 - \$100r$$
$$GX = X_f Y^f + X_\varepsilon \varepsilon = 0.1 Y^f + \$4\varepsilon$$
$$IM = IM_y Y = .2Y$$
$$NX = GX - IM$$
$$\varepsilon = 100 + 10(r^f - r)$$

Suppose further that the government follows a balanced-budget rule: Government purchases G are equal to government tax collections tY. Derive the IS for this economy: real GDP as a function of all the unspecified variables in the economy. Is the level of real GDP along the IS curve more or less sensitive to changes in interest rates than it was in problem 1? Why?

The Term Premium and Expected Future Interest Rates

What determines the value of the *term premium* — the gap between short-term and long-term interest rates? To start thinking about this question, consider once again a simple two-period model in which the periods are "now" and the "future." Bankers make long-term loans that fall due in two periods. Bond traders buy and sell long-term bonds that fall due in two periods. The real interest rate paid on these long-term loans and bonds is the long-term real interest rate r. Bankers also make short-term loans (and bond traders also buy and sell short-term bonds) that mature in just one period.

Someone thinking about buying a long-term bond (or making a long-term loan) knows that for each real dollar invested in such financial instruments today, he or she will after two periods have

$$\text{Gross return} = 1 + r + r$$

Each period they will receive the long-term real interest rate on their investment, r.

Someone thinking about buying a short-term bond today (or making a short-term loan) knows that for each real dollar invested in such financial instruments today, she or he will after the end of the first period (the one that is going on "now") have $1 + r_n^s$: r for the real interest rate, s because it is the rate paid on a short-term loan, and n because it is the interest rate paid in the now period. But the person's capital will then, at the start of the second period (the one that will happen in the future), be lying idle. The natural thing to do then will be to invest it again in another short-term bond (or make another short-term loan — this time at the short-term interest rate that will prevail in the future, r_f^s.

So after two periods someone who chooses today to invest money in short-term securities will have

$$\text{Gross return} = 1 + r_n^s + r_f^s$$

for each real dollar that she or he invested at the start of the first period.

What will a flint-eyed money-maximizing rational bond trader do? The first complication is that he or she doesn't know today what the future short-term real interest rate r_f^s will be when the time to reinvest the principal arrives. The best he or she can do is form an expectation now — E_n — of what the future short-term real interest rate will be: $E_n(r_f^s)$.

Thus the bond trader has to decide whether to invest for the long-term or for the short-term (and then, later, to reinvest). The returns from investing for the long-term will be greater if

$$\text{Long-term gross return} = 1 + 2r > 1 + r_n^s + E_n(r_f^s) = \text{short-term return}$$

Or, defining $E_n(\Delta r)$, the expected change in the short-term real interest rate, as the difference between expected future short rates $E_n(r_f^s)$ and current short rates r_f^s

$$\text{Expected change in short rates} = E_n(\Delta r^s) = E_n(r_f^s) - r_n^s$$

The returns from investing for the long-term will be greater if

$$r - r_n^s > \frac{E_n(\Delta r^s)}{2}$$

And the bond trader will probably decide to invest for the long-term. If

$$r - r_n^s < \frac{E_n(\Delta r^s)}{2}$$

then the returns from investing for the short-term will be greater, and the trader will probably decide to invest for the short-term.

In equilibrium there are *both* short-term and long-term bonds held and short-term and long-term loans made. So in equilibrium the typical bond trader and bank loan officer must think that the expected returns from long-term and short-term financial investments are roughly equal. In equilibrium,

$$r - r_n^s = \frac{E_n(\Delta r^s)}{2}$$

The term premium $r - r^s$ is equal to the expected change in short-term interest rates over the life span of the loan, weighted by the proportion of the loan's time span over which the changed short-term interest rate will apply. In other words, *the term premium tells you how bond traders expect short-term interest rates to move in the future.*

If financiers are buying two-year bonds at, say, 5.75 percent — when they could instead buy three-month T-bills every quarter for two years — then they must believe that either portfolio strategy will average out to about 5.75 percent over two years, or else they would all be crowding into one security or the other. Demand for the one would rise; demand for the other would fall. And the interest rates on them and on loans of that duration would change until once more it looked to bond traders that the two strategies were equally attractive. Similarly, if bond traders are buying three-month T-bills at, say, 4 percent when they could instead buy two-year bonds at 5.75 percent, then they must expect that higher short-term rates a year and a half in the future — say, 7.5 percent — will balance out today's low rates to average out to 5.75 percent.

This is the *expectations theory of the term structure:* The long-term interest rate is the average of what bond traders expect future short-term rates to be for the duration of the long-term loan. The term premium tells us how much bond traders are expecting the average short-term interest rate to rise (or fall) over the duration of the long-term loan.

From the standpoint of governments that seek to control interest rates, this dependence of today's long-term interest rate on expectations of what the short-term interest rate will be tomorrow is very inconvenient. All the changes in today's interest rate that the central bank can undertake today will have only a limited effect on long-term interest rates unless bond traders are convinced that policies once adopted will be continued. Thus central banks guard their reputation for *credibility* and *consistency* above everything else. They can preserve their ability to move the economy along the IS curve by changing interest rates only if bond traders' expectations of the future, and thus today's long-term interest rates, react predictably to changes in interest rate policy.

Extending the Sticky-Price Model: More Analytical Tools

CHAPTER

QUESTIONS

What is money-market equilibrium?

What is the LM curve?

What determines the equilibrium level of real GDP when the central bank's policy is to keep the money stock constant?

What is the IS-LM framework?

What is an IS shock?

What is an LM shock?

What is the relationship between shifts in the equilibrium on the IS-LM diagram and changes in the real exchange rate?

What is the relationship between shifts in the equilibrium on the IS-LM diagram and changes in the balance of trade?

What is the aggregate supply curve?

What is the aggregate demand curve?

The IS curve as presented in Chapter 10 is enough to enable us to think about business cycles, as long as the central bank uses open market operations to set the real interest rate. But not all central banks peg interest rates. Not all central banks that peg interest rates today pegged them in the past. So the analysis of Chapter 10 is not complete, because it lacks a theory of what determines the real interest rate when it is not the interest rate but the money stock that is fixed. Moreover, even when central banks do peg interest rates, they usually peg not real but nominal interest rates. To think through the relationship between nominal and real interest rates, we need to understand the determinants of inflation.

Thus this chapter adds more analytical tools to extend the sticky-price model. We first derive an LM curve to serve as a sibling to the IS curve. The LM curve tells us how interest rates are determined when the stock of liquid money is fixed. The LM curve joins the IS curve in the IS-LM framework and diagram, which provides our analysis of the determinants of real GDP and the interest rate when the money stock is fixed.

Second, we examine in more detail the international side. We examine the effects of changes in the economy's equilibrium on international economic variables, and the effects of changes abroad on the domestic economy's equilibrium.

Third, we begin the process of understanding what determines the price level and the inflation rate in the sticky-price macroeconomic model. We summarize all the previous sections of Part IV in an aggregate demand (AD) relationship that tells how aggregate demand is associated with the price level and the inflation rate. We also present a model of aggregate supply (AS) to understand the relationship between real GDP and the price level. Putting these two together generates the AS-AD framework, which allows us to analyze not just the level of real GDP but also how changes in real GDP affect the price level.

11.1 THE MONEY STOCK AND THE MONEY MARKET: THE LM CURVE

Money Market Equilibrium

Recall from Chapter 8 three facts about business and household demand for money, where "demand for money" is economist-speak for the quantity of readily spendable liquid assets held in one's portfolio:

- **Money demand** is proportional to total nominal spending $P \times Y$.
- Money demand has a time trend, the result of slow changes in banking-sector structure and technology.
- Money demand is *inversely* related to the nominal interest rate.

The quantity of money demanded is inversely related to the nominal interest rate because the nominal interest rate is the opportunity cost of holding money. **Real money balances** earn zero interest, and over time they lose their power to purchase real, useful goods and services at the rate of inflation π. If money balances were sold and the proceeds put into some other investment, they would earn the prevailing market real interest rate r. Thus the expected opportunity cost of holding wealth in the form of money is the nominal interest rate $i = r + \pi^e$: the sum of the real interest rate r and the expected inflation rate π^e.

To keep our model simple, we ignore the time trend in velocity and write the demand for money as the function

$$\frac{M^d}{P} = \frac{Y}{V_0 + V_i \times (r + \pi^e)}$$

Because the left side is the nominal money stock divided by the price level, this equation represents real money demand — a demand for an amount of liquid power to purchase goods and services, rather than a demand for a stack of dollar bills. This equation shows that money demand is proportional to real GDP Y: The higher the real GDP, the more real money balances people wish to hold. The plus sign in front of the V^i parameter means that velocity is an increasing function of the nominal interest rate, and thus money demand is a decreasing function of the nominal interest rate. The higher the nominal interest rate, the higher the opportunity cost of holding money, and the lower the real quantity of money demanded, as Figure 11.1 shows.

In a sticky-price model, the price level P is predetermined and thus fixed. It cannot move instantly (as it could and did in the flexible-price model of Chapter 8) to make the money supply M^s equal to money demand M^d. Since the price level cannot move instantly to keep the money market in equilibrium, the nominal interest rate must adjust instead. So given the nominal money supply, the price level, and the level of real GDP, the economy's money market can be in **equilibrium** only if the nominal interest rate is

$$i = (r + \pi^e) - \frac{(Y \times P)/M^s - V_0}{V_i}$$

The nominal interest rate $i = r + \pi^e$ must be the level at which the money supply and money demand curves in Figure 11.1 cross. This must hold whether the money supply is automatically determined by the monetary system or is explicitly controlled by the central bank.

Suppose money supply is less than money demand, so that households and businesses want to hold more liquid money balances than exist. Businesses and

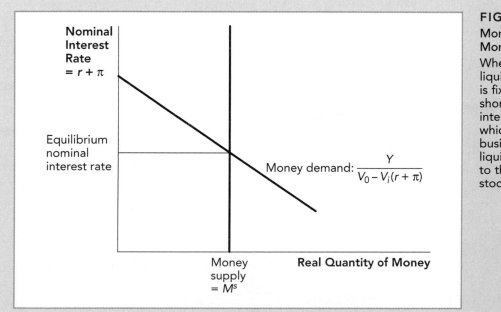

FIGURE 11.1
Money Demand and Money Supply
When the stock of liquid monetary assets is fixed, the equilibrium short-term nominal interest rate is that at which households' and businesses' demand for liquid money is equal to the (fixed) money stock.

households go to their banks and try to borrow to boost their cash holdings. Banks respond by raising the interest rates they charge for loans. As the nominal interest rate rises, the quantity of money demanded by households and businesses falls because the opportunity cost of holding money has risen. When the nominal interest rate has risen far enough that the quantity of money demanded is equal to the money supply, and households and businesses are no longer trying to increase their liquid money balances, there is no more upward pressure on the nominal interest rate.

Now suppose instead that money supply is greater than money demand, so that businesses and households are holding more liquid money balances than they want. They take these liquid money balances and deposit them at the bank. With more cash in their vaults as reserves, banks seek to make more loans, and in order to induce people to borrow they cut interest rates. As the nominal interest rate falls, the quantity of money demanded rises because the opportunity cost of holding money has fallen. When the nominal interest rate has fallen enough so that the quantity of money demanded is equal to the money supply, there is no more downward pressure on the nominal interest rate.

The LM Curve

If the money stock is constant, then the fact that demand for money depends on real GDP Y means that the equilibrium nominal interest rate varies whenever real GDP Y varies. At each possible level of total income Y, there is a different curve showing money demand as a function of the nominal interest rate, as Figure 11.2 shows. With a fixed money supply, each of these money demand curves produces a different equilibrium nominal interest rate. If real GDP Y rises and the money supply M^s does not, the nominal interest rate must rise too if the money market is to remain in equilibrium. With higher incomes, households and businesses want to hold more money. But if the money supply does not increase, then in aggregate their money holdings

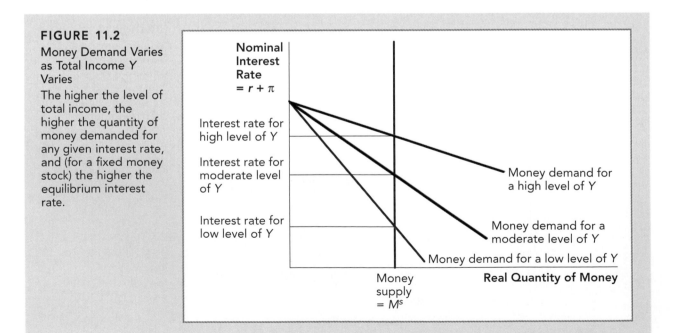

FIGURE 11.2

Money Demand Varies as Total Income Y Varies

The higher the level of total income, the higher the quantity of money demanded for any given interest rate, and (for a fixed money stock) the higher the equilibrium interest rate.

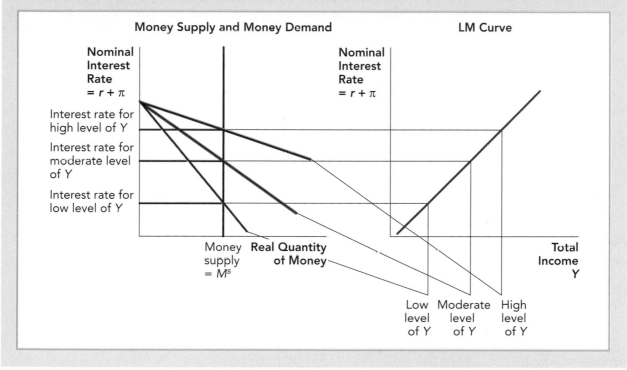

FIGURE 11.3
From Money Demand to the LM Curve
The LM curve on the right tells us what the nominal interest rate will be for each value of national income Y.

cannot grow. Something must curb their demand for liquid cash holdings and so keep money demand equal to money supply, and that something is a higher nominal interest rate, a higher opportunity cost of holding money.

Consider another diagram with the nominal interest rate $i = r + \pi$ on the vertical axis and the level of total income Y on the horizontal axis. For each possible value of Y on the x axis, plot the point whose y axis value is the equilibrium nominal interest rate, as in Figure 11.3. The result is the **LM curve**, the economy's current level of the real money stock M^s/P. The LM curve slopes upward: At a higher level of real GDP Y, the equilibrium nominal interest rate is higher.

The equation for the LM curve is simply the money demand function rewritten with the real GDP by itself on the left side:

$$Y = [V_0 + V_i \times (r + \pi^e)] \times \frac{M}{P}$$

This equation tells us that monetary policy changes that increase the nominal money supply shift the LM curve to the right: the same equilibrium nominal interest rate i corresponds to a higher level of real GDP Y. Monetary policy changes that decrease the nominal money supply shift the LM curve in and to the left. Similarly, a decline in the price level boosts the real money supply (M/P) and shifts the LM curve out to the right. A rise in the price level decreases the real money supply (M/P) and shifts the LM curve in to the left.

The IS-LM Framework

As long as we know the expected inflation rate, the fact that the nominal interest rate is equal to the real interest rate plus the **expected inflation rate** means that we can plot the IS and LM curves on the same set of axes, as in Figure 11.4. This is called the **IS-LM diagram**. The equilibrium level of real GDP and of the interest rate is at the point where the IS curve and the LM curve cross. At that level of real GDP and total income Y and the real interest rate r, the economy is in equilibrium in both the goods market and the money market. Aggregate demand is equal to total production, so inventories are stable (that's what the IS curve indicates); and money demand is equal to money supply (that's what the LM curve indicates). Box 11.1 shows how to calculate the economy's equilibrium position for some specific parameter values of the sticky-price model.

FIGURE 11.4

The IS-LM Diagram

What is the economy's equilibrium? It is the point at which the IS and LM curves cross. Along the IS curve, total production is equal to aggregate demand. Along the LM curve, the quantity of money demanded by households and businesses is equal to the money stock. Where the curves cross, both the goods market and the money market are in balance.

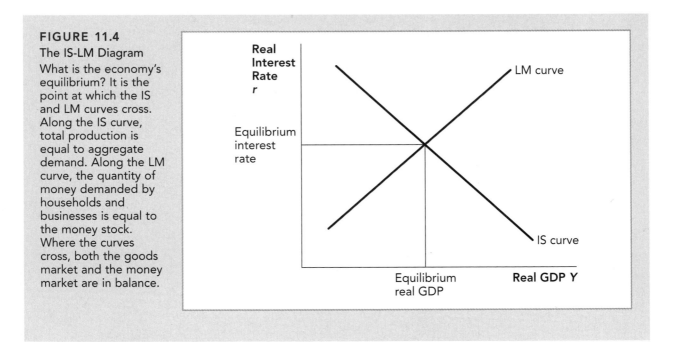

IS-LM EQUILIBRIUM: AN EXAMPLE

Suppose that the economy's marginal propensity to expend (MPE) is 0.5, that the initial level of baseline autonomous spending A_0 is $5,000 billion, and that a 1-percentage-point increase in the real interest rate will reduce the sum of investment and net exports by $100 billion. Suppose further that the inflation rate π is constant at 3 percent per year, and that the initial LM curve is

$$Y = \$1,000 + \$100,000 \times (r + \pi)$$

Then the economy's initial IS curve will be

$$Y = \frac{A_0}{1 - MPE} - \frac{I_r + X_\varepsilon \varepsilon_r}{1 - MPE} \times r = \frac{\$5,000}{1 - 0.5} - \frac{\$10,000}{1 - 0.5} \times r = \$10,000 - \$20,000 \times r$$

The initial equilibrium of the economy is at the one point that is on both the IS and the LM curves. Where is that point? Find it by substituting the LM-curve expression for Y into the IS curve:

$$Y = \$10,000 - \$20,000 \times r = \$1,000 + \$100,000 \times (r + 3)$$
$$\$6,000 = (\$20,000 + \$100,000) \times r$$
$$r = 0.05 = 5\%$$

If r equals 5 percent per year, then the equilibrium point for real GDP Y is $9,000 billion, as Figure 11.5 shows.

FIGURE 11.5
IS-LM Equilibrium Example

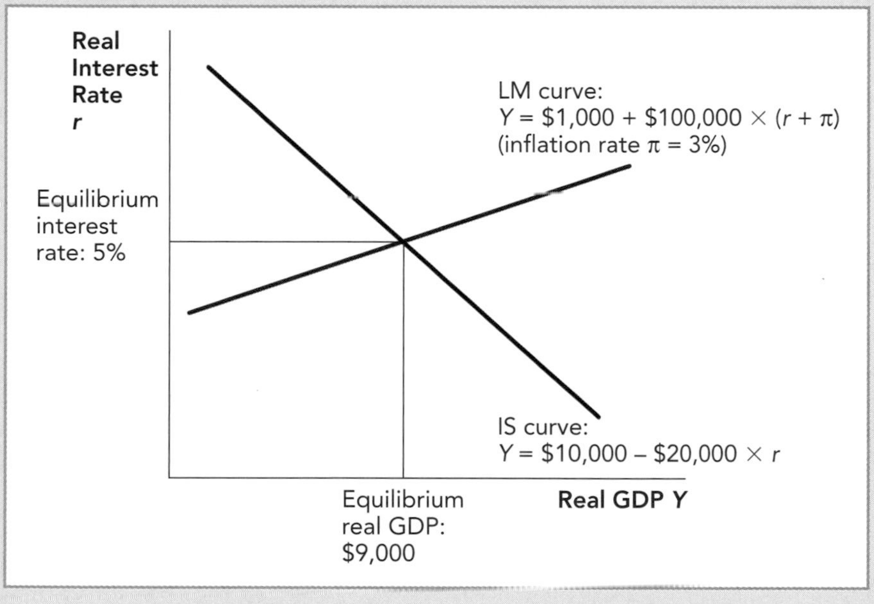

IS Shocks

Any change in economic policy or the economic environment that increases autonomous spending, such as an increase in government purchases, shifts the IS curve to the right. If the money stock is constant, it moves the economy up and to the right along the LM curve on the IS-LM diagram, as Figure 11.6 shows. The new equilibrium will have both a higher level of real interest rates and a higher equilibrium level of real GDP.

Exactly how the total effect of an expansionary shift in the IS curve is divided between increased interest rates and increased real GDP depends on the slope of the LM curve. Box 11.2 provides an example of how to calculate exactly what the effects are. If the LM curve is nearly horizontal (or if the central bank is targeting the money stock — in which case there is no LM curve as such) there will be little or no increase in interest rates. The increase in equilibrium real GDP will be the same magnitude as the outward shift in the IS curve. If the LM curve is very steeply sloped,

FIGURE 11.6
Effect of a Positive IS Shock

An expansionary shift in the IS curve raises both real GDP Y and the real interest rate r.

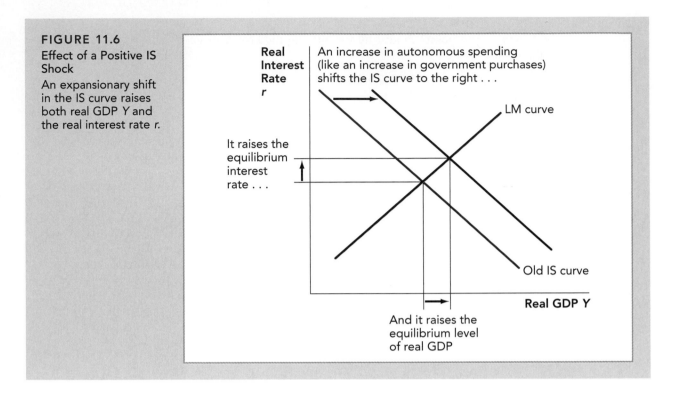

there will be a big effect on interest rates and little effect on real GDP. The LM curve will be steeply sloped if demand for money is extremely interest *inelastic*, and it takes a large change in interest rates to cause a small change in households' and businesses' desired holdings of money.

AN IS SHOCK: AN EXAMPLE

Suppose that, as in Box 11.1, the economy's IS curve is

$$Y = \frac{A_0}{1 - MPE} - \frac{I_r + X_\varepsilon\varepsilon_r}{1 - MPE} \times r = \frac{\$5,000}{1 - 0.5} - \frac{\$10,000}{1 - 0.5} \times r = \$10,000 - \$20,000 \times r$$

and its LM curve is

$$Y = \$1,000 + \$100,000 \times (r + \pi)$$

with the inflation rate π constant at 3 percent per year. Thus the initial equilibrium is as in Box 11.1, with real GDP Y at $9,000 billion and the real interest rate r at 5 percent.

Now suppose that there is a positive real shock to the economy: There is no immediate increase in potential GDP, yet new technological breakthroughs lead businesses to become more optimistic and generate an increase in baseline investment I_0 (and thus in baseline autonomous spending A_0) of $150 billion. What happens to the economy's equilibrium level of output and interest rates?

The new IS curve is

$$Y = \frac{A_0 + \Delta I_0}{1 - MPE} - \frac{I_r + X_\varepsilon\varepsilon_r}{1 - MPE} \times r = \frac{\$5,000 + \$150}{1 - 0.5} - \frac{\$10,000}{1 - 0.5} \times r = \$10,300 - \$20,000 \times r$$

Thus the IS curve shifts out and to the right by $300 billion — the magnitude of the shift in baseline autonomous spending times the multiplier.

The LM curve remains unchanged at

$$Y = \$1,000 + \$100,000 \times (r + \pi)$$

So, with inflation constant at 3 percent per year, the new equilibrium can be found by setting the values of Y produced by the IS and LM curves to be equal to each other:

$$Y = \$10,300 - \$20,000 \times r = \$1,000 + \$100,000 \times (r + 3)$$
$$\$6,300 = (\$20,000 + \$100,000) \times r$$
$$r = 5.25\%$$

With the real interest rate r equal to 5.25 percent per year, the annual equilibrium for real GDP Y equals $9,250 billion. A $300 billion outward shift in the IS curve has led to an increase of 0.25 percent in the real interest rate and a $250 billion increase in real GDP. The higher interest rate has "crowded out" one-sixth of the shift in autonomous spending, as Figure 11.7 shows.

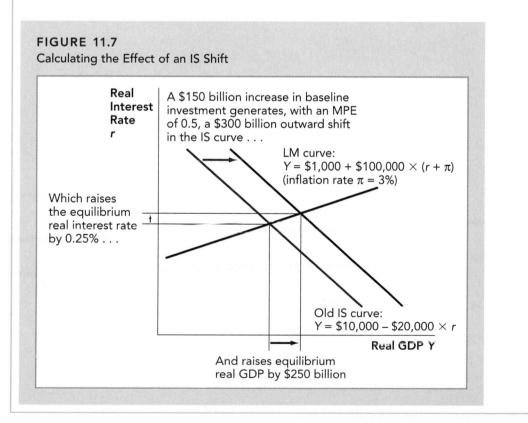

FIGURE 11.7
Calculating the Effect of an IS Shift

Real Interest Rate r

A $150 billion increase in baseline investment generates, with an MPE of 0.5, a $300 billion outward shift in the IS curve . . .

LM curve:
$Y = \$1,000 + \$100,000 \times (r + \pi)$
(inflation rate π = 3%)

Which raises the equilibrium real interest rate by 0.25% . . .

Old IS curve:
$Y = \$10,000 - \$20,000 \times r$

Real GDP Y

And raises equilibrium real GDP by $250 billion

LM Shocks

An increase in the money stock will shift the LM curve to the right. The larger money supply means that any given level of real GDP will be associated with a lower equilibrium nominal interest rate. Such an outward LM shift will shift the equilibrium position of the economy down and to the right along the IS curve, as Figure 11.8 shows. The new equilibrium position will have a higher level of equilibrium real GDP and a lower interest rate. Box 11.3 provides an illustrative example of such an expansionary LM shift. Conversely, a decrease in the money supply or any other contractionary LM shock that shifts the LM curve in and to the left will shift the economy up and to the left along the IS curve, resulting in higher equilibrium interest rates and a lower equilibrium value of real GDP.

FIGURE 11.8

Effect of an Expansionary LM Shock

An expansionary shift in the LM curve raises real GDP *Y* and lowers the equilibrium interest rate *r*.

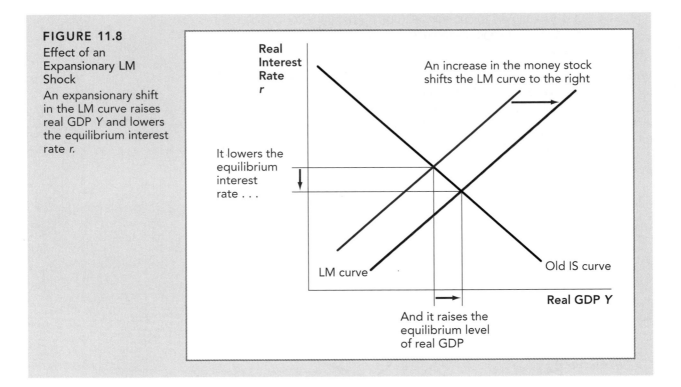

CALCULATING THE EFFECT OF AN LM SHOCK: AN EXAMPLE

Suppose that, as in Boxes 11.1 and 11.2, the economy's marginal propensity to expend (MPE) is 0.5, the initial level of baseline autonomous spending A_0 is $5,000 billion, and a 1-percentage-point increase in the real interest rate reduces the sum of investment and net exports by $100 billion. Then the economy's initial IS curve is the same:

$$Y = \frac{A_0}{1 - MPE} - \frac{I_r + X_\varepsilon\varepsilon_r}{1 - MPE} \times r = \frac{\$5,000}{1 - 0.5} - \frac{\$10,000}{1 - 0.5} \times r = \$10,000 - \$20,000 \times r$$

Suppose further that the economy's initial LM curve is represented by the equation

$$Y = \$1,000 + \$100,000 \times (r + \pi)$$

and that the inflation rate π is constant at 3 percent per year. Thus the initial equilibrium of the economy is with real GDP Y at \$9,000 billion and the real interest rate r at 5 percent.

Now suppose the central bank conducts an expansionary open market operation. It buys bonds for cash and increases the supply of money in the economy, shifting the LM curve to

$$Y = \$2,200 + \$100,000 \times (r + \pi)$$

So, with inflation constant at 3 percent per year, the new equilibrium can be found by setting the values of Y produced by the IS and LM curves to be equal to each other:

$$Y = \$10,000 - \$20,000 \times r = \$2,200 + \$100,000 \times (r + 3)$$
$$\$4,800 = (\$20,000 + \$100,000) \times r$$
$$r = 0.04 = 4\%$$

With the real interest rate r equal to 4 percent per year, annual equilibrium real GDP Y equals \$9,200 billion — a \$200 billion increase in the equilibrium level of annual real GDP, as shown in Figure 11.9.

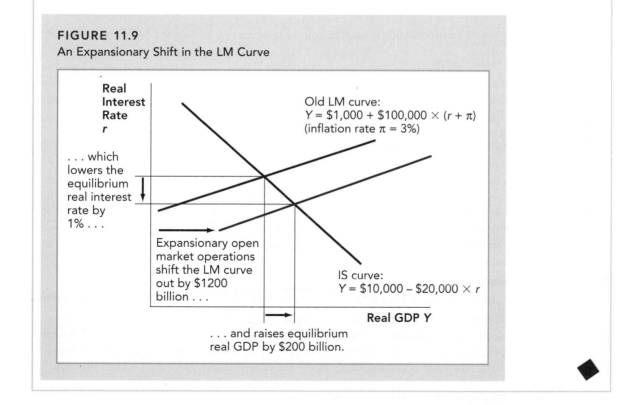

FIGURE 11.9
An Expansionary Shift in the LM Curve

Note the difference between how the money market works in this sticky-price model and in the flexible-price model presented in Part III. In the flexible-price model, the real interest rate balanced the supply and demand for loanable funds flowing through the financial markets. Changes in the money stock had no effect on either the real or the nominal interest rate. Instead, the price level adjusted

FIGURE 11.10
IS-LM Framework with an Interest Rate Target
When the central bank targets and fixes the interest rate, we can think of the LM curve as a horizontal line.

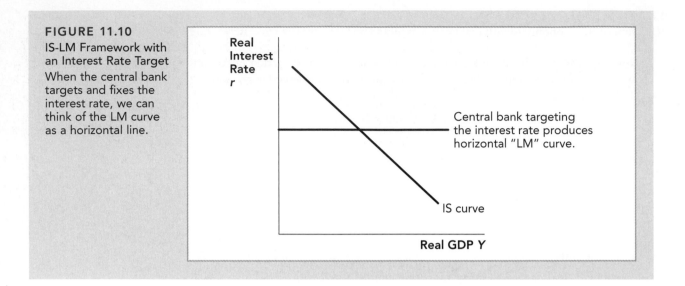

upward or downward to keep the quantity of money demanded equal to the money supply.

Here in the sticky-price model the price level is . . . sticky. It cannot adjust instantly upward or downward. So an imbalance in money demand and money supply does not cause an immediate change in the price level. Instead, it causes an immediate change in the nominal interest rate.

Interest Rate Targets

The intersection of the IS and LM curves determines short-run equilibrium values of real GDP when the money stock is fixed. It provides a flexible and useful framework for analyzing the expenditure-driven determination of output, money market equilibrium, and interest rates. Even the case in which the central bank is targeting the interest rate can be viewed in the IS-LM framework, as in Figure 11.10. An interest rate target can be seen as simply a flat, horizontal LM curve at the target level of the interest rate.

Classifying Economic Disturbances

The IS-LM framework allows economists to classify shifts in the economic environment and changes in economic policy into four basic categories, two that affect the LM curve and two that affect the IS curve. A surprisingly large number of economic disturbances affect aggregate demand and can be fitted into the IS-LM framework.

Changes That Affect the LM Curve

First, any change in the nominal money stock, in the price level, or in the trend velocity of money will shift the LM curve's location. Second, any change in the interest sensitivity of money demand — in how easy households and businesses find it to economize on their holdings of real money balances — will change the slope of the LM curve. Moreover, the fact that the IS-LM diagram is drawn with the *real*

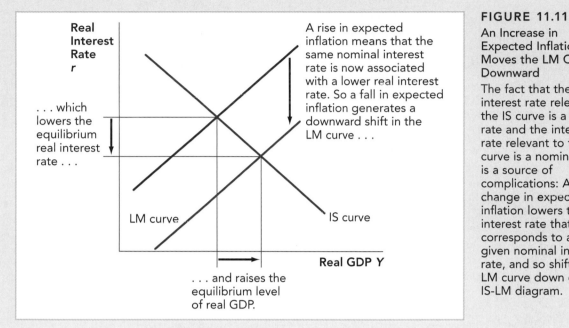

FIGURE 11.11

An Increase in Expected Inflation Moves the LM Curve Downward

The fact that the interest rate relevant to the IS curve is a real rate and the interest rate relevant to the LM curve is a nominal rate is a source of complications: A change in expected inflation lowers the real interest rate that corresponds to any given nominal interest rate, and so shifts the LM curve down on the IS-LM diagram.

interest rate — the *long-term, risky, real* interest rate — on the vertical axis has important consequences. The LM curve is a relationship between the short-run nominal interest rate and the level of real GDP at a given, fixed level of the real money supply:

$$Y = (V_0 + V_i \times i) \times \frac{M}{P}$$

As long as the spread between the short-term, safe, nominal interest rate i in the LM equation and the long-term, risky, real interest rate r in the IS equation is constant, there are no complications in drawing the LM curve on the same diagram as the IS curve.

But what if the expected rate of inflation π^e, the risk premium, or the term premium between short- and long-term interest rates changes? Then the position of the LM curve on the IS-LM diagram shifts either upward (if expected inflation falls, or if the risk premium rises, or if the term premium rises) or downward (if expected inflation rises, or if the risk premium falls, or if the term premium falls). Figure 11.11 illustrates what happens to the position of the LM curve if the expected inflation rate rises.

Thus changes in financial market expectations of future Federal Reserve policy, future inflation rates, or simply changes in the risk tolerance of bond traders shifts the LM curve. The IS-LM equilibrium is affected not only by disturbances in the money market but by broader shifts in the financial markets that alter the relationship between the nominal interest rates on short-term safe bonds and the real interest rate paid by corporations undertaking long-term risky investments.

Changes That Affect the IS Curve

Shifts in the IS curve are probably more frequent than shifts in the LM curve, for more types of shifts in the economic environment and economic policy affect planned expenditure than affect the supply and demand for money. Any change in the effect of a shift in interest rates on investment spending will change the slope of the IS curve. So will any change in either the sensitivity of exports to the exchange rate or the sensitivity of the level of the exchange rate to the level of domestic interest rates.

Furthermore, anything that affects the marginal propensity to spend — the MPE — will change the slope of the IS curve and the position of the IS curve as well. Any shift in the marginal propensity to consume C_y will change the MPE. Thus if households decide that income changes are more likely to be permanent (raising the marginal propensity to consume) or more likely to be transitory (lowering the marginal propensity to consume), they will raise or lower the MPE. Changes in tax rates have a direct effect on the MPE. So do changes in the propensity to import. Thus, for example, the imposition or removal of a tariff on imports to discourage them will affect the position and the slope of the IS curve.

Finally, changes in the economic environment and in economic policy that shift the level of autonomous spending shift the IS curve. Anything that affects the baseline level of consumption C_0 affects autonomous spending — whether it is a change in demography that changes desired savings behavior, a change in optimism about future levels of income, or any other cause of a shift in consumer behavior. Anything that affects the baseline level of investment I_0 affects autonomous spending — whether it is a wave of innovation that increases expected future profits and desired investment, a wave of irrational overoptimism or overpessimism, a change in tax policy that affects not the level of revenue collected but the incentives to invest, or any other cause. Changes in government purchases affect autonomous spending.

In sum, almost anything can affect the equilibrium level of aggregate demand on the IS-LM diagram. Pretty much everything *does* affect it at one time or another. One of the principal merits of the IS-LM is its use in sorting and classifying the determinants of equilibrium output and interest rates.

RECAP   THE MONEY STOCK AND THE MONEY MARKET: THE LM CURVE

Money demand is inversely related to the nominal interest rate because the nominal interest rate is the opportunity cost of holding money. Money demand is proportional to real GDP because the larger output is, the more liquid assets are needed to make sure that transactions run smoothly. The fact that money demand depends positively on national income Y and negatively on the nominal interest rate i means that equilibrium in the money market holds if and only if $Y = [V_0 + Vi \times (r + \pi^e)] \times (M/P)$. For a fixed value of the real money stock M/P, this equation defines the LM curve — an upward-sloping relationship between real GDP Y and the nominal interest rate $r + \pi^e$. If expected inflation π^e is constant, we can think of the LM curve as a relationship between real GDP Y and the real interest rate r, and draw it on the same axes as the IS curve to make the IS-LM diagram.

11.2 THE EXCHANGE RATE AND THE TRADE BALANCE

The IS-LM Framework and the International Sector

The IS-LM Framework and the Exchange Rate

In our sticky-price model, the real exchange rate ε is equal to speculators' opinion of its baseline fundamental value, ε_0, minus a parameter ε_r times the difference between the real domestic interest rate (r) and the foreign interest rate abroad (r^f):

$$\varepsilon = \varepsilon_0 - \varepsilon_r(r - r^f)$$

Thus the effects of changes in domestic conditions on the value of the real exchange rate are easy to predict. As long as the domestic real interest rate does not change,

FIGURE 11.12

IS-LM and the Exchange Rate

Rightward shifts in the IS and inward shifts in the LM curve will lower the exchange rate and the value of foreign currency, and reduce net exports.

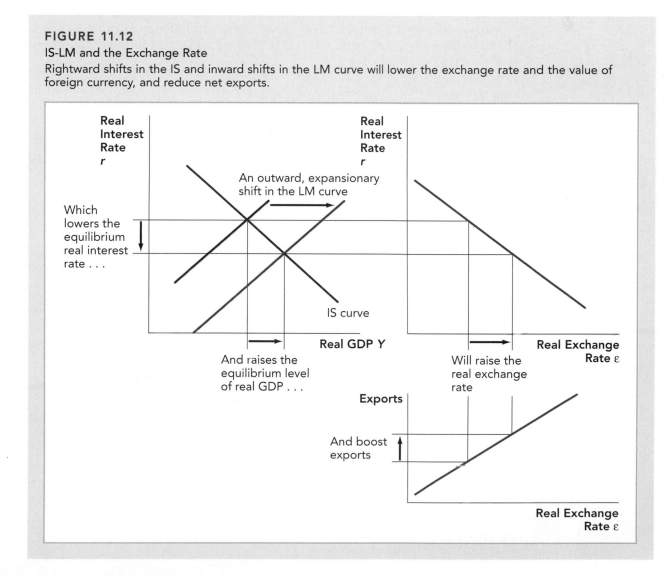

domestic conditions will have no impact on the exchange rate. If the exchange rate shifts, it will do so for other, external reasons.

Changes in the IS and LM curves that *do* change the domestic real interest rate will change the real exchange rate, however, by an amount equal to the parameter ε_r times the shift in the domestic interest rate. A rightward expansionary shift in the IS curve and a leftward contractionary shift in the LM curve both lower the value of the exchange rate. A leftward contractionary shift in the IS curve and a rightward expansionary shift in the LM curve will both raise the value of the exchange rate, as Figure 11.12 shows.

The effects of a change in domestic conditions on the real exchange rate are straightforward. The change in the exchange rate is proportional to the change in the real interest rate:

$$\Delta\varepsilon = \varepsilon_r \times \Delta r$$

What determines the size of the proportionality factor ε_r, and thus the interest sensitivity of the exchange rate? It is a function of foreign exchange speculators' willingness to bear risk and their assessment of how long differentials between domestic and foreign interest rates will persist. If speculators think differences in interest

FIGURE 11.13

Effect of Change in Domestic Conditions on the Exchange Rate and the Balance of Trade

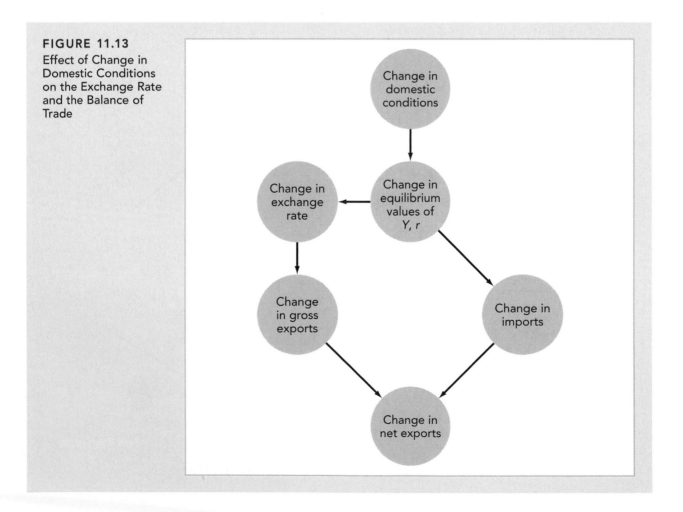

rates will last a long time, the interest sensitivity of the exchange rate will be high. If speculators fear bearing risk, the interest sensitivity will be small.

The IS-LM Framework and the Balance of Trade

The effects in the IS-LM framework of changes in domestic conditions on the balance of trade are a little more complicated. Changes in r affect the exchange rate, which affects gross exports. Changes in total income Y affect imports. Figure 11.13 sketches out the chief causal links.

The effect on net exports is the difference between the effect of a change in the interest rate on gross exports (remember: the higher the domestic interest rate, the lower the value of the exchange rate and the lower the value of gross exports) and the effect of a change in real GDP on imports:

$$\Delta NX = \Delta GX - \Delta IM = -(\varepsilon_r \times \Delta r) - (IM_y \times \Delta Y)$$

As the economy moves up or to the right (or both) on the IS-LM diagram, net exports fall. Box 11.4 provides an illustrative example of how to calculate the effect of a shock to the economy on the overall balance of trade.

AN LM SHOCK AND THE BALANCE OF TRADE: AN EXAMPLE

Suppose that the economy's marginal propensity to expend (MPE) is 0.5, that the marginal propensity to import IM_y is 0.15, that the initial level of baseline autonomous spending A_0 is \$5,000 billion, and that a 1-percentage-point increase in the real interest rate reduces investment spending by \$80 billion, and reduces the value of the exchange rate by 10 percent. Suppose further that each 1 percent increase in the exchange rate increases net exports by \$2 billion. Then the economy's initial IS curve is

$$Y = \frac{A_0}{1 - MPE} - \frac{I_r + X_\varepsilon \varepsilon_r}{1 - MPE} \times r = \frac{\$5,000}{1 - 0.5} - \frac{\$8,000 + 1,000 \times \$2}{1 - 0.5} \times r = \$10,000 - \$20,000 \times r$$

If the economy's initial LM curve is

$$Y = \$1,000 + \$100,000 \times (r + \pi)$$

and if the inflation rate π is constant at 3 percent per year, then the initial equilibrium of the economy is with an annual real GDP of \$9,000 billion and a real interest rate of 5 percent.

Now suppose the central bank conducts expansionary open market operations to shift the LM curve out to

$$Y = \$2,200 + \$100,000 \times (r + \pi)$$

The new equilibrium can be found by setting the values of Y produced by the IS and LM curve to be equal to each other:

$$r = 4\%$$
$$Y = \$9,200$$

The IS-LM diagram equilibrium has shifted, as shown in Figure 11.14, with a \$200 billion increase in the equilibrium level of annual real GDP and a 1-percentage-point decline in the real interest rate.

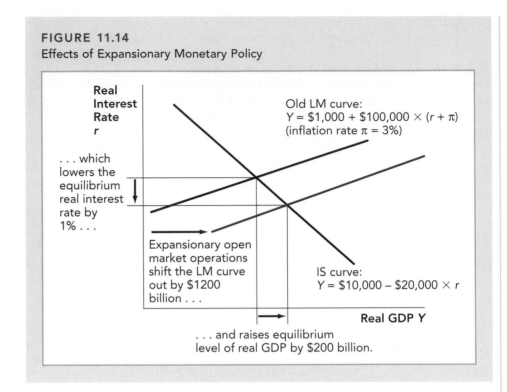

FIGURE 11.14
Effects of Expansionary Monetary Policy

Real
Interest
Rate
r

Old LM curve:
$Y = \$1{,}000 + \$100{,}000 \times (r + \pi)$
(inflation rate $\pi = 3\%$)

. . . which
lowers the
equilibrium
real interest
rate by
1% . . .

Expansionary open
market operations
shift the LM curve
out by $1200
billion . . .

IS curve:
$Y = \$10{,}000 - \$20{,}000 \times r$

Real GDP Y

. . . and raises equilibrium
level of real GDP by $200 billion.

The decrease in the real interest rate increases the real exchange rate by

$$-\varepsilon_r \times \Delta r = -10 \times (-0.01) = 0.10$$

and the rise in the real exchange rate increases gross exports by

$$X_\varepsilon \times \Delta\varepsilon = \$200 \times 0.1 = +\$20$$

The $200 billion increase in real national income increases imports by

$$IM_y \times \Delta Y = 0.15 \times \$200 = \$30$$

Thus the LM shock changes annual net exports by the difference between the two:

$$\Delta NX = \Delta GX - \Delta IM = \$20 - \$30 = -\$10$$

It shrinks net exports by $10 billion a year.

International Shocks and the Domestic Economy

Three different types of international shocks will affect the IS-LM equilibrium. The first is a shift in foreign demand for domestic exports — the result, usually, of changes in foreign real GDP. The second is a shift in the foreign real interest rate, and the third is a change in foreign exchange speculators' view about the fundamental value of the exchange rate.

An increase in foreign demand for home-country exports will affect the domestic economy in the same way as any other expansionary IS shock. The increase in export demand is an increase in baseline autonomous spending A_0. It shifts the IS curve rightward by an amount $\Delta A_0/(1 - MPE)$. This rightward IS shift raises the equilibrium level of real GDP and, to the extent that the LM curve is upward-sloping, raises the real interest rate. The increase in the real interest rate would make exports more expensive to foreigners, and put some countervailing downward pressure on exports. The increase in the equilibrium level of real GDP would raise demand for imports. Figure 11.15 shows the major links in the causal chain.

If the Federal Reserve is targeting the real interest rate, then the change in real GDP Y generated by a rise ΔY^f in foreign total income is straightforward to calculate. The effect on real GDP Y is simply the rise in foreign incomes times their propensity to spend on our exports times the multiplier:

$$\Delta Y = \frac{X_f \times \Delta Y^f}{1 - MPE}$$

which can also be written, if we replace the MPE by the parameters that determine it:

$$\Delta Y = \frac{X_f \times \Delta Y^f}{1 - C_y(1 - t) + IM_y}$$

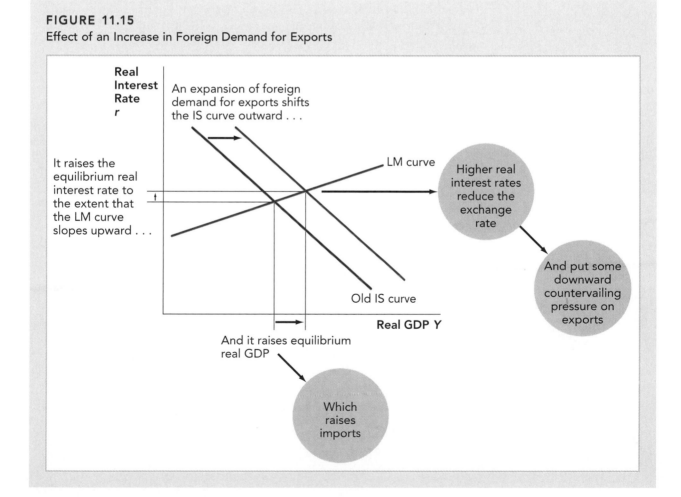

FIGURE 11.15
Effect of an Increase in Foreign Demand for Exports

The change in net exports is the difference between the change in gross exports produced by the expansion in foreign demand, and the change in imports produced by the rise in domestic national income:

$$\Delta NX = \Delta GX - \Delta IM$$

This difference can be written as a function of domestic and foreign national income:

$$\Delta NX = X_f \times \Delta Y^f - IM_y \times \Delta Y$$

And we already found the term to calculate the change in domestic national income, so we can put that in to obtain

$$\Delta NX = X_f \times \Delta Y^f - IM_y \times \frac{X_f \times \Delta Y^f}{1 - MPE}$$

$$= (X_f \times \Delta Y^f) \times \left(1 - \frac{IM_y}{1 - MPE}\right)$$

As long as the multiplier times the propensity to import is less than 1, an increase in foreign incomes will raise net exports.

The second type of international shock, an increase in the foreign interest rate r^f, also has an immediate impact on the domestic economy but through different channels. An increase in the foreign interest rate raises the value of the exchange rate, and so boosts exports. The increase in exports shifts the IS curve to the right, leading to a higher level of equilibrium real GDP and — to the extent that the LM curve is upward-sloping — to higher real interest rates. The consequences of such a shift are similar to those of an increase in foreign incomes save for the direction in which the exchange rate moves.

The third type of international shock is a sudden change in speculators' expectations ε_0 of the long-run fundamental exchange rate. Consider an upward shock to ε_0. It would have effects identical to an increase in interest rates overseas: The exchange rate would rise, the IS curve would shift outward, equilibrium real GDP would increase, and — to the extent that the LM curve is upward-sloping — the domestic real interest rate would increase as well. Box 11.5 works through an example of such a change in exchange market speculators' expectations.

A CHANGE IN INTERNATIONAL INVESTORS' EXPECTATIONS: AN EXAMPLE

Suppose that the economy's LM curve is represented by the equation

$$Y = \$1,000 + \$100,000 \times (r + \pi)$$

and that the inflation rate π is constant at 3 percent per year. Suppose further that the economy's marginal propensity to expend (MPE) is 0.5, that the marginal propensity to import IM_y is 0.15, that the initial level of baseline autonomous spending A_0 is $5,000 billion, that a 1-percentage-point increase in the real interest rate reduces investment spending by $40 billion and reduces the value of the exchange rate by 10 percent, and that each 1 percent increase in the exchange rate increases net exports by $6 billion. Then the economy's initial IS curve is

$$Y = \frac{A_0}{1 - MPE} - \frac{I_r + X_\varepsilon \varepsilon_r}{1 - MPE} \times r = \frac{\$5,000}{1 - 0.5} - \frac{\$8,000 + 1,000 \times \$2}{1 - 0.5} \times r = \$10,000 - \$20,000 \times r$$

The initial equilibrium has annual real GDP at $9,000 billion and a real interest rate of 5 percent.

Consider a sudden upward shock of 10 percent, as foreign exchange speculators lose confidence in the value of the domestic currency, changing their opinions ε_0 of the long-run fundamental value of the real exchange rate. Such a shock shifts the IS curve to the right, raising the level of real GDP on the IS curve for a given, fixed level of the real interest rate by an amount

$$\frac{X_\varepsilon \times \Delta\varepsilon_0}{1 - MPE}$$

The shifted IS curve is then

$$Y = \frac{A_0 + \Delta A_0}{1 - MPE} - \frac{I_r + X_\varepsilon \varepsilon_r}{1 - MPE} \times r = \frac{A_0 + X_\varepsilon \times \Delta\varepsilon_0}{1 - MPE} - \frac{I_r + X_\varepsilon \varepsilon_r}{1 - MPE} \times r$$

$$= \frac{\$5,000 + \$6 \times 10}{1 - 0.5} - \frac{\$8,000 + \$10 \times 200}{1 - 0.5} \times r = \$10,120 - \$20,000 \times r$$

The new equilibrium can be found by setting the values of Y produced by the IS and LM curve to be equal to each other:

$$\$1,000 + \$1,000 \times (r + \pi) = Y = \$10,120 - \$200 \times r$$
$$\$6,120 = \$1,200 \times r$$
$$r = 5.1\%$$
$$Y = \$9,100$$

Equilibrium annual real GDP increases by $100 billion as the raised exchange rate boosts exports, and the domestic real interest rate rises by 0.1 percent.

The increase in the domestic real interest rate means that the final change in the real exchange rate, which is

$$\Delta\varepsilon = \Delta\varepsilon_0 - (\varepsilon_r \times \Delta r)$$
$$= 10 - (10 \times 0.1) = +9$$

is less than the 10 percent magnitude of the initial shock: higher domestic real interest rates have offset some of the effect of the change in foreign exchange speculators' opinions. The increase in the domestic real interest rate also means that some domestic investment has been "crowded out" by the interest rate effects of the export boom:

$$\Delta I = -I_r \times \Delta r = -\$40 \times 0.1 = -\$4$$

The total effect on gross exports from the net change in the exchange rate is

$$\Delta GX - X_\varepsilon \times \Delta\varepsilon = \$6 \times 9 = +\$54$$

Subtract the total change in imports, which is

$$\Delta IM = IM_y \times \Delta Y = -0.15 \times \$100 = \$15$$

the total change in net exports from the shift in expectations is +$39 billion.

> ### RECAP   THE EXCHANGE RATE AND THE TRADE BALANCE
>
> The effects of a change in domestic conditions on the real exchange rate are straightforward. The change in the exchange rate is proportional to the change in the real interest rate. What determines the size of the proportionality factor? It is a function of foreign exchange speculators' willingness to bear risk, and their assessment of how long differentials between domestic and foreign interest rates will persist. If speculators think differences in interest rates will last for a long time, the interest sensitivity of the exchange rate will be high. If speculators fear bearing risk, the interest sensitivity of the exchange rate will be small.

11.3 AGGREGATE DEMAND

The Price Level and Aggregate Demand

What happens to the level of real GDP as the price level rises? If the nominal money supply is fixed, then an increase in the price level reduces real money balances and shifts the LM curve back and to the left. The equilibrium real interest rate rises, and the equilibrium level of real GDP falls, as Figure 11.16 shows.

Suppose we draw another diagram, this time with the price level on the vertical axis and the level of real GDP on the horizontal axis. We use this new diagram to plot what the equilibrium level of real GDP is for each possible value of the price level. For each value of the price level, we calculate the LM curve and use the IS-LM diagram to calculate the equilibrium level of real GDP. As Figure 11.17 shows, we find — if the nominal money supply is fixed — a downward-sloping relationship be-

FIGURE 11.16

An increase in the Price Level Shifts the LM Curve Left (If the Nominal Money Supply Is Fixed)

For a fixed level of the nominal money stock, an increase in the price level is a contractionary shift in the economy. The higher the price level, the lower the real money stock. The lower the real money stock, the further left the LM curve moves. The further left the LM curve, the lower real GDP is.

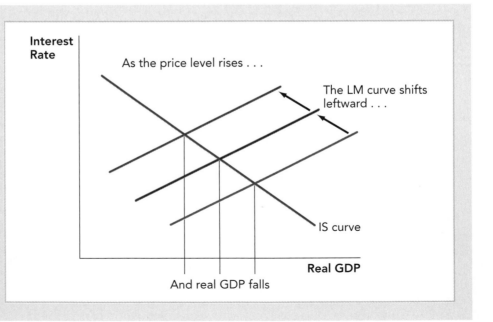

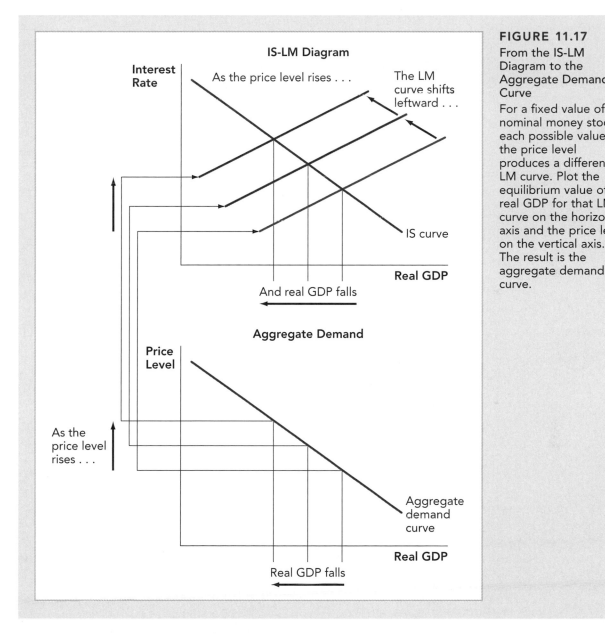

FIGURE 11.17
From the IS-LM Diagram to the Aggregate Demand Curve

For a fixed value of the nominal money stock, each possible value for the price level produces a different LM curve. Plot the equilibrium value of real GDP for that LM curve on the horizontal axis and the price level on the vertical axis. The result is the aggregate demand curve.

tween the price level and real GDP. With the nominal money stock held fixed, a rise in the price level increases the real money stock, and shifts the LM curve to the left because the position of the LM curve depends on the value of the real money stock. A leftward shift in the LM curve reduces the equilibrium level of real GDP and increases the interest rate. The lower the price level, the higher real money balances are, the lower the interest rate is, the higher aggregate demand is, and the higher the equilibrium level of real GDP is. Economists call this curve — according to which a lower price *level* means higher aggregate demand — the **aggregate demand curve**.

In this aggregate demand curve we can see how, over time, adjustments in prices and wages might carry the economy from the sticky-price model equilibrium back to the flexible-price equilibrium in which real GDP is equal to potential output. If real GDP is less than potential output, prices might fall over time, and falling prices would carry the economy down and to the right along the aggregate demand curve, increasing real GDP. If real GDP is greater than potential output, prices might rise over time, and rising prices would carry the economy up and to the left along the aggregate demand curve, reducing real GDP.

Monetary Policy and Aggregate Demand

Modern central banks, however, do not fix the money stock and then sit by passively watching the business cycle. So the derivation of the aggregate curve in the previous section must change for modern macroeconomies. Once we recognize that modern central banks play an active role in managing the macroeconomy, the analysis of aggregate demand is somewhat different. Modern central banks pay a lot of attention to the inflation rate. When the inflation rate rises, the central bank tends to increase the real interest rate to try to reduce aggregate demand and cool off inflation.

The Stanford economist John Taylor, on leave since 2001 at the Treasury Department as Undersecretary for International Affairs, has a simple model of how central banks act, called the *Taylor rule*. According to the Taylor rule, the central bank has a *target* value π' for the inflation rate, and an estimate r^* of what the normal real interest rate should be. If inflation is higher than its target value, the central bank raises the real interest rate above r^*. Whenever inflation is lower than its target value, the central bank lowers the interest rate below r^* according to the rule

$$r = r^* + \phi'' \times (\pi - \pi')$$

where the parameter ϕ'' (the Greek letter "phi" with a double prime symbol) determines how aggressively the central bank reacts to inflation.

We take the Taylor rule, the model of how the central bank acts, and substitute its expression for the determinants of the real interest rate into the IS-curve equation

$$Y = \frac{A_0}{1 - MPE} - \frac{I_r + X_\varepsilon \varepsilon_r}{1 - MPE} \times r$$

to obtain

$$Y = \left[\frac{A_0}{1 - MPE} - \frac{I_r + X_\varepsilon \varepsilon_r}{1 - MPE} \times r^* \right] - \frac{\phi'' \times (I_r + X_\varepsilon \varepsilon_r)}{1 - MPE} \times (\pi - \pi')$$

This equation is too complex to work with, so once again it is useful to simplify. Define Y_0 to be the level of real GDP when the real interest rate is at its long-run normal value r^*:

$$Y_0 = \frac{A_0}{1 - MPE} - \frac{I_r + X_\varepsilon \varepsilon_r}{1 - MPE} \times r^*$$

And define a new parameter ϕ', "phi prime," to be

$$\phi' = \frac{\phi'' \times (I_r + X_\varepsilon \varepsilon_r)}{1 - MPE}$$

Then we can write our combination of the Taylor rule and the IS curve in the simple-looking form

$$Y = Y_0 - \phi' \times (\pi - \pi')$$

which is called the *monetary policy reaction function*, shown in Figure 11.18.

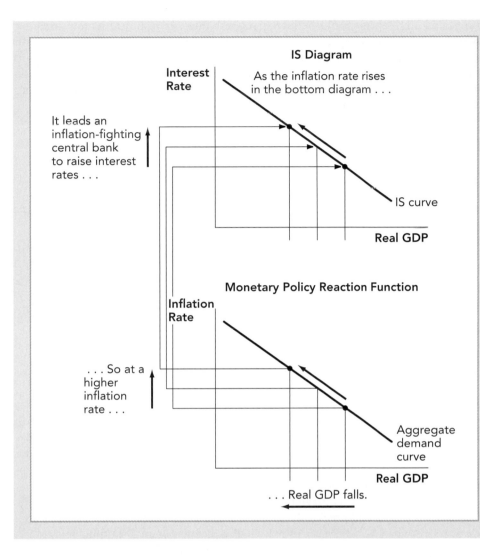

FIGURE 11.18
The Monetary Policy Reaction Function
The actions of an inflation-fighting central bank lead to the same kind of downward-sloping relationship between prices and output as in the previous section. But in this case it is a higher inflation rate, not a higher price level, that is associated with lower real GDP.

This monetary policy reaction function looks akin to the aggregate demand curve of the previous section. When prices increase — in this case, when inflation is higher than the central bank wants it to be — real GDP declines. There are, however, differences. The aggregate demand curve of the previous section was a relationship between the price *level* and real GDP. This monetary policy reaction function is a relationship between the inflation rate and real GDP. The previous aggregate demand curve assumed that the Federal Reserve sat like a potted plant while the business cycle proceeded. The monetary policy reaction function assumes that the Federal Reserve is engaged in the economy, trying to manage it to keep inflation close to the inflation target, and is a good model of how central banks actually behave.

This monetary policy reaction function offers a glimpse, once again, into how adjustments in prices and wages might carry the economy, over time, from the sticky-price equilibrium with potentially high unemployment and a gap between GDP and potential output back to the flexible-price equilibrium in which real GDP is equal to potential output. If real GDP is less than potential output, inflation might fall over time, and the central bank's reducing interest rates in response to low inflation would carry the economy down and to the right along the monetary policy reaction function, increasing real GDP. If real GDP is greater than potential output, inflation might rise over time, and the central bank's raising interest rates in response to high inflation would carry the economy up and to the left along the aggregate demand curve, reducing real GDP.

RECAP   AGGREGATE DEMAND

What happens to the level of real GDP as the price level rises? If the nominal money supply is fixed, then an increase in the price level reduces real money balances and shifts the LM curve back and to the left. The equilibrium real interest rate rises, and the equilibrium level of real GDP falls. If the central bank fixes the interest rate, in all likelihood it will follow a policy of raising real interest rates when inflation rises. In either case, higher prices (or inflation rates) are associated with lower values of real GDP. Economists call this relationship the *aggregate demand* relationship.

11.4 AGGREGATE SUPPLY

Output and the Price Level

Inflation is an increase in the general, overall price level. An increase in the price of any one particular good — even a large increase in the price of any one particular good — is not inflation. Inflation, then, is an increase in the price of just about everything. Together, the prices of all or nearly all goods and incomes rise by approximately the same proportional amount.

Whenever real GDP is greater than potential output, inflation is likely to be higher than people had previously anticipated. Thus inflation is likely to accelerate. Conversely, whenever the level of real GDP is below potential output, inflation is likely to be lower than people had previously anticipated. The inflation rate is likely to fall toward zero — and perhaps prices will begin to fall in deflation.

Economists call this correlation between real GDP (relative to potential output) and the rate of inflation (relative to its previously expected value) the short-run *aggregate supply* curve. One way to write the short-run **aggregate supply curve** is

$$\frac{Y - Y^*}{Y^*} = \theta \times \frac{P - P^e}{P^e}$$

That is, the proportional deviation of real GDP Y from potential output Y^* is equal to the parameter θ (the Greek letter "theta"), which represents the slope of the short-run aggregate supply function, times the proportional deviation of the price level P from its anticipated level P^e. But since the inflation rate π is simply the proportional rate of change of the price level, we can replace the expression $(P - P^e)/P^e$ with the actual inflation rate π minus the expected inflation rate π^e:

$$\frac{Y - Y^*}{Y^*} = \theta \times (\pi - \pi^e)$$

Figure 11.19 plots this version of the short-run aggregate supply curve.

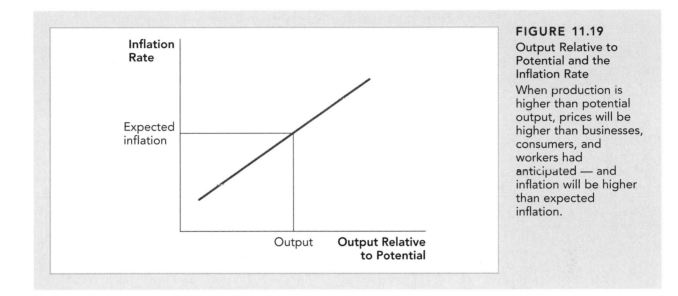

FIGURE 11.19
Output Relative to
Potential and the
Inflation Rate
When production is
higher than potential
output, prices will be
higher than businesses,
consumers, and
workers had
anticipated — and
inflation will be higher
than expected
inflation.

Whatever form of the aggregate supply function we use, we can combine it with
the aggregate demand or monetary policy reaction function to see not just the equilibrium level of real GDP but also what the economy's price level and inflation rate
will be, as Figure 11.20 shows. The aggregate supply curve slopes upward because a
higher inflation rate calls forth the more intensive use of resources and thus a higher
level of production. A higher inflation rate either reduces the real money stock by
raising the price level directly and thus increases the real interest rate, or induces the
central bank to raise the real interest rate, and so cuts aggregate demand. Where aggregate supply and aggregate demand are equal — where the two curves cross — is
the current level of real GDP and the current inflation rate.

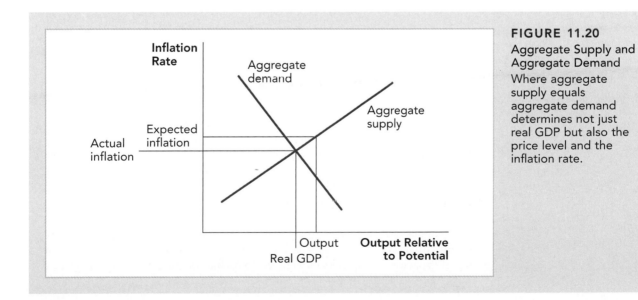

FIGURE 11.20
Aggregate Supply and
Aggregate Demand
Where aggregate
supply equals
aggregate demand
determines not just
real GDP but also the
price level and the
inflation rate.

Short-Run Aggregate Supply

There are many possible reasons why high levels of real GDP should be associated with higher inflation and a higher price level.

First, when demand for products is stronger than anticipated, firms raise their prices higher than they had previously planned. When aggregate demand is higher than potential output, demand is strong in nearly every single industry. Nearly all firms raise prices and hire more workers. Employment expands beyond its average proportion of the adult population and the unemployment rate falls below the "natural" rate of unemployment — the rate at which the rate of inflation is stable. High demand gives workers extra bargaining power, and they use it to bargain for higher wage levels than they had previously planned. Unions threaten to strike, knowing that firms will have a hard time finding replacement workers. Individuals quit, knowing they can find better jobs elsewhere. Such a high-pressure economy generates wages that rise faster than anticipated. Rapid wage growth is passed along to consumers in higher prices and accelerating inflation. Thus high real GDP generates higher inflation.

Second, when aggregate demand is higher than potential output, individual economic sectors and industries in the economy quickly reach the limits of capacity: Bottlenecks emerge. Confronted with a bottleneck — a vital item, part, or process where production cannot be increased quickly — potential purchasers bid up the price of the bottlenecked item. Since a car is useless without brakes, car manufacturers will pay any price for brake assemblies if they are in short supply. Such high prices signal to the market that the bottleneck industry should expand, and triggers investment that in the end boosts productive capacity. But developing bottlenecks lead to prices that increase faster than expected — thus to accelerating inflation.

To some degree the puzzle is not why high levels of real GDP (and low levels of unemployment) are associated with higher prices and inflation, but why the association is as weak as it is. In the model of Chapter 8, after all, changes in total nominal spending show up exclusively as changes in prices and not at all as changes in real GDP. But that is a subject for the next chapter.

RECAP   AGGREGATE SUPPLY

Economists call the positive correlation between real GDP (relative to potential output) and the rate of inflation (relative to its previously expected value) the aggregate supply curve. For a number of reasons, high levels of real GDP should be associated with higher inflation and a higher price level. First, when demand for products is stronger than anticipated, firms raise their prices higher than they had previously planned. And when aggregate demand is higher than potential output, demand is strong in nearly every single industry. Second, high demand gives workers extra bargaining power, and they use it to bargain for higher wage levels. Third, when aggregate demand is higher than potential output, individual economic sectors and industries in the economy quickly reach the limits of capacity: Bottlenecks emerge, and purchasers quickly bid up the price of the bottlenecked item and pass it along to consumers.

Chapter Summary

1. The money market is in equilibrium when the level of total incomes and of the short-term nominal interest rate is just right to make households and businesses want to hold all the real money balances that exist in the economy.

2. When the central bank's policy keeps the money stock fixed — or when there is no central bank — the LM curve consists of those combinations of interest rates and real GDP levels at which money demand equals money supply.

3. When the central bank's policy keeps the money stock fixed — or when there is no central bank — the point at which the IS and LM curves cross determines the equilibrium level of real GDP and the interest rate.

4. The IS-LM framework consists of two equilibrium conditions: The IS curve shows those combinations of interest rates and real GDP levels at which aggregate demand is equal to total production; the LM curve shows those combinations of interest rates and real GDP levels at which money demand is equal to money supply. Both equilibrium conditions must be satisfied.

5. An IS shock is any shock to the level of total spending as a function of the domestic real interest rate. An IS shock shifts the position of the IS curve. An expansionary IS shock raises real GDP and the real interest rate.

6. An LM shock is a shock to money demand or money supply. An LM shock shifts the position of the LM curve. An expansionary LM shock raises real GDP and lowers the interest rate.

7. Anything that affects the level of the real interest rate on the IS-LM diagram affects the real exchange rate. Increases in the real interest rate reduce the value of the real exchange rate, holding other things constant.

8. However, a number of different international shocks affect the real exchange rate as well as and in addition to changes in the domestic real interest rate. A collapse in foreign exchange speculators' confidence in the currency raises the real exchange rate. So does an increase in the real interest rate abroad.

9. The aggregate supply curve captures the relationship between aggregate demand and the price level. The higher real GDP is, the higher the price level and the inflation rate are likely to be.

10. The aggregate demand relationship arises because changes in the price level and inflation rate cause shifts in the determinants of aggregate demand — either directly as changes in the price level change the money stock, or indirectly as changes in the inflation rate change the interest rate target of the central bank.

11. Together the aggregate supply and aggregate demand curves make up the AS-AD framework, which allows us to analyze the impact of changes in economic policy and the economic environment not just on real GDP but also on the price level and the inflation rate.

Key Terms

money demand (p. 300)

real money balances (p. 300)

money market equilibrium (p. 301)

LM curve (p. 303)

IS-LM diagram (p. 304)

expected inflation rate (p. 304)

aggregate demand curve (p. 321)

aggregate supply curve (p. 324)

AS-AD diagram (p. 325)

Analytical Exercises

1. What are the *qualitative* effects, in the IS-LM model, of each of the following changes?
   a. An increase in firms' optimism about future profits.
   b. A sudden improvement in banking technology that makes checks clear two days faster.
   c. A wave of credit card fraud that leads people to use cash for purchases more often.
   d. A banking crisis that diminishes banks' willingness to accept deposits.
   e. A sudden military spending program.

2. What are the qualitative effects of an increase in real GDP on the rate of inflation?

3. Suppose that the expected rate of inflation suddenly jumped. What would happen — with no other changes in the economic environment — to the IS-LM equilibrium? Would equilibrium real GDP go up or down? Would the equilibrium real interest rate go up or down?

4. Suppose that the *term premium* — the gap between short-term and long-term interest rates — suddenly

went up. With no other changes in the economic environment, what would happen to the IS-LM equilibrium? Would equilibrium real GDP go up or down? Would the equilibrium real interest rate in the IS curve go up or down?

5. In what directions would you advise a government to change its fiscal and monetary policies if it wanted to make sure that net exports were positive — that it was running a trade surplus?

Policy Exercises

1. In 2000 the unemployment rate averaged 4.1 percent. Back in 1995 it averaged 5.6 percent. Real GDP in 1999 stood some 15.8 percent above real GDP in 1995. Assuming that the *natural rate of unemployment* remained unchanged between 1995 and 1999, how much of this growth in real GDP over those four years was due to increases in potential output? How much was due to "cyclical" factors — fluctuations in unemployment?

2. Between 1980 and 1986 U.S. net exports shifted from +$10 billion (in 1992 dollars) to –$164 billion. The unemployment rates in 1980 and 1986 were almost identical. Almost all observers agreed that this shift in the trade deficit was driven by shifts in the U.S. domestic condition. Which of the following do you think happened between 1980 and 1986?
   a. The LM curve shifted right and the IS curve shifted right.
   b. The LM curve shifted right and the IS curve shifted left.
   c. The LM curve shifted left and the IS curve shifted right.
   d. The LM curve shifted left and the IS curve shifted left.

3. Suppose that the Federal Reserve is wondering whether it should follow a policy of stabilizing the money stock or one of stabilizing the real interest rate. First, suppose that all shocks to the economy are shocks in autonomous spending: Which policy leads to smaller shifts in real GDP in response to shocks? Second, suppose that all of the shocks to the economy are shocks in the parameters of money demand — to the parameters L_0 and L_i in the money demand equation

$$\left(\frac{M}{P}\right)^d = \frac{Y}{V_0 + V_i \times (r + \pi)}$$

and in the LM equation

$$Y = [V_0 + V_i \times (r + \pi)] \times \frac{M}{P}$$

Which policy is now best in terms of leading to smaller shifts in real GDP? Third, suppose that the only shocks to the economy are changes in assessments of expected inflation π. Now what is your answer?

4. Suppose that money demand is interest insensitive. That is, suppose that the money demand function is

$$\left(\frac{M}{P}\right)^d = \frac{Y}{V}$$

with no dependence on the interest rate at all. What, then, is the LM curve for this economy? What effect does an increase in government purchases have on the level of real interest rates and the equilibrium level of annual real GDP?

5. Suppose that the economy's LM curve is given by the equation

$$Y = \$1,000 + \$100,000 \times (r + \pi)$$

and that the inflation rate π is constant at 3 percent per year. Suppose further that the economy's marginal propensity to expend (MPE) is 0.6, that the marginal propensity to import IM_y is 0.25, that the initial level of baseline autonomous spending A_0 is $5,000 billion, that a 1-percentage-point increase in the real interest rate reduces investment spending by $40 billion and reduces the value of the exchange rate by 10 percent, and that each 1 percent increase in the exchange rate increases net exports by $6 billion.
   What is the effect on the domestic economy's equilibrium of a sudden 30 percent increase in the exchange rate as foreign exchange speculators lose confidence in the economy?

The Phillips Curve and Expectations

QUESTIONS

What is the Phillips curve?

How has the natural rate of unemployment changed in the United States over the past two generations?

What determines the expected rate of inflation?

How can we tell how expectations of inflation are formed — whether they are static, adaptive, or rational?

How useful is the aggregate demand–aggregate supply framework — the IS-LM model and the Phillips curve — for understanding macroeconomic events in the United States over the past two generations?

How do we connect the sticky-price model of this part, Part IV, with the flexible-price model of Part III?

This chapter has two major goals: to complete the construction of the sticky-price model begun in Chapter 9, and to link the sticky-price macroeconomic model analysis of Part IV with the flexible-price macroeconomic model analysis of Part III. The key to accomplishing both of these is an analytical tool called the Phillips curve. The Phillips curve, a version of the aggregate supply relationship, describes the relationship between inflation and unemployment according to which a higher rate of unemployment is associated with a lower rate of inflation.

12.1 AGGREGATE SUPPLY AND THE PHILLIPS CURVE

Unemployment

So far in this book one of our six key economic variables, the unemployment rate, has been largely absent. In Part II, the long-run growth section, unemployment was not a significant factor. In Part III, the flexible-price macroeconomic model section, there were no fluctuations in unemployment. Wages and prices were flexible, and so labor supply balanced labor demand.

Now it is time to bring unemployment to center stage. Back in Chapter 2 we studied **Okun's law**, the simple yet strong relationship between the unemployment rate and real GDP. Letting u stand for the rate of unemployment and u^* for the economy's natural rate of unemployment at which there is neither upward nor downward pressure on inflation, and letting Y stand for real GDP and Y^* for potential output, Okun's law is

$$u - u^* = -0.4 \times \frac{Y - Y^*}{Y^*}$$

Because of Okun's law, we do not have to separately keep track of what is happening to real GDP (relative to potential output) and to the unemployment rate. Using Okun's law, you can easily go back and forth from one to the other. It is usually more convenient to work with the unemployment rate than with the output gap — real GDP relative to potential output — if only because the unemployment rate is easier to measure. Box 12.1 presents examples of how to use Okun's law to go back and forth.

FORMS OF OKUN'S LAW: A TOOL

As we saw in Chapter 2, Okun's law relates the unemployment rate u (relative to the natural rate of unemployment u^*) to real GDP Y (relative to potential output Y^*). When real GDP Y is equal to Y^*, then the unemployment rate u is equal to the natural rate of unemployment u^*. When real GDP Y is different from Y^*, unemployment u will be different from the natural rate of unemployment u^* by an amount

$$u - u^* = -0.4 \times \frac{Y - Y^*}{Y^*}$$

When real GDP is above potential output, unemployment will be relatively low. When real GDP is below potential output, unemployment will be relatively high. The percentage point gap between unemployment and its natural rate will be two-fifths the magnitude of the percentage point gap between real GDP and potential output.

We can reverse Okun's law to put the output gap between real GDP and potential output on the left-hand side:

$$\frac{Y - Y^*}{Y^*} = -2.5 \times (u - u^*)$$

It can sometimes be more useful to write Okun's law in its year-to-year change form. Once again we use the Greek capital letter delta Δ as a symbol for the annual change in a variable. If the natural rate of unemployment u^* is constant, and if we identify the proportional rate of growth of potential output with the trend rate of population growth n plus the trend rate of productivity growth g, then we can derive the year-to-year change form of Okun's law from the equation above. We start with

$$\Delta u - \Delta u^* = -0.4 \times \frac{\Delta Y - \Delta Y^*}{\Delta Y^*}$$

Since the natural rate of unemployment u^* is constant, this is equivalent to

$$\Delta u = -0.4 \times \left(\frac{\Delta Y}{Y^*} - \frac{\Delta Y^*}{Y^*} \right)$$

Using the definition of the proportional rate of growth of potential output:

$$\Delta u = 0.4 \times \left[\frac{\Delta Y}{Y^*} - (n + g) \right]$$

This equation tells us that in any year the unemployment rate will fall (or rise) by an amount equal to 0.4 times the gap between the proportional growth rate of real GDP minus n plus g, the proportional growth rate of potential output.

Alternatively, we can put the change in real GDP proportional to potential output on the left-hand side:

$$\frac{\Delta Y}{Y^*} = (n + g) - 2.5 \times \Delta u$$

All these forms of Okun's law can be useful at one point or another in helping us to go back and forth between movements in the unemployment rate and changes in real GDP.

Moreover, the unemployment rate is of special interest because a high unemployment rate means low social welfare (see Box 12.2).

COSTS OF HIGH UNEMPLOYMENT: POLICY ISSUES

BOX 12.2

In a typical U.S. recession, unemployment rises by 2 percentage points. By Okun's law, that means that the **output gap** — real GDP relative to potential output — falls by some 5 percent. Five percent is about four years' worth of growth in output per worker. Moreover, recessions are not permanent; with rare exceptions, they are over in a year or two and are followed by periods of rapid growth that return real GDP to its pre-recession growth trend. Even the steepest post–World War II recession raised the unemployment rate by only 4 percentage points, and it took only three years after the recession trough for unemployment to fall back to a normal level.

Yet people fear a deep recession much more than they appear to value an extra four years' worth of economic growth. For example, the memory of the 1982 recession has substantially altered Americans' perceptions of how the economy works, how much they dare risk in the search for higher wages, and how confident they can be that their jobs are secure.

Why do episodes of high recession unemployment have such a large psychological impact? The most likely answer is that recessions are feared because they do not distribute their impact equally. Workers who keep their jobs are only lightly affected, while those who lose their jobs suffer a near-total loss of income. People fear a 2 percent chance of losing half their income much more than they fear a certain loss of 1 percent. Thus it is much worse for 2 percent of the people each to lose half their income than for everyone to lose 1 percent. It is the unequal distribution of the **costs of high unemployment** that makes recessions so feared — and that makes voters so anxious to elect economic policy makers who will successfully avoid them.

Three Faces of Aggregate Supply

In the last part of Chapter 11, we looked at the aggregate supply relationship. Looking at it one way, we saw that when real GDP is greater than potential output, the price level is likely to be higher than people had expected. In this case aggregate supply relates the price *level* (relative to the previously expected price level) to the *level* of real GDP (relative to potential output):

$$\frac{Y - Y^*}{Y^*} = \theta \times \frac{P - P^e}{P^e}$$

Looking at it a second way, we saw aggregate supply as a relationship between the inflation *rate* (relative to the previously expected inflation rate) and the *level* of real GDP (relative to potential output):

$$\frac{Y - Y^*}{Y^*} = \theta \times (\pi - \pi^e)$$

Because inflation this year minus what inflation was expected to be is the same as the proportional difference between the price level now and what the price level was expected to be, these are different ways of looking at the same economic process.

We can use Okun's law to look at aggregate supply in yet a third way. Because

$$\frac{Y - Y^*}{Y^*} = -2.5 \times (u - u^*)$$

we can substitute the right-hand side of the equation above for $(Y - Y^*)/Y$ in our aggregate supply function

$$-2.5 \times (u - u^*) = \theta \times (\pi - \pi^e)$$

If we rearrange to put the inflation rate by itself on the left-hand side:

$$\pi = \pi^e - \frac{2.5}{\theta} \times (u - u^*)$$

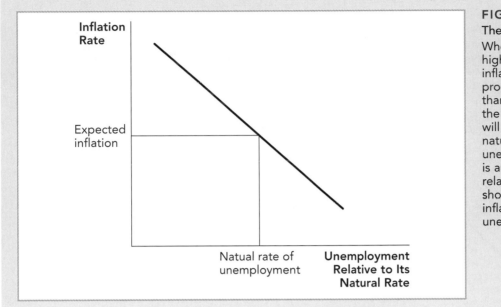

FIGURE 12.1
The Phillips Curve
When inflation is higher than expected inflation and production is higher than potential output, the unemployment rate will be lower than the natural rate of unemployment. There is an inverse relationship in the short run between inflation and unemployment.

and then define the parameter β (the Greek letter "beta") as β = 2.5/θ, the resulting function is

$$\pi = \pi^e - \beta \times (u - u^*)$$

This function is called the Phillips curve, after the New Zealand economist A. W. Phillips, who first wrote in the 1950s of the relationship between unemployment and the rate of change of prices. We will usually want to add an extra term to the Phillips curve:

$$\pi = \pi^e - \beta \times (u - u^*) + \varepsilon^s$$

where ε^s represents supply shocks — like the 1973 oil price increase — that can directly affect the rate of inflation.

Figure 12.1 sketches the **Phillips curve** on a graph with the unemployment rate on the horizontal axis and the inflation rate on the vertical axis. As you can see, it is an inverse relationship between inflation and unemployment. Figure 12.2 plots the Phillips curve alongside the other two ways of expressing the aggregate supply function. The underlying economic meaning is the same no matter which form — output-price level, output-inflation, or unemployment-inflation — you use. From this point on, however, we will almost always use the unemployment-inflation Phillips curve form. It is simply more convenient than the other forms.

The Phillips Curve Examined

The slope of the Phillips curve depends on how sticky wages and prices are. The stickier they are, the smaller the parameter β is, and the flatter the Phillips curve is. The parameter β varies widely from country to country and era to era. In the United States today it is about 0.5. When the Phillips curve is flat, even large movements in the unemployment rate have little effect on the price level. When wages and prices

FIGURE 12.2

Three Faces of Aggregate Supply

You can think of aggregate supply either as a relationship between production (relative to potential output) and the price level, between production (relative to potential output) and the inflation rate, or between unemployment (relative to the natural rate of unemployment) and the inflation rate. These are three different views of what remains the same single relationship.

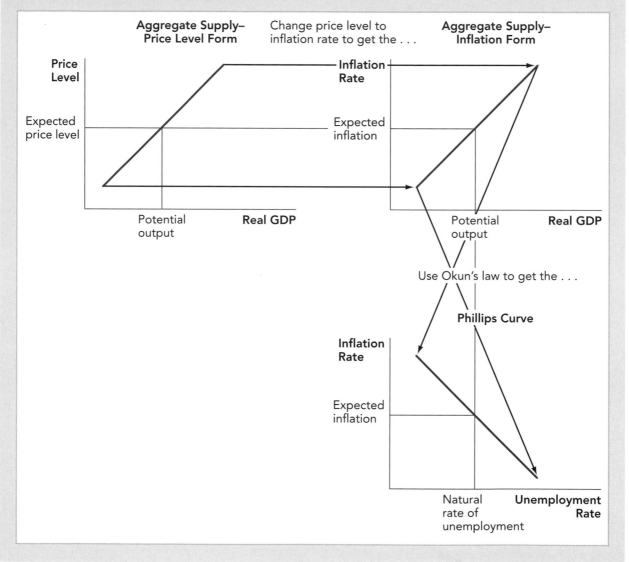

are less sticky, the Phillips curve is nearly vertical. Then even small movements in the unemployment rate have the potential to cause large changes in the price level.

Whenever unemployment is equal to its natural rate, inflation is equal to **expected inflation**. Thus we can determine the position of the Phillips curve if we know the **natural rate of unemployment** and the expected rate of inflation. A higher natural rate moves the Phillips curve right. Higher expected inflation moves the Phillips

FIGURE 12.3
Shifts in the Phillips Curve
When expected inflation changes, the position of the Phillips curve changes too.

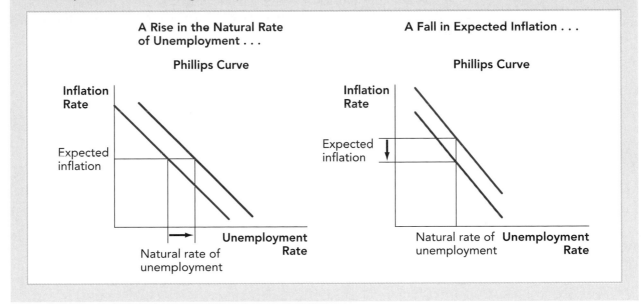

curve up. (See Figure 12.3.) If the past 40 years have made anything clear, it is that the Phillips curve shifts around substantially as *both* expected inflation and the natural rate change. Neither is a constant. The current natural rate of unemployment u^* is between 4.5 and 5 percent. The current rate of expected inflation π^e is about 2 percent per year. But both will be different in the future. One other important factor affects the position of the Phillips curve. Adverse supply shocks (like the 1973 tripling of world oil prices) move the Phillips curve up. Favorable supply shocks (like the 1986 worldwide declines in oil prices) move the Phillips curve down.

RECAP   AGGREGATE SUPPLY AND THE PHILLIPS CURVE

The Phillips curve is an inverse relationship between inflation and unemployment. It is the most convenient form of the aggregate supply relationship, so it is the one that we use. The Phillips curve tells us that when unemployment is below its natural rate, inflation is higher than expected inflation; conversely, when unemployment is above its natural rate, inflation is lower than expected inflation. The stickier wages and prices are, the flatter the Phillips curve is. When the Phillips curve is flat, even large movements in the unemployment rate have little effect on the price level. When wages and prices are less sticky, the Phillips curve is nearly vertical. Then even small movements in the unemployment rate have the potential to cause large changes in the price level.

12.2 AGGREGATE DEMAND AND INFLATION

In Chapter 11 we combined the IS curve with the Taylor rule for setting monetary policy and produced an aggregate demand function that showed how real GDP depended on the inflation rate. This **monetary policy reaction function (MPRF)** is

$$Y = Y_0 - \phi' \times (\pi - \pi')$$

However, we would prefer an aggregate demand equation with the unemployment rate on the left-hand side so we can use it along with the Phillips curve. So we use Okun's law to replace real GDP with the unemployment rate on the left-hand side:

$$u = u_0 - \phi \times (\pi - \pi')$$

where the parameter ϕ is the product of three different things, as is shown at great length in Box 12.3:

- How much the central bank raises the real interest rate in response to a rise in inflation.
- The slope of the IS curve — how much real GDP changes in response to a change in the real interest rate.
- The Okun's law coefficient — how large a change in unemployment is produced by a change in real GDP.

Together, this unemployment form of the aggregate demand relationship and the Phillips curve equation, which is

$$\pi = \pi^e - \beta(u - u^*) + \varepsilon^s$$

FIGURE 12.4
Equilibrium Levels of Unemployment and Inflation

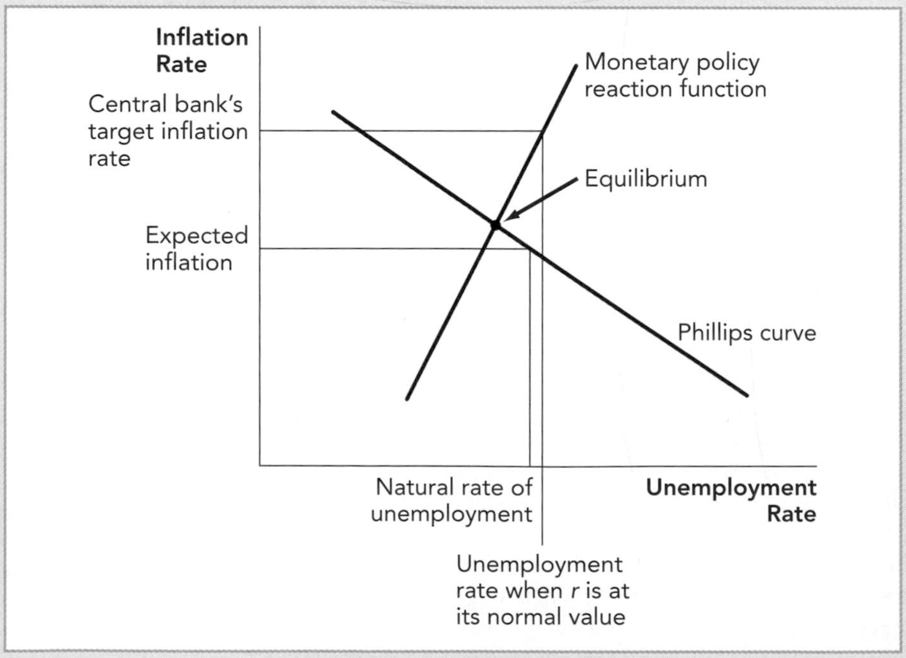

allow us to determine what the inflation and unemployment rates will be in the economy. (And when we have determined the unemployment rate, Okun's law allows us to immediately calculate real GDP as well.) Once again, the economy's equilibrium is where the curves cross: The Phillips curve determines inflation as a function of the unemployment rate, the MPRF determines the unemployment rate as a function of the inflation rate, and the two must be consistent, as Figure 12.4 shows.

As we have seen before, the position of the Phillips curve depends on:

- u^*, the natural rate of unemployment.
- π^e, the expected rate of inflation.
- ε^s, any current supply shocks affecting inflation.

The position of the aggregate demand curve, the MPRF, depends on

- u_0, the level of unemployment when the real interest rate r is at what the central bank thinks of as its long-run average rate.
- π', the **central bank's target level of inflation**.

All five of these factors together, along with the parameters θ and β — the slopes of the monetary policy reaction function and of the Phillips curve — determine the economy's equilibrium inflation and unemployment rates. Box 12.4 takes a more detailed look at precisely how.

FROM INCOME-EXPENDITURE TO THE PHILLIPS CURVE AND THE MPRF: SOME DETAILS

We have spent little time on the deeper parameters and functions that underpin the parameter, β, that governs the slope of the Phillips curve. The most we can say is that $\beta = 0.4/\theta$, where θ is the proportional amount of extra productive effort called forth by an extra 1 percent rise in the price level. Each of the competing reasons for an upward-sloping aggregate supply curve mentioned in Chapter 11 hopes to account for why θ is what it is. But none would claim to be able to do so yet.

By contrast, four chapters' worth of detail underpins the parameter θ, which governs the slope of the monetary policy reaction function.

$$u = u_0 + \phi \times (\pi - \pi')$$

The determinants of ϕ are:

$$\phi = \frac{1}{2.5} \times \phi'' \times (I_r + X_\varepsilon \varepsilon_r) \times \frac{1}{1 - [C_y \times (1 - t) - IM_y]}$$

All four of these terms have been analyzed at considerable length. The first term,

$$\frac{1}{2.5}$$

comes from Okun's law. It is the change in the unemployment rate produced by a 1 percent change in real GDP relative to potential output.

The second term,

$$\phi''$$

comes from central bankers' distaste for inflation. It is the amount by which central bankers raise the real interest rate when inflation is 1 percent per year higher.

The third term,

$$I_r + X_\varepsilon \varepsilon_r$$

comes from Chapter 10. It is the interest sensitivity of autonomous spending. It incorporates both the effect of interest rates on investment spending and the effect of interest rates on the exchange rate and hence on exports spending too.

The fourth and last term,

$$\frac{1}{1 - [C_y \times (1 - t) - IM_y]}$$

comes from Chapter 9. It is the multiplier — 1 divided by 1 minus the MPE. Most of the work of the preceding three chapters is encapsulated in this single parameter ϕ.

SOLVING FOR EQUILIBRIUM INFLATION AND UNEMPLOYMENT: SOME DETAILS

From our aggregate demand relationship, the MPRF:

$$u = u_0 + \phi \times (\pi - \pi')$$

and our aggregate supply relationship, the Phillips curve:

$$\pi - \pi^e - \beta(u = u^*) + \varepsilon^s$$

it is straightforward to find, algebraically, the economy's unemployment rate and inflation rate. Substitute the second Phillips curve equation into the monetary policy reaction function and solve for the unemployment rate:

$$u = \left(\frac{1}{1 + \phi\beta} u_0 + \frac{\phi\beta}{1 + \phi\beta} u^*\right) + \frac{\phi}{1 + \phi\beta} (\pi^e - \pi') + \frac{\phi}{1 + \phi\beta} \varepsilon^s$$

And substitute the first monetary policy reaction function equation into the Phillips curve and solve for the inflation rate:

$$\pi = \left(\frac{1}{1 + \phi\beta} \pi^e + \frac{\phi\beta}{1 + \phi\beta} \pi'\right) + \frac{\beta}{1 + \phi\beta} (u^* - u_0) + \frac{1}{1 + \phi\beta} \varepsilon^s$$

We see that the unemployment rate is equal to
- A weighted average of the natural rate of unemployment u^* and the unemployment rate u_0 when the central bank has set the real interest rate to its normal average value r^* (the greater the product of the slope parameters θ and β, the higher the relative weight on the natural rate u^*).
- A term that depends on the difference between the expected rate of inflation π^e and the central bank's target rate of inflation π'; when the first is higher than the second, unemployment is higher because the central bank has raised interest rates to fight inflation.
- A term that depends on current supply shocks ε^s.

We see that the inflation rate is equal to
- A weighted average of the expected rate of inflation π^e and the central bank's target rate of inflation π' (the greater the product of the slope parameters ϕ and β, the higher the relative weight on the target rate π').
- A term that depends on the difference between the natural rate of unemployment u^* and the unemployment rate u_0 when the central bank has

set the real interest rate to its normal average value r^*; when the first is higher than the second, inflation is higher because there is an inflationary bias to demand when the real interest rate is at its normal average value r^*.

• A term that depends on current supply shocks ε^s.

We can use this framework to analyze the effects of a shift in policy on the economy's equilibrium. For example, consider a depression abroad that lowers demand for exports. If the central bank takes a hands-off approach to this fall in exports and does not lower its estimate of r^*, the normal value for the real interest rate, then this change in the economic environment causes a rise in u_0, the unemployment rate when the real interest rate is at its normal value r^*, by an amount Δu_0. Since none of the other parameters of the inflation-unemployment framework change, the effect on the equilibrium levels of unemployment and inflation can be calculated immediately as

$$\Delta u = \frac{1}{1 + \phi\beta} \Delta u_0$$

Substitute the first monetary policy reaction function equation into the Phillips curve and solve for the change in the inflation rate:

$$\Delta\pi = \frac{-\beta}{1 + \phi\beta} \Delta u_0$$

The fact that the central bank has not reacted to the fall in export demand by lowering its r^* means that the monetary policy reaction function has shifted to the right, as Figure 12.5 shows, and the economy's equilibrium has moved down and to the right along the Phillips curve.

FIGURE 12.5
Effects of a Fall in Exports
A fall in exports with no countervailing change in the central bank's view of the normal target interest rate r^* shifts the MPRF right, raises the equilibrium unemployment rate, and lowers the inflation rate.

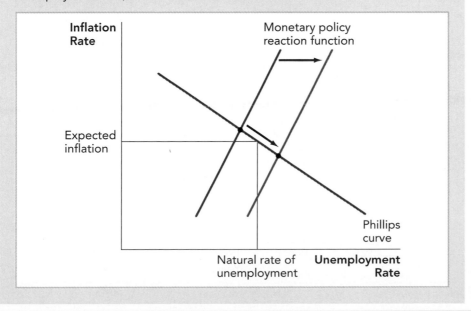

RECAP   AGGREGATE DEMAND AND INFLATION

We need a form of the aggregate demand function expressed in terms of the unemployment rate in order for the function to be useful alongside the Phillips curve. So we write an unemployment-rate version of the monetary policy reaction function (MPRF), which was set out in Chapter 11 as follows: $u = u_0 + \phi \times (\pi - \pi')$. The unemployment rate u is equal to u_0, the unemployment rate when the real interest rate is at what the central bank estimates is its normal value, plus a parameter ϕ times the difference between the current inflation rate π and the central bank's target inflation rate π'. This MPRF arises because the central bank raises the real interest rate above normal whenever inflation accelerates, and so higher inflation produces lower demand and higher unemployment.

The parameter θ is the product of three different things: (1) how much the central bank raises the real interest rate in response to a rise in inflation; (2) the slope of the IS curve — how much real GDP changes in response to a change in the real interest rate; and (3) Okun's law — how large a change in unemployment is produced by a change in real GDP.

12.3 THE NATURAL RATE OF UNEMPLOYMENT

In English, the word "natural" normally carries strong positive connotations of normal and desirable, but a high natural rate of unemployment is a bad thing. Unemployment cannot be reduced below its natural rate without accelerating inflation, so

FIGURE 12.6
Fluctuations in Unemployment and the Natural Rate
The natural rate of unemployment is not fixed. It varies substantially from decade to decade. Moreover, variations in the natural rate in the United States have been much smaller than variations in the natural rate in other countries.

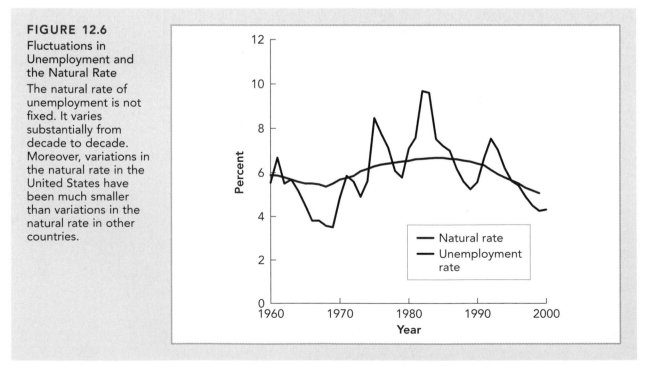

Source: Author's calculations and 2001 edition of *The Economic Report of the President* (Washington, DC: Government Printing Office).

a high natural rate means that expansionary fiscal and monetary policy are largely ineffective as tools to reduce unemployment.

Today, most estimates of the current U.S. "natural" rate of unemployment lie between 4.5 and 5.0 percent. But all agree that uncertainty about the level of the natural rate is substantial. And the natural rate has fluctuated substantially over the past two generations, as Figure 12.6 shows. Broadly, four sets of factors have powerful influence over the natural rate.

Demography and the Natural Rate

First, the natural rate changes as the relative age and educational distribution of the labor force changes. Teenagers have higher unemployment rates than adults; thus an economy with a lot of teenagers will have a higher natural rate. More experienced and more skilled workers find job hunting an easier experience, and take less time to find a new job when they leave an old one. Thus the natural rate of unemployment will fall when the labor force becomes more experienced and more skilled. Women used to have higher unemployment rates than men — although this is no longer true in the United States. The more educated tend to have lower rates of unemployment than the less well educated. African Americans have higher unemployment rates than whites.

A large part of the estimated rise in the natural rate from 5 percent or so in the 1960s to 6 to 7 percent by the end of the 1970s was due to changing demography. Some component of the decline in the natural rate since then was due to the increasing job-hunting experience of the very large baby-boom cohort. But the exact, quantitative relationship between demography and the natural rate is not well understood.

Institutions and the Natural Rate

Second, institutions have a powerful influence on the natural rate. Some economies have strong labor unions; other economies have weak ones. Some unions sacrifice employment in their industry for higher wages; others settle for lower wages in return for employment guarantees. Some economies lack apprenticeship programs that make the transition from education to employment relatively straightforward; others make the school-to-work transition easy. In each pair, the first increases and the second reduces the natural rate of unemployment. Barriers to worker mobility raise the natural rate, whether the barrier be subsidized housing that workers lose if they move (as in Britain in the 1970s and the 1980s), or high taxes that a firm must pay to hire a worker (as in France from the 1970s to today).

However, the link between economic institutions and the natural rate is neither simple nor straightforward. The institutional features that many observers today point to as a source of high European unemployment now were also present in the European economies in the 1970s, when European unemployment was low. Once again the quantitative relationships are not well understood.

Productivity Growth and the Natural Rate

Third, in recent years it has become more and more likely that a major determinant of the natural rate is the rate of productivity growth. The era of slow productivity growth from the mid-1970s to the mid-1990s saw a relatively high natural rate. By contrast, rapid productivity growth before 1973 and after 1995 seems to have generated a low natural rate.

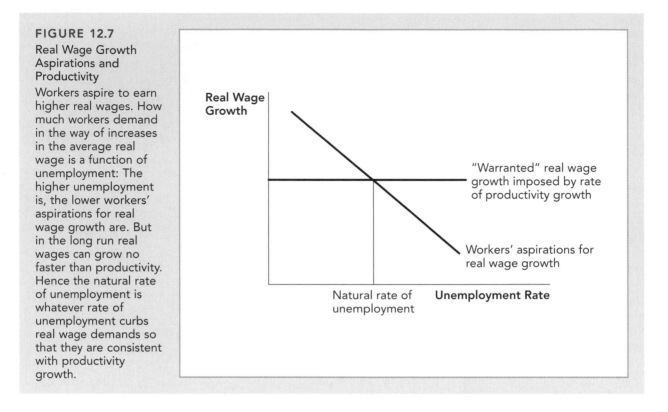

FIGURE 12.7
Real Wage Growth Aspirations and Productivity
Workers aspire to earn higher real wages. How much workers demand in the way of increases in the average real wage is a function of unemployment: The higher unemployment is, the lower workers' aspirations for real wage growth are. But in the long run real wages can grow no faster than productivity. Hence the natural rate of unemployment is whatever rate of unemployment curbs real wage demands so that they are consistent with productivity growth.

Why should a productivity growth slowdown generate a higher natural rate? A higher rate of productivity growth allows firms to pay higher real wage increases and remain profitable. If workers' **aspirations for real wage growth** depend on the rate of unemployment, then a slowdown in productivity growth will increase the natural rate. If real wages grow faster than productivity for an extended period of time, profits will disappear. Long before that point is reached, businesses will begin to fire workers and unemployment will rise. Thus if productivity growth slows, unemployment will rise. Unemployment will keep rising until workers' real wage aspirations fall to a rate consistent with current productivity growth, as shown in Figure 12.7.

The Past Level of Unemployment and the Natural Rate

Fourth and last, the natural rate will be high if unemployment has been high. Before 1980 western European economies had unemployment rates lower than the 5 to 6 percent that the United States averaged back then. But the mid-1970s brought recessions. European unemployment rose, but did not fall back much in subsequent recoveries. Workers left unemployed for two or three years had lost their skills, lost their willingness to show up on time, and lost their interest in even looking for new jobs. Thus the natural rate rose sharply in Europe with each business cycle. By the late 1990s European unemployment averaged 8 percent, and inflation was stable (see Figure 12.8). **Long-term unemployment** appears especially poisonous for an economy.

This laundry list of factors affecting the natural rate is incomplete. Do not think that economists understand much about why the natural rate is what it is. Almost every economist was surprised by the large rise in the natural rate in western Europe

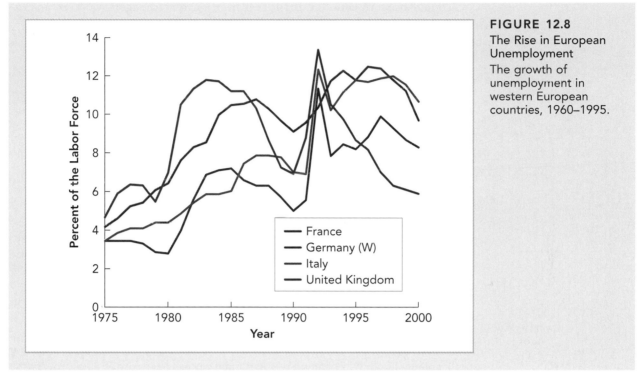

FIGURE 12.8
The Rise in European Unemployment
The growth of unemployment in western European countries, 1960–1995.

Source: Olivier Blanchard and Justin Wolfers, "The Role of Shocks and Institutions in the Rise of European Unemployment" (Cambridge: NBER Working Paper 7282, 2000).

over the past quarter century. Almost every economist was surprised by the sharp fall in America's natural rate in the 1990s. And economists cannot confidently account for these shifts even in retrospect.

RECAP   THE NATURAL RATE OF UNEMPLOYMENT

The natural rate of unemployment is not a constant. It has fluctuated substantially over the past two generations, and it will continue to fluctuate. Four sets of factors drive fluctuations in the natural rate of unemployment. First, the natural rate changes as the relative age and educational distribution of the labor force changes. Second, countries with inflexible labor markets are likely to have high natural rates of unemployment. Third, faster productivity growth brings a lower natural rate with it. Fourth, the natural rate will be high if unemployment has been high in the past and large numbers of workers have become discouraged.

12.4 EXPECTED INFLATION

The natural rate of unemployment and expected inflation together determine the location of the Phillips curve because it passes through the point where inflation is equal to expected inflation and unemployment is equal to its natural rate. Higher expected inflation would move the Phillips curve upward. But who does the expecting? And when do people form expectations relevant for this year's Phillips curve?

Economists work with three basic scenarios for how managers, workers, and investors go about forecasting the future and forming their expectations:

- **Static expectations** of inflation prevail when people ignore the fact that inflation can change.
- **Adaptive expectations** prevail when people assume the future will be like the recent past.
- **Rational expectations** prevail when people use all the information they have as best they can.

The Phillips curve behaves very differently under each of these three scenarios.

The Phillips Curve under Static Expectations

If inflation expectations are *static,* expected inflation never changes. People just don't think about inflation. In some years unemployment will be relatively low; in those years inflation will be relatively high. In other years unemployment is higher, and then inflation will be lower. But as long as expectations of inflation remain static (and the natural rate of unemployment unchanged), the trade-off between inflation and unemployment will not change from year to year (see Figure 12.9).

If inflation has been low and stable, businesses will probably hold static inflation expectations. Why? Because the art of managing a business is complex enough as it is. Managers have a lot of things to worry about: what their customers are doing, what their competitors are doing, whether their technology is adequate, and how applicable technology is changing. When inflation has been low or stable, everyone has better things to focus their attention on than the rate of inflation. Box 12.5 discusses the classic example of how the economy behaves under static expectations: The 1960s.

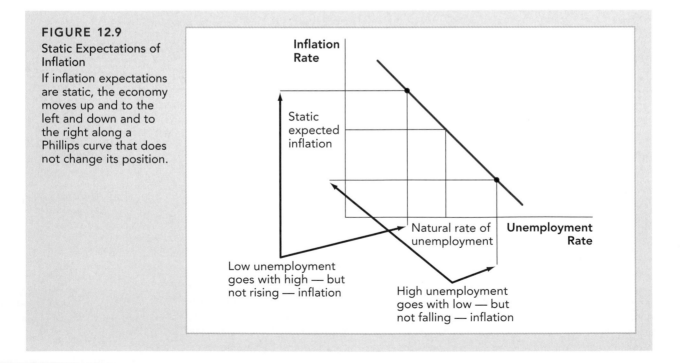

FIGURE 12.9

Static Expectations of Inflation

If inflation expectations are static, the economy moves up and to the left and down and to the right along a Phillips curve that does not change its position.

STATIC EXPECTATIONS OF INFLATION IN THE 1960s: AN EXAMPLE

The standard example of static expectations is expectations of inflation in the 1960s. When unemployment was above 5.5 percent, inflation was below 1.5 percent. When unemployment was below 4 percent, inflation was above 4 percent. This Phillips curve, shown in Figure 12.10, did not shift up or down in response to changes in expected inflation during the decade. Instead, the economy moved along a stable Phillips curve.

But inflation expectations remained static — and the Phillips curve unchanged — only when inflation was low and steady: As inflation rose and became more variable at the end of the 1960s, firms and workers began changing their expectations to *adaptive* ones. And in the early 1970s increases in expected inflation shifted the Phillips curve upward.

FIGURE 12.10
Static Expectations and the Phillips Curve, 1960–1968

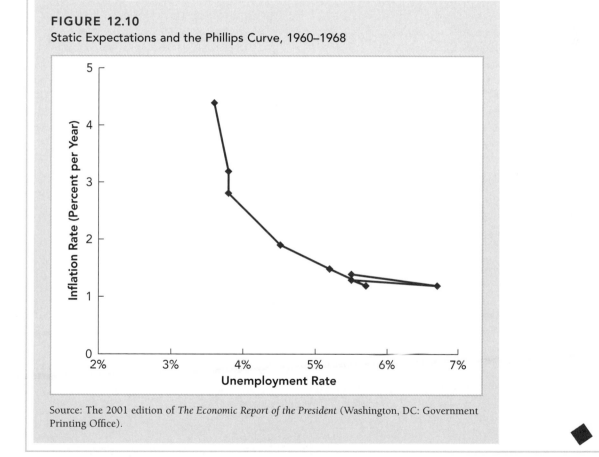

Source: The 2001 edition of *The Economic Report of the President* (Washington, DC: Government Printing Office).

The Phillips Curve under Adaptive Expectations

Suppose that the inflation rate varies too much for workers and businesses to ignore it completely. What then? As long as inflation last year is a good guide to inflation this year, workers, investors, and managers are likely to hold *adaptive* expectations and forecast inflation by assuming that this year will be like last year. Adaptive forecasts are good forecasts as long as inflation changes only slowly; and adaptive expectations do not absorb a lot of time and energy that can be better used thinking about other issues.

Under such adaptive inflation expectations, the Phillips curve can be written

$$\pi_t = \pi_{t-1} - \beta(u_t - u_t{}^*) + \varepsilon_t^s$$

where π_{t-1} stands in place for π_t^e because expected inflation is just equal to inflation last year. Under such a set of *adaptive expectations,* the Phillips curve will shift up or down depending on whether last year's inflation was higher or lower than the previous year's. Under adaptive expectations, inflation accelerates when unemployment is less than the natural unemployment rate, and decelerates when unemployment is more than the natural rate. Hence this Phillips curve is sometimes called the accelerationist Phillips curve. Box 12.6 presents an example of this "acceleration." And Box 12.7 discusses the dilemmas of economic policy under adaptive expectations.

A HIGH-PRESSURE ECONOMY UNDER ADAPTIVE EXPECTATIONS: AN EXAMPLE

Suppose the government tries to keep unemployment below the natural rate for a long time in an economy with adaptive expectations. As a result, inflation will be higher than expected inflation year after year, and so year after year expected inflation will rise. Specifically, suppose that the government pushes the economy's unemployment rate down 2 percentage points below the natural rate, that the β parameter in the Phillips curve is ½, and that last year's inflation rate was 4 percent. Because each year's expected inflation rate is last year's actual inflation rate, and because:

$$\pi_{t-1} + \beta \times 2 = \pi_t$$

FIGURE 12.11
Accelerating Inflation

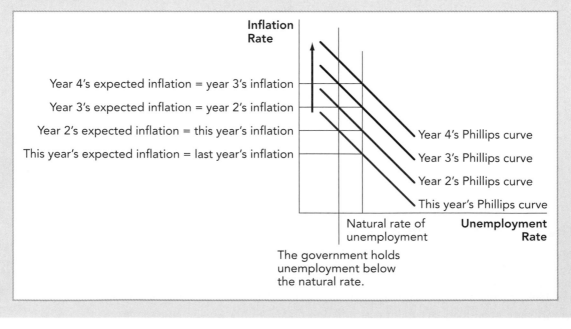

inflation rates are as follows:

This year's inflation rate will be	$4 + \frac{1}{2} \times 2 = 5$
Next year's inflation rate will be	$5 + \frac{1}{2} \times 2 = 6$
The following year's inflation rate will be	$6 + \frac{1}{2} \times 2 = 7$
The inflation rate the year after that will be	$7 + \frac{1}{2} \times 2 = 8$

as shown in Figure 12.11.

As long as expectations of inflation remain adaptive, inflation will increase by 1 percent per year for every year that passes. But expectations of inflation will not remain adaptive forever if the inflation rate keeps rising.

ADAPTIVE EXPECTATIONS AND THE VOLCKER DISINFLATION: POLICY ISSUES

At the end of the 1970s the high level of expected inflation gave the United States an unfavorable short-run Phillips curve trade-off. Between 1979 and the mid-1980s, the Federal Reserve under its chair Paul Volcker reduced inflation in the United States from 9 percent per year to about 3 percent.

FIGURE 12.12
The Phillips Curve before and after the Volcker Disinflation

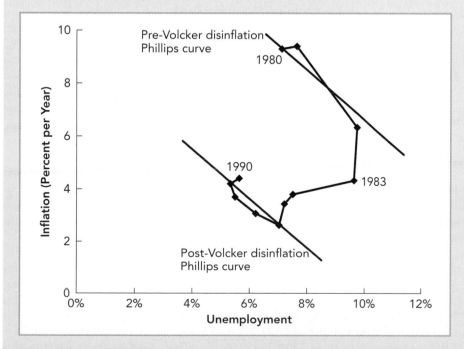

Source: The 2001 edition of *The Economic Report of the President* (Washington, DC: Government Printing Office).

Because inflation expectations were adaptive, the fall in actual inflation in the early 1980s triggered a fall in expected inflation as well. The early 1980s also saw a downward shift in the short-run Phillips curve, which gave the United States a much more favorable short-run inflation-unemployment trade-off by the mid-1980s than it had in the late 1970s, as shown in Figure 12.12.

To accomplish this goal of reducing expected inflation, the Federal Reserve raised interest rates sharply, discouraging investment, reducing aggregate demand, and pushing the economy to the right along the Phillips curve. Unemployment rose, and inflation fell. Reducing annual inflation by 6 percentage points required sacrifice: During the disinflation unemployment averaged some $1\frac{1}{2}$ percentage points above the natural rate for the seven years between 1980 and 1986. Ten percentage point-years of excess unemployment above the natural rate — that was the cost of reducing inflation from near 10 to below 5 percent.

The Phillips Curve under Rational Expectations

What happens when government policy and the economic environment are changing rapidly enough that adaptive expectations lead to significant errors, and are no longer good enough for managers or workers? Then the economy will shift to "rational" expectations. Under rational expectations, people form their forecasts of future inflation not by looking backward at what inflation was, but by looking forward. They look at what current and expected future government policies tell us about what inflation will be.

Economic Policy under Rational Expectations

Under rational expectations the Phillips curve shifts as fast as, or faster than, changes in economic policy that affect the level of aggregate demand. This has an interesting consequence: anticipated changes in economic policy turn out to have no effect on the level of production or employment.

Consider an economy where the central bank's target inflation rate π' is equal to the current value of expected inflation π^e, and where u_0, the unemployment rate when the real interest rate is at its normal value, is equal to the natural rate of unemployment u^*. In such an economy, the initial equilibrium has unemployment equal to its natural rate and inflation equal to expected inflation.

Suppose that workers, managers, savers, and investors have rational expectations. Suppose further that the government takes steps to stimulate the economy: It cuts taxes and increases government spending in order to reduce unemployment below the natural rate, as shown in Figure 12.13, and so reduces the value of u_0. What is likely to happen to the economy?

If the government's policy comes as a *surprise* — if the expectations of inflation that matter for this year's Phillips curve have already been set, in the sense that the contracts have been written, the orders have been made, and the standard operating procedures identified — then the economy moves up and to the left along the Phillips curve in response to the shift in aggregate demand produced by the change in government policy (Figure 12.14).

But if the government's policy is *anticipated* — if the expectations of inflation that matter for this year's Phillips curve are formed after the decision to stimulate the economy is made and becomes public — then workers, managers, savers, and in-

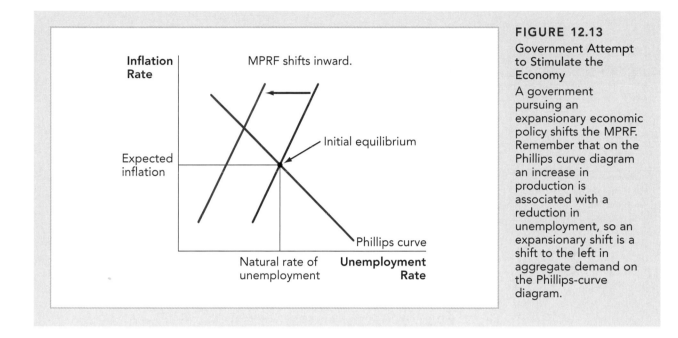

FIGURE 12.13
Government Attempt to Stimulate the Economy

A government pursuing an expansionary economic policy shifts the MPRF. Remember that on the Phillips curve diagram an increase in production is associated with a reduction in unemployment, so an expansionary shift is a shift to the left in aggregate demand on the Phillips-curve diagram.

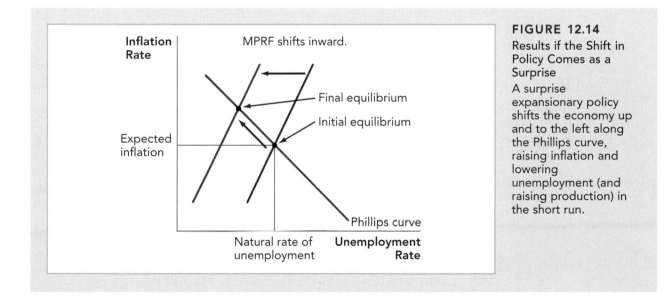

FIGURE 12.14
Results if the Shift in Policy Comes as a Surprise

A surprise expansionary policy shifts the economy up and to the left along the Phillips curve, raising inflation and lowering unemployment (and raising production) in the short run.

vestors will take the stimulative policy into account when they form their expectations of inflation. The inward shift in the MPRF will be accompanied, under rational expectations, by an upward shift in the Phillips curve as well (see Figure 12.15). How large an upward shift? The increase in expected inflation has to be large enough to keep expected inflation after the demand shift equal to actual inflation. Otherwise people are not forming their expectations rationally.

Thus an anticipated increase in aggregate demand has, under rational expectations, no effect on the unemployment rate or on real GDP. Unemployment does not

FIGURE 12.15

Results if the Shift in Policy Is Anticipated

If the expansionary policy is anticipated, workers, consumers, and managers will build the policy effects into their expectations: The Phillips curve will shift up as the aggregate demand curve shifts in, and so the expansionary policy will raise inflation without having any impact on unemployment (or production).

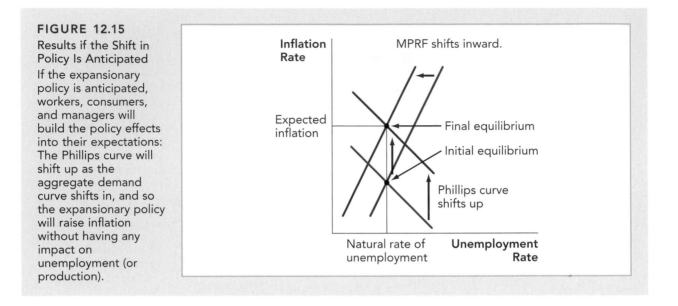

change: It remains at the natural rate of unemployment because the shift in the Phillips curve has neutralized in advance any impact of changing inflation on unemployment. It will, however, have a large effect on the rate of inflation. Economists sometimes say that under rational expectations "anticipated policy is irrelevant." But this is not the best way to express it. Policy is very relevant indeed for the inflation rate. It is only the effects of policy on real GDP and the unemployment rate — effects that are associated with a divergence between expected inflation and actual inflation — that are neutralized.

When have we seen examples of rational inflation expectations? The standard case is that of France immediately after the election of the Socialist President Francois Mitterand in 1981. Throughout his campaign Mitterand had promised a rapid expansion of demand and production to reduce unemployment. Thus when he took office French businesses and unions were ready to mark up their prices and wages in anticipation of the expansionary policies they expected. The result? From mid-1981 to mid-1983 France saw a significant acceleration of inflation, but no reduction in unemployment. The Phillips curve had shifted upward fast enough to keep expansionary policies from having any effect on production and employment.

What Kind of Expectations Do We Have?

If inflation is low and stable, expectations are probably static: It is not worth anyone's while to even think about what one's expectations should be. If inflation is moderate and fluctuates, but slowly, expectations are probably adaptive: To assume that the future will be like the recent past — which is what adaptive expectations are — is likely to be a good rule, and is simple to implement.

When shifts in inflation are clearly related to changes in monetary policy, swift to occur, and are large enough to seriously affect profitability, then people are likely to have rational expectations. When the stakes are high — when people think, "had I known inflation was going to jump, I would not have taken that contract" — then every economic decision becomes a speculation on the future of monetary policy. Because it matters for their bottom lines and their livelihoods, people will turn all their skill and insight into generating inflation forecasts.

Thus the kind of expectations likely to be found in the economy at any moment depend on what has been and is going on. A period during which inflation is low and stable will lead people to stop making, and stop paying attention to, inflation forecasts, so expectations of inflation tend to revert to static expectations. A period during which inflation is high, volatile, and linked to visible shifts in economic policy will see expectations of inflation become more rational. An intermediate period of substantial but slow variability is likely to see many managers and workers adopt the rule of adaptive expectations.

Persistent Contracts

The ways that people make contracts and form and execute plans for their economic activity are likely to make an economy behave *as if* expectations in it are less rational than expectations in fact are. People do not wait until December 31 to factor next year's expected inflation into their decisions and contracts. They make decisions about the future, sign contracts, and undertake projects all the time. Some of those steps govern what the company does for a day. Others govern decisions for years or even for a decade or more.

Thus the "expected inflation" that determines the location of the short-run Phillips curve has components that were formed just as the old year ended, but also components that were formed two, three, five, ten, or more years ago. People buying houses form forecasts of what inflation will be over the next 30 years — but once the house is bought, that decision is a piece of economic activity (imputed rent on owner-occupied housing) as long as they own the house, no matter what they subsequently learn about future inflation. Such lags in decision making tend to produce "price inertia." They tend to make the economy behave as if inflation expectations were more adaptive than they in fact are. There will always be a large number of projects and commitments already under way that cannot easily adjust to changing prices. It is important to take this price inertia into account when thinking about the dynamics of inflation, output, and unemployment.

RECAP EXPECTED INFLATION

Higher expected inflation shifts the Phillips curve upward. Lower expected inflation shifts the Phillips curve downward. Thus the dynamics of how expectations evolve are key to understanding the economy. Economists work with three basic scenarios for how managers, workers, and investors go about forecasting the future and forming their expectations: *Static expectations* of inflation prevail when people ignore the fact that inflation can change. *Adaptive expectations* prevail when people assume the future will be like the recent past. *Rational expectations* prevail when people use all the information they have as best they can.

The Phillips curve behaves very differently under each of these three scenarios. Under static expectations the Phillips curve doesn't shift, so changes in policy have powerful effects on unemployment and real GDP. Under rational expectations the Phillips curve shifts immediately and drastically in response to policies so that anticipated changes in policy have powerful effects on inflation, but not on unemployment and real GDP. And adaptive expectations are in the middle.

12.5 FROM THE (STICKY PRICE) SHORT RUN TO THE (FLEXIBLE PRICE) LONGER RUN

Rational Expectations

Our picture of the determination of real GDP and unemployment under sticky prices is now complete. We have a comprehensive framework to understand how the aggregate price level and inflation rate move and adjust over time in response to changes in aggregate demand, production relative to potential output, and unemployment relative to its natural rate. There is, however, one loose end. How does one get from the short-run sticky-price patterns of behavior that have been covered in Part IV to the longer-run flexible-price patterns of behavior that were laid out in Part III?

In the case of an anticipated shift in economic policy under rational expectations, the answer is straightforward: You don't have to get from the short run to the longer run; the longer run is now. An inward (or outward) shift in the monetary policy reaction function on the Phillips curve diagram caused by an expansionary (or contractionary) change in economic policy or the economic environment sets in motion an offsetting shift in the Phillips curve. In the absence of supply shocks, inflation is

$$\pi = \pi^e - \beta \times (u - u^*)$$

If expectations are rational and if changes in economic policy are foreseen, then expected inflation will be equal to actual inflation:

$$\pi = \pi^e$$

which means that the unemployment rate is equal to the natural rate, as shown in Figure 12.16. The economy is at full employment. All the analysis of Chapters 6, 7, and 8 holds immediately.

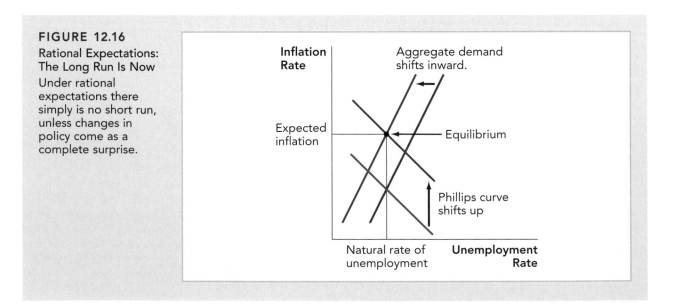

FIGURE 12.16

Rational Expectations: The Long Run Is Now

Under rational expectations there simply is no short run, unless changes in policy come as a complete surprise.

Adaptive Expectations

If expectations are and remain adaptive, then the economy approaches the long-run equilibrium laid out in Chapters 6 and 7 gradually, as is shown in Figure 12.17. An expansionary initial shock that shifts the aggregate demand relation inward on the Phillips curve diagram generates a fall in unemployment, an increase in real GDP, and a rise in inflation. Call this stage 1. Stage 1 takes place before anyone has had any chance to adjust their expectations of inflation.

FIGURE 12.17

Adaptive Expectations Convergence to the Longer Run

Under adaptive expectations, shifts in policy have strong initial effects on unemployment and production, but those effects slowly die off.

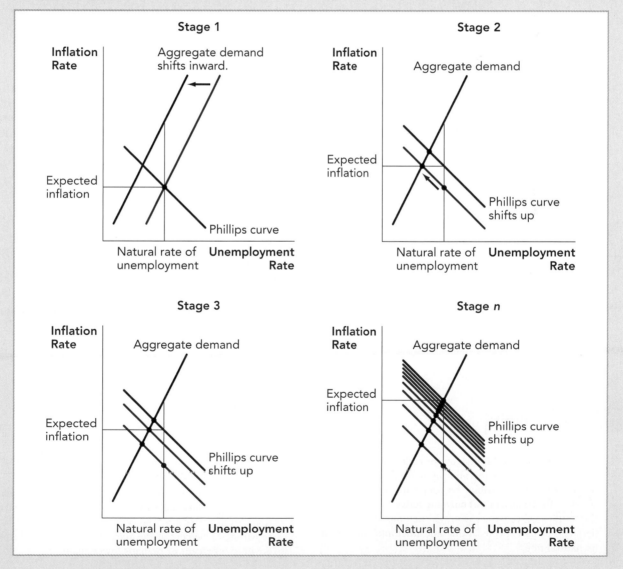

To reach stage 2, workers, managers, investors, and others look at what inflation was in stage 1 and raise their expectations of inflation. The Phillips curve shifts up by the difference between actual and expected inflation in stage 1. If the aggregate demand relation does not shift when plotted on the Phillips curve diagram, between stage 1 and stage 2 unemployment rises, real GDP falls, and inflation rises.

Moving toward stage 3, workers, managers, investors, and others look at what inflation was in stage 1 and raise their expectations of inflation. The Phillips curve shifts up by the difference between actual and expected inflation in stage 2. If the aggregate demand relation does not shift when plotted on the Phillips curve diagram, between stage 2 and stage 3 unemployment rises, real GDP falls, and inflation rises. As time passes the gaps between actual and expected inflation, between real GDP and potential output, and between unemployment and its natural rate shrink toward zero.

Under adaptive expectations, people's forecasts become closer to being accurate as more time passes. Thus the "long run" arrives gradually. Each year the portion of the change in demand that is not implicitly incorporated in people's adaptive forecasts becomes smaller. Thus each year a larger proportion of the shift is "long run," and a smaller proportion is "short run."

Static Expectations

Under static expectations, the long run never arrives: the analysis of Chapters 6 through 8 never becomes relevant. Under static expectations, the gap between expected inflation and actual inflation can grow arbitrarily large as different shocks affect the economy. And if the gap between expected inflation and actual inflation becomes large, workers, managers, investors, and consumers will not be so foolish as to retain static expectations.

RECAP   STICKY PRICES OR FLEXIBLE PRICES?

The amount of time that must pass before the relevant framework shifts from the sticky-price Part IV framework to the flexible-price Part III framework depends on the type of inflation expectations held in the economy. Under static expectations, Part III is never relevant. Under rational expectations, Part III is always relevant.

Chapter Summary

1. The location of the Phillips curve is determined by the expected rate of inflation and the natural rate of unemployment (and possibly by current, active supply shocks). In the absence of current, active supply shocks, the Phillips curve passes through the point at which inflation is at its expected value and unemployment is at its natural rate.

2. The slope of the Phillips curve is determined by the de-

gree of price stickiness in the economy. The stickier prices are, the flatter the Phillips curve is.

3. The natural rate of unemployment in the United States has exhibited moderate swings in the past two generations: from perhaps 4.5 percent at the end of the 1950s to perhaps 7 percent at the start of the 1980s, and now down to 5 percent or perhaps lower again.

4. Three significant supply shocks have affected the rate of

inflation in the United States over the past two generations: the (inflationary) oil price increases of 1973 and 1979, and the (deflationary) oil price decrease of 1986.

5. The principal determinant of the expected rate of inflation is the past behavior of inflation. If inflation has been low and steady, expectations are probably *static*, and the expected inflation rate is very low and unchanging. If inflation has been variable but moderate, expectations are probably *adaptive* and expected inflation is probably simply equal to last year's inflation. If inflation has been high, or has been moderate but varied extremely rapidly, then expectations are probably *rational* and expected inflation is likely to be households' and businesses' best guesses of where economic policy is taking the economy.

6. The best way to gauge how expectations of inflation are formed is to consider the past history of inflation. Would adaptive expectations have provided a significant edge over static ones? If yes, then inflation expectations are probably adaptive. Would rational expectations have provided a significant edge over adaptive ones? If yes, then inflation expectations are probably rational.

7. How fast the flexible-price model becomes relevant depends on the type of inflation expectations in the economy. Under static expectations, the flexible-price model never becomes relevant. Under adaptive expectations, the flexible-price model becomes relevant gradually, in the long run. Under rational expectations the long run is now: the flexible-price model analysis is relevant always and immediately.

Key Terms

Okun's law (p. 330)

output gap (p. 331)

costs of high unemployment (p. 332)

Phillips curve (p. 333)

expected inflation (p. 334)

natural rate of unemployment (p. 334)

monetary policy reaction function (MPRF) (p. 336)

central bank inflation target (p. 337)

real wage aspirations (p. 342)

long-term unemployment (p. 342)

static expectations (p. 344)

adaptive expectations (p. 344)

rational expectations (p. 344)

Analytical Exercises

1. What is the relationship between the three views of aggregate supply? Why do economists tend to focus on the Phillips curve to the exclusion of the other two views?

2. Under what circumstances will a government expansionary fiscal or monetary policy do nothing to raise GDP or lower unemployment?

3. Under the circumstances in which an expansionary government policy fails to raise GDP or lower unemployment, what would the policy manage to do?

4. If expectations of inflation are *adaptive*, is there any way to reduce inflation without suffering unemployment higher than the natural rate? What would you advise a central bank that sought to reduce inflation without provoking high unemployment to do?

5. What do you think a central bank should do in response to an adverse supply shock? How does your answer depend on the way in which expectations of inflation are being formed in the economy?

Policy Exercises

1. What factors do you think have led the natural rate of unemployment to be so high in Europe today?

2. What factors do you think have led the natural rate of unemployment to be so low in the United States today?

3. Do you think that inflation expectations in the United States today are static, adaptive, or rational? Why?

4. Suppose that the economy has a Phillips curve

$$\pi_t = \pi_t^e - \beta \times (u_t - u_t^*)$$

with the parameter $\beta = 0.5$ and the natural rate of unemployment u^* equal to 6 percent. And suppose that the central bank's reaction to inflation, the IS curve, and Okun's law together mean that the unemployment rate is given by

$$u_t = u_{0t} - \phi \times (\pi_t - \pi_t')$$

with the central bank's target level of inflation π' equal to 2 percent, the parameter ϕ equal to 0.4, and the normal real rate of interest level of aggregate demand corresponding to a value of u_0 of 6 percent. Suppose that initially — this year, in the year zero — expected inflation is equal to actual inflation.

a. What is the initial level of unemployment?

b. Suppose that the government announces that in year one and in every year thereafter its expansionary policies will reduce u_0 to 4 percent, that this announcement is credible, and that the economy has *rational expectations* of inflation. What will unemployment and inflation be in year one? What will they be thereafter?

c. Suppose that the government announces that in year one and in every year thereafter its expansionary policies will reduce u_0 to 4 percent, that this announcement is credible, and that the economy has *adaptive expectations* of inflation. What will unemployment and inflation be in year one? What will they be thereafter?

d. Suppose that the government announces that in year one and in every year thereafter its expansionary policies will reduce u_0 to 4 percent, that this announcement is credible, and that the economy has *static expectations* of inflation. What will unemployment and inflation be in year one? What will they be thereafter?

5. Suppose that the economy this year, in the year zero, is the same as presented initially in question 4.

a. What is the initial level of unemployment?

b. Suppose that the central bank raises its target inflation rate for next year — year one — to 4 percent, and announces this change. Suppose the economy has *rational expectations* of inflation. What will happen to unemployment and inflation in year one? What will happen thereafter?

c. Suppose that the central bank raises its target inflation rate for next year — year one — to 4 percent, and announces this change. Suppose the economy has *adaptive expectations* of inflation. What will happen to unemployment and inflation in year one? What will happen thereafter?

d. Suppose that the central bank raises its target inflation rate for next year — year one — to 4 percent, and announces this change. Suppose the economy has *static expectations* of inflation. What will happen to unemployment and inflation in year one? What will happen thereafter?

6. Suppose that the economy this year, in the year zero, is as depicted in question 4 initially.

a. What is the initial level of unemployment?

b. Suppose that the natural rate of unemployment u^* falls to 4 percent in year one and remains at that level indefinitely. And suppose that this fall in the natural rate of unemployment does not come as a surprise. Suppose the economy has *rational expectations* of inflation. What will happen to unemployment and inflation in year one? What will happen thereafter?

c. Suppose that the natural rate of unemployment u^* falls to 4 percent in year one and remains at that level indefinitely. And suppose that this fall in the natural rate of unemployment does not come as a surprise. Suppose the economy has *adaptive expectations* of inflation. What will happen to unemployment and inflation in year one? What will happen thereafter?

d. Suppose that the natural rate of unemployment u^* falls to 4 percent in year one and remains at that level indefinitely. And suppose that this fall in the natural rate of unemployment does not come as a surprise. Suppose the economy has *static expectations* of inflation. What will happen to unemployment and inflation in year one? What will happen thereafter?

Macroeconomic Policy

PART V

We now have all the tools we need to understand business cycles: Part III showed how to analyze business cycles in a flexible-price macroeconomy. Part IV showed how to analyze business cycles in a sticky-price macroeconomy, and how to understand when the flexible-price model and when the sticky-price model is the best one to use.

Part V uses the tools built up earlier in this book to conduct a guided tour of the major issues in modern macroeconomic policy. Chapter 13 considers stabilization policy: how the government attempts to keep unemployment low, growth steady, inflation low, and recessions shallow. Chapter 14 moves on to consider fiscal policy, and the effect of the government's taxes, spending, and national debt on the level of investment and long-run growth. Chapter 15 focuses on the international economy: how a government should try to manage its interconnections with the other economies of the world.

After these first three chapters, the two that follow them step back and take an even broader view. Chapter 16 discusses how the macroeconomy has changed over the past century, and how the changes in the macroeconomy have affected macroeconomic policy. Chapter 17 considers the discipline of macroeconomics: How has it changed in the past, and how is it likely to change in the future?

Stabilization Policy

CHAPTER

QUESTIONS

What principles should guide stabilization policy?

What aspects of stabilization policy do economists argue about today?

Is monetary policy or fiscal policy more effective as a stabilization policy?

How does uncertainty affect the way stabilization policy should be made?

How long are the lags associated with stabilization policy?

Is it better for stabilization policy to be conducted according to fixed *rules*, or to be conducted by authorities with substantial *discretion*?

Part IV of this book set out the sticky-price model in which short-run changes in real GDP, unemployment, interest rates, and inflation are all driven by changes in the economic environment and by shifts in two kinds of government policy: fiscal policy and monetary policy. Changes in *fiscal policy* shift the IS curve out and back. Central-bank-driven changes in interest rates and moves of the LM curve — *monetary policy* — raise and lower real interest rates, and cause the economy's equilibrium to move along the IS curve.

These policies and the economic environment together set the level of aggregate demand. They move the economy along the Phillips curve, raising and lowering inflation and unemployment. Changes in expectations of inflation, changes in the natural rate of unemployment, and supply shocks shift the position of the short-run Phillips curve, and thus play a powerful role in determining the options open to government.

It is in this context that the government tries to manage the macroeconomy. It attempts to *stabilize* the macroeconomy by minimizing the impact of the shocks that cause business cycles. The first part of this chapter looks at the institutions that make macroeconomic policy: the Federal Reserve, which makes monetary policy, and the Congress, which makes fiscal policy (subject to the president's veto). After looking at the institutions it will be time to look at how macroeconomic policy is actually made, and at how well it works.

13.1 ECONOMIC POLICY INSTITUTIONS

Monetary Policy Institutions

Monetary policy in the United States is made by the Federal Reserve, which is our central bank. In other countries the central bank bears a different name. The most common is the name of its country: The central bank of country X is probably named the Bank of X.

The principal policy-making body of the Federal Reserve system is its *Federal Open Market Committee* (FOMC). It is the FOMC that lowers and raises interest rates, and that increases and decreases the money supply. The Federal Reserve's *Board of Governors* can alter bank regulations, and can and raise or lower the interest rate at which the Federal Reserve itself lends to banks and businesses. But most of the time the FOMC plays the leading role within the Federal Reserve.

Today the Federal Reserve is the most important organization making macroeconomic policy. Because monetary policy is the most powerful tool for stabilizing the economy, the Federal Reserve plays the leading role in stabilization policy. Fiscal policy plays second fiddle. This institutional division of labor is probably the correct one. Over the past 50 years in the United States, monetary policy has proved to be more powerful, faster-acting, and more reliable than fiscal policy.

The Federal Reserve

The Federal Reserve has a central office and 12 regional offices. Its central office is the Board of Governors, composed of a chair, a vice chair, and five governors, all of them nominated by the president and confirmed by the Senate. The Board of Governors' offices are in Washington, DC.

The Federal Reserve's 12 regional offices are the 12 Federal Reserve Banks. They are scattered around the country in San Francisco, Minneapolis, Dallas, Kansas City, St. Louis, Chicago, Cleveland, Atlanta, Richmond, Philadelphia, New York, and Boston.

The members of the Board of Governors and the presidents of the 12 regional

FIGURE 13.1
Structure of the Federal Reserve System

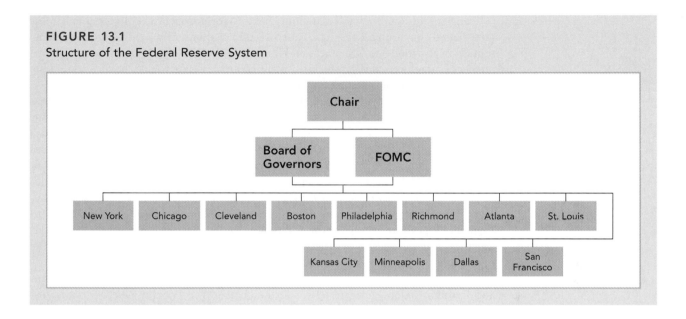

Federal Reserve Banks meeting together make up the Federal Open Market Committee (FOMC), the principal policy-making body (see Figure 13.1). The chair, the vice chair, the other five governors, and the president of the Federal Reserve Bank of New York are always voting members of the FOMC. The 11 presidents of the other Federal Reserve Banks alternate. At any moment four are voting members and seven are nonvoting members of the FOMC (see Figure 13.2).

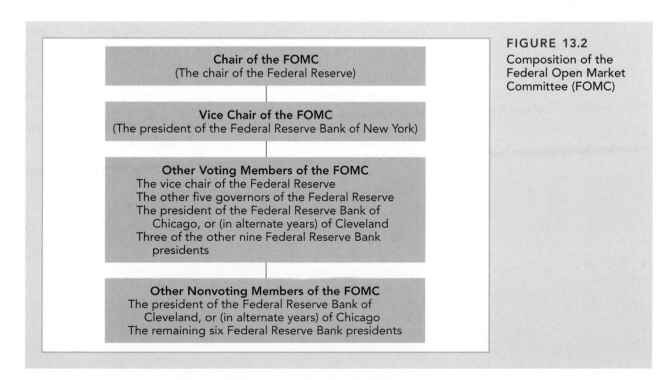

FIGURE 13.2
Composition of the Federal Open Market Committee (FOMC)

The Federal Reserve was created just before World War I. Its congressional architects feared that a unitary central bank based in Manhattan would pay too much attention to the interests of bankers and financiers and not enough attention to the interests of merchants and producers. A near-century of experience, however, suggests that they were wrong: Bankers in St. Louis think like bankers in New York.

The Federal Reserve failed to handle its first great crisis, the Great Depression that started in 1929. Depending on whom you believe, the Federal Reserve either did nothing to help cure the Great Depression, or it made things much worse and played a major role in causing the Great Depression. Since World War II, however, the Federal Reserve has done a much better job: There has been no repeat of the Great Depression.

The Federal Reserve's performance in the 1970s is generally regarded as inadequate. The 1970s were a decade of rising inflation and relatively high unemployment. Today, after two straight decades in the 1980s and 1990s of very successful monetary stabilization policy, the prestige of the Federal Reserve is high. It has almost unlimited freedom to conduct monetary policy as it wishes. Few outside the organization want to challenge its judgments or decisions.

The FOMC meets a little less often than once a month to set interest rates. It can and frequently does delegate power to the chair of the Federal Reserve to alter interest rates between meetings if circumstances require. And it can hold emergency meetings on short notice.

The FOMC tries to reach its decisions by consensus. If a consensus cannot be achieved, the members of the FOMC are more likely to postpone the issue than to make a decision that a substantial minority of its members oppose. However, once the FOMC decides on a change in policy, that change is implemented *immediately*. It takes only minutes for interest rates to shift in response to FOMC decisions. Indeed, interest rates often change in advance of the actual FOMC meeting as speculators attempt to make money by betting on what they believe the Federal Reserve will do.

The chair of the Federal Reserve Board is the chair of the FOMC: Alan Greenspan was confirmed to another four-year term as chair of the Federal Reserve Board in the summer of 2000. The president of the Federal Reserve Bank of New York is the vice chair of the FOMC: William McDonough has served in those roles since 1993.

The FOMC changes interest rates by carrying out open-market operations. In an expansionary open-market operation, the Federal Reserve buys government bonds. Such a transaction reduces the amount of interest-bearing government bonds available for investors to hold. This reduction in supply raises the price of short-term government bonds — and an increase in the price of a bond is a decline in its interest rate. When the Federal Reserve buys government bonds it pays for them by crediting the purchasers with deposits at the regional Federal Reserve banks. Commercial banks use these deposits to satisfy the reserve requirements imposed on them by bank regulators. The more reserves a bank has, the more deposits it can accept and the more loans it can make. With more banks trying to make more loans, the interest rates that banks charge on loans drop. Thus purchases of government bonds by the Federal Reserve are expansionary open-market operations, and lower interest rates. Contractionary open-market operations work in reverse, and raise interest rates.

Open-market operations are not the only policy tools the Federal Reserve has. The Board of Governors can alter legally required bank reserves, and it can lend money directly to financial institutions. But these are used very rarely. Almost always the FOMC can use open-market operations to set interest rates at whatever it wants them to be.

Note the qualifier "almost always." There is only one important restriction on the Federal Reserve's power to set interest rates. The Federal Reserve cannot reduce the nominal interest rate on any Treasury securities below zero. If a Treasury bill carried an interest rate less than zero, then no one would want to buy it: It would be more profitable to simply hold cash instead.

It is possible to envision situations in which this inability of the Federal Reserve to push nominal interest rates below zero has destructive consequences. If prices are expected to fall — if it is a time of anticipated deflation, so that the expected inflation rate is negative — a nominal interest rate that is close to but not less than zero may still be a relatively high *real* interest rate, because the real interest rate r is the difference between the nominal interest rate i and the expected inflation rate π^e.

$$r = i - \pi^e$$

If the expected inflation rate is sufficiently far below zero, the real interest rate will be high, and investment low, no matter what the FOMC does. As Box 13.1 discusses, this may be relevant to Japan's economic stagnation over the past decade.

RECAP   MONETARY POLICY INSTITUTIONS

The most important kind of stabilization policy is monetary policy, carried out by the Federal Reserve, the United States' central bank. The principal policy-making body of the Federal Reserve is the Federal Open Market Committee — the FOMC. The FOMC decides what the level of short-term safe nominal interest rates will be, and how fast the money stock will grow. The head of and the most important decision maker in the Federal Reserve is the chair. Alan Greenspan was reappointed to another four-year term as chair of the Federal Reserve in the summer of 2000.

JAPAN'S LIQUIDITY TRAP: A POLICY

The possibility that monetary policy might lose its power because expected deflation kept *real* interest rates high used to be dismissed as a theoretical curiosity irrelevant to the real world. But since the mid-1990s the Japanese economy has looked very much as though it might be caught in such a "liquidity trap." Real GDP has been far below potential output. Nominal interest rates on short-term government bonds have at times fallen to 0.04 percent — that is four-hundredths of 1 percent a year; the annual interest on $100 invested at such an interest rate would be four cents. (See Figure 13.3.) But a combination of expected deflation, high risk premiums, and steep term premiums meant that businesses found that the real interest rate they had to pay to borrow money was quite high.

This situation continues today. From banks' perspective there are few creditworthy borrowers. Yet from businesses' perspective there is little affordable capital. Japan's stagnation has dragged on for nearly a decade.

What is to be done? Two obvious policies might improve matters. The first is fiscal expansion: Cut taxes or increase spending to shift the IS curve to the left and raise the level of aggregate demand even if real interest rates are relatively high. The second is to create expectations of inflation by announcing that monetary policy will be expansionary not just now but for the indefinite future.

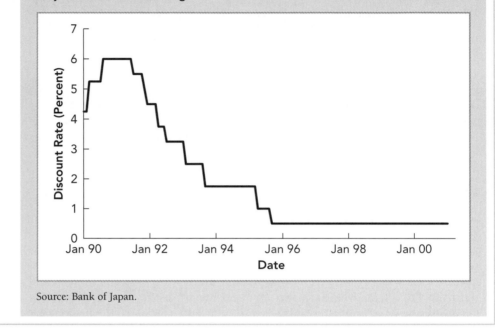

FIGURE 13.3
Japan's Liquidity Trap in the 1990s: Nominal Safe Interest Rates
The graph shows the official discount rate of the Bank of Japan. Despite a decade of extremely low interest rates on government bonds in Japan, investment has not boomed. Why not? Because risk premiums and expected deflation have made businesses believe that the real interest rates at which they can borrow remain high.

Source: Bank of Japan.

Fiscal Policy Institutions

Fiscal policy in the United States today is managed by Congress (subject to the veto of the president). Congress passes laws which the president then signs (or vetoes — and Congress then overrides or fails to override the vetoes). Congress's tax laws determine the taxes imposed by the federal government. Congress's spending bills determine the level of government purchases. Together these taxes and government purchases make up the government's fiscal policy.

Tax and spending levels are set in a combined bureaucratic-legislative process called the *budget cycle,* outlined in Figure 13.4. The federal government's year for budget purposes — its fiscal year — runs from October 1 of one year to September 30 of the next. The budget period from October 1, 2000 to September 30, 2001, for example, is called "fiscal 2001."

Some broad classes of expenditure, called "mandatory," are the result of open-ended long-term government commitments, and continue whether or not Congress explicitly appropriates money for them in the current year. Social security, Medicare, Medicaid, unemployment insurance, food stamps, and so forth fall into this category of so-called mandatory spending. Other broad classes of expenditure, called "discretionary," must be explicitly appropriated by Congress in each fiscal year. Defense spending, the National Park Service, NASA, the National Institutes of Health, highway spending, education spending, and so forth fall into this category of so-called

FIGURE 13.4

The Budget Process

The process by which Congress and the president make fiscal policy is arcane and byzantine.

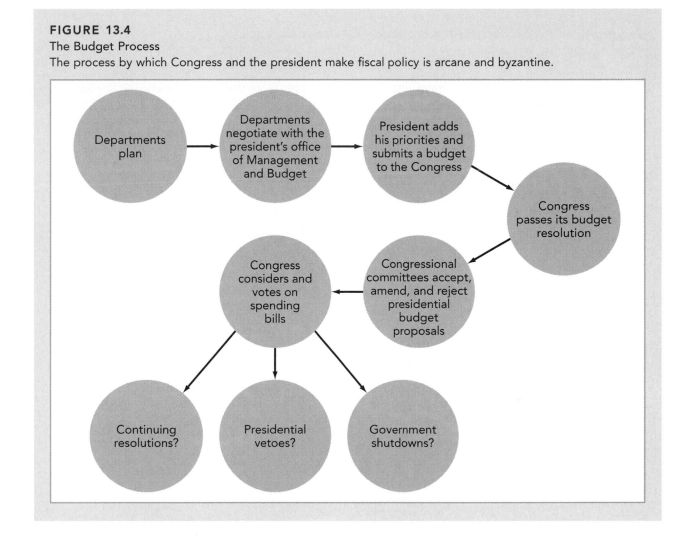

discretionary spending. Figure 13.5 shows major areas of spending relative to GDP over the last four decades. Figure 13.6 details nondefense discretionary spending.

Early in one fiscal year the executive branch departments and agencies that administer federal programs begin planning for the next. Throughout the fall they negotiate with the president's Executive Office — the Office of Management and Budget. The result of these negotiations, modified by the president's own priorities, becomes the president's budget submission to Congress in January.

Congress considers the president's budget request, conducts its own internal debates, and by the end of April is supposed to have passed a *budget resolution* giving spending targets for broad classes of expenditure. Using the budget resolution as a guide, Congress alters and amends the laws that control mandatory spending, alters and amends the tax code, and passes the appropriations bills necessary for discretionary spending. By the end of September all of the appropriations bills are supposed to have been passed, so that the new fiscal year can begin with the pieces of the government knowing how much should be spent and on what over the next 12 months.

FIGURE 13.5

Major Federal Government Expenditures by Category, 1960–2000

The past four decades have seen the level of federal government spending as a share of GDP remain roughly constant, but the composition of federal spending has changed remarkably. Spending on national defense and international affairs has fallen from nearly 10 to a little more than 3 percent of GDP. Spending on health and social security has risen from about 2.5 to 8 percent of GDP. Net interest rose sharply from 1 to 3 percent of GDP as a result of the deficits of the 1980s, and has since begun to decline. Income security — unemployment insurance, welfare, and so forth — rose from 1.5 percent of GDP in the 1960s to 3.5 percent by the deep recession years of the early 1980s, and has been cut since. And "other" — everything else the government does, from the FBI to the National Park Service, the National Institutes of Health, and the interstate highway system — rose from 3 to 5 percent of GDP between 1960 and 1980, and has since been cut back to 2.5 percent.

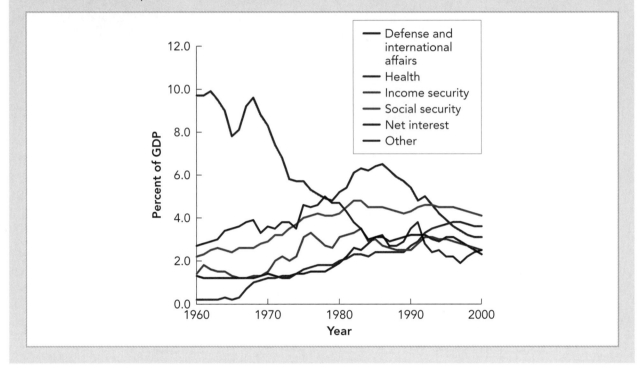

Source: Congressional Budget Office.

More often than not, however, Congress fails to pass or the president vetoes one or more appropriations bills. In that case the government continues more or less on autopilot if Congress passes and the president signs a *continuing resolution* until the appropriations bill is passed. If they don't, the government "shuts down." Discretionary spending is cut back to the bone. Nonessential employees are sent home. The Washington Monument and other major tourist attractions are closed. Government office buildings are inhabited by only a skeleton crew of key functionaries and unpaid interns until Congress and the president reach agreement, and pass and sign the appropriations bills necessary for the government's discretionary spending programs to go forward.

However, even during a government shutdown, most of what the government does continues. Mandatory spending does not have to be explicitly appropriated every year, and continues even if there is total gridlock in Washington.

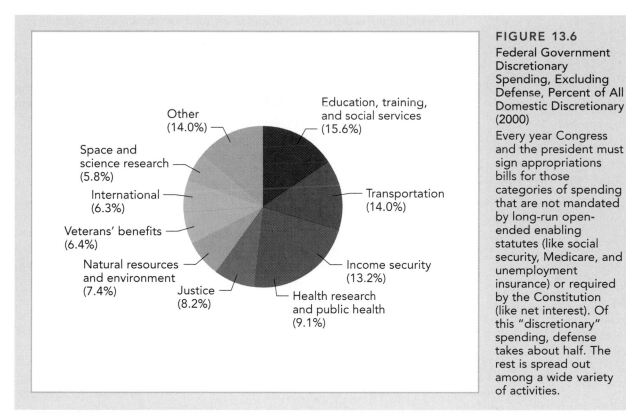

FIGURE 13.6
Federal Government Discretionary Spending, Excluding Defense, Percent of All Domestic Discretionary (2000)

Every year Congress and the president must sign appropriations bills for those categories of spending that are not mandated by long-run open-ended enabling statutes (like social security, Medicare, and unemployment insurance) or required by the Constitution (like net interest). Of this "discretionary" spending, defense takes about half. The rest is spread out among a wide variety of activities.

Chart labels:
- Education, training, and social services (15.6%)
- Other (14.0%)
- Space and science research (5.8%)
- International (6.3%)
- Veterans' benefits (6.4%)
- Natural resources and environment (7.4%)
- Justice (8.2%)
- Health research and public health (9.1%)
- Income security (13.2%)
- Transportation (14.0%)

Source: Congressional Budget Office.

The lesson to draw from this overview is that making fiscal policy in the United States is complicated, baroque, and time-consuming. The **inside lag** — the time between when a policy proposal is made and when it becomes effective — for fiscal policy is measured in years. By contrast, the inside lag associated with FOMC-decided changes in monetary policy is measured in days, weeks, or at most two months. The FOMC can turn on a dime. Congress and the president cannot. This is a key advantage that makes the Federal Reserve more effective at undertaking stabilization policy to manage aggregate demand.

The History of Economic Policy

The government did not always see itself as responsible for stabilizing the economy and taming the business cycle. It accepted this responsibility in the Employment Act of 1946, which did the following:

- Established Congress's Joint Economic Committee.
- Established the president's Council of Economic Advisers.
- Called on the president to estimate and forecast the current and future level of economic activity in the United States.
- Announced that it was the "continuing policy and responsibility" of the federal government to "coordinate and utilize all its plans, functions, and resources . . . to foster and promote free competitive enterprise and the general welfare; conditions under which there will be afforded useful employment for those

able, willing, and seeking to work; and to promote maximum employment, production, and purchasing power."

Passage of the Employment Act marked the rout of the belief that the government could not stabilize the economy and should not try to do so. In the old view, monetary and fiscal policies to fight recessions would keep workers and firms producing in unsustainable lines of business and levels of capital intensity, and would make the depression less deep only at the price of making it longer.

This doctrine that in the long run even deep recessions like the Great Depression would turn out to have been "good medicine" for the economy drew anguished cries of dissent even before World War II. John Maynard Keynes tried to ridicule this "crime and punishment" view of business cycles, concluding that he did not see how "universal bankruptcy could do us any good or bring us any nearer to prosperity." Indeed, it was largely due to Keynes's writings, especially his *General Theory of Employment, Interest and Money,* that economists and politicians became convinced that the government could halt depressions and smooth out the business cycle. But Keynes was not alone. For example, Ralph Hawtrey, an adviser to the British Treasury and the Bank of England, called worry about government action the equivalent of "crying, 'Fire! Fire!' in Noah's flood." But you still can see traces of this view in economics in places (like the real business cycle theories discussed at the end of Chapter 7).

The high-water mark of confidence that the government could and would manage to use its macroeconomic policy tools to stabilize the economy came in the

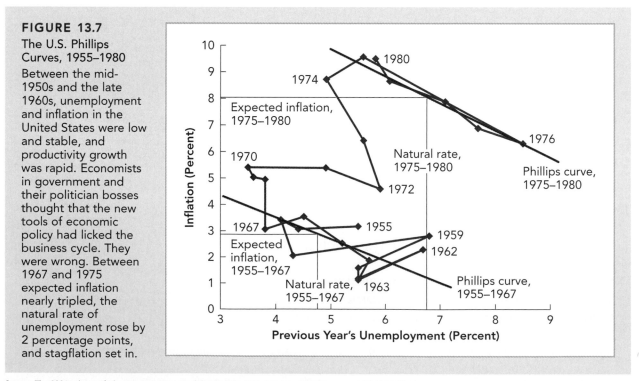

FIGURE 13.7

The U.S. Phillips Curves, 1955–1980

Between the mid-1950s and the late 1960s, unemployment and inflation in the United States were low and stable, and productivity growth was rapid. Economists in government and their politician bosses thought that the new tools of economic policy had licked the business cycle. They were wrong. Between 1967 and 1975 expected inflation nearly tripled, the natural rate of unemployment rose by 2 percentage points, and stagflation set in.

Source: The 2001 edition of *The Economic Report of the President* (Washington, DC: Government Printing Office).

1960s. In that decade President Johnson's chief economic adviser, Walter Heller, wrote of the *New Dimensions of Political Economy* that had been opened by the Keynesian revolution. The Department of Commerce changed the title of its *Business Cycle Digest* to the *Business Conditions Digest* — because, after all, the business cycle was dead.

The 1970s, however, erased that confidence. Economists Milton Friedman and Edward Phelps had warned that attempts to keep the economy at the upper left corner of the Phillips curve would inevitably cause an upward shift in inflation expectations — that even if expectations had truly been static during the 1950s and early 1960s, they would become adaptive if unemployment were pushed too low for too long. Friedman and Phelps were correct: The 1970s saw a sharp upward shift in the Phillips curve as people lost confidence in the commitment of the Federal Reserve to keep inflation low, and raised their expectations of inflation. (See Figure 13.7.) The result was *stagflation:* a combination of relatively high unemployment and relatively high inflation. The lesson learned was that attempts to keep unemployment low and the level of output stable were counterproductive if they eroded public confidence in the central bank's commitment to keep inflation low and prices stable.

The 1970s ended with many economists convinced that "activist" monetary policy did more harm than good, and that the United States might be better off with an "automatic" monetary policy that fixed some control variable like the money stock on a stable long-run growth path. But the sharp instability of monetary velocity since the start of the 1980s (see Figure 13.8) has greatly reduced the number of advocates of an automatic central bank that lets the money stock grow by a fixed proportional amount every year.

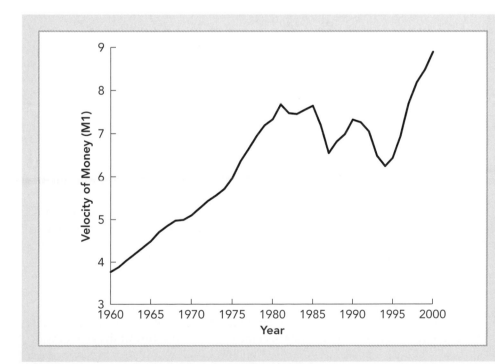

FIGURE 13.8
The Velocity of Money
Before 1980 monetarists argued that the velocity of money was stable and predictable. It had a constant upward trend as new technology was introduced into the banking system, and nearly no other fluctuations. Keep the money supply growing smoothly, they argued, and the smooth trend of velocity will keep the economy stable. They too were wrong. After 1980 the velocity of money became unstable indeed.

Source: The 2001 edition of *The Economic Report of the President* (Washington, DC: Government Printing Office).

RECAP   ECONOMIC POLICY INSTITUTIONS

Before the Great Depression, the government viewed the business cycle much like people today view hurricanes and tornadoes. They are catastrophes, and the government should help those who suffer, but it makes no sense to ask the government to prevent or manage them. Largely as a result of the writings of the British economist John Maynard Keynes, this attitude vanished during the Great Depression and World War II. After World War II, economists and politicians believed that the government could and should prevent great depressions and smooth out the business cycle. Overconfidence in the government's ability to manage the macroeconomy vanished in the 1970s, a decade of both relatively high unemployment and relatively high inflation. Today we have a more limited confidence in the government's ability to stabilize and manage the business cycle.

13.2 THE POWER AND LIMITS OF STABILIZATION POLICY

Economists today arrange themselves along a line with respect to their views as to how the central bank (the Federal Reserve) and fiscal authorities (the president and Congress) should manage the economy. At one end are economists like Milton Friedman, who holds that activist attempts to manage the economy are likely to do more harm than good. Government should settle on a policy that does not produce disaster no matter what the pattern of shocks or the structure of the economy. This end of the spectrum holds that most of the large business cycles and macroeconomic disturbances experienced in the past century were the result of well-intentioned but destructive economic policy decisions based on faulty models of the economy (see Box 13.2).

THE STRUCTURE OF THE ECONOMY AND THE LUCAS CRITIQUE: THE DETAILS

Economist Robert Lucas has argued that most of what economists thought they knew about the structure of the economy was false. Expectations of the future have major effects on decision making in the present: workers' nominal wage demands, managers' investment decisions, households' consumption decisions, and practically every other economic decision hinge, in one way or another, on what is expected to happen in the future. And expectations depend on many things — including the policies followed by the government. Change the policies followed by the government, and you change the structure of the economy as well.

Thus, Lucas argued, the use of economic models to forecast how the economy would respond to changes in government policy is an incoherent and mistaken exercise. Changes in policy would induce changes in the structure of the economy and its patterns of behavior that would invalidate the forecasting exercise. Economic forecasts based on a period in which inflation expectations were *adaptive* would turn out to be grossly in error if applied to a period in which inflation expectations were *rational.* Forecasts of consumption spending based on estimates of the marginal propensity to consume when changes in national income were permanent would lead policy makers astray if applied to forecast the effects of policies that cause transitory changes in national income.

This *Lucas critique* is an important enough insight that for it Robert Lucas was awarded the Nobel Prize in 1995.

At the other end of the spectrum are those who hold that shocks to the economy are frequent and substantial. They believe that appropriate government policy can do a lot to stabilize the economy — to avoid both high unemployment and high inflation.

This economic policy debate has been going on for generations. It will never be resolved, for the differences are inevitably differences of emphasis rather than sharp lines of division. Even the most "activist" economists recognize the limits imposed on stabilization policy by uncertainty about the structure of the economy and the difficulties of forecasting. Even the greatest believer in the natural stability of the economy — Milton Friedman — believes that the economy is naturally stable only if government policy follows the proper policy of ensuring the smooth growth of the money stock.

Uncertainty about the Economy

Because economic policy works with long and variable lags, stabilization policy requires that we first know where the economy is and where it is going. If future conditions cannot be predicted, policies initiated today are as likely to have destructive as constructive effects when they affect the economy 18 months or two years from now.

In general economists take two approaches in trying to forecast the near-term future of the economy. The first approach is to use large-scale macroeconometric models — more complicated versions of the models of this book. The second approach is to search for **leading indicators:** one or a few economic variables not necessarily noted in this book that experience tells us are strongly correlated with future movements in real GDP or inflation. Taking over a former U.S. government task, a private economics research group called the Conference Board now publishes a monthly index of leading economic indicators — ten factors averaged together that many economists believe provide a good guide to economic activity nine or so months in the future.

Of the components that go into the index of leading indicators (see Box 13.3), perhaps the most broadly watched is the stock market. The level of the stock market is a good indicator of the future of investment spending because the same factors that make corporate investment committees likely to approve investment projects — optimism about future profits, cheap sources of financing, willingness to accept risks — make investors eager to buy stocks and to buy stocks at higher prices. We can read likely future decisions of corporate investment committees from the current value of the stock market. But the stock market is far from perfect as a leading indicator: As economist Paul Samuelson likes to say, the stock market has predicted nine of the past five recessions.

WHAT ARE LEADING INDICATORS? THE DETAILS

The index of leading indicators contains 10 different components. The index used to be constructed by the Commerce Department's Bureau of Economic Analysis. As a cost-saving move, it was privatized: It is now compiled and reported by the Conference Board, a nonprofit economic research group. The Conference Board weights all 10 of these components to try to create the best possible index of leading indicators. The current weighting factors applied to the components of the index are shown in Table 13.1.

TABLE 13.1
Components of the Leading Indicators Index

Code	Component	Weighting
BCI-1	Average weekly hours, manufacturing	0.181
BCI-5	Average weekly initial claims for unemployment insurance	0.025
BCI-8	Manufacturers' new orders, consumer goods and materials	0.049
BCI-32	Vendor performance, slower deliveries diffusion index	0.027
BCI-27	Manufacturers' new orders, nondefense capital goods	0.013
BCI-29	Building permits, new private housing units	0.018
BCI-19	Stock prices, 500 common stocks	0.032
BCI-106	Money supply, M2	0.308
BCI-129	Interest rate spread, 10-year Treasury bonds minus federal funds	0.329
BCI-83	Index of consumer expectations	0.018

The Money Supply as a Leading Indicator

The leading indicator that has been most closely watched is the *money supply*. Before the instability of the 1980s *monetarists* used to claim that the appropriate measure of the money stock is the only leading indicator worth watching. If the central bank can guide the money stock to the appropriate level through open-market operations, then success at managing the economy will immediately and automatically follow.

As we saw in Chapter 8, there is no sharp, bright line separating assets that are easy to spend from other assets. A dollar bill is clearly "money" in economists' sense of being readily spendable purchasing power. But what about a 90-day certificate of deposit with an interest penalty if you cash it in before it matures? Each place you draw the line gives you a particular total dollar amount of the assets that make up the economy's "money" — a different monetary aggregate. In order from the smallest to the largest, with each a superset of the one before, the most often used measures are called by the shorthand names M1, M2, M3, and (biggest of all) L.

These four monetary aggregates do not behave the same. During 1992, for example, M1 — the narrow measure — grew by more than 13 percent while M3, the broad measure, grew by less than 1 percent, as shown in Figure 13.9. As gauged by M1, monetary policy in 1992 was expansionary: the Federal Reserve's monetary policy was forcing M1 to grow rapidly, pushing down interest rates and boosting

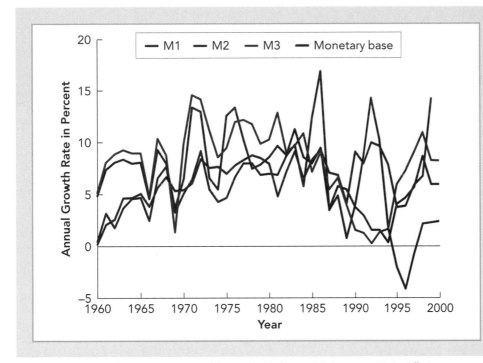

FIGURE 13.9
Different Measures of the Money Stock Behave Differently
The graph shows the different annual growth rates of money stock measures. Since 1980 these different measures have ceased to move together. A year like 1996 in which M1 falls can also see M3 grow, with a difference between the two of more than 10 percentage points per year.

Source: The 2001 edition of *The Economic Report of the President* (Washington, DC: Government Printing Office).

demand. But as gauged by total M3, monetary policy in 1992 was contractionary. The Federal Reserve was keeping M3 stable, pushing up interest rates and deepening the 1990–1992 recession.

Different measures of the money stock say different things about monetary policy. Republican Party critics of Alan Greenspan continue to blame his tight money policies for George H.W. Bush's defeat in the presidential election of 1992: During that year M3 grew by less than 1 percent. Supporters of Greenspan point to the extraordinarily rapid growth of M1 (and short-term real interest rates of less than zero) as evidence of a recession-fighting monetary policy that was strongly stimulative. To say that the money stock is the single most important leading indicator is unhelpful if different measures of "the" money stock say different things.

It is much harder to be a monetary economist than it used to be (see Box 13.4).

THE MONEY MULTIPLIER: DETAILS

The Federal Reserve's open-market operations change the monetary base: One more dollar's worth of Treasury bills sold to the public means one dollar of cash or reserve deposits fewer in the hands of the public. The effects of Federal Reserve open-market operations on the money supply are less direct, and less certain. Changes in the monetary base cause amplified changes in the *money supply* through a process called the *money multiplier,* μ.

When someone deposits $100 in cash in a bank, the Federal Reserve requires the bank to set aside some portion of that deposit as a reserve to satisfy the Fed that the

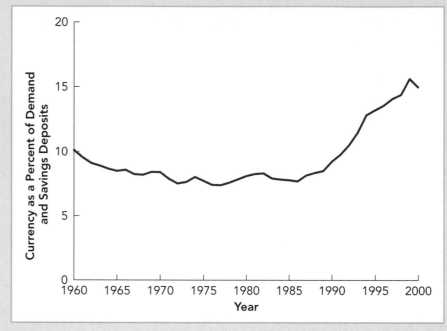

FIGURE 13.10
Changes in the Currency-to-Deposits Ratio
The currency-to-deposits ratio was fairly stable up until the mid-1980s. Since then it has risen substantially. Its sharp increase mean that changes in the money stock are not highly correlated with changes in the monetary base produced by Federal Reserve open-market operations.

Source: The 2001 edition of *The Economic Report of the President* (Washington, DC: Government Printing Office).

bank is liquid and can meet its daily demands for funds. Suppose — for simplicity's sake — that the current reserve requirement is 10 percent, so the bank takes $10 of the newly deposited cash and itself deposits it in the nearest regional Federal Reserve Bank as a *reserve deposit*. The bank then loans out the remaining $90 to collect interest. The borrower receiving the $90 loan typically redeposits it into some other banks. That second wave of banks set aside 10 percent of what they have received — $9 — as their reserves, and loan out the remaining $81. This cycle repeats over and over.

In the end, the Federal Reserve's 10 percent reserve requirement means that an initial injection of $100 in cash into the banking system leads to an increase in total banking system–wide deposits of $100/10% = $1,000, and an increase in banks' own reserve deposits at the Federal Reserve of $100. Thus if the Federal Reserve injects, say, $10 billion into the economy in an open-market operation — by purchasing bonds for cash — it triggers a potential increase of as much as $100 billion in the total money supply. We then say that the economy has a money multiplier of 10.

In practice, the increase in the money supply will be less. Borrowing households and businesses who seek to keep a fixed currency-to-deposits ratio will keep some of the money in cash, so not all money loaned out by banks in one wave will be redeposited in the next. And banks will keep some excess reserves — not all that they could legally lend will be. The money multiplier depends on three factors: the reserve requirements the Federal Reserve imposes on banks, the proportional amount of excess reserves to deposits that banks seek to keep, and the ratio of currency to deposits in which households and businesses prefer to hold their money. If you know these three factors, then you can calculate that the money multiplier μ is

$$\mu = \frac{(curr/dep) + 1}{(curr/dep) + (req/dep) + (exc/dep)}$$

where (curr/dep) is households' and businesses' desired holding ratio of currency-to-deposits, (req/dep) is the ratio of required reserves imposed by the Fed, and (exc/dep) is the ratio of excess reserves that banks desire to hold to total deposits.

Once you know the money multiplier, you can calculate the economywide stock of liquid money assets M by multiplying the monetary base B directly controlled by the Fed by the money multiplier μ:

$$M = \mu \times B$$

If any of the three factors determining the money multiplier shifts, the money multiplier will shift as well — and the money supply will change even if the Federal Reserve has not undertaken any open-market operations and has left the monetary base completely alone:

$$\Delta M = B \times \Delta\mu$$

Do the factors determining the money multiplier shift? Yes, they do. Figure 13.10 shows how one of these three factors — the currency-to-deposits ratio — has varied since 1960. ◆

Long Lags and Variable Effects

Even if economists have good, reliable forecasts, changes in macroeconomic policy affect the economy with long lags and have variable effects. Estimates of the slope of the IS curve are imprecise: This isn't rocket science, after all. Economists are estimating the reactions of human beings to changes in the incentives to undertake different courses of action. They are not calculating the motions of particles that obey invariant and precisely known physical laws.

Moreover, changes in interest rates take *time* to affect the level of aggregate demand and real GDP. It takes time for corporate investment committees to meet and evaluate how changes in interest rates change the investment projects they wish to undertake. It takes time for changes in the decisions of corporate investment committees to affect the amount of work being done that builds up the country's capital stock. It takes time for the changes in employment and income generated by changes in investment to feed through the multiplier process and have their full effect on equilibrium aggregate demand. Thus the level of total product now is determined not by what long-term real risky interest rates are now, but by what they were more than a year and a half ago.

As more than one member of the FOMC has said, making monetary policy is like driving a car that has had its windshield painted black. You guess which way you want to go by looking in the rearview mirror at the landscape behind. Box 13.5 gives an example of how hard driving then becomes.

THE LIMITS OF STABILIZATION POLICY: A POLICY

Suppose that the target level of real GDP that the central bank hopes to attain is $10,000 billion, but that the central bank staff forecasts that if interest rates are kept at their current levels the real GDP will be only $9,500 billion. Reducing the interest rate will boost real GDP. But there is uncertainty about how far it will be boosted. Suppose that there is one chance in four that a 0.01 percent reduction — a one basis-point reduction — in the interest rate will not boost real GDP at all, one chance in two that a 0.01 percent reduction in the interest rate will boost real GDP by $2 billion, and one chance in four that a one basis-point reduction in the interest rate will boost real GDP by $4 billion.

What should the central bank do? In this particular example, the answer is that it should do only half as much as it would if there were no uncertainty about the effects of its policies. The point is general: If the effects of policy are uncertain, do less than you otherwise would, and be cautious.

Assume that the central bank tries to make the expected value (in billions) of $(Y - \$10,000)^2$ as small as possible. The best situation is to actually have real GDP Y equal to $10,000 billion, and bigger deviations are proportionately worse. Then we can solve the central bank's problem. We can calculate the amount Δr by which it should reduce the real interest rate.

If the central bank reduces the real interest rate by Δr, there is

- One chance in four that $Y = \$9,500$.
- One chance in two that $Y = \$9,500 + (\$200 \times \Delta r)$.
- One chance in four that $Y = \$9,500 + (\$400 \times \Delta r)$.

In the first case, the squared deviation of Y from $10,000 is

$$(-\$500)^2 = \$250,000$$

In the second case, the squared deviation of Y from $10,000 is

$$[(\$200 \times \Delta r) - \$500]^2 = 250,000 - (200,000 \times \Delta r) + [40,000 \times (\Delta r)^2]$$

In the third case, the squared deviation of Y from $10,000 is

$$[(\$400 \times \Delta r) - \$500]^2 = 250,000 - (400,000 \times \Delta r) + [160,000 \times (\Delta r)^2]$$

Since there is one chance in four of each of the first and third cases, and one chance in two of the second case, the total expected value (in billions) of $(Y - \$10,000)^2$ is

$$0.25 \times (250,000) +$$
$$0.50 \times \{250,000 - (200,000 \times \Delta r) + [40,000 \times (\Delta r)^2]\} +$$
$$0.25 \times \{250,000 - (400,000 \times \Delta r) + [160,000 \times (\Delta r)^2]\} =$$
$$250,000 - (\$00,000 \times \Delta r) + [80,000 \times (\Delta r)^2]$$

When Δr equals 0, this expected value of $(Y - \$10,000)^2$ is $250,000. When Δr equals 0.5 percent, this expected value of $(Y - \$10,000)^2$ is $170,000. When Δr equals 1 percent, this expected value of $(Y - \$10,000)^2$ is $130,000. And when Δr equals 1.5 percent, this expected value of $(Y - \$10,000)^2$ is $130,000 too. The minimum value of the expected square of the deviation of Y from $10,000 billion comes for a value of Δr equal to 1.25 percent, which makes the expected square of the deviation of Y from $10,000 billion equal to $125,000 billion.

Suppose that we didn't take any account of uncertainty. Suppose that we simply said that the expected value of the increase in real GDP produced by a 1-percentage-point cut in interest rates is $200 billion, and that we have a $500 billion output gap to close. Then we would have set Δr at 2.5 percent — twice as large a change in the interest rate as the 1.25 percent that turned out to be the best a central bank trying to get real GDP as close as possible to $10,000 billion could do.

Why the difference once one recognizes the uncertainty in the effects of policy? Because active policy to close the output gap has the additional effect of adding yet more variation to real GDP. The stronger the shift in policy, the more uncertain are its effects and the more likely it is that the policy will be counterproductive. This extra risk is the reason that the best thing for the central bank to do in this example is to cut interest rates not by 2.5 percent but by only 2⅖ percent.

The point, however, is quite general. When there is uncertainty about the effects of your policies, do less, and be cautious about undertaking bold policy moves.

RECAP   THE POWER AND LIMITS OF STABILIZATION POLICY

During the 1970s, especially, economists and policy makers painfully learned that the ability of the government to successfully conduct stabilization policy was limited by three factors. First, it became clear that any loss by the public of their belief that the central bank was committed to low inflation produced *stagflation* — a combination of relatively high unemployment and relatively high inflation. Second, a lack of accurate forecasts combined with the long and variable lags with which economic policies take effect means that monetary and fiscal policy must be slow to respond to sudden falls in production and rises in unemployment. Third, because economic policies have uncertain effects, policies to aggressively fight recessions may well wind up being counterproductive. Good policy makers must be cautious policy makers.

13.3 MONETARY VERSUS FISCAL POLICY

Relative Power

At the end of the World War II era, most economists and policy makers believed that the principal stabilization policy tool would be *fiscal policy*. Monetary policy had proved to be of little use during the Great Depression: Risk premiums and term premiums were too high and too unstable for changes in the short-term nominal safe interest rates controlled by central banks to have reliable effects on production and employment. In contrast, changes in government spending and in taxes were seen as having rapid and reliable effects on aggregate demand. But over the past 50 years opinion has shifted. Today the overwhelming consensus is that monetary policy has proved itself faster acting and more reliable than discretionary fiscal policy.

When Congress tries to stabilize the economy by fiscal policy — by passing laws to change levels of taxes and spending — it cannot realistically hope to see changes in the level of output and employment in less than two years after the bill is first introduced into Congress. It takes time for the bill to move through the House of Representatives. It takes more time for the bill to move through the Senate, and for the conference committee to reconcile the different versions. Yet more time must pass before the operating departments in the executive branch of government can change actual spending or write new rules for administering the tax system once Congress has authorized the fiscal change. And it takes more time for the change in government purchases or in net taxes to have its full effect through the multiplier process (see Box 13.6).

Monetary policy lags are shorter. The FOMC can move rapidly; once its decisions are made they affect long-term real interest rates on the same day. There are substantial lags between when interest rates change and when output reaches its new equilibrium value: Monetary policy still takes more than a year to work. But **monetary policy lags** are shorter than those associated with **discretionary fiscal policy.**

The fact that the Federal Reserve's decision and action cycle is shorter than that of the president and Congress means that the Federal Reserve can, if it wishes, neutralize the effects of any change in fiscal policy on aggregate demand. As a rule, today's Federal Reserve does routinely neutralize the effects of changes in fiscal policy. Swings in the budget deficit produced by changes in tax laws and spending appropriations have little impact on real GDP unless the Federal Reserve wishes them to.

THE KENNEDY-JOHNSON AND THE REAGAN TAX CUTS: A POLICY

Believers in discretionary fiscal policy claim the 1964 Kennedy-Johnson tax cut as a success: It stimulated consumption spending and the economy. It was widely perceived as a permanent tax cut that would raise everyone's permanent income. But critics see it as a fiscal policy failure. Discussed in 1961 and proposed in 1962, it was not enacted until 1964 and had little effect on the economy until 1965–1967.

In 1961–1962 the unemployment rate was in the range of 5.5 to 6.7 percent. Maybe there was a case for thinking that unemployment was above its natural rate. But by 1965–1966 the unemployment rate was in the range of 3.8 to 4.5 percent, inflation was about to become a serious problem, and Johnson's advisers were already calling for tax increases to try to reduce aggregate demand and control inflation.

The deficits that followed the 1981 Reagan tax cut certainly shifted out the IS curve. But did they raise the level of national product? Almost surely not. The Federal Reserve did not want to see national product expanding so fast as to set inflation rising again. Thus the Reagan deficits led to tighter monetary policy, higher interest rates, and lower investment — not to higher employment and total product. The rule that prevails today and probably will prevail for the next generation is that the Federal Reserve offsets shifts in aggregate demand created by the changing government deficit.

Fiscal Policy: Automatic Stabilizers

There is, however, one kind of fiscal policy that does work rapidly enough to be important. The so-called fiscal **automatic stabilizers** swing into action within three months to moderate business cycle–driven swings in disposable income and so moderate the business cycle.

Whenever the economy enters a recession or a boom, the government's budget surplus or deficit begins to swing in the opposite direction. As the economy enters a boom, tax collections and withholdings automatically rise because incomes rise. Spending on social welfare programs like food stamps falls because higher employment and higher wages mean that fewer people are poor. Thus the government budget moves toward surplus, without Congress passing or the president signing a single bill. And if the economy enters a recession, tax collections fall, social welfare spending rises, and the government's budget swings into deficit.

As unemployment rises and national income falls, taxes fall by about 30 cents for every dollar fall in national product. Spending rises by about 7 cents for every dollar fall in national product. A $1 fall in national product produces a fall of only 70 cents in consumers' disposable income. Thus automatic stabilizers provide more than $1's worth of boost to aggregate demand for every $3 fall in production.

Such fiscal automatic stabilizers would be large enough to reduce the marginal propensity to spend from about 0.6 to about 0.4. This would imply a reduction in the size of the multiplier from about 2.5 to about 1.67. Business cycles could be considerably larger if these automatic stabilizers did not exist, if the Federal Reserve found itself unable to compensate for their disappearance, and if their disappearance did not lead to counteracting changes in the marginal propensity to spend.

How Monetary Policy Works

For monetary policy to work, the Federal Open Market Committee (FOMC) must first recognize that there is a problem. It takes three to six months for statistical agencies to collect and process the data, for the Federal Reserve to recognize the state of the economy, and for it to conclude that action is needed. To this recognition lag add a policy formulation lag. The FOMC is a committee that moves by consensus. Members who have taken positions out on various limbs need time to climb down. More than six months can elapse between the start of a recession and decisive FOMC action to lower interest rates to try to increase aggregate demand.

Once the Federal Reserve acts, the response of financial markets is immediate. At the latest, interest rates shift the very day the trading desk at the New York Federal Reserve Bank receives new instructions. Often interest rates change in advance of the policy change. Because the Federal Reserve moves by consensus, traders can often guess what it is going to do beforehand. However, it takes over a year for changes in interest rates to change national product and unemployment.

This means that the Federal Reserve is essentially powerless to smooth out fluctuations in less than a year. The average recession in the post–World War II United States has lasted less than 18 months. This means that by the time monetary policy changes initiated at the beginning of the recession and aimed at reducing its size have their effect on the economy, the recession is likely to be nearly over (see Box 13.7).

MONETARY POLICY INSTRUMENTS: A POLICY

Today the Federal Reserve focuses on controlling interest rates. In the past it has occasionally let interest rates be more volatile and focused on controlling the rate of growth of the *money supply* — also called the money stock — which is the economy's total supply of liquid assets.

Should the Federal Reserve target real interest rates — try to keep them stable, perhaps allowing them to climb when inflation threatens and to fall during a recession? Or should it focus on keeping the money stock growing smoothly because the money stock is a good leading indicator, and stabilizing the growth path of this indicator is a good way to stabilize the economy as a whole?

It depends.

If the principal instability in the economy is found in a shifting IS curve, then targeting interest rates will do little or nothing to reduce the magnitude of shocks to the economy. Better to have a monetary policy *reaction function* that reacts to leading indicators and outcomes. But if the instability lies instead in the relationship between the money stock and real output (the result of volatile money demand is volatile) or in a shifting relationship between the monetary base and the money supply (because the currency-to-deposits and reserves-to-deposits ratios vary), then targeting interest rates is wiser.

In recent years instability has been primarily in the velocity of money and the sign of the money multiplier. The money multiplier has fluctuated unexpectedly and widely in the 1980s and 1990s, chiefly because of unexpected fluctuations in the currency-to-deposits ratio. Since 1980, the Federal Reserve's control over the monetary base has not been enough to allow the Federal Reserve to exercise control over the money supply. And the velocity of money has fluctuated as well. By contrast, the position of the IS curve has been relatively stable.

Thus in the past two decades it has been better for the Federal Reserve to have as its monetary target the level of interest rates than the growth of the money supply.

13.4 RULES VERSUS AUTHORITIES

In the late 1940s Chicago School economist Henry Simons set the terms for a debate over macroeconomic policy that continues to this day. He asked, Should macroeconomic policy be conducted "automatically," according to rules that would be followed no matter what? Or should macroeconomic policy be left to authorities — bodies of appointed officials — provided with wide discretion over how to use their power and given general guidance as to what goals to pursue?

Competence and Objectives

The first reason for automatic rules is that we fear that the people appointed to authorities will be incompetent. If people are appointed because of friendships from the past, or because of their ability to rally campaign contributions for a particular cause, there is little reason to think that they will be skilled judges of the situation or insightful analysts. Better then to constrain them by automatic rules. Even if those appointed to authorities are well intentioned, they may fail to find good solutions to macroeconomic problems. The stream of public discourse about macroeconomics is polluted by a large quantity of misinformation.

A second reason for fixed rules is that authorities might not have the right objectives. To institute a good rule it is only necessary for the political process to make the right decision once — at the moment the rule is settled. But an authority making decisions every day may be more likely to start pursuing objectives that conflict with the long-run public interest. The state of the economy at the moment of the election is a powerful influence on citizens' votes. Thus politicians in office have a personal power incentive to pursue policies that will sacrifice the health of the economy in the future in order to obtain good reported economic numbers during the election year (see Box 13.8).

THE POLITICAL BUSINESS CYCLE AND RICHARD NIXON: A POLICY

The most famous example of the political business cycle at work comes from the American politician Richard Nixon's episodic autobiography, *Six Crises,* published in 1962. Looking back on his defeat in the 1960 presidential election by John F. Kennedy, Nixon wrote that

"Two other developments [that] occurred before the [Republican Party C]onvention . . . [had] far more effect on the election outcome. . . .

"Early in March [1960], Dr. Arthur Burns. . . called on me. . . . [He] expressed great concern about the way the economy was then acting. . . . Burns' conclusion was that unless some decisive government action were taken, and taken soon, we were heading for another economic dip, which would hit its low point in October, just before the elections. He urged strongly that everything possible be done to avert this development . . . by loosening up on credit and . . . increasing spending for national security. The next time I saw the President, I discussed Burns' proposals with him, and he in turn put the subject on the agenda for the next cabinet meeting.

"The matter was thoroughly discussed by the Cabinet. . . . [S]everal of the Administration's economic experts who attended the meeting did not share [Burns's] bearish prognosis. . . . [T]here was strong sentiment against using the spending and credit powers of the Federal Government to affect the economy, unless and until conditions clearly indicated a major recession in prospect.

"In supporting Burns' point of view, I must admit that I was more sensitive politically than some of the others around the cabinet table. I knew from bitter experience how, in both 1954 and 1958, slumps which hit bottom early in October contributed to substantial Republican losses in the House and Senate. . . .

"Unfortunately, Arthur Burns turned out to be a good prophet. The bottom of the 1960 dip did come in October. . . . In October. . . . the jobless rolls increased by 452,000. All the speeches, television broadcasts, and precinct work in the world could not counteract that one hard fact."

By 1972 Richard Nixon was president, and he had appointed Arthur Burns to be chair of the Federal Reserve. The year 1972 saw very good economic statistics — at the price of a sharp acceleration of inflation in subsequent years. Given the smoking gun provided by Nixon in *Six Crises,* many have diligently searched for evidence that the Federal Reserve made economic policy in 1971 and 1972 not in the public interest but to enhance the private political interest of Richard Nixon.

However, things are more complicated. Economist Herbert Stein pointed out that Nixon administration economic policy was in fact less expansionary than many Democratic politicians and economic advisers wished: The claim that Burns was leaning to the expansionary side of the center of gravity of opinion is simply not correct. And once Arthur Burns had become chair of the Federal Reserve, Nixon administration officials found him to be truly and annoyingly independent.

The verdict is that Richard Nixon dearly wished for the Federal Reserve to tune economic policies in a way that would enhance his reelection chances, but that the institutional independence of the Federal Reserve worked. White House political pressure in 1971–1972 led to little if any change in Federal Reserve policy. ◆

The substitution of technocratic authorities — like the Federal Reserve — in the place of presidents, prime ministers, and finance ministers provides some insulation.

The fear that politicians will have objectives different from the long-run public interest has led many to advocate that monetary policy be made by *independent* central banks. If stabilization policy is to be made by authorities, it should be made by authorities placed at least one remove from partisan politics (see Box 13.9).

BOX 13.9

IS THERE A POLITICAL BUSINESS CYCLE? THE DETAILS

Few would dispute that politicians seek to tune the macroeconomy to their political advantage. The Bush administration tried to persuade Federal Reserve chair Alan Greenspan to pursue a more expansionary monetary policy in 1991 to produce better economic numbers for the George Bush reelection campaign in 1992, going as far as threatening not to nominate Greenspan for a second term as Federal Reserve chair. But it was unsuccessful. Richard Nixon certainly believed when he appointed Arthur Burns to be Fed chair that Burns would still be the loyal partisan supporter he had been in 1960 — contemplating this appointment, Nixon referred to the "myth of the autonomous Fed" and laughed.

But how successful are governments at manipulating the political business cycle? It is not clear. It is true that in the United States since 1948, the fourth year of a president's term — the presidential election year — has seen annual real GDP growth average 0.6 percent more than the average of nonpresidential election years. But there is a 15 percent probability that at least that large a difference would emerge from random chance and sampling variation alone. Faster growth in presidential election years is suggestive, but not conclusive.

Moreover, other ways of looking at the data deliver even less evidence. Out of 12 post-1948 presidential terms, fully six — Johnson, Nixon-Ford, Carter, Reagan II, Bush, and Clinton I — saw slower economic growth in the politically relevant second half of the term than in the first half of the term. This alternative way of looking at the data provides not even a suggestion of evidence one way or another. And it is important when analyzing any situation not to choose to look at the data in only the way that makes one's preferred conclusion appear the strongest.

There is, however, stronger evidence not of a politically motivated component to the business cycle but of a politically influenced component to the business cycle. In all seven post-WWII presidential terms in which Republicans have occupied the White House, growth in the second year of a presidential term has been lower than average real GDP growth over that term. By contrast, in only one of the six terms in which Democrats have occupied the White House has second-year growth been lower than average, as shown in Figure 13.11.

The odds against this pattern happening are astronomical: There is less than one chance in a thousand that it could be the result of random sampling variation.

Economist Alberto Alesina interprets this pattern as showing that the political parties have — or had, for Clinton is the Democratic president for whom the pattern of growth fits the Republican model — different views of the relative costs of unemployment and inflation. Republicans have more tolerance for unemployment and less tolerance for inflation than Democrats do. Hence when Republicans come into office the Federal Reserve feels more free to try to push inflation down to a lower level. Because a considerable portion of inflation expectations relevant for the second year of a presidential term were formed back before the result of the election is known, actual inflation in the second year of a term is less than expected inflation and so economic growth is relatively low.

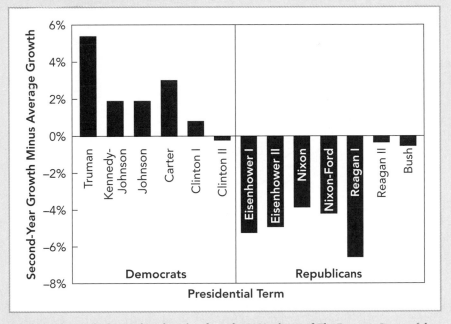

FIGURE 13.11

The Politically Influenced Business Cycle: Relative Growth in the Second Year of Presidential Terms

Economic growth (real GDP) tends to be rapid in the second year of the term of a Democratic president. Economic growth tends to be slow — or negative — in the second year of the term of a Republican President.

Source: Author's calculations based on data from the 2001 edition of *The Economic Report of the President* (Washington, DC: Government Printing Office); replicating an analysis conducted by Alberto Alesina and Nouriel Roubini, "Political Business Cycles in OECD Economies" (NBER: Working Paper 3478, 1990), http:/papers.nber.org/W3478; subsequently published in the *Review of Economic Studies* 59, October 1992, pp. 663–688.

CENTRAL BANK INDEPENDENCE: A POLICY

A number of economists have investigated the relationship between macroeconomic performance and the degree to which central banks are insulated from partisan politics. They have examined the legal and institutional framework within which central banks in different countries operate, and constructed indexes of the extent to which their central banks are independent.

Alberto Alesina and Lawrence Summers concluded that the more independent a central bank, the better its inflation performance. More independent central banks presided over lower average inflation and less variable inflation. Moreover, countries with independent central banks did not pay any penalty. Countries with independent central banks did not have higher unemployment, lower real GDP growth, or larger business cycles.

Interpreting this correlation is not straightforward. Perhaps the factors that lead countries to have independent central banks lead them to have low inflation. Perhaps independent central banks do reduce economic growth, but only countries likely to have high economic growth for other reasons are likely to have independent central banks. Nevertheless, at least the post-1950 experience of the industrialized countries strongly suggests that insulating central banks from partisan politics delivers low inflation without any visible macroeconomic cost (see Figure 13.12).

FIGURE 13.12

Inflation and Central Bank Insulation from Politics

Countries whose central banks are more independent — rate higher on an average index of independence — have lower average inflation rates.

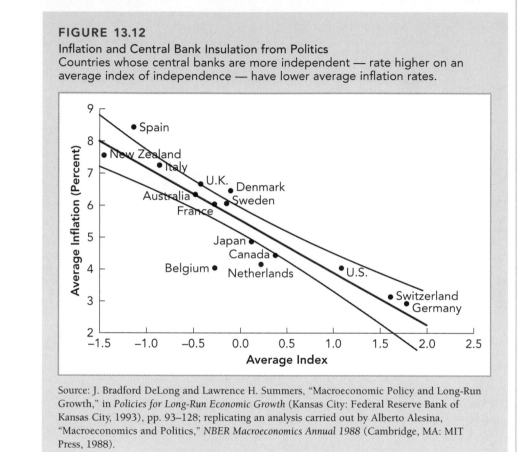

Source: J. Bradford DeLong and Lawrence H. Summers, "Macroeconomic Policy and Long-Run Growth," in *Policies for Long-Run Economic Growth* (Kansas City: Federal Reserve Bank of Kansas City, 1993), pp. 93–128; replicating an analysis carried out by Alberto Alesina, "Macroeconomics and Politics," *NBER Macroeconomics Annual 1988* (Cambridge, MA: MIT Press, 1988).

Credibility and Commitment

There is always a temptation for the central bank to pursue a more expansionary monetary policy: More expansionary policy raises national product and reduces the unemployment rate. Moreover, it has little impact on inflation in the short run in which expectations of inflation are more or less fixed. In the short run, expansionary monetary policy does always seem to be a central bank's best option. Suppose firms and unions agree on large nominal wage and price increases. Then in the short run it is best for the central bank to accommodate inflation and expand the money supply. To fight inflation by raising interest rates would generate a recession, and inflation would continue anyway. Suppose instead that firms and unions decide on wage and price restraint. Expansionary monetary policy is still better — inflation will be low, and the economy will boom.

In either case, pursuing a more expansionary monetary policy produces a better short-run outcome. Moreover, announcing that monetary policy will be more restrictive produces a better short-run outcome as well, for by announcing that fighting inflation is job one, the central bank may influence the expectations of workers, managers, investors, and households.

So why — given the obvious short-run benefits of a more expansionary monetary policy — should anyone ever believe that a central bank will aim for low inflation?

Yet in the long run, a central bank is wiser to keep low inflation as its top priority. Central banks benefit if workers, firms, and investors all believe that future inflation will be low. A central bank that succumbs to the temptation to make inflation higher than expected loses its credibility. All will soon recognize that the central bank's talk is cheap, and that it has a strong incentive once expectations for a period are formed to make inflation and money growth higher than expected. So the central bank will find that its words about future policy are ignored in the process of setting expectations. And expectations of inflation will be sky-high.

Economists give this conflict the awkward name "**dynamic inconsistency**": What it is good to have workers, managers, investors, and employers believe that you will do in the future is not what seems best to do when the future becomes the present. Many economists have argued that this dynamic inconsistency problem is a strong point on the side of rules rather than authorities: You don't have to worry about a rule breaking its word. Others have pointed out that central banks that are concerned with their long-term reputation and credibility appear to have little problem resisting the temptation to make inflation and money growth higher than the firms and workers in the economy had expected. And they have little problem acquiring credibility, which they do in many ways including

- Complaining that inflation may be rising.
- Refusing to admit even the possibility that monetary expansion might reduce unemployment.
- Repeatedly declaring that price stability is the primary objective.

The most important way to acquire credibility is to possess a history of past successful control of inflation.

Modern Monetary Policy

Whether monetary policy is guided by strict and rigid rules or made by authorities using their discretion to come up with the best policy for the particular — unique — situation, one question remains: What sort of rule should be adopted, or how should the authority behave? What sort of *guidelines* for monetary policy should those who set the rules or those who staff the authorities follow?

Economists believe that one set of rules to avoid are those that command the central bank to attain values for real economic variables, like the rate of growth of real GDP or the level of the unemployment rate. The rate of growth of real GDP is limited in the long run by the rate of growth of potential output. The level of the unemployment rate is controlled in the long run by the natural rate of unemployment. A central-bank target of too high a rate of real GDP growth, or too low a level of the unemployment rate, is likely to end in upward-spiraling inflation. A policy that targets *nominal* variables — like the nominal money stock, or nominal GDP, or the inflation rate — is robust, in the sense that it does not run the risk of leading to disaster if our assessment of the macroeconomic structure of the economy turns out to be wrong.

One proposal is for the central bank to choose a target for the inflation rate (call it π'), to estimate what the real interest rate should be on average (call it r^*). It would then raise interest rates when inflation is above and lower interest rates when inflation is below this target. A 1-percentage-point increase in inflation would cause the central bank to raise real interest rates by an amount represented by the parameter ϕ'':

$$r = r^* + \phi'' \times (\pi - \pi')$$

An activist central bank concerned with unemployment as well might also reduce the real interest rate when unemployment is above the natural rate, and raise it whenever unemployment falls below the natural rate, with a 1-percentage-point increase in unemployment causing the central bank to reduce real interest rates by an amount represented by the parameter γ:

$$r = r^* + \phi'' \times (\pi - \pi') - \gamma \times (u - u^*)$$

Stanford University macroeconomist John Taylor (now undersecretary of the treasury for international affairs in the Bush administration) put this *Taylor rule* forward as a description of how the Federal Reserve has typically operated, and as a way of adding some structure and order to the process by which monetary policy is made. Former Federal Reserve Vice Chair Alan Blinder, for example, has said that in making monetary policy he found the framework set out by John Taylor to be extremely helpful. He did not intend for the rule to be followed exactly. For example, if fiscal policy is unusually tight (or loose) then the federal funds rate should be lower (or higher) than the Taylor rule prescribes.

The Taylor rule provides a way to think about how strongly the Federal Reserve should move to counter shocks to the economy. Do you believe that the Federal Reserve should act more aggressively to boost the economy when unemployment is high? Then you are arguing for a larger parameter γ in the Taylor rule. Do you believe that the Federal Reserve reacts too strongly to cool the economy when inflation rises? Then you are arguing for a smaller parameter ϕ'' in the Taylor rule.

13.5 EXTREME SITUATIONS: FINANCIAL CRISES

Open-market operations are not the only tool by which the government affects the economy. Because the long-term interest rate is an average of expected future short-term interest rates, expectations of future Federal Reserve policy — closely tied to central-bank credibility — are also important influences on aggregate demand today. Even more important, however, are the existence of *deposit insurance* to insulate bank depositors from the effects of financial crises, and the expectation that should a financial crisis become deep enough the Federal Reserve will act as a lender of last resort. In extreme situations such alternative policy levers become important tools to try to stem depressions.

For nearly 400 years market economies have undergone *financial crises* — episodes when the prices of stocks or of other assets crash, everyone tries to move their wealth into safer forms at once, and the consequent panic among investors can lead to a prolonged and serious depression. Managing such financial crises has been one of the responsibilities of monetary policy makers for more than a century and a half.

A financial crisis — like the financial panics in East Asia in 1998 — sees investors as a group suddenly (and often not very rationally) become convinced that their investments have become overly risky. As a result, they try to exchange their investments for high-quality bonds and cash. But as everyone tries to do this at once, they create the risk that they hoped to avoid: Stock and real estate prices crash, and interest rates spike upward as everyone tries to increase their holdings of relatively safe, liquid assets.

The sharp rise in real interest rates that occurs in a financial crisis can severely reduce investment, and send the economy into a deep depression. Moreover, once the crisis gathers force, the ability of monetary policy tools to boost investment may well be limited. Financial crises are accompanied by steep rises in risk premiums. They are often accompanied by sharp rises in term premiums as well, as investors decide that they want to hold their wealth in as liquid a form as possible. And financial crises frequently generate deflation as well.

All of these drive a large wedge between the short-term nominal safe interest rates that the central bank controls and the long-term real interest rate relevant for the determination of investment and aggregate demand. The central bank may have done all it can to reduce interest rates, and it may not be enough: Real interest rates may remain high.

Lenders of Last Resort

In such a situation a central bank can do a lot of good easily by rapidly expanding the money supply, so that the increase in the demand for liquid assets to hold doesn't lead to a spike in interest rates and a crash in other asset prices. It can also do a lot of good by lending directly to institutions that are fundamentally *solvent* — that will, if the crisis is stemmed and resolved rapidly, be able to function profitably — but that are temporarily *illiquid* in the sense that no one is willing to lend to them because no one is confident that the crisis will be resolved. Such a *lender of last resort* can rapidly reduce risk and term premiums as it reduces safe short-term nominal interest rates, and end the financial crisis.

The problem is that a central bank can also do a lot of harm if it bails out institutions that have gone bankrupt, and thus encourages others in the future to take excessive risks hoping that the central bank will bail them out. Thus the central bank has to (*a*) expand the money supply and lend freely to institutions that are merely illiquid — that is, caught short of cash but fundamentally sound — while (*b*) forcibly liquidating institutions that are insolvent, those that could never repay what they owe even if the panic were stemmed immediately. This is a neat trick, to save one without saving the other.

A central bank can take institutional steps in advance to reduce the chance that the economy will suffer a financial crisis, and reduce the damage that a financial panic will do. The first and most obvious is to do a good job as a supervising regulator over the banking system. Depositors will panic and pull their money out of a bank when they fear that it is bankrupt — that it no longer has enough capital, and that the capital plus the value of the loans that it has made are together lower than the value of the money it owes to its depositors. If banks are kept well capitalized, and if banks that fail to meet standards for capital adequacy are rapidly taken over and closed down, then the risk of a full-fledged financial panic is small.

The potential problem with this strategy of supervision and surveillance is that it may be politically difficult to carry out. Bankers are, after all, often wealthy and influential people with substantial political connections. Bank regulators are midlevel civil servants, subject to pressure and influence from politicians.

Deposit Insurance and Moral Hazard

The most recent major financial crisis in the United States, the Great Depression, was also the most destructive. Banks closed; at the beginning of 1933, more than one in three of the banks that had existed in 1929 had closed its doors. When banks failed, people who had their money in them were out of luck; years might pass before any portion of their deposits would be returned. Hence fear of bank failure leads to an immediate increase in households' and businesses' holdings of currency relative to deposits. In the Great Depression this flight from banks reduced the money supply.

With 6,000 banks failing in the first three years of the Depression, more and more people felt that putting their money in a bank was not much better than throwing it away. Since a rise in the currency-to-deposits ratio carries with it a fall in the money multiplier, fear of bank failures shrank the money stock. That only deepened the Depression. Something had to be done to prop up depositors' confidence.

One of the reforms of President Franklin D. Roosevelt's New Deal program in the 1930s was the institution of deposit insurance provided by the Federal Deposit Insurance Corporation — the FDIC. If your bank failed, the government would make sure your deposits did not disappear. The aim was to diminish monetary instability by eliminating bank failure–driven swings in the money supply and interest rates.

Since the 1930s, federal deposit insurance has acted as a *monetary automatic stabilizer*. A financial panic gathers force when investors conclude that they need to pull their money out of banks and mutual funds because such investments are too risky. Deposit insurance eliminates the risk of keeping your money in a bank — even if the bank goes belly-up, your deposit is still secure. Thus there is no reason to seek to move your money to any safer place. Deposit insurance has broken one of the important links in the chain of transmission that used to make financial panics so severe.

The availability of deposit insurance and the potential existence of a lender of last resort do not come for free. These institutions create potential problems of their own — problems that economists discuss under the heading of *moral hazard*. If depositors know that the Federal Deposit Insurance Corporation has guaranteed their deposits, they will not inquire into the kinds of loans that their bank is making. Bank owners and managers may decide to make deliberately risky high-interest loans. If the economy booms and the loans are repaid, then they make a fortune. If the economy goes into recession and the risky firms to which they have loaned go bankrupt, they declare bankruptcy too and leave the FDIC to deal with the depositors. It becomes a classic game of heads-I-win-tails-you-lose.

The principal way to guard against moral hazard is to make certain that decision makers have substantial amounts of their own money at risk. Making risky loans using government-guaranteed deposits as your source of funding is a lot less attractive if your personal wealth is the first thing that is taken to pay off depositors if the loans go bad. Hence deposit insurance and lenders of last resort function well only if there is adequate supervision and surveillance: only if the central bank and the other bank regulatory authorities are keeping close watch on banks, and making sure that every bank has adequate capital, so that it is the shareholders' and the managers' funds, rather than those of the FDIC, that are at risk if the loans made go bad.

RECAP MACROECONOMIC POLICY IN PRACTICE

Given a macroeconomic model, it is easy to calculate what fiscal and monetary policies will bring the economy to full employment. Nevertheless the making of macroeconomic policy in practice is extraordinarily difficult. Policy makers must guard public confidence in their commitment to low inflation, work without good forecasts of where the economy is going, and use tools that have uncertain and variable effects on total spending. Economists disagree even over such fundamental issues as whether the central bank should be tightly constrained by policy rules or not. And in the extreme situations of financial crises, economic policy makers face a choice between large-scale bankruptcy, the possible unraveling of the financial system, and deep depression on the one hand; and rewarding those who have made overspeculative and overleveraged bets on the other.

Chapter Summary

1. Macroeconomic policy should attempt to stabilize the economy: to avoid extremes of high unemployment and also of high and rising inflation.

2. Long and variable lags make successful stabilization policy extremely difficult.

3. Economists arrange themselves along a spectrum, with some advocating more aggressive management of the economy, and others concentrating on establishing a stable framework and economic environment. But compared to differences of opinion among economists in the past, differences of opinion today are minor.

4. In today's environment, monetary policy is the stabilization policy tool of choice, largely because it operates with shorter lags than does discretionary fiscal policy.

5. Nevertheless, the fiscal "automatic stabilizers" built into the tax system play an important role in reducing the size of the multiplier.

6. Uncertainty about the structure of the economy or the effectiveness of policy should lead policy makers to be cautious: Blunt policy tools should be used carefully and cautiously lest they do more harm than good.

7. The advantage of having economic policy made by an authority is that the authority can use judgment to devise the best response to a changing — and usually unforeseen — situation.

8. The advantages of having economic policy made by a *rule* are threefold: First, rules do not assume competence in authorities where it may not exist; second, rules reduce the possibility that policy will be made not in the public interest but in some special interest; third, rules make it easier to avoid so-called dynamic inconsistency.

9. Dynamic inconsistency arises whenever a central bank finds that it wishes to change its previously announced policy in an inflationary direction: It is always in the central bank's short-term interest to have money growth be higher, interest rates lower, and inflation a little higher than had been previously expected.

10. Today, however, central banks are by and large successful in taking a long-term view. They pay great attention to establishing and maintaining the credibility of their policy commitments.

Key Terms

inside lag (p. 367)

Lucas critique (p. 370)

leading indicators (p. 371)

monetary policy lags (p. 378)

discretionary fiscal policy (p. 378)

automatic stabilizers (p. 378)

authorities (p. 380)
rules (p. 380)

political business cycle (p. 381)
credibility (p. 384)

dynamic inconsistency (p. 385)

Analytical Exercises

1. What is the Lucas critique? How would the Lucas critique suggest that you should design a policy to try to reduce annual inflation from 10 percent to 2 percent?

2. What is "dynamic inconsistency"? Why does dynamic inconsistency strengthen the case for having policy rules rather than having authorities with discretionary power over economic policy?

3. Under what circumstances do you think that the Federal Reserve should shift from targeting the interest rate to targeting the money stock growth rate?

4. What would be the economic advantages and disadvantages of eliminating federal deposit insurance?

5. Why do economic policy makers think it important to get the best available forecasts?

Policy Exercises

1. Suppose that the economy's Phillips curve is given by

$$\pi = \pi^e - \beta \times (u - u^*)$$

with β equal to 0.4 and u^* equal to 0.06 — 6 percent. Suppose that the economy has for a long time had a constant inflation rate equal to 3 percent per year. Suddenly the government announces a new policy: It will use fiscal policy to boost real GDP by 5 percent relative to potential — enough by Okun's law to push the unemployment rate down by 2 percent — and it will keep that expanded fiscal policy in place indefinitely.

Suppose that agents in the economy have *adaptive expectations* of inflation — so that this year's expected inflation is equal to last year's actual inflation. What will be the course of inflation and unemployment in this economy in the years after the shift in fiscal policy? Track the economy out 20 years, assuming that there are no additional shocks.

2. Suppose that all conditions given in question 1 are the case. In addition, suppose that for each 1 percentage point that the inflation rate rises above 3 percent, the central bank raises nominal interest rates by 2 percentage points — and that each 1-percentage-point increase in real GDP moves the economy along the IS curve sufficiently to shrink real GDP by 1 percent.

As in question 1, suppose that agents in the economy have *adaptive expectations* of inflation — so that this year's expected inflation is equal to last year's actual inflation. What will be the course of inflation and unemployment in this economy in the years after the shift

in fiscal policy? Track the economy out 20 years, assuming that there are no additional shocks.

3. Suppose that all conditions in question 2 are the case, except that β equals 0.5 and that for each 1 percentage point the inflation rate rises above 3 percent, the central bank raises real interest rates by 1 percentage point. Again, suppose that each 1-percentage-point increase in real interest rates moves the economy along the IS curve sufficiently to shrink real GDP by 1 percent.

Finally, suppose that agents in the economy have *rational expectations* of inflation — so that this year's expected inflation is what an economist knowing the structure of the economy and proposed economic policies would calculate actual inflation was likely to be.

What will be the course of inflation and unemployment in this economy in the years after the shift in fiscal policy? Track the economy out 20 years, assuming that there are no additional shocks.

4 Suppose that an expensive government program is proposed: it is to spend money helping unemployed workers find new jobs, learn new skills, and possibly move to cities where unemployment is low. What effect is this program likely to have on the location of the Phillips curve in the long run?

5. Why do economists today tend to believe that monetary policy is superior to discretionary fiscal policy as a stabilization policy tool? In what circumstances that you can imagine would this belief be reversed?

The Budget Balance, the National Debt, and Investment

CHAPTER

QUESTIONS

From the standpoint of analyzing stabilization policy, what is the best measure of the government's budget balance?

From the standpoint of analyzing the effect of changes in the national debt on long-run growth, what is the best measure of the government's budget balance?

What is the typical pattern that the U.S. national debt follows over time?

How has experience in the past generation deviated from this traditional pattern of debt behavior?

What are the reasons that we should worry about a rising national debt?

What are the reasons that we shouldn't worry too much about a rising national debt?

14.1 INTRODUCTION

The *national debt* — the amount of money that the government owes those from whom it has borrowed — changes each year. In a year when government spending is less than tax collections, the difference is the **government surplus.** The national debt shrinks by the amount of the surplus. In a year when government spending is greater than tax collections, the difference is the **government deficit.** The national debt grows by the amount of the deficit. Call the debt D and the deficit d (and recognize that a surplus is a negative value of d). Then the relationship between the **debt and the deficit** is

$$\Delta D = d$$

where Δ (the Greek capital letter "delta") is, as before, a standard symbol for change. The change in the debt from year to year is equal to the deficit.

A government spending more than it collects in taxes (including the inflation tax noted in Chapter 8) must borrow the difference in order to finance its spending. A government borrows by selling its citizens and foreigners bonds: promises that the government will repay the principal it borrows with interest. These accumulated promises to pay make up the national debt.

Economists are interested in the debt and the deficit for two reasons. First, the deficit is a convenient and often handy — though sometimes treacherous — measure of fiscal policy's role in stabilization policy. It is an index of how government spending and tax plans affect the position of the IS curve. Second, the debt and deficit are closely connected with national savings and investment. A rising debt — a deficit — tends to depress capital formation. It lowers the economy's long-run steady-state growth path and reduces the steady-state GDP per worker. Moreover, a high national debt means that taxes in the future will be higher to pay higher interest charges. Such higher taxes are likely to further discourage economic activity and reduce economic welfare.

What to do about the national debt is one of the current flashpoints of American politics. The United States ran its national debt up by an enormous amount during the high-deficit Reagan and first Bush administrations. One of the main questions facing American voters and politicians now that the era of deficits is over is: What (if anything) should be done to undo the rise in the debt? Should the government run large surpluses in order to push the debt down to its late-1970s level (or even lower) — as Democratic politicians have argued in recent years? Or should the government cut taxes and not worry as much about reducing the national debt — as Republican politicians have argued in recent years? At the moment this issue hangs in the balance.

14.2 THE BUDGET DEFICIT AND STABILIZATION POLICY

The Budget Deficit and the IS Curve

An increase in government purchases increases aggregate demand. It shifts the IS curve out and to the right, increasing the level of real GDP for each possible value of the interest rate. A decrease in government tax collections also increases aggregate demand, also shifts the IS curve out. The government's budget deficit is equal to pur-

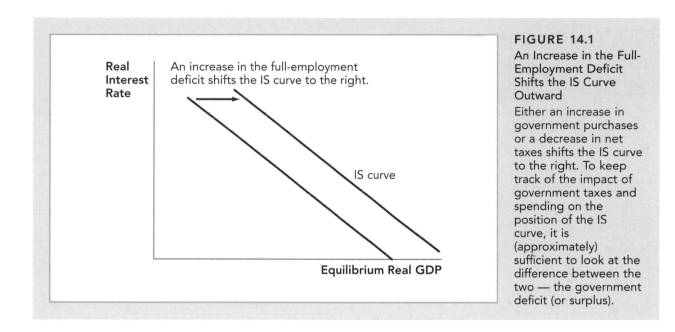

FIGURE 14.1
An Increase in the Full-Employment Deficit Shifts the IS Curve Outward
Either an increase in government purchases or a decrease in net taxes shifts the IS curve to the right. To keep track of the impact of government taxes and spending on the position of the IS curve, it is (approximately) sufficient to look at the difference between the two — the government deficit (or surplus).

chases minus net taxes. Why bother with two measures of fiscal policy — purchases and taxes — when you can just keep track of their difference?

This drive for simplification is the reason for focusing on the government's budget balance as a measure of fiscal policy. But it turns out that the right measure of budget balance is not the government's actual deficit (or surplus), as Box 14.1 explains. Instead, the right measure of fiscal policy is the **full-employment** or **cyclically adjusted deficit (or surplus)**: what the government's budget balance would be if the economy were at full employment. (See Figure 14.1.)

THE DEFICIT AS AN INDEX OF FISCAL POLICY: THE DETAILS

To see how the budget deficit can be used as an index of the effect of government policy on real GDP, return to the IS curve–based analysis of the determinants of real GDP that was conducted in Chapters 9 and 10. The effect on real GDP of a change in government spending is proportional to the value of the multiplier $1/(1 - MPE)$ (or $1/[1 - C_y(1 - t) + IM_y]$):

$$\Delta Y = \frac{1}{1 - C_y(1 - t) + IM_y} \times \Delta G$$

If the economy starts out at full employment with real GDP equal to potential output Y^*, then a change in tax rates has an effect on real GDP proportional to the product of the multiplier, the marginal propensity to consume C_y, and potential output Y^*:

$$\Delta Y = \frac{-1}{1 - C_y(1 - t) + IM_y} \times C_y Y^* \Delta t$$

Thus if both government purchases and tax rates change, the effect on real GDP will be given by the sum of these two formulas, which is

$$\Delta Y = \frac{1}{1 - C_y(1 - t) + IM_y} \times (\Delta G - C_y Y^* \, \Delta t)$$

Use ΔT^* to stand for the change in *full-employment tax collections* $Y^* \, \Delta t$, and add and subtract this change in full-employment tax collections from the right-hand side:

$$\Delta Y = \frac{1}{1 - C_y(1 - t) + IM_y} \times [(\Delta G - \Delta T^*) + (1 - C_y)\Delta T^*]$$

And use Δd^* to stand for the change in the *full-employment deficit* $\Delta G - \Delta T^*$ (or, when spending is low, the full-employment surplus): the difference between government purchases and what tax collections would be if the economy were at full employment:

$$\Delta Y = \frac{1}{1 - C_y(1 - t) + IM_y} \times [(\Delta d^*) + (1 - C_y)\Delta T^*]$$

Changes in government policy shift real GDP by (a) the product of the multiplier with the sum of the change in this full-employment deficit, Δd^*, and (b) an extra term equal to the multiplier by $(1 - C_y)\Delta T^*$.

Where does this extra term come from? Changes in government purchases affect aggregate demand directly and immediately, while changes in tax collections (and transfer payments) affect aggregate demand only to the extent that they affect consumption spending. The degree of this asymmetry depends on how far C_y is from 1.

If we are willing to simplify by ignoring this final term, then the change in the *full-employment* deficit Δd^* is a good approximate index of how changing fiscal policy affects the position of the IS curve, and real GDP. Perhaps the final term can be ignored because C_y is close to 1. Perhaps the final term can be ignored because of other, unmodeled factors. In any event, economists often do use the change in the full-employment deficit as an index of changes in fiscal policy. ◆

Measuring the Budget Balance

Unfortunately, the government budget bottom line reported in the newspapers is either the "unified cash" balance or the balance excluding social security. The first of these bottom lines is the difference between the money that the government actually spends in a year and the money that it takes in. This balance is called "unified" because it unifies all of the government's accounts and trust funds (including social security). This balance is called "cash" because it does not take account of either changes in the value of government-owned assets or the future liabilities owed by the government: It is just cash in minus cash out. The second of these bottom lines is equal to the unified cash balance minus the revenues and plus the expenditures of the social security program. It takes the social security system "off budget."

Why is the full-employment budget balance a better index than either of the more frequently mentioned **cash balance** measures? Consider a situation in which the government does not change either its purchases or its tax rates, and so there is no change in government fiscal policy. But suppose that monetary policy tightens: Real interest rates are raised, and so the economy moves up and to the left along a stable IS curve (see Figure 14.2). As the economy moves along the IS curve, real GDP falls

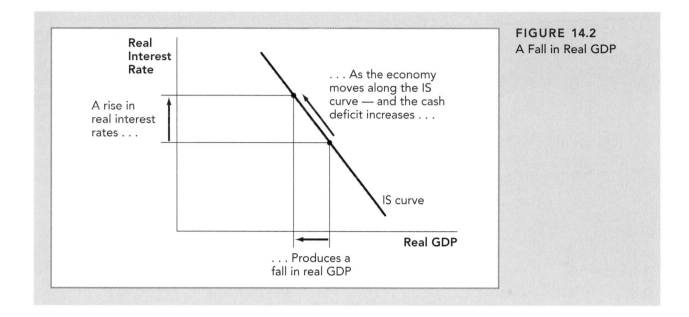

FIGURE 14.2
A Fall in Real GDP

and tax collections fall too. The government's cash deficit increases, even though there has been no change in government policy to shift the IS curve. The full-employment budget balance, however, remains constant. The fact that the cash

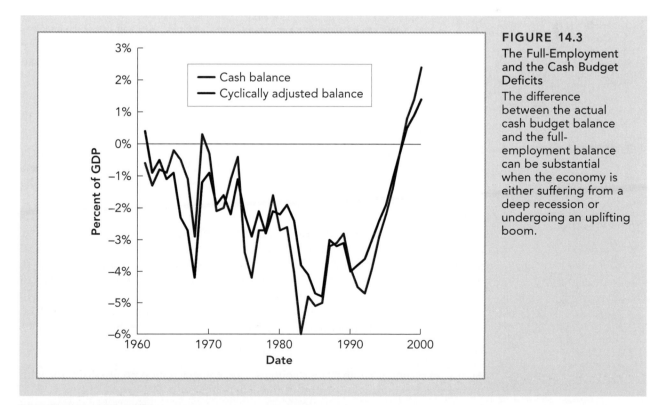

FIGURE 14.3
The Full-Employment and the Cash Budget Deficits
The difference between the actual cash budget balance and the full-employment balance can be substantial when the economy is either suffering from a deep recession or undergoing an uplifting boom.

Source: Congressional Budget Office.

budget balance changes as the economy moves along a constant IS curve means that it is not a good indicator of how the government's fiscal policy is affecting the location of the IS curve: The full-employment budget balance is better.

To turn the cash balance into the full-employment balance, we must adjust the budget deficit (or surplus) for the automatic reaction of taxes and spending to the business cycle, as done in Figure 14.3. When unemployment is high, taxes are low and social welfare spending high. The budget balance swings toward deficit. When unemployment is low, taxes are high and the budget balance swings toward surplus.

However, the cyclically adjusted budget deficit is not a perfect measure of the effect of taxing and spending on the position of the IS curve. And the standard budget deficit you see reported in the newspapers is not even a good measure of the effect of taxing and spending on the position of the IS curve.

RECAP   THE BUDGET DEFICIT AND STABILIZATION POLICY

The cyclically adjusted budget deficit is a good measure of the impact of the government's taxing and spending on aggregate demand. When the cyclically adjusted budget deficit rises, the IS curve shifts right as government policy becomes more stimulative. When the cyclically adjusted budget deficit falls, the IS curve shifts left as government policy becomes more contractionary.

14.3 MEASURING THE DEBT AND THE DEFICIT

In addition to cyclical adjustment, we could consider making three other adjustments to the reported budget balance. These adjustments matter, as Figure 14.4 shows.

Inflation

One adjustment economists make is to correct the officially reported cash budget balance for the effects of inflation. A portion of the debt interest paid out by the government to its bondholders merely compensates them for inflation's erosion of the value of their principal.

A good measure of the deficit should be a measure of whether the government is spending more in the way of resources than it is taking in: a measure of the change in the real debt that the government owes. At the end of the year the debt principal plus this inflation component of debt interest are together equal — in their power to purchase useful goods and services — to what the debt principal was at the start of the year. So the real interest that the government has paid on its debt is not equal to the nominal interest rate times the debt, $i \times D$, but to the real interest rate times debt, $r \times D$. The real deficit d^r is therefore related to the cash deficit d^c by

$$d^r = d^c - \pi \times D$$

Almost everyone who analyzes economic and budget policy prefers to work with these inflation-adjusted measures of the deficit and debt.

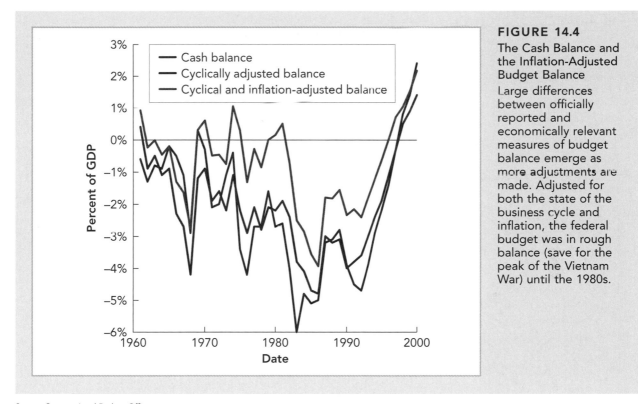

FIGURE 14.4
The Cash Balance and the Inflation-Adjusted Budget Balance

Large differences between officially reported and economically relevant measures of budget balance emerge as more adjustments are made. Adjusted for both the state of the business cycle and inflation, the federal budget was in rough balance (save for the peak of the Vietnam War) until the 1980s.

Source: Congressional Budget Office.

Public Investment

Yet another adjustment corrects for an asymmetry between the treatment of private and public assets. Private spending on long-lived capital goods is called "investment." A business that has total sales of $100 million, costs of goods sold of $90 million, and spends $20 million on enlarging its capital stock reports a profit of $10 million — not a deficit of $10 million. Standard and sensible accounting treatment of long-lived valuable assets in the private sector is definitely not to count their entire cost as a charge at the time of initial purpose, but instead to spread the cost out — a process called "amortization" — over the useful life of the asset. The government should do its accounting the same way, like a business, and amortize rather than expense its spending on long-lived assets.

There are periodic calls for a reform of the federal government budget to use *capital budgeting*. But few people use numbers based on capital budgeting. The principal reason that capital budgeting is resisted is political. Which government expenditures are capital expenditures? Aircraft carriers and nuclear weapons? The interstate highway system? Improvements to trails in the national parks? Head Start expenditures — money spent on educating poor children? (After all, it is an investment in their future.)

It is hard to see any long-run dividing line between government investment and government consumption expenditures that would be sustainable from a political point of view. Thus critics regard capital budgeting as simply too difficult to implement in a helpful way. Supporters, however, point out that not doing capital budgeting at all is, in a sense, worse than even the least helpful implementation. Nevertheless, relatively few of the uses to which budget balance numbers are put do correct for public investment. The fact that the numbers usually reported do not correct for public investment should be kept in mind: It tends to overestimate the real value of the outstanding national debt.

Liabilities and Generational Accounting

All of the issues surrounding capital budgeting appear again whenever the long-run future of the government's budget is considered. Back when I worked at the Treasury Department, some $10,000 a year was set aside for me in my Treasury pension account. It is as if my income had been $10,000 a year higher, and I had invested that extra $10,000 in U.S. government bonds. Bonds issued by the government appear on the books as part of the government's debt. But pension fund liabilities that the government owes to exworkers, such as me, do not.

Thus in a sense the right way to count the government's debt is to look not just at the bonds that it has issued but at all of the promises to pay money in the future that it has made. Indeed, a large chunk of the government's expenditures — those by the Medicare and social security trust funds, for example — are presented to the public in just this way. The social security deficit reported by the trustees of the social security system every spring is not the difference between social security taxes paid in and social security benefits paid out, but is instead the long-run, 75-year balance between the estimated value of the commitments to pay benefits that the social security system has made and will make, and the estimated value of the taxes that will be paid into the social security trust funds.

But the social security trustees' report covers just one program — albeit a big program. And great confusion is created by the fact that the social security systems expenditures and revenues are also included within the unified budget balance. Wouldn't it be better to bring all of taxation and spending within a long-run system like that currently used by social security?

Economists like Laurence Kotlikoff and Alan Auerbach say an emphatic yes. They propose — instead of the year-by-year budget balances — that the U.S. government shift to a system of "**generational accounting.**" Generational accounting would examine the lifetime impact of taxes and spending programs on individuals born in specific years, and provide a final balance that could be used for long-term planning. It is hard to escape the conclusion that Auerbach and Kotlikoff have a strong case. Yet few analysts of the budget use their generational accounting measures. Generational accounting is thus not part of the present state of macroeconomics, but I hope that it is part of its future.

14.4 ANALYZING DEBTS AND DEFICITS

Sustainability

The first question to ask about a government that is running a persistent deficit is: "Can it go on?" Is it possible for the government to continue running its current deficit indefinitely, or must policy change — possibly for the better, but also quite possibly for the worse?

The Steady-State Debt-to-GDP Ratio

The variable to look at to assess whether the government's current fiscal policy is sustainable is the time path of the ratio of the government's total debt to GDP, or the debt-to-GDP ratio, D/Y. Fiscal policy is *sustainable* if the debt-to-GDP ratio is heading for a steady state.

As in Chapters 4 and 5, we can analyze the debt-to-GDP ratio D/Y by looking to see if it heads for some steady-state value. At a steady-state value, both the numerator D and the denominator Y will be growing at the same proportional rate. We know that real GDP grows in the long run at a proportional annual rate $n + g$, where n is the annual growth rate of the labor force and g is the annual growth rate of the efficiency of labor.

What is the proportional growth rate of the debt, D? Adding time subscripts to keep things clear, the debt next year will be equal to

$$D_{t+1} = (1 - \pi)D_t + d$$

The real value of the debt shrinks by a proportional amount π as inflation erodes away the real value of the debt principal owed by the government, and grows by an amount equal to the officially reported cash deficit, d. As the economy grows, tax revenues grow roughly in proportion to real GDP and spending grows in proportion to real GDP too. So it makes sense to focus not on the deficit itself but on the deficit as a share of GDP, which we can call little delta (δ):

$$\delta = d/Y$$

Then the proportional growth rate of the debt is

$$\frac{D_{t+1} - D_t}{D_t} = -\pi + \delta \times \frac{Y_t}{D_t}$$

The debt-to-GDP ratio will be stable when these two proportional growth rates — of GDP and of the debt — are equal to each other:

$$n + g = -\pi + \delta \times (Y/D)$$

which happens when

$$\frac{D}{Y} = \frac{\delta}{n + g + \pi}$$

This is the steady-state level toward which the debt-to-GDP ratio will head (see Box 14.2). This is the level consistent with a constant cash-balance deficit of δ percent of GDP in an economy with long-run inflation rate π, and with long-run real GDP growth rate $n + g$.

THE EQUILIBRIUM DEBT-TO-GDP RATIO: AN EXAMPLE

Suppose that the economy is running a constant budget deficit of 4 percent of GDP year after year. Suppose further that the growth rate of the labor force is 2 percent per year, the growth rate of output per worker is 1 percent per year, and the inflation rate is 5 percent per year. What then will be this economy's **steady-state ratio of government debt to GDP?**

BOX
14.2

To determine the answer, simply plug the parameter values into the formula

$$\frac{D}{Y} = \frac{d}{n + g + \pi} = \frac{4\%}{2\% + 1\% + 5\%} = \frac{1}{2}$$

The steady-state debt-to-GDP ratio will be ½. If the current debt-to-GDP ratio is less than ½, the debt-to-GDP ratio will grow. If the current debt-to-GDP ratio is greater than ½, the debt-to-GDP ratio will fall.

Notice a similarity to the analysis of the equilibrium capital-output ratio way back in Chapter 4? The mathematical tools and models are the same, even though the phenomena in the world to which they apply are very different. Such recycling of a formal model in a different context is yet another trick economists use to try to keep their discipline and their models simple.

Is the Steady-State Debt-to-GDP Ratio Possible?

Why then do economists talk about deficit levels as being "unsustainable"? For any deficit as a share of GDP δ, the debt-to-GDP ratio heads for its well-defined steady-state value $\delta/(n + g + \pi)$.

This, however, is only half the story. The ratio of GDP to the debt that the government wants to issue heads for a stable value, yes. But are there enough investors in the world willing to hold that amount of debt? The higher the debt-to-GDP ratio, the riskier an investment financiers judge the debt of a country to be, and the less willing they are to buy and hold that debt.

A higher debt-to-GDP ratio makes investments in the debt issued by a government more risky for two reasons. First, revolutions — or other, more peaceful changes of government — happen. One of the things a new government must decide is whether it is going to honor the debt issued by previous governments. Are these debts the commitments of the nation, which as an honorable entity honors its commitments? Or are these debts the reckless mistakes made by and obligations of a gang of thugs, unrepresentative of the nation, to whom investors should have known better than to lend money for the thugs to steal? The holders of a government's debt anxiously await every new government's decision on this issue.

The higher the debt-to-GDP ratio, the greater the temptation for a new government to *repudiate* debt issued by its predecessor, hence the riskier it is to buy and hold a portion of that country's national debt.

Second, a government can control the real size of the debt it owes by controlling the rate of inflation. The (nominal) interest rate to be paid on government debt is fixed by the terms of the bond issued. The real interest rate paid on the debt is equal to the nominal interest rate minus the rate of inflation — and the government controls the rate of inflation.

Thus a government that seeks to redistribute wealth away from its bondholders to its taxpayers can do so by increasing the rate of inflation. The more inflation, the less the government's debt is worth and the lower the real taxes that have to be imposed to pay off the interest and principal on the debt. Whether a government is likely to increase the rate of inflation depends on the costs and benefits — and raising the rate of inflation does have significant political costs. But the higher the debt-to-GDP ratio, the greater the benefits to taxpayers of a sudden burst of inflation. When the debt-to-GDP ratio is equal to 2, a sudden 10 percent rise in the price level reduces the real wealth of the government's creditors and increases the real wealth of taxpayers by an amount equal to 20 percent of a year's GDP. By contrast, when the debt-to-GDP ratio is equal to 0.2, the same rise in the price level redistributes wealth equal to only 2 percent of a year's GDP.

Thus the government's potential creditors must calculate that the greater the debt-to-GDP ratio, the greater the benefits to the government of inflation as a way of writing down the value of its debt. The higher the debt-to-GDP ratio, the more likely it is that the government will resort to inflation. Thus the higher the debt-to-GDP ratio, the riskier it is to invest in a government's debt.

A deficit is *sustainable* only if the associated steady-state debt-to-GDP ratio is low enough that investors judge the debt safe enough to be willing to hold it. Think of each government as having a *debt capacity* — a maximum debt-to-GDP ratio at which investors are willing to hold the debt issued at reasonable interest rates. If this debt capacity is exceeded, then the interest rates that the government must pay on its debt spike upward. The government is faced with a much larger deficit than planned (as a result of higher interest costs). Either the government must raise taxes, or it must resort to high inflation or hyperinflation to write the real value of the debt down.

Effects of Deficits

Even if a given deficit as a share of GDP is sustainable, it still may have three types of significant effects on the economy. It may affect the political equilibrium that determines the government's tax and spending levels. It may, if the central bank allows it, affect the level of real GDP in the short run. And it will (except in very special cases) affect the level of real GDP in the long run.

The U.S. national debt today is below the level at which economists begin to watch the debt with anxious concern. There seems little chance that the deficit and debt will spiral upward out of control. The fears during the 1980s that the United States had put itself on a course for national disaster through a mounting national debt are now passed, as the government's cash balance is now in surplus.

The typical pattern the United States has followed is one of sharp spikes in the debt-to-GDP ratio during wartime, followed by paying off the national debt as a share of GDP during peacetime. It is easy to understand why governments usually run up large debts during wartime. Their survival, and perhaps the survival of their nation and their civilization, is at stake. So during major wars, governments use all the tools they have to gain control of resources for their fleets, armies, and airforces. And one of those tools is a substantial dose of government borrowing.

The great peaks in U.S. government debt as a share of total domestic product all come after the three major wars in which the U.S. has been engaged: the Civil War, World War I, and World War II. The minor peaks are mostly wartime peaks too: the initial level of debt as the federal government took over responsibility for state borrowing during the Revolutionary War, the uptick during the war of 1812, and a tiny uptick during the Spanish-American War at the end of the nineteenth century. (See Box 14.3 for some details.)

There are only two upward movements in the debt as a share of GDP not connected to wars: the rise in the national debt during the Great Depression of the 1930s, and the rise in the national debt during the Reagan and Bush presidencies of the 1980s (see Figure 14.6).

The reason that during peacetime the size of the government debt as a share of GDP falls is also straightforward. Economic growth raises real GDP and inflation

THE U.S. DEBT-TO-GDP RATIO: THE DETAILS

The United States ended the Revolutionary War with what was then thought of as a considerable national debt given the limited taxing capacity of late-eighteenth-century governments. The first secretary of the treasury, Alexander Hamilton, pressed hard and won congressional approval for the federal government to assume and pay the debts the individual states had incurred to fight the Revolutionary War. Hamilton believed that this assumption of the debt would make it easier for the federal government to borrow in the future. Moreover, he believed that if the government owed people money, there would be a strong interest group in favor of the continuation of the United States of America: Bondholders would like to be paid.

By the presidency of Andrew Jackson, however, virtually the entire debt run up first in the Revolutionary War and then in the War of 1812 had been repaid (see Figure 14.5). The Union debt run up during the Civil War was also repaid within a few decades. But then in quick succession came World War I, the Great Depression, and World War II, which together drove the U.S. national debt up to more than a year's GDP. Thereafter the growth of the economy, inflation, and more-or-less balanced budgets saw the debt fall relative to GDP until the coming of the 1980s with the Reagan tax cut and the resulting deficits and rapid increase in the debt once again.

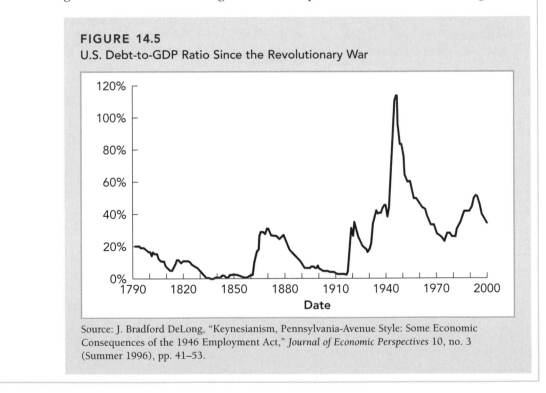

FIGURE 14.5
U.S. Debt-to-GDP Ratio Since the Revolutionary War

Source: J. Bradford DeLong, "Keynesianism, Pennsylvania-Avenue Style: Some Economic Consequences of the 1946 Employment Act," *Journal of Economic Perspectives* 10, no. 3 (Summer 1996), pp. 41–53.

provides an additional boost to nominal GDP. As long as the government's tax and spending programs are not grossly out of whack, in peacetime government debt tends to fall as a share of GDP. Before 1930 the government's tax and spending programs could not get out of whack in peacetime: There was barely any peacetime federal government. Since 1930, however, the peacetime federal government has in-

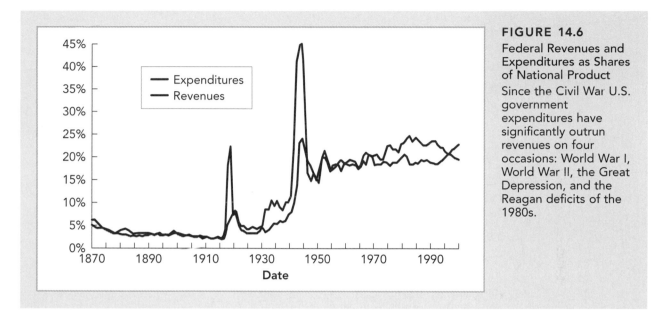

FIGURE 14.6
Federal Revenues and Expenditures as Shares of National Product
Since the Civil War U.S. government expenditures have significantly outrun revenues on four occasions: World War I, World War II, the Great Depression, and the Reagan deficits of the 1980s.

Source: J. Bradford DeLong, "Keynesianism, Pennsylvania-Avenue Style: Some Economic Consequences of the 1946 Employment Act," *Journal of Economic Perspectives* 10:3 (Summer 1996), pp. 41–53.

creased its share of the economy. Thus it was a surprise in the 1980s to see the emergence of substantial peacetime government budget deficits and a rising national debt-to-GDP ratio.

Partly because of higher spending on defense and other programs in the 1980s, partly because of substantial tax cuts, and partly because the productivity slowdown led real GDP growth to be smaller than previous forecasts, the Reagan presidency set in motion a series of deficits that ended by nearly doubling the burden of the federal government debt as a share of GDP. The rise in the debt was brought to an end by three factors:

- President Bush's economic advisers and the Democratic and Republican congressional leaders who persuaded him to go back on his campaign pledge of "read my lips, no new taxes" and to negotiate a serious deficit-reduction program including major reforms in congressional budget procedures in 1990.

- President Clinton, his economic advisers, and the Democratic members of Congress who made deficit reduction the highest priority of his administration in 1993.

- A healthy dose of good macroeconomic luck.

A fair but rough assignment of credit would give 40 percent to those who planned the 1990 deficit-reduction program, 30 percent to those who planned the 1993 deficit-reduction program, and 30 percent to sheer dumb good luck.

How important was the doubling of the debt as a share of GDP that took place in the 1980s and early 1990s? One view, held by a majority of economists, is that such large government deficits had three sets of effects. First, they had uncertain but probably destructive effects on the formulation of government spending and tax plans. Second, they had the potential to have *expansionary* effects on the economy in the short run. Third, they had contractionary effects on the economy in the long run. Thus the end of the era of deficits was, by the late 1990s, trumpeted by both political parties — by both then-President Clinton and then-Speaker of the House Gingrich — as an amazing and important political success, a policy accomplishment that would significantly improve the lives of Americans. Were they correct? On balance, probably yes.

Deficits: Political Consequences

One thread of political economic analysis holds that deficits have destructive political consequences: The possibility of financing government spending through borrowing makes the government less effective at advancing the public welfare. Electoral politics suffers from a form of institutional **voter myopia**: The benefits from higher government spending now are clear and visible to voters, and the costs of the higher taxes later that will be needed to finance the debt built up via deficit spending are distant, fuzzy, and excessively discounted. Moreover, the unborn and underage do not vote: Many of those who will be obligated to pay taxes to make interest payments on tomorrow's national debt do not vote today. The principle of "no taxation without representation" would seem to call for no long-term national debt — or, rather, for a national debt that is not larger than the government's capital stock.

Thus economists like Nobel Prize–winner James Buchanan have argued for a stringent balanced-budget rule. In Buchanan's view, only if political dialogue must simultaneously confront both the benefits of spending and the pain of the taxes needed to finance that spending can we expect a democratic political system to adequately and effectively weigh the costs and benefits of proposed programs.

Since the start of the 1980s, another argument has appeared: an argument for deficits created by tax cuts. The political system, its proponents argue, delivers steadily rising government spending unless it is placed under immediate and dire pressure to reduce the deficit. Therefore the only way to avoid an ever-growing inefficient government share of GDP is to run a constant deficit that politicians feel impelled to try to reduce. And should they ever succeed, the appropriate response is to pass another tax cut to create a new deficit. Only by starving the beast Leviathan that is government can it be kept from indefinite expansion.

The U.S. experience of the 1980s and 1990s tends to support James Buchanan's position, and to count against the alternative position. Few today are satisfied with the decisions about government spending and tax policy made in the 1980s and 1990s. Moreover, the deficits of the 1980s do not seem to have put downward pressure on federal spending. *Program* spending fell, but total spending rose because of the hike in interest payments created by the series of deficits in the 1980s. Because of the fact that interest payments are part of government spending, the deficits of the 1980s appear to have put not downward but upward pressure on the size of government.

Deficits: Short-Run Consequences

In the short run, the income-expenditure diagram tells us that a deficit produced by a tax cut stimulates consumer spending. A deficit produced by an increase in government spending increases government purchases. Either way, it shifts the IS curve out and to the right: Any given interest rate is associated with a higher equilibrium value of production and employment. If monetary policy is unchanged — if the LM curve does not shift — then output and employment rise in response to the tax cut. A deficit is expansionary in the short run.

Of course, the belief that deficits are expansionary — that they increase production and employment — in the short run hinges on the Federal Reserve's not changing monetary policy in response to the rise in the deficit. If the Federal Reserve does not want inflation to rise, it will respond to the rightward expansionary shift in the IS curve by tightening monetary policy and raising interest rates, neutralizing the expansionary effect of the deficit. Because the decision-making and policy implementation cycle for monetary policy is significantly shorter than the decision-making and policy implementation cycle for discretionary fiscal policy, the central bank can keep legislative actions to change the deficit from affecting the level of production and unemployment. The question is whether it will. The answer is yes. The central bank is trying its best to guide the economy along a narrow path without excess unemployment and without accelerating inflation. It has made its best guess as to what level of aggregate demand leads us along that path. In all likelihood its senior officials are uninterested in seeing the economy pushed away from that path by the fiscal policy decisions of legislators.

Deficits: Open-Economy Effects

Such an increase in the government's budget deficit also leads to an increase in the trade deficit. The outward shift in the IS curve pushes up interest rates. Higher interest rates mean an appreciated dollar — a lower value of the exchange rate and of foreign currency — therefore imports rise and exports fall.

Up to now we have implicitly assumed that the composition of aggregate demand has no effect on the productivity of industry. Businesses have been implicitly assumed to be equally happy and equally productive whether they are producing consumption goods, investment goods for domestic use, goods and services that the government will purchase, or goods for the export market. Yet this is unlikely to be true. Recall from your microeconomics courses that the point of international trade is to trade goods that your economy is especially productive at making for goods that your economy is relatively unproductive at making.

As large deficits that increase interest rates raise the value of the exchange rate, export industries — likely to be highly productive — shrink as exports shrink. This presumably reduces total productivity. Nobody, however, has a very sound estimate of how large these effects might be.

Long-Run Effects of Deficits

The Policy Mix: Deficits and Economic Growth

Higher full-employment deficits lead to low investment. On the IS-LM diagram, a deficit — whether from more government purchases or lower taxes — shifts the IS curve to the right, as shown in Figure 14.7. In any run long enough for the full-employment flexible-price model of Chapter 7 to be relevant, large full-employment deficits lead to lower total savings, higher real interest rates, and lower investment.

In the flexible-price context the analysis of persistent deficits is straightforward. Such deficits reduce national savings. Flow-of-funds equilibrium thus requires higher real interest rates and lower levels of investment spending.

Even in a sticky-price context it may well be that higher deficits reduce investment. The central bank can, and probably will, change monetary policy to neutralize the effect of the higher deficit on real GDP. The central bank chose its baseline monetary policy in order to try to strike the optimum balance between the risk of higher-than-necessary unemployment and the risk of rising inflation. The central bank does not want this balance disturbed by shifts in the IS curve, so it is highly likely to use monetary policy to offset the effect of the deficit-driven shift in the IS

FIGURE 14.7
Higher Full-Employment Deficits Reduce Investment

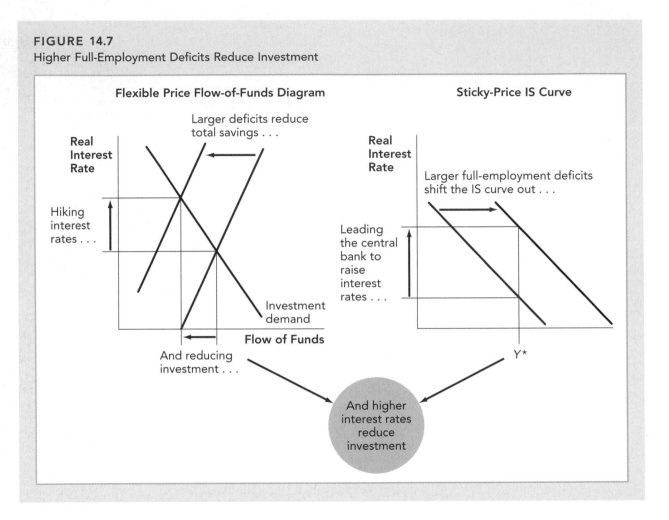

curve on the level of real GDP and employment. The IS curve shifts out, but interest rates rise, leaving real GDP unchanged and investment lowered.

Low investment reduces capital accumulation and productivity growth, putting the country on a trajectory to a lower steady-state growth path. Since the early 1960s, economists have argued that economic growth is fastest and the economy is best off when the policy mix pursued by the government and the central bank is one of tight fiscal policy (a government surplus) and loose monetary policy (a relatively low interest rate). Together this policy mix can produce full employment, high investment, and relatively rapid economic growth.

Over time, it has seemed that the U.S. government has the opposite bias. Certainly for a period of a decade and a half beginning with the Reagan tax cuts of the early 1980s, the U.S. economy had loose fiscal policy and tight monetary policy. Now the U.S. has a budget surplus and relatively high investment. Partly these are a result of good luck, but partly they are a result of politicians' taking economists' advice on the policy mix for the first time in more than a generation.

If the deficits continue for long, they will begin to have an effect on the economy's capital intensity. The reduction in national savings as a share of GDP will reduce the economy's steady-state capital-output ratio κ^*, which you will recall is equal to

FIGURE 14.8
Long-Run Effects of Persistent Deficits on Economic Growth

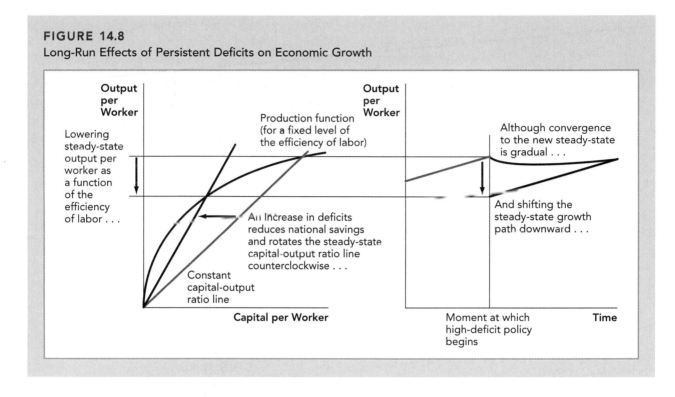

$$\kappa^* = \frac{s}{n + g + \delta}$$

the savings rate divided by the sum of the labor force growth, efficiency of labor growth, and depreciation rates.

A lower steady-state capital-output ratio implies a lower level of output per worker along the steady-state growth path for any given level of the efficiency of labor (see Figure 14.8). Thus a policy of persistent deficits will — as long as the rise in the deficit reduces national savings — reduce the long-run level of output per worker below what it would otherwise have been. (This, at least, is the conventional analysis of the interaction between deficits and long-run growth. It has been challenged by a group of professors centered on Harvard's Robert Barro — as discussed in Chapter 17 on the future of macroeconomics.)

Debt Service, Taxation, and Real GDP

But there are still more long-term effects. A higher deficit means a higher debt, which means that the government owes more in the way of interest payments to bondholders. Over time — even if the level of the deficit is kept constant — the increase in interest payment will require tax increases. And these tax increases will discourage entrepreneurship and economic activity. In addition to the reduction in output per worker resulting from the lower capital-output ratio, there will be an additional reduction in output per worker: The increased taxes needed to finance the interest owed on the national debt will have negative supply-side effects on production.

The interaction of macroeconomic policy, tax policy, incentives for production, and the level of real GDP deserves more space. No discussion of fiscal policy could be complete without noting, for example, a possible drawback of the progressive tax rates that create strong fiscal automatic stabilizers. The higher the marginal tax rate, the greater the danger that at the margin taxes will discourage economic activity — leading either to hordes of lawyers wasting social time executing negative-sum tax-avoidance strategies, to a shift away from aggressive entrepreneurship toward more cautious, less growth-promoting activities taxed at lower rates, or to a depreciated exchange rate (and thus less power to purchase imports) as capital flows across national borders to jurisdictions that have lower tax rates at the margin.

Thinking through these issues is complicated. Are government expenditures on infrastructure, basic research, and other public goods themselves productive? Do they raise total output by more than the increased tax rates threaten to reduce it? And what is the government's objective? After all, maximizing measured total output is the same thing as maximizing social welfare only if externalities are absent, and only if the distribution of total wealth corresponds to the weight individuals have in the social welfare function — with the tastes and desires of the rich being given more weight.

These topics are traditionally reserved for public finance courses, and are not covered in macroeconomics courses. But no one should think that an analysis of fiscal policy can start and end with the effects of discretionary fiscal policy and automatic stabilizers on the business cycle, and the effects of persistent deficits on national saving. There is much more to be thought about.

RECAP   ANALYZING DEBTS AND DEFICITS

A high government budget deficit has three types of significant effects on the economy. First, it will tend to swell the absolute size of the government in relation to GDP. Myopic voters will see the benefits of spending increases and not count the costs of future tax increases to finance them. Higher national debt levels increase interest payments, and the government must eventually raise taxes to make these interest payments. A high government budget deficit may — if the central bank allows it — raise real GDP in the short run by shifting the IS curve to the right. A high government budget deficit will in the long run slow economic growth, and lower real GDP below what it would otherwise have been.

Chapter Summary

1. The U.S. is usually a moderate-debt country. The level of the national debt with which U.S. politicians and voters are comfortable is not large relative to the debts of other countries. Only immediately after total wars does the U.S. national debt reach a high value relative to real GDP.

2. The 1980s and 1990s, however, saw steep rises in the national debt — unprecedented rises in peacetime. The era of deficits is now at an end. And the United States' national debt is still significantly below the level at which economists begin serious worrying about the consequences of the debt for the health of the economy.

3. From the standpoint of analyzing stabilization policy, the best measure of the government's stance is the full-employment deficit. The full-employment deficit is not a bad measure of the net effect of government policy on the location of the IS curve.

4. From the standpoint of analyzing the effect of changes in the national debt on long-run growth, the debt and deficit need to be adjusted for (a) inflation and (b) government investment. A third adjustment — for outstanding government liabilities — has been proposed and has some attractive features, but is not usually used.

5. Persistent deficits — a rising national debt — threaten to diminish national savings, reduce the level of output per worker along the economy's steady-state growth path, and retard economic growth.

6. Past deficits — a high ratio of current debt to GDP — threaten to reduce national prosperity because the higher taxes required to service the national debt act as a drag on economic activity.

Key Terms

deficit and surplus (p. 392)

debt and deficit (p. 392)

full-employment budget balance (p. 393)

cyclical adjustment (p. 393)

cash budget balance (p. 394)

inflation-adjusted budget balance (p. 397)

generational accounting (p. 398)

steady-state debt-to-GDP ratio (p. 399)

voter myopia (p. 404)

policy mix (p. 405)

Analytical Exercises

1. What is the typical pattern followed by the debt-to-GDP ratio in the United States over time?

2. How does the experience of the 1980s and 1990s differ from the typical U.S. pattern as far as the debt-to-GDP ratio is concerned?

3. Why are the deficits of the 1980s generally seen to have been a bad thing? What are the arguments that the deficits of the 1980s were a good thing?

4. Suppose someone asks you which measure of the government budget balance they should look at. How does your answer depend on the purpose for which they wish to use the budget balance?

5. Why might there be a long-run link between government budget deficits on the one hand and the inflation rate on the other?

Policy Exercises

1. Why might it make sense for a government to finance roads and other investments in public infrastructure through borrowing rather than through taxing today's taxpayers?

2. What effect in today's world do changes in tax and spending programs legislated by Congress and the president have on the level of real GDP in the short run?

3. What are likely to be the long-run effects of a fiscal policy that involves ever-present large budget deficits?

4. Today many politicians call for the government to exclude social security spending and taxes from the federal government budget. They argue that social security moneys should not be used to avoid recognizing the fact of possible deficits in other programs. What arguments can you think of to support the claim that the non-social-security budget balance is the more interesting and relevant measure? What arguments support the claim that the unified budget balance is the more interesting and relevant measure?

5. Suppose that in a debate you claim that large deficits lead to high interest rates and lowered investment spending, but your opponent claims that it is not fiscal policy that leads to high interest rates — it is too-tight monetary policy on the part of the central bank. How would you respond?

International Economic Policy

CHAPTER

QUESTIONS

How has the world organized its international monetary system?

What is a fixed exchange rate system?

What is a floating exchange rate system?

What are the costs and benefits of fixed exchange rates vis-à-vis floating exchange rates?

Why do most countries today have floating exchange rates?

Why has western Europe recently created a "monetary union" — an irrevocable commitment to fixed exchange rates within western Europe?

What were the causes of the major currency crises of the 1990s?

Up to this point this book has assumed that the economy's exchange rate is a **floating rate**, one that rises and falls freely as supply balances demand in the market for foreign exchange. This chapter changes the focus and considers alternative international monetary arrangements. How do such alternative arrangements — chiefly fixed exchange rate systems — work? What are the relative costs and benefits of fixed versus floating exchange rates? How did we arrive at our current system of largely floating exchange rates? And what difference does having this system make?

Our current system is unusual: for most of the past century the dominant regime for international exchange rates has been one of fixed, not floating, exchange rates. This chapter begins by sketching the economic history of the international monetary system in order to understand how we got here from there. It then analyzes how the economy works when the government fixes the exchange rate. The chapter concludes by analyzing some of the major international shocks to the world economy in the 1990s. Three separate major international financial crises (and a host of more minor crises) struck during that decade: the European crisis of 1992, the Mexican crisis of 1995, and the East Asian crisis of 1997–1998.

15.1 THE HISTORY OF EXCHANGE RATES

The Classical Gold Standard

What the Gold Standard Is

In the generation before World War I nearly all of the world economy was on a particular **fixed exchange rate** system: the **gold standard**. A government would *define* a unit of its currency unit as worth such-and-such an amount of gold. It would stand ready to buy or sell its currency for gold at that price at any time, in any amount. Such a currency was *convertible,* for it could be converted into gold freely (and gold could be converted into it freely). The currency's price in terms of gold was its *parity.*

When two countries were on the gold standard, their nominal exchange rate was fixed at the ratio of their gold parities. Someone wishing to turn British currency — pounds sterling — into U.S. currency — American dollars — could begin by taking British currency to the Bank of England and exchanging it for gold at the pound's parity. They would then ship the gold across the Atlantic to New York, take it to the U.S. Treasury office in New York, and exchange it for dollars.

At the post–World War II parities of the Bretton Woods "gold exchange" standard, the U.S. dollar was defined as equal to $1/35$ of a troy ounce of gold, and the British pound sterling was set equal to $1/15.58333$ ounce of gold. Thus the exchange rate of the dollar for the pound was £1.00 = $2.40. At the parities that had prevailed from 1879 to 1931 (with an interruption for World War I), the dollar-pound exchange rate was £1.00 = $4.86.

Suppose that supply and demand in the market for foreign exchange in 1910 had balanced not at £1.00 = $4.86 but at some other value — say £1.00 = $5.00. Someone with an idle pound sterling note could then get $5 for it if they sold it on the foreign exchange market. But with their $5 they could then buy enough gold at the U.S. Treasury to recover their original £1, and have 14 cents left over. So if the market exchange rate ever drifted up from £1.00 = $4.86 to £1.00 = $5.00, a huge mass of people selling pounds would enter the market and drive the exchange rate back to £1.00 = $4.86 as they attempted to carry out this **currency arbitrage**, outlined at greater length in Box 15.1.

Thus under the gold standard, nominal exchange rates were fixed at the ratio of

CURRENCY ARBITRAGE UNDER THE GOLD STANDARD: AN EXAMPLE

As long as central banks or treasuries stood ready to keep their currencies *convertible* at their gold parities, the ratio of two gold *parities* determined the nominal exchange rate. Why? Because of currency arbitrage. Anyone buying or selling one currency at any price other than the ratio of the two gold parities would find themselves facing an unlimited demand, and would soon find themselves losing a nearly unlimited amount of money.

Suppose that — as was originally envisioned under the Bretton Woods system — the U.S. Treasury stood ready to buy or sell gold from qualified parties at the price of $35 an ounce, that the British Treasury stood ready to buy or sell gold from qualified parties at the price of £15.58333 an ounce, but that the pound sterling was trading in the foreign exchange market not for the $2.40 that was the ratio of the gold parities, but instead for 10 percent more — $2.64.

Then someone with an ounce of gold could

- Trade it to the British Treasury for £15.58333.
- Then trade those pounds sterling for dollars in the foreign-exchange market and wind up with $38.50.
- Trade that $38.50 to the U.S. Treasury for 1.1 ounces of gold.
- Repeat the process as rapidly as possible, making a 10 percent profit each time the circle is completed.

Figure 15.1 shows these steps. Note that those who sell dollars for pounds at the rate of $2.64 = £1.00 are losing 10 percent of their value each time the circle is completed. The only things hindering this round-trip "arbitrage" process — as long as currencies remain convertible and parities remain fixed — are the costs of transporting and insuring the gold. Thus there can be very small fluctuations of exchange rates within the "gold points," but gold is cheap to transport and straightforward to insure: These fluctuations are minor indeed.

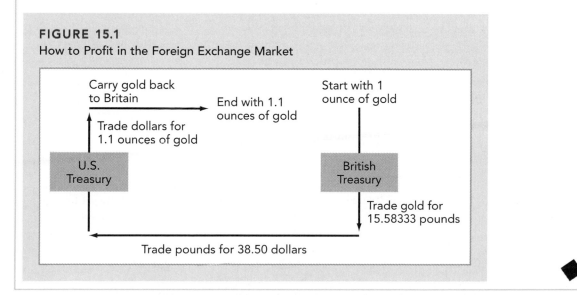

FIGURE 15.1
How to Profit in the Foreign Exchange Market

countries' gold parities, as Box 15.1 explains. The gold standard was a fixed exchange rate system.

This system grew up gradually. It originated when Sir Isaac Newton, in his government job as master of the mint in Britain, fixed the gold parity of the British pound sterling. Because the industrial revolution began in Britain, Britain became the largest trading nation in the world in the nineteenth century. Other countries' governments sought easy access to the British market for the products made by their citizens. A fixed gold parity meant the prices their countries' producers charged would appear stable to British customers. It also meant that British investors would not fear that depreciation and devaluation would erode the value of the principal that they had lent. Throughout the late nineteenth century, country after country joined the gold standard, as Figure 15.2 shows. By the eve of World War I the overwhelming fraction of world commerce and investment flowed between countries on the gold standard.

A Gold Standard Tends to Produce Contractionary Policies

Even in its turn-of-the-century heyday around 1900 it was already apparent that the gold standard had certain serious weaknesses as an international monetary system. The most important of these weaknesses was that the gold standard tended to be deflationary. In some circumstances it pushed countries to raise their interest rates to reduce production and raise unemployment. And it never provided a countervailing push to other countries to lower their interest rates to raise production and to lower unemployment.

To see why, we need to digress for a moment into the role played under a gold standard by a country's gold and other **foreign exchange reserves.** If the exchange rate is floating in country A, foreigners' earnings in currency A must be used to buy A's exports or be invested in country A: Nothing else can be done with them. Under a floating rate system a country's net exports *NX* plus net investment from abroad *NIA* must add up to zero:

$$NX + NIA = 0$$

The exchange rate moves up or down in response to the supply and demand for foreign exchange in order to make this so.

Under a gold standard things are different. There is an extra participant in the market: the country's treasury or central bank. One can do something else with foreign-currency earnings besides using them to buy imports or make investments abroad: Take them to the foreign country's treasury, turn them into gold, ship the gold back home, take the gold to the treasury there, and turn the gold into real spendable cash. Under a gold standard it is net exports plus net investment from abroad minus the flow of gold into your country — *FG* — that together add up to zero:

$$NX + NIA - FG = 0$$

What happens if a country finds that net exports plus net investment from abroad are less than zero? Its treasury will find itself losing gold, as a long line of foreigners come into its office, demand gold in exchange for currency, and then ship the gold out of the country. With each such transaction the country's gold reserves shrink. Eventually the government's gold reserves are gone.

At this point the country has a choice. One option is to abandon the fixed exchange rate system. It "closes the gold window," announces that the country will no longer buy back its currency at the established gold parity, abandons its fixed exchange rate, and lets the exchange rate float. The only other option is to solve its gold-outflow problem by making it more attractive for foreigners to invest. The way

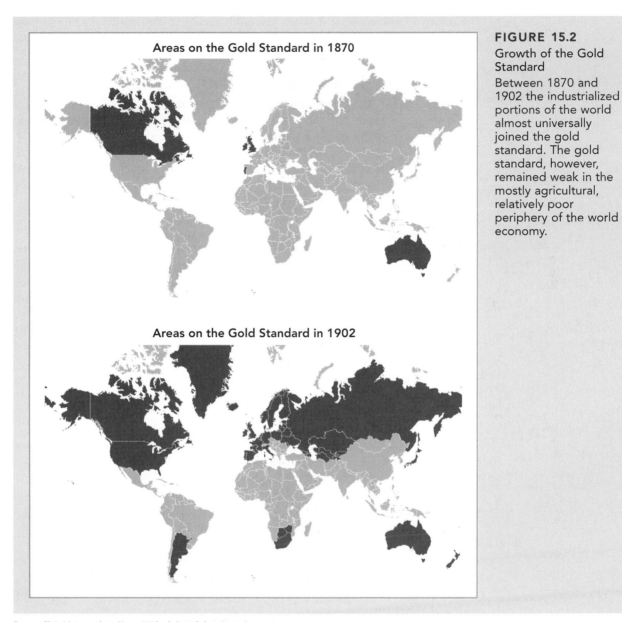

Areas on the Gold Standard in 1870

Areas on the Gold Standard in 1902

FIGURE 15.2
Growth of the Gold Standard
Between 1870 and 1902 the industrialized portions of the world almost universally joined the gold standard. The gold standard, however, remained weak in the mostly agricultural, relatively poor periphery of the world economy.

Source: Chris Meissner, http://econ161.berkeley.edu/~meissner/.

to increase net investment from abroad is to raise domestic interest rates. If net investment from abroad rises enough, gold will no longer flow out.

Thus under a gold standard countries running persistent balance-of-payments deficits — losing gold — must eventually raise interest rates to stay on the gold standard. However, surplus countries — those gaining gold — face no symmetrical crisis in which they must lower interest to stay on the gold standard. Their central banks can lower interest rates if they wish. But if they do not so wish, they can keep interest rates constant and watch their gold reserves grow.

This asymmetry means that a fixed exchange rate system like the gold standard puts periodic contractionary pressure on the world economy. Such pressure turned the interwar period into a disaster; the gold standard's contractionary pressure on countries to raise interest rates played a major role in generating the worldwide Great Depression of the 1930s.

The Collapse of the Gold Standard

The international gold standard was suspended when World War I began in 1914. Every country used inflation to help finance its massive war expenditures. Inflation was inconsistent with the gold standard. Under the gold standard attempted inflation simply leads everyone to immediately trade their currency for solid gold.

After World War I was over, politicians and central bankers sought to restore the gold standard. They believed that the pre–World War I system of a fixed exchange rate on the gold standard had been a success. They saw restoring it as an important step to restoring general economic prosperity. The gold standard had, after all, delivered 40 years of more rapid economic and industrial growth than the world had ever seen before.

It took more than half a decade to fully restore the gold standard. But the revived gold standard did not produce prosperity. Instead, in less than half a decade the Great Depression began, and the restored gold standard broke apart. The consensus of economic historians today is that the Great Depression had its principal origin in the United States, where for reasons not fully understood some combination of small shocks set off a downward spiral of destabilizing deflation. But a combination of mistaken policies and flaws in the functioning of the post–World War I gold standard then quickly amplified the Great Depression and propagated it around the world.

Economists Barry Eichengreen and Ben Bernanke argue that four factors made the post–World War I gold standard a much less secure monetary system than the pre–World War I gold standard:

- Everyone knew that governments could abandon their gold parities in an emergency. After all, they had done so during World War I. Thus everyone was eager to turn their holdings of currency into gold at the first sign of trouble. This meant countries had to maintain much larger gold reserves in order to keep the gold standard functioning.

- Everyone knew that governments had taken on the additional responsibility of trying to keep interest rates low enough to produce full employment.

- After World War I countries held their reserves not in gold but in foreign currencies. This was fine in normal times, but it meant that at the first sign of trouble not only would citizens show up trying to turn their currency into gold, but foreign central banks would do so too, greatly multiplying the magnitude of the gold outflow.

- The post–World War I surplus economies, the United States and France, did not lower their interest rates as gold flowed in.

These factors meant that as soon as a recession set in and gold drains began from countries with weak currencies, their governments found themselves under immediate and massive pressure to raise interest rates and lower output further if they were to stay on the gold standard. If they stayed on the gold standard, they guaranteed themselves high real interest rates and deep depression. If they abandoned the gold standard, they went against all the advice of bankers and gold standard advocates.

There was a clear divergence in the 1930s between those countries that abandoned the gold standard early in the Depression and those that stubbornly clung to gold, as shown in Figure 15.3. Those that clung to their gold parities found themselves forced to raise interest rates and contract their money supplies in order to

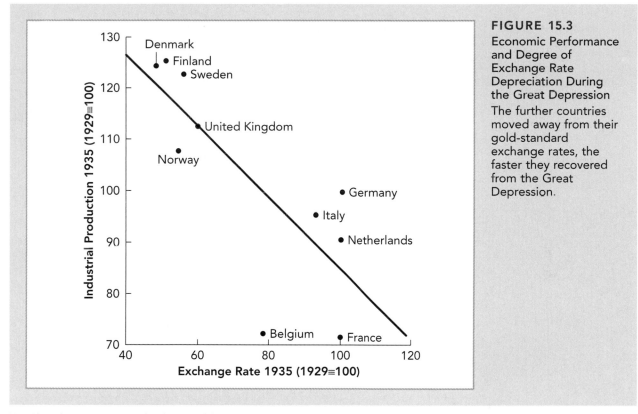

FIGURE 15.3

Economic Performance and Degree of Exchange Rate Depreciation During the Great Depression

The further countries moved away from their gold-standard exchange rates, the faster they recovered from the Great Depression.

Note: The exchange rate is in units of gold per unit of domestic currency.

Source: Barry Eichengreen and Jeffrey Sachs, "Exchange Rates and Economic Recovery in the 1930s," *Journal of Economic History* (December 1985), pp. 925–946.

avoid large gold losses that would rapidly exhaust their reserves. Those that abandoned the gold bloc and floated their exchange rates could avoid deflation, and avoid the worst of the Great Depression. By the middle of the 1930s the Great Depression was in full swing, and the gold standard was over.

The Bretton Woods System

After World War II, everyone took careful note of what they thought had gone wrong after World War I. Led by Harry Dexter White for the United States and John Maynard Keynes for Great Britain, governments tried to set up an international monetary system that would have all the advantages and none of the drawbacks of the gold standard. The system they set up came to be called the "Bretton Woods system," after a New Hampshire mountain resort town that was the location in late 1944 of a key international monetary conference.

Three principles guided this post–World War II international monetary system:

- In ordinary times, exchange rates should be fixed: Fixed exchange rates encourage international trade by making the prices of goods made in a foreign country predictable, and so have powerful advantages.

- In extraordinary times — whenever a country found itself in recession with a significantly overvalued currency that discouraged its exports, or found itself suffering from inflation because an undervalued currency raised the prices of imports and stimulated export demand — exchange rates should be changed. Such "fundamental disequilibrium" could and should be corrected by revaluing or devaluing the currency.

- An institution was needed — the International Monetary Fund — to watch over the international financial system. The IMF would make bridge loans to countries that were adjusting their economic policies. It would ensure that countries did not abuse their privilege of changing exchange rates. Exchange rate devaluation and revaluation would remain an exceptional measure for times of "fundamental disequilibrium," rather than becoming a standard tool of economic policy.

Our Current Floating-Rate System

The Bretton Woods system in its turn broke down in the early 1970s. The United States saw inflation accelerate in the 1960s. It found itself with an overvalued exchange rate and a significant trade deficit at the end of the 1960s. The United States sought to devalue its currency: to reduce the value of the dollar in terms of other currencies, so that exports would rise and imports would fall.

Policy makers in other countries thought that the United States should instead raise interest rates. Higher U.S. interest rates would make foreigners more willing to invest in the United States. The foreign currency committed to those investments could then be used to finance the excess of imports over exports that was the U.S. trade deficit. In the end the deadlock was broken by unilateral American action, and the Bretton Woods system fell apart.

Since the early 1970s the exchange rates at which the currencies of the major industrial powers trade against each other have been "floating" rates. The exchange rate is fixed by the government, but fluctuates according to the balance of demand and supply on that day in the foreign exchange market. There seem to be few if any prospects for a restoration of a global system of fixed exchange rates over the next generation. Thus this book has assumed as its standard case that exchange rates are free to float and are set by market forces.

Nevertheless, the older system is worth studying for three reasons. First, understanding the functioning of a fixed-rate system sheds light on how a floating-rate system works. Second, economic policy makers still debate the costs and benefits of a fixed-rate system relative to our current floating-rate system. Third, perhaps the pendulum will swing back in a generation and we will find ourselves once more in a fixed exchange rate system.

RECAP   HISTORY OF EXCHANGE RATES

In the generation before World War I nearly all of the world economy was on a fixed exchange rate system called the gold standard, under which nominal exchange rates were equal to the ratio of currencies' gold *parities*. The international gold standard was suspended when World War I began in 1914. After World War I attempts to rebuild the gold standard created a system vulnerable to shocks that played a key role in causing the Great Depression. Therefore, after World War II economists built a fixed exchange rate system — the Bretton Woods system — that they hoped would combine the advantages of fixed and floating rate systems. But this system collapsed in the early 1970s, and was followed by our current floating exchange rate system.

15.2 HOW A FIXED EXCHANGE RATE SYSTEM WORKS

We begin by distinguishing between two different economic environments in which a fixed exchange rate system works. The first is an environment of very high capital mobility, like the situation the advanced industrial countries face today. Foreign exchange speculators buy and sell bonds denominated in different currencies with a few presses on a keyboard. Hot money flows around the world nearly instantaneously in response to differences in expected rates of return. Governments find themselves in large part dancing to the tune called by international currency speculators

The second is an environment of lower capital mobility. The ability of individuals in one country to invest their money in a second is low and limited. Flows of capital out of one country into another are limited. And governments that are willing to do so can shift the exchange rate for a time by using their foreign exchange reserves to intervene in the foreign exchange market.

A fixed exchange rate is a commitment by a country to buy and sell its currency at fixed, unchanging prices in terms of other currencies. To carry out this commitment, the country's central bank and treasury must maintain *foreign exchange reserves*. If people come to your central bank or treasury under a fixed exchange rate system wanting to exchange your currency for pounds sterling or gold bars, the central bank or treasury must have the pounds sterling or the gold bars to trade to them.

But the foreign exchange reserves of a country are limited. With today's high degree of capital mobility the world has a great many potential foreign exchange speculators. All of them are seeking to make sure that their wealth is invested in the place that offers the highest expected return. Their decisions about where to invest their money are the result of a delicate balance between greed and fear, and all the foreign exchange reserves a government has cannot materially alter the balance of foreign exchange supply and demand for more than a day or two.

High Capital Mobility

Under high capital mobility, countries' foreign exchange reserves are all but irrelevant. The real exchange rate is set by the same exchange rate equation we have seen before, as greed balances fear in the mind of the typical foreign exchange speculator:

$$\varepsilon = \varepsilon_0 - \varepsilon_r (r - r^f)$$

Remember, in this equation ε_0 is foreign exchange speculators' beliefs about the long-run equilibrium value of the real exchange rate; $r - r^f$ is the difference between home and foreign real interest rates; and ε_r is a parameter that tells at what point fear balances greed: It tells how much extra speculators would be willing to bid up the value of dollar-denominated assets if those assets had an extra 1 percentage point per year interest rate differential. The higher the interest rate differential in favor of the home country, the lower the exchange rate (which, you recall, is defined as the value of foreign currency). (See Figure 15.4.)

Why must this equation for the exchange rate hold? Suppose that the government sets a fixed parity such that the fixed value of foreign currency ε^* is lower than given by the equation above. Foreign exchange speculators see foreign currency as a bargain. The extra interest return and potential capital gain from appreciation they get from investing their money in foreign currency–denominated assets more than offsets any risks. So foreign exchange speculators come to the government to sell it the

FIGURE 15.4

The Real Exchange Rate, Long-Run Expectations, and Interest Rate Differentials

When there is no differential between home and foreign real interest rates, the value of the real exchange rate is ε_0: what foreign exchange speculators believe and expect the long-run equilibrium value of the exchange rate to be. When home interest rates are higher than foreign interest rates, the value of the exchange rate is lower. When home interest rates are lower than foreign interest rates, the value of the exchange rate is higher.

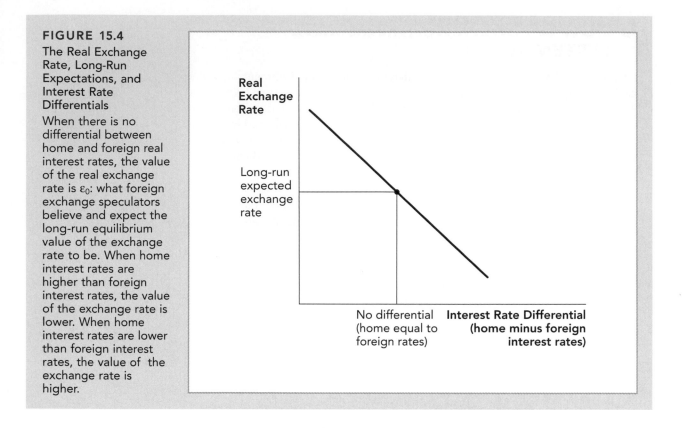

(overvalued) home currency and buy from it the (undervalued) foreign currency at the fixed exchange rate parity. The government spends down its reserves, buying its own currency in exchange for its stocks of other countries' currencies and of gold: It is a fixed exchange rate system after all.

The next day — or hour, or minute — the foreign exchange speculators do it again. And again. And again. The government rapidly runs out of reserves. When its reserves are gone, it can no longer buy and sell foreign currency for domestic currency at the fixed exchange rate parity because it no longer has any foreign currency — or gold — to sell. How long does this process take? Under high capital mobility, hours or days. There are lots of potential foreign exchange speculators. They are all eager to profit by betting against a central bank, especially a central bank that is carrying out its exchange transactions not for economic but for political reasons.

Thus if the government wants to keep the exchange rate at ε^*, its central bank must set interest rates so that the equilibrium value of the exchange rate produced by the equation

$$\varepsilon = \varepsilon_0 - \varepsilon_r(r - r^f)$$

corresponds to the desired fixed exchange rate value ε^*.

In order for this equation to hold, the central bank must set the domestic real interest rate r at

$$r = r^f + \frac{\varepsilon_0 - \varepsilon^*}{\varepsilon_r}$$

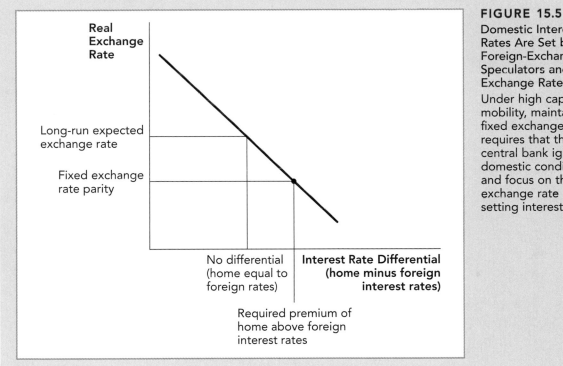

FIGURE 15.5
Domestic Interest Rates Are Set by Foreign-Exchange Speculators and the Exchange Rate Target
Under high capital mobility, maintaining a fixed exchange rate requires that the central bank ignore domestic conditions and focus on the exchange rate alone in setting interest rates.

Monetary policy no longer can play a role in domestic stabilization: You cannot ask the central bank to lower interest rates to fight unemployment or raise interest rates to fight inflation because the interest rate is already devoted to maintaining the fixed exchange rate system, as Figure 15.5 shows. Under a fixed exchange rate system with high capital mobility, not macroeconomic policy makers but international currency speculators determine the interest rate.

This means that international financial shocks coming from abroad are immediately transmitted to the domestic economy:

- An increase in foreign interest rates r^f requires an immediate, point-for-point increase in domestic interest rates — and a move up and to the left along the IS curve.

- An increase in foreign exchange speculators' view of the long-run fundamental value of the exchange rate ε_0 requires an immediate increase in domestic interest rates of $\varepsilon_0/\varepsilon_r$.

Figure 15.6 shows these effects.

Countries on fixed exchange rate systems find their interest rates tightly linked. This led John Maynard Keynes to warn in the 1920s against an attempt by Britain to return to the fixed exchange rate gold standard. It would, Keynes warned, force Britain to receive the full force of interest rate shocks delivered by the unstable U.S. economy. Earlier, when Britain was the leading industrial power before World War I, people expressed it differently: "When [the] London [money market] catches cold," they said, "Buenos Aires [or New York or Sydney] catches pneumonia."

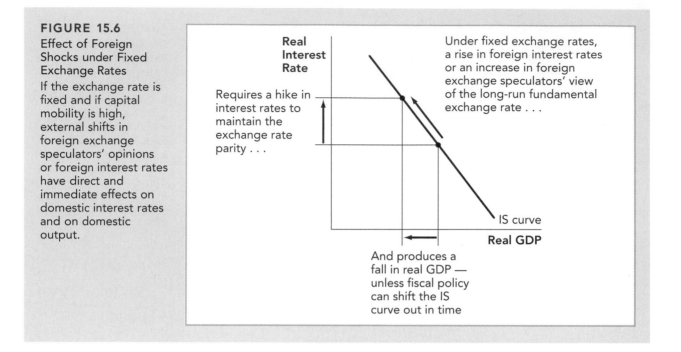

FIGURE 15.6

Effect of Foreign Shocks under Fixed Exchange Rates

If the exchange rate is fixed and if capital mobility is high, external shifts in foreign exchange speculators' opinions or foreign interest rates have direct and immediate effects on domestic interest rates and on domestic output.

Barriers to Capital Mobility

Now turn to the case of lower, as opposed to higher, capital mobility. Suppose that there are sufficient barriers to international financial flows to make it difficult and costly to move money across national borders. Thus the government's foreign exchange reserves are sizable relative to flows of capital. Capital mobility today is limited for many developing countries with "thin" financial markets. Capital mobility was limited for all countries only a few decades in the past. It may be limited in the future as well, either as future governments impose explicit controls on types of transactions or as small taxes on international transactions levied by future governments put sand in the wheels of international finance.

If capital mobility is low, the rate at which the government buys or sells its currency for foreign exchange has an impact on foreign exchange supply and demand and thus on the current exchange rate. The exchange rate is determined by foreign currency speculators' expectations, interest rate differentials, and also the speed at which the government is accumulating or spending its foreign exchange reserves (R):

$$\varepsilon = \varepsilon_0 - \varepsilon_r \times (r - r^f) + \varepsilon_R \times \Delta R$$

A change ΔR in foreign exchange reserves raises the value of the exchange rate by an amount equal to the slope of a demand parameter ε_R times the change in reserves. When the government is accumulating reserves, the value of foreign currency is higher than it would otherwise be: The government is in there buying foreign currency, raising the demand. When the government is spending reserves, the value of foreign currency is lower than it would otherwise be.

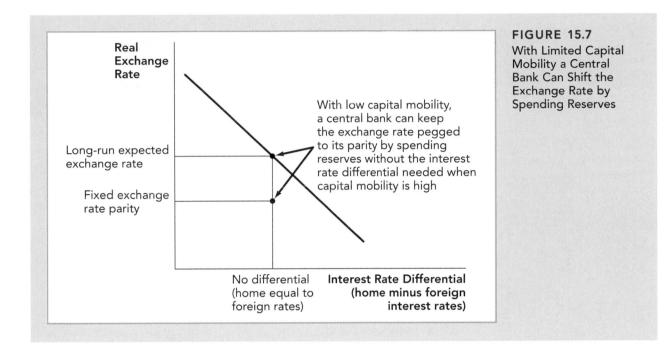

FIGURE 15.7
With Limited Capital Mobility a Central Bank Can Shift the Exchange Rate by Spending Reserves

Under such barriers to capital mobility, the central bank regains some freedom of action to use monetary policy for domestic uses. It does not have to directly and immediately transmit adverse shocks due to foreign exchange speculator confidence or foreign interest rates to the domestic economy in the form of higher interest rates and a recession. As long as it has reserves, it can choose to let them run down for a while rather than raising domestic interest rates (Figure 15.7). The domestic interest rate r is not

$$r = r^f + \frac{\varepsilon_0 - \varepsilon^*}{\varepsilon_r}$$

Instead, it is

$$r = r^f + \frac{\varepsilon_0 - \varepsilon^*}{\varepsilon_r} + \frac{\varepsilon_R}{\varepsilon_r} \times \Delta R$$

But the amount of freedom of action for monetary policy is limited by the sensitivity of exchange rates to the magnitude of foreign exchange market interventions performed by the central bank, and by the amount of reserves. The level of foreign exchange reserves must be positive:

$$R \geq 0$$

Policies that spend reserves cannot be continued forever, because once the government's foreign exchange reserves have fallen to zero it can no longer finance interventions in the foreign exchange market. (Note, however, that reserves can be replenished if they drop dangerously close to zero. That is what loans from the IMF, or from other major economy central banks, are for.)

> **RECAP   HOW A FIXED EXCHANGE RATE SYSTEM WORKS**
>
> In an environment of very high capital mobility, monetary policy no longer can play a role in domestic stabilization if you have a fixed exchange rate: International currency speculators rather than macroeconomic policy makers determine the value of your domestic interest rate. In an environment of low capital mobility, central banks have some freedom of action to set domestic interest rates to help the domestic economy, but their freedom of action is limited and is constrained by foreign exchange speculators and by limited foreign exchange reserves.

15.3 THE CHOICE OF EXCHANGE RATE SYSTEMS

Economists either applaud or deplore the breakdown of the Bretton Woods system and the resort to floating exchange rates, depending on their underlying philosophy. For some, like Nobel Prize–winner Milton Friedman, the exchange rate is a price. Economic freedom and efficiency require that prices be set by market supply and demand. They should not be set by the decrees of governments. Thus the replacement of the fixed exchange rate, administered-price Bretton Woods system by the floating exchange rate, market-price system of today is a very positive change.

For others, like Nobel Prize–winner Robert Mundell, the exchange rate is the value that the government promises that the currency it issues will have. A stable exchange rate means that the government is keeping the contract it has made with investors in foreign countries. To let the exchange rate float is to break this contract — and everyone knows that markets work only if people do not break their contracts. Thus the replacement of the fixed exchange rate, administered-price Bretton Woods system by the floating exchange rate, market-price system of today is a very negative change.

I think that the right answer is "It depends." High philosophy is all very well, but what should really matter are the details of how the choice of an exchange rate regime affects the economy.

Benefits of Fixed Exchange Rates

Under a floating exchange rate system, exporters and firms whose products compete with imported goods never know what their competitors' costs are going to be. Exchange rate–driven fluctuations in the costs to their foreign competitors are an extra source of risk, and businesses do not like unnecessary risks. The fact that exchange rates fluctuate discourages international trade, and makes the international division of labor less sophisticated than it would otherwise be. Fixed exchange rate systems avoid these costs, and encourage international trade by reducing exchange rate fluctuations as a source of risk. They avoid the churning of industrial structure — the pointless and inefficient shift of resources into and out of tradable goods sectors —

as the exchange rate fluctuates around its fundamental value. That is an important advantage. That advantage was behind the decision of nearly all western European countries at the start of 1999 to form a *monetary union:* to fix their exchange rates against each other irrevocably, so that even their national currencies will eventually disappear.

Fixed exchange rate systems avoid some political vulnerabilities as well. Large exchange rate swings are a powerful source of political turmoil. This political turmoil is avoided by fixed exchange rate systems.

Costs of Fixed Exchange Rates

Under fixed exchange rates, monetary policy is tightly constrained by the requirement of maintaining the exchange rate at its fixed parity. Interest rates that are too low for too long exhaust foreign exchange reserves, and are followed either by a sharp tightening of monetary policy or by an abandonment of the fixed exchange rate. A floating exchange rate allows monetary policy to concentrate on maintaining full employment and low inflation at home — on attaining what economists call **internal balance.** By contrast, under a fixed exchange rate system the level of interest rates must be devoted to maintaining **external balance** — the fixed exchange rate. And fixed exchange rates have the disadvantage of rapidly transmitting monetary or confidence shocks: Interest rates move in tandem all across the world in response to shocks. The central bank must respond to any shift in international investors' expectations of future profitability or future monetary policy by shifting short-term interest rates.

This is the cost-benefit calculation facing those who have to choose between fixed and floating exchange rates. Is it more important to preserve the ability to use monetary policy to stabilize the domestic economy, rather than dedicating monetary policy to maintaining a constant exchange rate? Or is it more important to preserve the constancy of international prices, and thus expand the volume of trade and the scope of the international division of labor?

Canadian economist Robert Mundell set out the terms under which fixed exchange rates would work better than floating ones with his concept of an "optimal currency area." Mundell said, the major reason not to have fixed exchange rates is that floating exchange rates allow adjustment to shocks that affect two countries differently. This benefit would be worth little if two countries suffer the same shocks, and react to them in the same way. It would also be worth little if factors of production possessed high mobility: Then the effects of shocks would be transient because labor and capital would rapidly adjust, and the benefits from different policy reactions to economic shocks would be small. (See Box 15.2.)

ARE WESTERN EUROPE AND THE UNITED STATES OPTIMAL CURRENCY AREAS? AN EXAMPLE

BOX
15.2

Today the two largest economic regions within which exchange rates are fixed are the United States and western Europe's "euro zone." California, for example, does not have a separate exchange rate vis-à-vis the rest of the United States. Almost all of the countries of western Europe are now committed to their common currency, the euro. Does this make economic sense? Or should there be a separate "California dollar" to allow California to have a different monetary policy than the rest of America?

Few economists today would maintain that western Europe's euro zone meets Robert Mundell's criteria for an optimal currency area. Shocks to the economy of Portugal are very different from shocks to the economy of western Germany. Southern Italy has few similarities in economic structure with Denmark. Vulnerability to different shocks would be relatively unimportant if factors of production were mobile. But the fact that different European countries have different languages means there is little chance that a boom in Denmark and a bust in Portugal will see large-scale migration to compensate.

Why then has western Europe embarked on monetary union? One reason is that some economists and policy makers hope that the benefits from economic integration are very large indeed — large enough to offset even substantial costs from adopting a common currency. But the main reason is that European monetary unification is not so much an economic as a political project: an attempt to knit Europe together as a single entity whether or not monetary union makes narrow economic sense.

Practically all economists today believe, by contrast, that the United States is an optimal currency area, although the U.S. economy's regions are no more subject to common shocks than western Europe's countries are. The mid-1980s saw the high dollar decimate midwestern manufacturing while leaving most of the rest of the country much less affected. The health of the economies of Texas and Oklahoma still depends substantially on the price of oil. Southern California's defense-industry boom and bust of the 1980s and early 1990s and northern California's high-tech boom of the 1990s make it clear that California is so big a state that its component parts experience very different economic shocks. But even though the United States' component parts experience different shocks, factor mobility across the United States is remarkably high. Capital and workers move to where returns and wages are high with remarkable speed — fast enough that it is hard to believe that different parts of the United States could gain substantially from following the different monetary policies that separate currencies and floating exchange rates would allow. ◆

As far as the United States, western Europe, and Japan are concerned, the issue of fixed versus floating exchange rates appears to have been decided: None of these three powers is willing to sacrifice its freedom of action in monetary policy. Within western Europe the answer also appears clear: Monetary union means that there is now one pan-European monetary policy, and Italy, for example, no longer retains the ability to use monetary policy to lower interest rates in Milan when unemployment is relatively high. Elsewhere in the world, the question is still under debate.

Moreover, fixed exchange rate systems have one more major disadvantage: They seem to make large-scale currency crises more likely. The decade of the 1990s has seen three major large-scale currency crises, all of which have threatened prosperity in the immediately affected countries, and all of which raised fears (initially at least) of their much wider spread to the world economy as a whole.

15.4 CURRENCY CRISES

The European Crisis of 1992

The first of the three major financial crises that hit the world economy in the 1990s came in the fall of 1992. In 1990 West German Chancellor Helmut Kohl reunified Germany, a country that had been divided since the end of World War II first into zones of occupation — French, British, American, and Russian — and then into two separate countries — East Germany and West Germany.

The two parts of Germany had very similar levels of economic development and economic structures before World War II. But since World War II they had diverged. West Germany had become one of the richest and most developed economies on earth, while East Germany had turned into a standard communist economy with dirty industry, inefficient factories, and inadequate infrastructure. Chancellor Kohl undertook a program of massive public investment to try to bring East Germany up to the West German standard as quickly as possible.

The expansion of German government purchases shifted the German IS curve to the right in the years after 1990. The German central bank, the Bundesbank, responded by raising real interest rates in order to keep real GDP in the range thought to be consistent with the Bundesbank's inflation targets (see Figure 15.8).

The rise in the real interest rate generated a rise in the German exchange rate vis-à-vis the dollar and the yen, and a sharp fall in net exports as capital flowed into Germany. The other countries of western Europe had then fixed their exchange rates relative to the German mark as part of the European Exchange Rate Mechanism (ERM). Britain, France, Italy, and other countries found themselves trapped: The rise in interest rates in Germany required that they too increase interest rates because r^f had risen in the equation

$$r = r^f + \frac{\varepsilon_0 - \varepsilon^*}{\varepsilon_r}$$

and r had to rise in response if the ERM was to be maintained. Without the surge of spending found in Germany and without the ability or desire to rapidly shift policy to run large deficits, such increases in interest rates threatened to send the other European economies into recession (see Figure 15.9).

Politicians in other European countries — Britain, Sweden, Italy, France, and elsewhere — promised that their commitment to their fixed exchange rate parity was

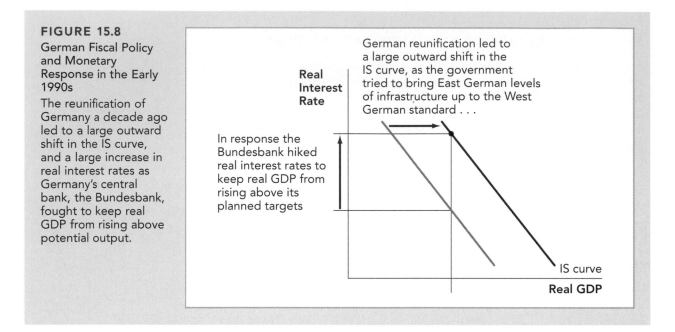

FIGURE 15.8
German Fiscal Policy and Monetary Response in the Early 1990s

The reunification of Germany a decade ago led to a large outward shift in the IS curve, and a large increase in real interest rates as Germany's central bank, the Bundesbank, fought to keep real GDP from rising above potential output.

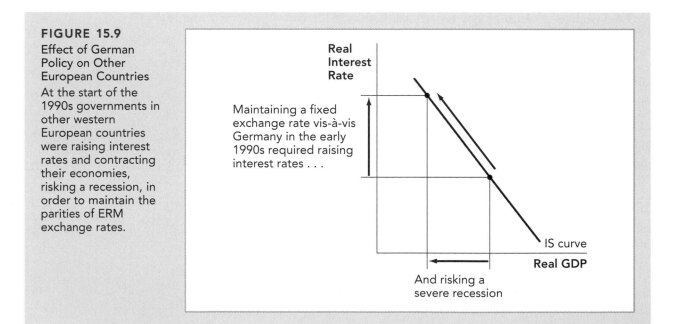

FIGURE 15.9
Effect of German Policy on Other European Countries

At the start of the 1990s governments in other western European countries were raising interest rates and contracting their economies, risking a recession, in order to maintain the parities of ERM exchange rates.

absolute. They promised that high interest rates and the risk of a domestic recession were prices worth paying for the benefits of a fixed exchange rate system within western Europe itself. But foreign exchange speculators did not believe they would keep their promise to maintain the fixed exchange rate parity when unemployment began to rise.

Thus foreign exchange speculators' expectations of the long-run fundamental real value of the exchange rate, ε_0, rose as well. This expectation that other European currencies would lose value vis-à-vis the German mark in the long run put their values under pressure in the short run as well.

The domestic real interest rate required to maintain the exchange rate parity, given by

$$r = r^f + \frac{\varepsilon_0 - \varepsilon^*}{\varepsilon_r}$$

was rising not just because of higher real interest rates in Germany but also because of foreign exchange speculators' more pessimistic expectations. The governments of much of western Europe found themselves in a trap. Different governments undertook different strategies:

- First, some tried to avoid the consequences of the shift in expectations. They spent reserves like water in the hope that a demonstrated commitment to maintain the parity would reverse the shift in speculator expectations. All this did was give international currency traders like George Soros the opportunity to make profits measured in the billions by betting on the abandonment of the fixed exchange rate. Economists Maurice Obstfeld and Ken Rogoff report that the British government may have lost $7 billion in a few hours during the September 1992 speculative attack on the pound.

- Second, some tried to demonstrate that they would defend the parity no matter how high the interest rate required to keep the exchange rate fixed. The Swedish government raised its overnight interest rate to 500 percent per year for a brief time. But all this did was reinforce speculators' opinion that the political and economic cost of keeping the exchange rate parity was too high for governments that sought to win reelection.

- Third, some abandoned their parity against the German mark, and let their currencies float as they turned monetary policy for a while to setting interest rates consistent with *internal balance*.

In less than two months what had seemed a durable framework of fixed exchange rates in western Europe had collapsed into a floating rate system.

But governments interested in long-run exchange stability within Europe regrouped. They proposed to try again to fix their exchange rates, with the European Monetary Union that began in January 1999. This time, however, they decided not to peg their exchange rates while keeping their national currencies (thus retaining at least the possibility of someday changing parities), but to eliminate their separate national currencies entirely: not fixed exchanged rates, but monetary union. The hope was to eliminate once and for all any fear or expectation that exchange rates might ever change again.

The Mexican Crisis of 1994–1995

In the winter of 1994–1995 the second of the major currency crises of the 1990s hit the world economy. The Mexican peso crisis came as a shock to economists and to economic policy makers. Previous speculative attacks on and collapses in the value of currencies had occurred for one of two reasons. In situations of limited capital mobility, governments with overvalued exchange rates and large inflation-financed budget deficits had suffered speculative attacks. And in cases like western Europe in

1992, currencies had suffered speculative attacks when speculators judged that the policies needed to maintain fixed exchange rates had become inconsistent with the government's political survival.

Mexico, however, fit neither of these two cases. The government's budget was balanced, so an outbreak of renewed inflation was not generally expected. The government's willingness to raise interest rates was not in question: In the end the government of Mexico raised real interest rates to 40 percent per year during the crisis. The Mexican peso was not clearly overvalued: In the winter of 1993–1994 the Mexican government had conducted large exchange rate interventions and had eased monetary policy to try to keep the value of the peso from rising. Yet the Mexican peso lost half of its value in four months starting in December of 1994. The peso fell from about 3.5 to about 7 to the U.S. dollar before recovering somewhat in the summer of 1995 (see Figure 15.10).

The sudden reversal of investor expectations about the long-run value of the Mexican peso was startling. At the start of 1994 Mexico had just joined the world's club of industrialized countries, the Organization for Economic Cooperation and Development (OECD). It had just entered into the North American Free Trade Agreement (NAFTA), which granted Mexico guaranteed tariff-free markets for its products in the largest consumer economy on earth. Expectations were that the Mexican peso would strengthen in real terms in the future, and that the profits from investing in Mexico were high.

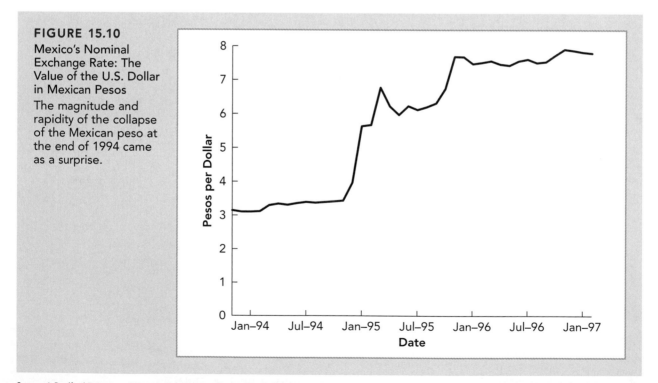

FIGURE 15.10

Mexico's Nominal Exchange Rate: The Value of the U.S. Dollar in Mexican Pesos

The magnitude and rapidity of the collapse of the Mexican peso at the end of 1994 came as a surprise.

Source: J. Bradford DeLong and Barry J. Eichengreen, "Between Meltdown and Moral Hazard: Clinton Administration International Monetary and Financial Policy," in Jeffrey Frankel and Peter Orszag, eds., *American Economic Policy in the 1990s* (forthcoming).

Optimism eroded in 1994. At the start of the year a guerrilla uprising in the poor southern Mexican province of Chiapas cast doubt on political stability. Further doubt was cast by a wave of assassinations killing, among others, Luis Donaldo Colosio, the presidential candidate of the ruling Party of the Revolution (Institutionalized) (PRI). During the presidential election year of 1994 itself, the central bank raised the money supply, causing some international investors to worry that macroeconomic policy was more political and less "technocratic" than they had thought. All of these events plus a wave of pessimism reduced foreign exchange speculators' estimates of the long-run value of the Mexican peso, and raised their assessment of the value of the long-run exchange rate, fundamental ε_0.

During 1994 the Mexican government spent $50 billion in foreign exchange reserves supporting the peso, believing at each moment that the adverse shift in expectations had to turn around. It did not. By the end of 1994 the Mexican government was out of foreign exchange reserves. And so it devalued the peso, and let it float against the dollar.

The devaluation of the peso had destructive consequences, however. First, a great many — naïve — investors in New York and elsewhere had believed the Mexican government when it said that it would do whatever was necessary to defend the value of the peso. The increase in the value of the Mexican exchange rate ε led to a further fall in the perceived fundamental value of the peso — a rise in the exchange rate fundamental ε_0 — which added to pressure for further depreciation and a further rise in the exchange rate ε. A more serious problem soon became clear: Much of the Mexican government's debt was indexed to the dollar in the form of securities called *tesebonos*. Each depreciation of the peso raised the peso value of the Mexican government's debt, increasing the temptation for the Mexican government to default on its debt, and the resulting financial distress led to further rises in foreign exchange speculators' opinions of ε_0.

The Mexican government seemed faced with a horrible choice. The first option was to raise interest rates to defend the peso, but adverse movements in foreign exchange speculator expectations meant that the level of interest rates that would be required by the formula

$$ r = r^f + \frac{\varepsilon_0 - \varepsilon^*}{\varepsilon_r} $$

was a level that would produce a Great Depression in Mexico. This first option would produce catastrophe.

The second option was to keep interest rates low and let the value of foreign currency rise much further. This would mean that Mexican companies — and the Mexican government — would be unable to pay their dollar-denominated and dollar-interest debts. Companies would declare bankruptcy. The government would default on its debt. Mexican exports would fall because foreign creditors would try to seize Mexican goods as soon as they left the country. Mexican imports would fall because foreign creditors would try to seize goods purchased by Mexico before they entered the country.

The result would be to delink Mexico from the world economy. Mexico's foreign trade would fall drastically. Meanwhile, international committees of lenders and creditors would thrash out a settlement of the bankruptcies with Mexican companies and the default with the Mexican government. This second option would produce catastrophe too. The Mexican government of Presidents Salinas and Zedillo had bet Mexico's economic future on increased integration with the world economy and the use of foreign capital to finance domestic industrialization.

The U.S. government and the IMF tried to give the Mexican government more options. The administration proposed loan guarantees to Mexico. But these guarantees fell through because neither then–Speaker of the House Newt Gingrich nor then–Majority Leader of the Senate Robert Dole nor other congressional leaders were willing to spend political capital on the issues. The administration then made direct loans to Mexico out of the U.S. Treasury's Exchange Stabilization Fund. These built Mexico's foreign-exchange reserves back to a level where it could support the peso to some degree without pushing domestic interest rates to Great Depression–causing levels.

These loans allowed the Mexican government to refinance its debt, and helped restore confidence that the Mexican government would not be forced into hyperinflation or resort to default. As time passed, Wall Street investors calmed down too. They recognized that Mexico was still the same country with relatively bright economic growth prospects, with promises of financial support if necessary from the U.S. Treasury and the IMF, and with NAFTA-guaranteed tariff-free access to the largest market for exports in the world. Thus the Mexican economic meltdown of 1994–1995 was a short, sharp recession that reduced Mexican real GDP by about 6 percent, but that was then followed by resumed economic growth.

The central lessons were two. First, the views of foreign exchange speculators could change radically with extraordinary speed. Second, developing countries that had not carefully prepared beforehand were extremely vulnerable to the shocks that such changes in international expectations could deliver.

The East Asian Crisis of 1997–1998

Two and a half years after the beginning of the Mexican crisis, the third international financial crisis of the 1990s hit the world economy. For 20 years before 1997 the economies of the East Asian Pacific rim had been the fastest-growing economies the world had ever seen. But in mid-1997 foreign investors began to worry about the long-run sustainability of the East Asian miracle and the growing overhang of non-performing loans in East Asian economies. They began to change their opinions of the fundamental long-term value ε_0 of East Asia's exchange rates.

In Thailand, Malaysia, South Korea, and Indonesia the values of domestic currency fell, and once again falling currency values caused a further swing in foreign exchange speculators' expectations of ε_0. Indonesia was hit the worst: Real GDP fell by one-sixth in 1998; the Indonesian currency, the rupiah, lost three-quarters of its nominal value against the dollar; and short-term real interest rates rose to 30 percent and nominal interest rates to 60 percent. Figure 15.11 shows the shock to two other currencies' exchange rates.

Once foreign exchange speculators began lowering their estimates of the long-run value of investments in East Asia, other, deeper problems in the Asian economies became apparent and were magnified. As East Asian exchange rates fell, it became clear that many of East Asia's banks and companies had borrowed heavily abroad in amounts denominated in dollars or yen. They had used those borrowings to make loans to the politically well connected, or to make investments that turned out not to be profitable in the long run.

The fact that East Asia's financial system was based on close links between governments, banks, and businesses — and that it was very difficult to obtain financial accounts from any East Asian organization — increased fear that more East Asian

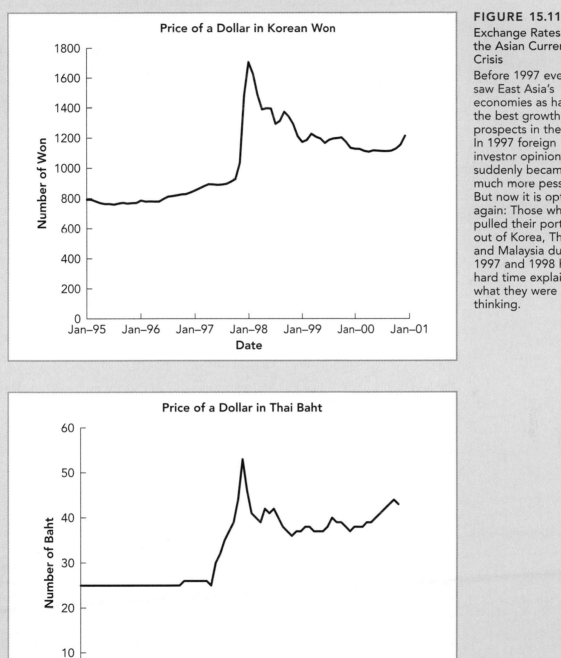

FIGURE 15.11
Exchange Rates During the Asian Currency Crisis
Before 1997 everyone saw East Asia's economies as having the best growth prospects in the world. In 1997 foreign investor opinion suddenly became much more pessimistic. But now it is optimistic again: Those who pulled their portfolios out of Korea, Thailand, and Malaysia during 1997 and 1998 have a hard time explaining what they were thinking.

Source: J. Bradford DeLong and Barry J. Eichengreen, "Between Meltdown and Moral Hazard: Clinton Administration International Monetary and Financial Policy," in Jeffrey Frankel and Peter Orszag, eds., *American Economic Policy in the 1990s* (forthcoming).

banks and companies were bankrupt than had been thought. This caused a further increase in foreign exchange speculators' views of the long-run exchange rate fundamental.

The vicious circle continued. Each loss of value in the exchange rate increased the burden of foreign-denominated debt and increased the likelihood of general bankruptcy. Each increase in the perceived burden of foreign-denominated debt caused a further loss of value in the exchange rate. Poor bank regulation had created a situation in which a small initial shock to exchange rate confidence could produce a major crisis. The shorter term the debt held by a country and its citizens, the more easily capital can flee — and the larger is the impact of the crisis.

As the Asian crisis developed, the IMF stepped in with substantial loans to boost foreign exchange reserves, made in return for promises to improve bank regulation and reform the financial system. The hope was that short-term loans would allow East Asian economies to avoid catastrophe until the pendulum of Wall Street expectations began to swing back. The hope proved sound. Since mid-1998, investors in New York and elsewhere have remembered that East Asia's economies had been the fastest-growing in the world in the previous generation, and were in all likelihood good places to invest.

Managing Crises

We can see the exchange-rate equation

$$\varepsilon = \varepsilon_0 - \phi(r - r^f)$$

as offering a country a menu of choices for its value of the real exchange rate ε and its value of the domestic real interest rate r. The higher the domestic real interest rate r, the more appreciated the exchange rate — that is, the lower is the value of ε, the real domestic-currency price of foreign exchange. If for any of many possible reasons international investors suddenly lose confidence in the future of a country's economy, their assessment of the exchange rate fundamental value ε_0 suddenly and massively depreciates.

Thus the menu of choices that a country has for its combination interest rate r and exchange rate ε suddenly deteriorates. If the interest rate r is to remain unchanged, the exchange rate must depreciate — the value ε of the real home-currency price of foreign exchange must rise a lot. If the exchange rate ε is to remain unchanged, then the domestic real interest rate r must rise a lot. Raising interest rates appears unattractive because it will create a recession. No domestic purpose would be served by such a recession: It is just the result of foreign investors' change of opinion.

Thus letting the exchange rate depreciate would seem to be the natural, the inevitable policy choice. A sudden panic by foreign exchange speculators is a sudden fall in demand for your country's products: International investors are no longer willing to hold your country's bonds at prices and interest rates that they were happy with last month. What does a business firm do when demand suddenly falls for the products it makes? It cuts its price. Perhaps a country faced with a sudden fall in demand for the products it makes should do the same: cut its price. The easiest way for a country to cut its price is to let its exchange rate depreciate. Such a depreciation of the exchange rate would in fact tend to stimulate exports, and production.

Yet throughout the 1990s, whenever international investors have suddenly turned pessimistic about investing in a country, observers have reacted with shock and horror when the exchange rate depreciates. Policy makers have sought to minimize the depreciation of the exchange rate. Observers have wrung their hands over such an economic catastrophe. This was the story in the collapse of the European monetary system in 1992, the collapse of the Mexican peso in 1994–1995, and the East Asian financial crisis of 1997–1998.

In all these cases the trigger of the crisis was a sudden change of heart on the part of investors in the world economy's industrial core — in New York, Frankfurt, London, and Tokyo. In Mexico in 1993 international investors poured some $25 billion into the economy; in Mexico in 1995 — even though the peso had been devalued by two-thirds, every piece of property and every business in Mexico was thus three times cheaper, and the country was the same country — international investors took perhaps $10 billion out of the country. In East Asia in 1996 international investors poured perhaps $70 billion into the region's economies. In 1998 the net private capital flow was about –$40 billion.

Economists will long dispute whether it was the relative optimism of investors before the crisis or the relative pessimism of international investors after the crisis that was the irrational speculative wave. The right answer is probably yes: Financial markets were excessively enthusiastic before the crisis, and were excessively pessimistic afterward. But why did such changes in international investor sentiment cause a crisis rather than an embarrassment? Why not let the exchange rate depreciate, and keep domestic monetary and fiscal policy aimed at maintaining internal balance?

The answer appears to be that large-scale depreciation is extremely dangerous: Your banks, businesses, and governments have borrowed massively abroad, and have done so not by promising to pay back their creditors in your home currency but by promising to pay them in foreign currencies — dollars, or yen, or euros, or pounds. Then a depreciation of the exchange rate bankrupts the economy: The foreign-currency value of all the domestic currency and businesses' assets are halved by the depreciation, while the dollar value of their liabilities is unchanged. Such an interlinked chain of general bankruptcies destroys the economy's ability to transform household savings into investment expenditures. The IS curve shifts far and fast to the left, just as the chain of bankruptcies caused by deflation shifted the IS curve far and fast to the left during the 1930s. Such chains of bankruptcies are the stuff of which Great Depressions are made.

Moreover, such a situation appears to arise most easily in the context of a fixed exchange rate. If the exchange rate is fixed for the moment, no one seems to worry that much about what currency loans are denominated in: After all, the exchange rate doesn't change, so six of one is half a dozen of the other. This may be the most damaging Achilles' heel of fixed exchange rate systems in our day: The knee-jerk belief that the system will continue indefinitely allows people to ignore important sources of risk that in currency crises have disastrous consequences.

Thus certain things should be done to reduce vulnerability to a crisis. Strongly discourage borrowers from borrowing in foreign currencies by taxing such loans. If you are going to accept free international capital flows (in an attempt to use foreign financing for your industrial revolution) then be sure that your exchange rate can float without causing trouble for the domestic economy. If your exchange rate must stay fixed (for inflation-fighting or other reasons), then recognize that an important part of keeping it fixed is having controls on capital movements.

But once the crisis has hit, good options are rare. As we saw above, not depreciating the exchange rate is no solution. To avoid depreciation, interest rates must rise. And high interest rates choke off investment and cause recession as well.

So is there a possible path to safety? Can you raise interest rates enough to keep the depreciation from triggering bankruptcy and hyperinflation, while still avoiding a high interest rate–generated recession? Can you depreciate the exchange rate enough to restore demand for home-produced goods without depreciating it so far as to bankrupt local businesses and banks?

Maybe.

The dilemmas are real. It is economic policy malpractice to claim that it is obvious that in a financial crisis, interest rates should not be raised and the exchange rate should be allowed to find its own panicked-market level even if banks and firms have large foreign-currency debts. It is economic policy malpractice to claim that in a financial crisis, interest rates should be raised high enough to keep the exchange rate from falling at all. It's not that simple.

So if sudden changes of opinion by international investors cause so much trouble, shouldn't we keep such sudden changes of opinion from having destructive effects? Shouldn't we use capital controls and other devices to keep international flows of investment small, manageable, and firmly corralled? Shouldn't we — as ruler Mahathir Muhammed did in Malaysia — impose capital controls?

Once again, maybe.

The first generation of post–World War II economists — John Maynard Keynes, Harry Dexter White, and their students — would have said "Yes, of course." Sudden changes of opinion on the part of international investors can cause enormous damage to countries that allow free movement of capital. Such sudden changes of opinion are a frequent fact of life. Therefore make it illegal, or at least highly restricted, to borrow from and lend to, invest in or withdraw investments from foreign countries.

The second and third generations of post–World War II economists had a different view. They regretted that capital controls kept people in the industrial core who could lend money away from people who could make good use of the money to expand economic growth. The balance of opinion shifted to the view that too much was sacrificed in economic growth at the periphery for whatever reduction in instability capital controls produced. Moreover, a regime of capital controls discouraged production and encouraged corruption. Often it was the cousin of the wife of the vice minister of finance who received permission to borrow abroad. Thus capital controls paved the way to kleptocracy: rule by the thieves.

So today we have the benefits of free international flows of capital. The ability to borrow from abroad does promise to give successful emerging market economies the power to cut a decade or two off the time it would take for them to industrialize. It promises to give investors in the world economy's industrial core the opportunity to earn higher rates of return. But this free flow of financial capital is also giving us one major international financial crisis every three years.

What is to be done will be one of the major economic policy debates of the next decade. Should we try to move toward a system in which capital is even more mobile than it is today but in which international financial crises may become an even more common occurrence? Or should we try to move toward a system in which capital is less mobile — more controlled — and in which some of the benefits of international investment are traded away in return for less vulnerability to financial crises? We don't have to have a global economy as vulnerable to currency crises as the economy of the 1990s has been.

RECAP CURRENCY CRISES

Three major (and many more minor) financial crises hit the world economy in the 1990s. The western European crisis of 1992 came about because foreign exchange speculators (correctly) doubted the commitment of other European countries to maintain their fixed parity with Germany as German interest rates rose. The Mexican crisis of 1994–1995 came about because foreign exchange speculators (incorrectly) doubted the commitment of the Mexican government to low inflation and economic reform, and because the fact that Mexico's government had borrowed heavily in dollars meant that a reduction in the value of the peso destabilized Mexico's finances. The East Asian crisis of 1997–1998 came about because foreign exchange speculators (correctly) feared that much recent investment in East Asia had been unproductive, (incorrectly) feared that the age of fast growth in East Asia was over, and because heavy dollar borrowings by East Asian companies meant that a reduction in the value of their currencies threatened to send much of East Asia's manufacturing and financial corporations into bankruptcy.

Chapter Summary

1. For most of the past century, the world has operated with fixed exchange rates — not, as today, with floating exchange rates.

2. Under fixed exchange rates, monetary policy has only very limited freedom to respond to domestic conditions. Instead, the main goal of monetary policy is to adjust interest rates to maintain the fixed exchange rate.

3. Why would a country adopt fixed exchange rates? To make it easier to trade by making foreign prices more predictable and less volatile. Fixed exchange rate systems increase the volume of trade, and encourage the international division of labor.

4. Nevertheless, in the past generation countries have usually concluded that freedom to set their own monetary

policies to satisfy domestic concerns is more important than the international integration benefits of fixed exchange rates.

5. An exception is western Europe, which is in the process of permanently and irrevocably fixing its exchange rates via a monetary union.

6. Wide swings in foreign exchange speculators' views of countries' future prospects have caused three major currency crises in the 1990s.

7. Such currency crises, although triggered by speculative changes in opinion, were greatly worsened by poor bank regulation and other policies that threatened to send economies subject to capital flight into a vicious spiral ending in depression and hyperinflation.

Key Terms

floating exchange rates (p. 412)

fixed exchange rates (p. 412)

gold standard (p. 412)

currency arbitrage (p. 412)

foreign exchange reserves (p. 414)

internal balance (p. 425)

external balance (p. 425)

currency crisis (p. 427)

Analytical Exercises

1. Why does a country's fixing the value of its currency in terms of gold also fix its nominal exchange rate?

2. Why do many economists think that a gold standard tends to put contractionary and deflationary pressure on economies that adhere to it?

3. What are the principal benefits of fixed exchange rates?

4. What are the principal costs of fixed exchange rates?

5. Why did the 1990s see so many international financial crises?

Policy Exercises

1. Suppose that foreign exchange speculators' believed value for the long-run equilibrium level of the real exchange rate suddenly rises by 30 percent, from 100 to 130. How does the interest rate increase required to keep the exchange rate constant in the face of this shift depend on the interest sensitivity of the exchange rate parameter ε_r? Under what circumstances would you think that the parameter ε_r would be large? Under what circumstances would it be small?

2. Look in the back of the book for the annual values of the U.S. real exchange rate. Suppose that the parameter ε_r is 10; then a swing of 1 percentage point in domestic real interest rates is associated with a 10 percent change in the exchange rate. By how much (and in which direction) would interest rates have to have changed in 1985 to push the real value of the U.S. exchange rate to the value it reached in 1990? By how much (and in which direction) would interest rates have to change today to push the real value of the exchange rate back to the value it reached in 1990? Would either of these shifts improve the condition of the domestic economy?

3. Suppose that a developing country with low capital mobility finds that foreign exchange speculators' views of the long-run value of its currency have suddenly shifted upward to 130, but that it wishes to maintain its pegged exchange rate ε^* of 100 and also keep domestic interest rates from rising above foreign interest rates. In the formula

$$r = r^f + \frac{\varepsilon_0 - \varepsilon^*}{\varepsilon_r} + \frac{\varepsilon_R}{\varepsilon_r} \times \Delta R$$

if $\varepsilon_R = 10$, $\varepsilon_r = 10$, and the relevant period of time is one month, how fast will the country lose reserves if it tries to maintain both its pegged exchange rate and the (relatively) low real interest rate? How high would it have to raise the domestic real interest rate above foreign rates to stop its loss of reserves?

4. Suppose you are asked to analyze whether Europe's monetary union was a mistake. What kinds of evidence would you look for to try to make up your mind?

5. Suppose you are asked whether some small Latin American country should *dollarize* — that is, fix its exchange rate with the United States once and for all by adopting the U.S. dollar as its own internal currency. What kinds of evidence would you look for to try to determine whether such dollarization is a good idea or not?

Changes in the Macroeconomy and Changes in Macroeconomic Policy

CHAPTER 16

QUESTIONS

How has the structure of the economy changed over the course of the past century?

How has the business cycle changed over the past century?

How has economic policy changed over the past century?

What are future prospects for successful management of the business cycle?

Why does unemployment in Europe remain so high?

Why does growth in Japan remain so low?

16.1 CHANGES IN THE MACROECONOMY

The Past

The structure of the macroeconomy is not set in stone. As time passes the economy changes. The patterns of aggregate economic activity studied in macroeconomics change too. Consumers' opportunities and spending patterns change, industries grow and shrink, the role of international trade steadily expands. The role of the government changes too, rising sharply during the New Deal era of the 1930s and the Great Society era of the late 1960s and early 1970s. It would be surprising indeed if the patterns of macroeconomic fluctuations remained unchanged as all these factors that underpin the macroeconomy change.

Over the past century the structure of modern industrial economies has changed, by some measures at least, more than in the entire previous millennium. Between the year 1100 and the start of the U.S. Civil War in 1860 the share of the labor force engaged in agriculture fell from perhaps 80 percent to perhaps 50 percent. But between the Civil War of the 1860s and the end of the twentieth century the share of the U.S. labor force engaged in agriculture fell from 50 percent to 2 percent, as shown in Figure 16.1. Today in America there are more gardeners, groundskeepers, and producers and distributors of ornamental plants than there are farmers and farm laborers.

The decline of agriculture is not the only major shift in the economy's occupational and industrial distribution. A century ago perhaps 40 percent of the labor force were engaged in mining, manufacturing, and construction: the nonagricultural industries that still required heavy lifting. Today perhaps 25 percent of the labor force are so engaged. The fall in relative employment in these industries has been offset by a rise in service-sector employment — both traditional services and what one might call information-intensive services.

Moreover, a hundred years ago the government's social insurance state was barely in embryo, the tax system was not at all progressive, and most households found it very difficult to borrow in order to see themselves through a year of low income and of unemployment. Today, by contrast, the American financial system lends immense amounts of money to all kinds of consumers. In standard economic theory, that should allow them to smooth their consumption spending. Households should be able to greatly reduce the impact of changes in their incomes on changes in consumption, and so reduce the marginal propensity to consume. Such reductions in the marginal propensity to consume *should* carry along with them a substantial reduction in the size of the multiplier. The same holds true for the fiscal automatic stabilizers of progressive taxes and social insurance, which appear to exert a powerful stabilizing force on the economy. They were not present a century ago.

The past century has also seen the rise of **financial automatic stabilizers** like deposit insurance. One major factor making depressions (most notably the Great Depression) larger in the distant past was the fear that your bank might fail, so you needed to pull your money out of the bank and hide it under your mattress. Such sudden increases in the demand for cash during financial panics caused interest rates to spike, investment to fall, and production to decline. Today the existence of a large deposit insurance system has all but eliminated this fear.

Still another change is in the pace and direction of material progress. Back in the late nineteenth century the bulk of improvements in labor productivity came from capital deepening: the buildup of the infrastructure and the factories of the country. In the twentieth century the bulk of improvements in labor productivity came from

FIGURE 16.1

Occupational Distribution of the Labor Force

A thousand years ago almost everyone was a farmer. Even in 1900, nearly one-third of the labor force was made up of farmers. Today the occupational distribution of the labor force is very different. The industries of the industrial revolution — manufacturing, mining, and construction — still employ a quarter of our labor force. But most of today's workers are in the service sector, many of them in information-intensive services.

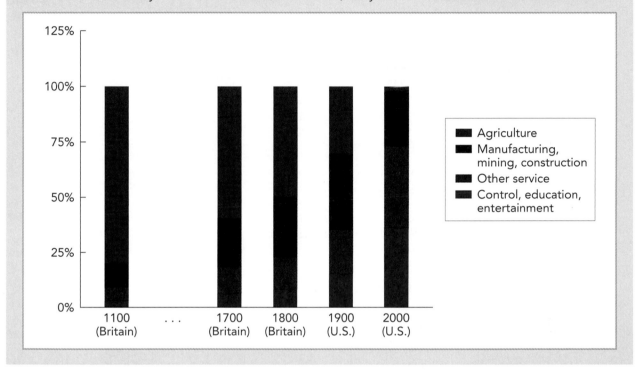

Source: Author's calculations from *Historical Statistics of the United States* (Washington, DC: Government Printing Office, 1975) and other sources.

improvements in the efficiency of labor as a result of improvements in science and technology: inventions and innovations in materials production, materials handling, and organization.

The share of economic activity oriented toward the future increased as well. Research and development became not a casual by-product of the rest of economic activity, but an organized branch of industry and a key component of investment. At least partly as a result, labor efficiency growth in the twentieth century proceeded at twice the pace of labor efficiency growth of the nineteenth century. And there are few if any signs that the pace of growth in the early twenty-first century will be slower.

Yet in spite of all of these changes in the structure of the economy, the U.S. economy's business cycle has continued. The patterns of the business cycle we see today would seem familiar to those who watched business cycles late in the nineteenth century. Everything else in the economy changes, yet the business cycle seems to remain largely the same. As Table 16.1 shows, there are some signs that fluctuations in unemployment have become smaller in recent years (and many signs that the Great Depression of the 1930s involved an extraordinarily violent business cycle). But the major lesson is that in spite of a number of structural changes that would

TABLE 16.1
Business Cycle Indicators

Period	Typical Swing in Unemployment	Typical Swing in Nonfarm Unemployment	Proportion of Time Spent in Recession
1870–1910	2.3%	4.4%	NA
1886–1915	2.9%	4.8%	22%
1901–1930	1.4%	1.9%	30%
1916–1945	7.2%	8.7%	28%
1931–1945	8.1%	10.1%	18%
1946–1975	1.2%	1.3%	19%
1976–1998	1.3%	1.3%	11%
1946–1998	1.5%	1.5%	15%

Source: Author's calculations from estimates provided by Christina Romer, "Spurious Volatility in Historical Unemployment Estimates," *Journal of Political Economy* 94, no. 1 (February 1986), pp. 1–37; and from *Historical Statistics of the United States* (Washington, DC: Government Printing Office, 1975).

seem likely to diminish the size of the business cycle, it remains and has remained largely the same.

Future Changes

We should not imagine that change is over: It will continue. We can already see some of the future changes that will transform the macroeconomy in the future.

The increase in **financial flexibility** that allows consumers to borrow will continue. The increase in financial flexibility will also make it more difficult to read the financial markets — and is thus likely to make monetary policy somewhat more difficult to conduct. International trade will continue to expand. The odds are that international investments will become easier to make, and so the speed at which capital flows across national borders will increase. And labor markets are likely to continue to change as well.

Consumption

Already **liquidity constraints** — the inability to borrow and the consequent fact that consumption spending is limited by income — play a relatively small role in determining consumption spending in America. They certainly play a much smaller role than at the beginning of this century, or even early in the post–World War II period. Economists' theories tell us that if liquidity constraints are absent, then the marginal propensity to consume should be very low. The level of consumption should depend on one's estimate of one's lifetime resources, and be affected by changes in current income only to the extent that changes in current income change one's estimate of lifetime resources.

Now economists' theories may overstate the case. Tying your current level of spending to your current level of income is a reasonable rule of thumb for managing one's affairs. And it just isn't worth the time spent to do better than one does by using reasonable rules of thumb. So the marginal propensity to consume may remain at some noticeable fraction, and increasing ease of borrowing may not lead the multiplier to completely disappear. Nevertheless, the multiplier is likely to grow still smaller over time. It will surely play a smaller role in the economy (and in economic policy, and in economics textbooks) in the future.

Globalization

The future is likely to see international trade continue to expand. The growth in trade, depicted in Figure 16.2, will also lower the multiplier: A greater portion of changes in domestic spending will show up as changes in demand for foreign-made goods. So the economy at home will be even less vulnerable to domestic shocks that disturb employment and output. However, increased international integration means that the domestic economy is more vulnerable to foreign shocks: Recession abroad that lowers demand for exports will have repercussions at home.

Accompanying the increase in international trade will be an increase in the magnitude of international financial flows. The odds are that international investments will become easier to make. And the odds are — as means of international communication increase — that investors in one country will become much more confident in making investments in another. So the speed with which capital flows across national borders will increase.

Yet in Chapter 15 we saw that increased flow of capital across national borders is a potential source of financial crisis and macroeconomic volatility. In the East Asian crisis of 1997–1998 a sudden shift in investors' expectations meant that $100 billion a year in international capital flows that had financed investment in East Asia was no longer there. That $100 billion a year had financed the employment of 20 million people working in investment industries, who dug sewer lines, built roads, erected buildings, and installed machines as both domestic and foreign investors bet that there was lots of money to be made in East Asia's industrial revolution. These 20 million East Asian workers had to find new jobs outside of investment industries.

The fall in the value of East Asian currencies has gone a long way to bringing the supply of and demand for foreign exchange back into balance. Falling exchange rates make East Asian goods more attractive to European and American purchasers. East Asia's economies are growing rapidly again.

But what caused the sudden sharp shift in investment patterns? Unfortunately for economists, and unfortunately for economics as a social science, we cannot find any disturbing cause proportional to the large effect. The shift in Wall Street's desires to

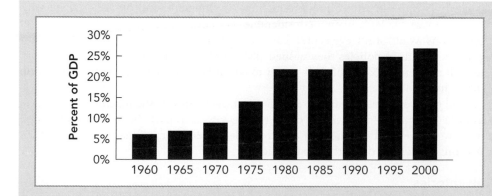

FIGURE 16.2

Globalization: Merchandise Imports as a Share of Total Goods Production

Since 1960 in the United States, the share of merchandise imports has quadrupled relative to total production of goods.

Source: The 2001 edition of *The Economic Report of the President* (Washington, DC: Government Printing Office).

invest in East Asia appears to have been impelled much more by the trend-chasing and herd instincts of Wall Streeters — a community of people who talk to each other too much, and whose opinions often reflect not judgments about the world but simply guesses about what average opinion expects average opinion to be — than by any transformation in the fundamentals of East Asian economic development.

And here we have reached the limits of economics. Economists are good at analyzing how asset markets work if they are populated by far-sighted investors with accurate models of the world and long horizons. Economists are even good at pointing out that such asset markets can be subject to multiple equilibria — situations in which it is rational to be optimistic and rational investors are optimistic if they think that everyone else is optimistic, and in which it is also rational to be pessimistic and rational investors are pessimistic if they think that everyone else is pessimistic. But that is all they can say.

Note that the process of international investment may still be worth supporting. It does promise powerful benefits: faster industrialization on the developing periphery, and higher rates of return for investors from the industrial core, as well as diversification to reduce risk. These benefits may well outweigh the costs of international financial crises. Nevertheless, it is likely that the next generation of business cycles will be judged to have gone well or ill depending on whether the financial crises generated by cross-border financial flows are handled well or badly.

Monetary Policy

The increase in financial flexibility that reduces the multiplier will also make it more difficult to read the financial markets, and probably to conduct monetary policy. Monetary policy works, after all, because the central bank's open-market operations change interest rates. These operations have large effects on interest rates because the assets traded — Treasury bills on the one hand, and reserve deposits at regional Federal Reserve banks on the other hand — play key roles in finance. Few substitute assets can serve the functions that they serve.

But as financial flexibility increases, any one kind of asset will become less and less of a bottleneck. There will be more ways of structuring transactions, and more kinds of financial instruments will be traded. Thus in the future, changes in the supply of Treasury bills likely will have less effect on interest rates than they do today. Open-market operations are likely to become somewhat less effective, and monetary policy somewhat more difficult to conduct, in the future.

Will this make much of a difference? Nobody knows. But monetary policy today is *plenty* effective at controlling production, employment, and prices — albeit with long and variable lags. Even a considerable reduction in the power of open-market operations would still leave central bankers with more-than-ample tools to carry out whatever kinds of policies they wished. The fear that increases in financial instability will rob central banks of their power to control economies is at least a generation in the future.

Will these ongoing and future changes in the structure of the macroeconomy have as little effect on the relative size of the business cycle as past changes appear to have had? To answer that question we need to look at the history of macroeconomic fluctuations, which we do in the next section.

Inventories

Fourth and last of the changes that we can foresee is that improvements in information technology will improve businesses' ability to control their inventories. Mismatches between production and demand — unanticipated large-scale inventory accumulation or drawdowns — have been a principal source of fluctuations in unemployment and output over the past century. There is reason to think that better information technology will reduce this component of macroeconomic instability.

But how large this reduction will be is, once again, something that nobody knows.

RECAP **CHANGES IN THE MACROECONOMY**

The future is likely to bring a continued increase in liquidity. People will find it easier and easier to borrow, hence their spending will be less closely tied to their current income, and the marginal propensity to consume will fall. International trade and financial markets are likely to become increasingly integrated, but at least as far as financial markets are concerned it is not clear that this is a good thing. It's likely that over time the power and effectiveness of monetary policy will decline as increased financial options erode the key role played by commercial bank deposits in finance. And firms will probably become better at managing their inventories, so that inventory fluctuation–driven business cycles will become a thing of the past.

16.2 THE HISTORY OF MACROECONOMIC FLUCTUATIONS

Estimating Long-Run Changes in Cyclical Volatility

Assessing changes in the size of the overall business cycle turns out to be harder than it looks. The obvious thing to do is to compare the cyclical behavior of real GDP and unemployment over the century. But good-quality data exist only for the post–World War II period. The pre–World War II data are much spottier. The Federal Reserve Board index of industrial production begins only in 1919. The Commerce Department GDP series begins only in 1929. The Bureau of Labor Statistics unemployment rate series begins only in 1940. And there is good reason to think that pre-1950 data are less reliable than post-1950 data.

Professor Christina Romer of the University of California–Berkeley has demonstrated that the procedures used to construct pre-1950 data tended to artificially inflate the cyclical volatility of the data. If you simply use the estimates reported in *Historical Statistics of the United States,* you will be comparing pre–World War II apples to post–World War II oranges. A consistent division of the past century-plus into recessions and expansions, as used in Table 16.2, shows little difference in the size of recessions. The average pre–World War I recession was almost exactly one month shorter than the average post–World War II recession.

We can reach a few solid conclusions about the changing cyclical variability of the American economy. The first and most obvious fact is the extraordinarily large size of the business cycle during the interwar period — the 1920–1940 period that came after World War I and before World War II. The Great Depression that began in 1929 was only the largest of three interwar business cycles. Other major contractions in economic activity took place in 1920–1922 and 1937–1938 (see Figure 16.3).

TABLE 16.2

Length of Recessions and Expansions since 1886

Pre–World War I recessions (months to trough) are almost exactly the same length as post–World War II recessions. Post–World War II expansions (months from trough to next peak), however, are half again as long as pre–World War I expansions.

1886–1916			1920–1940			1948–Present		
Year of Peak	Mos. to Trough	Mos. from Trough to Next Peak	Year of Peak	Mos. to Trough	Mos. from Trough to Next Peak	Year of Peak	Mos. to Trough	Mos. from Trough to Next Peak
1887	5	66	1920	14	26	1948	11	45
1893	13	23	1923	14	32	1953	10	39
1896	12	39	1927	9	21	1957	8	24
1900	8	31	1929	34	61	1960	10	106
1903	8	40	1937	10	18	1969	11	36
1907	11	19	1939	3		1973	16	58
1910	16	37				1980	6	12
1914	6	17				1981	16	92
1916	8					1990	8	
Avg.	9.7	34.0	Avg.	14.0	31.6	Avg.	10.7	51.5

Source: Christina Romer, "Remeasuring Business Cycles" (NBER Working Paper 4150), http://papers.nber.org/W4150, published subsequently in the *Journal of Economic History*, 54 (September 1994), pp. 573–609.

FIGURE 16.3

The Great Depression Relative to Other Business Cycles: U.S. Unemployment

Calculating fluctuations in unemployment according to a methodology consistent with the post–WWII data reveals that past unemployment estimates contained in *Historical Statistics of the United States* overstated the size of the depression of the 1890s.

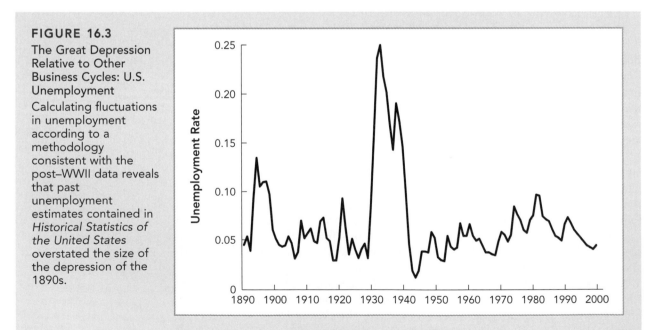

Source: The 2001 edition of *The Economic Report of the President* (Washington, DC: Government Printing Office); *Historical Statistics of the United States* (Washington, DC: Government Printing Office, 1975); and Christina Romer, "Spurious Volatility in Historical Unemployment Estimates," *Journal of Political Economy* 94, no. 1 (February 1986), pp. 1–37.

A second clear conclusion is that in the post–World War II era the business cycle, measured relative to the size of the economy, has been a little bit but not much smaller than before World War I. The shrinkage in the business cycle appears to be between 25 and 30 percent. The postwar business cycle is a somewhat smaller animal, but it would seem to be of the same species.

Thus many of the changes in the economy since 1900 must have roughly canceled each other out. The decline of agriculture as a share of employment and production (as a rule not very susceptible to the industrial business cycle) has been offset by the rise in importance of relatively acyclical services (also not very susceptible to the business cycle). An increase in the life span of capital equipment built with more durable materials might seem likely to increase cyclical volatility because more economic activity takes the form of long-term bets on the future. But this has apparently been offset by faster technological obsolescence, which reduces the effective economic life of investments in fixed capital. A smaller multiplier due to reduced liquidity constraints on households has presumably had some effect. But perhaps keeping spending proportional to income remains a useful rule of thumb even as credit becomes widely available, and so perhaps credit availability has not done as much to reduce the multiplier as economists' theories claim.

Economic Policy

How Economic Policy Has Worked

Yet if we look a little deeper, we see that business cycles today are not the same animals as they were before the Great Depression. The fall in the multiplier, the arrival of automatic stabilizers, and the increasing power of central banks have allowed monetary policy to offset many of the kinds of shocks that generated pre-Depression business cycles. The absence of significant stabilization springs from the fact that the increasing power of central banks has created a new class of shocks to the economy: recessions deliberately induced by monetary authorities to curb rising inflation. The post–World War II economy appears to have had fewer small recessions caused by shocks to the IS and LM curves. Stabilization policy has worked, in that it allows for the central bank working in combination with automatic stabilizers to react when the economy threatens to turn down into recession because of any sudden shock.

Before 1916 it was impossible for the U.S. government to have any effect on aggregate demand. Government purchases and net taxes were so small relative to economic activity that no fiscal policy variation short of fighting a major war could materially shift the IS curve, and change equilibrium real GDP. The pre–World War I government also lacked, until the founding of the Federal Reserve in 1914, the ability to affect the level of interest rates. Neither fiscal stabilization policy nor monetary stabilization policy as we know them today was possible before World War I.

By the end of World War II the power of stabilization policy and the government's commitment to manage aggregate demand were both firmly established. The war left the United States with a federal government that annually spent about one-fifth of GDP, and a government committed to countercyclical fiscal policy. Before World War II it had been a commonplace of political and policy-making discourse that taxes should be raised and spending cut to try to balance the budget in a recession. By the 1950s this doctrine was dead: The automatic stabilizers of the federal budget were in place.

The emergence of a significant progressive income tax made government revenues substantially procyclical, and the emergence of unemployment compensation, food stamps, and welfare led government spending to have a substantial automatic procyclical component as well. By the 1960s the federal government believed that it ought to be undertaking countercyclical discretionary fiscal policy as well (even though it has never been able to succeed in doing so). In monetary policy a similar shift had been accomplished near the beginning of the post–World War II period. By the early 1950s the U.S. Treasury and the Federal Reserve had agreed — in their Accord of 1951 — that the principal task of the Federal Reserve was to use monetary policy to stabilize the economy.

Since then the Federal Reserve has attempted to use monetary policy, within the limits placed on it by long and variable lags, to stabilize the economy and to moderate recessions. Both overall survey studies and detailed studies of cases like the interest rate cuts that followed the stock market crash of 1987 teach the lesson that the Federal Reserve has had considerable success in cutting short recessions and in accelerating growth in the early stages of the subsequent economic expansion.

There is no doubt that automatic stabilizers as well have played a role in moderating the business cycle. Yet a third innovation in economic policy — deposit insurance — has had effects that are harder to quantify. However, as Christina Romer observes, "the obvious starting point is the observation that financial panics were ubiquitous before World War I and almost nonexistent since World War II . . . there were major panics in 1890, 1893, 1899, 1901, 1903, and 1907 — all of them the source of substantial contractionary pressure on real GDP." Perhaps the effects of deposit insurance have been large as well: We are not really sure.

How Economic Policy Has Not Worked

But if economic policy since World War II has prevented or moderated many recessions, it has caused recessions as well. The existence of **policy-induced recessions** like those of 1981–1982 and 1990–1992 is what explains why there has not been a more dramatic reduction in the size of the business cycle over time. At least four times in the United States since World War II the Federal Reserve has engineered a recession, or has willingly accepted a substantial risk of a recession, in order to accomplish its policy goal of curbing inflation. It has had to curb an inflation rate that has crept upward into an uncomfortably high range.

If the prewar boom-and-bust business cycle was driven by, in John Maynard Keynes's phrase, the "animal spirits" of investors' shifts from optimism to pessimism and back again (and by financial panics), the post–World War II boom-and-bust business cycle has been driven by economic policies that have allowed rises in inflation, followed by the development of a consensus within the Federal Reserve that the rise in inflation must be reversed.

The minutes of the FOMC meetings identify seven moments since World War II at which the Federal Reserve took steps to reduce the growth rate of aggregate demand because inflation was thought to be too high. At each of these seven moments, therefore, the Federal Reserve risked a recession in order to try to reduce inflation. It sought to combat an inflationary cost-price spiral in spite of the fact that if it did so it would run the risk of incurring temporary unemployment.

Why have economic policy makers in the post–World War II era found themselves repeatedly driven to risk recession in order to fight inflation? In the late 1940s inflation was allowed to accelerate because the Federal Reserve had adopted the mission of keeping interest rates low to reduce the cost of financing the huge national debt incurred during World War II. The Federal Reserve was not satisfied with this mission, and in fact negotiated the Treasury–Federal Reserve Accord of 1951 to remove it from its list of policy objectives.

In the 1960s and 1970s inflation was allowed to accelerate for reasons that economists still debate. I have stressed historical accidents and the lingering memory of the Great Depression. The Stanford economist John Taylor stresses mistaken economic theories held in the early 1960s — in particular, the Phillips curve model of Samuelson and Solow constructed under the assumption that inflation expectations were and would remain static. Political scientists like Edward Tufte stress political business-cycle considerations.

At the first, surface level, the United States had an unstable macroeconomy in the 1970s because until the 1980s no influential policy makers — until Paul Volcker chaired the Federal Reserve — would place a sufficiently high priority on keeping inflation from rising. As long as inflation remained relatively low, it was not seen as a crisis, and so other goals took precedence among every group of economic policy makers. Thus presidents, members of Congress, and members of the Federal Open Market Committee were willing to accept the risk of increasing inflation to achieve other goals. Only after inflation had risen — only after it had reached the level of a political crisis — did a consensus develop that priorities needed to be changed, and steps were taken to reduce inflation.

Under this interpretation, the United States after World War II had a boom-bust, stop-go business cycle because the political system could pay attention to only one phenomenon at a time: When inflation wasn't a crisis, it wasn't an issue.

Only with the acceleration of inflation toward the end of the 1970s did political sentiment begin to shift. For rising inflation did become a severe political problem in 1979. And Paul Volcker was then nominated and confirmed as chair of the Federal Reserve in a political environment in which control of inflation — rather than reducing the unemployment rate — was the highest priority for economic policy. The Volcker-led Federal Reserve quickly signaled its intention to place first priority on controlling inflation by shifting its operating procedures to place a greater emphasis on money supply targets.

At a second, deeper level, the United States had a burst of inflation in the 1970s that required a painful recession cure in the 1980s because economic policy makers during the 1960s dealt their successors a bad hand: an unfavorable Phillips curve. Thus the policies of the 1960s left economic policy makers of the 1970s with a painful dilemma: either higher-than-usual inflation, or higher-than-usual unemployment. Bad cards coupled with bad luck made inflation in the 1970s worse than anyone expected it might be. And unsuccessful attempts to find a way out of this dilemma gave the economy the boom-bust cycle of the 1970s.

And at a third, deepest level, the truest cause of the inflation of the 1970s was the memory of the Great Depression. The Great Depression made it impossible for a while to believe that the business cycle was a fluctuation *around* rather than a shortfall *below* potential output and potential employment. The memory of the Great Depression made everyone skeptical of taking the average level of capacity utilization or the unemployment rate as a measure of the economy's sustainable productive potential.

Only after the experiences of the 1970s were economic policy makers persuaded that the flaws and frictions in American labor markets made it unwise to try to use stimulative macroeconomic policies without limit. Only after the experiences of the 1970s were policy makers persuaded that the minimum sustainable rate of unemployment attainable by macroeconomic policy was relatively high, and that the costs — at least the political costs — of even moderately high one-digit inflation were high as well.

It is somewhat depressing that the post–World War II gains from stabilization policy appear to have been relatively small. Nearly 50 years ago Milton Friedman warned that stabilization policy, if pursued overly aggressively by policy makers who did not understand its limits, could easily turn into destabilization policy. It looks as though his gloomy warning was very close to being correct. Yet important lessons may have been learned.

> **RECAP   PRE–WWII VERSUS POST–WWII BUSINESS CYCLES**
>
> The pre–WWII boom-and-bust business cycle was driven by investors' shifts from optimism to pessimism and back again. The post–WWII boom-and-bust business cycle has been driven by economic policies that have allowed rises in inflation, followed by a Federal Reserve–caused recession to reverse the rise in inflation. There is reason to hope that the modern Federal Reserve has learned how to eliminate or at least reduce the size of these inflation-fighting recessions. The magnitude of the business cycle has been much smaller since the mid-1980s.

The Great Depression

But if the business cycle has remained in spite of — and in part because of — active macroeconomic policy, it is important to remember that active macroeconomic policy has made a disaster on the order of magnitude of the Great Depression inconceivable. To see how bad things could get in an extreme situation when economic policy does not do its job, we need only to look back 70 years at the Great Depression.

The Magnitude of the Great Depression

The speed and magnitude of the economy's collapse during the first stages of the Great Depression was unprecedented: Nothing like it had been seen before, and nothing like it has been seen since. From full employment in 1929, real GDP fell until it was nearly 40 percent below potential output by 1933 (see Figure 16.4). Investment collapsed: By 1932 real investment spending was less than one-ninth what it had been three years before. And by 1933 unemployment had reached a quarter of the labor force.

In our analytical framework it is straightforward to understand why investment and real GDP fell so far so fast between 1929 and 1933. They did so because of an extraordinary rise in real interest rates. Real interest rates that had been 4 percent in 1929 spiked to nearly 13 percent by 1931, and stayed high throughout 1932 (see Figure 16.5). With such high real interest rates, naturally investment spending fell off.

After 1932 investment spending remained low, averaging less than half its 1929 value for the rest of the Great Depression decade even though real interest rates returned to more normal values. Why didn't the return of real interest rates to normal values cause a revival of investment? Because the magnitude of the Great Depression itself caused businesses to put off expanding their capacity. In 1933, with real GDP less than two-thirds of potential output, practically every business in the United States had excess capacity and hence no immediate incentive to invest at all. The

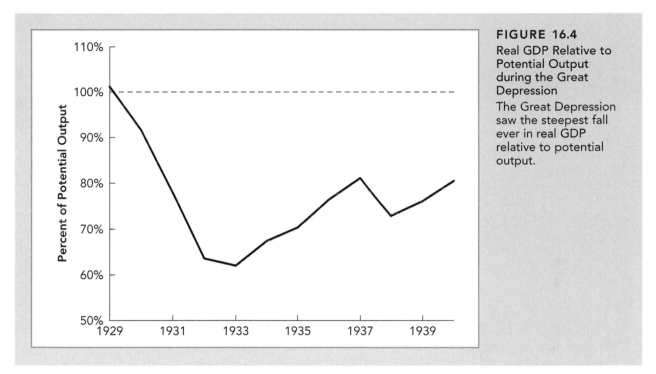

FIGURE 16.4

Real GDP Relative to Potential Output during the Great Depression

The Great Depression saw the steepest fall ever in real GDP relative to potential output.

Source: Author's calculations from *Historical Statistics of the United States* (Washington, DC: Government Printing Office, 1975).

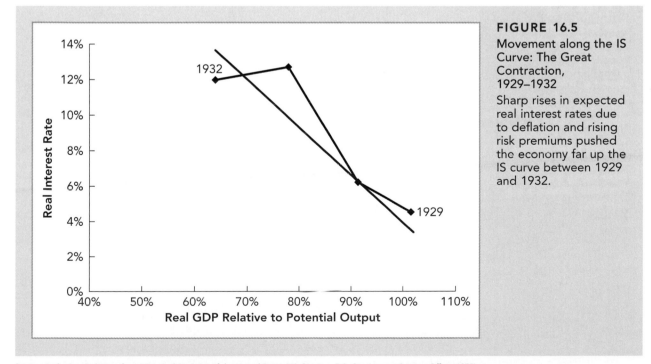

FIGURE 16.5

Movement along the IS Curve: The Great Contraction, 1929–1932

Sharp rises in expected real interest rates due to deflation and rising risk premiums pushed the economy far up the IS curve between 1929 and 1932.

Source: Author's calculations from *Historical Statistics of the United States* (Washington, DC: Government Printing Office, 1975).

very depth of the Great Depression caused a steep fall in the baseline investment co-efficient I_0 in the investment equation

$$I = I_0 - (I_r \times r)$$

Thus even a restoration of real interest rates to normal levels was not sufficient to re-store the economy to full employment.

Deflation and High Real Interest Rates

So why did real interest rates rise so high between 1929 and 1932? The immediate, proximate cause of high real interest rates was rapid deflation: rapid sustained falls in prices that, when combined with moderate nominal interest rates, produced very high real interest rates, as shown in Figure 16.6.

What caused the deflation? The first thing was the depth of the Great Depression itself: Falling production, employment, and demand produced steep falls in prices, which caused high real interest rates that reduced demand, production, and em-ployment still further. But it makes little sense to say that the Great Depression caused itself. There must have been an initial shock to start the downward spiral that was the Great Depression.

The Initial Shock

Economists have proposed many candidates for the shock that triggered the Great De-pression. Perhaps the stock market crash of 1929 reduced wealth and increased un-certainty, and caused a downward shift in the baseline level of consumption. Perhaps the availability of consumer credit in the 1920s caused a consumption spending boom

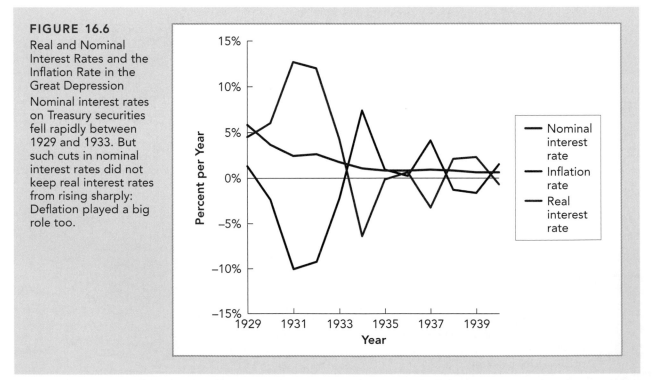

FIGURE 16.6

Real and Nominal Interest Rates and the Inflation Rate in the Great Depression

Nominal interest rates on Treasury securities fell rapidly between 1929 and 1933. But such cuts in nominal interest rates did not keep real interest rates from rising sharply: Deflation played a big role too.

Source: Author's calculations from *Historical Statistics of the United States* (Washington, DC: Government Printing Office, 1975).

that then came to a natural end. Perhaps there was excessive residential investment in the 1920s because builders failed to realize how the restrictions on immigration put into place in the mid-1920s would affect housing demand in the long run. Perhaps the recognition that the housing stock was too large triggered a downward shift in the baseline level of investment. Perhaps the Federal Reserve's 1928 increases in interest rates, an attempt to reduce stock market speculation, triggered the initial slump.

Practically any analyst soon reaches the conclusion that the response was disproportionate to the initial shock. Somehow the American economy at the end of the 1920s was very vulnerable in the sense that a small shock could cause a big depression. It is this disproportion between the hard-to-find initial shock and the subsequent depression that makes many economists fear that the economy will be unstable if not managed by appropriate government policies.

Consequences of the Price Level Decline

Economists have reached a consensus that a sufficiently aggressive and activist monetary policy could have stemmed the price decline, and so ended the Great Depression much earlier if undertaken rapidly and aggressively enough. Policies of massive federal deficits funded by money-printing, coupled with aggressive open-market operations to increase the monetary base could have, if carried far enough, produced inflation. And without the high real interest rates produced by deflation in the early 1930s, it is hard to see how there could have been a Great Depression.

Falling price levels reduce real GDP through two separate channels. The first is the real interest rate channel that we saw above: The real interest rate is the nominal interest rate minus the inflation rate, so deflation leads to high real interest rates, to a move up and to the left along the IS curve, and to falling real GDP and employment.

But there is a second channel as well. Unexpected falls in the price level redistribute wealth from debtors to creditors. Those businesses that are heavily in debt find that they cannot pay, and so they go bankrupt. Those financial institutions that have loaned to heavily indebted businesses find that their loans are worthless, and so they go bankrupt as well. Deflation destroys the web of credit that channels funds from savers through banks and other financial institutions to businesses wanting to invest. More than one-third of U.S. banks failed in the first years of the Great Depression. And without the web of financial intermediaries to channel investment through the financial markets, maintaining or restoring the flow of investment becomes very difficult.

These effects of deflation are long-lasting. Even after real interest rates have returned to normal, the deflation-driven destruction of the web of financial intermediation will continue to depress investment. So it was in the Great Depression.

16.3 MACROECONOMIC POLICY: LESSONS LEARNED

Stabilization

For almost all of your lives — "you" being the typical reader of this textbook — the business cycle has been relatively quiescent. A substantial difference in business-cycle behavior comes from dividing the post–World War II era into two periods with the breakpoint chosen at the end of the Volcker disinflation in the early 1980s. The pre-1984 years show much more business-cycle volatility than do the post-1983 years, as Table 16.3 indicates.

TABLE 16.3

Post-Volcker Stabilization of the U.S. Economy: Standard Deviation of Percentage Changes

Since the mid-1980s the U.S. economy has been astonishingly, remarkably stable. Typical business-cycle movements in the unemployment rate or in real GDP have been half the size they were from 1948 to 1984.

Series	1948–1984	1985–Present
Industrial production	5.7%	2.2%
GNP	2.8	1.3
Commodity output	5.3	3.6
Unemployment rate	1.2	0.6

Source: Christina Romer, "Changes in Business Cycles: Evidence and Explanations" (NBER Working Paper 6948, 1999), http://papers.nber.org/W6948.

One possibility is that the period since 1984 has been the result of good luck — that business-cycle macroeconomic performance has been good because there have not been many shocks nor any truly large shocks to the economy. But just as the relatively placid 1960s were followed by the disruptive 1970s, perhaps the 1990s will turn out to be followed by an equally turbulent decade.

Learning

A second possibility is that lessons have truly been learned from the experience of the 1960s and 1970s. The late 1980s and the 1990s were not only an era of relatively stable economic growth but also an era of low inflation. Recessions have been few and growth relatively steady since the early 1980s in large part because inflation has been firmly under control: A lack of inflation has meant that the Federal Reserve has not had to risk a recession to control inflation.

This leads to the hope that the monetary policy authorities have gained sufficient experience and expertise at using their policy tools to successfully carry out stabilization policy. Perhaps the first three decades of the post–World War II era saw little stabilization of the business cycle because of repeated policy mistakes: overoptimism with respect to the possible sustainable rate of economic growth, followed by recessions to demonstrate that the central bank was, after all, serious about controlling inflation.

Prospects

Perhaps the more recent era shows how much more stable our economic system can be with successful institutions that understand the limits of their power. But it is not clear whether the growth of aggregate demand has been smoother because economic policy makers have recognized the limits of what they can achieve, because of the skill of Paul Volcker and Alan Greenspan, because of better economic theories to guide policy, or simply because of good luck. It is clear that every time in the past a "new era" or a "new economy" has been proclaimed, the same old business cycle has soon returned.

The expansion of the 1920s led economists to hope that the newly constructed Federal Reserve had learned how to stabilize output by eliminating the fluctuations in interest rates that caused financial crises. Irving Fisher, the most prominent monetarist of his day, went so far as to claim on the eve of the 1929 crash that stock prices had reached a "permanent and high plateau." The prolonged expansion of the 1960s led the Department of Commerce to change the name of its *Business Cycle Digest* to the *Business Conditions Digest,* for it seemed silly to have a publication named after a phenomenon that no longer existed. Both President Eisenhower's and President Johnson's Council of Economic Advisers chairs, Arthur Burns and Walter Heller, agreed that substantial progress in economic science and policy making toward economic stability had opened up new dimensions of political economy.

One can be optimistic about the future of macroeconomic policy, and count up all the lessons that economists and policy makers have successfully learned over the course of the twentieth century.

One can be especially optimistic from the perspective of the United States today. From that perspective macroeconomic policy appears remarkably successful. Unemployment is very low, at levels that have not been seen in a generation. Inflation is also low, at levels that have not been seen in a generation either. The stock market is at record highs, both absolutely and relative to corporate earnings and dividends, suggesting that the market at least expects a very bright future. The increase in income inequality that was an extremely worrisome social trend in the United States appears to have stopped (although it has not reversed itself). And in recent years *measured* productivity growth has been rapid, suggesting that the political claims by Clinton administration officials in the early 1990s that deficit reduction would lead to a high-investment, high-productivity-growth, high-income-growth recovery were largely correct.

Nevertheless, it is likely that at some point the long expansion that began in the early 1990s will be followed by a recession. And what will follow in the way of management of the business cycle is ours to decide.

16.4 MACROECONOMIC POLICY: LESSONS UN- OR HALF-LEARNED

One can also be pessimistic about the future of macroeconomic policy. One can count up all the lessons that economists and policy makers have not learned, or have half-learned, or have learned and then forgotten over the course of the twentieth century. Certainly a look outside the United States, either at Japan, or at the financial-crisis-ridden emerging economies, or at Europe with its stubbornly high unemployment, does not lend strength to the claim that traditional business-cycle patterns have come to an end.

Lessons Unlearned: High European Unemployment

Europe at the end of the 1990s is not in a Great Depression. Nevertheless, unemployment rates in western Europe at the end of the 1990s are within hailing distance of the rates achieved during the Great Depression. Unemployment averages 10 percent in the zone of countries that now share the common currency of the euro (see Figure 16.7).

Up until the end of the 1970s, unemployment in western Europe had been lower — sometimes substantially lower — than unemployment in the United States. But

FIGURE 16.7
European Unemployment

The growth of unemployment in the 4 largest western European countries, 1975–2000.

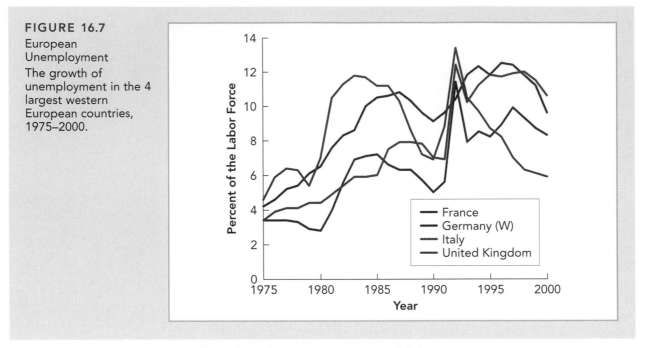

Source: The 2001 edition of *The Economic Report of the President* (Washington, DC: Government Printing Office).

starting in the 1970s European unemployment began to ratchet upward. Unemployment rose during recessions, yet it did not fall during economic expansions. During the recession of the Volcker disinflation at the start of the 1980s, western European and U.S. unemployment rates were about equal. But during the later 1980s and 1990s the trend of U.S. unemployment was down; the trend of European unemployment was stable or upward.

In the United States it is possible to understand the comovements of unemployment and inflation over 1960–2000 using the standard Phillips curve. The Phillips curve shifts out in the 1970s as everyone begins to expect higher inflation and demographic factors cause the natural rate of unemployment to rise. The Phillips curve shifts back in the 1980s and 1990s as people regain confidence in the Federal Reserve's commitment to low inflation and as changing demographic factors cause the natural rate of unemployment to fall. The story does not fit badly. Movements in the expected rate of inflation reflect changes in the economic policy environment. Movements in the natural rate of unemployment are relatively small, and can be linked to plausible factors.

In western Europe, by contrast, the accelerationist Phillips curve *never* fit the historical experience very well. Each policy episode from 1970 on — supply shocks, the Volcker disinflation, the recession of the early 1990s — seemed to shift the Phillips curve further out, and to further raise the natural rate of unemployment. It seemed as if this year's natural rate of unemployment was equal to whatever unemployment had happened to be last year.

The dominant view expressed in Europe in the early 1990s was that high European unemployment was the result of labor market rigidities. Europe possessed laws, restrictions, and regulations that made it too difficult for firms to hire new workers cheaply at a relatively low wage, and too difficult for firms to fire workers (and thus forward-looking firms were reluctant to hire workers). Thus it was too expensive to conduct a labor-intensive business in Europe or to adjust to changes in the economic environment.

According to this dominant view, high unemployment in Europe is an *equilibrium* level that is what economists call "**classical**": It arises not from any deficiency of aggregate demand, but simply from the fact that the state's regulations keep the labor market from clearing. The state's regulations boost the cost of employing the marginal worker far above the extra revenue the typical firm would gain from employing an extra worker.

But the "rigidities" in the European labor market were stronger in the 1960s — when European unemployment was very low — than they are today. It is not that the natural rate of unemployment in Europe has always been high; it is that each additional adverse shock that increases unemployment seems to increase the natural rate as well. Thus many economists who have examined European unemployment dissent from the conventional wisdom of the editorial writers and the politicians. They tend to see western Europe not as locked into high unemployment, but as in a reversible situation. Just as increases in unemployment in the 1970s and 1980s raised the natural rate of unemployment in Europe, so decreases in the rate of unemployment in the 2000s would in all likelihood lower the natural rate of unemployment in Europe.

A Grand Bargain?

Economists' views of western European unemployment thus suggest there is potential for much improvement. Have central bankers and governments shift to a more expansionary monetary policy. As demand expands, people will find that the natural rate of unemployment is falling. The falling natural rate of unemployment will create still further room for demand expansion, and for further unemployment rate reduction.

Central bankers may fear that the economists' view is wrong and that the conventional wisdom is right — that attempts to expand demand and reduce unemployment a little bit will lead to accelerating inflation as unemployment falls below its (high) current natural rate. Therefore begin the process with some steps to eliminate labor-market rigidities: Reduce employers' contributions to social security, reduce severance costs, transfer unemployment insurance money from the payment of benefits to assistance with job searching, and allow the minimum wage to fall. These steps should leave central bankers confident that there is room to expand demand in the context of a falling natural rate of unemployment.

But governments find that such steps to initiate the process of demand expansion can be portrayed as an attack on the standard of living of the unemployed — as an antiworker, antihuman policy. Only if governments are confident that reform of the social insurance system will be accompanied by stronger demand and higher employment will they be willing to undertake their part of the grand bargain. Otherwise they will fear that — with high interest rates and slow demand growth — social insurance system reform will merely change high classical unemployment to high Keynesian unemployment, and in the process create mass poverty. And only if central banks are confident that their expansionary monetary policies will be accompanied by social insurance system reform would it make sense for them to risk lower interest rates and a change in monetary policy.

Even if the conventional wisdom is right, such a grand bargain promises to make everyone — the currently unemployed, the currently employed who pay taxes to support the social insurance system, politicians dealing with high unemployment, central bankers accused of being out of touch with human experience — better off. And if the economists' view is right — if the principal determinant of a high natural rate of unemployment in Europe is the fact that unemployment has been high in Europe for a long time — then the benefits to such a grand bargain are overwhelmingly large.

Yet European politicians and central bankers have been unable to learn how to deal with their high, stubborn rates of unemployment.

Lessons Half-Learned: Japanese Stagnation

The End of the Bubble Economy

The standard analysis of how the Japanese economy entered its present period of stagnation is straightforward. The Japanese stock market and real estate market rose far and fast in the 1980s, to unsustainable "bubble" levels. And eventually the market turned, and both the real estate and stock markets collapsed.

When stock and real estate prices collapsed, it was discovered that lots of enterprises and individuals had borrowed heavily against their real estate and security holdings, putting up their real estate and their stocks as collateral. After the collapse, not only were those who had borrowed heavily bankrupt, but the banks and other institutions that had loaned them money were bankrupt as well: The value of the collateral they had accepted was no longer enough to repay the *lenders'* creditors.

One problem was that no one was exactly sure which institutions were bankrupt — which institutions had liabilities in excess of their assets. Thus no one was anxious to lend money to anyone: You might well never see your money again if the organization you loaned it to was one of those that had extended itself during the bubble economy of the late 1980s. A second problem was regulatory forbearance: the belief that the best way to solve the problem was to pretend that it did not exist, try to let business go on as usual, and hope that a few good years would allow all of the institutions that were "underwater" to make enough in profits to repay their debts even given the low value of the collateral that they had accepted.

These two problems together meant that investment spending was depressed. Financial institutions exist to channel money from savers with purchasing power to businesses that can use that purchasing power to expand their capital. But in the aftermath of the collapse of the bubble, no one really wanted to lend — for you could not know whether the organization wanted your money to invest, or to try to paper over some of its previous losses.

The situation was analogous to the collapse of investment spending in the Great Depression, where the chain of deflation and bankruptcies had similar effects. The collapse of the Japanese financial bubble of the 1980s depressed consumption and investment spending. Banks' and other institutions' large bets on the real estate market meant that the collapse of the bubble put them underwater — with assets and lines of business that were worth less than the debt they already owed that they had borrowed to speculate in real estate. Who will invest in a business — or a bank — if they fear that their money will be used not to boost profitability but instead to pay back earlier creditors?

Thus Japan has fallen into a decade of economic stagnation. Growth since 1990 has been almost zero, as Figure 16.8 shows. Unemployment has risen to levels previously unheard-of in Japan. The IS curve has shifted far to the left. And nothing seems to correct it: Even extremely low nominal interest rates are not sufficient to boost investment and aggregate demand. And for nearly an entire decade Japanese economic growth has been extremely slow and stagnant.

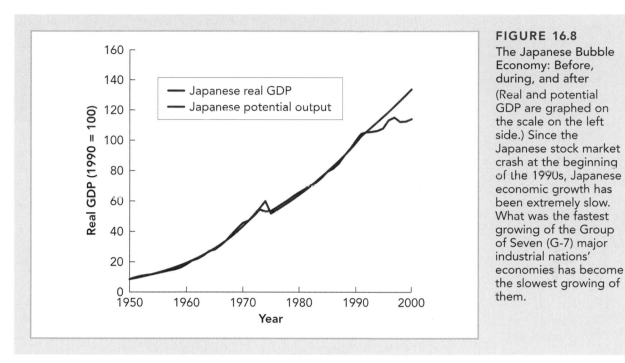

FIGURE 16.8
The Japanese Bubble Economy: Before, during, and after
(Real and potential GDP are graphed on the scale on the left side.) Since the Japanese stock market crash at the beginning of the 1990s, Japanese economic growth has been extremely slow. What was the fastest growing of the Group of Seven (G-7) major industrial nations' economies has become the slowest growing of them.

Source: Organization for Economic Cooperation and Development.

What should economic policy makers do in such a situation? The answer to what you should do in order to recover from such a state of depressed aggregate demand is "everything." You should have the government run a substantial deficit (although, as E. Cary Brown of MIT pointed out in the 1950s, it requires truly awesome deficit spending — on the order of deficit spending in World War II — to reverse a Great Depression like that in the United States in the 1930s or a Great Stagnation like that in Japan today). You should have the central bank push the interest rate it charges close to zero (to make it very easy and cheap to borrow money).

If that isn't enough you should try to deliberately engineer moderate inflation. If demand is depressed because people think investing in corporations is too risky, change their minds by making the alternative to investment spending even more risky. If the alternative is hoarding your money in cash, then eat away a share of its real purchasing power every year with inflation.

So far Japan has changed its fiscal policy to run big deficits (but, as any student of the Great Depression would suspect, they haven't been big enough). Japan has lowered its short-term safe nominal interest rates to within kissing distance of zero. But these haven't done enough good. The lessons of the Great Depression have been only half-learned.

Lessons Half-Learned: Moral Hazard

Even in the United States, it seems that some of the lessons on economic policy taught by the past century of experience have been only half-learned. Consider the problem of dealing with financial crises: those moments when large and highly leveraged financial institutions have failed or are about to, and when there is a genuine fear that a chain of bankruptcies is about to be triggered.

In such a situation the fear that the organization to which one might lend will fail greatly retards lending. The flow of funds through financial markets will slow to a trickle, as savers conclude that keeping their wealth close at hand in safe forms is a much better opportunity than lending it to organizations that are probably bankrupt. Thus such a financial crisis is likely to see the IS curve shift far and fast to the left as the level of investment spending collapses. If this leftward shift in the IS curve is not stemmed, there will be a recession and the financial crisis will rapidly become worse as businesses that were solvent at normal levels of production and sales find that the fall-off in demand has bankrupted them.

What to do in such a situation was first outlined by Bagehot a century and a quarter ago. The government needs to rapidly close down and liquidate those organizations that are fundamentally bankrupt. If they would be bankrupt even if production and demand were at normal levels relative to potential, then they should be closed. The government needs to lend money — albeit at a high, unpleasant, penalty rate — to organizations that would be solvent if production and demand were at normal levels, but that nevertheless suffer a cash crunch now.

The key is twofold: Government support is necessary in order to prevent a deep meltdown of the entire financial system. Government assistance must be offered on terms unpleasant enough and expensive enough that no one would wish in advance to get into a situation in which they need to draw on it. Moreover, the government must accept that its ability to distinguish between these two classes of institutions is imperfect, and that it will inevitably make mistakes.

Yet more and more in the political discussion over economic policy one hears the claim that government provision of liquidity and support in a financial crisis is dangerous — that it causes "moral hazard" because organizations place riskier and riskier bets counting on government support to bail them out if things go wrong. The right policy in a financial crisis is a completely hands-off one. A century and a quarter of experience suggests that this is only a half-truth. Moral hazard is a problem, but so is a Great Depression. The balancing point is hard to determine: Bank and financial regulators must impose rules that restrict the growth of moral hazard, assistance in times of financial crisis must be expensive and painful to the organization drawing on the government, and yet the worst outcome — a freezing-up of the financial system and a severe recession — must be guarded against. To focus on only one of these three rather than balancing between them is to recommend bad economic policy.

The Ultimate Lesson

It is strange that neither European nor Japanese governments appear to have learned the lessons that macroeconomists have to teach. It is also strange that fundamentals of crisis policy that seemed settled more than a century ago are still up for grabs in America's political debate. The principal lesson is that it seems very hard to learn the lessons of history.

Thus the future of economic policy seems likely to be similar to the past. Gross mistakes will be made, historical analogies will be misapplied, and economists and other observers after the fact (and sometimes during the fact) will find major policy mistakes made by governments and central banks to be inexplicable: We will genuinely be unable to figure out just what the people who made the decisions were thinking.

So do not mistake the steady hand on the monetary policy tiller and the relatively placid business cycle that the United States has experienced since the mid-1980s for the way things will be in the future.

**RECAP   MACROECONOMIC POLICY: LESSONS
UN- OR HALF-LEARNED**

Economists and economic policy makers have learned much over the past century, but many lessons appear unlearned or imperfectly learned. European unemployment remains stubbornly high in spite of the prospect that a two-handed approach to both stimulate aggregate demand and remove restrictions on aggregate supply would allow for more rapid growth and expanded employment without inflation. The Japanese government continues to fail to resolve what is now a decade-old financial crisis, thus keeping its economy stagnant. And the economic policy debate within the United States fails to note that financial crises pose a choice between evils and not a situation in which one single principle of economic governance — whether "avoid moral hazard" or "avoid chains of bankruptcies" — can be applied to the fullest. Perhaps the most important lesson is that the lessons of history are hard to learn.

Chapter Summary

1. The structure of the economy has undergone mammoth changes over the past century, yet these changes appear to have had relatively little impact on the size of the business cycle.

2. Stabilization policy as we know it was impossible a hundred years ago; yet it is now performed routinely and aggressively.

3. Since World War II, stabilization policy has had successes and failures. Its principal failure has been that it has generated recessions to fight inflation, and these policy-induced recessions have kept policy from successfully stabilizing the economy to a greater degree.

4. In the past two decades, stabilization policy in the United States has been very successful. Is this just good luck, or is it a pattern? We shall see.

5. Certainly from the U.S. perspective there is every reason to be optimistic about the future of macroeconomic policy, and of the macroeconomy.

6. From a European perspective there is less reason to be optimistic: European governments and central banks have not learned how to deal with their high levels of unemployment.

7. From a Japanese perspective there is less reason to be optimistic: The Japanese government has not learned how to deal with its financial meltdown.

8. Even from a U.S. perspective, it seems to be hard to learn the lesson that good economic policy during an economic crisis is not a matter of clinging to one principle, but of balancing the conflicting requirements of several valid principles.

Key Terms

stabilization policy (p. 440)

financial automatic stabilizers (p. 440)

financial flexibility (p. 442)

liquidity constraints (p. 442)

globalization (p. 443)

cyclical volatility (p. 445)

policy-induced recessions (p. 448)

classical unemployment (p. 457)

bubble economy (p. 458)

moral hazard (p. 459)

Analytical Exercises

1. What changing factors since the start of the twentieth century would make one expect business cycles to become larger?

2. What changing factors since the start of the twentieth century would make one expect business cycles to become smaller?

3. As the macroeconomy continues to change in the twenty-first century, do you expect business cycles to become larger or smaller?

4. Why has production become more stable in the United States since the early 1980s?

5. Why does unemployment remain high in Europe today?

Policy Exercises

1. How, in your view, is the way the Federal Reserve conducts monetary policy likely to change over the next generation?

2. If the government's share of GDP in spending shrinks over the next generation, what in your view is likely to happen to the size of the business cycle?

3. How, in your view, will increased ease of international trade and increased international capital mobility change the workings of the macroeconomy over the next generation?

4. What steps would you take to try to reduce European unemployment, and how might those steps backfire?

5. What steps would you take to try to end Japan's current depression, and how might those steps backfire?

The Future of Macroeconomics

CHAPTER

QUESTIONS

What might the future of macroeconomics bring? How might the macroeconomics taught two decades from now differ from the macroeconomics that is taught today?

What have been the principal changes in the way macroeconomics is taught over the past 20 years?

What additional changes took place in the 20 years before that — from roughly 1960 to roughly 1980?

What direction will macroeconomics take if the real-business-cycle research program is successful?

What direction will macroeconomics take if the new Keynesian research program proves successful?

How will economists understand the foundations behind the power of monetary policy?

The past 16 chapters of this book have given a historically informed long-run, growth-stressing, new Keynesian view of macroeconomics. But that is not all of macroeconomics — there are other currents of thought, and other live research programs. What is the past, and what might be the future of macroeconomics? This chapter takes a look back at the history of macroeconomics, and then looks forward and sketches a few outlines of what the future of macroeconomics might be.

If one thing is certain it is that we will know different (and, we hope, know more about) macroeconomics in a decade than we do today. What will be taught in macroeconomics courses in 20 years will not be the same as what is taught today.

17.1 THE PAST OF MACROECONOMICS

The Age of John Maynard Keynes

Macroeconomics as a discipline is to a remarkable extent the creation of John Maynard Keynes. His 1936 book *The General Theory of Employment, Interest, and Money* shifted economic research and macroeconomic thought into new and different directions that have led us where we are today. The *General Theory*'s extraordinary impact was in large part a result of the then-ongoing Great Depression. Other and previous approaches to understanding business cycles had little useful to say about it. Keynes had a lot to say.

Keynes's book emphasized (a) the role of expectations of future profits in determining investment, (b) the volatility of expectations of future profits, (c) the power of the government to affect the economy through fiscal and monetary policy, and (d) the multiplier process, which amplified the effects of both private-sector shocks and public-sector policies on aggregate demand. It swept the intellectual field, and shaped modern macroeconomics.

By a decade or so after World War II much of the analytical apparatus used in this textbook was already in place. The IS-LM model was developed by economists John Hicks and Alvin Hansen. Other economists developed the approaches used in this textbook to understanding consumption (Milton Friedman and Franco Modigliani), investment (Dale Jorgenson, James Tobin, and many others), and the relationship between interest rates and the money supply (James Tobin once again, along with many others). The difference between the behavior of the macroeconomy in the flexible-price long run and the fixed-price short run was clarified by many economists (here Franco Modigliani was again the major contributor). The Solow growth model that is the workhorse of Chapters 4 and 5 was developed by — no surprise — Robert Solow.

This is not to say that the bulk of this textbook stands as it would have been written back in 1960. Macroeconomics textbooks in 1960 had next to no discussion of the relationship between production and inflation. They had little discussion of expectations. The short run was seen as lasting for decades, and analysis of the long-run flexible-price model was rarely included in undergraduate courses. Textbooks in 1960 also downplayed monetary policy and emphasized fiscal policy: Investment was seen as responding little to changes in interest rates, and estimates of the multiplier were much higher than we believe today to be correct for now or for then.

The Age of Milton Friedman and Robert Lucas

Between 1960 and 1980 a good deal of the rest of the meat of this textbook was added to macroeconomic views. Powerful critiques of the then-established conventional wisdom of macroeconomics were made first by Milton Friedman and then by Robert Lucas, both of whom made their intellectual home at the University of Chicago.

Milton Friedman's critique of the then-dominant tradition in macroeconomics had four major parts. The first was that the standard models of the time greatly over-estimated the government's ability to manage and control the economy. Great uncertainty, long lags, and variable effects of policy actions placed extremely tight limits on the ability of the government to smooth out recessions and avoid periods of high unemployment. The second was that the standard models greatly overestimated the power of fiscal policy and greatly underestimated the power of monetary policy. The third was that the measurement of the money supply told you most of what you needed to know about how economic policy was working.

The fourth was the idea of the natural rate of unemployment, developed by Friedman and Edward Phelps in the second half of the 1960s. To the extent that macroeconomists in the early 1960s talked about aggregate supply and inflation at all, they tended to follow the lead of economists who took the location of the short-run Phillips curve to be fixed. A given level of unemployment would produce a fixed, unchanging rate of inflation with no feedback of past inflation on expected inflation and no shifts in the natural rate of unemployment. Friedman and Phelps argued that high past inflation would raise expected inflation, and that if unemployment were kept below its natural rate then the Phillips curve would shift upward over time, generating higher and higher inflation.

The "stagflation" of the 1970s proved Friedman and Phelps to be completely correct on their fourth point. In less than a decade the economics profession shifted to the "accelerationist" Phillips curve that we use today. Friedman's first and second points also became part of the received wisdom. Only the claim that the money supply was the sole important variable for understanding macroeconomic policy failed to win broad acceptance.

But Milton Friedman's **"monetarist"** critique was only the first half of the successful revisionist challenge to the doctrines of the post–World War II **Keynesians**. The "rational-expectations" macroeconomists — Robert Lucas, Thomas Sargent, Robert Barro, and others — argued that Keynesian economics had failed to think through the importance of expectations.

The rational-expectations economists assumed that people were doing the best they could to figure out the structure of the economy in which they lived. Because standard Keynesian models did not pay enough attention to expectations, the models failed to recognize that systematic changes in economic policy would change the parameters of the consumption and investment functions as well as the location of the Phillips curve. Thus macroeconomic models that took estimated consumption functions, investment functions, and Phillips curves as building blocks would blow up in the face of policy makers.

Once again the critique was incorporated into the mainstream quite rapidly. As MIT economist Olivier Blanchard puts it, the "idea that rational expectations was the right working assumption gained wide acceptance . . . not . . . because all macroeconomists believe that people, firms, and participants . . . always form expectations rationally . . . [but because] rational expectations appears to be a natural benchmark, at least until economists have made progress . . . understanding . . . actual expectations." By the mid-1980s the intellectual structure of the version of modern macroeconomics presented in this book was largely complete.

And since? The late 1980s and 1990s were a time of idea generation and exploration. They saw macroeconomists exploring and testing a large number of different ideas and models. It was an age in which the set of possible approaches expanded, but in which the mainstream policy-analytic position of macroeconomists did not shift much. If the past is any guide, such a period of exploration and experimentation will eventually be followed by another period of successful critique, during which the mainstream of macroeconomics will once again change substantially and rapidly as it did in the 1970s and early 1980s.

What might the future of macroeconomics bring?

RECAP   THE PAST OF MACROECONOMICS

John Maynard Keynes's 1936 book *The General Theory of Employment, Interest, and Money* swept the intellectual field, shaped modern macroeconomics, and set the groundwork on which the analytical apparatus used in this textbook was built. Milton Friedman's critique in the 1960s established that the then-standard models greatly overestimated the government's ability to manage and control the economy. Friedman's critique was reinforced by a further critique led by Robert Lucas that established that Keynesian economists had failed to think through the importance of expectations. Since the Lucas critique a lot of ideas have been generated and explored in macroeconomics, but the views held on economic policy issues today are as they were shaped by Keynes, Friedman, and Lucas.

17.2 THE FUTURE OF MACROECONOMICS: "REAL" BUSINESS CYCLES

One Possible Road

One place where the future of macroeconomics might lie is in the theory of "**real**" **business cycles**, briefly sketched in Chapter 7. The fundamental premise of this line of thinking is that all the other macroeconomists took a wrong turn a long time ago. It is more than half a century since economists turned away from the line of analysis of Joseph Schumpeter and toward that of the monetarists and Keynesians. One possibility is that this was, in the long run, a mistake.

John Maynard Keynes, Irving Fisher, Milton Friedman, Paul Samuelson, and all of the economists working in both Keynesian and monetarist traditions believe that there are two key elements to understanding business cycles. First, you need to understand the determinants of nominal aggregate demand. Second, you need to understand the division of changes in nominal aggregate demand into changes in production (and employment) on the one hand and changes in prices (inflation or deflation) on the other. Thus Keynesians and monetarists think about the velocity of money, the determinants of investment spending, the multiplier, crowding out, the natural rate of unemployment, the rate of expected inflation, the Phillips curve, and other related topics.

To real-business-cycle economists in the Schumpeterian tradition like Edward Prescott, most of this is a waste of time. There are changes in nominal aggregate demand, but their impact falls mostly on prices and only a little in output and employment. To understand the roots of real fluctuations — fluctuations in the real economy — you need to follow a different road.

The theory of real business cycles begins with the fundamental assumption that the same theory that determines what happens in the long run — the theory of economic growth — should also be applied to explain fluctuations in production and employment in the short run. It is not that real-business-cycle theorists assume that prices are never rigid, or that markets always clear, or that every price paid for every good balances supply and demand at that moment. Instead, real-business-cycle theorists assume that the price rigidities and patterns of sluggish adjustment that Keynesians and monetarists see are simply not very relevant. They assume that a reasonable first approximation is to suppose that the money supply and the level of potential output determine the price level, and that the level of potential output at any moment is more or less equal to actual real GDP. They believe strongly in the *classical dichotomy:* Real fundamentals effectively determine the values of real quantities like GDP even in the short run, and nominal variables (like the money stock) determine the values of nominal quantities (like the price level).

The Unevenness of Economic Growth

Some years there are adverse cost shocks — the tripling of world oil prices in 1973, for example. In such years it makes no sense to produce at what had been the normal level of economic output. The normal level balances social benefits and social costs: When social costs increase, the last 1 percent of output produced is certainly no longer worth the resources in people's time, used-up capital, depleted natural resources, and so on, that it consumes. So when an adverse cost shock hits the economy, a recession ought to follow and people ought to spend less time working: That's what an efficient economy would look like. Conversely, when a favorable cost shock hits the economy, it is advantageous to produce as much as possible: Because goods and services can then be produced at low cost, workers should work extra shifts and heavy demands should be placed on other resources.

But these are not the only "real" shocks to the economy's production possibilities that happen. Entrepreneurs have to guess at the future of technological development, and the value of new investment. There are moments when rapid technological innovation opens up new industries and new possibilities for investment. At such moments the stock market will be high, the returns to investment large, and so investment spending will be high and an efficient economy will be in a boom even though the new technologies have not yet increased real output. Current productivity is not especially high. But putting lots of new capital in place is uniquely profitable.

At other moments entrepreneurs will realize that they and those who came before them have been overly optimistic. Branches of industry that have been built up turn out to be unpromising. The socially optimal thing to do is not to invest, but instead to retrench: to cut back on investment spending and scrap capital until it becomes clear where there will be opportunities for profitable large-scale investment. Most of the work on real-business-cycle theory has concentrated on the effect of cost — supply — and productivity shocks on output. But shocks to future technologies are just as "real" in that they involve changes in the economy's long-run production possibilities. And they are large: Just look at the technology section of your newspaper, or visit Silicon Valley.

Is this theory of real business cycles a promising theory of economic fluctuations? Economists disagree. Perhaps fewer economists think that real-business-cycle theory is a progressive research program this year than thought so a decade ago, but that could change. Whether you think that real-business-cycle theory is promising depends on answers to three questions:

- Should the fact that a reduction in work hours shows up as some people becoming wholly unemployed change one's interpretation of what causes a decline in total hours worked?
- Should the fact that many wages and prices are not flexible lead one to assign a prominent role to monetary factors as causes of real fluctuations in output and employment?
- How large are technology shocks to the economy, anyway?

Problems of Real-Business-Cycle Theory

Unemployment

Real-business-cycle theory assumes that the total amount of hours worked at any moment is largely determined by how many hours it makes sense for people to work. The supply of hours worked is set at the point where the marginal displeasure of working an extra hour is just about equal to the marginal social product of an extra hour's work, given the marginal value of extra goods for consumption or for investment purposes.

When the marginal social product of labor is high — when labor is more than usually productive, or when there are extremely valuable opportunities to invest that an increase in work hours and thus of total product can take advantage of — workers are willing to work more hours. When labor is relatively unproductive, or when highly valuable investment opportunities are scarce, it makes sense for total work hours to fall. Instead of spending extra time on the job producing output of relatively little marginal value, take a week or two off and go on an extra vacation, or spend some extra time with the kids.

Such a willingness to work more hours when the incentive to work is relatively high and fewer hours when the incentive to work is relatively low is called an intertemporal substitution of labor. As an example, consider a student who needs to (a) take classes and (b) earn money to save toward some goal. It's hard to take classes and earn money at the same time, so the choice is between either working in the summer and taking classes in the winter, or working in the winter and taking classes in the summer. If the student works in the summer and gets paid at the end of the summer, then at the end of the winter the student will have $W_s(1 + r/2)$ dollars — the sum of his or her summer wage and the interest for half a year that he or she would earn by banking that money until it is needed at the end of the winter. If the student works in the winter, then at the end of the winter the student would have W_w dollars.

The real relative wage between the summer and the winter is thus equal to

$$\frac{W_s(1 + r/2)}{W_w}$$

The higher this quantity, the more likely the student is to choose summer rather than winter work. Thus the incentive to work hard now — accept lots of overtime, say — depends on three things: (a) the wage now, (b) the wage expected in the future, and (c) the real interest rate. Increases in the first and the third tend to lead people to postpone recreation and other nonwork uses of time to the future. Increases in the second tend to lead people to cut back on work effort now. If people are highly willing to shift their hours of work from season to season or from year to year, then one would expect fluctuations in current productivity and technological opportunities to lead to substantial fluctuations in employment.

But critics of real-business-cycle theory think that it makes little sense to analyze the total amount of hours worked in the economy as if it were like the decisions of a representative worker. They point out that people change their weekly work hours by relatively little. People in the labor force want to work. When total work hours fall it isn't because people have chosen to work shorter shifts and avoid overtime, it is because people have lost their jobs. The unemployment rate fluctuates substantially over the business cycle. And high unemployment in a recession is not a market-clearing phenomenon: People don't say they are "taking an extra vacation" or "out of the labor force because wages will be higher next year"; people say they are "unemployed."

Advocates of real-business-cycle theory say that this critique misses the point. People stay unemployed because they would rather spend more time searching for a better job that matches their skills and pays more than the job they could get today. And the job they could get today pays relatively little either because labor productivity is not high, or because there are no extremely valuable uses in investment or consumption for the good produced by an extra amount of work.

Technology and Real Business Cycles

According to real-business-cycle theories, production fluctuates because of the changing value of output and the changing productivity of the economy. When production technology improves, more is produced. When unique opportunities for investment open, more is produced. Perhaps recessions are times in which increases in costs — the tripling of oil prices in 1973, say — make it socially inefficient to run factories near capacity. Perhaps recessions are times in which everyone now recognizes that too much has been invested, and that it is better to cut back on investment than to continue to build up capital that adds little to the economy's productive capacity.

Critics of real-business-cycle theory concentrate their fire on the claim that the economy experiences large negative shocks to productivity. They claim that increases in costs like the 1973 oil shock are the exception rather than the rule. Critics tend to be silent on whether downturns in investment are to be understood as rational reactions to news about future growth and productivity, and have little to offer as alternative explanations of why investment fluctuates so much.

Money and Real Business Cycles

Real-business-cycle theorists tend to argue that monetary policy has little impact on production and employment, and that fluctuations in the money stock and interest rates are mostly reactions to changes already taking place in output and employment. But the Federal Reserve certainly believes that it affects the level of interest rates, that it makes decisions about the level of the money supply, and that its decisions cause changes in the level of production and output. Either everyone in the Federal Reserve's conference room is hopelessly deluded (and what they think are their decisions are instead the result of fluctuations in real activity that they do not consciously know about at the time they make their votes) or monetary policy has a powerful impact on production and employment.

Assessment

If I thought this line of research is truly the future of macroeconomics, I would have written a different book. Nevertheless these theorists make important points, especially those in what I see as the Schumpeterian wing of the real-business-cycle tradition. Economic growth is *not* smooth. It *does* proceed sector by sector. Shifts in investment — big backward-and-forward moves in the position of the IS curve — do arise out of changing beliefs about the current productivity of the economy and the future value of new investment.

The existence of real-business-cycle theory is a call for all economists to spend more time thinking about the determinants of investment fluctuations: either tying them to changes in productivity and the value of investment, or developing useful social-psychological theories of the shifts in animal spirits that cause such large movements in investment over time. My guess is that a lot of what is now called real-business-cycle analysis will be incorporated into mainstream macroeconomics over the next two decades as the theory of growth is integrated with the theory of business cycles, and as economists make progress in understanding why investment is so volatile.

> **RECAP** **THE FUTURE OF MACROECONOMICS: "REAL" BUSINESS CYCLES**
>
> Real-business-cycle theorists see booms as generated when rapid technological innovation opens up new industries and new possibilities for investment. At such moments the stock market will be high, the returns to investment large, and so investment spending will be high. Real-business-cycle theorists see recessions as generated when entrepreneurs conclude that those who came before them have been overly optimistic. The socially optimal thing to do is not to invest, but instead to retrench: to cut back on investment spending and scrap capital until it becomes clear where there will be opportunities for profitable large-scale investment.

17.3 THE FUTURE: NEW KEYNESIAN ECONOMICS

The second possible future for macroeconomics sees the continued development of the mainstream research program, as its weaknesses and incoherencies are slowly repaired.

Certainly the area of modern macroeconomics that is in least satisfactory shape is the area of aggregate supply. Why do changes in nominal aggregate demand show up as changes in the level of production and employment, and not just as changes in the level of prices? Since at least the 1930s, the mainstream of macroeconomics has attributed the sluggishness of aggregate supply — the fact that the Phillips curve has a slope, and is not vertical — to stickiness in wages and prices. Thus fluctuations in the nominal level of aggregate demand cause fluctuations in output and employment. But where does this stickiness and slow adjustment of wages and prices come from? After all, business cycles appear to be so unpleasant and costly to society as a whole that by now we should have found a way to greatly reduce the harmful macroeconomic consequences of **price stickiness**.

Thus a possible future direction for macroeconomics is a deep investigation into the sources of sluggish wage and price adjustment, and of aggregate supply. This research program has gained the name *new Keynesian economics*.

Menu Costs

Prices do not adjust immediately and completely in the short run because it is costly to change them. A restaurant must print up a new menu; a mail-order firm must send out a new catalog. Economists call these costs of changing prices **menu costs.** They are what lead firms to adjust prices once in a while — not, with a few exceptions, every second. In most cases such menu costs are small: It doesn't cost a firm very much to change its prices. But "small" does not mean "unimportant." As macroeconomists George Akerlof, Janet Yellen, and Greg Mankiw have stressed, it is entirely possible, in theory at least, for small menu costs at the level of an individual firm to have large effects on the economy as a whole.

A price adjustment or a failure to adjust prices on the part of one firm affects other firms. Whenever one particular business lowers its price, it frees up a little bit of nominal purchasing power. The extra nominal purchasing power that would have been spent buying that particular firm's product (but that wasn't spent because the price was lowered) is instead free to be spent on products made by other firms. As long as total nominal spending remains constant, a decline in one firm's price slightly increases demand for other firms' products. New Keynesian economists call this phenomenon an *aggregate demand externality.*

Because of such aggregate demand externalities, as long as total nominal demand is fixed, the economy as a whole benefits more by one firm's reduction in price than that one firm does. But the firm decides whether to cut its price depending on whether the benefit *to the firm* from cutting its price exceeds the menu costs the firm must pay. Thus the economy can get stuck in a situation in which no firm reduces its price — because no firm can see a private benefit in excess of its menu cost — even though the economy as a whole would benefit by vastly more than the sum of menu costs if all businesses were to reduce their prices.

Staggered Prices and Coordination Failures

Even if menu costs are not important, the fact that one firm's best choice for its price depends on the prices that other firms are charging may lead to sluggish adjustment in wages and prices even though individual prices are theoretically free to move without hindrance.

Macroeconomist John Taylor was the first to consider an economy in which large groups of workers sign three-year labor contracts. Those who negotiate their wages in years divisible by three will look forward at what demand and supply on the labor market is likely to be, but they will also look sideways, at firms that negotiated their labor contracts one or two years ago. Thus the wage negotiated this year will depend not just on what will happen but on what people one or two years ago — when the last set of contracts were signed — thought was likely to happen. The aggregate wage and price levels will thus exhibit inertia even without barriers to price flexibility when renegotiations occur, just because of the institutional structure of the economy.

Are such "**coordination failures**" caused by the fact that agents in the economy do not all make long-run decisions at the same time or are unable to commit to deciding in similar ways important causes of business cycles? Two decades ago economists thought that the answer was almost surely yes. Many studies were written comparing the U.S. system of wage negotiation with other, more centralized systems found in Germany and Japan that seemed less likely to lead to coordination failures.

Today, because of the relatively good macroeconomic performance of the U.S.

economy, theories that point out structural flaws in U.S. macroeconomic institutions receive little attention. The theoretical point, however, remains unsettled.

Assessment

At the moment these ideas about the microfoundations of price stickiness are at the stage of just-so stories: plausible and possible mechanisms, but only that. There are no convincing quantitative analyses of just how much sluggishness in wage and price adjustment is contributed by each possible cause. There are no tests of one theory against another, and no predictions of the magnitude of price inertia that should emerge from any of the possible theoretical causes. In this sense, the theory of aggregate supply today is in a position roughly analogous to the position of the theory of aggregate demand just before John Maynard Keynes.

I have no doubt that the mechanisms of business cycles should be a large part of the future of economics. We should be able to learn a lot about which models of business cycles are potentially useful by turning theories loose on perhaps the greatest macroeconomic laboratory available: the extant record of macroeconomic historical statistics. A robust and useful theory of business cycles should be able to account for the patterns seen in the long-run data for many countries.

My reading of the historical evidence is that business-cycle models that do not put monetary economics at the center of analysis are inconsistent with the evidence on the behavior of real exchange rates. Events like the comparative pattern of national recoveries from the Great Depression cannot be understood without placing prices that are sticky at the center of the analysis as well. Thus I think that the new Keynesian research program is likely to play a stronger role in the future of macroeconomics than the real-business-cycle research program. But I have been wrong before.

> **RECAP**   **THE FUTURE: NEW KEYNESIAN ECONOMICS**
>
> Why do changes in nominal aggregate demand show up as changes in the level of production and employment, and not just as changes in the level of prices? The mainstream of macroeconomics has attributed this to stickiness in wages and prices. But where does this stickiness come from? One possibility is that small costs of changing prices on the part of individual firms have large effects because a price adjustment or a failure to adjust prices on the part of one firm affects other firms through *aggregate demand externalities*. Another possibility is that prices and wages are sticky because agents in the economy do not all make long-run decisions at the same time.

17.4 DEBTS AND DEFICITS, CONSUMPTION AND SAVING

Debts and Deficits: Ricardian Equivalence

Chapter 14 detailed economists' standard view of debts and deficits. Fiscal deficits stimulate the economy in the short run as long as the central bank does not take action to neutralize the fiscal stimulus. In the long run, however, debts and deficits crowd out investment and shift the economy to a less favorable steady-state growth path.

But this standard view has been subject to a powerful challenge that may become an important part of the future of economics. Whether it is successful or not, this challenge is likely to change the way we think about how the government's budget affects the economy. This alternative view of the long-run (and also the short-run) effects of debts and deficits is called "Ricardian" after David Ricardo, who does not seem to have held the view; it should be called "Barrovian" after its most effective and powerful advocate, Harvard macroeconomist Robert Barro.

Robert Barro's View

Think of it this way: The government is, in a sense, our agent. It buys things for us (government purchases) and it collects money from us to pay for the things it buys on our behalf. The moneys it collects from us are called taxes. Sometimes the government collects as much from us as it buys on our behalf: Then the government budget is balanced. Sometimes the government collects less from us than it spends on our behalf: Then the government budget is in deficit, and the government makes up the deficit by borrowing money now and implicitly committing to raise taxes to repay the debt (interest and principal) at some time in the future.

Suppose that the government spends an extra $1,000 on your behalf and at the same time raises your taxes by $1,000. Because your after-tax income has gone down by $1,000, you cut back on consumption spending. Now suppose that the government spends an extra $1,000 on your behalf, but doesn't raise taxes — instead it borrows the $1,000 for one year, and announces that it is going to raise taxes next year to repay the debt.

What is the difference between these two situations? In one case, the government has collected an extra $1,000 in taxes from you this year. In the other case, the government has announced that it will collect an extra $1,000 in taxes from you next year. In either case you are poorer. In the first case you cut back on your consumption. Shouldn't you cut back on your consumption in the second case too — set aside a reserve to pay the extra taxes next year, and invest it, perhaps in the bonds that the government has issued? After all, the effect of the government policy on your personal private wealth is identical in the two cases.

Robert Barro would say yes. He would say that what matters for the determination of consumption spending is not what taxes are levied on you this year, but what all of the changes in government policy tell you about the value of the total stream of taxes this year, next year, and on into the future. Government policy thus ought to affect consumption only to the extent that it tells you how much the government is going to spend — and thus what will be the total lifetime tax bill levied on your wealth.

Counterarguments

Many economists point out that the theoretical elegance of Barro's view is broken by a number of different considerations, including the following:

Myopia. Perhaps people are not far-sighted enough to fully work out what an increased deficit in the present implies for their future taxes.

Liquidity constraints. Barro's argument implicitly assumes that it is easy for people to borrow and lend. If a good many people can't borrow and lend — they would spend more if only they could borrow it on reasonable terms —

then you would expect consumers to react to tax cuts by increasing consumption spending even if they knew full well that the government was going to recapture those tax cuts with tax increases later.

Beneficiaries and payers may differ. I am the beneficiary from increased spending this year, but the extra taxes that the government will exact two decades hence may well not be paid by me but by someone who isn't even in the labor force today.

But are any of these — or all of them together — really enough to make us confident that changes in the timing of taxes (holding government spending patterns constant) will have a big effect on overall consumption? Even if Barro's challenge to the conventional wisdom is unsuccessful, it will become clear that it is unsuccessful only when we have a much better understanding of how and why people divide their income between consumption and saving.

Consumption and Saving

In the early part of the twentieth century it was relatively easy to justify a relatively high marginal propensity to consume. Most households had little if any savings. Most households found themselves unable to borrow. Hence they were *liquidity constrained:* They wished to spend more today, but could not find anyone to lend them the liquid wealth to enable them to do so. Thus one would expect a boost to income today to generate a large rise in consumption spending. Add to this the fact that buying consumer durables is in a sense as valid a way of saving for the future as putting money in the bank; then a high marginal propensity to consume and a strong multiplier process seem easy to understand.

The past 50 years, however, have seen steady and large increases in the flexibility of the financial system. Few Americans today are without the ability to borrow to increase current consumption should they so wish. Those Americans whose liquidity is constrained today receive a very small portion of total income, and a small portion of increases in total income. Thus economists' theories would predict that the marginal propensity to consume would have dropped far by today, and that the multiplier process would be more or less irrelevant to aggregate demand. Nevertheless, consumption still declines significantly when the economy goes into recession.

This consumption puzzle is another substantial hole in today's current macroeconomic knowledge. Many economists are trying to close it. Some, like Johns Hopkins macroeconomist Chris Carroll, argue that typical consumers are both **impatient** and strongly **risk averse**. Risk aversion makes them unwilling to borrow. Impatience makes them eager to spend increases in income. Thus the fact that improvements in financial flexibility means that consumers could borrow doesn't mean that they will. Other economists focus on the persistence of income changes, and say that current income is a good proxy for permanent income and hence should be a strong determinant of consumption. Still others — led by Chicago economist Richard Thaler — argue that it is time for economists to throw the simple-minded psychological theory of utility maximization overboard, and to take seriously what psychologists have to say about how humans reason.

It is unclear how this hole in macroeconomists' understanding will be resolved. It is clear, however, that whatever answer is reached to the puzzles regarding consumption and saving will also have a powerful impact on the debate over debts and deficits.

17.5 DOES MONETARY POLICY HAVE A LONG-RUN FUTURE?

When the Federal Reserve uses open-market operations to affect interest rates, it does so because its purchases or sales of Treasury bills raise or lower the supply of bank reserves in the economy, and so make it easier or harder for businesses to borrow money. But total commercial bank reserves in the United States amount to less than half a percent of GDP. A typical open-market operation is a few billion dollars.

In the context of an economy in which annual GDP is more than $11 trillion and in which total wealth is something like $40 trillion, how is it that a swap of one government promise to pay (a Treasury bill) for another (a dollar bill) can cause big changes in the cost of borrowing money, and ultimately in the level and composition of economic activity?

This question has not been asked often enough in the past hundred years. Economists have tended to assume that monetary policy is powerful and that the reasons for its power are relatively uninteresting. They have by and large ignored the fact that to shift from an extremely tight monetary policy in which long-run nominal GDP growth is zero to a loose one in which long-run nominal GDP growth is 10 percent per year requires that the Federal Reserve increase purchases of Treasury bills by an average of only some $20 million a day.

Monetary policy is certainly powerful. But in at least one of the potential futures of macroeconomics the reasons for its power become very interesting indeed. For it is at least possible that the future evolution of the financial system might undermine the sources of influence that monetary policy today possesses.

The reasons that monetary policy has power today that economists usually bring forward rest on what Harvard macroeconomist Benjamin Friedman calls — politely — "a series of . . . familiar fictions: Households and firms need currency to purchase goods . . . nonbank financial institutions [cannot] create credit . . . [and] so on."

The standard explanation is that open-market purchases of Treasury bills increase the reserve balances held by the bank where the seller of the Treasury bills receives payment. Thus the total volume of reserves in the banking system as a whole rises, and the banking system responds to this increase in reserves by increasing total credit in the economy by more than 10 times the reserve increase. Because commercial banks must hold reserves, and because only the Federal Reserve can change the total amount of reserves, it has a uniquely strong ability to affect interest rates. In the standard story the central bank's power is further boosted because everyone in financial markets takes its actions today as a powerful signal of what its actions will be in the entire future.

This Federal Reserve power, however, would be of little use if nobody much cared about keeping deposits at commercial banks, and nobody used reserve-backed commercial bank deposits as transactions balances. Looking to the future, it's likely that more and more transactions will be carried out not through cash or check but through credit cards, debit cards, smart cash cards now used in Europe, or other forms of electronic funds transfer at points of sale.

Will the future hold a gradual weakening of central bank power? Macroeconomists know that central banks today are powerful and are likely to remain so for at least a generation. But forecasting beyond that point requires a deeper knowledge and better models of the sources of central bank power than macroeconomists currently possess. This is thus another area in which the macroeconomics taught in the future is likely to be substantially different from the macroeconomics taught in the past.

Chapter Summary

1. Modern macroeconomics has its origin in the Keynesian theories of the Great Depression and the immediate post-WWII era.

2. Modern macroeconomics was reforged by the monetarists under Milton Friedman in the 1960s and 1970s, and by the rational-expectations economists led by Robert Lucas in the 1970s and 1980s.

3. Perhaps the focus on aggregate demand will turn out in the long run to have been a false road. Perhaps a better theory of the macroeconomy can be built up out of the theory of real business cycles in the Schumpeterian tradition.

4. Perhaps the future of macroeconomics lies in a more detailed investigation of aggregate supply. Perhaps uncovering the reasons that prices are sticky will lead to the next wave of progress in macroeconomics.

5. The entire conventional analysis of debts and deficits is under challenge by Robert Barro, who argues that individuals are far-sighted and closely linked, and that they take action to neutralize the effects of many government policies.

6. The conventional analysis of consumption — the permanent income hypothesis — is also under challenge by more psychological approaches to understanding consumption.

7. The other possible interesting direction in which macroeconomics might evolve involves the future of monetary policy. How will the coming of the "new economy" and the changing institutional framework of transactions and settlements affect the power of monetary policy?

Key Terms

monetarism (p. 465)

Keynesianism (p. 465)

real business cycles (p. 466)

sticky prices (p. 470)

menu costs (p. 471)

staggered prices (p. 471)

coordination failures (p. 471)

Ricardian equivalence (p. 472)

myopia (p. 473)

liquidity constraints (p. 473)

impatience (p. 474)

risk aversion (p. 474)

Analytical Exercises

1. What are the principal pieces of real-business-cycle theory?

2. Why is it possible that real-business-cycle theory will play a much larger role in macroeconomics courses in the future than in the present?

3. In what areas do new Keynesian economists concentrate their research?

4. What is Ricardian equivalence? Why might it not be a good approximation to the way individuals actually behave?

5. Why do some economists fear that monetary policy is going to lose its effectiveness?

Epilogue

Macroeconomics is far from complete. It will not become complete in my or your or anyone's lifetime. One reason for this is that the subject is complicated. A second reason is that macroeconomists are pursuing an ever-changing and ever-moving target: As the economy changes, its macroeconomic behavior changes as well. Four centuries ago (if there had been a macroeconomics course then) the macroeconomics of harvest failures would have been a big topic. Today it isn't. Many of what we see as important topics today will be dismissed as irrelevant a generation or a century from now. And much of what those societies will need answers to is unimportant to us, or unknown to us.

But here at the end of the book is the place to quickly look back over the entire text. There are a great many things that macroeconomists do know. And this is the place to summarize them, before going on to discuss what macroeconomists don't know, and what I believe macroeconomists will never know.

WHAT ECONOMISTS KNOW . . .

. . . About the Current State of the Economy

Largely relying on government-collected statistics, economists know a substantial amount about the current state of the economy. They have good estimates of the level of potential output. They have good estimates of the current real wage level, of the amount of unemployment, and of the general state of the labor market. They have good estimates of the rate of inflation.

Economists' knowledge of the long-run pace of economic growth is, however, much more partial. The size and extent of the biases inevitably present in the national income and product accounts remain elusive. And economists' knowledge of the current state of the economy comes with a substantial lag: Economists know much more about the state of the economy last year than they do about the state of the economy today.

But all in all, the NIPA system — and the other largely government-collected economic statistics — give us a remarkable amount of knowledge about the current state of our economy. Certainly the amount of easily and publicly available information about the state of the American macroeconomy today dwarfs the knowledge that even the best-informed in previous centuries had, or even the knowledge that the leaders presiding over the centrally planned economies of the twentieth century had of the real state of affairs.

. . . About Long-Run Economic Growth

Economists also know a surprising amount about the preconditions of long-run growth. We know demography — Malthus, the population explosion, the demographic revolution, and the importance of education. We know that before the industrial revolution living standards were very low because in the race between human fertility, diminishing returns, and technological development the rate of technological progress was slow. We know that once human populations pass through a threshold level of material prosperity and literacy, population growth rates slow down drastically — the experience of western Europe suggests that negative population growth may be in humanity's future after the middle of the next century.

Economists understand the importance of a high rate of investment for achieving successful economic growth — both because capital goods amplify our skills and capabilities, and because much of modern technology that increases total factor productivity works only if it is accompanied by, embodied in, the right kinds of capital goods. A high rate of investment is key to a rapidly growing and relatively prosperous economy.

Economists also know that better *technology* — understood in both a broad and a narrow sense — is the single most important key to sustained progress in material standards of living. And here I believe economists have fallen down on the job: Macroeconomists know much less about the development and diffusion of this truly important source of growth, technology, than we should. But it is completely clear that a high rate of investment to generate a high capital-output ratio, a strong commitment to education to create a skilled and literate workforce (and a low rate of population growth), and better technology are the goals of economic policy as far as the long run is concerned.

Economists also know important things about how to achieve these goals of economic policy: The role of the government in economic development has become increasingly clear over the past generation. It is now clear that it is much easier to achieve successful long-run growth by relying on the market system to coordinate economic activity than by relying on central planning and central commands. Market economies appear to function well only if they are coupled with strong legal and institutional protections for private property. Overly mighty governments — governments that regard other people's things as the government's property — appear to be very bad for economic growth.

It is also clear that government policy needs to provide the market economy with the right incentives and signals if it is to function: Activities with negative externalities like pollution need to be penalized; activities with positive externalities like research and development need to be encouraged. Thus a government that protects property rights, promotes education, and promotes innovation seems important as a precondition for successful economic growth.

But our knowledge of economic growth is incomplete. The links between different kinds of investment and rates of total factor productivity growth and the mechanisms underlying the transfer of technology from rich countries to poor countries remain elusive.

. . . About Business Cycles, Unemployment, and Inflation in the Long Run

Economists know that market economies are robust things. In the long run — and exceptional circumstances like the Great Depression aside — the market economy does tend to return to a position of nearly full employment. Markets for goods and for labor do — absent large blockages — reach something like a supply-and-demand equilibrium. In a recession it is safe to predict that the next five years will bring a boom. In a gigantic boom it is safe to predict that the next five years will bring a slowdown.

Thus economists know that shifts in government spending will crowd out (or crowd in) consumption and investment. They know that shortfalls of national saving or booms in investment will bring inflows of capital and the trade deficits needed to finance them. They know that the central bank's policy is in the long run the absolutely crucial determinant of the price level and the inflation rate.

. . . About Business Cycles, Unemployment, and Inflation in the Short Run

Economists know that the basic Keynesian sticky-price model still provides a good guide to the basic determinants of the level of aggregate demand. And the aggregate supply–Phillips curve diagram still provides a guide — not necessarily a good guide, but the best one we have — to the relationship between the level of real aggregate demand and the rate of price increase.

Because aggregate demand is the principal determinant of the level of GDP in the short run, anything that affects aggregate demand affects employment and output: fiscal policy, monetary policy, expectations, shocks to components of demand, shocks to the financial markets, changes in the international environment — all of these produce shifts in the equilibrium level of output.

Economists know that aggregate demand interacts with aggregate supply — the Phillips curve — to generate the inflation rate. And economists know that the Phillips curve is extremely volatile. The natural rate of unemployment can undergo substantial shifts much more rapidly than the changing composition of the labor force would suggest is possible. The expected rate of inflation depends critically on expectations of the central bank's competence and commitment to price stability.

. . . About the Making of Macroeconomic Policy

Thus governments attempting to stabilize the economy face a hard task of damping out many kinds of shocks. Their task is made harder because shifts in economic policy have uncertain and delayed effects on spending: Policy affects output and prices with long and variable lags. Perhaps the first lesson of stabilization policy is that governments should not overestimate their power and attempt to do too much. The second lesson is that monetary policy is the most useful *discretionary* stabilization policy tool. And the third lesson is that automatic stabilizers — the fiscal automatic stabilizers in the government's budget and the financial automatic stabilizers of deposit insurance — are important factors that help limit the need for discretionary stabilization policy.

Economists have learned over the past two decades that peacetime inflation at a level high enough that it becomes an important part of voters' consciousness — inflation at a rate of even 10 percent per year — is politically unacceptable in modern industrial democracies. Voters appear to hate and loathe politicians who preside over such episodes of inflation. Why even moderate inflation should be viewed so negatively is somewhat of a mystery: Economists' attempts to model costs of inflation have a difficult time coming up with costs that justify the high political value of low inflation. It may be that people simply dislike the greater uncertainty that inflation generates. It may be that people are simply making a mistake — that they should not dislike inflation as much as they do.

But for whatever reason, it is clear that in a modern democracy, successful control of inflation must be a very high priority for public policy.

At the root, the ultimate determinant of inflation is growth in the money supply. Control the rate of growth of the money supply, and you control inflation. A central bank that loses sight of this goal will find itself unable to control inflation.

But that is not all that economists know about controlling inflation. We also know that controlling inflation is easy — can be accomplished at low cost — if and only if investors, managers, and workers have confidence in the central bank's commitment to control inflation. Central bank *credibility* is the most important asset in order to make control of inflation easy and cheap. Central bank *credibility* is the most valuable thing a central bank can have — and is the most costly thing to regain once it is lost.

Economists know that in the short run the level of GDP and of employment depends on the level of aggregate demand for goods and services. Thus a good macroeconomic policy that seeks to avoid unnecessary unemployment and inflation must walk a fine line. Aggregate demand must be high enough to eliminate unnecessary unemployment, but not high enough to generate accelerating inflation or (worst of all) to call into question the central bank's commitment to low inflation.

WHAT ECONOMISTS DON'T KNOW — BUT COULD LEARN

. . . About the Long-Run Relationship between Kinds of Investment and Productivity Growth

The list of what macroeconomists don't know is even longer than the list of things they do know. First, large chunks of the process of long-run economic growth remain a mystery. Macroeconomists cannot prescribe to poor countries the policy mix that would enable them to duplicate the rapid convergence of Japan or Italy to industrial-core status that we have seen since World War II. Macroeconomists cannot prescribe to rich countries how to maximize their rates of economic growth and appropriately discounted levels of economic welfare. Macroeconomists do not know what is the right degree of "openness" for the world economy. They do not know at what point we would get the most benefits from international trade and invest flows while suffering the lowest costs from international financial market–generated economic instability.

But in these areas, at least, macroeconomists can learn. The history of the world over the past century provides a lot of lessons about the sources of long-run growth and stagnation. And the future will continue to provide more such lessons. As long as economists are willing to take fresh looks at the world and revise their beliefs in response to new information, macroeconomists in a generation will know much more about long-run growth than we do today.

. . . About the Short-Run Determinants of Investment

Ultimately the key issue dividing the new Keynesian and the real-business-cycle schools of macroeconomists is the sources of shifts in investment. The most common large-scale macroeconomic shock hitting a modern industrial market economy is an inward (or outward) shift in the IS curve caused by an investment slump (or boom) accompanied by a fall (or a swift rise) in the stock market. Is this shock better thought of as optimal responses of the market to news about future profits and technological opportunities? If so, then the real-business-cycle research program will be the most fruitful over the next generation. Is this shock more accurately seen as one of the less-than-rational shifts in social-psychological opinion that John Maynard Keynes referred to as "animal spirits"? If so, then the new Keynesian research program is likely to pay the highest dividends over the next generation.

This question of the most important determinants of domestic investment booms is closely tied to the key issue in international finance. Why have international financial markets been so vulnerable to financial crises over the past decade? And what is the appropriate response to constrain governments from engaging in disturbing policies? Is it to reduce the magnitude of cross-border trade and financial flows, or to adopt more aggressive policies to intervene to support countries afflicted by financial crises?

The only true answer is that macroeconomists today do not really know. This area will be one of the major political flashpoints of the next generation. It will also be one of the major battlegrounds — and hopefully areas of the progress of knowledge — for macroeconomic theory over the next generation.

. . . About the Impact of Government Policy on the Economy

A lot is still not known about how and why government policy affects the economy. Macroeconomists still argue about the relative roles played in generating short-run business cycles of "monetary" shocks and "real" shocks. Macroeconomists for the most part feel there ought to be powerful benefits from eliminating noise in the price system. But these gains from achieving low and stable inflation have not hitherto been demonstrated. And it remains mysterious why voters seem so averse to inflation when its measured economic costs appear relatively low.

Thus many fundamental questions about government policy remain up for grabs. How aggressively should central bankers pursue stabilization policy? The answer to that question depends on the solutions to the mysteries noted in the paragraph above. How much should we worry about large government deficits? The answer turns on whether or not Ricardian equivalence is roughly correct, and that depends in turn on the determinants and motivations of households' consumption and savings decisions.

. . . About the Microfoundations of Macroeconomics

Thus we come to the final set of things that economists do not know — but might someday find out. Macroeconomists do not understand aggregate consumption and savings decisions in the economy. They do not understand what determines the large shifts in the natural rate of unemployment seen over the past 30 years. Nor do they understand what can be done to constructively lower the natural rate of unemployment, or even what the natural rate of unemployment should be. Clearly it is worthwhile for the average worker who loses a job to spend some time unemployed searching for a new job. But how much?

And last, what are the underlying reasons that wages and prices are slow to respond to shifts in aggregate demand?

These questions about the "microfoundations of macroeconomics" have been at the top of the agenda for economic research at least since the end of World War II. Looking back, it is somewhat depressing to realize how little progress has been made, and how much the live microfoundational issues of today are those that economists like Franco Modigliani were worrying about immediately after World War II.

WHAT ECONOMISTS WILL NEVER KNOW

Chasing an Ever-Moving Target

In the natural sciences there is a strong sense of progress toward a goal: knowledge advances, and the amount of unknowns left to be understood shrinks. In the social sciences it is not so clear that there is progress. More is known, yes. But we are chasing an ever-moving target: One economist's joke is that you can give the same exam every 20 years, as long as you remember that the right answers will change.

Macroeconomics is a science of what might be called *emergent* phenomena. The marginal propensity to consume, the slope of the IS curve, the velocity of money — these are not basic, unchanging, fundamental quantities that can be measured and described once and for all. They are, instead, summary rule-of-thumb characterizations of phenomena that *emerge* from the billions of economic decisions made by hundreds of millions of workers, consumers, and firms. Thus we should expect macroeconomic "truth" to change over time as our economy changes.

So if there is a final lesson, it is this: Keep an open mind. Recognize that some of the things taught in this book will turn out to be wrong, or incomplete. And recognize that the questions that people want macroeconomics to answer will change in the future as well, both because the economy will change and because macroeconomics is the handmaiden of policy, which is a sub-branch of politics. And as politics changes, the questions that policy makers will ask of macroeconomists will change as well.

GLOSSARY

A

accelerating inflation When inflation is rising yearly, so that this year's inflation is greater than last year's inflation, which is greater than inflation in the year before. Not only are prices rising, but they are rising at an increasing proportional rate. Accelerating inflation is typically found when the unemployment rate is lower than the natural rate of unemployment, or when the economy is hit by an adverse supply shock like a sharp oil price increase.

accelerationist Phillips curve Found when inflation expectations are adaptive, that is, the expected rate of inflation that determines the position of the Phillips curve is equal to last year's rate of inflation. Each extra percentage point rise in expectations of inflation shifts the entire Phillips curve upward by 1 percentage point. Thus if unemployment falls and remains below the natural rate, inflation will accelerate.

accommodation A strategy for economic policy in which the central bank does not counteract but reinforces the consequences of a shock. For example, consider an adverse supply shock that boosts inflation. A policy of accommodation would not increase real interest rates to fight inflation, but would instead allow real interest rates to fall and so further boost inflation.

AD-AS diagram *See* aggregate demand–aggregate supply diagram.

adaptive expectations Expectations of the future formed by assuming the future will be like the past. Usually applied to expectations of inflation: Adaptive inflation expectations forecast future inflation by assuming it will be equal to inflation in the recent past. Adaptive expectations of inflation are one of the three cases economists typically analyze; the other two are static inflation expectations and rational inflation expectations.

aggregate demand Also called planned expenditure. Total spending — by consumers, investing firms, the government, and the international sector — on final goods and services. When considering the details of national income accounting, there are differences between aggregate demand, national product, GDP, and national income caused by differences in their exact definitions. At the eagle's eye level of analysis used in most of this book, however, the circular flow principle means that aggregate demand, national product, GDP, and national income are all equal.

aggregate demand–aggregate supply diagram Abbreviated AD-AS diagram. It plots real GDP (relative to potential output) on the horizontal axis and the price level (or the inflation rate) on the vertical axis. On this diagram the aggregate demand curve shows how planned expenditure varies with the price level (or the inflation rate); the aggregate supply curve shows how firms' total production varies with the price level (or the inflation rate). Equilibrium is where the curves cross, and thus where production is equal to sales, inventories are stable, and there is neither upward nor downward pressure on production or prices.

aggregate demand curve A downward-sloping relationship between aggregate demand and the price level, plotted on the AD-AS (or aggregate demand–aggregate supply) diagram. This inverse relationship is produced because (*a*) a higher price level means a lower money stock, higher interest rates, lower investment spending, and lower aggregate demand; or (*b*) a higher price level means that inflation is high, and a central bank wishing to control inflation has raised interest rates to reduce aggregate demand.

aggregate demand line Usually called the planned expenditure line. Found on the income-expenditure (or Keynesian cross) diagram that shows aggregate demand on the vertical and national income on the horizontal axis. An important part of the sticky-price, short-run business-cycle model. The planned expenditure line shows total spending — aggregate demand — as a function of the level of national income. The slope of the planned expenditure line is the MPE — the marginal propensity to expend income on domestic goods. The intercept of the planned expenditure line is the level of autonomous spending.

aggregate supply The quantity of final goods and services that firms produce given their existing stocks of plant, equipment, and other capital, and given the prevailing wage and price levels. In the flexible-price business-cycle model of Chapters 6 through 8 (and in the growth model of Chapters 4 and 5), wages and prices adjust so that in equilibrium, aggregate supply is equal to the economy's potential output. In the sticky-price model of Chapters 9 through 12, aggregate supply in the short run is an increasing function of the inflation rate (and thus of the price level).

aggregate supply curve The curve on the AD-AS (aggregate demand–aggregate supply) diagram that shows the dependence of firms' production on the inflation rate (and thus on the price level): the higher the inflation rate, the more goods and services are produced. The aggregate supply curve and the Phillips curve are different ways of expressing the same economic relationship.

analytic geometry The idea that graphs and equations are two different ways of expressing the same concepts. It allows lines and curves on a graph to represent algebraic equations — and algebraic equations to represent lines and curves on a graph. In economics, it is the use of graphs and diagrams as an alternative to equations and arithmetic for expressing economic relationships. In mathematics, it is the branch of mathematics that relates geometry and algebra. Often called Cartesian geometry because much of it was invented by Rene Descartes.

animal spirits Waves of optimism and pessimism — perhaps irrational or self-confirming — about the future of the economy that affect investment spending. Shifts in animal spirits push stock market and other asset prices up and down, and lead businesses to increase and decrease how much they spend on investment. A term often used by John Maynard Keynes as part of his argument that private investment spending was inherently unstable, and that strong stabilizing monetary and fiscal policies were needed to control the natural fluctuations of the business cycle.

anticipated monetary policy Found when workers, managers, and investors have rational expectations of inflation. Anticipated monetary policy is then those shifts in the money stock or interest rates that they had anticipated in advance. Under rational expectations, anticipated changes in monetary policy have no effect on production or unemployment, but they do have powerful effects on prices.

appreciation An increase in value, usually on the part of a currency. The opposite of depreciation. When an appreciation is sudden and is the result of an explicit change in policy by a government, it is called a revaluation. An appreciation of foreign currency is an increase in the value of the exchange rate. By contrast, an appreciation of the dollar is a fall in the value of the U.S. exchange rate.

arbitrage Earning profits by buying a good or an asset in one place (or time) and selling it in another place (or time) where its price is higher. In this book, arbitrage is used to derive equilibrium conditions in financial markets: In equilibrium, no arbitrage opportunities are left for financiers to exploit. Thus, for example, any differential in interest rates paid on investments at home and investments abroad must be offset by an expected change in the exchange rate.

automatic stabilizers In a recession, tax revenues automatically decline as incomes fall, and social insurance spending automatically rises as more people qualify for food stamps, unemployment insurance, and other social welfare expenditures. The government budget automatically swings toward a deficit, providing a stimulus to aggregate demand, whenever private demand drops. Similarly, it automatically swings toward a surplus, reducing aggregate demand, whenever private demand rises. The structure of the government's tax and spending programs thus automatically provides a degree of stabilization to aggregate demand. These fiscal automatic stabilizers are the only form of fiscal policy in the United States that works rapidly and effectively to reduce the size of the business cycle.

autonomous consumption Written C_0. That component of consumption spending that is independent of the level of national income. You can think of it as the level that consumption spending would be if household income were to fall to zero.

autonomous spending Written A. Those components of planned expenditure or aggregate demand that are independent of the level of national income. A higher level of autonomous spending is an upward shift in the aggregate demand line on the income-expenditure diagram. A higher level of autonomous spending increases equilibrium aggregate demand by an amount equal to the boost in autonomous spending times the multiplier. Autonomous spending A, is equal to autonomous consumption C_0, plus investment I, government purchases G, and gross exports GX: $A = C_0 + I + G + GX$.

B

bads The opposite of "goods." Elements produced by an economy that diminish consumers' welfare, and that would constitute a subtraction from GDP in some better, future system of social accounts to measure economic welfare. Bads include congestion (waiting in traffic jams), pollution, increases in crime (which increase measured GDP to the extent that they trigger greater expenditures on security), and the depletion of valuable resources (which are thus removed from the wealth of future generations).

Bagehot rule The principle that in a financial crisis the government needs to keep functioning those financial institutions and other businesses that are fundamentally sound and to — rapidly — close down and liquidate those organizations that are fundamentally bankrupt. If they would be bankrupt even if production and demand were at normal levels relative to potential, then they should be closed. If they would be solvent if production, demand, and asset prices were at their normal levels, the government needs to lend them as much money as they need to keep functioning through the crisis — albeit at a high, penalty rate.

balance of payments account The accounting system used to measure and comprehend a country's economic relations with the rest of the world. The balance of payments account has three parts: The current account tracks a country's imports and exports of goods and services; the capital account tracks a country's gross investment of capital abroad and foreigners' gross investment of capital at home; and, under a fixed exchange rate system, the official settlements account tracks changes in governments' exchange reserves.

balanced budget When the government's tax receipts equal its spending. Since there are many possible ways of accounting for tax receipts and for spending, the concept of a balanced budget is a fuzzy one.

balanced growth When a country has converged to its long-run steady-state growth path, and has a capital-output ratio equal to its equilibrium value κ^*, which is found by dividing the country's savings-investment rate s by the sum of the labor force growth rate n, the efficiency-of-labor growth rate g, and the capital depreciation rate δ: $\kappa^* = (s/(n + g + \delta))$.

bank assets The sum of a bank's reserves and the loans it has made (and thus that people owe it). Bank assets are equal to the sum of a bank's liabilities — its deposits and its borrowings — and shareholders' net worth.

bank deposits Sums of money that people and organizations have taken to and placed in the bank for convenience, safe-keeping, and profit. Deposits are usually classified as either checking-account deposits (which can be transferred to others by writing checks) and saving-account deposits (which must be withdrawn or transferred into some other form before they can be spent). But there are other forms as well: certificates of deposit or money market account deposits, for example.

bank liabilities How much a bank owes to other people and organizations. The sum of the deposits that people have made in the bank, any direct borrowings that the bank itself has undertaken, and any bonds that the bank itself has issued.

bank reserves Cash held in bank vaults, or money that banks have on deposit at the local branch of the Federal Reserve. A bank's reserves are the amount of money it can pay out to depositors easily and immediately, without selling less than perfectly liquid assets, calling in loans, or borrowing itself. Bank regulators require that banks maintain a specified level of reserves in proportion to the total deposits that they have accepted.

Changing reserve requirements is a way that the Federal Reserve affects the money supply.

bank run Before deposit insurance, when the depositors in a bank fear that it is insolvent, and so all at once demand that the bank liquidate their deposits for cash.

base year In the construction of an index, the year from which the weights assigned to the different components of the index are drawn. It is conventional to set the value of an index in its base year equal to 100.

behavioral relationship One of the two key kinds of equations that appear in economic models. (The "equilibrium condition" is the other kind.) A connection between economic variables that is the result of people's actions — how consumers change their spending in response to changes in income, how businesses change employment in response to changes in inventories, how foreign exchange speculators assess the length of time that interest rates in the United States will remain higher than interest rates abroad, and so forth.

bond A tradable financial instrument that is a promise by a business or a government to repay money that it has borrowed. A discount bond is a short-term promise to pay a fixed sum on the date that the bond matures. A coupon bond is a promise to periodically pay out coupon interest payments until the bond matures, and then to repay the bond's principal value at maturity.

bond market The set of places and communication links along which governments and others bid for, offer, and trade bonds. Economists often say that interest rates are determined by supply and demand in the bond market. These days the bond market is largely a computer network — numbers on bond traders' computer screens, and electronic offers to buy and sell.

bond rating Some financial information services rate bonds, thus telling investors how safe and secure an investment a particular bond is. The highest-rated bonds are rated AAA.

boom A situation in which production is above long-run trend and has been growing rapidly, in which employment is high and unemployment is low, and in which nearly everyone is optimistic about the future of the economy.

bubble economy When a country's stock and real estate markets have risen far and fast to unsustainable "bubble" levels that cannot be justified on the basis of fundamental values. Bubbles are driven by investors' belief in the "greater fool" theory: that even though they may be fools for buying stocks and bonds at overvalued prices, somewhere out there is a greater fool who will soon buy the securities from them at even higher prices. At some point, however, the greater fool theory turns out to be false, the markets turn, and values on the stock and real estate markets crash. Today when economists refer to *the* bubble economy, they are referring to Japan in the late 1980s.

budget balance The net state of the government's finances. When government spending equals tax receipts, economists say that the budget is in balance or that the budget balance is zero. When spending exceeds taxes, the government's budget is in deficit. When taxes exceed spending, the government's budget is in surplus.

budget deficit The difference between government spending and taxes when the first is larger than the second. In sticky-price short-run models, a budget deficit raises aggregate demand: The government's purchases of goods and services inject more spending power into the economy than the government's net taxes are withdrawing from the economy. In flexible-price models, a budget deficit lowers national saving and investment: Money that would otherwise have been borrowed by businesses and used to finance investment in new plant and equipment is borrowed by the government instead.

budget surplus The difference between the government's spending and the government's revenues when the second is larger than the first. In sticky-price short-run models, a budget surplus lowers aggregate demand: The government's purchases of goods and services inject more spending power into the economy than the government's net taxes are withdrawing from the economy. In flexible-price models, a budget surplus raises national saving and investment: The government's retirement of its debt injects purchasing power into financial markets that is then borrowed by businesses and used to finance investment in new plant and equipment.

Bureau of Economic Analysis A bureau in the U.S. Department of Commerce, charged with estimating macroeconomic data. The Bureau of Economic Analysis maintains the national income and product accounts, the NIPA.

Bureau of Labor Statistics A bureau of the U.S. Department of Labor, charged with keeping track of key labor market and living standard data. The Bureau of Labor Statistics calculates the unemployment rate and the consumer price index (CPI).

Burns, Arthur Chair of the Federal Reserve Board from 1970 to 1978. Before that, he had been a senior member of Richard Nixon's White House staff, chair of Eisenhower's Council of Economic Advisers, and president of the National Bureau of Economic Research. One of Richard Nixon's relatively few long-time friends.

business cycle A short-run fluctuation in the output, income, and employment of an economy. A *political business cycle* is one produced by policy actions implemented for political gain. A *real business cycle* is a boom generated not by stimulative monetary or fiscal policies or by the irrational animal spirits of investors, but by rapid technological innovation opening up new industries and new possibilities for investment.

business structures One of the components of investment spending. The construction of buildings, railroad tracks, bridges, or other things that are not machines, not inventory, yet improve the productive capacity of businesses.

C

Capital Produced goods, like machines, buildings, transportation infrastructure, or inventories, that amplify the economy's productive potential.

capital account That part of the international balance of payments that covers investment flows from one country to another. When gross investment in foreign countries by domestic citizens is greater than gross investment in the home country by foreigners, economists say that there is a capital outflow. When gross investment in foreign countries by domestic citizens is less than gross investment in the home country by foreigners, we say there is a capital inflow. The capital account and the current account must match: When there is a capital inflow, the current account must show a trade deficit — an excess of imports over exports — of equal magnitude; when there is a capital outflow, the current account must show a trade surplus — an excess of exports over imports — of equal magnitude.

capital accumulation Increases in a country's capital stock when gross investment is greater than depreciation.

capital deepening Increases in an economy's capital-labor ratio.

capital flight When a collapse of confidence in a country's economic policy leads investors to try to pull their investments out of a country and invest them somewhere else. Capital flight is associated with a sharp depreciation in the value of the currency, and poses very difficult economic policy choices.

capital flows Net investment by the citizens of one country in another — the "flow" of capital from one country to another. When there is a net outflow of capital from a country, the outflow is equal to its trade surplus — net exports. When there is a net inflow of capital into a country, the inflow is equal to its trade deficit — imports minus exports.

capital mobility The extent to which it is easy for investors to place their money in or pull their money out of other countries.

capital-output ratio The economy's capital stock divided by potential output. In the economic growth chapters, Chapters 4 and 5, the capital-output ratio is the key variable in the economic growth model. Over time, economies converge to steady-state growth paths along which the capital-output ratio is at a constant, equilibrium level. The equilibrium capital-output ratio is equal to the share of national product that is saved and invested, divided by the sum of the depreciation, labor force growth, and labor efficiency growth rates.

capital share The share of national income that is received as income by the owners of capital: the sum of profits, rent, and net interest divided by total national income. If the economy is competitive — without monopolies — and there are no major external benefits to investment in the economic growth process, then in equilibrium the capital share of an economy will be equal to the diminishing-returns-to-scale parameter of its aggregate production function.

capital stock The economy's, or sometimes a firm's, total accumulated stock of buildings, roads, other infrastructure, machines, and inventories. The greater the capital stock, the more productive the average worker. A substantial chunk of long-run economic growth is due to increases in the capital stock.

cash budget balance A way of measuring the government's budget balance called "cash" because it does not take account of changes in the value of government-owned assets or of the future liabilities owed by the government. It is just cash paid in minus cash paid out.

cash flow The difference between a business's revenues and its immediate cost of doing business. Cash flow is available for the business to either return to its shareholders in dividends, use to buy back its stock or its bonds on the financial market, or spend on increasing its capital stock through investment.

CBO *See* Congressional Budget Office.

central bank The arm of a national government that controls the money supply and the credit pattern of an economy, and usually oversees and regulates the banking system as well. The Federal Reserve system — the Board of Governors in Washington, DC, and the 12 regional Federal Reserve Banks in Boston, New York, Philadelphia, Cleveland, Richmond, Atlanta, Chicago, Kansas City, St. Louis, Dallas, Minneapolis, and San Francisco — is the United States' central bank.

certificate of deposit A type of bank account that is one step less liquid, and thus one step less moneylike, than a savings account. You give your money to the bank. In return it gives you a "certificate of deposit" that you can redeem after a fixed period of time to get your money back with interest. However, if you try to cash in your certificate of deposit early, you will suffer, as the advertisements all say, "substantial penalties for early withdrawal."

chain-weighted index An index constructed not by choosing one particular year as the base year and calculating the index value for every year using the base-year weights, but by "chaining" together year-to-year changes. That is, each year-to-year change in the index is calculated using that particular year as the base year. These calculated changes in the index are then linked together to create the index level values. Chain-weighted indexes avoid problems that fixed-weight indexes develop as time passes and the base-year weights used to construct the index become less and less relevant.

checking account deposits Often called "demand deposits" because the bank pays them out whenever the depositor demands (usually by writing a check that the check recipient's bank then presents to the depositor's bank). Because it is so easy to use checking account balances to pay for goods and services, checking account deposits are included in every possible measure of the money stock.

circular flow The central, dominant metaphor in macroeconomics, and the way of looking at the macroeconomy that underlies the national income and product accounts. Every economic transaction is made up of a flow of goods or services, and of an offsetting flow of purchasing power in the opposite direction. Every economic agent has an income and an expenditure, and the two must match. Thus purchasing power flows from businesses to households and back in a circular fashion.

classical dichotomy When real variables (like real GDP, real investment spending, or the real exchange rate) can be analyzed and calculated without thinking about nominal variables (like the price level or the nominal money stock). If the classical dichotomy holds, then economists also say that money is *neutral* — changes in the money stock do not affect the real variables, income, production, and employment in the economy. They also say that money is a veil — a covering that does not affect the shape of the face underneath.

classical unemployment When unemployment arises not because aggregate demand is too low, but because government regulations or market power keep the labor market from clearing and keep labor demand by firms below labor supply.

closed economy An economy in which international trade is so small a share of national product that exports and imports can be ignored. Contrast with an open economy, in which trade and capital flows have important effects on real GDP and other economic variables.

commodity futures A contract that allows you to "lock in" today the price at which you will buy or sell a commodity in the future. The contract can then itself be traded, and depending on how prices move a contract that allows you to buy a commodity — euros, say — at a low price can itself be very valuable. Businesses and investors can use such commodity futures contracts to avoid bearing various forms of risk. Other businesses and investors use such commodity futures to gamble.

comparative statics A method of analysis to determine the effect on the economy of some particular shift in the environment or policy. First look at the initial equilibrium position of the economy without the shift; then look at the equilibrium position of the economy with the shift; and finally see the difference in the two equilibrium positions as the response to the shift.

Congressional Budget Office Abbreviated CBO. The place to go to look for forecasts of the government's tax and spending programs, and what they mean for the economy.

consumer confidence How optimistic or pessimistic are consumers about the economy? The University of Michigan and the Business Conference Board conduct surveys of consumer confidence. The more confident consumers are, the higher consumption is likely to be for any given level of GDP. Consumer confidence is a powerful determinant of autonomous consumption.

consumer price index Abbreviated CPI. The most commonly used measure of the cost of living. It measures the cost of a slowly changing basket of consumer goods. The change in the CPI is the most frequently used measure of inflation. Because of difficulties in getting good measurements of components of the cost of living, the CPI probably contains a slight bias. A plurality of economists believe that the CPI overstates true changes in the cost of living by between 0.5 and 1.0 percentage points per year.

consumer prices The average prices paid by households for the goods they buy as consumers. Consumer prices are distinguished from investment-goods prices, the prices paid by the government, and export prices.

consumption function The relationship between baseline consumption, the amount households would spend on consumption goods if they had no income at all (C_0); the marginal propensity to consume (C_y); and disposable income (Y^D). $C = C_0 + (C_y \times Y^D) = C_0 + [C_y \times (1 - t)Y]$

consumption per worker A measure of the consumption of the workforce — the consumption component of GDP divided by the labor force for the national economy.

consumption spending Spending on goods and services purchased and used by consumers. Consumption spending is the major component of national product, equal to about two-thirds of the total. Consumption spending does not include purchases of existing houses or the construction of new houses. The purchase of an existing house is an asset. Housing construction is counted in investment.

contractionary policy The opposite of expansionary policy: shifts in government spending, taxation, or monetary policy that reduce aggregate demand and tend to reduce national product, income, employment, and inflation. A contractionary fiscal policy increases net taxes or reduces government spending. A contractionary monetary policy is usually an open-market operation by which the Federal Reserve sells bonds for cash, thus reducing the money supply and raising short-run interest rates.

convergence Applied to a set of countries, the tendency for productivity and real wage levels to draw together. Applied to one country, the tendency for it to approach a steady-state growth path with a constant capital-output ratio determined by the country's investment, technology, population growth, and depreciation rates.

coordination failures Failures of firms to change prices to respond quickly to the marketplace or in concert with other firms. Such things as long-term price and labor contracts produce a kind of inertia.

cost-of-living escalators Provisions in contracts that automatically raise wages or prices as official price indexes rise.

countercyclical Something that moves in the opposite direction from the business cycle; something that is low when national product is above potential output, and vice versa. The unemployment rate is countercyclical, as is the government's budget balance.

coupon bond A bond that pays its holder not only its principal value at maturity but also a periodic interest payment called a "coupon."

CPI *See* consumer price index.

CPS *See* Current Population Survey.

credibility The degree to which the public believes in the policy action taken by some institution of government (e.g., the Fed, Congress, or the president). As long as people in an economy believe that the central bank will act to keep inflation low, it is possible that the economy will be able to have both relatively full employment and relative price stability. But if the central bank does not have this credibility, either unemployment will be high or inflation will be high — or both.

currency The sum of paper money and coins. Currency is one of the major components of the money stock. It is the form of money that is easiest to use to buy goods and services.

currency arbitrage A situation, operating under the gold standard, whereby people buying or selling one currency at any price other than the ratio of the two gold parities would find themselves facing an unlimited demand, and would soon find themselves losing a nearly unlimited amount of money.

currency board An exchange rate system in which the central bank gives up its power to conduct domestic open-market operations, and commits to buying and selling foreign currency at the official exchange rate only. Under a currency board, a country's stock of high-powered money is equal to its foreign exchange reserves. Establishing a currency board system is a way that a central bank can gain credibility: It not only fixes its exchange rate in terms of foreign currency, but it abandons the key lever — open-market operations — that it would use should it wish to begin a policy of inflation.

currency confidence The condition where people, domestic or foreign, have faith in the continuing value of one country's currency relative to one or more other currencies.

currency crisis A situation where a country's currency is in serious trouble relative to the exchange rates of other countries. The most common problems facing that country are the prospect of hyperinflation or the need for significant devaluation.

currency-to-deposits ratio How much individuals and firms wish to hold in currency for every dollar that they hold in the form of bank deposits. When people are nervous about the stability or liquidity of the banking system, the currency-to-deposits ratio will rise, pushing the money multiplier and the money stock down and perhaps causing a recession.

current account In the balance of payments, the account that keeps track of a country's exports and imports. When exports exceed imports, economists say that there is a current account or trade surplus. When imports exceed exports, economists say that there is a current account or trade deficit. The current account and the capital account must match: Whenever there is a capital inflow, the current account must show a trade deficit — an excess of imports over exports — of equal magnitude; whenever there is a capital outflow, the current account must show a trade surplus — an excess of exports over imports — of equal magnitude.

Current Population Survey Abbreviated CPS. The survey undertaken by the Labor Department's Bureau of Labor Statistics to estimate the unemployment rate.

cyclical unemployment The difference between the current unemployment rate and the current value of the natural rate of unemployment. Cyclical unemployment is associated with deviations of national product from potential output.

cyclically adjusted What the value of an economic variable would be if unemployment were at its average rate, and the business cycle were in neither a boom nor a depressed state.

cyclically adjusted budget deficit Also called the high-employment budget deficit. An estimate of what the budget deficit would be if national product were at potential output and unemployment were equal to the natural rate. This measure removes shifts in the budget deficit that are due to the operation of the economy's automatic stabilizers.

D

debt The national debt of a country is the sum total of all past deficits the government has run. The government owes interest on the national debt — thus taxes must be higher when the debt is higher. And the fact that investors hold the bonds issued by the government that are the national debt means that they have less to use to finance private investment that boosts the country's capital stock.

deficit The amount by which government spending on goods, services, and transfer payments exceeds tax revenues in a given year. A national debt is created when the government borrows to cover the shortfall.

deflation When the price level falls for some substantial period of time. The opposite of inflation: a decrease in the overall price level. Deflation is rarely seen today, but in the Great Depression the deflation of 1929–1933 was a major factor contributing to the depth of the Depression: The falling price level bankrupted firms and banks that were in debt, and so reduced total aggregate demand.

demand deposits Checking account deposits. Called demand deposits because the bank pays them out whenever the depositor demands (usually by writing a check). Checking account deposits are part of what economists call the money stock because it is so easy to use checking account balances to pay for goods and services.

demographic transition A period in history which sees a rise in birth rates and a sharp fall in death rates as material standards of living increase above "subsistence" levels. (But after a while birth rates start to decline rapidly too. The end of the demographic transition sees both birth and death rates at a relatively low level, and the population nearly stable.)

dependent variable The variable alone on the left-hand side of an equation. The variable whose value is determined by the values of the variables on the right-hand side, and that changes when the variables on the right-hand side change.

deposit insurance A promise by the government or the central bank that bank failures will not freeze consumers' or firms' bank deposits and thus their ability to spend. Deposit insurance in the United States was instituted by Franklin Roosevelt's New Deal, and has reduced the risk of a classic financial crisis. (But it also obligated U.S. taxpayers to bail out many bankrupt savings and loan associations in the late 1980s.)

depreciation rate The rate at which capital wears out, rusts, or becomes obsolete and is scrapped. Because of depreciation, the economy's capital stock does not grow by the full value of gross investment. It grows by the amount of net investment — the difference between gross investment and depreciation.

depression The word used for an economic downturn, a fall in national product and a rise in unemployment, before "recession" was coined as a euphemism. Today the meaning of "depression" is confined to a very severe downturn.

devaluation In a fixed exchange rate system, a reduction in the value of a country's currency so that it takes more units of the home country's currency to purchase one unit of foreign currency. An action taken by a central bank or treasury to decrease the official price of a country's currency relative to the price of other currencies — or in terms of gold. (Revaluation is the opposite action.)

diminishing returns Doubling the number of workers on a farm, or doubling the value of the capital each employee uses in a factory does not generally double production but raises it by some smaller amount. Moreover, as more factors are added, smaller and smaller increases in production are generated. Such diminishing returns prompted nineteenth-century literary critic Thomas Carlyle to call economics "the dismal science."

discounting Figuring out how much money you would have to put aside today and invest at the prevailing interest rate in order to obtain a specified sum at some particular point in the future. We calculate the profitability of investments by discounting future profits from investments and comparing the discounted present value to the cost of the investment.

discouraged workers Potential workers who have left the labor force because they do not believe they can find worthwhile jobs. Discouraged workers return to the labor force when the labor market tightens. Many think that official unemployment rates understate the problem because of the existence of discouraged workers.

discretionary policy Discretionary policy is policy that is not automatic in the sense that automatic stabilizers swing into action without anyone making an explicit decision. Discretionary monetary policy is made by the FOMC's decisions to change interest rates. Discretionary fiscal policy is made by Congress's and the president's decisions to change levels of spending and of taxes.

disinflation A reduction in inflation, a reduction in the rate at which prices are increasing — but not so great a reduction as to cause deflation. Usually seen in the context of the Volcker disinflation, the 1979–1984 fall in the U.S. inflation rate carried out by the Federal Reserve during the term of Chair Paul Volcker.

disposable income What is left of income after taxes have been paid. The difference between national income and net taxes. Even when national income is unchanged, changes in the government's tax and transfer programs change disposable income and so are likely to change consumption spending. Disposable income $Y^D = Y - T = (1 - t)Y$ where Y is total income, T is taxes, and t is the tax rate.

divergence The tendency for a per capita measurement (e.g., incomes or standards of living) in various countries to become less equal over a period of time.

dividends Payments by a corporation to its shareholders on a regular, periodic basis. Dividends are the primary way that a firm rewards those who have invested in its common stock by returning a portion of the firm's profits to its investors.

domestic investment The same as "investment" in the national income and product accounts. Distinguished from foreign investment, which is investment by one country's citizens in the economy of another country.

durable manufacturing That part of the economy's manufacturing sector that makes durable goods — long-lived goods like refrigerators, large turbine generators, structural steel, and washing machines.

dynamic inconsistency A situation where a central bank succumbs to the temptation to make inflation higher than expected and thereby loses its credibility. That central bank will find that its words about future policy are ignored in the process of setting expectations, and expectations of inflation will be sky-high.

E

East Asian crisis The remarkably deep and sudden financial crisis that hit East Asian economies in 1997 and 1998. The East Asian crisis came with the least warning of any financial crisis in the 1990s. In other crises — Britain's, Brazil's, or Mexico's — some observers at least had pointed out fundamental problems with the economy that made it vulnerable to a crisis. The East Asian crisis appeared to come out of a blue sky.

East Asian miracle Since the mid-1960s the economies of East Asia have grown more rapidly than any other group of economies, anywhere, anytime.

economic expansion A sustained increase in GPD bracketed on either side by a period of recession.

economic growth The process by which productivity, living standards, and output increase.

Economic Report of the President A "book" prepared once a year (in January) by the president's Council of Economic Advisers. It gives their view of the economy's accomplishments, problems, and opportunities.

efficiency of labor The skills and education of the labor force, the ability of the labor force to handle modern technologies, and the efficiency with which the economy's businesses and markets function. The efficiency of labor is very closely linked to an economy's total factor productivity.

elasticity The proportional response of one quantity to a proportional change in another quantity. If a 1 percent change in one variable generates a 1 percent change in the other, the elasticity is one. If a 1 percent change in one generates a 2 percent change in the other, the elasticity is two.

equilibrium Short-run equilibrium is a state of balance between supply and demand in a particular market, or in the economy as a whole. Long-run equilibrium requires that markets balance, and also that expectations of inflation and other quantities be correct.

equilibrium capital-output ratio In the economic growth chapters, Chapters 4 and 5, the equilibrium capital-output ratio is the key to understanding where the economy is headed: what its long-run dynamic trajectory will be. Over time, the economy will converge to its steady-state growth path along which the capital-output ratio is constant at its equilibrium level. This equilibrium capital-output ratio is equal to the share of national product that is saved and invested, divided by the sum of the depreciation, labor force growth, and labor efficiency growth rates.

equilibrium condition A relationship between two economic quantities that holds not because any one actor or group in the economy makes it hold, but because the operation of the system as a whole pushes the economy to a state in which the relationship holds. The requirement that aggregate demand equal total output on the income-expenditure diagram is an equilibrium condition: If it does not hold, then inventories are either rising or falling and so businesses are either cutting back or raising production and thus total output is either rising or falling toward aggregate demand.

establishment survey A survey of businesses and how many employees they have that is carried out by the Bureau of Labor Statistics. The establishment survey is not used to calculate the unemployment rate.

excess bank reserves Bank reserves held over and above those mandated by law because banks are not confident that they would be paid back if they made additional loans, or because banks believe that some loans they have already made are about to go into default, or because they believe depositors are about to withdraw deposits.

exchange rate The nominal exchange rate is the rate at which one country's money can be turned into another's. The real exchange rate is the rate at which goods produced in one country can be bought or sold for another's. The definition of the exchange rate is either the value of home currency, or the price of foreign currency, depending on the textbook.

expansionary policy Increases in government spending, decreases in net taxes, or increases in the money stock that lower interest rates. Expansionary policies raise aggregate demand, national product, employment, and inflation.

expectations Everyone in the economy makes plans about what to do that depend on what they think the future will be like. Economists focus on this dependence of behavior on beliefs about the future: investors', consumers', employers', and workers' expectations are a principal determinant of economic behavior. As a shorthand, economists usually collapse the range of different and conflicting expectations held by people into a single average number — for example, expectations of inflation.

expectations theory of the term structure The theory that the long-term interest rate is an average of today's short-term interest rate and of the short-term interest rates that are expected to prevail in the future.

expenditure side That part of the national income and product accounts made up of total expenditure — on consumption spending, investment, net exports, and government purchases.

exports Total goods and services produced at home and sold to purchasers in foreign countries. Exports are an addition to aggregate demand for home-produced products.

external balance When the trade surplus (or deficit) of a country is equal to the value of investors' new long-term investments abroad (or foreigners' new long-term investments here). A lack of external balance means that something — usually the exchange rate, but possibly interest rates or the level of GDP — is about to change.

F

Federal Open Market Committee The principal decision-making body of the Federal Reserve. The FOMC meets roughly every other month, decides on the level of short-term interest rates, and directs the open-market operations that the New York Federal Reserve Bank carries out on behalf of the Federal Reserve system.

Federal Reserve The United States' central bank. The institution conducts monetary policy and regulates banks. Its open-market operations change the money stock and peg short-term nominal interest rates. The Federal Reserve consists of a Board of Governors (seven, one of whom is chair) and 12 regional Federal Reserve Banks.

Federal Reserve Banks The 12 regional banks — located in New York, Chicago, Cleveland, Boston, Philadelphia, Richmond, Atlanta, St. Louis, Kansas City, Dallas, Minneapolis, and San Francisco — that are the local branches of the Federal Reserve system.

Federal Reserve Board The Washington, DC–based head office of the United States' central bank, the

Federal Reserve system. The board consists of seven governors, one of whom is chair and one of whom is vice chair. The chair is appointed to a four-year term by the president with the advice and consent of the Senate.

final goods and services Products that are not themselves used by businesses to make other products. Products that are either (*a*) bought by consumers, (*b*) bought by firms or individuals as investments that increase their capital stock, (*c*) bought by foreigners (in excess of intermediate goods bought by domestic producers), or (*d*) bought by the government.

financial flexibility A situation in which a large number of different financial instruments are traded on thick and liquid markets. This means that any one kind of asset has less and less potential to become a bottleneck.

financial markets The stock market, the bond market, the short-term borrowing market, plus firms' borrowings from banks. The markets in which the flow of money from savers seeking a return to investors seeking money to finance purchases takes place.

financial panics Sudden falls in stock market and bond market prices, and rises in interest rates, driven at least in part by the fear that other people are about to panic and sell.

fine-tuning The hope that the Federal Reserve, Congress, and the president could together adjust fiscal and monetary policy so as to keep the economy always near full employment — as you tune a radio to get the strongest signal.

fiscal automatic stabilizers In a recession, tax revenues automatically decline as incomes fall, and social insurance spending automatically rises as more people qualify for food stamps, unemployment insurance, and other social welfare expenditures. The government budget automatically swings toward a deficit, providing a stimulus to aggregate demand, whenever private demand drops. Similarly, it automatically swings toward a surplus, reducing aggregate demand, whenever private demand rises. The structure of the government's tax and spending programs thus automatically provides a degree of stabilization to aggregate demand. These fiscal automatic stabilizers are the only form of fiscal policy in the United States that works rapidly and effectively to reduce the size of the business cycle.

fiscal policy Changes in government purchases or in net taxes that affect the level of aggregate demand. Increases in purchases or in transfer payments are expansionary policy; increases in taxes are contractionary policy.

fixed exchange rate system A system of international monetary arrangements by which central banks buy and sell in foreign exchange markets so as to keep their relative exchange rates fixed. Before 1971 the industrial world was on a fixed exchange rate system called the Bretton Woods system.

fixed investment Investment to build houses and apartments, infrastructure, offices, stores, and other buildings, plus investment in machinery and equipment. The other important component of investment is inventory investment.

fixed-weight indexes Indexes formed by taking a weighted average of different quantities, where the weights are fixed and unchanging over the span of years for which the index is constructed.

flexible prices When wages and prices in an economy are not sticky, but move smoothly and rapidly to keep supply equal to demand in the labor market and in the goods market. Under flexible prices, real GDP is equal to potential output and unemployment is equal to its natural rate. Under flexible prices, changes in monetary and fiscal policy do not affect the level of real GDP, but they do affect its composition, and they affect the price level as well.

floating exchange rate system A system of international monetary arrangements by which central banks let exchange rates be decided by supply and demand, so that they "float" against one another as supplies and demands vary. Floating systems can be "clean" — if central banks truly leave the markets alone — or "dirty" — if central banks try at times to nudge exchange rates in one direction or another.

flow of funds The process by which savings — whether private, government, or international — are transformed into purchasing power useful for businesses undertaking investment spending. The flow of funds through financial markets is the center of macroeconomic analysis in the flexible-price full employment model of Chapters 6 and 7.

flow variable An economic quantity measured as a flow per unit of time. GDP, investment spending, and inflation are examples of flow variables. The unemployment rate, the capital stock, and the price level are not flow variables — they are stock variables.

FOMC *See* Federal Open Market Committee.

foreign currency The money of any country save the one you happen to live in. When domestic exporters earn foreign currency by exporting, they have to figure out what to do with it — it's no good in this country, after all. So they need to trade it either to someone who needs foreign currency to buy imports, or someone who wants foreign currency to make an investment abroad.

foreign exchange market The decentralized trading around the world of assets denominated in one currency for assets denominated in another: deutschmarks or dollars, pounds or yen. Exchange rates are set in the foreign exchange market.

foreign exchange reserves Foreign currency–denominated assets held by a country's central bank or treasury to use in foreign exchange interventions. Under a fixed exchange rate system, a government must maintain sufficient foreign exchange reserves so that it can satisfy the people who wish to trade home currency for foreign currency.

foreign trade The purchase of commodities made in other countries. Imports and exports.

formulation lag The lapse of time between the moment that makers of economic policy recognize that a shock has affected the economy, and the moment at which their policy response begins to be implemented. The time it takes to formulate policy.

fractional reserve banking A banking system — like the one we have — in which banks hold in their vaults only a portion of deposits they accept as reserves, and lend the rest to customers who pay interest.

frictional unemployment The unemployment generated by firms taking time to fill vacancies and workers taking time to find the right job. Frictional unemployment is the labor market counterpart of goods inventories in the goods market: It boosts output and workers' incomes by giving them the opportunity to find jobs that match their skills.

Friedman, Milton One of the four most influential macroeconomists of the twentieth century (the other three being John Maynard Keynes, Irving Fisher, and Robert Lucas). Leading exponent of monetarism, and one of the first to recognize the dominant role potentially played by the Federal Reserve in stabilization policy.

future value The inverse of present value — the value that a sum of money or a flow of cash would have at some date in the future, if it were invested and compounded at the prevailing rate of interest.

G

GDP *See* gross domestic product.

GDP deflator The ratio of nominal GDP to real GDP. The second most used estimate of the overall price level (the consumer price index is the most-used estimate).

generational accounting A way of looking at the government's tax and spending plans not individual year by individual year, but all at once. Generational accounting attempts to set out the total lifetime impact of government policy on an individual's resources and obligations.

globalization The ongoing process by which barriers to the free flow of commodities, capital, and information across countries are reduced.

GNP *See* gross national product.

gold standard The particular fixed exchange rate system dominant for more than a half century before the Great Depression. A system by which central banks preserve fixed exchange rates by always being willing to buy or sell their currencies at fixed rates in terms of the precious metal gold.

golden rule In growth theory, when an economy's savings rate is equal to its capital share. In such a case the steady-state growth path has a higher level of consumption associated with it than any other steady-state growth path with the same path over time of the efficiency of labor.

goods market Economists sometimes divide the economy into four "markets" — the labor market where firms hire and pay workers; the money market where people buy and sell liquid assets; the bond market where people buy and sell stocks; and the goods market where people (and firms, and the government) buy and sell final goods and services.

goods market equilibrium In the flexible-price model, when prices have adjusted to make total aggregate demand for goods equal to potential output. In the sticky-price model, when firms have responded to their increasing or decreasing inventories by adjusting production to aggregate demand so that inventories are stable.

government purchases Government spending on goods or services (including the wages of government employees). Much government spending is not purchases but is instead transfer payments: payments like social security or food stamps that do not buy any good or service for the government.

Great Depression From 1929–1941, the deepest depression the United States has ever experienced. At its nadir in 1933, more than a quarter of the labor force was unemployed.

gross domestic product Abbreviated GDP. The most commonly used measure of product, output, and income. The total amount of final goods and services produced. By the circular flow principle, equal to the total income earned through domestically located production. Also equal to total expenditure on domestically produced goods and services.

gross investment Spending on investment goods that includes spending to simply replace worn-out or obsolete pieces of capital, or to keep existing capital in working condition. Subtract depreciation from gross investment to obtain net investment, the net increase in the economy's capital stock.

gross national product Abbreviated GNP. Equal to GDP minus the income earned by foreign-owned factors of production located in the United States, plus income of U.S. factors of production located abroad. GNP used to be the most-used measure of national product, but the government lost confidence in its ability to estimate the difference between GNP and GDP.

growth rate Almost always the annual growth rate of GDP, or of GDP per worker. How much real economic product is increasing from year to year.

H

high-employment budget deficit Alternatively the cyclically adjusted budget deficit. An estimate of what the government's budget deficit would be if national product were equal to potential output and unemployment were equal to the natural rate. This measure removes shifts in the budget deficit that are due to the operation of the economy's automatic stabilizers.

high-powered money Usually called the monetary base. The sum total of currency and of bank reserves on deposit at the Federal Reserve. The money stock is equal to the monetary base times the money multiplier.

high-pressure economy Another example of hydraulic metaphors: an economy in which the "pressure" of economic activity is high. Unemployment is low, production is often higher than potential output, workers are being pulled into the labor force, and inflation is often rising.

hyperinflation Extremely high inflation, so high that the price mechanism breaks down. Under hyperinflation people are never sure what the true value of their money is, and spend a great deal of time and energy trying to spend their cash incomes as fast as possible before they lose value. One rule of thumb is that inflation of more than 20 percent per month is hyperinflation.

I

implementation lag The time that passes between when a monetary or fiscal policy action is completed by the Federal Reserve or Congress, and when the action affects real GDP, unemployment, and inflation.

imports Goods and services produced in and purchased from other countries. Imports are a reduction in aggregate demand: Consumption and investment spending that are diverted to imports are not part of aggregate demand for domestically produced goods and services.

imputed rent Some people rent apartments from landlords. Other people own houses or condominiums. National income accountants were worried at the idea that if a tenant bought an apartment or a house from his or her landlord, real GDP would go down. So they invented "imputed rent" — the rent that those who live in owner-occupied housing pay as tenants to themselves as landlords — and include imputed rent in their calculations of GDP.

income-expenditure diagram The tool for figuring out what the equilibrium level of aggregate demand and national product is. If national product is too low, it is to the left of equilibrium on the income-expenditure diagram, and inventories are rapidly being exhausted. If national product is too high, it is to the right of equilibrium and inventories are being involuntarily built up.

income side That part of the national income and product accounts made up of total income — earned by workers, received by investors, paid to landlords, and residual economic profits left for entrepreneurs and risk-bearers.

independent variable A variable on the right-hand side of an equation. A variable whose value helps determine the value of the variable on the left-hand side, and that, when it changes, makes the variable on the left-hand side change.

index number A number that isn't a set sum, value, or quantity in well-defined units (like dollars, people, or percent) but that is a quantity relative to a base year given an arbitrary index value of 100. Index numbers are usually weighted averages of a large number of individual components, and the weights can either be fixed or chained.

industrial economies Those economies that have finished the process of industrialization — the United States, Britain, Germany, Japan, France, Canada, Italy, and the smaller economies at roughly the same stage of economic development.

industrial revolution The transformation of the British economy between 1750 and 1850 when largely handmade production was replaced by machine-made production, a change made possible by technological advance. Following the initial British industrial revolution, other countries have in turn undergone their own industrial revolutions.

inflation An increase in the overall level of prices in an economy, usually measured as the annual percent change in its consumer price index.

inside lag The lapse of time between the moment that a shock begins to affect the economy and the moment that economic policy is altered in response to the shock. The inside lag has two parts — the recognition lag, during which makers of economic policy do not yet recognize the shock, and the formulation lag, during which makers of economic policy are designing the policy response.

insider-outsider theory A theory of how cyclical unemployment that persists for too long becomes transformed into structural unemployment. Workers who remain unemployed gradually lose their skills and their attachment to the labor force. And unions bargain to raise the wages of current members, not to find jobs for exmembers.

interest The periodic sums that you pay to "rent" the money that you have borrowed.

interest rate The price, measured in percent per year, paid for borrowing money. Conversely, the return earned by saving, and the relative price at which purchasing power can be transferred from the present to the future.

intermediate goods Goods that are not final goods and services. Goods that are bought by businesses as inputs into some further process of production. Intermediate goods are excluded from product-side counts of GDP: To include them would lead to double counting the same economic product twice, once in the intermediate good and once again in the final good that the intermediate good was used to produce.

internal balance When unemployment is equal to its natural rate, inflation is unchanging, and GDP is equal to potential output. Under a fixed exchange rate system, monetary policy cannot be used to pursue internal balance because the level of interest rates must be devoted to maintaining the fixed exchange rate.

international division of labor Resource-rich countries produce and export natural resources and resource-based products, industrialized economies export capital-intensive high-technology manufactures, and other countries export labor-intensive manufactures. All gain by concentrating their production in those sectors in which their economy is most efficient.

inventory investment A change in the stock of goods that make up firms' inventories: materials and supplies, work in progress, goods in storage, and finished goods that have not yet been sold. Fluctuations in inventory investment are primarily involuntary, the result of quarter-by-quarter differences between national product and aggregate demand.

investment The buildings and goods (both machines and inventories) purchased to add to the economy's stock of capital, plus (sometimes) government creation of infrastructure, plus residential construction.

investment accelerator The dependence of the level of business investment on the level of production. It arises from firms' preference to use internally generated rather than externally raised funds to finance investment, and from other causes. A strong accelerator increases the value of the Keynesian multiplier.

investment function How investment spending depends on the interest rate. Investment considered as a function of the interest rate. The relationship between the baseline level of investment (I_0), the real interest rate (r), and the responsiveness of investment to a change in real interest rates (I_r): $I = I_0 - (I_r \times r)$.

investment requirements The share of GDP that must be devoted to investment spending in order to keep an economy's capital-output ratio from falling.

investment spending That portion of total spending

(approximately 20 percent) devoted to increasing business capacity and the economy's capital stock.

investor optimism The principal determinant of baseline investment I_0. When investors are optimistic, I_0 is high. Fluctuations in investor optimism — what John Maynard Keynes called investors' "animal spirits" — are a principal cause of the business cycle.

IS curve The downward-sloping relationship between the (real, long-term) interest rate and the equilibrium level of national product and aggregate demand. The IS curve summarizes the information about equilibrium national product in an entire family of income-expenditure diagrams, one for each possible value of the interest rate.

IS-LM diagram A diagram with the interest rate on the vertical axis and the level of national product on the horizontal axis, used to determine what values of the interest rate and of national product together produce equilibrium in the money market — supply of money equal to money demand — and equilibrium in the goods market — aggregate demand equal to national product. Whenever the central bank does not set the interest rate but instead sets the money stock, you need to look at the IS-LM diagram to determine the economy's equilibrium.

K

Keynes, John Maynard One of the four most influential macroeconomists of the twentieth century (the other three being Milton Friedman, Irving Fisher, and Robert Lucas). To Keynes we owe the income-expenditure aggregate-demand framework that still dominates intermediate macroeconomics courses and textbooks.

Keynesian cross diagram The income-expenditure diagram by another name. The tool for finding equilibrium aggregate demand and national product. Principally used in the derivation of the multiplier: the amplified response of changes in equilibrium aggregate demand and national product to fluctuations in autonomous spending.

Keynesian multiplier The change in national income and aggregate demand that follows from a one-dollar change in any component of autonomous spending, such as government purchases. To find the value of the multiplier, subtract the economy's marginal propensity to expend from 1, and then take that number's inverse.

Keynesianism The school of thought, developed from the ideas of John Maynard Keynes, that emphasizes (*a*) the role of expectations of future profits in determining investment; (*b*) the volatility of expectations of future profits; (*c*) the power of the government to affect the economy through fiscal and monetary policy; and (*d*) the multiplier process, which amplifies the effects of both private-sector shocks and public-sector policies on aggregate demand.

L

labor force The sum of those who are employed and those who are actively looking for work. The unemployment rate is defined as the number of unemployed divided by the labor force.

labor market equilibrium When the only kind of unemployment is "frictional" unemployment, and there is neither cyclical nor structural unemployment. When, save for those in the process of changing jobs, the economy is at full employment.

labor productivity National product divided by the number of workers (or alternatively, by the total number of hours worked). Such a measure of output per worker is probably the best available measure of long-term economic growth.

labor unions Organizations of workers that attempt to bargain with employers for higher wages and better working conditions by threatening to strike. Multiyear union contracts have been seen as important causes of price inertia.

lags The time between when a policy proposal is made and when it becomes effective in changing the economy in some way. Lags can arise during *recognition* of a condition, *formulation* of a policy, or *implementation* of that policy. The first two are *inside* lags, because they occur inside the government. The last is sometimes called the *outside* lag.

leading indicators A number of variables correlated with future movements in real GDP or inflation. Many economists believe these indicators can be relied on as a good guide to economic activity nine or so months ahead. Some key indicators are stock prices, new manufacturing orders, the money supply, and the index of consumer expectations.

lender of last resort When the government steps in and lends money to organizations that are thought to be fundamentally sound, but that are critically short of cash in a financial crisis.

life-cycle consumption Consumption is depressed below income in peak earning years because people are saving for retirement. Before and after peak earning years, consumption is raised above income either as parents pay for upbringing or as retirees spend their savings.

liquid assets Forms of wealth that can be readily and cheaply converted into spendable form. Forms of wealth that can be easily used to finance purchases.

liquidity Applied to assets, whenever they can be easily, quickly, and without cost turned into money.

liquidity constraints A *liquidity constraint* is an inability to borrow. When consumers suffer from liquidity constraints, their consumption spending is limited by their current income, and the marginal propensity to consume is likely to be high.

liquidity crisis When banks or other institutions cannot make the payments they owe because they lack cash, but when nobody (or few people) doubts that they will be solvent and profitable if the current financial crisis is successfully resolved.

LM curve The positive relationship between national income and the interest rate that emerges from considering a whole family of money demand–money supply diagrams, a different diagram for each possible level of national income. Plotted along with the IS curve on an IS-LM diagram, it determines the levels of national income and of the interest rate consistent with goods-market and money-market equilibrium.

loanable funds The total flow of resources available — private savings, government savings, and international savings — to finance investment spending and capital accumulation.

long-run growth The path of economic growth once the business-cycle fluctuations have been removed. The long-run pace of growth of potential output.

long-term interest rate The interest rate required if you are going to borrow money not for a short term of months but for a long term of decades.

long-term real interest rate The interest rate required if you are going to borrow money not for a short term of months but for a long term of decades, adjusted for inflation by subtracting the inflation rate from the nominal interest rate.

Lucas, Robert One of the four most influential macroeconomists of the twentieth century (the other three are John Maynard Keynes, Irving Fisher, and Milton Friedman). The leader of the rational-expectations school of macroeconomics for nearly two decades.

Lucas critique The assertion that much analysis of the effects of economic policy is badly flawed because it does not take proper account of how changing policies induce changes in people's expectations.

M

M1, M2, M3 Different measures of the money stock — of the total stock of assets in the economy that are liquid enough to be readily used to finance purchases.

macroeconomics The subject of the course you are taking: business cycles, the determinants of inflation and unemployment, and probably long-run growth and effects of government fiscal policy. Macroeconomics is contrasted with microeconomics — the study of what goes on in individual markets within the economy.

marginal product of capital The increase in potential output from a unit increase in the economy's capital stock. Often calculated as equal to $\alpha Y/K$ (α, the share of national income received by owners of capital, divided by the capital-output ratio K/Y).

marginal product of labor Abbreviated MPL. The increase in potential output from a 1-unit increase in the supply of labor to the economy. Often calculated as $(1 - \alpha)Y/L$ (the share of national income received by workers, $1 - \alpha$, times average labor productivity Y/L).

marginal propensity to consume Abbreviated MPC. The increase in consumption spending resulting from a one-dollar increase in disposable income. The parameter C_y in the consumption function $C = C_0 + C_y(1 - t)Y$, where C_0 is baseline consumption, t is the tax rate, and Y is total national income.

marginal propensity to expend Abbreviated MPE. The increase in total spending — on consumption goods through the marginal propensity to consume and on net exports — from a one-dollar increase in national income. In the model of Chapters 9–12, $MPE = C_y(1 - t) - IM_y$, where C_y is the marginal propensity to consume, t is the tax rate, and IM_y is the share of income spent on imports. Note, however, that in more complicated models MPE may be different: Changes in national income may have other effects as higher firm profits lead to higher investment spending and as higher household incomes lead to lower social insurance spending.

maturity The date or the number of years in the future at which a bond's interest payments cease and its principal sum is returned to the lender.

median The middle one of something. The value such that half or more are as large or larger, and half or more are as small or smaller.

medium of exchange A commodity or an asset that almost everyone will accept as payment for a transaction. The most important function of money.

menu costs The costs to a firm of changing the price(s) of a good(s) or service(s). They lead firms to adjust their prices infrequently.

microeconomics That field of economics that deals with the behavior of the individual elements in an economy with respect to the price of a single commodity and the behavior of individual households and businesses.

mixed economy An economy in which markets control the allocation of resources and of labor to industries and firms, but in which the government plays a not overwhelming but significant role: providing social insurance and social welfare benefits on a large scale, trying to stabilize the macroeconomy, and enforcing contracts. Post-WWII mixed economies have been extraordinarily successful at generating economic growth.

model A construct that aims to establish relationships — usually quantitative — between and among economic variables. Economists describe the process of reducing the complexity and variation of the real-world economy into a handful of equations "building a model."

monetarism The theory, very popular in the 1970s and the early 1980s, that fluctuations in interest rates had little impact on money demand, so that stabilizing national product and employment could be carried out in a smooth and straightforward fashion by stabilizing the rate of growth of the money stock.

monetary automatic stabilizers Named by analogy with the fiscal automatic stabilizers produced by the structure of the government's budget. Features of the financial system that tend to cushion and prevent declines in the money stock that would otherwise occur during a financial crisis. For example, deposit insurance is a monetary automatic stabilizer: It prevents bank deposits and the money stock from dropping when people begin to fear that a depression may bankrupt the bank they use.

monetary base Often called high-powered money. The sum total of currency and of bank reserves on deposit at the Federal Reserve. The money stock is equal to the monetary base times the money multiplier.

monetary policy How the supply of money or the interest rate varies with economic conditions like inflation, unemployment, and the exchange rate. The rules of thumb that the Federal Reserve uses to decide what instructions it is going to give the Federal Reserve Bank of New York.

monetary transmission mechanism How changes in the money supply or in interest rates affect spending on consumption, investment, and other components of aggregate demand; and thus lead to changes in national income and product.

money A word that economists use in a technical sense. To an economist, "money" means only "wealth in the form of readily spendable purchasing power." Cash, plus balances in checking accounts, plus whatever other assets are held primarily as a way to keep purchasing power on hand to spend rather than as long-term investments.

money balances How much money — wealth in the form of readily spendable purchasing power — consumers and firms actually hold at a given moment.

money demand How much money — wealth in the form of readily spendable purchasing power — consumers and firms wish to hold at the given levels of national income and of interest rates.

money demand curve A curve — drawn for a given and fixed level of national income — that shows how consumers' and firms' demand for money varies with the interest rate: The higher the interest rate, the lower money demand is. On the money demand–money supply diagram, the point where the money demand curve is equal to the supply of money determines the market-clearing interest rate.

money illusion When managers, workers, and others fail

to recognize that some of the change in their nominal income and revenue is a result of inflation, and is not a change in their real income and revenue.

money multiplier The change in the money stock that follows a one-dollar change in the monetary base; the ratio between the money stock and the monetary base. Increases in the reserves-to-deposits ratio or in the currency-to-deposits ratio reduce the money multiplier.

money supply How much in the amount of liquid assets the Federal Reserve has allowed the banking system to create.

money supply curve The money supply considered as a function of the interest rate. In general the higher the interest rate, the lower are the excess reserves that the banking sector holds and the higher is the money stock.

money supply–money demand diagram The building block of the LM curve, the diagram with the interest rate on the vertical and the quantity of money supplied and demanded on the horizontal axis.

moral hazard The danger of imprudent, improper, or dishonest behavior in economic situations where actions are not easily or routinely monitored. A possible drawback of deposit insurance and of lender of last resort activities.

MPC *See* marginal propensity to consume.

MPE *See* marginal propensity to expend.

MPL *See* marginal product of labor.

multiplier The change in national income and aggregate demand that follows from a one-dollar change in any component of autonomous spending, such as government purchases. To find the value of the multiplier, subtract the economy's marginal propensity to expend from 1, and then take that number's inverse.

myopia Short-sightedness. A failure to look far enough ahead into the future. For example, "voter myopia" is the theory that voters react to the immediate economic situation, rather than to what has happened in the further past or what is likely to happen in the future.

N

NAIRU Acronym for the nonaccelerating inflation rate of unemployment, which is the same as the natural rate of unemployment. The rate of unemployment when inflation is equal to expected inflation. The rate around which unemployment tends to fluctuate, and at which (because actual and expected inflation are equal) there is neither upward nor downward pressure on inflation.

national income The total incomes from all work and asset ownership in an economy. Leaving aside differences in accounting definitions, national income is equal to national product (for the only way incomes can be earned is by producing products) and is equal to total expenditure, or aggregate demand (for all incomes flowing to individuals must be expended one way or another).

national income and product accounts Abbreviated NIPA. The system that government statisticians use to measure, estimate, and check data on the flow of economic activity.

national income identity The requirement — built into the national income and product accounts — that total income add up to total expenditure, and that both be equal to the total value added produced by businesses: $C + I + G + NX = Y$, where C is consumption spending, I is investment spending, G is government purchases, NX is net exports, and Y is total national income.

national product The total value of all final goods and services produced in an economy. Leaving aside differences in accounting definitions, national product is equal to national income (for the only way products can be produced is by paying people to make them) and is equal to total expenditure, or aggregate demand (for every product is ultimately purchased).

national product per worker A synonym for labor productivity. It is probably the best measure of an economy's development. Other measures — national product per adult or per capita — fail to take account of the changing mix of market and household production, or imply that adults who spend their money on raising children are impoverished compared to adults who buy videos.

national saving The sum of private saving and government saving — or since the government is usually not saving but running a deficit, private saving minus the government deficit. Domestic investment is equal to national saving plus net investment in this country by foreigners.

national savings identity A consequence of the national income identity: that private savings $(Y - C - T)$ plus the government's budget surplus $(T - G)$ plus the net inflow of capital $- NX$ is equal to investment: $(Y - C - T) + (T - G) - NX = I$, where Y is total national income, C is consumption spending, T is net taxes, G is government purchases, NX is net exports, and I is investment spending.

natural rate of unemployment A synonym for NAIRU: the rate of unemployment where actual and expected inflation are equal, and there is no downward or upward pressure on inflation. Milton Friedman coined the phrase "natural rate"; those who did not like the hint in the word "natural" that such unemployment was a good thing preferred the colorless acronym NAIRU.

net domestic product Another measure of total production, obtained by subtracting capital depreciation from GDP.

net exports The difference between exports and imports. Net exports have to be added to the sum of consumption, investment, and government purchases in order to arrive at aggregate demand, because exports are an addition to and imports a subtraction from aggregate demand for domestically produced goods and services.

net investment The difference between gross investment and depreciation. Net investment is the increase in the economy's capital stock — the stock of buildings, infrastructure, machines, and inventories that amplify worker productivity.

net national product Abbreviated NNP. Yet another measure of the economy's total output. Net national product subtracts depreciation from gross domestic product, and also subtracts payments that foreigners receive for the use of foreign-owned productive resources located in this country. Net national product is from a conceptual point of view the best estimate of national product.

net taxes The difference between taxes collected by the government and transfer payments received by households and businesses. Net taxes are the impact of the government's fiscal policy on the disposable income of the private sector. A fall in net taxes raises disposable income, and thus consumption spending. Net taxes are the variable T in the models of this book.

New Deal President Franklin D. Roosevelt's programs during 1933 to 1941 to attempt to pull the economy out of the Great Depression. Of mixed success.

New York Federal Reserve Bank The most important of the 12 banks that are the regional branches of the Federal Reserve. The bank that carries out the open-market operations that the Federal Reserve uses to change interest rates.

NIPA *See* national income and product accounts.

NNP *See* net national product.

nominal A quantity that is not adjusted for inflation, or for changes in the price level.

nominal exchange rate The exchange rate not adjusted for the changes in countries' relative price levels over time.

nominal GDP Real GDP times the price level as measured by the GDP deflator. Nominal GDP is the total current-dollar value of final goods and services produced.

nominal interest rate The interest rate measured in terms of money: how many dollars you have to pay in the future in exchange for one dollar borrowed today; the nominal interest rate is equal to the real interest rate plus the inflation rate.

nominal wage The average level of money wages paid in an economy; the money cost to an employer of an average worker.

nondurable manufacturing Manufacturing that produces relatively short-lived products. Demand for nondurable manufactures is fairly steady — since they wear out, there is always a stable source of replacement demand.

O

OECD *See* Organization for Economic Cooperation and Development.

official settlements account International transactions that are neither current account transactions (payments for imports or exports) nor capital account transactions (payments for investments in other countries) but the purchase or sale of foreign currency assets by governments, or central banks.

Okun's law A fall in the unemployment rate of 1 percentage point is associated with a 2.5 percent rise in national product relative to potential output. This association is called Okun's law: Periods of high (or low) unemployment relative to the natural rate are the same as periods of low (or high) national product relative to potential output.

100 percent reserve banking A banking system — never seen in the real world, but sometimes used in economics textbooks as a baseline case — in which banks accept deposits but cannot make loans. When they accept deposits they must either (*a*) hold them in cash in their vaults or (*b*) redeposit the money in their own accounts at the central bank.

open economy An economy without substantial tariffs on imports or restrictions on international investments. Alternatively, an economy where imports, exports, and international capital flows are relatively large shares of national product and are important determinants of fluctuations in employment and output.

open-market operation The principal way that central banks affect interest rates; the purchase (or sale) of short-term government bonds to increase (or decrease) the money supply, and push interest rates down (or up). Open-market operations are not the only tool that central banks have to affect money supplies and interest rates, but they are by far the most often used.

Organization for Economic Cooperation and Development (OECD) Originally a club of all countries that received Marshall Plan aid from the United States, plus the United States and Canada. Now a club of the industrialized countries that is used to collect data and try to coordinate economic policy.

P

participation rate The fraction of adults who are in the labor force. The participation rate is procyclical, because discouraged workers drop out of the labor force when unemployment is relatively high. The participation rate has grown steadily over time, as gender roles have changed and the boundary between market and household work has shifted.

permanent income The level of income that households regard as likely to persist in the future. Their income minus any transitory windfalls that they do not expect to receive again in the future.

Phillips curve The downward-sloping relationship between unemployment and inflation. The old-fashioned (incorrect) flavor implied unemployment could be permanently reduced at the price of a small (permanent) rise in inflation. The location of the more satisfactory "accelerationist" Phillips curve depends on expectations of inflation: the higher expected inflation, the higher the unemployment rate needed to keep inflation at any particular level.

planned expenditure function The relationship $E = C + I + G + NX$ used to build aggregate demand for domestically produced products from the determinants of each of its components: consumption spending (C), investment spending (I), government purchases (G), and net exports (NX).

planned expenditure line Found on the income-expenditure (or Keynesian cross) diagram that shows aggregate demand on the vertical and national income on the horizontal axis. An important part of the sticky-price short-run business-cycle model. The planned expenditure line shows total spending — aggregate demand — as a function of the level of national income. The slope of the planned expenditure line is the MPE — the marginal propensity to expend income on domestic goods. The intercept of the planned expenditure line is the level of autonomous spending.

policy mix The combination of monetary and fiscal policies being followed by a country's government and central bank.

potential growth rate The growth rate of potential output. The growth rate at which the economy's unemployment rate is neither rising nor falling.

potential output The level at which national product would be if expectations were correct, and if unemployment were equal to its natural rate. Potential output grows smoothly over time as technology advances, as net investment augments the capital stock, and as the labor force grows.

present value How much money you would have to put aside and invest today (at prevailing interest rates) in order to match a specified sum or pattern of cash flows in the future. Thus the value in today's dollars (calculated using prevailing interest rates) of a sum or sums of money to be received in the future.

price inertia Inflation can be slow to accelerate and also slow to decline because many decisions on changes in prices and wages are made with a long advance lead.

price level The average level of nominal prices in the economy. Changes in the price level are inflation (or deflation). The concept of the price level is meant to abstract from shifts in relative prices like a rise in the relative price of oil or a fall in the relative price of

computers, and to capture changes in the value of the unit of account in which goods are priced, workers are paid, and contracts are written.

price stability The goal of central banks. An inflation rate so low that no one worries about it.

private saving Equal by definition to households' disposable incomes minus their consumption spending. Note that earnings not paid out but retained by corporations and then reinvested are counted in disposable income. Hence private saving includes both saving done directly by households and saving done on their behalf by firms whose stock they own.

procyclical Varying with the business cycle. A procyclical variable tends to be high when national product is high relative to potential output. Investment, especially investment in inventories, is procyclical; employment is procyclical; and inflation is procyclical. Unemployment is countercyclical.

producers' durable equipment One of the major components of business investment. The machines that embody the technologies of the industrial revolution bought by businesses: computers, fax machines, large turbine generators, metal presses, and other capital goods that are not structures and not part of inventories.

production function The relation between the total amount of national product produced, and the quantities of labor and capital (and the level of technology) used to produce it. The production function tells us how the productive resources of the economy — the labor force, the capital stock, and the level of technology that determines the efficiency of labor — can be used to produce and determine the level of output in the economy. In the Cobb-Douglas form of the production function: $Y^* = (K)^\alpha (L \times E)^{1-\alpha}$, potential output ($Y^*$) is determined by the size of the labor force (L), the economy's capital stock (K), the efficiency of labor (E), and a parameter α that tells us how fast returns to investment diminish.

productivity Usually a synonym for labor productivity: total national product divided by the number of workers, or by the number of hours worked. Sometimes used for total factor productivity: the amount of national product divided by the number of weighted units of labor and capital used in production.

productivity growth The rate at which the economy's full-employment productivity expands from year to year as technology advances, as human capital increases, and as investment increases the economy's physical capital stock.

productivity slowdown Around 1973, the rate of productivity growth in the United States and other economies suddenly slowed. The causes of this slowdown still remain somewhat a mystery. The most likely explanation is bad luck: a number of small negative factors all affecting the economy at once, each with its own separate causes. The productivity slowdown era appears to have come to an end in the mid-1990s.

profits Income earned by entrepreneurs and equity investors. What is left over from the receipts of an enterprise after it has paid for (*a*) intermediate goods and materials, (*b*) wages, salaries, and fringe benefits, (*c*) rent, and (*d*) interest.

purchasing power parity Valuing production in different countries as if the relative exchange rate gave you equal purchasing power in each country; sometimes also used for the theory that exchange rates ought to fluctuate around the values that correspond to purchasing power parity.

Q

quantity theory of money The core belief of monetarism: the belief — strongly pushed by Milton Friedman in the 1960s and 1970s — that money demand is insensitive to changes in interest rates and that the velocity of money is nearly constant. If true, then successful stabilization policy would require little more than stabilizing the rate of growth of the money stock.

R

rational expectations Expectations about the future formed by using all information about the structure of the economy, and the likely course of government policy. When people in an economy have rational expectations, it is extremely difficult for shifts in economic policy to cause anything other than shifts in the rate of inflation or the price level. Contrasted with static expectations and adaptive expectations.

real Adjusted for inflation; either divided by the price level, or with the inflation rate subtracted from it.

real appreciation A rise in the value of the nominal exchange rate under a floating-rate system that is greater than the ongoing difference in inflation rates between the home country and other countries. An increase in the relative price of domestic-made goods in terms of foreign-made goods.

real balances The purchasing power of the money — wealth in the form of readily spendable purchasing power — that consumers and firms actually hold at a given moment. Equal to nominal money balances divided by the price level, and thus adjusted for inflation.

real business cycle A boom generated when rapid technological innovation opens up new industries and new possibilities for investment. At such moments the stock market will be high, the returns to investment large, and so investment spending will be high as well. An adverse supply shock — like the sudden and

extreme rises in oil prices in the 1970s — can generate a real-business-cycle recession as well.

real depreciation A fall in the value of the nominal exchange rate under a floating-rate system that is greater than the ongoing difference in inflation rates between the home country and other countries. A reduction in the relative price of domestic-made goods in terms of foreign-made goods.

real devaluation A reduction in the value of the exchange rate under a fixed-rate system that is greater than the ongoing difference in inflation rates between the home country and other countries.

real exchange rate The exchange rate adjusted for changes in relative price levels. The price of foreign-made goods measured relative to the price of domestic-made goods.

real GDP Inflation-adjusted gross domestic product; the most commonly used measure of national product, output, and income. The total income earned through domestically located production. Equal as well to total expenditure on domestically produced goods and services. Real GDP can be calculated by dividing nominal (or money) GDP by the price level.

real interest rate The nominal interest rate minus the inflation rate. The real interest rate measures how expensive it is in terms of goods to borrow purchasing power. It answers the question: "How much more power to purchase goods and services in the future must I offer in order to borrow a fixed amount of power to purchase goods and services today?"

real money balances The total stock of nominal money balances in the economy divided by the price level. Money demand is usually thought of as a demand for real money balances: If the price level doubles while interest rates and (real) national income remain the same, then nominal money demand should double as well in order to keep real money demand constant.

real wage The wage paid to the average worker divided by the price level.

real wage growth The change in the wage paid to the average worker divided by the price level. Found by taking the rate of increase of nominal wages, and subtracting the inflation rate.

recession A fall in the level of GDP for at least six months, or two quarters of the year. The National Bureau of Economic Research announces and dates recessions. They sometimes, but rarely, deviate from this simple definition.

recognition lag It takes time for the Bureau of Labor Statistics and the Bureau of Economic Analysis to compile and analyze data about the economy. The recognition lag is the lag between when a process begins and when those making economic policy recognize that it is going on. Recognition lags are on the order of three to six months.

representative agent A simplification often made in macroeconomics that assumes all participants in the economy are the same (i.e., that the differences between businesses and workers do not matter much for the issues under study). Macroeconomists will analyze a situation by examining the decision making of a single *representative agent* and then generalize to the economy as a whole from what would be his or her decisions.

reserve requirements The amount of money that the central bank requires other banks to maintain either as cash in their vaults or at the central bank for each dollar of deposits that they hold. Reserve requirements are one of the principal determinants of the money multiplier. Their adjustment is a rarely used tool of central banks.

reserves-to-deposits ratio The ratio of bank reserves to bank deposits; partly the result of mandated government regulations, and partly the result of banks' desire to avoid getting caught short and of fear that those they lend to will not pay the money back. One of the two determinants (along with the currency-to-deposits ratio) of the money multiplier.

residential investment New construction of residences, both single-family homes and apartment buildings. An important component of total investment, and the principal nonbusiness component of investment. Fluctuations in residential investment are an important source of the business cycle.

revaluation When a central bank raises the value of its currency under a fixed exchange rate system.

Ricardian equivalence The hypothesis that households will cut consumption whenever they see a government deficit, anticipating higher future taxes that will be raised to pay off that deficit. Named for the nineteenth-century economist David Ricardo, but should be named after its principal advocate, the late-twentieth-century economist Robert Barro.

risk averse When individuals and institutions are unwilling to invest in ventures with a reasonable expected return, but also with a substantial probability of disaster.

risk premium The higher interest rate that lenders charge some of their borrowers because they fear that the borrower may not repay their money. Risk premiums are measured relative to the interest rates that the U.S. government can borrow using Treasury bills.

rules Monetarists believe that central banks should operate by setting fixed rules for how fast they will allow the money supply to grow. Only by setting policy according to fixed rules, they argue, can the central bank minimize uncertainty and let the private sector do its job.

rules versus authorities The debate, started by the early Chicago School economist Henry Simons, over whether macroeconomic policy should be conducted "automatically," according to rules that would be followed no matter what, or determined by authorities with the discretion to respond to specific circumstances as they saw fit.

S

sacrifice ratio The number of percentage points of unemployment in excess of the natural rate times the number of years such excess unemployment must be endured to reduce annual inflation permanently by 1 percentage point.

safe interest rate The interest rate on assets where there is no significant probability of default.

Samuelson, Paul Nobel Prize–winning MIT economist. The person whose late-1940s economics textbook set the mold for the economics textbooks that you use.

savings rate The share of total GDP that an economy saves. Usually calculated as the difference between the private savings rate and the government's budget deficit.

savings-and-loan crisis In the United States in the late 1980s, perhaps $200 billion worth of deposits in savings and loan associations were lost in a run of bad and risky investments, mostly in real estate and in high-yield bonds.

seasonal adjustment Over a year, employment and production undergo seasonal fluctuations about as large as in a typical business cycle. They build up in the fall in preparation for the Christmas rush. They fall in the summer as vacations are taken. Seasonal adjustment removes these seasonal variations from economic data to give a better idea of the longer-term evolution of the economy.

seignorage The tax implicitly levied on an economy's private sector by the government's exercise of its power to print more money.

services Commodities that are not (or are only incidentally) physical objects but are instead useful processes or pieces of information. Services are contrasted with goods — commodities that are principally useful physical objects.

shareholders Those who own the common stock issued by a company, and so are entitled to vote for its directors and other officers at the company's annual meeting, and to receive dividends (if any).

short-term interest rate The interest rate paid to borrow money for the short term — three to six months.

short-term nominal interest rate The interest rate paid to borrow money for the short term — three to six months. A nominal interest rate is not adjusted for inflation. The short-term nominal interest rate is important because it is the interest rate that has the greatest impact on money demand.

stabilization policy Policy aimed at avoiding recessions and undue inflation by keeping total aggregate demand growing smoothly, and unemployment near its NAIRU. Stabilization policy is countercyclical policy.

stagflation The coexistence of recession and rising inflation, or of recession and relatively high inflation. Politicians on whose watch economies suffer from stagflation usually lose their jobs at the next election.

static expectations Barely deserve the name of "expectations" at all — visions of the future that do not change at all in response to changes in the current economic situation. Contrasted with adaptive expectations and rational expectations.

statistical discrepancy A fudge factor added to reconcile two measurements of the same quantity that should be equal by definition, but that are not equal as measured. The national income and product accounts are full of statistical discrepancies. The statistical discrepancy in the international trade sector is often the largest.

steady-state capital-output ratio The value of the capital-output ratio to which an economy with constant investment and population growth rates converges over time. The steady-state capital-output ratio is calculated by dividing the investment share of national product by the sum of the population growth, technology growth, and depreciation rates.

steady-state growth path The path toward which national product per worker tends to converge as the capital-output ratio converges to its steady-state value. In analyzing long-run growth it is often easiest to first calculate an economy's steady-state growth path, and then to use the fact that the economy tends to converge to that path.

sticky prices When wages and prices do not move smoothly and immediately to keep supply equal to demand in the labor and goods markets. With sticky prices, inventory adjustment is the principal determinant of short-run equilibrium.

stock market The market on which the shares of common stock that carry ownership of companies are bought and sold. A company's bondholders have a right to be paid their interest and principal out of a company's operating profits. A company's stockholders have the right to elect the company's board of directors and to decide what to do with the rest of its profits. A relatively high stock market indicates optimism about future profits, and is likely to be accompanied by a high level of investment.

stock variable An economic quantity or variable that is measured not as a flow over some period of time but as a stock that exists at a single moment in time. For example, the capital stock and the money supply are "stock variables." GDP, consumption, and the government deficit are "flow variables." The capital stock and the money supply can be measured in dollars. But when you speak of GDP, consumption, or the government deficit, you must always be measuring — implicitly or explicitly — in dollars per year.

structural deficit A synonym for cyclically adjusted or high-employment government budget deficit. The government runs a structural deficit when its budget deficit exists not because real GDP is less than potential output, but because taxes are too low or spending too high to balance the budget even when real GDP equals potential output and unemployment is at its natural rate.

structural unemployment Unemployment that is not "cyclical" and not "frictional." Cyclical unemployment goes away when output expands and real GDP reaches the level of potential output. Frictional unemployment serves as the economy's inventory of workers and is part of the normal process of workers changing jobs and finding good matches. Structural unemployment is the result of (*a*) a real wage level stuck too high for supply to balance demand in the labor market, (*b*) poor labor-market tax and regulatory policies that drive a large wedge between the earnings that workers receive and the costs firms must pay to employ them, (*c*) other policies that make it difficult for workers to move to where the jobs are and for jobs to move to where the workers are, or (*d*) a gross mismatch between the educational and skill levels of the labor force and the levels that employers require. Structural unemployment has been high in western Europe for two decades, was high in the United States during the Great Depression, and is frequently high in the developing world.

structures Buildings, docks, bridges, and every other component of investment that is neither a piece of machinery and equipment nor a component of inventories. One way of looking at investment is to divide it into spending on machinery and equipment, changes in inventories, and spending on structures — residential, business, and government structures.

supply shocks Changes — usually large, sudden changes — in the productivity of the economy. Supply shocks can take the form of a large, sudden change in the price of a key raw material, as happened in the oil shocks of the 1970s. The sudden rise in the price of oil gave businesses a powerful incentive to use less oil and energy and more labor and capital in production; thus the economy's output per worker and its potential output dropped. The sudden rise in the price of oil also set in motion compensating price rises in other sectors, and led to higher inflation. The supply shocks of the 1970s were a major contributing factor to the stagflation of that decade. Rapid changes in technology can be seen as supply shocks as well.

surplus A shortened form of "government surplus." The amount by which the government's taxes exceed its spending.

T

taxes Payments by citizens to the government. Transfer payments are subtracted from gross taxes to calculate net taxes, or taxes less transfer payments. Net taxes are the measure of how much purchasing power is removed from the private sector by the government's fiscal policies.

taxes less transfers A synonym for "net taxes." The difference between total gross taxes collected by and transfer payments issued by the government. Taxes less transfers is a measure of how much purchasing power the government's fiscal policies remove from private households. Taxes less transfers is the variable T in the models of this book and is equal to $t \times Y$, the tax rate t times national income Y.

technological progress Invention and innovation in the broadest sense — including innovations in organization and control — that boost economic productivity over time.

technology transfer The rapid advance in total factor productivity possible in developing countries as they adopt the more productive technologies already well known in the world economy's industrial core. Since most of the difference between productivity levels across countries is due to differences in total factor productivity and the efficiency of labor, successful technology transfer is at the heart of successful economic development.

term structure The relationship between the lifetime — the maturity — of bonds and the interest rates buyers receive from holding bonds until their maturity. "Term structure" is a synonym for "yield curve." The term structure of interest rates usually has an upward slope: The interest rate on long-term bonds is higher than the interest rate on short-term bonds. When the interest rate on short-term bonds is higher, economists say that the term structure is inverted, and an inverted term structure is one sign of a possible future recession.

time inconsistency In macroeconomics, the temptation for central banks to make total nominal spending a little higher than people had expected, for once expectations have been formed, contracts made, and wages and prices set, there appear to be only benefits and no costs to a little more total nominal spending. With total nominal spending a little higher than had been expected, output and employment boom. And since wages and prices have already been set, there is little corresponding increase in inflation. Of course, if a central bank establishes a pattern of always making total spending a little higher than anticipated, people will come to expect such action, and the result will be high and destructive inflation. In the long run the central bank wants to gain and keep a reputation for keeping inflation low. Thus what the central bank would like to do in the short run (goose the economy a bit) is inconsistent with what it needs to do in the long run (maintain its credibility as an inflation fighter).

total factor productivity Total factor productivity is not labor productivity — not real GDP Y divided by the labor force L. Total factor productivity is not capital productivity — not real GDP Y divided by the capital stock K. Instead, total factor productivity is real GDP Y divided by a geometric weighted average of the factors of production, where each factor's weight is the share of national income that is paid to it. Total factor productivity is very closely related to the efficiency of labor E: In the Solow growth model of Chapter 4, total factor productivity is equal to $E^{1-\alpha}$. Total factor productivity is the best measure of the technological level and the overall efficiency of an economy.

total savings Private savings (by businesses and households) plus public savings (the government's surplus, and public savings are negative when the government runs a deficit) plus the capital inflow (the net amount of money that foreigners are committing to buying up property and assets in the home country, equal to minus net exports). Total savings are equal to total investment. Total savings are distinguished from national savings, which are equal to private savings plus the government surplus (leaving out the capital inflow); and total savings are distinguished from private savings, which are just the savings directly undertaken by households plus the business savings undertaken by firms on behalf of the households that are their owners.

trade balance A synonym for net exports, equal to gross exports minus imports.

trade deficit When gross exports are less than imports, and thus when net exports are negative. A country runs a trade deficit when international demand for goods and services it produces is less than home demand for goods and services produced abroad. A trade deficit is a subtraction from aggregate demand for domestically made products. A trade deficit is also necessarily associated with an equal capital inflow: net investment by foreigners in the home country.

trade surplus When gross exports are greater than imports, and thus when net exports are positive. A country runs a trade surplus when international demand for goods and services it produces is greater than home demand for goods and services produced abroad. A trade surplus is a boost to aggregate demand for domestically made products. A trade surplus is also necessarily associated with an equal capital outflow: net investment by home-country citizens in foreign countries.

transfer payments Spending by the government that is not a purchase of goods or services but instead simply a transfer of income from taxpayers to program recipients. Payments to contractors who have built highways or to bureaucrats who have sold their labor time to the government are not transfer payments. Payments to food stamp recipients, social security recipients, or unemployment insurance recipients are transfer payments. Transfer payments are included in the NIPA not as government purchases but under the "taxes" category. Transfer payments are subtracted from gross taxes to arrive at net taxes.

transitory income The difference between a household's current income and its permanent income. A household's transitory income is any portion of its current income that is seen as a windfall, and is not expected to continue in the future. Households tend to spend most of changes in their permanent income and to save most of changes in their transitory income. The marginal propensity to consume out of transitory income is much lower than the marginal propensity to consume out of permanent income.

Treasury bill A short-term bond issued by the United States Treasury. A U.S. government bond with a maturity — a period between the date at which the bond is issued and the date at which its principal comes due — of a year or less. A Treasury bill is a discount bond. It has no explicit payment of interest associated with it, and pays a positive interest rate to investors solely because it is initially sold at a discount to — for less than — its principal value. Federal Reserve monetary policy is carried out almost exclusively by open-market operations in Treasury bills.

Treasury bond A long-term bond issued by the United States Treasury. A U.S. government bond with a maturity — a period between the date at which the bond is issued and the date at which its principal comes due — often years or more. A Treasury bond is a coupon bond: Not only does the government pay the holder the bond's principal at its maturity, but it pays the holder periodic "coupon" interest payments throughout the bond's lifetime.

Treasury note A medium-term bond issued by the United States Treasury. A U.S. government bond with a maturity — a period between the date at which the bond is issued and the date at which its principal comes due — between one and ten years. A Treasury note is a coupon bond: Not only does the government pay the holder the note's principal at its maturity, but it pays the holder periodic "coupon" interest payments throughout the note's lifetime.

twin deficits During the 1980s the U.S. government budget deficits and trade deficits mirrored each other: When one rose, the other rose; when one fell, the other fell; they were "twins." The argument was made that the first was driving the second: that high U.S. trade deficits

were the result of large government budget deficits, and that the cure for the trade deficit was for the government to get its fiscal house in order and balance its budget, and not to impose tariffs and import restrictions on goods coming into the United States. In the 1990s the U.S. government budget and trade deficits were no longer twins: By the end of the decade the U.S. government was running a surplus, and the trade deficit was larger than it had ever been before. Why? Because the "twin deficits" doctrine was too simplistic: It would have been more accurate to say that a large trade deficit is the result of a large net capital inflow into the United States, and while a government budget deficit that raises domestic interest rates is one factor that can cause such a capital inflow, there are others as well. In the 1990s the inflow of capital into the United States was driven by investor optimism and high rates of investment in America.

U

unemployment rate The share of the labor force who are looking for but have not found an acceptable job. The labor force is calculated by adding (*a*) the number of people who told the Current Population Survey interviewers that they were at work and (*b*) the number of people who told the CPS interviewers they were looking for work but had no job. The number of unemployed is calculated as the number of people who told the CPS interviewers they were looking for work but had no job. The unemployment rate is the number of unemployed divided by the labor force. The conventionally measured unemployment rate is usually seen as an underestimate of the amount of unemployment in the economy. The unemployment rate fails to take account of discouraged workers — those who want to work but are not looking for a job now because they don't think they can find one. It also makes no allowance for those who are working part-time for economic reasons — people who want a full-time job, but have found only a part-time one.

unionization rate The share of an economy's workforce that belongs to a labor union. In the United States the unionization rate has been falling slowly but steadily since World War II, so that private-sector unionization rates are now about one-third what they are in western Europe.

unit of account One of the three functions that economists traditionally ascribe to money: Money is a medium of exchange, a store of value, and a unit of account. To say that a form of money — the U.S. dollar, say — is a unit of account is to say that a great many contracts are written promising to exchange such-and-such a good or service for such-and-such a number of dollars. The fact that a form of money is a unit of account means that changes in that form of money's value — inflation or deflation — can have powerful effects on the distribution of income and the level of production. Falling prices — deflation — increase the real wealth of creditors: The amount of money they are owed buys more real goods and services when the price level is lower. Rising prices — inflation — increase the real wealth of debtors: The quantity of real goods they must sell to raise the money to pay off their debt is lower when the price level is higher. As John Maynard Keynes wrote in 1923, "the fact of falling prices injures entrepreneurs; consequently, the fear of falling prices causes [them to] . . . curtail . . . their operations" and leads to reduced production and high unemployment.

V

value added The difference between the material costs a business incurs in production by buying raw materials and intermediate goods and the revenue it earns when it sells its products. *Value added* is equal to the sum of (*a*) employee compensation (wages, salaries, and benefits), (*b*) capital costs (depreciation and interest), and (*c*) profits.

variable lags Part of a phrase from economist Milton Friedman: "monetary policy works with long and *variable lags*." It reflects the idea that shifts in government policy will have powerful effects on aggregate demand, but that how long it takes such policy shifts to have their effects is not fixed but varies from time to time, country to country, and case to case. Because changes in economic policy work with long and variable lags, caution in changing economic policies helps avoid doing more harm than good.

velocity of money The rate at which the economy's money stock "turns over" in an economy, equal to nominal expenditure or income divided by the money stock. If an economy has $1 trillion of monetary assets and annual nominal national income of $10 trillion, economists say that money has an *income velocity* of ($10 trillion)/($1 trillion) = 10. The velocity of money is a measure of how often the average monetary asset is used as a means of payment, and thus changes hands, over the course of a year. The higher the interest rate, the greater the velocity of money. A higher interest rate gives businesses and households an incentive to economize on their use of money — that proportion of their wealth they hold in liquid and readily spendable but low interest-earning form.

Volcker, Paul Chair of the Federal Reserve Board from 1979–1987. His tenure saw the highest unemployment rates in post–World War II U.S. history, and the reduction of inflation from near 10 percent per year to less than 4 percent per year.

W

wage indexation When unions or workers negotiate with managers for wage levels that rise automatically when the price level rises. If (say) a steelworkers' contract provides them with an extra 1 percent increase in wages for each 1 percent rise in the CPI, economists say that their wages are *indexed* to the CPI. The more prevalent wage indexation is in an economy, the steeper its Phillips curve and the larger the change in inflation produced by any shift in the unemployment rate. When wage indexation is prevalent, changes in prices will immediately and automatically trigger corresponding changes in wages.

Y

yield curve The relationship between the interest rate you earn for lending or are charged for borrowing money and the length of time of the loan contract. "Yield curve" is a synonym for "term structure." A *yield curve* diagram is drawn with the interest rate for a given risk category of bonds on the vertical axis, and the bonds' maturity — the time until the borrower repays the principal — on the horizontal axis. The yield curve usually slopes upward: You pay a higher interest rate to borrow and earn a higher interest rate to lend for a longer term because longer-term investments bear higher risk. Whenever the yield curve slopes downward — whenever short-term interest rates are higher than long-term rates — economists say that the yield curve is inverted. An inverted yield curve is a sign of a possible future recession.

yield-to-maturity The interest rate you will earn over the life span of a bond if you buy it today and hold it until it reaches its maturity and the issuer pays you back the bond's principal. Note that if the bond's current price is different from its face (or principal) value, the *yield-to-maturity* will be different than the coupon interest rate. Consider a five-year bond with a principal value of $100 that pays annual coupon interest of 5 percent, or $5 a year. If you paid $100 for this bond, its yield-to-maturity would be the coupon interest rate of 5 percent per year. But if you buy the bond for $85, its yield-to-maturity is 8.84 percent. Remember: The lower the price of a bond, the higher the interest rate it pays.

INDEX

A

Abstractions, 63
Accelerationist Phillips curve, 346
Accounting definitions, 69
Adaptive expectations, 73
    convergence to long run, 353–354
    in high-pressure economy, 346–347
    Phillips curve under, 345–348
    and Volcker disinflation, 347–348
Adverse cost shocks, 467
Adverse supply shock, 208
After-tax disposable income, 250
Aggregate demand, 67
    changes due to real business cycles, 210
    and circular flow, 259
    compared to real GDP, 260
    components, 186, 251, 252
    dependent factors, 186
    effect of price level changes, 320–322
    equation, 251–253
    and fiscal policy changes, 194–199
    GDP and level of, 249
    in income and expenditure framework,
        248–250
        autonomous spending, 251–255
        consumption function, 249–251
        marginal propensity to expend,
            251–255
    and inflation, 336–340
    interest rate-investment relationship,
        270–271
    and interest rates
        dependence on, 281
        difficulties of controlling by, 285–287
        exports and autonomous spending,
            275–277
        fluctuations in investment, 271
        investment and real rate, 271–275
    and inventory adjustments, 257–260
    in IS curve, 277–280
    in IS-LM diagram, 304
    and monetary policy, 322–324
    moving along IS curve, 284–287
    multiplier effect, 261–265

Aggregate demand—*Cont.*
    planned expenditure function, 253
    and shifts in IS curve, 283–284
    short-run aggregate supply and, 326
    and sticky prices, 248
Aggregate demand curve, 321
Aggregate demand externality, 471
Aggregate supply
    aspects of, 332–333, 334
    equal to aggregate demand, 187–189
    monetary policy reaction function, 325
    output and price level, 324–325
    and Phillips curve, 330–332
    short-run, 326
Aggregate supply curve, 324–325
Agriculture, decline of, 440
Akerlof, George, 471
Alesina, Alberto, 383, 384
Algebra, 80–83
Algebraic equations, 70–71
Analytical geometric diagrams, 71
Analytic Geometry (Descartes), 70
Animal spirits, 165, 448
Appreciation of currencies, 20, 21, 174
Apprenticeship programs, 341
Appropriability of research, 146
Approximations, 39
Arbitrage
    currency, 412, 413
    international, 134
Argentina, 6–7, 88
Aspirations for real wage growth, 342
Assembly lines, 128
Auerbach, Alan, 398
Authority for economic policy, 380–386
Automatic rules, for economic policy,
    380–386
Automatic stabilizers
    financial, 440
    fiscal policy, 264, 378–379
    monetary, 388
    success of, 448
    tax rates and, 407–408
Autonomous spending, 251–255
    and exports, 275–276

Autonomous spending—*Cont.*
    and investment, 271
    in IS curve, 278–280
    and real interest rate, 277
    shifted by IS curve, 312

B

Baby-boom generation, 129
Bads, 56
Bagehot, Walter, 460
Bagehot rule, 460
Balanced-budget rule, 404
Balanced growth, 75, 76
Balanced-growth equilibrium
    output per worker, 77–80
Balance of trade
    in IS-LM framework, 313–320
    and LM shocks, 315–316
Bank of Japan, 24
Banks
    reserve requirements, 225
    sales of government bonds, 362
Barro, Robert, 465, 474
Base year, 32
Base year values, 51
BEA; *see* Bureau of Economic Analysis
Behavioral relationships, 62
    in economic models, 73–80
    production function, 74
Bernanke, Ben, 416
Blanchard, Olivier, 465
Blinder, Alan, 386
Bond prices, and interest rates, 168
Bonds, 35–36
    interest rate on, 37–38
    and term premium, 295–296
    yield curves, 272
Booms, 8, 241
Boskin, Commission, 131
Bottlenecks, 326
Bretton Woods system, 21, 412, 413,
    417–418, 424
British pound, 412–414
Brown, E. Cary, 459

Bubble economy, in Japan, 24, 459
Buchanan, James, 404
Budget; *see* Government budget
Budget constraint, 177–178
Budget cycle, 364
Budget resolution, 365
Bureau of Economic Analysis, 12 22, 43,
    52, 53–54, 372
Bureau of Labor Statistics, 14, 40, 445
    Current Population Survey, 44
    on labor force, 45
    price indexes, 43
Burns, Arthur, 381, 382, 455
Bush, George H. W., 291, 373, 382, 392,
    403
Business Conditions Digest, 369, 455
Business Cycle Digest, 369, 455
Business cycles, 8, 445; *see also* Real-
        business-cycle theory
    assessing changes in size of, 445–447
    conditions creating, 246
    economic policy failures, 448–450
    economic policy successes, 447–448
    economists' knowledge of, 479–480
    effectiveness of economic policies,
        447–450
    in future macroeconomic theory, 472
    Great Depression, 450–453
    indicators, 442
    and inventory adjustments, 255–260
    and IS curve, 287–292
    multiplier process, 248
    persistence of, 440–442
    phases of, 241
    political, 381–383
    recessions and expansions 1886–1997,
        446
    and sticky-price model, 237, 241–242
Business expenditures, 67
Business sector, 67

C

Capital accumulation, 95–97
Capital budgeting, 397
Capital consumption, 165
Capital controls, 436
Capital deepening, 440–441
Capital flight, 400
Capital flow
    cross-border, 443
    impact of real interest rate rise,
        196–197
    projected expansion of, 443–444

Capital inflow, 187–189
Capital intensity, 88
    determinants, 89
    source of long-run growth, 89
Capital-labor ratio, 74, 75
Capital mobility
    barriers to, 422–423
    versus capital controls, 436
    high, 419–421
    low, 419
Capital-output ratio, 76, 98
    global patterns, 139–140
    growth of, 102–103
    steady-state, 111–115
    in steady-state growth equilibrium,
        103–105
    steady-state growth path, 109
Capital per worker growth, 98–101
Capital stock, 90
    depreciation of, 96–97
    growth in, 98–99
Carroll, Chris, 474
Carter, Jimmy, 131, 382
Cash budget balance, 394–396
Cecchetti, Steve, 225
Central banks, 224, 300; *see also* Federal
        Reserve System
    barriers to capital mobility, 422–423
    dangers in bailouts, 387
    dynamic inconsistency in policy, 385
    expansionary monetary policy, 315–316
    foreign exchange reserves, 419
    future prospects, 475–476
    independence of, 383–384
    lenders of last resort, 387–388
    Taylor rule, 322–323
Central bank's target level of inflation,
        336–337
Chain weighting, 43
Churchill, Winston, 135
Circular flow, 65–69
    measures of, 67–69
    as metaphor, 63
    of purchasing power, 63, 67
Circular flow diagram, 65–67
Circular flow model
    aggregate demand equals aggregate
        supply, 187
    aggregate demand in, 259
    and inventory adjustments,
        255–260
    statistical discrepancy, 68–69
Civic responsibility, 5–6
Classical dichotomy, 219, 467

Classical flexible-price assumptions,
        154–156
Classical unemployment, 457
Clinton, Bill, 22–23, 291, 382, 403, 404
Clinton administration, 455
Closed economy, 264–265
Cobb-Douglas production function, 74,
        154
    analysis equation, 160
    equation, 75, 90
    level of output per worker, 101
    marginal product of labor for, 157
    in standard growth model, 90–93
Coincidence of wants, 220
Colosio, Luis Donaldo, 431
Commodity prices 1895-1997, 127
Communist countries, 135–139
Companies
    investment spending, 165–169
    reasons for investment spending, 166
Comparative statics, 193–194
Computer paradox, 131
Conference Board, 372
Consumer price index, 35, 41, 43
    as Laspeyres index, 40, 42
    purpose of, 40
Consumers, impatient and risk averse, 474
Consumption
    in macroeconomic theory, 474
    projected changes in, 444
Consumption function, 163, 164–165
    calculating, 251
    equation, 249
    and flexible-price logic, 242–244
    and marginal propensity to consume,
        249–250
Consumption goods, 14
Consumption smoothing, 180
Consumption spending, 67
    component of aggregate demand,
        249–251
    consequences of fall in
        for flexible-price model, 242–244
        in sticky-price model, 244–245
    determinants, 186
    household decisions, 161–163
    marginal propensity to consume,
        163–165
    marginal utility of consumption,
        178–181
    and national income, 162
    permanent and transitory income,
        178–181
        budget constraints, 177–178

Consumption spending—*Cont.*
  portion of aggregate demand, 248
  in real GDP, 53
  and real interest rate, 181–182
Continuing resolution, 366
Contractionary monetary policy, 414–416
Contracts, and expectations, 351
Convertible currencies, 413
Coordination failures, 471–472
Copyrights, 145–146
Costs of high unemployment, 331–332
Countercyclical discretionary fiscal policy,
  448
Creeping inflation, 17
Cross-border capital flows, 443
Crowding-out effect, 307
Cultural literacy, 4
Currency; *see* Appreciation of
      currencies; Depreciation of
      currencies
Currency arbitrage, 412, 413
Currency crises; *see* Financial crises
Currency speculation, 202–207; *see also*
      Foreign exchange speculators
Currency-to-deposits ratio, 374
Current Population Survey, 14, 44
Cyclical adjustments, 396
Cyclical volatility, 445–447

D

Data, importance of, 28
Debt capacity of government, 401
Debt repudiation, 400–401
Default, 273
Deficit; *see* Government deficit
Deficit-reduction program, 22–23
Deflation, 8, 16
  in Great Depression, 452
DeLong, J. Bradford, 109, 124, 384, 402,
      403, 430
Demand for loanable funds, 189
Demand for money; *see* Money demand
Demographics, 141
  of natural rate of unemployment, 341
  of unemployment, 46
Demographic transition, 122–124
Department of Commerce, 10, 68, 372,
      445, 455
Department of Labor, 14
Depletion of natural resources, 56
Deposit insurance, 386
  as monetary automatic stabilizer, 388
  as moral hazard, 388

Depreciation, 54, 165
  of capital stock, 96–97
  example, 95–97
  in steady-state capital-output ratio, 113
Depreciation of currencies, 20, 21, 174,
      434
Depressions, 8
  unemployment, 14–15
Descartes, René, 70, 76, 79
Destabilization, 6
Devaluation of currencies, 418
Devaluation of dollar, 174
Developmental states, 143, 147
Diagrams, 64, 71
Diminishing returns to capital, 79
Diminishing returns to scale, 73–74, 79
Discouraged workers, 45
Disinflation, 8, 347–348, 456
  in early 1980s, 17
Disposable income, 162
  after-tax, 250
Distribution of income, 72
Divergence of modern economic growth
  examples, 132–139
  sources of, 139–140
Dole, Robert, 432
Domestic economy
  effects of expansionary monetary policy,
      315–316
  and international shocks, 316–319
Domestic spending
  consumption spending
      household decisions, 161–163
      marginal propensity to consume,
      163–165
      and real interest rate, 181–182
  determinants, 186
  government purchases, 169
  investment spending, 165–169
  permanent and transitory income
      budget constraints, 177–178
      marginal utility of consumption,
      178–181
Dornbusch, Rudiger, 23, 109
Dorwick, Steven, 124
Dow Jones Industrial Average, 34

E

Earnings per share, 20
East Asian financial crisis, 25, 206–207,
      443
East Asian miracle, 137
Economic activity, indicators of, 10–12

Economic data; *see* Data
Economic disturbances
  affecting IS curve, 312
  changes affecting LM curve, 310–311
Economic growth; *see also* Long-run
      growth
  accelerating or decelerating, 6
  in capital-output ratio, 102–103
  convergence of G-7 economies, 136
  determining pace of, 98
  effect of long-run deficits on, 406–407
  in emerging markets, 25
  end of Malthusian era, 122–125
  former Communist countries, 135–139
  growth of capital per worker, 98–101
  long-run, 478–479
  output per worker, 101–102
  prior to Industrial Revolution,
      120–122
  real-business-cycle theory, 467
  relative or absolute stagnation, 142
  Sweden and Argentina, 7
  in U.S. 1800–2000, 125–132
  unequal results, 142–143
  unevenness of, 467–468
  worldwide
      cause and effect, 141
      divergence of, 132–139
      global patterns, 139–140
      OECD nations, 134–135
      rich versus poor nations, 133
      sources of divergence, 139–140
Economic models; *see also* Flexible-price
      model; Standard model;
      Sticky-price model
  building, 72–73
  examples, 77–80
  focus on expectations, 73
  opportunity cost, 72–73
  representative agents, 72
  solving
      advantage of algebra, 80–83
      behavioral relationships, 73–80
      equilibrium condition, 73–80
Economic news, 5
Economic policy
  central bank independence, 383–384
  comparisons of monetary and fiscal
      policies, 377–378
  competence and objectives, 380–384
  credibility and commitment, 384–385
  dynamic inconsistencies in, 385
  economists' knowledge of, 480–481
  and expected inflation, 350–351

Economic policy—*Cont.*
  failures, 448–450
  in financial crises, 386–388
  fiscal policy automatic stabilizers,
    378–379
  flaws in
    European unemployment,
      455–458
    Japanese stagnation, 458–459
    moral hazard, 459–460
  with government deficits, 405–407
  growth policy, 6–7
  history of, 367–369
  irrelevant under rational expectations,
    350
  lags and variable effects, 375–377
  lessons learned on stabilization,
    453–455
  for long-term growth
    promoting education, 143–144
    role of government, 146–147
    savings and investment, 143
    technological advances, 144–146
  modern monetary policy, 385–386
  money multiplier in, 373–375
  moral hazard in, 388
  policy mix, 405–407
  and political business cycles, 381–383
  and political popularity, 6
  power and limits of stabilization policy,
    370–377
  and quality of life, 9
  under rational expectations, 348–350
  by rules or authority, 380–386
  stabilization, 7–8, 264
  successes, 447–448
  uncertain impact of, 482
  workings of monetary policy,
    379–380
Economic policy debate, 370–371
Economic policy institutions
  fiscal policy, 364–367
  monetary policy, 360–363
Economics; *see also* Macroeconomics
  circular flow concept, 65–69
  dominant concepts, 63–64
  rhetoric, 63–64
  as science, 60–62
  use of abstractions, 63
Economic statistics, 10–12
Economic value added, 51–52
Economic variables, 28–29; *see also*
    Macroeconomic variables
Economies of scale, 48

Economists
  areas of ignorance
    impact of government policy, 482
    investment-productivity link, 481
    microfoundations of
      macroeconomics, 482
    areas of knowledge
      business cycles, 479
      current state of economy, 478
      economic policy, 480–481
      inflation, 479
      long-run economic growth, 478
      unemployment, 479
  characteristics, 60–61
  in early macroeconomics, 464
  patterns of thought, 69–83
    building models, 72–73
    on equilibrium, 70
    focus on expectations, 73
    on markets, 70
    solving models, 73–80
    using graphs and equations, 70–71
  in recent macroeconomics, 464–466
  short-term determinants of investment,
    481–482
  simplifying by, 62–63
Economy
  economists' knowledge of, 478
  leading indicators, 371–375
  Lucas critique, 370–371
  move toward equilibrium, 258
  moving to IS curve, 281–282
  open versus closed, 264–265
  political business cycles, 381
  uncertainties about, 371–372
  using IS curve to understand, 283–292
Economy-wide GDP deflator, 40
Education, 141
  commitment to, 128
  for economic growth, 143–144
Efficiency of labor, 88, 91
  and education, 144
  improvements since 1800, 122
  in standard growth model, 95
Eichengreen, Barry J., 109, 416, 417, 430
Eisenhower, Dwight D., 455
Emerging markets, 25
Employment
  fluctuations in, 7–8
  and output, 159–161
Employment Act of 1946, 367–368
Engerman, Stan, 140
Entrepreneurs, investment by, 467
Equations, 70–71

Equilibrium, 63, 70; *see also* Steady-state
    growth equilibrium
  flow of funds, 189–190
  full-employment, 186–193
  goods market, 256
  in income-expenditure diagram, 256
  labor market, 158–159
  moving economy toward, 258
  search for, 97–98
  sticky-price, 255–261
Equilibrium condition, 62
  capital-output ratio, 76
  in economic models, 73–80
Equilibrium debt-to-GDP ratio, 399–400
Equilibrium price level, 244
Equilibrium real interest rate, 191–193
  and fiscal policy change, 194–195
Europe
  application of Phillips curve to, 456
  currency crisis in 1992, 427–429
  high unemployment, 455–458
  labor market rigidities, 457
  long-term unemployment, 342–343
  macroeconomic situation, 23–24
  monetary union, 425–426
  optimal currency area, 425–426
  unemployment policy problems,
    457–458
European Central Bank, 23
European Exchange Rate Mechanism, 427
European Monetary Union, 23, 429
Euro zone, 425–426
Exchange-rate equation, 434
Exchange rates; *see also* Fixed exchange
      rates; Floating exchange rates;
      Nominal exchange rate; Real
      exchange rate
  Bretton Woods system, 417–418
  choice of systems, 424–426
  and currency crises, 427–437
  depreciation during Depression, 417
  determinants, 173–174
  as economic variable, 20–21, 28–29
  effect of foreign interest rate changes,
    200–202
  equation, 174
  and high capital mobility, 419–421
  history of gold standard, 412–417
  impact of currency speculation,
    202–207
  impact of real interest rate rise,
    196–197
  index numbers, 32–34
  internal/external balance, 425

Exchange rates—*Cont.*
  in IS-LM framework, 313–320
  and optimal currency areas, 425–426
  overall, 32–34
  samples of, 32
  and speculator expectations, 318–319
  in 2000, 23
Excludability of technology, 145
Expansionary monetary policy
  effects of, 315–316
  temptation to pursue, 384–385
Expansions, 8
Expectations
  focus of economists, 73
  and Great Depression, 61–62
  and price stickiness, 245–246
  types of, 73
Expectatons theory of the term structure,
    296
Expected inflation, 232
  in IS-LM framework, 304
  kinds of expectations, 344–350
  and persistent contracts, 351
  and Phillips curve, 334–335, 343–351
  short- and long-run, 352–354
Expenditure-weighted index, 40
Experimental method, 60–61
Exports
  and autonomous spending, 275–277
  effects of increase in foreign interest
    rates, 316–318
  and exchange rates, 29–31
External balance, 425

F

Factors of production, 65
Federal Deposit Insurance Corporation,
    388
Federal Open Market Committee, 224,
    284, 360–362
  composition of, 361
  functions, 362
  monetary policy operations, 379–380
  recession risks, 448
Federal Reserve Banks, 360–361
Federal Reserve System, 360–363
  as central bank, 224
  control of interest rates, 284–287
  decisions and action cycle, 378
  disinflation policy, 347–348
  and economic slowdown 2000–2001,
    22–23
  economic stabilization, 448

Federal Reserve System—*Cont.*
  future prospects, 475–476
  history and performance of, 362
  index of industrial production, 445
  interest rate increase 1929, 453
  interest rate targeting, 284–285
  lack of action in 1960s, 288
  and monetary base, 373–375
  monetary policy 1980–1989, 64
  monetary policy instruments, 379–380
  monetary policy prospects, 455
  monetary policy reaction function,
    323–324
  open-market operations, 224–225, 284,
    286
  policies in 1970s, 288
  policies in 1980s, 289
  policies in 1990s, 291
  reserve requirements, 225
  restrictions on, 363
  structure and functions, 360–363
  and Taylor rule, 386
Federal Reserve System Board of
    Governors, 360–361
Final goods and services, 14, 65
Finance, insurance, and real estate
    expenditures, 52
Financial automatic stabilizers, 440
Financial crises, 206–207
  and capital controls, 436
  in East Asia 1997–1998, 432–434,
    443
  economic policy for, 386–388
  in Europe 1992, 427–429
  management of, 434–436
  in Mexico 1994–1995, 429–432
  moral hazard problem, 388
  role of central banks, 387–388
Financial flexibility, 442, 444
Financial markets
  flow of funds through, 187–189
  surplus of purchasing power, 189
Financial transactions, 188
Fiscal policy
  as automatic stabilizer, 264, 378–379
  compared to monetary policy,
    377–378
  countercyclical discretionary, 448
  government deficit as index of,
    393–394
  impact of changes in flexible-price
    model, 194–199
  and IS curve, 360
  in 1980s, 289

Fiscal policy—*Cont.*
  sustainability, 399
  tax cuts, 378
  tax incentives for production,
    407–408
Fiscal policy institutions, 364–367
Fiscal year, 364
Fisher, Irving, 455, 466
Fixed exchange rates, 21
  and barriers to capital mobility,
    422–423
  benefits of, 424–425
  costs of, 425–426
  gold standard, 412–417
  high capital mobility, 419–421
  monetary policy under, 421
Flexible-price logic, 242–244
Flexible-price model
  assumptions, 154, 241
  as classical dichotomy, 219
  comparative statics analysis
    changes in fiscal policy, 194–199
    international disturbances, 200–207
    investment shocks, 199–200
    nature of, 193–194
  consequences of fall in spending, 244
  consumption and real interest rate,
    181–182
  domestic spending
    budget constraint, 177–178
    consumption spending, 161–165
    government purchases, 169–170
    investment spending, 165–169
  effect on savings of fall in spending,
    243
  full-employment equilibrium, 186–193
  impact of supply shocks
    oil prices, 207–209
    real business cycles, 209–212
  international trade, 170–174
    exchange rates in, 173–174
    gross exports, 171–172
    net exports and imports, 172–173
  key questions, 154
  marginal utility of consumption,
    178–179
  and national debt, 405
  permanent and transitory income
    budget constraint, 177–178
    consumption, 178–179
  potential output and real wages
    labor market, 156–160
    production function, 154–156
  real interest rate, 270

Floating exchange rates, 21, 412
  current system of, 418
  domestic benefits, 425
  drawbacks, 424–425
Flow of funds
  decline in confidence in exchange rate, 205
  effect of adverse supply shock, 209
  effect of foreign interest rate changes, 203
  excess supply of savings, 190
  through financial markets, 187–189
  and financial transactions, 188
  and increase in government purchases, 195
  in investment boom, 200
  in Schumpeterian analysis, 211
Flow of funds equilibrium, 189–190
Flow variables
  inflation rate, 43
  interest, 37
  real Gross Domestic Product as, 49
FOMC; see Federal Open Market
    Committee
Ford, Gerald, 382
Ford, Henry, 128
Fordism, 128
Forecasts
  qualitative, 28
  quantitative, 28
Foreign exchange market, 29–31
Foreign exchange reserves, 419
Foreign exchange speculators, 202–207, 419–420
  in East Asian crisis, 432–434
  effect of expectation changes, 318–319
  in European currency crisis, 429
Foreign interest rates, effect of increase in, 200–202, 318
Free-trade policies, 143
Frictional unemployment, 14
Friedman, Benjamin, 475
Friedman, Milton, 177, 369, 370, 424, 450, 464–466, 466
Full employment, 160; see also Flexible-price model; Natural rate of unemployment
  in flexible-price model, 243
Full-employment budget balance, 394–396
Full-employment deficit, 393, 394
  impact on investment, 405–406
Full-employment equilibrium, 186–193
  as classical dichotomy, 219

Full-employment equilibrium—*Cont.*
  comparative statics analysis
    effect of fiscal policy changes, 194–199
    international disturbances, 200–207
    investment shocks, 199–200
    nature of, 193–194
  and flow of funds, 187–189
  impact of supply shocks
    oil prices, 207–209
    real business cycles, 209–212
  and interest rates, 186–187
  solving the model, 191–193
Full-employment tax collections, 394

G

GDP deflator, 35
  economy-wide, 40
  as Paasche index, 50
GDP-deflator-based inflation rate, 43
General Theory of Employment, Interest, and Money (Keynes), 368, 464
Generational accounting, 398
Germany
  fiscal and monetary policies in 1990s, 428
  hyperinflation in, 218, 234
  reunification of, 427
Gingrich, Newt, 404, 432
Globalization, projected changes in, 444
Gold exchange standard, 412; see also
    Bretton Woods system
Gold parity, 413
Gold standard
  collapse of, 416–417
  contractionary monetary policy, 414–416
  and currency arbitrage, 412, 413
  description of, 412–414
  growth 1870–1902, 415
Goods and services, 49
  in consumer price index, 40
  for consumption spending, 53
  imputations, 52
  for investment spending, 53
  weighted by base-year values, 51
Goods market equilibrium, 256
Gorbachev, Mikhail, 138
Government
  cause of hyperinflation, 233–234
  changing role in economy, 440
  core competencies, 147
  debt capacity, 401

Government—*Cont.*
  debt repudiation, 400–401
  economic policy history, 367–369
  fiscal automatic stabilizers, 264
  fiscal policy institutions, 364–367
  growth policy, 6–7
  investment policy, 168
  as kleptocracy, 147
  monetary policy institutions, 360–363
  role in economic growth, 146–147
Government budget
  balanced-budget rule proposal, 404
  cash budget balance, 394–396
  continuing resolution, 366
  cyclical adjustments, 396
  measuring balance, 394–396
  process, 365–366
  unified cash balance, 394
Government budget cycle, 364
Government budget surplus, 67, 188
  significance for economists, 392
Government deficit; see also
    National debt
  Barro's view, 473
  created by tax cuts, 404
  critique of Barro's view, 473–474
  debt service, 407–408
  effects of, 401–408
  index of fiscal policy, 393–394
  inflation measure, 396–397
  and IS curve, 392–394
  liabilities and generational accounting, 398
  long-run effects, 405–408
  open-economy consequences, 405
  political consequences, 404
  and public investment, 397–398
  real GDP and, 407–408
  Ricardian equivalence, 472–474
  short-run economic consequences, 404–405
  significance for economists, 392
  and stabilization policy, 392–396
  sustainability, 398–401
  and taxation, 407–408
Government expenditures
  beneficiaries versus tax payers, 474
  capital budgeting, 397
  discretionary categories, 367
  general categories of, 366
  and IS curve, 283–284
  mandatory versus discretionary, 364–366
  public investment, 397–398
  as share of national product, 403

Government purchases, 14, 52
  boom in, 197–199
    compared to aggregate demand, 251
    in domestic spending, 169–170
    and fiscal policy changes, 194–199
    in GDP, 55
    in real GDP, 53
Government revenues, as share of national
    product, 403
Graphs, 64, 70–71
Great Depression, 8, 126, 445
    bank failures, 388
    compared to other business cycles, 446
    deflation and high interest rates, 452
    exchange rate depreciation, 417
    and expectations, 61–62
    and inflation of 1970s, 449
    Keynesian revolution, 368–369
    magnitude of, 450–452
    price level decline, 453
    stock market crash of 1929, 452–453
Greenspan, Alan, 291, 362, 373, 382, 454
Gross Domestic Product, 68; *see also* GDP
    deflator; Nominal GDP; Real GDP
    components, 54
    definition, 50
    depreciation in, 54
    effect of supply shocks, 207–209
    and flexible-price logic, 242–244
    forecasts for emerging markets, 25
    government purchases in, 55, 169
    in Great Depression, 450–452
    gross exports in, 170–171
    growth 1993–1998, 131
    imputations, 52
    and intermediate gods, 50–52
    and inventories, 52
    investment spending percentage of, 165
    in IS curve, 278–280
    and level of aggregate demand, 249
    and net national product, 54
    omissions from, 55–56
    ratio to national debt, 399–401
    replacement investments, 54
Gross Domestic Product per capita,
    national comparisons, 138
Gross Domestic Product per worker, 110
    and years of schooling, 140
Gross exports, 53–54, 170–172
Gross investment spending, 53
Gross investment, 165
Gross national product, 48
Growth multiplier, 106, 108
Growth-of-a-power rule, 39

Growth-of-a-product rule, 39
Growth-of-a-quotient rule, 39
Growth policy, 6–7
Growth rate, 75
G-7 economies
    convergence of, 136
    productivity slowdown, 120–121

H

Hall, Robert, 140
Hamilton, Alexander, 402
Hansen, Alvin, 464
Hawtrey, Ralph, 368
Heller, Walter, 369, 455
Heston, Alan, 133, 138, 140
Hicks, John, 277, 464
High-powered money, 225–226
High-pressure economy, under adaptive
    expectations, 346–347
Hiring policy, 158
Historical Statistics of the United States,
    445
Hoover, Herbert, 168
Household production, 55
Households
    disposable income, 162
    income, 67
    income measures, 139
    liquidity constraints, 474
    savings by, 162
    spending decisions, 161–163
Household sector, 67
Housing, 52
Hubbard, Glenn, 225
Hyperinflation, 16
    caused by government, 233–234
    costs of, 233–234
    in Germany, 218, 234

I

Imperfect information, 247
Imports, 53, 172–173
    and exchange rates, 29–31
Imputed rent, 52
Income, permanent or transitory,
    177–181
Income distribution, 72
    worldwide, 133
Income-expenditure diagram, 253, 277
    equilibrium in, 256
    and goods market equilibrium, 256
    inventory adjustments, 257

Income-expenditure framework
    building up aggregate demand, 248–250
        autonomous spending, 251–255
        components, 251
        consumption function, 249–251
        marginal propensity to expend
    multiplier in, 261–265
    planned expenditure function, 253
    sticky-price equilibrium, 255–261
Income redistribution, 400–401
Income tax cuts
    deficits created by, 404
    in Kennedy-Johnson years, 287–288, 378
    in Reagan years, 378, 406
Indexing to combat inflation, 233
Index number, 32–34, 40–43
    equation, 33
Index number problem, 43
Index of leading indicators, 372
Indonesia, 432
Industrial economies
    changes since 1860, 440
    changing structures, 440
Industrialized economies, 124
Industrial Revolution, 120
    characteristics, 124–125
Inflation, 218
    acceleration in 1960s-70s, 449
    adaptive expectations, 345–348
    and aggregate demand, 336–340
    central bank's target level of, 336–337
    costs of, 231–235
        hyperinflation, 233–234
        moderate expected inflation, 232
        moderate unexpected inflation,
            232–233
    creeping, 17
    decline in 1990s, 291
    definition, 324
    economists' knowledge of, 479–480
    and GDP, 326
    and interest rates, 229–231
    in late 1960s, 288
    and money supply growth, 228
    and national debt, 400
    in 1980s, 289–290
    political repercussions, 233
    and price level, 40–44
    in quantity theory of money, 226–227
    rational expectations, 348–350
    and real exchange rate, 30–31
    static expectations, 344–345
    trotting, 17
    U.S. measures of, 44

Inflation-adjusted budget balance, 396–397
Inflation-adjusted purchasing power, 183–184
Inflation rate, 4; *see also* Expected inflation rate; Phillips curve
  and consumer price index, 43
  as economic variable, 16–20, 28–29
  effect on money demand, 229
  equilibrium rate, 336, 338–339
  as flow variable, 43
  and Okun's law, 332–333
  Taylor rule, 322–323, 386
Inflation-rate targeting, 386
Inflation tax, 233–234
Inflation-unemployment trade-off, 23, 64;
  see also Phillips curve
Innovation, 144–145
Institutional voter myopia, 404
Institutions, and natural rate of unemployment, 341
Interest, as flow variable, 37
Interest rate differentials, 420
Interest rates, 37–40; *see also* IS curve; IS-LM *entries*
  and aggregate demand, 270–271
    exports and autonomous spending, 275–277
    fluctuations in investment, 271
    investment and real rate, 271–275
  changes in foreign rates, 202
  controlled by Fed, 284–287
  crowding-out effect, 307
  dependence of aggregate demand on, 281
  determinant of exchange rate, 173–174
  as economic variable, 17–19, 28–29
  Fed restrictions, 363
  and flow of funds, 187–189
  flow of funds equilibrium, 189–190
  and full-employment equilibrium, 186–187
  future expected, 295–297
  gap between nominal and real, 273
  in Great Depression, 452
  under high capital mobility, 419–421
  and investment spending, 166
  in IS curve, 277–280
  in Japan, 24
  with limited capital mobility, 422–423
  mathematical tools, 39
  in monetary policy, 379–380
  and money demand, 228–229
  prices and inflation, 229–231

Interest rates—*Cont.*
  and real GDP 1960–1999, 287
  risky, 272–274
  safe, 273
  and stock and bond prices, 168
  Taylor rule, 386
  term premium, 286–287, 295–297
Interest-rate targeting, 284–285, 310, 379–380
Intermediate goods, 50–52
  government purchases, 55
Internal balance, 425, 429
International arbitrage, 134
International disturbances
  increase in foreign interest rates, 200–202
  loss of confidence in currency, 202–207
International Monetary Fund, 206, 432
  in East Asian crisis, 434
  founding of, 418
International monetary system
  Bretton Woods system, 417–418
  current floating-rate system, 418
  gold standard, 412–417
International savings, 187–188, 191
International shocks
  change in speculator expectations, 318–319
  and domestic economy, 316–319
  increase in demand for foreign exports, 316–318
  increase in foreign interest rates, 318
International trade
  in flexible-price model, 170–174
  with gold standard, 412–417
  gross exports, 170–172
  imports and net exports, 172–173
  in IS-LM framework, 313–320
  J curve, 172
  projected expansion of, 443–444
Invention, 144–145
Inventories
  and GDP, 52
  projected changes in, 444–445
  rising and falling, 257–258
Inventory adjustment process
  in circular flow model, 255–260
  funds market equilibrium, 256
  income-expenditure diagram, 257
Inventory investment, in 1990s, 258
Inverted yield curve, 18
Investment
  components of, 53
  example, 96–97

Investment—*Cont.*
  policies to encourage, 143
  private versus governmental, 397
  reduced by government deficits, 405–406
  shift in patterns of, 443–444
  short-run determinants, 481–482
  in standard growth model, 96–97
Investment boom, 131
  international consequences, 201
Investment effort, 89, 102–103, 113
Investment function, 166–167
  equation, 271
  relevant interest rate, 273, 274
Investment goods, 14
Investment-productivity relationship, 481
Investment requirements, 89, 102–103, 113
Investment shocks, 199–200
Investment spending, 165–169
  compared to aggregate demand, 251
  determinants, 186
  effect of foreign interest rate changes, 202
  effect of rise in savings, 243
  and fiscal policy changes, 194
  flexible-price versus sticky-price models, 270–271
  in IS curve, 277–280
  kinds of, 165
  meaning of, 165
  opportunity cost, 271
  and present value concept, 183–184
  and real business-cycle theory, 210
  in real GDP, 53
  reasons for, 166
  reasons for fluctuations, 166
  relation to stock market, 168
  role in autonomous spending, 271
  as share of real GDP, 270
  sources of fluctuation in, 271
  stock market indicator, 275
Investors, changes in optimism, 199–200
Iraqi invasion of Kuwait, 291
Iron Curtain countries, 135–139
IS curve, 336
  analysis of economic fluctuations, 287–292
  disturbances affecting, 312
  effect of marginal propensity to expend, 312
  and fiscal policy changes, 360
  and government deficit, 392–394

IS curve—*Cont.*
government spending and, 283–284
in Great Depression, 452
meaning of, 277–280
and monetary policy, 360
moving along, 284–285
moving economy toward, 281–282
position of, 281
shifts in, 283–284
slope of, 280
Taylor rule, 322–323
IS-LM diagram, 304
and aggregate demand curve, 321
government deficits in, 405
IS-LM equilibrium, 304–305
IS-LM framework
and balance of trade, 315–316
classifying economic disturbances
changes affecting LM curve,
310–312
interest rate targets, 310
IS shocks, 305–307
LM shocks, 308–310
exchange rates in, 313–315
international shocks and domestic
economy, 316–319
origin of, 464
IS shocks, 305–307

J

Jackson, Andrew, 402
Japan
bubble economy, 459
economic stagnation, 458–459
liquidity trap, 363–364
macroeconomic situation, 24–25
J curve, 172
Johnson, Lyndon B., 180–181, 369, 382,
455
Jones, Charles, 140
Jorgenson, Dale, 464

K

Kennedy, John F., 147, 381
Kennedy-Johnson tax cut, 378
Keynes, John Maynard, 165, 246, 248,
265, 368, 417, 421, 436, 448, 464,
466, 472
Keynesian revolution, 368–369
Keynesian sticky-price analysis, versus
classical assumption, 155
Kleptocracy, 147

Kohl, Helmut, 427
Kotlikoff, Laurence, 398
Kuwait, 291

L

Labor demand, 156–158
and real wages, 159
Labor force, 45, 90
baby-boom generation, 129
occupational distribution, 441
and population growth, 94–95
Labor force growth, 94–95
in GDP per-worker levels, 110
and steady-state capital-output ratio,
111–112
Labor force participation, by gender, 56
Labor market, 70
employment and output, 159–161
at full employment, 160
hiring policies, 158
and labor demand, 156–158
rigidities in Europe, 457
Labor market equilibrium, 158–159, 243
Labor supply, 158–159
Labor unions, and natural rate of
unemployment, 341
Lags
fiscal versus monetary, 377–378
in monetary policy effects, 378
in policy effects, 371, 375–377
La Porta, Rafael, 140
Laspeyres index, 40, 42
Layard, Richard, 109
L definition of money, 226, 372–373
Leading indicators, 371–372
index of, 372
money supply as, 372–375
stock market, 35–36
unemployment rate, 44
Liabilities of government, 398
Liquidity
equation, 244
of money, 219
Liquidity constraints, 442, 473–474
Liquidity trap in Japan, 363–364
LM curve
derivation, 302–303
economic changes affecting, 310–311
effect of price level changes, 320–322
money market equilibrium, 300–302
LM shocks, 308–310
and balance of trade, 315–316
Loanable funds, 189

Loanable funds market, determination of
interest rates, 270
Loan default, 273
Long run, versus short run, 246,
352–354
Long-run economic growth
economists' knowledge of, 478–479
end of Malthusian era, 122–125
before Industrial Revolution, 120
in modern United States, 125–132
policies for
education, 143–144
role of government, 146–147
savings and investment, 143
technological advance, 144–146
pre-modern, 121–122
relative and absolute stagnation, 142
significance of, 85, 88
sources of
capital intensity, 89
technology, 88
standard growth model, 89–97
analysis of, 98–103
efficiency of labor, 95
population growth, 94–95
production function, 90–93
savings and investment, 96–97
Long-term interest rate, 271–272
and term premium, 295–297
Long-term unemployment, 342–343
Lopez-di-Silanes, Florencio, 140
Lucas, Robert, 370–371, 464–466
Lucas critique, 370–371
Lump-sum taxes, 264

M

Macroeconomic fluctuations; *see also*
Business cycles; Recessions
effectiveness of economic policy,
447–450
Great Depression, 450–453
long-run changes in cyclical volatility,
445–447
Macroeconomic policy; *see* Economic
policy
Macroeconomics
in age of Friedman and Lucas, 464–466
in age of Keynes, 464
and civic responsibility, 5–6
contrasted with microeconomics, 9–10
and cultural literacy, 4
current state of economists' ignorance,
481–483

Macroeconomics—*Cont.*
current state of economists' knowledge, 478–481
definition, 4
as emergent phenomena, 483
Friedman's critique, 465
future of
consumption and saving, 474
government debt and deficits, 472–474
in monetary policy, 475–476
new Keynesian economics, 470–472
real-business-cycle theory, 466–470
Keynesian revolution, 368–369
microfoundations of, 482
patterns of economic thought, 69–83
reliance on quantitative models, 62–64
as science, 60–62
and self-interest, 4–5
significance of IS curve, 277–280
significance of long-run growth, 85
Macroeconomic variables, 4
exchange rates, 20–21
inflation rate, 16–20
interest rates as, 17–19
key, 28–29
key indicators, 12–22
real GDP, 12–14
stock market, 19–20
unemployment rate, 14–15
Macroeconomy, 4
changes in past centuries, 440–442
economic statistics and activity, 10–12
in emerging markets, 25
of Europe, 23–24
future changes
consumption, 442–443
globalization, 443–444
inventories, 444–445
monetary policy, 444
in Japan, 24–25
of United States, 22–23
Maddison, Angus, 7, 13
Mahathir, Muhammad, 436
Malaysia, 432, 436
Malthus, Thomas R., 121
Malthusian age
description of, 121–122
end of
demographic transition, 122–124
Industrial Revolution, 124–125
technology, 122
Mankiw, N. Gregory, 471
Mao Zedong, 137

Marginal product of labor, 156–158
equation, 156
Marginal propensity to consume, 163–165, 179–181, 249–250
Marginal propensity to expend, 251–255
calculating, 254–255
in calculating aggregate demand, 281
and IS curve, 312
and value of multiplier, 261–262
Marginal social product of labor, 468
Marginal tax rate, and economic activity, 408
Marginal utility of consumption, 178–181
Market basket of goods and services, 40
Market-clearing level of wages, 155
Markets, 63, 70
contrasting views of, 9
Market transactions, 220
Marshall Plan, 135
Marx, Karl, 135
Mass production, 128
Mathematical tools, 39
McDonough, William, 362
M1 definition of money, 226, 372–373
M2 definition of money, 226, 372–373
M3 definition of money, 226, 372–373
Medium of exchange, 220
Menu costs, 247
in new Keynesian economics, 471
Metaphors, 63
Mexican bailout, 432
Mexican financial crisis, 206–207, 429–432
Microeconomics, 4
contrasted with macroeconomics, 9–10
definition, 9
Microfoundations of macroeconomics, 482
Miller, G. William, 288
Mishkin, Rich, 225
Mitterand, Francois, 350
Model-building, 62–63, 72–73
Model-T Ford, 128
Modigliani, Franco, 464
Monetarist critique, 465
Monetarists, 372
Monetary aggregates, 372–373
Monetary automatic stabilizer, 388
Monetary base, 224–225
expanding or contracting, 286
Fed changes in, 373–375
Monetary policy, 224–225
activist versus automatic, 369
and aggregate demand, 322–324

Monetary policy—*Cont.*
compared to fiscal policy, 377–378
expansionary, 315–316, 384–385
under fixed exchange rates, 421, 425–426
under gold standard, 414–416
instruments of, 379–380
and IS curve, 360
lags in effects, 378
lessons learned on, 454–455
and liquidity trap, 363–364
modern, 385–386
operations of, 379–380
projected changes in, 444
questionable future of, 475–476
and real-business-cycle theory, 469
Taylor rule, 386
Monetary policy institutions, 360–363
Monetary policy reaction function, 380
and aggregate supply, 325
and Phillips curve, 336–338
and real GDP, 323–324
Monetary union, Europe, 425–426
Money, 218–221
and costs of inflation, 231–235
and exchange rates, 20–21, 29–34
and interest rates, 37–40
interest rates and price of, 17–19
liquidity equation, 244
as liquid wealth, 219
medium of exchange, 220
neutrality of, 219
opportunity cost of holding, 221–222, 229, 300
and price levels, 222–226
in real-business-cycle theory, 469
unit of account, 220–221
usefulness of, 220
Money demand
in economic disturbances, 310–312
equation, 229
and inflation rate, 229
and interest rates, 228–229
and LM curve, 302–303
and money supply, 301–302
and nominal interest rate, 228–229, 300–302
in quantity theory of money, 221
Money demand equation, 300–301
Money illusion, 247
Money market, 70
in IS-LM framework, 304–310
in LM curve, 302–303
Money market equilibrium, 300–302

Money multiplier, 373–375
  fluctuations in, 380
Money stock/supply
  components, 219
  currency-to-deposits ratio, 374
  definitions of, 225–226
  in economic disturbances, 310–312
  effects of increase in, 230–231
  and inflation rate changes, 227
  in IS-LM framework, 304–310
  as leading indicator, 372–375
  in LM curve, 302–303
  measures of, 219, 372–373
  in monetary policy, 379–380
  and money demand, 301–302
  money market equilibrium, 300–302
  nominal variable, 219
  in quantity theory of money, 224–226
Moral hazard
  deposit insurance, 388
  as flaw in economic policy, 459–460
Moving along the IS curve, 284–285
MPE; see Marginal propensity to expend
Multiplier, 244, 248
  changing size of, 264–265
  determining size of, 261–264
  in income-expenditure framework,
      261–265
  and open economy, 264–265
  with proportional taxation, 264
  reduced by financial flexibility, 444
  related to output, 271
  and slope of IS curve, 280
  value of
      example, 263–264
      and marginal propensity to expend,
          261–262
      and planned expenditure function,
          261
Multiplier effect, 262
Mundell, Robert, 424, 425–426

N

National debt
  Barro's view, 473
  critique of Barro's view, 473–474
  end of rise in, 403
  GDP ratio to, 402
  inflation measure, 396–397
  liabilities and generational accounting,
      398
  policy mix, 405–407
  and public investment, 397–398

National debt—*Cont.*
  repudiation of, 400–401
  Ricardian equivalence, 472–474
  service on, 407
  significance for economists, 392
  steady-state debt-to-GDP ratio, 399–401
  sustainability, 398–401
National income, 48, 68, 69
  components, 161
  consequences of fall in spending, 244
  and consumption spending, 162
National income and product accounts,
      10–12, 48, 68, 478
  definition of total expenditure, 259–260
  failure to account for environmental
      protection, 128–129
  imputations, 52
  and inventories, 52
  omissions from, 55–56
  transfer payments in, 169
National income identity
  effect of foreign interest rate increases,
      201–202
  effect of investment shocks, 199–200
  effect of supply shocks, 208
Natural rate of unemployment, 240,
      340–343, 465; *see also* Full
      employment entries
  demography of, 341
  institutions and, 341
  and past unemployment levels,
      342–343
  and Phillips curve, 334–335
  and productivity growth, 341–342
Natural resources, 128
  depletion of, 56
  scarcity, 122
Natural sciences, 60
Neoliberalism, 147
Net domestic product, 48, 54
Net export function, 194
  and fiscal policy change, 194–195
Net exports, 53–54, 172–173
  and capital flow, 187–189
  compared to aggregate demand, 251
  determinants, 186
  equation, 173
  in real Gross Domestic Product, 53
Net investment, 165
Net national product, 48
Net output, 54
Net taxes, 161–162, 169
Neutrality of money, 219
New Deal, 388

New Dimensions of Political Economics
      (Heller), 369
New Keynesian economics, 470–472,
      481–482
  aggregate demand externality, 471
  assessment of, 472
  menu costs, 471
  staggered prices and coordination
      failure, 471–472
Newton, Isaac, 414
Nixon, Richard M., 6, 381–383
Nolling, Willheim, 109
Nominal exchange rate, 20, 29–31
  under gold standard, 412, 413
Nominal GDP, 12, 49–50
Nominal interest rate, 17, 37–38
  compared to real rate, 273
  in expected inflation, 232
  Fed restrictions, 363
  in Great Depression, 452
  and money demand, 228–229
  opportunity cost of holding money, 229
  related to money demand, 300–302
Nominal prices, 247
Nominal variables, 219
North American Free Trade Agreement,
      430

O

Obstfeld, Maurice, 429
Oil price increases, 129, 207–208, 467
Okun's law, 46–48
  and inflation rate, 332–333
  and unemployment rate, 330–331
Okun's law coefficient, 336
Open economy, 264–265
Open-market operations, 224–225, 284,
      286, 362
  future prospects, 475
  lessened effect of, 444
Opportunity cost, 72–73
  of holding money, 221–222, 229, 300
  of investment project, 271
Optimal currency areas, 425–426
Organization for Economic Cooperation
      and Development, 430
  economies of, 134–135
Organization of Petroleum Exporting
      Countries, 129, 207–208
Output
  and aggregate supply, 324–325
  determined by autonomous spending
      and multiplier, 271

Output—*Cont.*
   and employment, 159–161
   as function of labor hired, 157
   and marginal product of labor, 156–158
Output gap, 331–332
Output per worker, 75
   calculation of, 107
   Cobb-Douglas production function,
      91–93
   growth of, 101–102
   growth since 1870, 126
   prior to 1500, 120
   rate of growth, 130
   steady-state, 79–80
      algebraic calculation, 78–79
      arithmetic calculation, 77
   steady-state growth path, 105–108
   in U.S. 1973–1995, 128

P

Paasche index, 40–42
   and Gross Domestic Product deflator,
      50
Parameters, 75
   of Cobb-Douglas production function,
      90–92
Part-time workers, 46
Patents, 145–146
Percentage per year, 37
Permanent income, 177–181, 182
Peso devaluation, 431
Phelps, Edward, 465
Phillips, A. W., 333
Phillips curve, 23, 63, 64, 291
   accelerationist, 346
   under adaptive expectations,
      345–348
   and aggregate supply/unemployment,
      330–332
   criticism of, 449
   description of, 333–335
   and disinflation, 347–348
   and expected inflation, 343–351
   Friedman's critique, 465
   in long- and short-run, 352–354
   and monetary policy reaction function,
      336–338
   under rational expectations, 348–350
   and stagflation, 369
   under static expectations, 344–345
   in U.S. 1955–1980, 368
   in U.S. versus Europe, 456
Phleps, Edward, 369

Planned expenditure function, 253
   and autonomous spending, 275–276
   and value of multiplier, 261
Policy-induced recessions, 447, 448
Political business cycles, 381–383
Political popularity, 6
Poor countries, 133
Population explosion, 121
Population growth, 111–112, 141
   from 5000 BC to 1800 AD, 120
   expected rates 1997–2015, 123
   global projections, 144
   since 1000 AD, 121
   in standard growth model, 94–95
Positive-technology shock, 211
Post-Communism, 138
Potential output
   aggregate demand exceeding, 326
   decline in 1970s, 288
   equation, 154
   and labor market, 156–160
   production function, 154–156
   in United States 1960–2000, 240
Premodern growth, 121–122
Prescott, Edward, 466
Present value, and investment spending,
      166, 183–184
Price changes
   with imperfect information, 247
   menu costs, 247, 471
   nominal versus real, 247
Price-earnings ratio, 20
Price indexes; *see also* Consumer price
      index; Producer price index
   calculating, 41
   chain weighting, 43
   and substitution bias, 42
Price inertia, 351
Price level, 218–219
   and aggregate demand, 320–322
   and aggregate supply, 324–325
   calculation, 223–224
   and consumer price index, 40
   decline in Great Depression, 453
   equation, 230
   index numbers, 40–43
   and inflation, 40–44
   and inflation rate, 43
   measures of, 35
   and money, 222–226
   short-run aggregate supply and, 326
Prices; *see also* Sticky prices
   classical assumption, 154–156
   in hyperinflation, 233–234

Prices—*Cont.*
   and interest rates, 229–231
   real versus nominal, 247
   staggered, 471–472
Principal, 17
Pritchitt, Lant, 132
Private investment, 397
Private savings, 187, 191
Problem-of-measurement argument,
      128–129
Producer price index, 40
Production
   bottlenecks, 326
   consequences of fall in spending,
      244–245
   economies of scale, 48
   fluctuations in, 7–8
   and inventory adjustments, 255–260
   value added in, 51–52
Production function, 71; *see also* Cobb-
      Douglas production function
   definition, 90
   equation, 74, 90
   example, 93
   in flexible-price model, 154–156
   output per worker, 77–80
   in standard growth model, 90–93
Productivity
   computer paradox, 131
   improvements in, 440–441
   patterns of growth, 142
   relationship to investment, 481
   in steady-state capital-output ratio, 113
   and work hours, 468
Productivity growth, 126
   and natural rate of unemployment,
      341–342
Productivity multiple, 127
Productivity slowdown, 128–132
   effects of, 130–131
   end of, 131
   explanations of, 129–130
   in G-7 countries, 129
   measurement problems, 128–129
Product price levels 1895–1997, 127
Profits equation, 156
Progressive income tax, 447–448
Proportional change, 39
Public good, 145
Public investment, 397–398
Public savings, 187, 191
Purchasing power, 63, 67, 301
   in hyperinflation, 233–234
   inflation-adjusted, 183–184

Purchasing power—*Cont.*
  and interest rates, 17–19
  surplus of, in financial markets, 189
Purchasing power parity, 134

Q

Qualitative forecasts, 28
Quality of life, 9
Quantitative forecasts, 28
Quantitative models, 62–64
Quantity equation, 222
  to calculate price level, 223–224
  and inflation rate, 226–227
Quantity of imports demanded, 173
Quantity theory of money
  inflation in, 226–227
  and money demand, 221
  and money stock, 224–226
  and price level, 222–224
  quantity equation, 222
  velocity of money, 222
Quintiles, household income, 139

R

Rational expectations, 73
  long-run results, 352
  Phillips curve under, 348–350
Rational-expectations macroeconomists,
    465
Reagan, Ronald W., 289, 291, 382, 392,
    403
Reagan tax cut, 378
Real business cycles, 209–212
Real-business-cycle theory, 466–470
  assessment of, 469–470
  early theorists, 466–467
  fundamental assumption, 467
  problems with
    money stock, 469
    technology, 469
    unemployment, 468–469
  on sources of shifts in investment,
    481–482
  unevenness of economic growth,
    467–468
Real exchange rate, 20
  calculating, 31–32
  characteristics of, 29–31
  definition, 30–31
  formula, 32
  J curve, 172
  and purchasing power parity, 134

Real exchange rate—*Cont.*
  and quantity of imports demanded,
    173
  and volume of gross exports, 171–172
Real GDP, 48–56, 49–50
  and aggregate supply, 332–333
  calculating, 49
  compared to aggregate demand, 260
  components, 53–54
  and components of spending, 161
  as economic variable, 12–14, 28–29
  effect of budget deficit on, 393–394
  effect of price level changes, 320–322
  as flow variable, 49
  in full-employment economy, 160
  growth rate in 1990s, 240
  and high price/inflation levels, 326
  and inflation rate, 227
  and interest rates 1960–1999, 287
  investment as share of, 270
  in IS-LM diagram, 304–305
  in Japan 2001, 24
  monetary policy reaction function,
    323–324
  and money demand, 301
  and Okun's law, 47
  and unemployment rate, 46–48,
    330–332
Real GDP per worker, 13, 14, 74
  in United States 1960–2000, 240
Real interest rate, 17, 300; *see also* IS
    curve; IS-LM *entries*
  and autonomous spending, 277
  calculating, 38–40
  compared to nominal rate, 273
  and consumption spending, 181–182
  effect of fall in spending, 243
  effect of supply shocks, 208
  effect on exchange rate and capital flow,
    196–197
  and exchange rates, 203
  in flexible-price model, 270
  in Great Depression, 452
  interest rate differentials, 420
  in investment boom, 199–200
  and investment function, 166–167
  and investment spending, 166, 183,
    271–275
  in IS-LM diagram, 304–305
  mathematical tools, 39
  and real business-cycle theory, 210
  relevance to investment spending, 272
  and shifts in economy, 284
  in sticky-price model, 271

Real interest rate—*Cont.*
  Taylor rule, 322–323
  in U.S. 1960–2000, 18
Real money balances, 300
Real prices, 247
Real stock price indexes, 19
Real variables, 219
Real wage
  business cycle unemployment, 212
  growth aspirations, 342
  and hiring policy, 159
  and labor market, 156–160
  production function, 154–156
Recessions, 8, 241
  and gold standard, 416
  of late 1990s, 291, 292
  persistence of, 448
  policy-induced, 447, 448
  unemployment, 14–15
  unemployment rates in, 331–332
Replacement investment, 54
Representative agents, 72
Research and development, 144–145
  copyright protection, 145–146
Reserve deficit, 374
Reserve requirements, 225, 373–374
Revaluation, 418
  of dollar, 174
Rhetoric of economics, 63–64
Ricardian equivalence, 472–474
Rich countries, 133
Risk aversion, 474
Risk premium, 35
  and interest rate, 273, 274
Risky interest rate, 272–274
Rivalry in technology, 145
Rogoff, Ken, 429
Romer, Christina, 15, 446, 454
Roosevelt, Franklin D., 388
Rostow, W. W., 147
Roubini, Nouriel, 383
Rules for economic policy, 380–386
Russian government default, 273

S

Sachs, Jeffrey, 140, 417
Safe interest rate, 273
Salinas y Gotari, Carlos, 431–432
Samuelson, Paul A., 71, 449, 466
Sargent, Thomas, 465
Savings, 67
  effect of fall in consumption, 245
  effect of fall in spending, 243

Savings—*Cont.*
  effect of interest rates, 181–182
  effect of supply shocks, 208
  excess supply of, 190
  by households, 162
  in macroeconomic theory, 474
  policies to encourage, 143
  in standard growth model, 96–97
Savings rate, 95–97
  example, 114
  in steady-state capital-output ratio,
    113–115
Schooling, 140
Schumpeter, Joseph A., 209, 211, 466
Sciences, 60–62, 144–145
Seigniorage, 233–234
Self-interest, 3–4
Shleifer, Andrei, 140
Short-run aggregate supply, 326
Short run versus long run, 246, 352–354
Short-term interest rates, 271–272
  and term premium, 295–297
Simons, Henry, 380
Six Crises (Nixon), 381
Smith, Adam, 121
Social sciences, 28, 60
Social security deficit, 398
Sokoloff, Ken, 140
Solow, Robert, 131, 449, 465
Solow model; *see* Standard growth model
Soros, George, 429
South Asian Development Bank, 147
South Korea, 432
Speculator expectations, 318–319
Spending multiplier, 261
Stabilization policies, 6, 7–8
  amid economic uncertainties,
    371–372
  and budget deficit, 392–396
  effectiveness of, 447–448
  examples, 376–377
  fiscal, 264
  lessons learned on, 453–455
  power and limits of, 370–377
Stagflation, 369, 465
Staggered prices, 471–472
Stagnation, 142
Stalin, Josef, 137
Standard and Poor's 500 index, 19, 20, 34
Standard growth model, 89–97
  analysis of, 97–115
    pace of growth, 98–103
    steady-state capital-output ratio,
      111–115

Standard growth model—*Cont.*
  analysis of—*Cont.*
    steady-state growth equilibrium,
      103–110
  efficiency of labor, 95
  population growth, 94–95
  production function, 90–93
  savings and investment, 96–97
Standard of living
  and long-run growth, 88
  Malthusian view, 121–122
  in post-Communist areas, 138
  and productivity slowdown, 130–131
  since 1800, 120
  in U.S. 1895–1997, 126–127
Static expectations, 73
  and long run, 354
  Phillips curve under, 344–345
Statistical discrepancy, 68–69
Steady-state balanced growth, 98
Steady-state balanced-growth capital-
    output ratio, 139–140
Steady-state balanced growth equilibrium,
  90
Steady-state balanced growth path, 110
Steady-state capital-output ratio
  depreciation and production growth,
    113
  labor-force growth, 111–112
  savings rate, 113–115
Steady-state debt-to-GDP ratio,
  399–401
Steady-state growth equilibrium
  capital-output ratio, 103–105
  growth multiplier, 106, 108
  output per worker, 105–108
Steady-state growth path, 105–108
  pace of, 109–110
Steady-state output per worker
  arithmetic calculation, 77
  geometric calculation, 79–80
  steady-state, 78–79
Stein, Herbert, 381
Sticky-price equilibrium, 255–261
Sticky-price model, 237, 241–242
  and aggregate demand, 320–324
  aggregate demand and inflation,
    336–340
  and aggregate supply, 324–326
  exchange rates and trade balance,
    313–320
  and expected inflation, 343–351
  exports and autonomous spending,
    275–277

Sticky-price model—*Cont.*
  income-expenditure framework,
    248–261
    building up aggregate demand,
      248–255
    inventory adjustment process,
      255–260
    sticky-price equilibrium, 255–261
  interest rates and aggregate demand,
    270–277
  investment and real interest rate
    long-term rate, 271–272
    risky rate, 272–274
  IS curve, 277–292
  IS-LM framework, 304–310
  LM curve, 300–313
  money stock and money market,
    300–313
  multiplier in, 261–265
  and national debt, 405–406
  and natural rate of unemployment,
    340–343
  real interest rate, 271
  role of investment, 270–271
  as short-run analysis, 246
  from short run to long run, 352–354
  sources of investment fluctuation, 271
  using IS curve to understand economy,
    283–292
Sticky prices, 241–248
  and aggregate demand, 248
  and business cycles, 241–242
  consequences of
    on expectations, 245–248
    and flexible-price logic, 242–244
    sticky-price logic, 244–245
  and menu costs, 247
  and money illusion, 247
  in new Keynesian economics,
    471–472
  reasons for, 246–248
Stock market
  crash of 1929, 452–453
  crash of 1987, 291
  as economic variable, 19–20, 28–29
  fears in 2000, 23
  in Great Depression, 61–62
  indicator of investment spending, 275
  information gained from, 36–37
  operation of, 34–37
  relation to investment spending, 168
  useful knowledge about, 35–36
Stock market indexes, 35
Stock prices, and interest rates, 168

Stocks, 35–36
    calculating value of basket of, 36
    value equation, 36
Stock variable, unemployment rate, 45
Structural unemployment, 70
Substitution bias, 42
Sukarno, 147
Summers, Lawrence H., 383, 384
Summers, Robert, 133, 138, 140
Supply and demand, 74–75
Supply shocks, 207–209
Surplus; *see* Government surplus
Sustainable deficits, 398–401
Sweden, 7, 88

T

Tax-avoidance strategies, 408
Tax cuts, 287–288, 378, 406
    deficits created by, 404
Taxes
    as automatic stabilizer, 264
    lump-sum, 264
    paid by households, 161–162
    proportional, 264
    Vietnam War surtax, 180–181
Tax rates, and automatic stabilizers,
        407–408
Taylor, John, 322, 386, 449, 471
Taylor rule, 322–323, 386
Technocratic authorities, 381–382
Technological advances
    components, 144–145
    invention and innovation, 144–145
    patents and copyrights for, 145–146
    rivalry versus excludability, 145
Technology
    and end of Malthusian era, 122
    of Industrial Revolution, 124–125
    Malthusian view, 121–122
    of mass production, 128
    and real-business-cycle theory, 209–212
    in real-business-cycle theory, 469
    source of long-run growth, 88
Technology level, 74, 88
Term premium, 286–287, 295–297
Term structure of interest rates,
        expectations theory of, 296
Tesebonos (Mexican bonds), 431
Thailand, 432
Thaler, Richard, 474
Tobin, James, 464
Total income, 68
Total savings, 187

Total spending
    components of, 161
    determinants, 186
    in NIPA, 259–260
Tract on Monetary Reform (Keynes), 246
Transfer payments, 169
Transitory income, 177–181
Treasury bills, 18
Treasury notes, 18
Treasury yield curve, 37
Trotsky, Leon, 5
Trotting inflation, 17
Tufte, Edward, 449

U

Unemployment, 44–48; *see also* Natural
        rate of unemployment
    business cycle pattern, 212
    classical, 457
    costs of, 331–332
    economists' knowledge of, 479–480
    effect on taxes and spending, 379
    frictional, 14
    kinds of, 45
    long-term in Europe, 342–343
    in real-business-cycle theory, 468–469
    in sticky-price model, 244–245
    structural, 70
Unemployment rate; *see also* Natural rate
        of unemployment; Phillips curve
    and aggregate supply, 330–332
    calculating, 44–46
    decline in 1990s, 291
    by demographic groups, 46
    as economic variable, 14–15, 28–29
    equation, 45
    equilibrium rate, 336, 338–339
    in Europe, 23–24, 455–458
    natural, 240
    and Okun's law, 46–48, 330–331
    past levels of, and natural rate, 342–343
    in recession of 1982, 9
    in 1990s, 23
    as stock variable, 45
    in 2000, 9
    in United States 1950–2000, 45
    in United States in 20th century, 15
Unexpected inflation, 232–233
Unified cash balance, 394
United States dollar
    devaluation, 174
    under gold standard, 412
    revaluation, 174

United States economy, 62
    application of Phillips curve to, 456
    business cycles 1960–2000, 8
    debt-to-GDP ratio, 402
    demographics of unemployment, 46
    economic data 2000–2001, 11
    end of Bretton Woods system, 418
    gross exports 1980–1990, 171
    growth 1800–1973, 125–127
    growth 1870–1973, 127–128
    growth since 1973, 128–132
    inflation rate 1890–2000, 16–17
    investment boom 1992–1999, 131
    macroeconomic situation, 22–23
    measures of inflation, 44
    national debt, 401–402
    optimal currency area, 425–426
    Phillips curve 1955–1980, 368
    post-World War II inflation, 218
    potential output 1960–2000, 240
    real exchange rate 1975–2000, 21
    real GDP per worker, 13, 240
    real interest rate 1960–2000, 18
    reasons for strength of, 128
    sources of economic weakness, 23
    standard of living 1895–1997, 126–127
    structural changes, 441–442
    unemployment rate 1950–2000, 45
    unemployment rate in 20th century, 15
    using IS curve to understand, 283–292
        economy of late 1970s, 288–289
        economy of 1960s, 287–288
        economy of 1980s, 289–290
        economy of 1990s, 291–292
    velocity of money before 1980, 369
    velocity of money 1960–1990s, 223
United States Treasury Exchange
        Stabilization Fund, 432
Unit of account, 220–221
Utility maximization, 178–181

V

Value added, 51–52
Variables, 28–29
    nominal versus real, 219
Velocity of money, 222
    fluctuations in, 380
    and inflation rate, 228
    and price level, 222–224
    in quantity theory, 222–224
    in U.S. before 1980, 369
    in United States 1960–1990s, 223
Vietnam War expenditures, 288–289

Vietnam War surtax, 180–181
Virtuous circles, 141
Vishny, Robert, 140
Volcker, Paul, 17, 18, 288, 347, 449, 454
Volcker disinflation, 347–348, 456
Voter myopia, 404, 409, 473

W

Wages
    classical assumption, 154–156
    market-clearing level, 155
    natural stickiness, 247

Wall Street Journal, 206
Warner, Andrew, 140
White, Harry Dexter, 417, 436
Williamson, Jeffrey, 124
Women in labor force, 56
Worker mobility, 341
Workers
    discouraged, 45
    part time, 46
Work hours, 468
Work incentives, 468–469
World War I, and end of gold standard,
    416

Y–Z

Yellen, Janet, 471
Yield curve, 17, 271, 272
    inverted, 18
    Treasury, 37
Zedillo, Ernesto, 431–432

U.S. Macroeconomic Data

Year	Real GDP (billions of chained 1996 dollars)	Real GDP per Worker (chained 1996 dollars)	Inflation (percent per year)	Unemployment (percent)	Long-Term Real Interest Rate (percent per year; corporate BAA bonds minus current inflation rate)	Real Exchange Rate (1982 = 100)	Real Stock Market Value (S&P Composite) (chained real 1996 index value)	Consumption (billions of chained 1996 dollars)
1959	2,318.96	33,918.26	1.1	5.5	3.95		262.25	1,470.7
1960	2,376.78	34,135.34	1.4	5.5	3.79		251.69	1,510.8
1961	2,432.25	34,520.06	1.1	6.7	3.98		295.32	1,541.2
1962	2,579.14	36,524.45	1.4	5.5	3.62		274.32	1,617.3
1963	2,690.08	37,449.15	1.1	5.7	3.76		303.78	1,684.0
1964	2,846.35	38,942.53	1.5	5.2	3.33		348.63	1,784.8
1965	3,028.40	40,674.18	1.9	4.5	2.97		370.77	1,897.6
1966	3,227.63	42,597.77	2.9	3.8	2.77		348.57	2,006.1
1967	3,308.11	42,769.71	3.1	3.8	3.13		364.66	2,066.2
1968	3,465.94	44,019.15	4.3	3.6	2.64		375.29	2,184.2
1969	3,571.41	44,236.80	4.9	3.5	2.91		354.62	2,264.8
1970	3,578.45	43,233.08	5.3	4.9	3.81		286.37	2,317.5
1971	3,697.99	43,824.36	5.0	5.9	3.56		322.05	2,405.2
1972	3,898.79	44,796.13	4.3	5.6	3.86	102	343.18	2,550.5
1973	4,123.81	46,112.64	5.6	4.9	2.64	113	319.73	2,675.9
1974	4,098.80	44,576.94	9.0	5.6	0.50	116	226.24	2,653.7
1975	4,084.74	43,558.95	9.3	8.5	1.31	122	215.24	2,710.9
1976	4,312.11	44,843.96	5.7	7.7	4.05	124	241.16	2,868.9
1977	4,512.12	45,572.86	6.4	7.1	2.57	120	218.13	2,992.1
1978	4,760.58	46,557.81	7.1	6.1	2.39	133	199.09	3,124.7
1979	4,912.16	46,799.40	8.3	5.8	2.39	134	197.15	3,203.2
1980	4,901.22	45,831.50	9.2	7.1	4.47	131	208.24	3,193.0
1981	5,020.76	46,201.92	9.3	7.6	6.74	111	205.31	3,236.0
1982	4,919.19	44,637.13	6.2	9.7	9.91	100	180.69	3,275.5
1983	5,132.49	46,010.68	4.0	9.6	9.55	95	232.88	3,454.3
1984	5,505.18	48,485.00	3.7	7.5	10.49	87	224.61	3,640.6
1985	5,716.92	49,513.85	3.2	7.2	9.52	84	253.55	3,820.9
1986	5,912.25	50,174.38	2.2	7.0	8.19	108	313.82	3,981.2
1987	6,113.05	50,999.44	3.0	6.2	7.58	123	369.72	4,113.4
1988	6,368.54	52,343.15	3.4	5.5	7.43	126	331.37	4,279.5
1989	6,592.00	53,217.49	3.8	5.3	6.38	118	387.70	4,393.7
1990	6,707.63	53,302.86	3.9	5.6	6.46	129	386.76	4,474.5
1991	6,676.38	52,842.03	3.6	6.8	6.20	129	419.56	4,466.6
1992	6,880.30	53,708.32	2.4	7.5	6.58	134	452.68	4,594.5
1993	7,062.35	54,662.16	2.4	6.9	5.53	124	479.97	4,748.9
1994	7,347.53	56,064.07	2.1	6.1	6.52	126	479.55	4,928.1
1995	7,543.64	57,017.51	2.2	5.6	6.00	136	552.21	5,075.6
1996	7,813.20	58,332.28	1.9	5.4	6.15	129	670.50	5,237.5
1997	8,159.32	59,864.30	1.9	4.9	5.96	117	856.72	5,423.9
1998	8,515.61	61,853.86	1.3	4.5	5.92	113	1,051.64	5,678.7
1999	8,875.80	63,686.03	1.5	4.2	6.37	109	1,266.90	5,978.8
2000						100		

Investment (billions of chained 1996 dollars)	Government (billions of chained 1996 dollars) Purchases	Net Exports (billions of chained 1996 dollars)	Short-Term Nominal Interest Rate (3 month T-Bills) (percent/year)	Long-Term Nominal Interest Rate (corporate BAA bonds) (percent per year)	Price Level (1996 = 100)	Government Budget Surplus (percentage of GDP)	Nominal S&P Composite Index	Labor Force
272.9	661.4	−34.2	3.405	5.05	21.9		57.38	68,369
272.8	661.3	−20.5	2.928	5.19	22.2		55.85	69,628
271.0	693.2	−18.4	2.378	5.08	22.4	−0.6	66.27	70,459
305.3	735.0	−25.8	2.778	5.02	22.7	−1.3	62.38	70,614
325.7	752.4	−22.0	3.157	4.86	23.0	−0.8	69.87	71,833
352.6	767.1	−15.0	3.549	4.83	23.3	−0.9	81.37	73,091
402.0	791.1	−26.4	3.954	4.87	23.8	−0.2	88.17	74,455
437.3	862.1	−39.9	4.881	5.67	24.5	−0.5	85.26	75,770
417.2	927.1	−49.2	4.321	6.23	25.2	−1.1	91.93	77,347
441.3	956.6	−66.1	5.339	6.94	26.3	−2.9	98.70	78,737
466.9	952.5	−70.2	6.677	7.81	27.6	0.3	97.84	80,734
436.2	931.1	−63.8	6.458	9.11	29.1	−0.3	83.22	82,771
485.8	913.8	−74.6	4.348	8.56	30.5	−2.1	98.29	84,382
543.0	914.9	−87.8	4.071	8.16	31.8	−2	109.20	87,034
606.5	908.3	−62.0	7.041	8.24	33.6	−1.1	107.43	89,429
561.7	924.8	−35.6	7.886	9.50	36.6	−0.4	82.85	91,949
462.2	942.5	−7.5	5.838	10.61	40.0	−3.4	86.16	93,775
555.5	943.3	−40.4	4.989	9.75	42.3	−4.2	102.01	96,158
639.4	952.7	−65.3	5.265	8.97	45.0	−2.7	98.20	99,009
713.0	982.2	−66.4	7.221	9.49	48.2	−2.7	96.02	102,251
735.4	1,001.1	−45.5	10.041	10.69	52.3	−1.6	103.01	104,962
655.3	1,020.9	10.0	11.506	13.67	57.0	−2.7	118.78	106,940
715.6	1,030.0	5.2	14.029	16.04	62.4	−2.6	128.05	108,670
615.2	1,046.0	−14.6	10.686	16.11	66.3	−4	119.71	110,204
673.7	1,081.0	−63.8	8.63	13.55	68.9	−6	160.41	111,550
871.5	1,118.4	−128.4	9.58	14.19	71.4	−4.8	160.46	113,544
863.4	1,190.5	−149.1	7.48	12.72	73.7	−5.1	186.84	115,461
857.7	1,255.2	−165.1	5.98	10.39	75.3	−5	236.34	117,834
879.3	1,292.5	−156.2	5.82	10.58	77.6	−3.2	286.83	119,865
902.8	1,307.5	−112.1	6.69	10.83	80.2	−3.1	265.79	121,669
936.5	1,343.5	−79.4	8.12	10.18	83.3	−2.8	322.84	123,869
907.3	1,387.3	−56.5	7.51	10.36	86.5	−3.9	334.59	125,840
829.5	1,403.4	−15.8	5.42	9.80	89.7	−4.5	376.18	126,346
899.8	1,410.0	−19.8	3.45	8.98	91.8	−4.7	415.74	128,105
977.9	1,398.8	−59.1	3.02	7.93	94.1	−3.9	451.41	129,200
1,107.0	1,400.1	−86.5	4.29	8.62	96.0	−2.9	460.42	131,056
1,140.6	1,406.4	−78.4	5.51	8.20	98.1	−2.2	541.72	132,304
1,242.7	1,421.9	−89.0	5.02	8.05	100.0	−1.4	670.50	133,943
1,393.3	1,455.4	−113.3	5.07	7.86	102.0	−0.3	873.43	136,297
1,566.8	1,486.4	−221.0	4.81	7.22	103.2	0.8	1,085.50	137,673
1,669.7	1,536.1	−322.4	4.66	7.87	104.8	1.4	1,327.33	139,368
						2.4		

TABLE 5.1
Economic Growth through Deep Time

Year	Population*	GDP per Capita†
–5000	5	$ 130
–1000	50	160
1	170	135
1000	265	165
1500	425	175
1800	900	250
1900	1625	850
1950	2515	2030
1975	4080	4640
2000	6120	8175

* Millions.

† In year-2000 international dollars.

Source: Joel Cohen, *How Many People Can the Earth Support?* (New York: Norton, 1995).

TABLE 5.2
Labor-Time Costs of Commodities, 1895–1997

Commodity	Time to Earn (Hours)*		Productivity Multiple
	1895	1997	
Horatio Alger books (6 vols.)	21.0	0.6	35.0
One-speed bicycle	260.0	7.2	36.1
Cushioned office chair	24.0	2.0	12.0
100-piece dinner set	44.0	3.6	12.2
Hairbrush	16.0	2.0	8.0
Cane rocking chair	8.0	1.6	5.0
Solid gold locket	28.0	6.0	4.7
Encyclopedia Britannica	140.0	4.0	35.0
Steinway piano	2400.0	1107.6	2.2
Sterling silver teaspoon	26.0	34.0	0.8
Oranges (dozen)	2.0	0.1	20.0
Ground beef (1 lb.)	0.8	0.2	4.0
Milk (1 gal.)	2.0	0.25	8.0
Television	∞	15.0	∞
Plane ticket: SFO-BOS	∞	20.0	∞
Antibiotic strep-throat cure	∞	1.0	∞
Dental x-ray	∞	2.0	∞
Laptop computer	∞	70.0	∞

* Time needed for an average worker to earn the purchase price of the commodity.

Source: 1895 Montgomery Ward catalogue.